REGRESSION THERAPY:

A HANDBOOK FOR PROFESSIONALS

Volume II

Other Releases from the Deep Forest Press

Meditation Tapes

Moonlight Meditation

This meditation assists the listener to contact a deep altered state through imaging of light and traveling through Nature: earth, river, and forest. In this deep state he is assisted in formulating affirmations regarding the body image and health, wisdom, love, tranquility, and productivity. The accompanying music is among the most beautiful that Steven Halpern has written.

The Golden Flower

Side 1: Meditation on the Golden Flower
Within the physical body is a Light Body, called by the ancient Chinese "the Golden Flower." This tape suggests appropriate meditational steps for experiencing it.

Side 2: Radiant Continuum
This tape takes the listener through his current lifetime, reviewing his choices concerning parents, birth, and inner lessons, and offering expanded perspective on his life patterns.

The Mind Mirror Video Tapes

In five video tapes the levels of brain wave functioning of senior therapists and their patients are recorded on a small screen and videotaped during the regression. Both the spread of brain wave levels and the synchronization of patient and therapist are observable.

REGRESSION THERAPY
A HANDBOOK FOR PROFESSIONALS

VOLUME II: SPECIAL INSTANCES
OF ALTERED STATE WORK

Winafred Blake Lucas Ph.D.

DEEP FOREST PRESS

First edition 1993

Published in the United States by

Deep Forest Press
P.O. Drawer 4
Crest Park, CA 92326

Cover art: Amanda Goodenough
Jacket design: Kasey Fansett
Photo credit: Mara Magliarditi
Press logo: William Abell

Library of Congress No. 92-097247
ISBN (2 Volumes) 1-882530-00-4
    (Vol 2) 1-882530-02-0

Printed by Jostens Press, Visalia, CA

Acknowledgments to Volume II

Grateful acknowledgement is made to the following for permission to quote previously published material:

Doubleday, a division of Bantam Doubleday Dell Publishing Group, Inc. for permission to quote from *The Unquiet Dead* by Edith Fiore. Copyright ©1987 by Edith Fiore. And from *Other Lives, Other Selves* by Roger Woolger. Copyright ©1987 by Roger Woolger.

Michael Gabriel and Marie Gabriel for permission to quote from *Voices from the Womb* by Michael Gabriel and Marie Gabriel. Copyright ©1991 by Michael Gabriel.

Alice Givens for permission to quote from *The Process of Healing* by Alice Givens. Copyright ©1990 by Alice Givens.

Harper Collins Publishers, Ltd, for permission to quote from *Multiple Man* by Adam Crabtree. Copyright ©1985 by Adam Crabtree.

Hickman Systems for permission to quote from *Mind Probe—Hypnosis* by Irene Hickman. Copyright ©1983 by Irene Hickman.

Gladys McGarey for permission to quote from *Born to Live* by Gladys McGarey. Copyright ©1980 by Gladys McGarey.

Samuel Sandweiss for permission to quote from *Sai Baba: The Holy Man and the Psychiatrist* by Samuel Sandweiss. Copyright © 1975 by Samuel Sandweiss, M.D.

Chet Snow for permission to quote from *Mass Dreams of the Future* by Chet Snow. Copyright ©1980 by Chet Snow.

Joel Whitton and Joe Fisher for permission to quote from *Life Between Life* by Joel Whitton and Joe Fisher. Copyright ©1980 by Joel Whitton and Joe Fisher.

The Association for Past-Life Research and Therapies for permission to reprint the following articles from *The Journal of Regression Therapy*:

Findeisen, Barbara. "Rescripting in Pre-and Peri-Natal and Early Childhood Problems," Vol. III, No. 1, 1988.
Givens, Alice. "The Child is Innocent," Volume IV, No. 1, 1989.
Loehr, Franklin. "Death Preview: A New Direction in Psychography," Vol. II, No. 1, 1987.
Lucas, Winafred. "Spontaneous Remissions," Vol. II, No. 2, 1987.
———. "The Weighing of the Heart and Other Hells," Vol. III, No. 2, 1988.
Motoyama, Hiroshi. "A Case of Possession in a Past Life Resulting in Physical Problems," Vol. II, No. 2, 1987.
Pecci, Ernest. "Exploring One's Death," Vol. III, No. 1, 1987.
Snow, Chet. "Death Comes to Marie-France," Vol. II, No. 1, 1987.

This book is dedicated to

Helen Wambach

whose innovative pioneer research revitalized

and grounded the concept of past-life experience.

We are in her debt.

Contents

Volume II - Special Instances of Altered State Work

Foreword

When I begin teaching my required course in Human Development to clinical psychologists in training, I draw a line on the board to represent what is usually considered the developmental continuum of a person's lifetime. I mark the beginning of the line on the left as physical birth and the end of the line on the right as physical death. I also extend the line to the left a few inches, using a dotted line, saying that this represents the period from conception to birth.

Then we discuss the picture. Is this all there is to a lifetime? Does human development occur outside of or beyond these parameters? Do any of you feel comfortable extending this dotted line back before conception? How about extending it to the right beyond physical death? Are there ways in which one can step outside of one's place on the lifetime's usual continuum in order to re-experience the past? Experience the future? Gain information from outside of the "skin encapsulated ego" and physical reality?

Soon I am extending the continuum, at their suggestion, even further in both directions and adding loops and arrows moving in and out of the level baseline. Terms are offered: "between lives," "interlife," "bardo," "devachan," "the afterlife," "the astral plane," "the soul," "soul growth," "rebirth," "karma," "fetal awareness," "past lives," "near-death experience," "out-of-body experience," "precognition," "channeling," "spirit communication," "spirit possession," and others.

Let me add that the scene I am describing to you is taking place at an alternative-type graduate school in the San Francisco Bay Area. I am not at all sure that any of these extensions and additions would be volunteered, or even tolerated, at present in any of the classrooms of the American Psychological Association's accredited clinical training programs in our mainstream higher education system.

We know that hypnotic age regression works. It is a widely acceptable practice, used in court to enhance recall of crime events and used in a wide variety of clinical situations with psychotherapeutic success. But how far back can a person be hypnotically regressed? That is, how far back do an individual's experiences go? Solid empirical evidence shows that we can regress people back to infancy and to their own births, with accompanying recall and deeply visceral and authentic re-living of those experiences. There is now a growing body of evidence that hypnotic age regression can take a person back into the prenatal experience in order to re-live experiences from that period as well. Through such a technique it has been found that a client can be helped to experience, re-live, own, make sense of, resolve, dispel, integrate, or transmute the cognitive-emotional and psychoenergetic fields involved. How far back can the client be taken? How far back do the memories go that represent that individual's real, lived experience?

For each professional, there is usually some threshold beyond which he or she will not comfortably venture. Before the third trimester? The second? The first? Before conception? I would presume that most of you who are holding this book at this moment have been able to hypnotically age-regress subjects or clients back to what appear to be a variety of prenatal periods, as well as into the strange realms of pre-conception, apparent between-life periods, and on into past lives. I think we are currently undergoing a paradigm shift in psychology, and in our science in general. One major arena within which this shift is taking place is in this gradual extending of our understanding of the traditional lifeline continuum of a person into these new areas as well as into post-death transpersonal (soul evolution) domains.

This book has assembled a fascinating, and valuable assortment of conceptualizations and clinical case-descriptions by fellow therapists. Their work involves inducing in clients a shift in consciousness to an altered state that enables them to connect with problematic and as yet unresolved prior experiences within this extended evolutionary scheme of our human nature.

It is not the primary intention of this book to convince the still-skeptical psychological mainstream that hypnotic age regression can successfully venture into the realms of the prenatal, interlife and past lives, spirit possession, or projections into the future, or to try to prove that such experiential realms exist. It is Dr. Lucas' intention to provide clinicians who are genuinely open to or who have already experienced such realms with their clients with a useful set of case studies from fellow therapists about how they do their work so that they might better be able to help their clients in the future. In this sense, Dr. Lucas is a dedicated and inspired pioneer in her efforts to provide more clinicians with a deeper understanding of how altered state and age-regression psychotherapy can be utilized, especially in these extended experiential realms of our development continuum.

I would hope as part of the paradigm shift in our science that ten years from now the textbooks and classroom activities that will be used to teach human personality and development and the theories and techniques of psychotherapy will include the kinds of extended understanding and approaches that Dr. Lucas has pioneered and advocated throughout her professional career and that she has brought together in this book.

Jon Klimo, Ph.D.
Rosebridge Graduate School, Concord, California
August, 1992

Preface

This second volume is an outgrowth of the original volume on past-life therapy. While a patient is in an altered state, his recovery of past lives constantly touches prenatal and birth experiences, childhood traumas, death and the interlife, and attaching entities. Books describing the general background of these areas have been available, but reports of therapeutic techniques using such altered states are few. Many therapists work routinely in these areas, but they have been slow to share their knowledge.

Recently a few books have described emerging theories and suggested therapeutic approaches. Michael Gabriel's *Voices from the Womb* establishes initial concepts for the prenatal field. Alice Givens' *The Process of Healing* covers altered-state work in childhood and child abuse. Joel Whitton's *Life Before Life* presents initial assumptions of the interlife. Annabelle Chaplin's early conceptualization of the phenomenon of releasement, presented in *The Bright Light of Death,* has been extended by Edith Fiore in *The Unquiet Dead,* and more recently in *Multiple Man: Explorations in Possession and Multiple Personality* by Adam Crabtree. *Mass Dreams of the Future* documented the years of research of Helen Wambach and Chet Snow on future progression.

These books have established a core of psychotherapeutic theory, but the experience of other therapists is needed to confirm and extend these conceptions and to present innovative techniques of psychotherapy. To begin to meet this need I have assembled some mini-treatises in the hope that these will enable therapists to move more confidently into such extended areas of altered-state work and to encourage them to publish further. Many articles in this volume are reprinted from *The Journal of Regression Therapy,* which is an excellent clearing house for new theories and techniques.

As in Volume I, I have not struggled to achieve a non-sexist style. I have again respected the orientation of the contributors and the designation of "C" for client and "P" for patient. In addition, where appropriate "E" has been used to indicate communications of entities as they are reported by patients.

Here also I am indebted to Chet Snow for his candid reaction to the material and for his consistent support in the long effort to complete this book. My secretary Teri Stanton has come early and stayed late and slugged through snow and ice to keep updated versions coming off our computer. Joanne Garland again put final editing of all the articles and compilation of an index ahead of the pressing concerns of her busy life. Her enthusiasm for and belief in the value of the material has encouraged me more than she can ever know. Thank you, Joanne.

The contributors themselves patiently responded to the continuous stream of requests for detailed information on their articles and biographies. I am sure they have wondered if the book would ever come to completion, and it is with relief that I can finally tell them it is finished. My special appreciation goes to Marilyn Porter, my Jostens editor, for her patience and warm cooperation in preparing these complicated volumes for press, and to artist Kacey Fansett for her sensitive artistic presentation.

Winafred Blake Lucas, Ph.D.
Crest Park, California

Contributors

Afton L. Blake, Ph.D. completed her doctorate at the California School of Professional Psychology and is a director and in private practice at the Brentwood Psychotherapy Center. Her current interest in transformational imaging and regression therapy is grounded by years of training in psychoanalysis and Psychosynthesis. Another focus for her is working with single mothers.

Robert Bontenbal, M.A., took his graduate degrees at the University of Amsterdam in Political Science and Urban Planning. During his academic years he read extensively in the field of past-life therapy and in 1984 completed a training course under Dr. Hans ten Dam, the moving force in past-life training in Holland. Following this he began working in the past-life field and became a founder of the Dutch Association of Past-Life Therapy. Currently he is one of the four leaders of its two-year training program and serves as the editor of its bulletin.

Adam Crabtree, M.A. is a psychotherapist in Toronto, Canada, with a background in philosophy and languages. He is the founder and director of the Willow Workshops, which provide seminars for professionals, and he co-founded Stress Analysis Consultants, a firm that offers seminars on a management level. He is a lecturer at St. John's University in Minnesota and at Humber College and McMaster University in Ontario. His recent book, *Multiple Man: Explorations in Possession and Multiple Personality*, provides a sound foundation for releasement work.

Hazel M. Denning, Ph.D. has pursued a dual track of academic competence and a long-standing interest in transpersonal areas. She earned two master's degrees, then finished her doctorate when she was 76 with an impressive study of the release of long-standing guilt through past-life work. She was one of the founders of the Association for Past-Life Research and Therapies, served as its president for two years and its Executive Director for many more. She travels widely, lecturing and giving workshops around the world. She designed and administered a comprehensive exploration of the healing potential of regression work. She served as Consulting Editor of *The Journal of Regression Therapy* during its early years.

Claire Etheridge, Ph.D. is president and founder of the Institute for Advanced Studies, a non-profit, continuing education organization focused on healing, enlightenment, and spirituality. She is a Diplomate in both Clinical Psychology and Psychological Hypnosis and served on the faculty of Pepperdine University and the University of California at Irvine. She is known for her innovative approaches in the areas of prenatal psychology, multiple personalities, and clinical hypnosis.

Barbara Findeisen, M.A. M.F.C.C., a graduate of Stanford University, is an experienced past-life therapist and one of the pioneers in pre- and perinatal psychology. Her video film, "Journey to Be Born," has made a significant contribution to this field. She gives workshops throughout Europe and has established a therapy center in Stockholm, Sweden. She is founder and director of the Pocket Ranch, a transpersonally-oriented treatment and conference center in northern California.

Edith Fiore, Ph.D. is a licensed clinical psychologist with a practice in Saratoga, California. She established herself as one of the pioneers in regression therapy with her popular book *You Have Been Here Before.* Always on the cutting edge, she next documented the area of attachment and possession in *The Unquiet Dead.* A recent book, *Encounters,* describes the treatment of patients who have had UFO experiences. Throughout the publication of *The Journal of Regression Therapy* she has been both a valued member of the Editorial Board and a frequent and popular contributor.

Michael Gabriel, M.A. is a certified hypnotist. Currently he is an instructor at West Valley College in Saratoga, California and a director of Wellhouse Prenatal and Past-Life Seminars. His private practice focuses both on current-life issues and on perinatal and past-life experiences. Recently he co-authored *Voices from the Womb* with his wife, Marie.

Alice M. Givens, Ph.D., a licensed psychologist, was the Director of Religious Education in the Unitarian Church for 15 years, and also served on the staff of the Alhambra Psychiatric Hospital and the Ingleside Hospital. Since 1975 she has been in private practice. Currently she specializes in working with deep fear and trauma, especially in adults who have been victims of child abuse. Her recent book, *The Process of Healing,* explores altered-state work in childhood.

Hugh W. Harmon, Ph.D. is a psychologist and hypnotherapist. His original graduate work was in medicine, but after a course in medical school on hypnotherapy he was so much more impressed with the power of the mind than with chemical healing that he shifted focus and completed his doctorate in psychology at the University of Southern California. Currently he heads a private clinic in Palm Desert and also directs a state-authorized school for hypnotherapy and regression. His research concentrates on incest and molestation cases. He has a book in press that deals with "turning emotional lead into psychic gold."

Irene Hickman, D.O. began her professional career as a physician, but her disillusionment with the limitations of physical medicine led her to try out hypnotherapy as an adjunctive technique. Striking successes with this method led to her specialization in this approach, and eventually she moved into regression therapy. Her book *Mind Probe—Hypnosis,* now in its third printing, is a documentation of her constructs and techniques. She designed *The Journal of Regression Therapy* and edited its first issue for the Association for Past-life Research and Therapies. She remains on the Editorial Staff as a Consulting Editor. Her home is in Kirksville, Missouri.

Louise Ireland-Frey, D.D. was born in Idaho, grew up in Colorado, and earned her M.D. from Tulane University. She practiced medicine briefly in Wichita, Kansas, before retiring due to failed health. A 16-hour course in self-hypnosis improved her health so dramatically that she took several hundred hours of professional training and workshops in hypnosis and in 1981 began a new career as a hypnotherapist. She has four sons: a gemologist, a musician, and two medical doctors. Her home is in Cedar Edge, Colorado.

Barbara P. Lamb, M.F.C.C. has had extensive experience in dance therapy and Tai Chi. Her interest in regression therapy is an outgrowth of the transformational work she did in Psychosynthesis and Spiritual Hypnosis. She is a former co-director of Greensleeves Association, a counseling group in Claremont, and is currently in private practice there. For many years she has worked with patients on issues involving loss, grieving, and death and dying and has heard many testimonies of spirit visitations.

Franklin Loehr, D.D. was director of research at the Religious Research Foundation in Grand Island, Florida until his death in 1988. He began his research with past lives in the 50's and developed an approach that he called Psychography. His best known book is *The Power of Prayer on Plants,* which was the outcome of years of research. *Diary after Death,* a charming and thought-provoking description of what happens on the other side, grew out of his experience with what he called the Death Preview, described in his article.

Winafred B. Lucas, Ph.D. became aware of the new discipline of clinical psychology in the early 30's while studying Sanskrit in Munich. Later she completed a doctorate in psychology and became a diplomate of the American Board of Professional Psychology. She spent a decade each on therapy with children, treatment of adolescents, transformational imaging, and finally on regression therapy and releasement work. She edited *The Journal of Regression Therapy* from 1987 to 1990.

Ann Hubbel Maiden, Ph.D. is a licensed California psychologist who founded and directs both the Marina Counseling Center and the Transpersonal Psychotherapy Training Program in San Francisco and is a faculty member and lecturer at the California Institute of Integral Studies and at the John F. Kennedy University. Her experiences in India and Tibet researching birth practices are described in her forthcoming book, *Tibetan Birth Wisdom.* Currently she travels in Europe, Japan, Korea, and China gathering material for a second book, *Options for Healthy Birth.*

Gladys T. McGarey, M.D. is a physician, lecturer, writer, and mother of six. She has practiced medicine for nearly 50 years and has enriched her medical knowledge through the study of ancient and alternative healing methods, including research in the Edgar Cayce psychic readings. She was co-founder of a home childbirth program and of the ARE Clinic in Phoenix and served as president of the American Holistic Medical Association. Her book *Born to Live* was one of the earliest books to document a holistic approach to childbirth. Recently she helped found the Scottsdale Holistic Medical Group, where she is a practicing physician.

Hiroshi Motoyama, Ph.D. graduated from Tokyo University of Education with doctoral degrees in philosophy and clinical psychology. He is both a scientist trained in empirical methodology and a psychic who has experientially gained deep philosophical knowledge. He is the head priest of the Tamamitsu Shrine in Tokyo and is well versed in Yoga treatises. His scientific endeavors resulted in the establishment of the Institute for Religious Psychology, a research facility, and the International Association for Religion and Parapsychology. He has authored over 30 books and has traveled widely throughout the world. A central theme of his work is the study of parapsychological phenomena and their relation to religion. He has conducted controlled experiments in extrasensory perception and psychokinesis. In recognition of his important work in this field, UNESCO selected him in 1974 as one of the world's 10 foremost parapsychologists. He is a valued current member of the Editorial Board of *The Journal of Regression Therapy.*

Kenneth J. Naysmith, Ph.D. has held a lifelong interest in spiritual and non-orthodox methods of healing. As a young man he spent seven years in a Hindu monastery and months with Tibetan lamas in the Himalayas. For many years he worked as a licensed clinical psychologist at the San Bernardino County Medical Center and the San Diego County Psychiatric Hospital. Currently he is a forensic psychologist with the State of California and has a part-time private practice in Berkeley, California. He is currently writing a book on new concepts in psychology.

Tineke Noordegraaf, M.M. studied medicine at the University of Amsterdam but failed to find in modern medicine the answers she was seeking. She spent several years traveling, primarily in Asia, searching for better answers. It is there that she became open to reincarnation. When she returned to Holland, she joined the training program initiated by Hans ten Dam, which confirmed her feeling that reincarnation therapy was the optimal synthesis between her analytical skills and her intuitive talents. Currently she helps direct the past-life training program in the Netherlands and with Rob Bontenbal gives workshops and presents the concept of past lives throughout Europe and the United States.

Ernest F. Pecci, M.D. began his career as a physician, but when his hope that science had the answers to people's problems was not realized, he began his search for new ways of investigating and healing, first progressing backward to early childhood, then to birth experience, and finally into past lives. He worked on a process for transforming early childhood decisions and wrote a book describing this: *I Love You/Hate You: A Treatise on the Parent-Child Struggle Within.* Currently he is Director of the Rosebridge Graduate Institute in Walnut Creek, California, an approved graduate school with transpersonal emphasis. He served as the second president of Association for Past-life Research and Therapies. During its early issues he served on the Editorial Board of *The Journal of Regression Therapy* and submitted many valuable articles.

Chet B. Snow, Ph.D. is a clinical psychotherapist, professional historian, and international lecturer with degrees from Columbia University, the International Institute for Advanced Studies, and the Sorbonne in Paris. In the early 1980's he met and studied with Dr. Helen Wambach until her death. Their joint research lead to his writing *Mass Dreams of the Future*. Currently he is president of the Association for Past-life Research and Therapies and divides his time between the home of his French wife and Scottsdale, Arizona. In process is a second book discussing the spiritual aspects of predicted earth changes. He has been a valuable member of the Editorial Board of *The Journal of Regression Therapy* since its inception and for a number of years served as Associate Editor.

Joel L. Whitton, M.D. Ph.D. is a professor in the Department of Psychiatry, Faculty of Medicine, at the University of Toronto in Canada, and Adjunct Professor, Department of Graduate Studies, York University, Toronto. He teaches and does research in Neuropsychiatry at the University of Toronto and trains and supervises students and Candidates in psychotherapy at the Center for Training in Psychotherapy in Toronto. For many years he has given scope to his interest in research by designing and carrying out studies in the retrieval of past lives. His exploration of the interlife, which grew naturally out of hypnotic investigations of previous lives, has been documented in a book written with Joe Fisher titled *Life Between Life*, which has been translated into ten languages and published in 27 countries. Currently he is writing a sequel to this book. For many years he has served on the Editorial Board of *The Journal of Regression Therapy*.

Roger J. Woolger, Ph.D. is a graduate of the C.G. Jung Institute in Zurich and holds degrees in psychology, philosophy, and religion from Oxford and London Universities. He has practiced his own integration of Jungian analysis and past-life therapy for over 15 years, formerly in Vermont and currently in New Paltz, New York. A widely known teacher and author, he has taught on the faculties of the University of Vermont, Vassar College, and Concordia University in Montreal. His book *Other Lives, Other Selves* is a classic in the field. With Jennifer Woolger he later co-authored *The Goddess Within*. In addition to his private practice he presents experiential and training workshops in the United States and Europe. He has served on the Editorial Board of *The Journal of Regression Therapy* since its inception and has been a major contributor.

Chapter I

Regression to Prenatal and Birth Experiences

A surprising finding emerges from scanning an increasing number of birth and death experiences—birth is approached with far more reluctance than is death. Few patients find birth to be something they look forward to eagerly. The more common reaction is regret, reluctance, or even refusal. Birth in a sense promises blood, sweat, tears, and a ceaseless chain of choices.

Irene Hickman

In the pre- and perinatal areas everything the mother experiences, and through her the experiences of others, is recorded by the fetus without its knowing that the intensity of these feelings is in reality being experienced by mother and people around her. Thoughts and feelings by the mother and others both draw and reflect traumas from past lives of the fetus and at the same time aggravate these traumas by becoming attached to current feelings and thoughts of the fetus. Birth reinforces this attachment: almost all present problems are manifested there.

Tineke Noordegraaf
Rob Bontenbal

If we were locked into the patterns of emotion and thought that are set in place during our gestation, we would be prisoners of our history, controlled by a forgotten past. However, bringing our prebirth memories to consciousness through regression leads to a liberation from early negative experiences and to increased autonomy and freedom of choice. We can jettison our subconscious scripts. When the therapy is concluded, emotional limitations are lifted and the potential for personal fulfillment is increased.

Michael Gabriel

Bibliography

Chamberlain, David. *Babies Remember Birth.* Los Angeles, CA: Jeremy P. Tarcher, Inc., 1986.

Cheek, David. "Techniques for Eliciting Information Concerning Fetal Experience." Paper presented at the meeting of the Society for Clinical and Experimental Hypnosis, Los Angeles, California, 1977.

———. "Maladjustment Patterns Apparently Related to Imprinting at Birth." *The American Journal of Clinical Hypnosis,* Vol. 18, No. 2.

Findeisen, Barbara. Rescripting for Pre- and Perinatal and Early Childhood Regression Work." *The Journal of Regression Therapy,* Vol. III, No. 1, 1988.

Gabriel, Michael and Marie Gabriel. *Voices from the Womb.* Lower Lake, CA: Aslan Publishing, 1992.

Givens, Alice. "The Alice Givens Approach to Prenatal and Birth Therapy," *The Journal of Pre- and Perinatal Psychology,* Vol. 1, No. 3.

McGarey, Gladys T. *Born to Live.* Phoenix, AR: The Gabriel Press, 1980.

Orr, Leonard and Sandra Ray. *Rebirthing in the New Age.* Berkeley, CA: Celestial Arts, 1977.

Rank, Otto. *The Trauma of Birth* N.Y.: Robert Brunner Publishers, 1952.

Riley, Clara (Claire Etheridge). "The Emotional and Psychological Effects of Prenatal Physical Trauma." *The Journal of Pre- and Perinatal Psychology,* Vol. 1, No. 1, 1986.

———. "Transuterine Communication in Problem Pregnancies." *The Journal of Pre- and Perinatal Psychology,* Vol. 1, No. 3, 1987.

Turner, John Richard. "Birth, Life and More Life: Reactive Patterning Based on Prebirth Events." In P.G. Fedor-Freybergh and M. Voegel (eds). *Prenatal and Perinatal Psychology and Medicine.* Carnforth Parthenon Publishing, 1991.

Verney, Thomas. *The Secret Life of the Unborn Child.* New York: Delta Publishing Co., 1981.

Wambach, Helen. *Life Before Life.* New York: Bantam Books, 1979.

Watkins, Helen. "The Development of Ego States in the Fetus Following an Attempted Abortion: A Case Study." Paper presented at the meeting of the Society for Clinical and Experimental Hypnosis, Los Angeles, California, 1977.

———. "Treating the Trauma of Abortion," *The Journal of Pre- and Perinatal Psychology,* Vol. 1, No. 2, New York: Human Sciences Press

Regression to Prenatal and Birth Experiences

Introduction

Each individual experiences a plethora of emotional and physical events in his multiple lifetimes. The patterns that he is to work on in a current life make their initial imprint during the prenatal period and at birth. Scanning such patterns before they become covered with later events facilitates their transformation. However, many therapists who work skillfully with past lives fail to make use of uterine and birth experiences and do not see them as the clear-cut revelation of patterns that they are. They also do not make use of the potential of soul patterns to be transformed on any level—not just in past lives but also in prenatal and birth experiences or in early childhood.

Because the prenatal and birth states lie between past lives and current childhood, entry into them can be made from either direction—from childhood backward or from past lives forward. The continuous spectrum of experience is deepened as it is moved in either direction to expose additional levels of the pattern. Prenatal levels can also be contacted directly through an affect bridge or a body state.

Findeisen and Woolger often begin with the prenatal and birth states and move backward into other lifetimes that shed light on these experiences. Hickman starts with either past lives or childhood and moves the pattern into the prenatal state. Gabriel, Woolger and Noordegraaf and Bontenbal use the affect bridge, and Givens and Etheridge use various other bridges to go directly to prenatal memories. When I work with patients who are uncomfortable in altered states, I have them first unearth troubling childhood recollections and then move backward in prenatal exploration to find the earlier, often more starkly clear expression of the same pattern, extending the exploration to past lives if that is helpful.

Patients who assume that such memories are unavailable can be requested to "make up a story." They hesitate to describe their impressions because they are convinced that such impressions are invented, but making up a story enables them to risk sharing these. As in other forms of regression work, whether what is remembered is "true" remains unimportant as long as the energy field carrying the pattern is tapped and transformation and healing take place.

Just as therapists differ in their method of contacting prenatal and birth experiences—and sometimes use different approaches with different patients—they also vary in their procedures for exploring these. Most therapists use feeling states to expand and deepen such memories rather than depend on a cognitive approach. Transformational techniques range from simple recall (and usually repetition until the charge is decathected) to more involved techniques, such as rescripting and reframing. Givens, Hickman, and Woolger are convinced that, as is the case in past lives, traumatic experiences must be fully lived through on an emotional level in order for healing to occur. Findeisen and Gabriel often have a patient rescript a disastrous prenatal event or a difficult birth into a more positive experience, guiding the rescripting so that it moves under the direction of the Higher Self. Etheridge and I stress cognitive reframing to dissolve unproductive patterns and open the way for the creation of helpful ones.

Research into the prenatal period and birth has been more comprehensive than in any other area of regression work. Because such memories can often be validated, exploration of prenatal and birth memories has appeal for the researcher. Moreover, this research does not require such a stretching, or even disintegration, of one's belief system as do past lives. Thomas Verney and Stanislav Grof, who have explored this area, are already marginally credible to the professional community, and findings in most prenatal and birth work stretch only slightly the conceptions of psychoanalysis regarding the compulsive repetition of patterns. The difficult question as to what vehicle carries the memories of very early perceptions has as yet no generally accepted answer.

Freud suggested that the prenatal state was characterized by an "oceanic feeling of bliss" that invoked a wish to "return to the womb." Our contributors often discovered, on the contrary, patterns of distress that were later to emerge in childhood and that had been initiated in former lifetimes. Is a blissful womb experience a fantasy? Our current recovery of intra-uterine memories suggests that it is. We find, instead, early statements of rejection and trauma and difficult lessons that invite therapeutic exploration and transformation.

These scripts of anxiety and violence may be stamped into the personality of the fetus at any point during the nine months of gestation or while the child is being born. They may have many sources and leave deep gouges in the psyche. Some of them, such as acceptance or rejection of the sex of the child or an uncompleted abortion attempt, are considered unimportant and passed over lightly. Our material suggests, however, that unborn babies sense clearly whether they are wanted or not, whether their sex is acceptable, and that those who experience uncompleted abortion attempts go through violent emotional upset.

As we move into an understanding that the fetus is influenced by the thoughts and feelings of the mother and often takes them to be its own, we are confronted by the implication that the mother must take responsibility for what she thinks and feels during her pregnancy—an onerous extra burden on her during an already stressful time. We will not be able much longer to disregard the impact of the mother's feelings on the fetus by the comfortable assumption that such feelings have no effect, any more than we can now excuse child abuse, as many abusers formerly did, on the assumption that the child does not know what is happening and so what happens doesn't matter. There are far-reaching implications in current findings. We are obtaining extended knowledge of good and evil and are leaving our Eden of ignorance behind.

Induction into Prenatal and Birth Experience

This induction includes elements from several of the contributors in this section, with especial recognition to Barbara Findeisen.[1]

The Planning

You are planning this current lifetime, and with you are Guides who are helping you choose. Can you see them? What are they saying? Are you eager to come into this lifetime or are they urging you? What do you say to each other as you decide about this lifetime? It is at this time that you will be deciding on the lesson you wish to learn in this lifetime that will help you along on your soul journey. Do you decide on this lesson or do your Guides have some suggestions?

You need parents who will help you to learn this lesson. They won't necessarily be the ones who will make you feel the most comfortable or make your childhood the happiest, but you will choose them because they are good teachers for you, though undoubtedly you will grumble later when you have forgotten why you chose them. Why do you choose your mother? Have you known her in another lifetime? Why do you choose your father? Have you known him in another lifetime? And what about your siblings? Are you going to be a boy or a girl? Why?

You have something to say about your physical body sheath, though you will probably be limited by how you have treated your body in earlier lifetimes. What are your physical strengths and vulnerabilities going to be? How will they help you in your soul's journey? The choice of your body is important because your body is going to be your laboratory in which you learn to handle the energies of life. Nothing can take the place of this form of learning, so observe carefully what you choose for your body and why.

Prenatal Experience

Now you have made the choices and must leave the Light. It is hard, after you have garnered wisdom in other lifetimes, to have to be limited again by the body of a baby. Are you reluctant to do this or do you look forward to the chance to grow further? Where are you while this new sheath for your soul is forming? Are you inside it, aware of each cell as it presses forward to the completion of human form? Or do you hover outside, waiting until the last minute to take possession, perhaps joining your body only in the moment of birth?

What does your mother feel when she knows she is pregnant? Is she happy about you? Or is she frightened? Does she feel overwhelmed with all that is involved in having a child?

How does your father react when he learns your mother is pregnant? Is he happy? Or dismayed? Or perhaps overwhelmed, too, with the thought of so much responsibility?

Go through the stages of your growth in the uterus. Do you feel bonded with your mother? Are your parents happy together or do they argue? What is the emotional climate in which you begin this sojourn? Remember that you have chosen this way in order to learn as much as possible. If your mother is overwhelmed by her own pain and cannot spare any light for you, you will have to find love and light by your own strength alone, and perhaps that has something to do with the lesson you have chosen.

Now the new body is complete. If you have not entered it before or if you have only flitted in and out trying it out, now you must embrace it and go through the experience of forgetting all the lifetimes back of lifetimes which have been strung like pearls on your soul's necklace of experiences. Finally you are going to have only the here and now of your baby self. You have to win back all that you have previously experienced but have forgotten, slowly thinning out the fog of your forgetting.

Birth

The birth is beginning. It is a long journey.

Here the therapist works to uncover specific traumas in the stages of the birth process. These differ with each individual. Body work and breathing exercises are helpful in recovering the memories and experiences.

Finally you are born. What does your mother say? How does she respond to you? Do you feel wanted and cherished? Do you feel bonded with your mother? And if your father is there, how does he feel about you? Is it a safe world?

What patterns have you brought with you from your experiences in the uterus and from the birth process that both reflect the nature of your previous soul path in other lifetimes and set the pattern of what you will experience in this one?

Spend time tracing these patterns and core issues and tying in past-life, prenatal, birth, and current experiences.

Prenatal Regression Therapy

by

Michael Gabriel, M.A. and Marie Gabriel, M.P.A.

Introduction

Experiences *en utero* have profound and enduring consequences; they are intensely felt and become deeply imprinted. *En utero* we assimilate emotions and form patterns of response that set a direction for our lives and that initiate the basic pattern or scripts by which we function as adults.

To understand these critical formative experiences we must understand the unique nature of the prenatal infant. The unborn infant is completely surrounded by and unable to escape from, the emotional energy of his mother. He lives within her. She is his environment, his universe. Her physical and emotional state is experienced as his own—he has not developed a separate identity or ego to distinguish himself from her. This prenatal experience is all the more significant because it occurs before verbal skills, thought, or memory are developed. A client hypnotically regressed to the prenatal period realizes, "I am feeling what my mother is feeling. I am accepting my mother's emotions as my own." The infant's experience in the womb is joyous or traumatic, depending on the feeling he receives from his mother.

These experiences continue to impact the personality throughout life if there is no intervention, but it is possible to examine them in an altered state and reverse emotional patterns and attitudes that were formerly unrecognized and unconscious. Regression to the prenatal experience allows healing of such traumatic imprints to take place.

The Nature and Functioning of the Prenatal Infant

Extensive work in regression to the prenatal state has revealed these principles:

1. In the womb, we do not have a sense of self. We have not yet developed a separate identity or autonomy.

2. We are receptive, or reactive, to the emotions and energies of our mother, who constitutes the total physical environment in which we live. We do not initiate actions through the exercise of our will or personal determination.

3. We tend empathetically to absorb the mother's, and occasionally the father's, emotions.

4. We have little ability to distinguish between the feelings of others and our own feelings.

5. We are vulnerable to the parental emotions that encompass us. We have no way to escape or distance ourselves from emotions that we find unpleasant or threatening. We are not able to define the emotions as good or bad, desirable or undesirable. We have no psychological skills for deflecting, containing, modifying, or releasing negative emotions.

6. We have little sense of time or the process of change. We do not recognize that experiences change, cease, or are replaced by other experiences. The present moment, whether joyous or painful, seems eternal.

7. Within our limited capacities we adapt to the prenatal environment. Our emotions, attitudes, self-esteem, and self-expression are given definition by these adaptions to our prenatal experience, and following birth our psychological development is strongly influenced by them. The prenatal experience propels life in a particular direction.

Psychological Adaptions during Gestation

Because the prenatal infant feels with intensity but lacks defenses and methods of escape, he is forced to try to deal with the pressure of the emotions and conditions encompassing him. He does so by making a psychological adjustment to the situation in a way that enables him to deal with the conditions and energies within the womb, especially his mother's emotional energies. The adaptation chosen will often define the emotional patterning and personality development that follows birth. Such an adaptation becomes generalized as a way of responding to life's problems.

As the infant matures into adulthood, he develops a more complex personality, a defined structure for responding to life experiences and initiating actions. He becomes more individualized and develops a sense of identity. Nevertheless, he frequently retains at his core the primal emotions associated with the intense experiences felt while in the womb. Experiences that he was unable to assimilate there become reference points for subsequent behavior, and as long as these habitual patterns remain unexamined and unevaluated, they continue to influence the life of the adult.

There are five significant patterns of prenatal adaptation:

Becoming self-reliant

This is an adaption made by some prenatal infants who have not received nurturing from their mother and lack the feeling of being protected by her. They take responsibility for themselves, even to the extent that sometimes they become aggressively self-reliant. These infants lack a feeling of living in a supportive, caring world and strive to confront life through their own efforts.

Assuming responsibility for parents

Other unborn infants, prompted by empathy, adapt by taking responsibility for their distressed or burdened parent(s) and making an inner commitment to assist them. On a more subtle level, the infant is also prompted by his survival instinct, since he needs his parents in order to survive. Often these infants feel a sense of guilt for burdening the parents.

After birth some infants actively help their parents by supporting them emotionally and trying to ease their distress. Others, more passive, become "good children"; they are well-behaved and avoid causing trouble. The pattern carries into adulthood where these people seek out others, often partners, in order to "rescue" them.

Withdrawing from life into safety

Some infants adopt an opposite resolution and withdraw from their parents and life into inner isolation, separating themselves from the emotional currents of the family. Although they succeed in avoiding distressing emotions, they cut themselves off from the positive emotions of love, nurturance, and belonging. These infants become adults who live in their minds and are poorly connected with the life energies of the body, energies such as love, expressiveness, sexuality, creativity. For them, the world of emotions and feelings is threatening; and often without even knowing or fully registering that they are doing so, they live deprived of loving, nurturing relationships.

Selective response

A fourth response consists of rejecting the specific source of the prenatal infant's pain. The infant may reject the unloving mother and form an emotional alliance with the father. Later, this rejection generalizes into a distrust of all women and disconnection from them.

Compensatory response

When conditions in the womb are difficult, the unborn infant may adapt by making a compensatory response, such as determining to maintain a forward-moving, extroverted energy rather than becoming closed down or introverted. Those who have adapted in this way often strive to earn good grades in school; later they seek recognition through professional status. A fragile self-esteem underlies their drive for achievement, and their feeling of worth, since it is dependent upon success, is conditional.

There are other forms of compensation. If a prenatal infant is not of the desired gender, that infant may compensate by developing the kind of personality his parents desire in their child. A girl, whose parents would have preferred a boy, may become a tomboy.

Therapeutic Processes for Healing Prenatal Trauma

If we were locked into the patterns of emotion and thought that are set in place during our gestation, we would be prisoners of our history, controlled by a forgotten past. However, bringing our prebirth memories to consciousness through regression leads to a liberation from early negative experiences and to increased autonomy and freedom of choice. We can jettison our subconscious scripts. When the therapy is concluded, emotional limitations are lifted and the potential for personal fulfillment is increased.

There are four steps for resolving prenatal wounds and changing the consequent behavior patterns.

Recall of pertinent experiences

In this process, the adult examines his early patterns, including those that were present before and during birth. This review brings out of obscurity hidden but highly influential formative experiences. It gives words to situations for which the infant could have no words, allowing these situations to be clearly recognized, understood, and evaluated by the adult mind.

Reframing: educating the infant within

In reframing, events are reinterpreted by applying adult understanding and insight to them. The regression process teaches the adult-self to view family dynamics more comprehensively and to develop a more accurate understanding of the motives, psychology, and interactions of the family members.

The adult-self speaks to and forms a relationship with the emotionally centered prenatal infant-self. The adult's ability to convey logical information to the infant has limitations similar to those encountered when an attempt is made to educate a four-year-old child to the meaning of divorce. However, because the presence, energy, feelings, and understanding of the adult can affect the prenatal infant-self, a door is opened to an effective resolution of the infant's emotional distress.

Releasing emotions

Putting emotions into words helps to relieve them and re-living and understanding early experiences release feelings of anger, protectiveness, shame, hostility, vulnerability, hurt, inadequacy, and blame. We become neutral and give up emotional alliances and attachments.

Rescripting

With the release of the limiting biases, the client becomes free to re-experience his history in the light of a new, more adult perception of the situation and to build a new personal psychology. Rescripting allows the emotional and thought patterns to be restructured. The client is provided with alternative responses to the pattern that has been repeated throughout his life.

Rescripting Techniques

Experiencing gestation as the child of "ideal parents"

The infant is given the experience of being free of the original birth parents, with whom he associates detrimental influences. He experiences a gestation surrounded in love and nurtured and validated by "ideal" parents (imagined parents who fully appreciate and support him). He traverses each month of the gestation and then matures through childhood, adolescence, and adulthood in a positive interaction with these ideal parents. He is given the opportunity to feel that he is trustful, open, adventuresome, and loved by others, experiencing a positive sense of life and relating that models his later development. Most clients are able to experience this supportive environment and to envision living in a more vital way in alignment with their intrinsic soul energies.

Experiencing the gestation and full expression of the underlying love the parents held for their unborn infant and for each other

Though parents love their infants, they often fail to express the full measure of their love. Psychological limitations such as fear, hurt, a sense of unworthiness, and strict ideals about how life should be lived often restrict the way parents express their love for each other and for their infant. Rescripting is designed to bypass such limitations. In this process the parents and children live out the true, often powerful underlying love within the family, the love that created the marriage and family and that enables the infant to feel that he is part of a loving family group. The infant, when he is in touch with this underlying truth, becomes able to experience the environment of the womb as nurturing. Some clients become more open to this experience after they have healed some of their hurt through the process of "ideal parents."

Separating from the parents' identity and emotions

This process, the opposite of the one just described, is used to rescue the prenatal infant from parents who feel ill will toward it. The client cuts the psychic cords to his parents. This allows him to recognize and claim himself as a separate identity with his own intrinsic qualities and potential. In this process he visualizes and experiences in detail his development and maturation in a different context.

Re-living the prenatal experience while accompanied by one's own adult self, an adult friend, or a spiritual guide

In this therapeutic process the infant-self is guided through early life experiences by the more mature and knowledgeable adult-self. The adult speaks to the prenatal infant-self still present within him and becomes an empathetic, loving adult to the inner child. The infant then feels a supportive presence and experiences the benefits of developing in a secure environment, and he matures through the stages of life with this feeling of support. The "infant-within" is experienced as a psychic entity with his own ways of responding and his own pattern of development. As the relationship continues, the infant-within no longer feels isolated but is safe enough fully to express himself.

In a variation of this process, the infant allies with a "friend" or with a guardian angel or guide, rather than with the adult-self. This variation is useful when the client is identified with his child-self and, since he has little confidence in his own adult functioning, is not able to be an effective adult role model to his inner child.

Re-living the prenatal experience from the level of one's own spiritual identity

This can be done by bringing into the womb the light and energy of the spiritual dimension in which we live before incarnating—where we experience wholeness, peace, and unity. Keeping the consciousness aware that there is a spiritual home allows the client to feel less vulnerable while re-living the gestation.

A slightly different process brings the client back to the point of being a spirit who has not yet taken a body. He can then re-live the prenatal experience with an awareness of being this spirit, maintaining connection with the spiritual Self and keeping an awareness of his intrinsic identity.

Bringing light energy into the wounded area of one's self

This process involves imaging healing light being brought into the area of one's being that feels wounded and bringing about healing through the subtle energy of the light. The wound can be experienced as emotional, physical, or psychic. Even though it may not be identified as part of the physical body, such a wound can be sensed.

Case 1. Anna's Prenatal Adaptation

The following case study provides an example of how one client made an adaptation by taking responsibility for her parents. Anna's presenting problem was her feeling of being overburdened yet unable effectively to change her life. She was not happy in her marriage and said that her husband of 20 years required that she alone be responsible for all the family duties, including the care of their four children. She did so but resented it. The same pattern was manifested at her job. Because of her feeling of responsibility for the effectiveness of the program she co-directed, she worked extra unpaid hours. In neither situation did her discontent result in her taking action to effect a change.

We first spent some sessions investigating her fear that some harm would befall one of her children. In a hypnotic regression Anna traced this feeling of nervousness and fear back to her experiences *en utero:*

P: *I am completely engulfed in darkness and feeling so nervous that I'm just about ready to die. I just want it to go away. I don't know what it is.*

T: *Let's have you trace that feeling back to its origin.*

P: *I'm getting a figure of a fetus. There's a lot of darkness around it....*

She reported that her mother felt happy in the early part of the pregnancy, but about the eighth month, the situation changed.

P: *Things get more burdened. The pregnancy gets hard on her. It's harder and harder for her to keep going.*

T: *Why is that?*

P: *Because something's going wrong physically. Her body's getting sick. My being there is affecting my mother's health. My poisons are taking over.*

T: *Your poisons are taking over?*

P: *Poisons from the womb. (Toxemia.) She's getting really weak, like maybe she'll die. I can't do anything about it! I'm just paralyzed. My being here is creating more problems. So they've got to think of a way to get me out of here. It seems very frantic and desperate.*

T: *And then what happens?*

P: *They take her to the hospital. There are needles and IV's and machines.*

T: *And what do you experience while this is going on?*

P: *It's my fault. I shouldn't have come here. I have to hurry up and be born, but I don't want to. I just have to wait until they do something. All I know is if I don't get born, she's going to get worse.*

T: *Then what happens?*

P: *They come in and pull me out with instruments and hands. I don't like it! It's cold and impersonal and I resent it. I'm mad at them. They just do what they want to me, and I don't like it. I just feel resentful and helpless.*

Anna felt guilt: "My poisons are taking over.... It's my fault." Her prenatal adaptation was to take responsibility for her mother's condition. Yet she felt powerless to change the situation: "I just have to wait until they do something." Her current life pattern of *feeling responsible yet powerless to change her circumstances* was coming into focus. As an adult she continued to repeat the pattern of this stressful experience *en utero*.

We investigated Anna's experience after birth. Her pain and helplessness were exacerbated.

P: *I'm so alone. Everyone is taking care of my mom, but no one is taking care of me. My mom is just lying there; she doesn't know what's going on. I'm wanting to be close to my mother.*

Anna was affected by her parents' interaction with each other after her birth and this intensified her adaptation:

> P: *I feel a lot of nervousness. It has to do with my father. He's worried about my mother because she's older (age 45). He feels that it was too much for her to have me because she almost died, and now he feels I'm going to be too much for her to deal with.*
>
> T: *When he becomes very concerned for her, how does she respond?*
>
> P: *By feeling nervous and anxious and trying to be strong so that she can prove it's okay. She's afraid he'll get upset or mad if she can't handle it. She feels worn out, but she can't let anyone know.*
>
> T: *So he's concerned for her, but she feels burdened by him. How does this affect you?*
>
> P: *I'm feeling like I have to be really cute and happy, keep everybody in balance. I'm trying to prove to my father that it is okay. I feel so responsible. I can't rely on anyone else, or expect anyone else to take care of me. I may want that, but I need to be independent and strong so I don't put any burdens on my father and mother.*

Throughout the regression we hear Anna's theme: "I feel so responsible." Her adaptation to both the prenatal and post-birth periods provided clear parallels to her life situation when she came into treatment. She felt overburdened with responsibility for her family and her job. She built up resentment, yet felt helpless and victimized, unable to change her situation.

Anna's subsequent therapy took place in stages. After recovering the prenatal and birth experiences she rescripted them so that she no longer felt responsible for her mother's toxemia, which she came to realize resulted from her mother's carelessness about diet and general health needs during pregnancy. She became able to visualize herself interacting with her family members in a more balanced way and without feeling an inappropriate sense of responsibility. She later went back to the spiritual dimension and identified herself as a whole and complete being. Currently, she is able to maintain boundaries between herself and the energies of those around her, including her mother. She has come into a comfortable sense of her own identity.

Case 2. Jane's Birth Experience

Jane's traumatic birth experience, during which she experienced stark terror, led to a misunderstanding that colored her entire life. She described what had started out as a normal birth:

> P: *I feel pressure like waves. I'm being pushed real hard, and I'm in the middle of all this confusion.*
>
> T: *Okay, let's move you forward a bit. What's happening now?*

P: *The nurse is near my mother. The nurse is telling her something. She's tying my mother's legs together with some kind of strap.*

T: *Why does she tie your mother's legs together?*

P: *The doctor is not here.... He was told he would not be needed until later. The nurse is panicked—the birth is coming too soon!*

T: *Breathe deeply now.... That's it.*

P: *I'm feeling an incredible pressure, but I'm stuck here. I feel like I'm being crushed. I am caught in the birth canal and can't get out! The feeling of being closed in is horrible! A rush of anger comes from my mother. (Pause.) I'm getting angry! How could she do this to me? I feel anger and panic all mixed together. Am I going to die? Maybe she doesn't want me. (Jane begins crying intensely.)*

T: *Can you go on? What happens next?*

P: *Now its changing...it's better, easing up...a different kind of pressure. The doctor is here. I'm moving now. I'm not going to die! At last I am born!*

    After I get born, I feel a great outpouring of love from my mother, but it confuses me—she was angry at me and didn't want me. How can I trust her? I want to love her, but I also want to punish her. I'm angry about what happened.

Jane recognized in this session that the claustrophobia she had experienced throughout her life, the sudden fear she felt whenever she found herself in a small enclosure, was a direct consequence of her experience while in the birth canal. She was repeatedly playing out the terror of being confined in the birth canal and dying there. She was also hypersensitive to being slighted or disliked by others. If her own mother didn't want her and was even trying to harm her, which was her assumption during the traumatic birth, why would anyone else care for her?

The first regression had been an intense and emotional one, but Jane's second re-living was easier for her because she had released some of her emotion during the earlier recall, and this time she was able to experience her birth more objectively.

T: *Now move ahead to the time when your mother's legs were strapped together by the nurse.*

P: *The nurse had told the doctor that he wasn't needed until later, so she became frantic when the birth started going fast. So she ties my mother's legs together. My mother is panicking. She doesn't know what to do, and she is very distressed. My mother is furious.*

T: *Breathe deeply, feel her anger, feel whom the anger is directed toward.*

P: *She's angry at the nurse! My mother really fears harm toward me. I assumed that her anger at the nurse was anger toward me. That was a serious mistake.*

This case illustrates the four processes I use for resolving prenatal wounds. Jane was able to *recall* her difficult birth experience, including her intense fear of death and her anger because she thought that her mother intended to harm her. She saw how those emotions had influenced her life. She was then able to *release* some of the emotional "charge" that had accumulated around her birth by bringing the birth into conscious awareness and re-living it. Once she had re-experienced her birth, she was able to go back, view her birth more objectively, and *reframe* it, using adult understanding and evaluation to interpret her experience. She was able to recognize that as an unborn infant she had misinterpreted the situation—the anger her mother felt had been directed not toward her but toward the nurse—and this misinterpretation had had significant consequences.

This revelation allowed for *rescripting*: Jane re-experienced and re-lived her birth in the light of what had actually happened. She reconnected with her mother's deep love for her and felt a sense of completion. "I am connecting with her basic unqualified love for me. I know I am wanted," she concluded, and as she said this, she released a deep level of her hurt. In subsequent sessions she intensified this positive pattern and became able to remain connected with her mother's love for her as she progressed through her prenatal experiences, birth, and childhood.

Rescripting processes can lead to more effective modes of behavior. Active imagination and mental imagery are able to imprint a new and positive image of the prebirth experience and establish a different emotional tone to replace the negative qualities of the original experience. These techniques make use of the client's inner potential for wholeness and integration and provide affirmative life-giving energy.

Case 3. Dora Releases Her Inferiority

Dora received two intertwined messages from her mother during her impressionable prenatal period—the message "I love you" and the message her mother was in actuality saying of herself, "I'm not good enough." Dora took her mother's self-hatred and absorbed it as her own. She feared that if she let go of her self-disparagement, she would also be letting go of her mother's love. I pointed out that the two messages need not be joined, that her mother's sense of inferiority and insufficiency were not connected with her love for her child. Dora recognized that she needed to go back to gestation and incorporate that understanding as a body experience.

Because Dora had expressed enthusiasm over returning to the spiritual dimension in which she had existed prior to incarnation I decided to use the rescripting technique of re-living the prenatal experience from the level of her own spiritual identity. "I can't wait to learn all the things I'm supposed to be learning. I have a voracious appetite for that. I feel tremendous zeal for this life," Dora told me.

I directed Dora back to the prior dimension where she had existed before she came into her body, and from there she progressed to her experience *en utero*. She reported that at the beginning of her gestation she was clear of her mother's mixed message about love and self-hatred.

P: *The message was zinging around me, but I wasn't yet absorbing it.*
T: *Who were you before you started to absorb that?*
P: *I'm too busy growing and developing to be aware of anything else; all I'm doing is dividing cells like mad.*
T: *And who is the spirit in the cells that are dividing?*
P: *I get a very loving, whole spirit.*
T: *Why don't you rest in that for a few minutes. Just be your spirit before you get all enmeshed in the physical.*
P: *I am open and eager and loving, really excited about coming into this life. Very loving.*
T: *Very loving and not feeling inferior?*
P: *No, I don't have any sense of that inferior feeling at all!*
T: *Now experience what it feels like to be loving without being inferior.*
P: *It's a new sensation. There's a lot of strength there! I'm feeling whole and complete.*

Dora was able to rescript her prenatal period, re-living her entire gestation with a sense of being a whole, complete, and loving spiritual being. By recognizing that her mother's inferiority was not her own and by becoming more aligned with her spiritual identity, Dora changed her feelings of inferiority to feelings of self-appreciation.

As therapists we seek to assist our patients to release the constraints of fear, guilt, anger, blame, poor self-esteem, and excessive responsibility so that they can fulfill their potential for love and creative expression. We reinforce the fundamental life energy that is seeking to be manifested. The rescripting process allows the client, by using active imagination, to live through distressing experiences in a way that is optimal for him. It is important to reinforce new patterns by repetition so that they can replace outgrown patterns.

Rescripting in the prenatal state transcends the limitations of our personal psychology and expresses the longing of our spirit to engage harmoniously with our parents, with whom we have a soul connection and whom we love. Through expressing this higher level of spiritual truth and union, healing can take place. We then allow the power of who we are as spiritual beings to become dominant in our lives. In physical form we strive to be the radiant spirits and immortal beings that we truly are.

Prenatal and Birth Reprogramming

by

Alice Givens, Ph.D.

Introduction

The embryonic and fetal stages of life demonstrate that there is a part of us that records all of our experience from the instant of conception through our birth and beyond. It is recorded as if Mother's experience is our own. The words, feelings, and events of Mother's life are stored in the unconscious awareness and accepted without censorship. There is no conscious awareness in the fetal state of life that is able to make judgments on the validity of beliefs or conclusions to accept them or reject them. All is accepted as fact and as a basis for living.

Words are recorded in the prenatal state when the unconscious does not know that words exist or that they have any meaning, but there is no doubt that the words are recorded and can be reproduced at a later date. The fetus records the mother's feelings, thoughts, and words, as well as the words that Mother hears or reads. All of her experience becomes the experience of the child. The fetus can also hear voices and sounds from outside Mother's body, and these words are recorded but do not have meaning until after the child becomes verbal.

Early psychoanalysts viewed the prenatal period as limitless passive bliss, but my work suggests that the prenatal is often a time of pain and trauma because in pregnancy the tiny fetus shares Mother's body pain and experience. Mother thinks and worries about the responsibility of the baby growing within her, and when the baby isn't wanted because of lack of money or for other reasons, there can be extreme pain to mother and baby. The mother may attempt to abort the developing child. Even before birth the tiny personality suffers the extreme trauma that accompanies being a member of the human species.

Mother's habitual feelings of fear, anxiety, anger, depression, or of satisfaction and well-being, have programmed her child from the instant of conception. A depressed or fearful toddler can continue the programming of its prenatal time; if an adult is chronically depressed and suffering, it is invariably found that the same feeling has dominated the prenatal period.

Traumatic events, such as attempted abortion, that have occurred during pregnancy, have a lasting effect. Expectant mothers may try a variety of methods to abort their babies—by ingesting various medications and herbs, by exhausting themselves through running, working, shoveling, or sitting in hot baths, and by inserting sharp instruments into their uterus. These attempts often fail without the mother being aware that her thoughts and feelings are recorded in the unconscious mind of the fetus. Mother has increased her own stress by adding guilt and shame to her fear and dread, and her desperation and anguish, in addition to the physical trauma, affect the fetus. In this kind of prenatal period there is only pain, anger, violence, and physical trauma: that the fetus survives is miraculous.

If Mother has a chronic physical illness or any serious maladies, they affect and program her unborn child. Often this influence continues after birth, but the strongest messages occur during the prenatal and birth experiences because there is no escape from them. The fetus feels Mother's illness and pain and physical discomfort, as well as her pain during birth, as if it were its own.

Attitudes about the body in our Western culture have strongly influenced our thinking about pregnancy and childbirth. As a result of the advent of the technological age and the development of modern medicine, the human being has come to be viewed as a machine, and doctors have been demoted to the role of mechanics who cut the body, repair it properly, and inject the right chemicals into it to enable it to function smoothly. Until recently, the existence of a consciousness in relation to our organs or our illness was not seriously considered by the medical profession, and if the conscious and unconscious minds of adults were not recognized, there could certainly be no belief in the unconscious memories of children, infants, and of the fetus and embryo.

Prenatal and delivery room practices have ignored the needs of the infant and its reaction to the effects of the position of the mother, the lights, medications, anesthetic, and surgical procedures. Women giving birth in a hospital have had to give up their dignity and autonomy. They have been forced to obey the decisions and rules of medical personnel or be considered "difficult." The infant in the mother's body has not been perceived as a real baby until it emerges into open space and is seen, heard, and felt as a separate entity. After that, treatment of the fetus and newly born infant focuses on maintenance and ignores the more comprehensive welfare of the baby and mother. Demands of enlightened women who are aware of the inappropriateness of this approach are changing these practices.

Under all emotions and attitudes—anger, depression, futility, indifference, confusion—we find fear. If we dig down through the confusion, the illusions and the delusions, the sadness and despair, the desperate need for control, the anger and rage, fear emerges, and, if the emotional impact has been particularly serious, we may find stark terror. When intense fear is chronic in a patient, I usually find that it has begun in the prenatal period with Mother's fear (or even further back in other lifetimes, with a restatement of the fear pattern in the pre-natal state and a further replication in the birth process). I look for this early statement of the fear pattern in these months before birth and often find it continued and amplified in the delivery room, where it can be Mother's fear or can come from medical personnel.

This fear, that lies at the bottom of every kind of psychological problem and of many physical illnesses, is especially evident in the birth process. Birth is a time in which physical symptoms and body ailments become locked in. Many sinus, throat, and breathing problems originate there. The cone for ether or gas that is so often put over Mother's face produces a feeling of suffocation or of dying. The words in her mind that are recorded with the infant are, "I can't breathe. I'm dying." Then, if there are long delays in birth or if there are umbilical cord complications, the baby has feelings of suffocation and death. The breathing difficulties at the moment of birth are often reinforced by the words of the medical personnel: "He's not breathing." "She can't breathe." "Help her breathe."

It is important to know that a large portion of the anxiety and pain that characterize some patients may have originally belonged to someone else. It is difficult to release a feeling that was someone else's until it is recognized as not being one's own. Anger, rage, fear, and guilt were often originally Mother's or Father's. The infant, the toddler, and most especially the fetus, internalized it as its own because it possessed no critical faculty to recognize the feelings as belonging to someone else. An infant accepts the crying or screaming of others as its own crying or screaming. The arm that touches it is its own. Mother's throat crying is its own throat. Before birth, mother's body is its body: they are one and the same. The same identification is made with the people attending the birth. If a crisis occurs and the nurse and doctor feel fear and panic, then it becomes the baby's fear and panic. In childhood, this is to some extent true, also, and the younger the child, the greater is the acceptance of someone else's feelings as its own.

The fact that we have internalized other people's feelings and beliefs is extremely important in regression therapy. It is necessary to be back in the scene where the feelings and hypnotic beliefs originated and feel how they were internalized. A patient re-living his birth needs to recognize, for instance, that the terror he is feeling is actually coming from the words of the nurse in the delivery room. The nurse might be saying, "Help me! He can't breathe! Hurry up!" Her crisis is added to the infant's body feelings. By repeating her words and expressing his own fear, the patient diminishes the energy of the fear.

Many serious problems stem back to survival issues or what were felt as survival issues in Mother's body and during birth. Mother may think, "If I have this baby, I'll die.... Somebody come and help me.... They'll never help me." Feelings of suffocation and extreme pain in birth are matters of life and death to the baby, also, who has taken on Mother's feeling. In the unconscious mind paralyzing fear goes back to a terror as great as that of ceasing to exist. Though later at birth some protective process shuts off the memory of prenatal life and past lives from our conscious awareness, the fear, the rage, and the frustration remain and must eventually be recognized, re-experienced, and dealt with.

The etiology of fear may be found on any level of soul activity but the experiences in the prenatal and birth processes most often pinpoint the problem. The information, feelings, and body pain of these periods are stored up or taped into our unconscious minds in the same way that they are implanted on past lives and childhood. These unresolved feelings from past experiences *en utero* or in the birth process are stimulated into repetition by later incidents because the problems have not been resolved and because we must keep trying to obey directives from an unconscious past that keeps giving us inappropriate signals. Present-day problems often cannot be resolved unless we go into this archaic material.

Identical methods are used to recover prenatal memories and to re-live a birth. The patient is directed to a specific feeling or event, such as the hardest contraction in the birth or the prenatal time when hopelessness was most intense, depending on the present feeling experienced by the patient. The patient is asked to repeat the words, then is directed on to the next words. Saying the words until the feeling is depleted is a necessary part of therapy. The objective of going back to the beginning of this life is to release the trauma, and words are often what have locked that trauma in place.

The more extreme the psychic or physical pain in the prenatal period and birth, the more difficult it is to get the patient to break through the barrier or the protection set up by the unconscious mind. It can be the prenatal period that is most painful, particularly in cases where the mother is unmarried or the father is abusive. However, the most difficult suffering seems to occur during birth, and this is hardest to reach, often because of the physical trauma that was set up by past medical practices, including the administration of an anesthetic such as ether that triggered Mother's fear of death when the mask was put on her face. The medical trauma of birth, combined with Mother's fear of loss of control and her helplessness, can cause the feeling to be so painful that it requires a number of therapy sessions to work through it.

The retrieval of such material is difficult because, when directed back to the source of the fear, our minds automatically try to evade it in order to avoid the pain that goes with feeling it. Sometimes the pain becomes so great that we block it out by seeing everything as grey or black or blank. In such a case we may skip over the trauma of fear and place ourselves in a later incident. In other cases the pain becomes so great that we may go into a state of catatonia that resembles unconsciousness—the brain has its own anesthesia when the suffering becomes too great to be borne. In order to circumvent all the methods the mind has of avoiding pain and terror, the therapist must identify the trauma and recognize when the patient is in danger of going blank or becoming catatonic because the pain is too great. The event must be put into context and related to current behavior and feelings by repeating all the words that were said or felt in the past. The words must be said in first person, present tense, in order for the fear and pain to be re-lived. It is essential to take the patient through the trauma of fear over and over until the frightening incident can be viewed without anxiety.

Fear and pain must be thoroughly re-lived and felt. Even knowing that current panic originates in the past doesn't take care of it. We cannot resolve the issues relating to fear with the cognitive, analytical, and critical part of the mind, and there is no simple way of getting rid of it, such as analyzing it or going into meditation. In order to resolve fears that prevent people from working or relating, creating or having fun, it is necessary to go back and feel the pain and yell through it. To weaken and remove the overwhelming power of fear, we must go back to its source, re-experience it, feel it, and define it by putting it in its proper context. With therapeutic help patients can recognize that their pain may have come from others and that *they have no obligation to keep it.*

In dealing with feelings or trauma, I use the terms "giving it up," "releasing it," "letting it go." This is not a magical or mysterious process. Releasing the trauma, or giving it up, occurs as a result of re-living the incident. Trauma that is stored in the unconscious mind contains energy, and as it is re-lived and expressed in regression therapy, the energy is released, whether it relates to childhood, infancy, or to prenatal and birth memories. Such traumatic experiences usually need to be experienced or re-lived two or three times. Feelings are expressed by crying, screaming, saying all the words that the trauma would say if it were talking. The client knows when the feeling is expressed and no more is there. The release of trauma can be observed by the therapist as the words are repeated and the feeling diminishes. The repetition of words until the feeling that is bound into them is depleted releases the tension in the patient's body.

The patient needs to go back to the experience with a trusted, skilled person because the unconscious mind will allow the experience into awareness only under conditions that it perceives as safe. A requirement for success is the therapist's conviction that it is possible to release disturbing emotions by re-living them. His or her attitude must say, "I know that experience is there, and you will go directly to it." These words are not necessarily spoken, but the method and the messages given convey that kind of certainty. In addition, the therapist needs to have worked through the trauma and pain in his/her own life, in prenatal and birth as well as the rest of life. There can be no expectation of the patient going into prenatal experience unless the person leading him into it has felt the experience personally. If we evade our own trauma, we cannot expect to lead others through theirs.

Following are assumptions regarding the prenatal period:

1. The embryo is an individual person from the moment of conception.

2. The fetus sees, hears, tastes, and feels months before birth.

3. The basic foundation for personality is shaped *en utero*. The fetus feels Mother's feelings and records all of Mother's experiences as its own.

4. Because the fetus feels Mother's feelings, it is affected by Mother's body discomfort as well as Mother's emotions.

5. Temporary pain or anxiety has no lasting effect upon the unborn child's personality; however, Mother's serious and chronic body problem, or chronic anxiety, panic, anger, and depression, do have lasting effects, damaging the child's physical and emotion health for all of life.

6. Father, and the whole family system, have a significant effect on the unborn child as a result of the effect on Mother.

7. There is evidence that the fetus learns in utero; however, the important learning for this tiny one is that which affects physical and emotional health. For this reason, the health of the marriage partnership between Mother and Father is most vital.

Case 1. Origin of Ongoing Depression and Nausea

Symptoms such as nausea and depression, like other chronic feelings or body conditions, can be traced to a prenatal origin. Breathing and throat problems often stem back to the birth experience. Fatigue and weakness, back and neck problems, and chronic pain will be found in Mother's experience in her pregnancy, as well as in the birth. All is recorded in the unconscious mind of the infant, and bringing this material into awareness begins the release of it. The repetition of the words and the feelings lets it go forever.

When Ernest first came to see me because of depression he sat slumped over, staring at the floor, and I could barely hear his words. Going to work had become an impossible task for him. He must have once been a handsome young man, but he had changed. Now there was a dark stubble of whiskers on his face, and he was so thin his bones stuck out. Continuously nauseous, he had trouble eating and holding food down, and he slept very little. Both he and his family felt hopeless about his condition. He had been hospitalized several times, but extensive tests had revealed no reason for either his nausea or his depression.

Though Ernest had little understanding of the nature of psychotherapy, he was willing to talk openly about his life. He told me how his father and mother had both worked and he and his brothers had had heavy responsibilities. Father often became drunk and during those times would whip the boys, so Ernest would hide under his bed or in his closet. In spite of the cruel details of his childhood home life, he insisted that he loved his parents. In one breath he said what he thought he should feel and that he loved his parents, but in the next breath he described the reality as it actually had been in an angry, cruel, and frightening home.

His father's death six months before his first psychotherapy appointment had immediately preceded the beginning of his depression. He was aware that he was going through the same thing that his father had experienced and that in a sense he had taken over his father's life, and I agreed that his father's death had increased his earlier problems. Our task was to go back and find the origin of these problems and then determine why Father's death had suddenly made them insurmountable. There must also be some reason in the past why Ernest's stress took the form of nausea and eating problems. In other clients, depression caused headaches, neck pain, chronic back problems, and numerous other physical reactions, but Ernest's symptom was nausea. I suspected that the original programming for this problem would lie in the prenatal, since this is true for almost all chronic, stress-related body complaints.

I listened to a description of his feelings and then, after telling him to lie down and close his eyes, sent him back with a repetition of his own words.

> T: *Ernest, you're back in your mother's body now during the nine months before you were born. Sometime during that nine-month period your mother felt the same way you do now. She feels so sick and depressed that she wants to die. Say the first words that come to you.*
>
> P: *(Lies silently.)*
>
> T: *(Repeating.) She feels so sick and depressed that she wants to die. Say the first words that come to you.*
>
> P: *I have a headache and my stomach hurts...I'm so tired of throwing up.*
>
> T: *Go on, Ernest, and say the next words. All of Mother's thoughts are recorded in your mind.*
>
> P: *I feel sick and nervous...why did I have to get pregnant again?... It's too much...I can't eat anything...(leaning over, vomiting) Oh, how awful I feel...this nausea will never end...sick, sick, sick, how can I live? I want to die.*

He was saying the same words with which I had sent him back to the prenatal, so I had him repeat them until the emotion was gone and the feelings of sickness and despair were released. He had been programmed from the beginning to respond to stress with nausea. (Most women have sick feelings in the stomach during several weeks of pregnancy. However, few have them for the whole nine months.)

We now needed to ascertain why his reaction to his father's death had started the depression and sick feelings. We talked about his childhood and went back into several scenes where Father had been drunk and had beat him. Ernest was unable to express any anger over this and became even more depressed. But finally, after crying and talking about his father, he finally gave a clue to the aetiology of the sudden depression.

P: *It's my fault he died.*
T: *Were you with him when he died?*
P: *No. I was there the night before. He was terribly sick. (Staring at the floor as he speaks.)*
T: *Did you know he was going to die?*
P: *The doctor told us he would go soon.*
T: *What happened, Ernest, that makes you say that you killed him?*
P: *(Crying again so that he can hardly speak.) The night before he died, the last time I saw him, I took him a marijuana cigarette to smoke because I thought it would relax him. He had had some strokes and couldn't speak or move on one side of his body. I held the cigarette for him. I thought it might give him an hour or so of good feeling.*
T: *Did it help him that night?*
P: *He seemed to feel better for a while.*
T: *What makes you think you killed him?*
P: *My sister said the marijuana killed him.*
T: *Ernest, the truth is that the marijuana probably did relax him for a while, but it had nothing to do with his death. Your sister was speaking in ignorance. Go and talk to your doctor about it. I'm not a medical expert, so I cannot give you medical advice but only an opinion.*

Ernest left that day planning to talk to his medical doctor about giving his father marijuana before his death. But we were not at the source of his depression, which stemmed from intense fear and anger at his father, both in childhood and throughout his life. The fear and anger were overlaid with guilt, which came from prenatal messages and from the final incident of his father's death.

When Ernest returned the next week, he felt a little better because the medical doctor had verified my opinion. However, I knew there was still more work to do. Deep depression does not respond to simple logic. So I had him lie down and go back to the origin of his guilt feelings about his father. I expected him to go to an incident in his childhood, but he returned to the prenatal. His mother was talking to Father, switching from despair to rage.

> P: *She's crying.... Help me!...Can't you see I'm sick?... It's all finished. I know you've been with another woman. Get out! Get the hell out of here!... She's mad and trying to hit him.... You son of a bitch!... He's going out now with his clothes and she's screaming.... Don't ever come back! I never want to see you again.*
>
> T: *Say the next words. Father is gone now. If Mother's feelings were talking, what would they be saying?*
>
> P: *She's lying on the bed.... What have I done? What will I do now? I can't live without him. My temper will ruin me. Why do I get so angry? I might as well die here all alone.*

Mother was in deep despair after feeling her anger. While Ernest was still in her body, we went through several similar scenes. In each one Mother was enraged at Father because he was drunk and out with other women. Some scenes were more violent than others, but they all ended with Mother feeling sick and depressed.

> P: *Leave me alone. I want to die.... This baby'll be deformed.... Let me die. I feel too bad to live.*

Ernest's desperate feelings were programmed in the prenatal: his fear and anger, then his guilt, depression, and nausea. Then scenes in childhood where his father was drunk, abusive, and violent were repeated. His father's death had made the resolution of his feelings more difficult. The problem was not only Ernest's conception of his role in his father's death but also the guilt at being angry with him when he was dead.

As Ernest re-lived scenes in childhood when he was beaten and kicked by his father and hid in closets and under beds, he finally began to accept his anger and recognize that it was normal. This made it easier for him to express the angry feelings and re-evaluate the guilt that accompanied them. He began to accept himself as a worthwhile, respectable person.

We reworked this prenatal and childhood material intensively until one day Ernest came in and said that he had gained five pounds since our last session, his nausea had ceased, and he was planning on going back to work.

Case 2. Making Fear of Loss Come True

Betty was a pretty young woman in her late twenties with curly brown hair and a warm smile. Her first parting from a loved one occured at age two when her mother was put in a mental institution. Betty never saw her again, and after four years with her grandparents she was put up for adoption. Her most painful childhood memory was of being given away to strangers at the age of six. She never recovered from the unloved and lonely feeling that she experienced at that time and was not able to develop a feeling of being close and accepted by her new parents; because she had experienced no commitment from any of her early loved ones, she had developed no expectation of loyalty and care.

Betty came to see me because she was constantly involved in miserable relationships with men. She could not be interested in anyone unless he was already committed or had decided not to marry or have a long-term relationship; a man who was available did not interest her. She tried over and over to go out with men who were single and attractive, but she never seemed to have fun with them. Her life had been a long stream of unhappy partings. Always there had come a time when the relationship seemed hopeless and finally ended.

When she began her prenatal regression into the body of a woman who had later been put in a mental institution for life, I felt sure we would find fear and instability in Mother's thoughts and feelings. Patterns of broken relationships and non-commitment usually begin, or reproduce, earlier templates in the prenatal.

Betty's greatest fear when she came to see me was that she was going to be left again. Whenever anyone, and especially a man she was going with, was late, she was sure that person would never come back, that she would never see him again. She began her regression by going back to a time in the nine months before she was born when her mother had the same fear: "He'll never come back." I chose this fear because it was the pattern of her childhood and had permeated all her relationships.

The basic process of regression therapy is the same, whether the regression is to childhood or to the prenatal state and birth. Whatever the direction, there must be a purpose, and the words and direction must be specific. While searching for the incident where her mother had said, "He'll never come back," Betty lay quietly with her eyes closed for a few minutes.

P: *He's gone.*
T: *Say it again.*
P: *Why is he always gone when I need him?*
T: *Say it again.*

I had Betty repeat the words as many times as necessary to release the feeling that went with them. It is the underlying fear and trauma that hold the old messages in place, and the reason for re-living the prenatal and birth is to release the old programming. Throughout all our sessions I kept repeating, "Say it again," and "Again." When the next phrase came out, I said, "And the next words." The patient needs to be directed forward continuously because material does not come from conscious memory but from an unconscious recording of the experience.

P: *I hate you for going away and leaving me.*
T: *Say the next words.*
P: *You might as well stay away.*
T: *And the next words.*
P: *I'm lonely when you're gone.*
T: *The next words.*
P: *I love you. I'm afraid I'll lose you forever.*

Betty began to cry with what were really her mother's tears, and I told her to say the words over and over so that she could give up the pain and grief that went with them. It did not matter whether Mother's feeling actually fit the reality of the situation because Mother's feeling was the only reality for the tiny fetus in her body.

P: *I feel total despair.*
T: *And say the next words.*
P: *Where can I go...what can I do?*
T: *And the next words.*

If the patient is silent for several minutes, I say, "Just let the next words drift in to you," or, "If Mother's feeling was talking now, what would it say?"

P: *He'll never come back.*
T: *The next words.*
P: *I want to die here all alone.*
T: *The next words.*
P: *I've lost him...I can't live this way.*
T: *What position is Mother's body in while she's thinking these thoughts?*
P: *She's standing up.*
T: *Is she inside or outside?*
P: *She's inside, looking out the kitchen window. She can see the kids playing out there.*
T *If Mother's feeling was talking while she's looking out the window, what would it be saying?*
P: *I don't want to go on having babies and be here all alone.*

All through the pregnancy Mother was alone, and her abandoned, desperate feelings continued. In many pregnancies, sad feelings are mixed with intervals of satisfaction and fun, but not so with Betty's mother. Perhaps it was her endless despair that drove her into an institution later. It was our task to remove this despair from Betty's unconscious, both from the prenatal experience and from its continuation as the mother was on the way to the hospital and experienced the birth.

Birth is a particularly vulnerable time for the tiny infant. There is Mother's pain, which is registering in the baby's unconscious as its own, and there is the pain, suffocation, and pressure in the infant's body. All this is being locked in with the words that Mother is thinking and the words that are being said in the room.

P: *(On the way to the hospital) Please don't leave me alone...I don't want to go through this all alone.*
(In the delivery room) I need you.... Why aren't you with me...I'm all alone.... Nobody cares...I want to die.

Though Betty's mother seemed to have few physical complications, her constant hopelessness and despair provided Betty's early programming for her life. The despair she knew at this time was reinforced in childhood when her mother was taken away from her when she was two years old, and again when she was adopted at the age of six.

After we worked with the prenatal and birth memories, we went through the childhood scenes, and gradually Betty relinquished her feeling that no one could ever be trusted to stay with her. She stopped setting up situations to prove that these feelings were valid. Shortly afterwards, she found a boyfriend who was interested in a permanent relationship.

Tracing the Karmic Source of Prenatal Programs

by

Roger Woolger, Ph.D.

Introduction

The mother's consciousness during pregnancy provides the occasion for the reactivation of psychic patterns or samskaras previously laid down in the child's psyche in a past lifetime. The incoming soul is attracted to a mother and father who will help mirror his or her unfinished karmic business during pregnancy and birth. A child is drawn to a mother and father, not so much out of choice but because the life scripts of certain parents will restimulate old karmic residues within the unconscious psyche and provide a new opportunity for their resolution.

The consciousness of the mother plays its part. There is a growing consensus among therapists doing experiential work involving prenatal and birth memories that even if the fetal infant has no ego-consciousness before or at birth, the unconscious mind of the fetus is awake and is influenced by the mother's attitude. From the moment of conception onward, like a computer recording a program, the fetus absorbs many of the mother's thoughts and feelings, as well as images or surrounding events. However, in the absence of an ego to discriminate, the fetus cannot distinguish between its own feelings or ideas and those of its mother. Not just single thoughts but whole scenes between mother, father, doctor and others are imprinted in the unconscious of the fetus, with the effect of re-establishing patterns, originally initiated in earlier lifetimes, that later in this one can become debilitating complexes. Part of the work of therapy has to be to release these old patterns or programs and find new and more helpful ones.

Recent research by Dr. Gerhard Rottman in Austria on how fetal consciousness directly reflects the mother's emotional state during pregnancy has identified four types of mothers who hold different conscious and unconscious attitudes toward their babies while they are pregnant. Ideal Mothers want their babies on both conscious and unconscious levels. Catastrophic Mothers don't want them on either level. Ambivalent Mothers want their babies on a conscious level but reject them on an unconscious level, and Cool Mothers think they don't want them but unconsciously do. An incoming soul still dominated by catastrophic memories of violent deaths, deprivation, or abandonment will be attracted to the Catastrophic Mother. The mother's feelings that she doesn't want her child will be an exact mirror of the incoming soul's negative thoughts such as, "I don't really want to be here. Nobody wants me." All but the Ideal Mother unconsciously attract candidates for one or more of the many unpredictable birth traumas that so often surround pregnancy and birthing.

Because the thoughts and feelings and events that comprise the experience of the mother can act to trigger the karmic patterns that are already in the consciousness of the infant *en utero*, the infant is not a purely passive victim, helplessly taking on all of its mother's ambivalence, fear, and negativity. Not only is the fetal consciousness selective, absorbing from all that the mother does, thinks, and feels primarily those tapes it has already played in other lifetimes, but it is also engaged in a sort of deep rumination over the still-unfinished business of other lives that it will have to deal with after it is born. For the most of the early gestation period the impact of the mother's consciousness, rather than the actual physical experience of the fetus, is the triggering mechanism for its reactions and reflections unless there are physical complications. But in the final stages of pregnancy, beginning with the onset of labor, the fetus begins to experience intense physical sensations in addition to the mother's reaction to labor and the impending birth. The compression of the last month and the contractions of labor have the effect of triggering violent past-life memories and archetypal and visionary experiences in the fetal consciousness that are not necessarily connected to the mother's consciousness.

Whenever there is severe trauma in the struggle to be born, the form of the trauma commonly proves to be an exact and faithful symbolic mirror of accumulated past-life death experiences in all their attendant terror and stress. Each individual drama of birth seems to be an occasion for these unresolved past-life complexes to be revived in the unconscious of the child. Whether or not we choose our parents, there is certainly a huge psychic magnetism that seems to draw the raw karmic stuff of a potential new personality to a womb that will remind it of the work that lies ahead. Therefore, realizing that the individual drama of birth seems to be an occasion when unresolved past-life complexes are revived in the unconscious of the child, we cannot put the responsibility or blame for difficult births solely on the hospital, the doctor, or the mother.

Case: A Battered Life as the Continuation of a Karmic Pattern

When first hearing of the story of a young man named Chris, it was hard to feel that the responsibility for his difficult and battered life was really his. The son of a harsh father and an alcoholic mother, Chris grew up on a farm, accustomed to fights, abuse, and flying fists. At 12 years of age his first attempt to run away landed him in a reform school and started a pattern of self-destructive behavior and personal violence. He was always in fights and frequently in automobile accidents, either as the cause of them or as a victim. He was jailed several times and wandered in and out of a dismal spiral of depression, alcohol, and suicidal attempts. His sense of victimization escalated when his infant son died early of infant crib death.

During Chris's many attempts at therapy, he repeated one wretched litany: "I'm all alone." His first attempt to go back to where this struck a chord took him to a scene following his birth.

> *P: I'm all alone. It's cold. She never comes. It's a nurse. She doesn't care. Nobody wants me...bright lights. Things attached to me. They don't want me. I don't want to be here. I wanna die. I wanna die!*

Chris was a premature baby and was racked with pain and despair. I suggested he go back to just prior to being born, and the confused stream of consciousness which resulted commingled his mother's words with his own thoughts.

> *P: I'm so scared. So scared. I don't want it. I don't want this kid. It's too much trouble. I don't want to be here. I don't want to be inside. I deserve to live. Let me live. It's too much trouble. I'll hurt myself, then I don't have to have a kid. I'll stab myself. Kill me! I'll drink myself to death.*

Chris next tuned in to Christmas and the snow. His mother was talking to her own mother on the phone.

> *P: Ma, help me! I'm gonna have this baby. I don't want it. God help me. I don't want this child. I can't win. Ma, I'm gonna hurt myself!*

Chris perceived his mother in the bathroom with a knife. His infant thoughts became entangled with his mother's drunken, hateful monologue.

> *P: She's in the bathroom—with a knife. She's going to hurt herself. She's punching her stomach.*

In the bathroom the mother's thoughts were half on killing herself, half on killing the baby inside her. She beat on her own stomach, with Chris inside, and contemplated cutting herself and him with a knife but didn't use it. After the desperate phone call to her mother, she fell down the stairs in a drunken stupor.

> P: *Now she's falling. Oh, it hurts! She's at the bottom of the stairs. Help me!*

The fall brings on labor and the mother is rushed to the hospital.

> P: *We're in a car. She's half awake. I'm starting to come out. I don't want to be here. There's blood!*
>
> *A nurse is talking. "She's losing blood. We've got to hurry. It's coming. Oh, it's so small. It's not going to make it. She's weak, too."*
>
> *I'm so little. She doesn't do anything. She doesn't care. Now I'm all alone. I'm in this box.... My belly hurts. I don't want to be here. I don't want to be here!*

Chris was born three months early and hooked to intravenous feeding tubes, where he stayed for nearly three months.

As we worked through this material I helped him detach as far as possible from this mother's negative and violent thoughts about him. For one thing, he started to realize that he had always seen himself as "too much trouble." Most of all he heard how deeply ingrained in his unconscious was his mother's death wish toward herself and him. Her phrases, "I'll hurt myself. I'll stab myself" led to flashbacks of adolescent falls and devil-may-care flirtations with death. He realized that he had unconsciously been trying to fulfill her abortive and suicidal thoughts for most of his life.

To help process the misery encapsulated in his lonely experience in the incubator, he explored phrases from that unhappy part of his life. He started repeating the phrases "I'm all alone. I don't want to be here. I want to die." These phrases took him directly into a past life that resonated with this loneliness.

> P: *I'll never get out. I'm sick.... It's a dungeon. I'm chained to a wall. They've left us. Deserted us. The English, the bloody English! The swine! I'll never get out now. I can't last much longer. I'll never make it. It's so cold. They've forgotten, don't care. I'm dying."*

Beaten, sick with dysentery, left for dead, he hung in chains, festering hatred for his brutal captors. The suffering he remembered in the cold damp dungeon fused with that of the unwanted and abandoned baby in the incubator.

From one past memory of sickness we went to another where Chris found himself a very sickly adolescent in an Indian tribe in the American

Northwest. Because he was too weak to be trained as a warrior, his father disowned him, while the medicine man proclaimed his sickness to be evil.

> P: *I don't want to be here. I'm too much trouble. I've failed.*

The tribe was under siege from white soldiers and food had dwindled during the winter. His father left him out to die in the tribal burial grounds. As he died alone and enfeebled, his thought turned against his father and mother.

> P: *She didn't want me. You (Father) didn't want me. I'm no good. I deserve to die.*

This Indian death merged with another death in a tribal experience in the Old World where he was an old man left out to die in a cave. He was eaten by a bear while still half-alive, a repetition of the pattern of abandonment, violence, and aloneness.

We searched for the karmic origin of the victimization and violence in Chris's lives that had been so accurately mirrored in the perinatal dramas attending his birth. While exploring further images of violence, particularly involving knives, two more past lives surfaced that helped us to understand. In the first he was a little boy in China whose father worked on the dock and had little time for him, and whose mother was a prostitute.

> P: *She's cruel. She makes me stand guard, while she screws them. I hate that bitch. She tells me to stay away from her. She's always trying to seduce me, too. I hate her. I hit her with my fists until she leaves me alone. What a whore!*

Chris's anger boiled at the memory, his fists clenched, and his knuckles whitened. I directed him to see what came of his anger. Almost immediately a terrible image emerged.

> P: *I'm 13 or so now. Stronger. God, I hate her—and women. I'm not at home. I sleep on the docks. I steal. I'm a criminal now. I'm in this house, robbing this woman. She's pregnant. I kill her with my knife—I cut her heart out—and then her baby. All the time I'm thinking of my mother. Oh God, the blood! What have I done? I didn't want to do it, but I hated her so much.*

The intrauterine memories of his mother with the knife wove in and out of this appalling scenario, and a grim sense of justice slowly began to dawn on Chris.

A final past-life memory was of an Eskimo man who was characterized by sociopathic behavior within his tribe. He was married to a shrewish woman whom he had come to hate, and in retaliation he forced himself sexually on as many of the tribe as he could get to yield to him. Eventually he murdered his wife, which brought the vengeance of the whole tribe upon him. They staked him out in the cold and left him to die, and again a bear came, this time a polar bear that was responsible for his bloody end.

In Chris's experience the interweaving of the same patterns of violence, even to the detail of the knife, and the unnourishing and disruptive relationship with women appeared in various past lives, in the prenatal and birth experiences, and in his current lifetime from infancy on. His hatred for women, which he experienced so intensely in this life, persisted from lifetime to lifetime, returning in thoughts of violence and vengeance and often in sadistic action and finally drew him to experience *en utero* the mirror of all his past brutality. This pattern of violence had been deeply ingrained in him psychically, and there was much work of self-acceptance and self-forgiveness to be done. Being aware of what he had gone through gave him a new context for seeing himself. Now he must choose whether to go on blaming his violent parents—who are only a reflection of his own nature—or to take full responsibility for that portion of darkness within himself that he was born to work with.

Awareness en Utero

by

Hugh Harmon, Ph.D.

Not many decades ago it was common belief that intelligent life was not in a fetus until the third trimester. Even today there are some who argue that a spirit/intelligence is not present until just before birth. It is my experience that spirit/intelligence is present at the time of fertilization of the egg and probably even before its inception into physical form. I further believe the spirit/intelligence is capable of coming into and leaving the embryo or fetus anytime during the gestation period.

With the thousands of regressions that I've done, I have found that there may be one in a thousand who under hypnosis does not recover a time *en utero* and this is usually because there has been a walk-in, that is, an exchange of spirit/intelligence. So, almost without fail a person is able to recall his or her experiences while still within the mother's womb.

In nearly all of the regressions I have conducted, people have told me many things that have happened, often in extraordinarily vivid detail, to both them and their mothers, as well as to others around their mothers. They have frequently seen both parents even before they entered the mother's body. It is not unusual to report mother and father having sex, with the spirit/intelligence fully aware that this particular act of sex is going to result in its conception. People report being around or in the egg at the time of fertilization. They discuss seeing or feeling the spermatozoa and the initial contact with the egg. Sometimes the patient reports to me that he welcomes the contact; sometimes, however, he resents or resists it. People have stated in regression that they can feel the multiplication of cells; others describe the growth of the embryo in great detail.

This could, of course, be imagination. However, even those persons, and there are many, who feel or state that they do not believe this memory is possible, proceed, to their great surprise, to give detailed accounts of their time in the womb. The most stubborn individuals will then protest that they must have "made it all up." Yet, we've also asked little children before the age of four if they remember being in Mommy, and they will talk about the sounds they heard or what it felt like to be in Mommy when she was doing different things they can relate to, like what it was like when Mommy would be taking a bath.

The amount of detail people go into when they are regressed to the womb is also, in my opinion, quite convincing. In addition to the vivid description of what happened during the gestation period, during the growth from egg to embryo to fetus to baby, they will report, verbatim, on conversations held around or about them, describe the clothing people were wearing, even the thoughts people were thinking. There have been instances of physical hurt, such as feeling the blows someone was directing to the mother and reports on how it feels when the mother takes different medications or stimuli, how it affects them in the womb. They often state that they are aware, *en utero*, whether they are loved or unloved, wanted or unwanted, by one or both parents.

Case 1. Recalling a Birth with Hypnosis

I had a woman come to me whose mother, 30 years before, had used hypnosis for her birth. We regressed this woman, curious to find out what it had been like for her at birth. She first went back to when her father was told about the pregnancy. In regression she stated that she was there in the womb and was aware that her father was worried and unhappy about the pregnancy. To her conscious knowledge, her father had never told that to anyone, but she saw it clearly in his thoughts and she stated in regression, "I think it's because he does not have enough money." Her father, as it happens, is a multi-millionaire today, and when he was asked about this later, he verified his concern and unhappiness when told of his wife's pregnancy. At that time he had immediately wondered where he was going to find the money for the delivery. The patient in regression went on to describe her birth and added that after her birth the OB nurse took her away from her mother, insisting that the baby must be taken to the nursery. Her mother, the patient reported, immediately jumped off the delivery table and followed the nurse down the hall, finally catching up with her and struggling with her to take the baby back so she could nurse her. The mother later verified the story, stating that she had nearly forgotten the incident, but yes, now that she was reminded, she recalled both it and the fact that she had won—she had taken back her daughter to nurse her on the delivery table.

Case 2. Anticipating an Unhappy Family Situation

In the regression of another young woman, it was found that she was aware of the sexual contact between her mother and father and the union of egg and the sperm. She was further aware that her mother was in a quandary when she discovered the pregnancy. Her mother loved children and already had three, but she was unhappy with her marriage and had been trying to figure a way out of it when she received the news that she was pregnant. This was described by my patient in great detail. She announced that her father was happy about the pregnancy. However, her three older siblings were angry and upset about another baby being on its way. The father was an abusive man and all of them had suffered an uncomfortable childhood and didn't want to see another baby come into their world and create more problems. The patient became so distressed with the unhappiness she was sensing that she asked to terminate the regression. Later, she spoke with all the members of her family, and all of the things she had experienced were validated, including articles of clothing the woman had reported seeing, *en utero*, on members of the family, clothing long since discarded and that this woman had no way of knowing about.

Case 3. Experiencing the Mother's Sexual Assault

In another case a man reported instances of physical abuse while *en utero*. He related several occurrences when his father would force his mother into sex, hitting her on the stomach. He could feel the hitting sensation as the blow went through her abdomen. He reported, in great agitation, that his father was raping his mother both vaginally and anally and described, in heart-wrenching detail, how his mother screamed and writhed and how it felt to him, the embryo, inside.

Case 4. Remembering a Difficult Birth

In a regression with a medical doctor, the real physical pains and injuries occurring at his birth were reviewed. This physician had rushed into my office one day requesting an immediate regression, stating that it was important that it be done right way. Fortunately this was possible. When regressed, the doctor reported that his father was not happy when he heard there was to be a baby in the family. It was during the Depression, and his father, he stated, was having financial difficulties. The mother, however, was happy. He stated also that, while he had always been told his birth had occurred at the hospital with a drunken doctor in attendance, he could see now he was being born at home with a midwife delivering him.

He was, he said, in a breech position. (The baby boy, rejected by his father who did not want him, was blocking his own way out.) The midwife, not knowing how to handle a breech delivery, started pulling on the one leg of the baby she had managed to get out. When the leg broke, she reached in and grabbed the other leg and pulled. In the regression, he began screaming, saying his head was hooked on the pubic bone. "You're pulling my head off! You're pulling my head off!" he screamed. Then he stopped screaming and in the authoritative tones of the doctor he is now, he severely reprimanded the midwife. "Stop that, you stupid woman! Don't you know how to deliver a baby yet? Push that baby around this way." He then described how to turn the baby's head and ease it out of the birth canal even as he would interrupt himself to scream, "Stop pulling my head off—you're killing me!"

After the regression, this physician reported that he had indeed been born with a broken leg, double curvature of the spine, wry neck and other injuries. His regression had been extremely vivid and revealing and was contrary to his conscious beliefs about his birth. He later called to report that he had confronted his mother, who had finally confirmed the details of his birth as he had seen them in his regression. He did not return, however, nor did I ever discover what had driven him to seek a regression he professed not to believe in.

Case 5. Remembering Birth with a Twin

A woman wanted her son to see me but thought she ought to check me out first herself. I suggested a regression and she felt that that would be interesting. In hypnosis I suggested that she go to the time of conception. She immediately reported that she was having fun rolling down the fallopian tube. Suddenly she saw little swimmers coming up toward her and then swimming all around her. She laughed and described the spermatozoa all bumping into her and felt one get really strong and attach itself and then enter through the skin of the egg.

She began to multiply, feeling joyous and happy, and as she was describing her growth she said, "Oh, something funny's happening. There's a part of me that's getting bigger than the other parts of me." She began a detailed description, saying she was experiencing that part as getting bigger and bigger and then separating into a second part of the egg and pulling away from her and growing on its own.

As she and this other part grew, she realized it was another baby, and a male. Identical twins, which mean coming from the same egg, are always supposed to be of the same sex, but this time, in her memory, this identical twin from the same egg was a brother. She described each of their growths and how they played, how they touched and held each other as they were growing, and how when his foot would get in her face, for instance, she would twist around the other way.

The birthing process was exciting for her until her brother, who was born first, left. She felt an absolute state of terror at his leaving. Then she said, "Whoops, here I go, too!" and she followed her brother out of the birth canal.

This was certainly an entertaining and lively description of the *en utero* experience from a woman who didn't believe that such a memory, or active intelligence in the womb, was possible. She confirmed afterward that she indeed had a twin brother, whom she had always, of course, thought was a fraternal twin. "But it was so real," she remarked, "my feeling of it all being a part of me until he began to pull away and split off into a separate self."

There are many instances of regression where we can validate the experiences remembered *en utero*. (It is also interesting to note that we can often determine who the natural father was, if there is any doubt about it, simply by taking the person back to the moment of his conception.) Just as in law we allow the weight of the evidence to convince us, I am, after thousands and thousands of regressions, convinced that there is clear and concise communication with our life *en utero*.

Treating Psychological Problems through Prenatal Recall

by

Claire Etheridge, Ph.D.

With the advent of hypnotherapy, especially as a tool for regression, therapists have begun to hear reports that have made sense only within the context of prenatal recall. Such a hypothesis is often verified by the patients' mothers, who frequently add, "How did he/she know that? I never told anyone in my life."

At present, it cannot be proved that prenatal consciousness exists or that a person's prenatal recollections are true. The validity of a person's early memories, while in hypnosis or otherwise, can always be questioned, even when verified by a third party. What is certain is that therapeutic change occurs after a person re-lives his/her traumatic early experiences and heals the memories of them with the help of a qualified therapist. Patients who seem to abreact with puzzling emotional states that cannot be resolved by conventional techniques are often helped by such an exploration.

In remembering prenatal experience patients show that the feelings of the mother have been absorbed into their own consciousness in a kind of emotional contagion. By re-living these prenatal emotions and understanding how the distressing experiences of that time, and especially the experiences of the mother that they have absorbed, are falsely related to the present, patients can be freed from disabling symptoms. This is particularly true in the case of pervasive fear that seems unrelated to post-birth biographical happenings.

Case 1. Skin Rash Revealing Very Early Prenatal Fear

This regression was significant because it went back to conception and included details that are ordinarily not expected to be available to recall. The content of such experiences is often difficult to communicate because there is no adequate vocabulary.

This subject, Bess, began by recalling an event that had occurred near the beginning of pregnancy and had initiated a pattern of fear that resonated throughout her life. As in many cases, this destructive pattern was perpetuated by an inaccurate assessment of the meaning of what had happened. When this faulty connection between two happenings that were actually unrelated was reframed, the pattern of fear was released.

Bess had experienced therapy years before but had returned because of a rash that had broken out over her arms and did not respond to medical attention. I thought it might be the result of current stress in her life and decided to take a Gestalt approach and have the skin describe its problem while Bess was in an altered state.

T: *(I would like to speak with your skin...) I understand you broke out all over your arms. What was that all about? What were you saying?*

P: *I'm trying to write...I'm trying to send messages. I have no other way to speak, I was trying to say things.*

T: *What were you trying to say?*

P: *Oh, trying to reveal all the trouble we have in here now. Get it from the inside to the outside.*

The skin described how it wanted to let "all the wants" break out. It had tried to make itself cold and numb, but the "wants" broke out onto the surface of the rash. I asked to talk to the "wants."

P: *See. I'm not supposed to want. I'm...I'm dealing with a really important aloneness.... Sometimes I'm it and sometimes I'm outside of it looking at it because as soon as I think about it I become it, and it's very, very lonely, and very frightened, and very, very, very, small. (Voice sounds frightened.) But no, wait, it's big, I'm small.*

T: *It's big, you're small?*

P: *Right. I'm much smaller.*

T: *Okay. How little are you?*

P: *I'm about...about half the size of a big toe.*

T: *And what are your body proportions?*

P: *Oh, mostly head. Mostly head—just an indication of anything else.*

T: *And what are you aware of?*

P: *Fear.*

T: *Yes...and what about it?*

P: *Oh, it. It's...oh...I have...I have a little voice. Don't move! Don't think! Don't cry! Don't want! Don't want! It never comes true. It never is there. It never, never is there.*

T: *There is something to be afraid of, you said. What is happening? What is trying to happen or is going to happen? Can you go back and be that little-bitty person, that little-bitty you?*

P: *Can't breathe. I can't breathe. It's...my throat's all blocked up.*

T: *What's happening?*

P: *There's a rhythm. It stops...(sharp cry). There has to be a rhythm. I made it outside of my body 'cause it was hurting.*

T: *And where are you outside your body.*

P: *Uh...I'm inside. The rhythm, the beat, is a little above me, so that it won't bring the nerves into play and the muscles. It's a slender connection but it will do.*

Apparently she had gone into a temporary dissociation. Probably this functioned as a self-protective mechanism so that the nerves registering the fear would not affect the rudimentary heartbeat. She became aware of the electromagnetic field that surrounded her body. Because of her panic state, her connection to the body was tenuous at this point.

T: *And where is your body?*

P: *Oh...Jesus...it's...I can't see a thing. I'm surrounded. Closed in. There's an electrical field. And...my body is in a state of absolute panic. Just panic. Like...like a fragile connection.*

T: *A fragile connection. All right now, what is happening outside your body that's got that little body so scared?*

P: *Can't...mustn't...I mustn't move...mustn't want.*

T: *You mustn't want?*

P: *Every...every...every time I want something...this is really physical. It's nerves. It's not even emotional. It's want. It's air. It's food. It's want. Whenever I want something, I get cut off. (Pause) If I don't want, if I'm very still...I...will stay alive?*

T: *Yes, you will stay alive.*

P: *So—I was very still....*

T: *And what you wanted at that time...was to live?*

P: *Yes. But—it makes so much sense. I want...I think this has happened to me in every way from the very beginning. Want, and then disconnections as soon as I want it and then being able to survive.*

T: *The pattern was laid down when you were very, very tiny, and what you wanted was to live, and you did live.*

P: *I did live.*

T: *And it's okay to go ahead and experience what you experienced. Then these contractions came, and your little body was all nerves and in an awful lot of pain.*

P: *Uh-huh.*

T: *And you were still, and you did keep living.*

P: *Uh-huh.*

T: *But now there's a part of you that knows what was happening to disturb you in that dark, closed-in place that's supposed to be very safe.*

P: *Yes. There is a part of me that knows. This is connected with not seeing or hearing. Everything else is away. That's why it was so fragile, because I felt only like a life-form—just something to stay alive with.*

The pattern of fear and being still unable to survive was laid down from a physical trauma but generalized to an emotional belief that subsequently expressed itself in behavior in life. We made an effort to determine just what the physical trauma was that had set everything off but could come up with only an approximation.

> T: *And what was happening? What happened to that environment to cause those contractions? Part of you knows.*
>
> P: *Well, there's a couple of pictures. Like a soft, round shape, like a pillow, sort of.*
>
> T: *A soft, round shape like a pillow.*
>
> P: *Whenever I think of the shape, I will see it being punched in. It's a blow. Like a small bomb going off. And it caves in. I'm very afraid of it. Of that picture.*
>
> T: *Is it like something being hit? And something caves in?*
>
> P: *You know, it's almost like it was my belly, or something, but it's outside of me. It's...I don't know if it's because I'm outside, or if...*

In the conversation after the session, the best we could reconstruct at this time was that her mother had been at a parade early in the pregnancy and then became caught in the crush of the crowd. Bess confused her belly with her mother's belly in the event. In the following session further hypotheses emerged.

At this point in the dialogue Bess shifted again to her awareness of the electromagnetic field.

> P: *I got something else.*
>
> T: *Oh. Tell me.*
>
> P: *It's like yellow, but it's not yellow. It's like when you put a connector on a battery and there's a shower of sparks. Like an electrical spark field.*
>
> T: *An electrical field of some sort?*
>
> P: *Yes. Some of it goes blue, too. I don't have any idea what it is or what it means. It's just there. It's not seen, it's just there.*
>
> T: *You're not seeing, you just have an awareness that it's there.*
>
> P: *Yes. And the awareness has colors. There's a lot of awareness of color that isn't seeing. It has to do with the connection that's maintained. The reason I made a picture of it is because most of my being is busy with it, making sure it is there. I have, like, two awarenesses. There is one, and there's some kind of blow or some kind of sock in the stomach. But if I'm very still and just be, then I'm all right. They're separate, they're separate. Want is separate. But it was simultaneous. I got it mixed up.*
>
> T: *I see. You got the wanting to live mixed up with the wanting to be still.*
>
> P: *Yes...and yes...and...and I was getting some kind of flak from the outside, and I felt that if I stopped wanting, that was how to survive the flak. But the flak and the wanting were different.*

T: *They were different.*

P: *Yeah. Yeah. I'll die if I want something. This is cross-connected. "I'll die" turned into, "It's no use." And feeling like I needed to be very still and not send out any impulses at all in order to survive connects with being a baby or a very small child. Being a small child and wanting to be touched or loved, which is being alive—which is staying alive, because I have to be touched to stay alive.*

T: *Yes.*

P: *Uh-huh.*

Here Bess became aware of her confusion of the pattern of "be still to survive" and "don't want anything if you are to survive." As she became aware of how she had mixed up the two admonitions, she could begin to restructure her affirmations and release the pattern that had so detrimentally affected her as she grew up.

P: *And wanting that and feeling that if I want it I got hit. And besides it wasn't ever going to be there. I got touched, but if I asked for it or wanted it, I got hit.*

T: *So again as a child growing up, if you wanted something you felt you were punished for wanting.*

P: *Yes. And survival...I couldn't want. I couldn't make myself not want, but I could make myself be very still and keep it inside.*

T: *That was a fallacious idea in the first place.*

P: *Yes, it was ridiculous.*

T: *And so I want you to know it's safe to want now.*

P: *Okay. It's safe to want now.*

T: *Yes. You don't have to be afraid you're going to be hit. You don't have to be afraid you're going to lose your life.*

P: *I believe that. Thanks, Doc.*

T: *I hope you can make a picture of those images you saw without seeing.... You can relax now. You worked very hard today. Just let yourself relax and rest.*

The following week the patient brought in the pictures she had drawn of the writing on her arms and of the "electrical field" she had perceived. We talked about these for a while and then I asked if there was anything else she had to say to me.

P: *Yeah, I'd like to stop. I'd like not to hold in the wants. I'd like to stop itching and burning. I'd like to stop trying to hold it all in. I don't think I need to make pictures anymore.*

T: *You may stop itching and burning any time you choose. You may stop holding it all in any time you choose. It's not necessary anymore. Now that*

*you are getting it outside by talking and drawing, you don't have to draw
pictures on your skin anymore.*

P: I feel better today.

T: *(After a pause) What is happening now?*

P: *I'm looking for pain. Seeing where it hurts...I found some pain.*

T: *You want to tell me about it?*

P: *Yeah. It's small today. It's not nearly as big as it's been. Little flakes of it
in the chest right on the bone and the left wrist... The skin is trying to be
numb...it's either all itch and burn or it's all numb. I have a lot of trouble
with coordination.*

T: *Last week we were dealing with fear. I'd like to talk to that part of Bess
that is afraid.*

P: *(Sounds frightened, cannot catch her breath, emits a loud cry.)*

T: *I'd like to suggest that you give your fear a voice and express it in that way.
I think you'll find it a little more comfortable.*

P: *(Voice is suddenly whispering and dry.) I don't want to be here.*

T: *Describe what it's like where you are.*

P: *I have a weight. I can't see. I have a weight pressing down on my nose and
my eyes.*

T: *Wait a minute. How big are you?*

P: *Small.*

T: *How small? Compared to what?*

P: *Coat button.*

T: *And is it light or dark where you are?*

P: *It's dark. It's very dark.*

T: *And is it wet or dry?*

P: *It's soft, and it isn't wet or dry. It's just soft.*

T: *All right now, I'd like to suggest that you go back a little bit in time before
you had something over your nose and eyes, before the fear.*

P: *Okay.*

T: *Now how are you?*

P: *There's a light. I'm—there isn't anything but this light.*

T: *Where is it?*

P: *Everywhere. It's all there is. Just this light and me.*

T: *How big are you?*

P: *Oh small. Oh small.*

T: *Compared to what?*

P: *Compared to the light. I don't know about size.*

T: *You don't know about size. You're just coming from the light.*

P: *Yes.*

T: *You look peaceful.*

P: *I feel...at peace.*

At the time of this session I did not know what Bess meant by "the
light," "no size," and "growing," but now I feel that she was representing her
consciousness at conception, when "the soul is at one with the light."

Following this memory, which predated even the very early memory of the preceding session, I moved Bess forward in order to reprocess the trauma that had occurred. Many times in healing a memory, whether prenatal or otherwise, it is important to go back in time before the fear or trauma occurred and then have the patient move forward into the fear. The repeated recall brings up additional details and helps the pattern that has been responsible for the distortion to emerge more clearly.

T: *How much time goes by as you grow until your first fear?*
P: *Two weeks.*
T: *And what happens at your first fear?*
P: *Interruption. Interruption—static—like when a heart misses a beat. Like when somebody slams on the brakes.*
T: *What caused this interruption?*
P: *Fear.*
T: *Where did the fear come from?*
P: *Outside.*
T: *What happened outside?*
P: *I don't know.*
T: *Part of you does now.*
P: *I don't want to know. (Sharp cry.)*
T: *It isn't necessary to go through it. You can just observe it and perceive it like on a screen.*
P: *I fear.*
T: *Yes, I know, fear. It's coming from the outside. I want to know what is it that's coming from the outside to cause the fear. You can experience it in whatever comfortable way you wish.*
P: *I hear a train and a lot of blueness. Outside is a lot of blueness. No, that isn't the fear. That's just there. I don't...see, I don't...I don't want to see or hear.*
T: *I know you don't want to see or hear, but sometimes it's necessary, so in whatever tolerable way you can, just recite the source of the pain, as if you were a narrator.*
P: *(Sudden transition to adult voice) I...I see crowds. I see...I see an elbow. This was the first blow. There were others. This is the first blow. It comes from an elbow.*
T: *Whose elbow?*
P: *Blue jacket. Don't know. Doesn't mean anything. Blue jacket. Elbow. Blow. Some kind of immediate nervous reaction. There isn't really very much there but nerves. And there's an interruption that happens with the blow. (Then, as though it were a sudden revelation) Fa-all.*
T: *Are you breathing?*
P: *Everything is breathing.*
T: *So. The fear all started with a blow of the elbow, and there were more blows and then a fall and then your heart started skipping beats.*

P: *More like—more like synapses misfiring. You know the electro-magnetic thing? Well, something's wrong there.*

T: *All right, but that was when you were just two weeks old, and it was a big fright. But this is now. And you have a lot of circuits now. Even if one doesn't work, another one will. You don't have to be afraid now. You're wired up very well with lots of provisions.*

P: *I won't die if I'm not afraid?*

T: *You won't die if you're not afraid. In fact, you will live better. You don't need to be afraid anymore. This week I want you to be aware of how well your heart beats and how all your circuits are put together and of all the extra safety mechanisms that have now been built in that you didn't have when you were two weeks old, and be aware of all the electricity that you carry with you and all the energy that you carry with you, and you yourself will see and know and perceive that you can live safely without fear.*

P: *Okay.*

T: *And if you have any fear left, draw me a picture of it.*

The following week Bess reported that she had become aware throughout the week that she was reaching out to make friends and had less debilitating fear than ever in her life. She said that she felt stronger, more assured, and safe.

Our impression from these sessions dealing with her very early prenatal experiences was that a blow from the outside must have caused both physical disturbance and the fear. The fear had followed Bess throughout her life, inhibiting her performance and interpersonal relationships and causing stress reactions. After she re-experienced the fear and discovered its fallacious generalizations, she became aware that she felt less stress, was stronger, more assured, and for the first time considered herself to be safe. A number of sessions working over the same material were needed to bring about a full release.

As treatment progressed, Bess became a healthier, happier person. She subsequently went back to college, graduating with a straight "A" average, and was awarded a full scholarship to graduate school. Her relationships became more stable, satisfying, and secure as she learned to live without the previous debilitating fear.

Case 2. Fear of Losing One's "Home"

Joanna, a successful business woman in her early forties with two teen-aged children, came to me in a state of panic over her decision to divorce her husband. He had had affairs throughout their marriage and had currently moved out and was living with someone else, but she found herself ambivalent over letting him go. She didn't want to spend the rest of her life with him, but she still felt she was doing the wrong thing to separate.

T: *What do you want to happen?*
P: *I would like to keep the house. I'm so angry at him!*

This was her first mention of her concern about keeping her house, a theme that was to emerge as the crucial focus for her problems.

Later, in a flood of material about her childhood, she suddenly brought up the possibility that her mother had tried to abort her. I encouraged her to elaborate on this, not seeing the connection with her current problem but knowing that there was one.

P: *I feel helpless (bursting into tears). I feel like I can't take care of myself. I feel like something terrible is about to happen.*

I encouraged her to talk about times when she had felt this way as a child, and she recalled being left at a neighbor's house while her mother went to work and also reported feeling deserted and alone when she had various childhood illnesses. When her mother had contracted tuberculosis, Joanna had been afraid Mother would die. When Joanna was three years old her mother was hospitalized and Joanna was almost sent away, which could be translated as "losing her home," but her father couldn't let her go and hired a housekeeper instead.

This material led to a reiteration of her fear that if she got a divorce, she would lose her home. She felt she could not tolerate this eventuality, even though it would be financially advantageous to sell.

T: *Go back in time to when you are feeling like you are losing your home.*
P: *I'm imagining myself in the womb. I feel...tension. The womb is unbending, not pliable. I'm going to have extreme difficulty in being born. My mother resented being pregnant. She didn't want another baby. She wanted to abort me.*
T: *How does your mother feel?*
P: *She feels frightened. Terrible fear...she's frightened. She's talked to a friend who had an abortion and is telling my mother how to do it. Get a coat hanger. Use soda and vinegar and purge. She tried it.*
T: *What are you feeling?*
P: *Oh, my God! I'm being rocked around! It's like being pulled down by a wave in the ocean...I'm hanging on for dear life!*

She continued in this vein until the pressure subsided.

Her description of the womb experience in the abortion attempt as "like being pulled down by a wave in the ocean" parallels descriptions reported by other therapists.[2]

After the recollection, she realized that not only had she feared for her home at age three but earlier she had feared for her first home, her mother's womb. The attempted abortion had laid the groundwork for her irrational fear of losing her home in the divorce, and that was why she could not let go of her marriage. It was true that if she had lost her first home she would not have survived, but the feeling had been transferred inappropriately to her current situation. "Home" had come to represent "survival." The unearthing of the problem took Joanna many weeks of therapy and was followed by an extended period of working through, but she finally became able to let go of the marriage and sell the house, freeing herself emotionally and profiting financially.

Case 3. Pre-natal Source of a Weight Problem

Amy, a woman in her early thirties who was happily married and successful in her chosen career, came to me for some-short term therapy to help her curb her intense cravings for food. She had attended Weight Watchers for three years and had eliminated from her diet the foods she was allergic to and therefore had a tendency to crave, but she could not escape from her obsessive thought that no amount of food would ever be enough. She was also disturbed by her inability to respond to her mother's love for her.

She felt that there was something in her past that might have triggered both these problems, and we began to explore this. After briefly touching on the diaper stage of her childhood, she went back to a uterine experience. During the first session she moved only briefly into this unfamiliar area.

> P: *I'm in the womb. I'm "head-up" and I'm looking through my mother's belly. I see rosy, flesh-blood colored light. Something big and round is outside and I'm afraid. The fear is very physical. I feel tightness through my legs and back and shoulders. I feel a band of tightness just under my waist on my stomach. It's hard to breathe. I feel stiff, frozen.*

In the next session she was more comfortable and without much prompting she began to describe the feelings of an experience her mother had gone through.

P: *I have feelings in my stomach, and I don't know where I am. It feels constricted around my stomach. My stomach is being pushed into my back. My mouth is dry. I move and float around, except my stomach...it is still and held in, pushed up like I was sucking my stomach in under my ribs. I feel very alone and unconnected. My stomach feels like there's a snarling animal gnawing at me, at my stomach, like being hungry, like having my stomach all hurt and empty.*

It's weird being here. Real strange being in this little place. Neat to roll around. All nice and fluid and rubbery except my stomach. It's stuck there—the cord goes in there.

I want to know what's going on with my mother. She seems distracted. I want her attention. She's like...pulling it away..it comes in the cord. Or is it her attention? The cord and the attention seem the same.... My feet are down. It feels awkward. I feel my back curve along around her stomach. The cord is a little looser now, but it feels kinda dry.

There's something going on with my mother. She's all involved in something emotional about her father. She's distracted from me and I'm mad! 'Cause I'm here and she's pretending I'm not! Going about her business like she's not pregnant. She's all tight. She's reaching out to her father. Her father is reaching back to comfort her. He sees just dimly now. I feel his hand on her stomach. I see his head, the dark print of it through the colored lights. She's just not paying attention in here! His hand is nice, but she's not here so I just have to take it alone.

I wish it wasn't like this. It's sad to be like this. I miss her a lot. She's not bad, she's just distracted and I'm all alone because of it. And I'm so little.

T: *What was it like before your mother became so distracted?*

P: *Just growing little cells. I kind of watch it. She doesn't know what's happening. It sneaks up on her. She's happy 'cause she wants me. She just feels strange with me. I just get too big for her, I guess. When the cells are first dividing the nourishment just comes. It's okay now.*

(Long pause.) She had some drugs. She was flying on an airplane and she was afraid of flying. She was afraid of losing me. Now my stomach is sinking. She's upset. She's not breathing real good! She's holding her stomach tight and I'm grey and dark, kinda bumping around. I'm holding myself all tight, too! We're all just a bunch of nerves.

Mom, I'm getting hungry! I'm still and clumsy. Now my head is down. I don't like this grey color.

T: *What's going on with your nourishment.*

P: *Now I've got it, but I want more! I want more! I want it to be rich and full! Fill up my stomach and roll through my veins! I keep trying to suck it in my stomach. Pull it up the cord to my stomach! It's bulky and dry and not there very much. I'm hungry! I keep being hungry! I don't like this!*

I just learn to live with it. Just stay hungry. My mother stays distracted until birth. She really wants me at birth. It feels good. She's very loving at birth. I want to come out. I feel my spine stretching and growing. But it's cold! But my mother loves me a lot. She's the only one I really see. There's lots of hustle and bustle and they are doing strange things to her, but she doesn't let it bother her or distract her—she's just loving me. I feel good and connected again. I'm lying on her heart and she's holding me and it's warm.

Amy had confused her mother's distraction and lack of focus on her with her experience of malnourishment, and this confusion led to feelings of ambivalence toward her mother. Her malnourishment had initiated the overeating behavior. The cause of the malnourishment was unclear but seemed to have been the result of an abnormal stiffness of the umbilical cord that may have been caused by the prescription drug her mother had taken during the pregnancy to help her with the airplane flight. The inadequacy of the food supply that resulted from the stiffness of the umbilical cord had set off feelings of both physical and emotional deprivation. Once Amy realized that the problem was biological in nature, she was able to disconnect her false association, reconcile her ambivalent feelings toward her mother and modify her eating habits. She continued to attend Weight Watchers and was finally able to lose the necessary weight and more easily adhere to an appropriate diet.

Some time later Amy wrote me an interesting letter that confirmed many of our suppositions:

I talked with Mother about what I had remembered and told her about the experience of her love and wanting me at the birth and at the beginning. She said it wasn't a surprise because they had been working so hard to start me. She had been delighted. She was very moved by what I said.

She told me that at the end of March, three or four months into her pregnancy, her father got sick. She went to see him and that's when she first started taking a prescription drug. I realized later that I had no direct memory or experience of the drug. I just know that it was there.

My mother said her father was very happy she was pregnant. He put his hand on her stomach and I kicked. That was the first movement that Mother felt. The doctor didn't believe her; it was too early. I recall Mother had told me about her father putting his hand on her stomach. That was something I knew consciously. I did have the memory of her father's hand on her stomach, or rather, of a hand on her stomach, and now I know it was her father's. I also know now how intimately the baby experiences what is going on with the mother.

Mother never saw her father again after the March visit. He died on either May 13 or 15. Her grandmother died on the other day, and another relative died on one of those two days.

When I told my mother about the memory of being head up, she said yes, I was. She thinks the doctor turned me around. She said that when I was born, they put me in her arms as soon as the cord was cut.

After the session it was a great, wonderful relief for me to know that my mother wasn't doing anything bad to me. She was just upset and distracted. I feel pure and delicate and fresh.

Amy

A Re-evaluation of Relationships in the Prenatal Period

by

Rob Bontenbal, M.A. and Tineke Noordegraaf, M.D.

Introduction

The period from the moment of conception until birth starts is filled with recorded experiences. First, there is the so-called mother-tape, on which can be found everything that the mother is experiencing during her pregnancy: it is "the world according to mother." Then there are two tapes of the child—that of the embodied part that records the emotional (E) and somatic (S) experiences of the fetus during its stay in the uterus, and another tape of the unembodied part that gives information on the state of consciousness of the new incarnate.

In the pre- and perinatal areas everything mother experiences, and through her others, is recorded by the fetus without its knowing that the intensity of these feelings is in reality being experienced by mother and people around her. Thoughts and feelings by mother and others both draw and reflect traumas from past lives of the fetus and at the same time aggravate these traumas by becoming attached to current feelings and thoughts of the fetus. Birth reinforces this attachment: almost all present problems are manifested there. In addition to pinpointing early expressions of major traumas that have to do with intimacy, rejection, love, and many other aspects of relationships, a fifth matrix, the moment of bonding, has proven to be essential.

The client needs to re-live what happened during conception, pregnancy, at birth, at the moment of bonding, and in infancy in order to understand why certain symptoms emerge in his/her current experience. Processing these helps him to detach from inappropriate feelings and thoughts about father, mother, grandparents, friends, neighbors, midwife, doctor, nurse, or anyone who played an important role in those periods. Without recovering the moments when these attachments were initiated and without detaching from them, it is difficult to integrate past-life traumas.

When the therapist suspects that prenatal or birth or infancy traumas are involved or when the client has used a variation of phrases indicating disturbance in mother's state during the prenatal time, the use of single words is one way to trace the E and S of these traumas because single words or simple phrases have been used at this early time to express feelings. We have found that the Grof-matrices of the birth experience are helpful for working in this area, although we use the MES bridge and MES processing techniques instead of holotropic breathing.[3]

Case: A Re-evaluation of Mother and Father

In this case TR signifies interventions by Rob Bontenbal and TT refers to those by Tineke Noordegraaf.

The following regression was conducted following a spring conference of the Association for Past-Life Research and Therapies. The subject was a registered nurse who had attended the conference because of her interest in the transpersonal field. We were limited to a single session, so extensive processing of the material was not possible. However, the subject had gone through many years of working on herself. She was a competent and stable professional person with uncommon courage, and we felt that she would be able to process her own recall advantageously.

We used no formal induction but the MES bridge, "I am unreal," to take her into the trauma that needed to be investigated.

T-R: *What do you want to work on?*

C: *Feeling as if my mother wanted to kill me.... It leads to such sadness.*

T-R: *You realize there will only be this session and you will have to process whatever comes up. Tell me something about yourself.*

C: *I married a young physician and immediately had a child. I realized almost from the beginning that the marriage wasn't good for me, that it would not work out. But I kept on having children, six of them, and I felt I couldn't leave. I thought I had chosen and I had to stay. But I finally got out. I still feel bad about it. I've had a lot of therapy, but it hasn't helped very much.*

T-R: *In therapy you didn't find the core issue?*

C: *No, but I felt I was unreal.*

T-R: *Say, "I am unreal."*

C: *(Repeats several times. Begins to cry.) It's ridiculous to feel sad so easily.*

T-T: *Say, "I feel sad."*

C: *(Repeats.)*

T-T: *Feel how sad you are. Feel where in your body you are most sad.*

C: *(Crying.) Everywhere. (Finally points to chest.)*

T-R: *Is there anything connected to your sadness?*

C: *My mother cried all the time. I just feel so bad.*

T-R: *Move backward in time to where you had these same feelings of being so sad.*

C: *I was walking along the street by myself. I had gone to the feature with my twin sister. She wanted to stay to see it again, but I was afraid of what my mother would say, so I said we couldn't stay. And we met my older sister and my mother and they said, "Why didn't you stay?" They made fun of me. (Deep sobbing.) It was horrible.*

T-R: *Say again, "It's horrible."*

C: *(Deep sobbing.)*

T-R: *What is the most horrible thing?*

C: *They laugh at me.*

T-R: *They laugh at me.*

C: *(Deep sobbing.)*

T-T: *Take a deep breath and listen to them again.*

C: *(Wild sobbing.) I feel just so bad.*

T-T: *Take the feeling back, way back to the time when the feeling connected with, "I feel just so bad." Connect with the very first time.*

C: *I don't have anything. Nothing comes.*

T-T: *Say, "I don't have anything."*

C: *It's terrible. There's nothing there. I can't remember anything. (Deep sobbing.)*

T-T: *Nothing's there.*

C: *Nothing's there.*

T-T: *One sentence, one emotion.*

C: *A little thing.*

T-T: *Let the one thing come with feelings.*

C: *It seems like I'm in the womb with my sister. Nothing is there.*

T-T: *You're in the womb with your sister. And your mother is thinking nothing is there. What is it like when mother feels nothing?*

C: *I feel nothing. I don't know why.*

T-T: *What does mother do in order to feel nothing?*

C: *I don't know.*

T-R: *Listen to the words, "I don't know."*

C: *My mother didn't know how to handle it. She didn't know what to do.*

T-R: *Let it all come out.*

C: *(Deep sobbing.)*

T-R: *What goes through mother's mind?*

C: *It's devastating.*

T-T: *Repeat as if your mother is thinking it. Realize this is mother's feeling. Let it all come out.*

C: *It's devastaing.*

T-R: *It's so devastating to be pregnant.*

C: *She finds it so terrible to be pregnant.*

T-R: *Find if there's any moment of doubt in your mother's feeling about going on with the pregnancy.*

T-T: Breathe into your deepest feeling....

T-R: Find a word.

C: I can't, I can't. I just can't. Oh! I keep thinking of something else. My sister told me that my mother had an abortion before my older sister was born. Maybe she thought of it while she was carrying us. It keeps coming in.... I keep feeling my father had a sexual experience.

T-R: What impression do you have of your father?

C: Having sex with my mother.

T-R: What is her feeling?

C: I feel nothing.

T-R: Repeat that.

C: I feel nothing.

T-T: Feel how much of that mother had to say to herself.

C: She feels terrible! (Cries.) I feel terrible, terrible, terrible!

T-R: Keep repeating in. (Presses her chest until she screams.) Terrible!

T-T: I feel terrible.

C: I feel terrible. But it keeps coming back, that terrible feeling. It keeps coming back.

T-T: (Repeats a number of times.)

C: She just feels terrible.

T-T: Breathe through it. It keeps coming in. Mother can't push it away.

T-R: (Takes her feet and shakes them.) Release the tension.

C: (Wild screaming.)

T-T: Release the feelings for mother.

T-R: (Coaches deep breathing.) Cleanse yourself from all these feelings.

C: (Gradually releases.)

T-R: How is father feeling?

C: Very angry.

T-R: What does he say?

C: Bitch! You bitch! (Wild screams.)

T-R: How does mother feel?

C: She feels nothing.

T-T: Let a number come up to know what month of pregnancy this is.

C: Two comes up.

T-R: How do you feel now?

C: Squished.

T-R: Repeat that.

C: (Repeats a number of times.)

T-R: What happens with mother?

C: She's squished.

T-R: What comes to mind about "squished"?

C: My father on top of her.

T-R: Father's on top of mother and she feels squished.

C: She doesn't like it.... I don't like it. (Repeats.)

T-T: Feel how unreal mother makes herself. Feel how much of that feeling is from mother. Go into the feeling and breath it out, now that you know

it is mother's feeling.... Breathe it back—that wooden feeling—breath it
back to your father. See how much that feeling of being unreal belongs
to your mother.

C: My God! (Deep breathing.) It hurts. There's a sadness.

T-T: Why is she so sad?

C: Because she didn't feel anything. It must be bad to feel. It's not Christian
to feel. It's against God.

T-T: What is she forbidding herself?

C: Forbidding the good feelings.

T-R: To feel real.

T-T: Go to the moment you took over her "It's forbidden."

C: It's forbidden.

T-T: Go to the point where she forbids herself. Which feelings are forbidden?

C: It's forbidden to feel angry...or sad.

T-T: What's most forbidden when having sex with father?

C: To have any feelings about it.

T-T: Say it as mother.

C: I won't. I won't. I mustn't enjoy sex.

T-R: Why?

C: She thought it was bad.

T-T: She thought it was bad feeling good. Which feelings does mother refuse
to have?

C: Maybe that's why she hated me—because I was so sexual. Maybe she
knew.

T-T: What is mother feeling about herself.

C: That's she's bad.

T-T: And she's bad because she feels good.

C: She hates herself because she had some good feelings sometimes and
they're forbidden.

T-T: Go to the words that mother still believes.

C: It's a sin. (Repeats.)

T-T: Breathe everything of those words out that you don't believe. Breathe
them out of your system. Breathe it out. You no longer believe those
words: "It's a sin." It no longer belongs to you.

T-R: Move your body. Stretch yourself. Get it out of your system.

T-T: Keep breathing. Get it all out. All the consequences. Come on, get it out.

C: (Wild gagging.)

T-T: Get it out. It doesn't belong to you any more. (Hands her a towel.) Get
it out.

C: (Gagging and vomiting.)

T-T: Get it out. (Helps client to get cleaned up.)

T-T: How do you feel?

C: Peaceful. My body is tight.

T-R: (Vibrates her feet.)

T-T: (Puts hand above client's diaphragm and runs energy.) Breathe it out.

C: Something up there. (Touches shoulder.)

T-R: Concentrate on that feeling.
C: Something flat. I want to shake it off.
T-R: Does it hurt?
C: Just a shadow.
T-R: Look at the specific part of your shoulder. What impression are you getting?
C: Ball, black ball. Not large.
T-R: If you could bring the black ball to where it belongs, where would it go? Bring it back to where it belongs.
C: I don't know if it's mother's or father's.
T-T: Do you want to get rid of it?
C: Yes.
T-T: Throw the ball in the direction it came from.
T-R: Where does the ball belong?
C: Down somebody's throat? A mouth.
T-T: Mother's or father's?
C: Mother's
T-T: What is father doing to the throat of mother?
C: He's choking her.
T-T: Get that feeling that father's choking mother.
C: Only thing I can think of is oral sex.
T-T: Go to the feelings. The only thing you need to do is to breathe into it and understand it. Go into the feelings and breathe through it. Breathe through it.
C: (Gags.)
T-T: Do whatever you need to clear your throat. Get it out.
C: (Gags and spits up.)
T-T: Good. Let's open up. I feel the repressed anger is connected here. Breathe through it and understand it. It keeps coming up. Get rid of all the consequences.
C: (Deep breathing.) There's a little pain right there. (Rubs under right ear on neck.)
T-T: Is it mother or father?
C: Mother.
T-T: What's father doing to cause her pain.
C: He's touching her there.
T-T: What's causing the pain? What is connected to pain?
C: Stop! Stop!
T-T: What's father doing that she wants him to stop?
C: Rubbing with his penis.
T-R: Breathe with the whole of your breath and see if there's any feeling still there.
C: I'm quite comfortable now. (Said after several minutes.)
T-R: Quite comfortable?
C: (Laughs.) Yes.

T-R: Release all the strong feelings about mother and father.... You were very strong and brave. Thank yourself for doing well.... Now let yourself come back into the room in San Diego. (Counts from one to five.) Take your time.

Follow-Up

Several weeks after the regression the client reported that she was still processing the shift in perception about her parents. She had always seen her father as kind and caring and her mother as a controlling person, a crybaby, always the victim. Now she realized that her mother had good reason to be distressed with her life. When the mother had her first child she was told not to have further children or her life would be at risk. This threat, added to the economic pressures of the Depression, probably made her ambivalent about the new pregnancy. The client had always thought her mother had made her father's life miserable, but now she saw it the other way around.

She was struggling particularly with the new sexual information. She realized how vulnerable a woman is during pregnancy, and the unconscious memories of how her mother had suffered from the sexual pressures of her father, now that the memories had become conscious, helped her understand her lifelong resistance to being feminine. She was able to face more candidly the distorted sexuality of her father, who had needed sex so much during the pregnancy that he had forced her mother to accept his oral approach. The client was shaken by this, but it opened her memory to a game of "bear" that her father had played with her and her sisters, where he chased them around on the rug and then grabbed them and fondled them sexually. Though she was feeling pain and distress over men's insistence on entitlement to their "sexual stuff," she had an increasing feeling of well-being and for the first time honored the memory of her mother on Mother's Day.

Several months afterward she wrote about her continuing growing freedom and peace:

I see my mother and father in an almost totally opposite way. It's especially unbelievable how I saw my mother. I had no idea that her life was hard and that my father must have forced her to have sex when it was so repulsive to her. She must have enjoyed some of it but felt that she was so bad for enjoying it that she then felt terrible. Seeing my mother totally different lets me be more feminine, less controlled, less tough on myself and less strict. I believe all my sexual experiences were somehow the flip side of my mother's repressed, distasteful feelings about sex.

Seeing my mother so differently makes me aware that my perceptions of other people, incidences, experiences may be very different from what I think they are in the moment. And every time I say "I don't know," I remember that that's one of the statements I made in the regression and is tied to mother and her not wanting to know or remember.

My body moves. My hips move, and I walk along with more movement—not holding my hips strictly in place. It's a funny feeling to be walking along and feel me moving more freely—I like it. I suppose this has to do with being less restricted about looking sexual.

Last night as I turned over to go to sleep I had this horrible, anxious, almost terrifying feeling. It is a familiar, terrifying feeling, the same one I felt during the regression. I've had this feeling a lot of my life and now I'm very aware of it as it emerges. I can now say, "Go away, feeling, you don't belong to me. There's no reason for me to feel you." As I say this, the most wonderful feeling of joy is right there in me. I can hardly believe these feelings can be so close together, one immediately replacing the other.

I still have a lump in my throat. I'd like to open up my throat, get out whatever needs to be gone through to open up. But I'm feeling much more peaceful, even if my throat does get clogged up! I'm able to get into more peace, less struggle, and feel good, really good more of the time.

Life is much more joyous, more than it's ever been. The move to the hills away from the city has been great. Being able to be outside a lot is nice, and having a garden, flowers, etc., is wonderful. Being by the bay is nice, too. With the move and regression life is quite different and wonderful.

Rescripting Destructive Birth Patterns

by

Barbara Findeisen, M.F.C.C.

Introduction

Issues around birth and life *en utero* create a template on which later life experiences are laid. It is as if our first impressions last and form the basis of our feelings about life, about being in a body, and about relationships. Our uterine life within the womb and within the psyche of the mother is our first relationship. If it is positive, children have a basic sense of trust in themselves and in the world. If it is negative, the basic instinct is one of fear and mistrust of the world. Einstein was once asked, "What is the most important question?" He answered, "Is the Universe friendly?" Our first learned answer to that question influences every aspect of our lives.

Birth and death are intertwined. Both are experiences of separation at the physical level. Both are experiences of going through a dark tunnel and emerging into the light. Both affirm the continuity of the basic self. A difficult time *en utero* or a dangerous experience at birth often create in consciousness an especially thick veil between our limited this-time existence and an understanding of our more extended and joyous consciousness. It is as though we get stuck in our physical bodies because we have been so traumatically involved with them. However, these experiences are not difficult for everyone. Many babies perceive the uterus as a haven, a place of contentment, abundance, love, and even play, and never experience the "poisonous uterus" image retained by those whose births were traumatic. People who are troubled enough to seek therapeutic help probably have experienced trauma, and they can be helped to transform even these very early and deep noxious templates.

In beginning an exploration of the uterine state, I use imagery to take the client back to just before conception for this lifetime. This time is experienced as one of pure energy, of peace and calm joy. I then suggest that the client observe both parents and recount what awareness there is of each one. We then visualize the conception. It is amazing how often this can be recalled vividly. Then the client is encouraged to tune into the mother's thoughts when she finds that she is pregnant, including the timing and emotional climate of her communication of her pregnancy to the father, and the general atmosphere of anticipation or dismay over the fact of the pregnancy. The unborn child is aware of the discussion about the pregnancy and may misinterpret what is said.

From there we move through all stages of uterine development and birth, becoming aware of the thoughts and feelings of the parents and others in the immediate environment. Often the client discovers that the feelings that he or she accepted into consciousness were actually the mother's feelings, and they do not reflect the way the client originally felt. Many babies *en utero* begin to feel guilty for being alive; they become aware of the mother's resentments that arise from the extra pressure of pregnancy. These babies become *en utero* therapists, deciding that it is they who must be the caretakers. (Perhaps the saying that gifted therapists are born, not made, is literally true!) During this portion of the regression, the therapist looks constantly for connections that are related to current situations. It is especially important to correct misconceptions that occurred when the fetus had taken for itself some verbalization that was actually meant for another in the environment (as when a distraught mother says to the father, "Just leave and never come back!"). Many such incidents and verbalizations can be recovered in regression work with the *en utero* personality. Often these recollections can be verified by asking surprised parents if some particular thing happened or was verbalized.

The general experience of the growth process in the uterus is followed, including the feeling of the uterus getting crowded, and finally the birth process itself. Birth, even at its easiest, is a time of stress. It sets a pattern for handling all later stresses. From the first relationship with the mother, a child learns the nature of relationship in general and from the nature of this early set follows the general direction of his attitudes, feelings, philosophy and approach to life. These attitudes can be modified, but not until we know how we originally structured them.

The re-living of the process of birth can be deepened by the therapist asking questions that open up the experience, such as "What are the first signs that the birth is beginning? What feelings are there?" Building up of pressure is noted, as are any problems that may have occurred in the birth process. Especially important are the decisions and promises that the person makes at this time. For instance, when the contractions begin but the cervix is not open, there may be a sense that there is no way out. Common experiences related to this stage have to do with feeling helpless, hopeless, trapped, alone, and filled with existential despair. Any past-life memory of being enclosed or trapped or being completely helpless or in despair becomes attached to this stage of labor and is easy to manifest later. Claustrophobia is generally related to this experience.

The next stage of birth is the struggle through the birth canal while the cervix is open. Contractions of up to one hundred pounds of pressure push the baby, creating a feeling of enormous struggle for survival. Often anoxia occurs. Difficult births are experienced in terms of violence and torture and later may, in the individual's unconscious, connect sex with aggression. Many sexual problems, especially sadomasochism, seem related to this period. Here the child becomes not only a victim but an active participant. This stage marks the borderline between the agony of birth and the ecstacy of freedom. The prevailing feeling during this part of the birth is rage. If birth is delayed and the child is not allowed to emerge according to his own timing, such a delay may set a lifelong pattern of not being able "to get through" anything.

If a separation occurs at this time, the bonding is a crippled one that is difficult to heal later. Clinical theory has suggested that it is this failure of early bonding that leads to development of the sociopathic personality. Inadequate early bonding may create a troublesome relationship between mother and child that may continue for a lifetime—and, as we believe, influence future lifetimes. If it is true that we choose our parents for karmic lessons, this negative pattern is only reinforced by the failure to bond. Eventually, in future lifetimes, this emotional wound will be healed, but meanwhile current failure in birth and bonding handicaps our learning path. Ancient lives of rejection, difficult and painful relationships and separations are all reactivated when a child and a mother do not bond well at birth or are actually separated. During this early phase, such traumas seem to be stamped deeply into the psyche, probably because it has no defenses in that early stage. It is not strange, therefore, that individuals who endured such initial separation or rejection grow up to be highly defensive.

Patterns that can influence one's childhood emerge clearly when the events just following birth are observed. It is important to help the client notice where the mother is, what is said and to whom, especially about the sex of the child, whether there is a preference (which the fetus always knows and which sets some of the expectation of his/her relationship with the parents), whether nursing takes place and how soon, whether there are stroking and eye contact. All of these early events lead to decisions that continue to function at an unconscious level until they are unearthed and examined and, if need be, re-evaluated.

Case 1. An Inhospitable World

When Anna first came to me she was in a suicidal depression, actively planning to disappear physically. She did not want to be here. Such a script usually has a long history and may have lain dormant for years, exerting an unconscious influence over behavior and feelings. In a crisis it may assume control over the individual unless it has been uncovered, re-experienced, and changed. Anna came to me in just such a crisis.

We began her regression in her prenatal state. She at first experienced the womb as safe and comfortable.

C: The light is here with me.

I moved her forward to when her mother learned she was pregnant.

C: *Oh, she doesn't want me here! She's scared. She doesn't want me! She wants me to leave....*

En utero, Anna's relationship with her mother disintegrated into one of little trust. She began to believe that she could not depend upon her mother.

T: *What's happening to your mother?*
C: *She's saying,"I don't want this baby. I don't want to get married. I'm too young. I'm not ready. I don't like him." (Sobbing.) She wants to kill me. It's all my fault. I'm bad.*

Here are seen the beginning of feelings of guilt and self-hate. Throughout Anna's stages of uterine life and through her birth process we continued to look for sources of later pathology.

T: *Move ahead and tell me what happens as your body grows.*
C: *It's black and cold in here and I'm scared. I don't like it in here.*
T: *What's frightening your mother?*
C: *He's scary. He's frightening her, and she can't do anything. She can't protect me. Maybe if I'm very still, she will forget I'm here.*

The baby is affected *en utero* as much by the mother's moods and feelings as by what she is eating and drinking. Anna's reaction to being frightened was to continue her script of being invisible in order to be safe, with the not surprising result that later as a child she became shy and withdrawn and fearful of her father.

C: *I can't breathe. I can't breathe. My head—they are crushing my head. They are killing me!*

Anna experienced a traumatic premature birth during which her mother was drugged and not able to help her. She was pulled from the birth canal with forceps. Subsequently she manifested severe respiratory problems. Again she learned that life was dangerous and that people wanted to hurt her.

> *T: What happens after you come out?*
> *C: I'm all alone. I'm in a box. No one is here. No one wants me (crying).*

Her mother was not able to be with Anna through the critical bonding time after birth. She was placed in an incubator for many weeks, which reinforced her initial script that no one wanted her. This early failure in bonding occurs often. After what is frequently a life-threatening struggle with stress and fear, the newborn finds himself alone, feeling abandoned, and with no human comfort. Basic life attitudes of compulsive independence or dependence, trust or mistrust, are begun in those precious first hours after birth. It is not the nature of the script but its compulsiveness that will cause later problems. One such event doesn't necessarily determine a lifelong pattern, but it lays a foundation. Later events either reinforce it or cause it to fade.

As Anna grew, she generalized her mistrust to almost everyone. She learned that her world was a dangerous and inhospitable place: post-natal life was a continuation of her uterine scripting. She became quiet, separate, and tried to take care of herself. She learned to suppress her needs and feelings and to ask for nothing—to "disappear" as much as she could. If she couldn't disappear physically, she disappeared psychologically and emotionally. Her childhood in a dysfunctional family with a sadistic and cruel father reinforced her script to go away, which she eventually translated into suicidal terms.

Such scripts can be changed by rescripting or reframing, using a higher power to assist in the transformation. To be a valid and healing experience, such rescripting must move in the direction of the Higher Self. To prepare for such rescripting, I had Anna review her pre- and perinatal experiences until we felt she had released most of the painful memories and had a clear picture of what had occurred. After that we were able to change the damaging scripts and to reframe what had happened to her.

In order to connect with a strong positive experience, we were fortunate that we could return to the beginning of her first regression, where she had clearly felt the presence of the Light. She realized that she had felt it was *her Light*, was her.

> *T: Go back to the time you felt your Light. Do you remember?*
> *C: Yes...my Light...yes, it's here again. I thought I had lost it (crying). It's back.*
> *T: Keep the Light with you as we move through these early experiences. Take the Light with you and go to where your mother discovered you were in her body.*
> *C: I wanted to be there. I wanted to come.... It's not my fault she is upset. I didn't ruin her life. She didn't have to stay with him. She could have done something else. It's not my fault.*

T: *Continue to move forward. Be sure you take your Light. Tell me what you see.*

C: *Oh...she wanted to die. She wanted me to die, too, but I wanted to live...I wanted to live. Those were her feelings, not mine!*

This was a dramatic turning point in Anna's healing process. She said over and over, "*She* wanted to die!...*I* wanted to live." Her script continues to be, "I want to live; this is my life and it is safe for me to be seen." No longer the lost child, she has found herself and is continuing to work with the child within, to love herself and to create in her inner and outer world a safe place in which to live and share her talents.

Case 2. Uncompleted Abortion

A 30-year-old woman, Carol, came into therapy suffering from feelings of inferiority to the point where she seriously considered suicide. She felt as though she shouldn't be here. She was painfully shy, unable to relate to people, and kept a low profile. University educated, she was a competent programmer. Aside from a few work-related contacts she spent her time alone.

The event in this lifetime, triggering her feeling that she shouldn't be here, occurred shortly after conception. In the regression her body trembled with terror and her teeth chattered as she turned and twisted on the mat.

T: *Can you describe what you are experiencing?*

C: *It's as though something is trying to scrape me away, to kill me.*

T: *How are you responding to this feeling?*

C: *I'll be good. I'll be quiet. I'll never be a bother.*

She recovered several past-life experiences of being honored, singled out as special, and then ceremonially sacrificed. Apparently the abortion attempt restimulated her memory of sacrificial deaths, both in Egypt and in South America. This encouraged her obsession with keeping a low profile.

Carol had always wanted to live, both in those lifetimes and in this one. This positive feeling was reinforced by re-living a lifetime in Greece as a temple dancer. She participated in the rituals there and recognized that lifetime as one of beauty, grace, and fulfillment with no sacrifice involved.

As Carol understood the strength of her own desire to survive and be here, she began to feel positive and accepting of herself for the first time. In therapy she gradually reclaimed her rights to be alive, to have needs, to be able to attend social gatherings safely, and make friends. Currently she is engaged and is planning to be married to a man she met in her office.

Case 3. Rescripting Guilt

Helen was heavily burdened with guilt. She had spent her life adapting to others' wishes and needs by denying herself and then taking care of everyone in her life. She wanted to "let go of the past" and end the chronic feeling of guilt that lay over her life like a heavy blanket. She wanted to learn how to be comfortable with power, especially her own. Her rescripting took several forms, both conscious psychological rescripting and transformational rescripting, processes that often take place together.

In a regression to her uterine life she sensed her mother's resentful anger at being pregnant. Helen felt that she was already a mistake, that she was "wrong" to be there. Later she felt she was "wrong" for being a female, another mistake. Her birth was breech, which almost killed her mother—another reinforcement of "I'm wrong, bad, a mistake"—she even comes out the "wrong" way. Her fear of her own power is there. Her low self-esteem, and the resulting script to adapt and take care of others, stemmed from these pre- and peri-natal experiences.

During a subsequent session, conducted with Helen lying on a mat on the floor, she regressed back to her birth and found herself crying that she didn't want to come out. In an instant, to my surprise, she physically reversed herself 180 degrees on the mat. Then, after a short rest, she felt herself being born "right."

Later I asked her about this. She carried no conscious memory of having "righted" herself. When she viewed the videotape of the session, she expressed amazement. At a physiological level, she had rescripted herself from being "wrong," a mistake, to being "right and okay to be here."

During her next regression, Helen found herself in a past life confronting a guilt-producing event that was to be re-stimulated by her birth in this lifetime, when she felt she had hurt her mother.

> C: *I'm in that room where I work with an older woman. She's angry—has been angry for a long time. She doesn't like anything I do. I know I'm not what she is saying. She's walking back and forth, talking real mean, lots of words. I'm arguing with her, trying to outshout her. I'm very angry; like I'm pushing her.... I'm hitting her.... I hit her.... I killed her! I can't believe it. I can't live with that. I couldn't have done that. It's not true.... I'm holding her. I'm sorry. I love you!... I despise myself."*

She continued relating the events of that lifetime following the murder. She ran away, and later she was killed by some passersby who discovered her in the woods where she was hiding.

Helen felt distraught as a result of this memory. The guilt over killing her teacher and friend, plus the guilt from early in this present life, felt overwhelming. Even though in this life she had tried to be exactly what her mother wanted and had adapted herself to always making her mother happy, she had never succeeded. Her script had enabled her to survive but only at the expense of her own identity and self-esteem. I used rescripting techniques to help release the guilt and anguish she was feeling.

She moved back to the scene wherein she hit and killed her friend. I suggested that she see if there was another way she could choose to deal with this situation.

C: *I could turn and walk out the door.*

T: *What would happen then?*

C: *She'd be furious for a while, and then she'd settle down and be okay. I don't have to fight her. There is power in walking out the door...real strength.*

T: *What would you want to communicate to her?*

C: *I want to do things the way you want—but the way I want, too. I deserve respect. Together we can do good things...she would understand that. She's sorry that I had to go away, and she's sorry for me...for what I did to me! She's forgiving me (Helen cries and sounds astonished). It feels humbling.... I tried to be God and judge myself.*

Through this process, Helen began to see power in a new and more positive way. She had consciously rescripted her attitudes about her own power, and realized that power can sometimes be having the courage to "walk out the door." Power is not to be feared and it is not necessarily characterized by anger in its expression. She now realized that she had choices in how to use her energy. As she said, "Real power is in knowing what to do."

The sense of forgiveness Helen gained through her regression proved to be transforming. She experienced a wave of compassion for herself and for her friend. Her script of guilt and adaptation then began to lose its power in her life. After the session ended she walked to the creek, listened to the water gurgling over the rocks, and then, alone on a hillside, danced in the warm February sunshine. She described herself as dancing and laughing like a child, in a way that she had never felt like doing before.

Rescripting comes directly from a transformational domain and is always healing, for it brings one into harmony with the Self that lies beyond and before roles and scripts.

Case 4. Etiology of Fear

The earlier that traumas occur and the more global the feelings are, the more entrenched is the neurosis that later develops. This is particularly true when fear is experienced early in uterine development. Diana, a sophisticated, intelligent woman from a family of physicians—father, husband, and sons—had awakened for as long as she could recall with feelings of panic.

Years of therapy had not been able to release her from the daily feeling of doom.

In a regression back to her earliest memory in the womb, she experienced a blissful state of peace and joy, but when I moved her forward to the time when her mother found out that she was pregnant, Diana instantly experienced the panic to which she awoke daily; the bliss changed abruptly to one of fear. She had no cognitive understanding of the source of this fear but felt only visceral surges of great danger.

We worked to bring the memory into consciousness where it could be seen and connected to the past and released in her present life. The next morning Diana did not feel the usual panic when she awakened. She had been able to leave the past experience where it had occurred.

When Diana left Pocket Ranch and returned home, her 80-year-old mother asked about her daughter's experience in California. As Diana tentatively brought up her birth regression and the fear that she had experienced early in the pregnancy, her mother gasped and told her that before conceiving Diana she had given birth to three children and the doctor had advised her never to get pregnant again because another pregnancy would kill her. When she discovered she was pregnant, she went into the panic that Diana had felt invading her safe and blissful womb-life. Diana's first feeling, therefore, was her mother's fear and she took it on and made it a part of her own psyche. Though her mother had chosen to take the risk and continue the pregnancy, Diana had for fifty-odd years compulsively and unconsciously repeated that original awakening to her mother's panic. She needed to become consciously aware of it in order to release it. Then it did not need to be re-experienced over and over like some shadow knocking on the door of her consciousness.

Case 5. Twin Bonding

Joy and Joni were identical twins. Joy came to me originally for severe anxiety and periodic suicidal depressions. The twins lived together in a symbiotic relationship. Joy was the older of the two. She was the responsible one who knew how to drive and had a car and a steady job. The twins harbored resentment toward each other but could not separate.

As we worked on Joy's relationship with her parents, she gradually became better able to handle her emotions, and her fears lessened. We went back to her birth to try to find the source of her resentment toward Joni.

Joy experienced being born in this life on a chilling December night on an Indian reservation in Arizona. In her struggle to be born she felt pain around her ankle, as though her twin sister were holding onto her and didn't want her to be born. Joy was the first one in the womb and had all along resented the other baby's presence but was aware of a feeling that she must take care of her twin. Almost immediately after her birth, Joy was taken from her mother and given to her father to hold while Joni, who was not expected, was born.

In a past-life regression Joy saw herself leading a younger sister up a steep mountain trail. The sister stumbled. Joy struggled to hold onto her hand, but the little girl slipped to her death. At the end of the trail, people severely blamed her for the death of her sister.

One evening I asked Joy to come to my office so that I could practice using my new video camera. She arrived with her twin sister, and the two wanted me to regress them together. They argued that since they had both been in the womb together, there was no reason that they couldn't be regressed at the same time. They regressed back in time and into the prenatal state quite easily.

Joy: (Very agitatedly) Baby, go 'way! Baby, go 'way!

Joni remains quiet as Joy becomes more and more upset about the presence of the other baby. When it is time to be born, Joy is determined to get away from her twin. As she twists and turns, Joni begins to cry and clings to Joy's ankle to keep her from leaving.

Strong bonds forged of ancient guilt, resentment, and fear of being abandoned had held these two girls together. They are still together, but new avenues of communication and caring, based on present needs and not on past experiences, now form the basis of their relationship. Joni does not have to fear that she will not survive if Joy lets go of her, and Joy no longer feels forced to be responsible for her sister. The old guilt and resentment are largely gone.

Reluctant Birthing

by

Irene Hickman, D.O.

Introduction

A surprising finding emerges from scanning an increasing number of birth and death experiences—birth is approached with far more reluctance than is death. Few patients find birth to be something they look forward to eagerly. The more common reaction is regret, reluctance, or even refusal.

Death comes in many forms: some brutal and gruesome, some by suicide, some a peaceful dying during sleep. Prior deaths often leave scars that make themselves felt in present-life patterns and reactions as well as attitudes. But although deaths are often violent and leave lingering emotional problems, the feeling immediately after is usually of freedom and few regrets. Birth, in contrast, requires the assumption of difficult or unpleasant limitations and responsibilities, as is recognized by the patient in the following case.

Case: Resistance to Being Born

Larry described a recent unsatisfactory past life in which he had had an unusual and hated name and had been controlled by a dominating mother. His death in his last lifetime had occurred in 1913 from pneumonia, just a short time after an unsuccessful attempt at suicide. Suicide attempts seldom lead to a positive experience in the lifetime to follow and intensify a natural resistance to being incarnated again. The suicide attempt in Larry's previous life had been initiated by his perception that he had moved into an impasse. He had also been depressed by his conviction that his wife didn't think him much of a man.

Following his death he apparently did not spend much time in the interlife, since little is recorded of any experience there. His current life began a scant year later, so evidently he rushed from that life to this one without having done much processing of the difficulties in the previous one.

Only his final sentence, where he longed to return "to the brownies—the little people," suggests any content for an interim experience.

The conflict over whether to be born, a conflict that flowed through Larry's awareness in the prenatal state, was intensified in the birth process, and in a sense was solved by default as he entered his body at the last possible moment. But his agreement to be involved in what happened to him, even if tortured and ambivalent, was at least a small step forward in his consciousness journey.

T: *It's now 1913...1913. What are you doing now?*

P: *I'm outside now, just trying to understand. That's funny. I can see a little girl. Her name is Mary Anne. She's going to have a brother.*

T: *Are you going to be that brother?*

P: *Yeah. That's the funniest thing. She's patting her mother's stomach. She says, "That's my brother in there." I'm in there but I'm outside too.*

T: *You want to be born?*

P: *If she's going to be my sister, I guess I want to be born. She's such a nice girl. I just decided that I want to be her brother. This is silly. Why should I want to be her brother?*

T: *You are going to be born. Describe your birth.*

P: *I'm up in the air watching.*

T: *You're watching yourself being born?*

P: *I see a funny looking little head coming out sideways. He's twisting sideways.*

T: *What else is happening?*

P: *I hear somebody screaming. It's all over and she's still screaming. Why doesn't she just relax?*

T: *Can you help her in any way?*

P: *I'm separated from her now. The doctor is cleaning me up. I'm a mess. He's drawing something away from my face and I'm breathing.*

T: *Did the doctor spank you?*

P: *He didn't spank me. He just held me in his hand and I started breathing.*

T: *When you started breathing, were you aware any more of who you were before, or who you are going to be?*

P: *There's some kind of trouble. I don't want to go in there.*

T: *Where?*

P: *In that body—that baby. It's just trouble all over again. Every time you go through this, it's just the same thing, over and over and over again.*

T: *You came to learn something.*

P: *What can you learn? People are stupid and they don't get smarter. No one likes you and they give you a funny name and you end up in the hospital, and it's all over, and then I have to face it again. I don't want to do it almost. I feel like I have to, but I don't want to do it.... But if I don't, he won't live. What a choice! (Pause.) Seems like everything is frozen. Nobody's moving. Everything stops while I am making up my mind. It's a big job. (Pause.) To get the courage to do it again. Why do it? It doesn't*

> *make any sense. You just go through it and through it.... If I could just learn something!*
>
> T: *What are they naming the baby?*
> P: *Don't hurry me. I'm not there yet. I don't know if I want to. I don't know. If I just thought there was any possibility of making this baby happy, I would. But that baby—what chance has he got more than anybody else?*
> T: *You have to be born.*
> P: *I've got to do something. I can't just sit here. If I don't, who will? Maybe somebody else will do it...I don't see anybody else around.*
> T: *Going in.... Let's move ahead a year.*
> P: *No, don't rush me. Just don't rush me. I'm just going in—going in. I'm just in. Let me rest for a minute. I hope it will work out. What chance does he have to learn something? This poor little baby—he didn't do anything to anybody. What can I do to help him better? To learn something? To not just muddle through? I don't know. I'm just a baby. I guess I'll have to give up. I had no choice to stay out there. I can't just stay out there. I want to be back with the brownies—the little people.*

Birth in a sense promises blood, sweat, tears, and a ceaseless chain of choices. This was a formidable and unwelcome demand, especially to a soul like Larry, who had failed to handle these adequately in his previous lifetime. Larry was also handicapped by the fact that he had apparently shortchanged his opportunities for learning in the interlife.[4]

The mention of the "brownies—the little people" suggests that interim experiences, even those with positive implications, do not always include teachings in "pavilions of light," so often described. Apparently souls are also drawn into less glamorous realms. However, Larry's yearnings for the "little people" gives an intimation that his experience with them had been positive, however limited that may have been.

This case also suggests that there is no set time for the soul to enter into the body. Larry was aware of his prospective body and what it went through at birth, but he managed to bypass suffering the difficulties of the experience by delaying entering the new body until it was well birthed, just as he had tried to bypass frustrations in his past life by his suicide attempt. Is this last-minute entrance of the soul into body a usual occurrence, or is it specific to Larry and others like him who are especially resistant to being born? In this account of Larry there is also the implication that if a soul decides not to be born, the infant body will be stillborn, an interesting speculation.

Regression of the Cautious Patient

by

Winafred B. Lucas, Ph.D.

Introduction

Many patients approach therapy expecting to work on current dilemmas by analyzing them with the therapist's help and deciding on more productive courses of action than those that have precipitated them into difficulties. This existential approach, which characterizes much of contemporary therapy, is effective if the roots of the problem do not stem from deeper, older sources. But unfortunately, as Freud pointed out, many negative forms of behavior were patterned far back in an individual's history and have become difficult to see because they have become covered over with the stresses and strains of the years. If this is true of sources of distress that lie in childhood, it is even more true of patterns initiated earlier in past lives or in prenatal and birth experiences.

The belief system of many patients interferes with recovery of these very early sources. Such patients, however, are usually willing to look at their early childhood memories, even though they protest that they can't remember early events, and they will allow themselves to be relaxed into an altered state through straightforward suggestions and instructions. In such a state they recover significant memories that facilitate understanding of their current attitudes and behavior. The wealth of these memories is often a surprise; patterns emerge with clarity, and often experiences that neither therapist nor patient have suspected, such as child abuse, become remembered.

This successful recovery of childhood memories acts as a springboard into prenatal recall, where the patterns that were revealed in childhood appear in even clearer form. The repetition of the pattern, often surprising to the patient, has a powerful impact, not only on the credibility of the memory but also on its therapeutic potential. The energy field of the recovered pattern becomes open to modification, which is accomplished through repetition, rescripting, and cognitive reframing techniques, as well as by working toward forgiveness of parents and self.

Repeating prenatal and birth experiences, once they are uncovered, significantly deepens them. With each new exploration, more details are retrieved and the pattern clarifies. It is like exploring an unknown land—each trip through it exposes new details and makes the general configuration of the landscape clearer. The process of reframing is also reinforced and deepened by repetition of the experience. Many times a too-hasty journey does not hold.

Background

This subject, Richard, had no experience with altered-state work, and his belief system did not include the concept of past lives. He was not introspective and agreed to explore in an altered mode only because he had reached a dead-end in conventional therapy and was adventurous enough to be willing to try something new. Our careful work on the aspects of his life of which he was aware had led him to feel he could trust me, a necessary ingredient of successful regression work. Although working in an altered state obviously made him feel insecure and even, perhaps, a little ridiculous, he approached it with courage and did his best.

As happens with patients who cannot move easily beyond ordinary states of consciousness, Richard needed to begin with childhood memories and work backward. My approach with him when he said in the beginning that he had no memories was to ask him to make up something, and this permission moved him through his resistance so that by the time we came to uterine memories he produced them easily. His childhood reminiscences had taken time, as they frequently do, but they proved to be valuable in themselves and they built a foundation for his uterine and birth memories. He could trust himself to produce these deeper recollections and let them flow, setting aside objections from his rational mind.

Richard's presenting problem was his marriage. He had been pressured by his wife, Martha, to come in to see me. Martha was an attractive, intelligent, and assertive woman who in our opening joint session accused Richard of lying about everything and not being open with her. She insisted that all successful marriages were characterized by complete openness. Richard did not defend himself but sat passively taking her attack, even occasionally conceding that she was right, which failed to satisfy her. He made no effort to rebut her additional accusation that their financial prosperity was due to her.

When I saw Richard alone he intimated that the money they had, which evidently was considerable, though initially built on a loan from his wife at the time of their marriage, had escalated due to his business sense. Both he and Martha had been married before. At the time of his divorce Richard had given his first wife what he had accumulated in order to provide for her and their two daughters. Martha's husband had been killed in a plane crash, and as a result of heavy insurance and a generous airline settlement, she and her two children had been left in a good financial situation. Richard failed to realize the part this course of events had played and looked upon himself as essentially a beggar.

The problem of lying, reported by Martha, was perceived to have begun at the time they were married, when Richard failed to tell Martha that he had a Jewish father. When she found this out, she became acutely distressed and constantly reproached him. He took her anger without protestation and appeared unable to find any way to defend or exonerate himself. Meanwhile, his tendency to shade or conceal the truth spread to other areas of his life, which drew further accusations. They had gone on year after year, with Martha constantly attacking, confronting, and reproaching, and Richard responding helplessly and apologetically.

Martha felt it was Richard who needed the therapy, and, evidently for the first time, he had agreed. The question he and I confronted first was why he subjected himself to such heartless and non-loving attacks, which had turned him off sexually (another of Martha's complaints). Richard could not bring himself to think that he deserved anything better than this defensive life. There were evidences of companionable and satisfying aspects to the marriage, but these were always implied rather than stated.

Regression to Childhood

Careful exploration gave no sufficient explanation of his passive attitude or his equivocation, nor did it throw any light on his economic anxiety. I suggested going back to his early childhood to seek information. Richard claimed that he could not remember anything about his childhood. However, in an altered state a flood of memories returned that supplied answers to some of the questions.

Early memories of childhood or the prenatal state can be retrieved by working backward through a patient's life, following some theme or statement, but this time I went directly to Richard's first year and moved forward. I hoped that recall of childhood would encourage him later to go back before birth. The fact that he had some impression about the circumstances of his infancy encouraged him to make a start, and as he sank deeper into an altered state, he was able to retrieve new memories.

T: *Tell me about your first year. If you can't remember, make it up.*
P: *I see my father with a fedora on his head. He doesn't have a mustache. He has round metal-framed glasses. He's smiling.*

T: *At you?*

P: *Yes. He's saying I am the apple of his eye. He's asking where I got all my blond curls. I see myself in a baby carriage.*

T: *Do you remember more about your father?*

P: *He's gone a lot. My mother has to go and get him. Not a lot of people have cars, but we have a Chevrolet. I don't think he ever drives because he is losing his eyesight.*

T: *What does he do?*

P: *He's a practicing physician, gives anesthetics—he's the only anesthesiologist in the hospital, so he works nights, too. My mother drives him, and the lady downstairs watches me.*

T: *Does your mother nurse you?*

P: *I never nursed—I think I went on the bottle right away.*

T: *In your second year of life, what are you experiencing?*

P: *We're on a picnic. We sit on the running board of the car. We eat lunch—I see it being handed to me—an egg sandwich.*

T: *What is your father doing?*

P: *I don't see him doing anything. I see my mother doing everything.*

T: *What are you feeling?*

P: *I'm happy—I'm happy with my parents.*

T: *How do you feel about your father?*

P: *I don't feel any threat. I'm totally satisfied.*

T: *Now you're in your third year. What are you experiencing?*

P: *Now I'm starting to get less happy because I'm never completely accepted by my peers. I don't play marbles well. They take all my marbles away. I'm not good at anything—I have the feeling my parents always protect me.*

T: *How does your mother deal with this?*

P: *She defends me. I am relieved but embarrassed. My mother says anybody who teases me is bad, and that relieves me but I don't like it. My parents dress me up. I don't want to be "pretty." They tell me I am the prettiest and the smartest. I have to live up to this but I don't know how.*

Altered-state work often lacks an accurate sense of time, and it is possible that Richard picked up feelings that belonged to slightly older periods.

T: *You are in your fourth year now. What are you experiencing?*

P: *I don't go to school until the first grade—there's no kindergarten. I fall out of a window and get hurt. I like sleigh riding.*

T: *How do you see your father now?*

P: *He's not home much—he's working. He's either just coming home or sitting in an armchair. He has glaucoma, restricted peripheral vision, but he can read. Most of the time he is smoking.*

T: *How do you feel about him?*

P: *I love both my parents, but I don't like the pressure they put on me to be pretty and smart. I feel like I'm always performing.*

T: *Is this the start of not being able to deal with pressure?*

P: *Yes, but I didn't know that then. It was just my mother...and her mother... We live in an apartment. For some reason I spend more time playing with girls than with boys. I am always afraid of being hurt. Boys play too rough. I'm afraid of conflict.... But I remember that years later when I was in the Navy and we were caught in a storm off Cape Shelbourne, I was a first lieutenant and went and lashed the mast, probably the most dangerous thing. It's conflict with physical hurt that can make me afraid.*

I see a marble game. One or more of the boys take my marbles and I never try to defend myself. Now I am at a seacoast in New Jersey in a cabin with a friend and I wet the bed. I'm constantly embarrassed by wetting the bed, by not being adept at ball games, by begin afraid when there's a conflict.

T: *What are you experiencing with your parents?*

P: *My parents are fighting.*

T: *How does this make you feel?*

P: *Frightened. My father is losing his eyesight and my mother is threatening to leave him. I feel he will become my responsibility. I beg her to stay.*

T: *How old are you?*

P: *Seven or older.*

Here Richard again skipped forward in his time sequence, as he had done when he recalled the Cape Shelbourne incident. He made a major effort to reframe incidents in the context of later events, experiencing his early years and processing them at the same time.

T: *What about your fifth year?*

P: *It is a transition time. My father is just quitting his medical practice—he's losing his eyesight. My mother is starting to work as a legal secretary. I remember good times with my parents, but I do so many things alone. My sister is born during this year.*

T: *Tell me about that.*

P: *I'm not sure if I will be happy or not to have a sister; I like the limelight. When my mother goes out to work, my father babysits us. I can't remember much of my sister except that once she had a white dress with red flowers. My main job was to look after my father. I can remember him doing the cooking. Or warming over things my mother made.*

T: *What is your relationship with your parents?*

P: *I'm confused. My mother is the dominant person. I am the light of her life. When I take care of my father, it is for her, not for him—a duty! I am being a good boy, relieving her of responsibility. It takes the pressure off her.*

T: *Do you have any fun?*

P: *In winter I can go ice skating on the tennis court.*

T: *Do you celebrate Christmas?*

P: *My parents get a tree and presents. The people two stories down get drunk. They have Scotties. We live on the third floor.*

T: *How do you spend your days?*

P: *I spend time walking through a vacant lot. Once I go to New Jersey to visit Mother's cousins.*

T: *What about food?*

P: *I am a terrible eater. I chew food and keep it in my cheek and my parents have to take it out.... The cousins I visit live in a house with tennis courts. I am the poor relation, but later my aunt's husband divorces her and she has nothing. I help support her now.*

Richard here brings in a process of cognitive reframing, correcting the childhood perception that he is a poor relation.

T: *Tell me about your sixth year.*

P: *I go right into the first grade. I am afraid to go to school—my mother has to take me. My penmanship is terrible—cramped little hand. We sit in funny little desks and carry our books home in a strap. I have to stay in knickers—I'm small for my age—don't grow up until high school.*

I don't know where it started, being petrified about getting bad grades. I hide any bad grades as long as possible. I must have got decent grades because I skipped a lot. But my father is never satisfied. He keeps saying, "You can do better. Why did you only get a B?" This is where I start to lie. My mother encourages me to hide things from my father. He can't see the report card so I don't tell him about the "B's." My mother keeps telling me not to upset my father. That's where the evasion starts. It seems to me that it is done for my mother.

T: *What would happen if you told him the truth?*

P: *My father would go berserk, just the way my wife does. Tell them something they don't want to hear and they go berserk. Both begin with "Why...?"*

T: *You married someone much like your father.*

P: *I didn't know before I married her. Her son told me later that she had always been that way. I never told my first wife anything that would upset her—I didn't want to seem inadequate. I don't like anything unpleasant.*

T: *What would you like to tell the little boy who's learning to lie?*

P: *It's a shame that pattern got started. It has caused me more grief that anything else. It has carried through in everything, including business. But lately I've been trying and I've come clean with a friend of mine. Also, I'm beginning to see that when business ventures go bad and others are shaken, I'm the steadying hand. I don't know why it's happening.*

In these memories, covered over for so long, lay the origins of many of Richard's difficulties and character traits. As is usual, when a memory is recovered, it seemed to him that he had always known it—he had retained it, but only on an unconscious level. Exploring the origin of the lying, a trait urged on him by his mother, made it possible for Richard to begin to be straightforward with people, realizing he was no longer a little boy whose father would rage at him. The longtime pattern of lying and evasion could not be dropped easily, however, as it had been multiply reinforced by the circumstances of his life, but he became free finally to reject the early programming and substitute other behavior more in line with his values.

Regression to the Prenatal Period

Since the childhood memories had come pouring out so freely, I suggested to Richard that we go a little further back and tune in on his prenatal and birth experiences. The extent of the memories he had recovered from a period he had considered unavailable to recall had so surprised him that, though it appeared obvious that he was neither completely comfortable nor enthusiastic, he made no protest.

T: *How does your mother feel about being pregnant? If you don't feel you remember, just say how you imagine it might be.*

P: *I see her with a little white dog. Bobbed hair. She's 26. She got pregnant when she was 25. It is a complicated time because my father has just learned he has glaucoma. He is concerned with how they can take care of a child economically, and the two of them talk about that all the time. But my mother is happy with her pregnancy—she wants an attractive baby.*

T: *Does she want a boy or a girl?*

P: *She doesn't care.*

T: *What happens when she first tells your father?*

P: *She thinks he'll be delighted. She goes to him and says, "I think we're going to have a baby. It's a month beyond when I should have had started my period." He kisses her and is delighted.*

T: *How does she feel during the pregnancy?*

P: *She's sicker than hell, throws up every moment. Everything's uncertain, but they want me, and I'm fine.*

T: *What are some other things they talk about?*

P: *They discuss the chief surgeon at the hospital, who is my uncle. He's drunk a lot and performed an operation while he was drunk—my father was the anesthesiologist. My father talks to my mother about this and says it isn't safe for my uncle to deliver their baby if he has been drinking. My father feels he should do something—the hospital is out of control—but he can't jeopardize his position. My mother says he's doing the right thing, but she keeps asking, "What are you going to do when your sight is gone?" He doesn't have an answer.*

T: *What about their relatives? Can they help?*

P: *My parents wanted to be out of their families. Both families were from a lower class and they thought if they moved away and struck out on their own, with my father's medical background they could become somebody. They didn't want to go back. Now they are all alone.*

Here we have the origin of Richard's feeling of economic panic. He says, "The two of them talk about it all the time," and because they have cut off their families, they have no one to fall back on. Nine months of worry over his father's impending loss of income because of his blindness not only initiated a pattern of economic anxiety in Richard but undoubtedly could have pulled up patterns of similar anxiety from other lifetimes.

Regression to Birth

In the account of this birth Richard recovered surprising detail but was involved only minimally on a feeling level. Would it have been helpful to have re-lived the experience more fully, or is Richard's approach of constant cognitive reframing sufficient for transformation? Until we have contradictory evidence it seems best to me to respect a patient's way of processing his material, especially when memories flow freely and are met with courage, as in Richard's case.

> T: *The time of your birth is approaching. Who starts the process?*
> P: *My mother—that's what I seem to be sensing. I'm sliding from place to place. It's mass confusion. I've got to get out and I'm not sure which way to go. I'm panicked and I've got to get out. It's a panic that builds up to a crescendo. I'm flailing around with my arms and legs. It's head first. I'm in a hurry. My Uncle Moe grabs my head and he's telling my father to get out of the room. I hear this commotion and I'm still in a major panic, and the confusion over why my father is put out doesn't help. I come out and I can finally breathe. I've always been worried about drowning. It feels good to be in the air because I can breathe. My mother's smiling—she has that bobbed hair. I don't know why I should be worried about drowning. They hand me to my mother and I wonder why they don't let my father back in.*
> T: *How do they feel about your being a boy?*
> P: *Oh, she wants me. But that is going to be it—she doesn't want any more children. I stay with my mother quite a while. That uncle becomes my godfather—it is a family affair. After a while I get put on a trolley and trundled out. I see my mother smiling—a radiant smile.*

Richard and I spent months processing these memories and tying into his current life the reframing he had done. The two major findings, of the source of his tendency to lie and equivocate and of the basis (or continuation) of his unrealistic perception of economic threat, made possible a reconceptualization that had to be integrated into his present life. The retrieval of the prenatal anxiety over money helped him to re-evaluate his financial status realistically and acknowledge that he is financially secure. Without this particular worry he is now a freer and more joyous man. He has become compassionate with himself and is gradually becoming able to be straight about the things in his life. These two changes have, in turn, strikingly modified his relationship with his wife. He can remain comfortably silent when she pressures him to tell her something that he knows would infuriate her. He has learned to walk out when the pressure she puts on him is too great, but he does this in a kindly way, reassuring her that he will be back when she feels quieter. Best of all, he and Martha are now able to experience with increasing frequency their basic compatibility and their shared potential for adventurous living.

No doubt Richard's two negative patterns—he has many positive ones, too—have deep roots and many expressions in former lives, and perhaps sometime he will want to recover the memories of these. Such a process might deepen his understanding, but if there is no such thing as time and one can enter a pattern at any level, the work he has done will be enough to reverse the unproductive programming.

Chapter II

Regression to Childhood

Children identify with their feelings as a part of themselves, and when their feelings are branded as bad or wrong, they accept this as a message that they are bad or wrong. In the period before children lose touch with themselves, they know intuitively and feel what is present but denied, and having to contort themselves to fit the picture of what seems to be wanted inflicts great harm on their authenticity.

Barbara Findeisen

Specific incidents in childhood reactivate or trigger a latent past-life story that belongs to the inherited or karmic level of the complex. These incidents carry a symbolic resonance with the specific past-life trauma that they trigger. The re-living of a past-life story may be even more painful and dramatic than the re-living of a current-life experience, but it has the potential of resolving and dissipating the energy that has been bound in the complex.

Roger J. Woolger

Bibliography

Armstrong, Thomas *The Radiant Child*. Wheaton, IL: The Theosophical Publishing House, 1985.

Bolduc, Henry Lee. "Regression to Childhood: Inductions and Transformations." *The Journal of Regression Therapy,* Vol. IV, No. 1, 1989.

Findeisen, Barbara. "Rescripting in Pre- and Perinatal and Early Childhood Regression to Childhood." *The Journal of Regression Therapy*, Vol. IV, No. 1, 1989.

Givens, Alice *The Process of Healing*. San Diego, CA: The Libra Press, 1990.

Hickman, Irene. "Principles and Techniques of Regression to Childhood." *The Journal of Regression Therapy,* Vol. IV., No. 1.

Miller, Alice *Prisoners of Childhood*. New York: Basic Books, 1981.

———. *Thou Shalt Not Be Aware*. New York: Farrar, Straus, Giroux, 1984.

Missildine, W.H. *Your Inner Child of the Past*. New York: Pocket Books, 1963.

Pearce, J.C. *Magical Child*. New York, Bantam Books, 1980.

Pecci, Ernest *I Love You/I Hate You*. Pleasant Hill, CA: TL Publishing, 1978.

Schubot, Errol. "Creative Source Therapy: Pathways for Healing the Inner Child." *The Journal of Regression Therapy,* Vol. IV, No. 1.

Whitfield, Charles L. *Healing the Child Within*. Deerfield Beach, FL: Health Communications, Inc., 1987.

Regression to Childhood

Introduction

An altered-state approach to childhood can uncover a panorama of emotional threads and patterns that ordinarily would remain too far under the surface to come to consciousness. Work in this state not only deepens and extends the usual scope of childhood memories but often corrects them. It is as much more comprehensive in the uncovering of such memories as slugging through a country, noting towns and fields and forests, is more revealing than flying over a landscape. Since each person retains in his deep unconscious a memory of all that he has experienced, there is no limit to the detail that he can recover in an altered state.

As in other areas of regression therapy, however, it is not the details that are important, interesting as these may be, but the repetition of patterns that are revealed through the details. Old patterns that have drawn the fetus to their repetition in the prenatal state and at birth and that may have impacted other lifetimes, now appear in infancy and childhood in the approximate form in which they will be lived out during the current lifetime. The continuation of prenatal patterns into childhood, especially scripts of isolation, loneliness, and loss, is striking.

In a broader perspective, childhood and prenatal experiences form only part of the pattern because, considered alone, they may give the impression of victimization or undeserved loneliness or flagrant injustice. To understand their appropriateness and their value as teaching situations it is helpful to know the individual's journey in other lifetimes and the judgments made and the intentions set in the interim state immediately preceding this life.

It is possible to transform patterns that were present in childhood without recall to other lifetimes by dealing with the patterns as sub-personalities. Long-standing patterns begin to crystallize into personality systems and function semi-autonomously at the age of three or four. These patterns are so specific that they may even be christened with names such as "the Bitch" or "the Victim" or "the Little Mother." Patients can become aware of a dominating energy pattern and can dialogue and reason with it and convince the sub-personality of its inappropriateness. In the therapeutic process the patient traces the pattern to its initial appearance in this life, understands its function in defending the organism, and releases it by demonstrating that the need for it has been outgrown, a variation of reframing.

An important aspect of altered-state recall of early childhood, as Findeisen points out, is its potential for providing a new opportunity for the child to be accepted as he is. Most children are loved conditionally—they are accepted if they meet standards parents have set up—and so grow up not accepting themselves. Grief and anger are particularly taboo in many families, and the child takes over the attitude and evaluation of the parents in these areas. The individual moves through his lifetime retaining a damaged perception of himself. The therapeutic ambiance provided by an unconditionally accepting therapist makes possible re-evaluation and finally self-acceptance.

Another major reframing that takes place in altered-state recall of childhood involves the patient's concepts of his parents. It seems a part of the human condition to feel that it is one's inalienable right to have perfect parents (whatever that may be!). Since, in fact, none of us is blessed with these, we deal with our disillusionment either by denying that our parents are imperfect or by being permanently angry at them and feeling victimized. In rejecting our parents because they are not perfect, we negate our opportunity to have what they *can* give, limited as this sometimes is, and in walking away from them we neglect the simple human kindness of appreciating what they may have tried to do. We leave them feeling that they are alienated after a lifetime of what they considered to be devotion to their children. Nothing embellishes life so much as a smidgen of kindness and warmth, which is lost when we hang onto resentments about our parents' imperfections. The deeper, more extended viewpoint of the altered state helps us to re-evaluate and reframe these distorted childhood perceptions. The case of Carrie, the young physician, demonstrates how, with painstaking work and taking account of the impact of a sub-personality, this reframing can be accomplished.

Childhood memories are usually the most available of all the memories with which regression therapy deals, not so much because they are the most recent—probably all memories theoretically are equally available—but because *we believe that we can contact them*. Also, if asked to "make up" a memory, enough details of childhood are consciously remembered to provide a framework. No elaborate induction is necessary beyond relaxation to bring the patient into an altered state where memories can be retrieved. Most therapists use simple bridges of feelings or physical states to elicit appropriate material.

To explore childhood the therapist can also use age regression to take the patient backward year by year, possibly continuing on through the prenatal period into past lives, as Irene Hickman does, or he can begin at birth and move forward. Prenatal, birth, and childhood feelings are becoming seen as a continuous pattern, and most therapists explore these periods in random order, sometimes weaving back and forth so that it is difficult to assign focus for an exploration other than the pervasive focus of the pattern being explored. Some of the cases reported in this section could as easily have been included in the prenatal section, and vice versa.

Again, some of our therapists, Givens, Hickman, and Woolger, stress intense re-experiencing of feelings, and others put at least equal stress on reframing. Probably both processes occur in any successful therapeutic intervention. Some re-experiencing of feelings is necessary to bring them to consciousness, the intensity of the experience depending in part on the individual patient. The therapist provides an environment where the patient feels it is safe to recover feelings, and by empathic responses and reflections he encourages these feelings to emerge and deepen, particularly where original taboos on feeling were repressive. Ordinarily each patient also deals with his material cognitively and reframes it, and the therapist with his broader perspective plays an important role in facilitating the reframing.

Reframing a Repressive Childhood

by

Barbara Findeisen, M.F.C.C.

Introduction

Regression to childhood makes possible a sort of reparenting. Few children feel themselves accepted for who they really are, with their angers, uncertainties, differences of opinion, and even—or especially—their insecurities. It is crucial for mental health in childhood that there is someone who hears what the child is saying and accepts the child's feelings. One person who is able to do that may prevent childhood traumas, large or small, from becoming knots that tie the individual to repeating his past again and again as he grows into adulthood; one significant person can confer reality to the child's experiences and enable him to let go and grow up. Instead, tragically, too frequently in dysfunctional families the child's reality is not only not heard but is actually denied. In alcoholic families, for example, one parent can act out violently, and the next day the entire family forms a conspiracy to pretend that nothing has happened.

Many children do not know what is real or how they feel or even what they want. What they see or feel is said to be wrong, or bad, or crazy, and they are punished if they question anything. Children identify with their feelings as a part of themselves, and when their feelings are branded as bad or wrong, they accept this as a message that they are bad or wrong. In the period before children lose touch with themselves, they know intuitively and feel what is present but denied, and having to contort themselves to fit the picture of what seems to be wanted inflicts great harm on their authenticity. The cost can literally be their own integrity and a forfeiture of their appropriate path. In time the façade comes to be the reality that must be protected at all costs, forming a pathological barricade that imprisons the souls of its members and knots their spirits into twisted patterns.

Regressing patients to childhood makes possible the unravelling and untangling of the threads that have colored and restricted their lives. Traumas are knots, fraught with repressed pain and avoided out of fear and the need to control. People who have not been accepted in childhood live like armed crustaceans, always on guard as the result of those traumas and the fear of confronting them, and society supports this repression and denial. "Don't cry," or "Be a big boy," or" No, you don't feel that way," or "We know what is best (about you)."

In actual childhood it is not enough to heal a child who is the product of such a dysfunctional family and send him back into such a system. Family therapists have long seen the need to heal the system. For the adult, however, when such a problem has been initiated by his early family's need to cover up anything that doesn't fit the perfect picture, recovering the experience, re-living it and then reframing it is therapeutic.

To be healthy and maximally productive each person must re-evaluate his childhood and have the experience of being accepted as he is. It is particularly necessary for the person himself to accept his earlier experiences of loss and hurt and to grieve over them: grieving is a natural function that heals loss and hurt. When hurts and losses cannot be experienced, shared and felt, they remain as knots in the fabric of our restricted lives.

Another knot that is often present is an unhealthy approach to dealing with anger. Children are often punished or abandoned ("Up to your room until you put a smile on your face!") if they express negative feelings. Here again, children are taught to lie, repress, or deny feelings, leading them to act them out against themselves or others in a variety of ways. Sometimes their emotions build up internally to such intensity that they explode and do damage to someone or something or to the person's own body.

One of the most common infringements on a person's integrity is child abuse—physical, sexual, emotional, or psychological. Abused children become defensive about everything that is theirs and have difficulty sharing. They need to protect themselves to a pathological degree and cannot allow anyone to enter into their space.

A different type of restrictive situation occurs in a family where everyone appears good—a "perfect family" to the outside world. This is an especially difficult scenario. There is no violence, no alcoholism, no overt dysfunctional behavior, and no divorce, but the child feels bad, unworthy, not okay. Since outsiders see everything as fine, the child internalizes guilt and blame for being "what is wrong."

A direct re-living of the memory of this childhood milieu is facilitated in several ways. First, the therapist must be accepting of the patient's feelings of confusion and non-validation. Creating a safe environment in therapy is the first basic step to enable the patient to feel that he/she dares to express old pains from childhood. Such acceptance provides a situation that the patient may never have experienced before. Secondly, he needs assistance in reframing the situation. Then the long transformation can begin, leading to the place where the patient feels okay in himself and no longer has to make apologies for being.

If, however, the therapist becomes the critical, controlling parent, then the abandoned and hurt inner child of the patient does not feel safe to be who he really is. Once again he must adapt to being some kind of person who is acceptable to the "parent" in the guise of the therapist. Alice Miller writes in her brilliant work, "The therapist then creates another crime of further burying the wounds and encouraging more layers of repression."[1]

Case: Recovering Power Lost in Childhood

Mary, a married woman in her early 40's, came into therapy because of a lack of boundaries that left her unable to say no to her children or stand up for her right to have an opinion or express a wish. She had struggled with this problem throughout her life and had finally come to a place where she didn't want any longer to live such a circumscribed life. She was not sure the attitude could be changed because, as do many others who have such a problem, she felt that it was a part of her personality, while in reality it had become her approach to life through learning and conditioning in childhood. The events of her early years had led her to limit and restrict her fulfillment and sense of satisfaction in life.

Mary had grown up with an engulfing mother who felt she owned her child. She told Mary how to feel, how to think, how to dress, and whom to have as friends. It was clear that Mary had spent a great deal of energy manipulating her life around this mother and learning to live with her. It was also clear that she not expect that her mother or anyone else would give her any space or respect her integrity.

Every human being has the right to define his/her own boundaries and to have the power to say yes or no, but children such as Mary, whose toys and rooms and tastes and thoughts have not been respected, come to feel that they have no right to their emotional, psychological, and physical space and often grow up unable to define their boundaries. They have been conditioned to believe that they don't have the right to their own belongings or their own opinions, and gradually they build walls around themselves, within which exist only frail skeletons of their personalities.

In spite of the indication that Mary's problem had undoubtedly started in early childhood, we approached these early years gradually and looked first at her marriage to uncover how her attitude had influenced her behavior there, and to what extent she had become the projection of her husband. We found that she fitted into whatever it was that her husband wanted her to be, as if she had no self. In a chameleon-like way she became what he and others expected her to be.

From her marriage we worked backward to an early time in her childhood.

T: *Where are you?*

C: *I am in my bedroom.*

T: *How old are you?*

C: *I am about four or five years old. I am really scared.*

T: *Tell me about it.*

C: *When Mama is shouting, she is real angry. She is angry at my sister. I am really scared. I want to hide under the covers.*

T: *Then what happens?*

C: *My big sister is screaming at my mama. She is screaming at my mama. She is trying to hit my mama. I am just so scared.*

C: *(Crying in a pitiful way.) My mama is packing a suitcase for my sister. She is putting clothes in it.*

T: *Now what's happening?*

C: *(Becomes more and more hysterical and tries to curl up in the corner of the therapy room.) My mama is putting my sister out and is throwing her suitcase after her outside the door. My sister is screaming. My mama is throwing her out the door.*

T: *Now what's happening?*

C: *I am too afraid. I am too scared. I'm afraid of what Mama might do to me if I'm not good.*

T: *Now what's happening?*

C: *My sister's outside and she's crying. She's screaming and banging on the door, and it's really cold outside.*

At this point Mary went to a level of nonverbal fear and terror and began to cry and tremble. I asked her if there was an earlier time in this lifetime when she had had similar feelings.

After a few minutes Mary found herself in her crib crying. She was hugging a little white rabbit she loved. She had been put in her crib for some fault, she didn't remember what, but she felt that it was a punishment. As she sat there crying and screaming and holding the white bunny, her mother burst into the room and grabbed the bunny from her, telling her to shut up. The mother then threw the bunny away and Mary never saw it again.

When a terrified child bonds to some kind of toy or animal and the parent takes that away, the child feels completely isolated and alone, as if a safe touchstone has been lost. Mary felt violated. Her own personal belonging had been taken away from her, and later, when she saw her mother throwing her sister out with her suitcase, it reinforced the fear that she did not have any right to say or possess anything. She had become afraid to say "I want this" for fear that what she desired or cared about would be taken away from her. She began to learn that it was better if she didn't confront her mother, didn't demand any rights because this would upset her mother so much that she would begin to scream that Mary didn't really care about her, that Mary wasn't grateful for all the mother had done for her.

Mary gradually became addicted to becoming whatever it was her mother wanted her to be.

In subsequent regressions Mary went back to even earlier times to find the roots of this particular pattern. She found that she was an unwanted child, that her mother already had a boy and a girl and felt her family was complete. So the seeds of her fear of being rejected or abandoned existed in her prenatal experience.

Then we went further back and found a still earlier experience in her last lifetime that connected her to threads of this pattern. She found herself in a speak-easy atmosphere in the 20's.

T: *What do you see around you?*

C: *It's smoky—there are a lot of people dancing. It looks like it's the '20's...kind of flappers. I am sitting at a table with some people. There is a man here that I am afraid of.*

T: *Why are you afraid of him?*

C: *He's giving me some drinks. He looks like one of that classic kind of mobster in the movies.*

T: *What's happening now?*

C: *Somebody comes in and talks and he leaves. I am getting up and going to the ladies room but actually what I really want to do is get out of here. I get my coat and go out the door and I leave. 1 am walking down the street and it's really cold. I am in a big city. I am a little bit tipsy. I am walking down the street.*

T: *Go to the next significant event.*

C: *I am in this apartment; it's kind of a fancy apartment. I get a suitcase out and I'm real busy putting a book...I am real frantic...I am trying to get some things packed. I want to get out of here. I am real scared. I am emptying drawers, putting things in the suitcase. I am so...Oh, my God! Oh, my God! He's here. He's here. He's coming in.*

T: *What is happening?*

C: *He says, "What are you doing?" I tell him, "I've had enough of this. I don't want to do this anymore. I'm leaving." He says, "You're not leaving me. Nobody ever leaves me. You can't say no to me." Then I say...I am scared. My God, I am so scared! I am so scared!...Then I say, "No. Well I am saying no to you. I am going to say no to you. I am getting out of here." I say...Oh, my god!...*

Mary started to scream and began to thrash about, crying and screaming and gagging. Then all of a sudden she was silent.

T: *What's happening now?*

C: *I'm looking down at that body. My God, he strangled me! He strangled me! He killed me for saying no to him. He killed me. I am beginning to feel a little bit less...beginning to feel...the scene is fading, it's fading, it's fading....*

As Mary processed this scene she was able to see how her fear of saying no had either originated in or been intensified by this incident when she had tried to say no to the gangster—when she had finally gotten up the courage to say no and been killed for it.

There may have been even earlier lifetimes where similar incidents happened, but Mary returned from that gangster lifetime to her childhood in this lifetime. She was sitting at the table when she about five years old, not wanting to eat asparagus.

C: *I am telling my mother that I don't like asparagus, that I don't like it. She is saying to me, "You don't know what you like. You eat it. I put it there, you eat it."*

I'm saying "No, I don't want to eat asparagus." I take the asparagus and I throw it at her. I pick it up and I throw it.

She picks me up out of the chair and she turns me over and she...Oh my God, she is beating me up with some instrument or something or other. It hurts like the dickens. Then she picks me up and throws me in the bedroom.

I am there all by myself crying and crying and crying, 'cause I really don't like asparagus and don't understand why I have to eat it. She comes in and says to me, "Don't you ever say no to me! I know what you like. I know what's good for you. I know what's best for you. Don't you ever say no to me again!" She is saying this to me over and over again. She is hitting me with something—I can't figure out what it is.

I'm rocking and I'm rocking, talking to myself. "Don't ever say no to your mommy. Just don't kill me! Just don't kill me, Mommy." Rocking...rocking...rocking..."Don't kill me!"

As I brought her out of this she began to cry.

C: *That poor child. That poor little girl. I really did think I was going to be killed. I keep hearing my mother saying, "Don't ever say no to me again."*

After this session Mary began to explore her boundaries and plan how she might begin to be able to say yes when she wanted something and no when she didn't want it. In pursuing this she returned in subsequent sessions to other childhood incidents that had furthered the pattern of negating herself. She had a memory of being accosted on her way home from school by some young hoods, teenagers, who chased her and eventually knocked her down, and one of them raped her. She didn't put up any protest. After they left she tried to put herself back together. She was missing buttons and her jacket had been lost and she was terrified about what her mother would say if she discovered the missing buttons. As she ran home she tried to smooth out her hair and wipe the smudges and tears away so that she could arrive home looking okay for her mother. Her fear of her mother overshadowed distress over the rape. Her mother didn't notice, and Mary never told anyone about the incident until she came to therapy.

When a behavior pattern is embedded with a strong bout of fear and the opportunity later comes for the person to break the pattern, the fear floods the person and freezes him/her into immobility. This was true of Mary. At first she seemed unable to break the pattern because of the old terrors and fears, but gradually she began to be able to say, "Yes, I want..." and "No, I don't want..." In the process she began to discover her authentic self. Previously she had not known what she really wanted except that she didn't want to be killed.

As her therapy drew to a close, we scanned her marriage again and became more aware of how, when she had been at the university, she had started going out with a strong and domineering man who decided to marry her. She was unable to say no, even though she didn't want to marry him, and went willingly, like a sheep to the slaughter, into a marriage where she didn't want to be, with somebody she didn't really love.

John Lennon wrote a song called "Whatever Gets You Through the Night." These patterns that we adopt do get us through the pain of our childhood, but they become prison walls and restrict our ability to love. As we come to genuinely appreciate the wounded infant within us, we are able to begin to love and accept the wounded parts from our childhood and not only feel more comfortable and more as though we are our own person, but we also find ourselves more able to love and accept others.

Childhood Depression and Fear

by

Alice Givens, Ph.D.

Introduction

A variety of patients in a therapist's office voice a dominant complaint of painful aloneness, depression, sadness, and fear. Underneath these feelings is often unacknowledged and pervasive anger. All such feelings are usually anchored in prenatal and early childhood experiences, but unless patients are directed to a specific age, which often cannot be pinpointed at the beginning of therapy, it may be unclear just where such painful feelings began. However, although difficult, it is not only possible but vital that the trauma connected with these early beginnings be re-lived. What is needed is a large component of patience reinforced by persistence.

When loneliness and hopelessness are pervasive, the patient and I may opt to examine the period of infancy because of the supposition that this is where these feelings began. The objective of the regression is expression of the feelings of this time. However, in the experience of the crib it is particularly difficult to elicit expression of emotion, especially in cases where there was no response to the infant's crying and the infant grew up to have nothing to say, having given up hope that any further crying or communication would help.

The patient is often silent at the beginning of a regression to infancy, and it requires skilled intervention to establish how old the child is or what the location is, though the latter is usually a crib. I often say, "Just let your feeling say words." Often the silence continues. The feeling of depression is so great that it seems to have no words. However, though the infant is in a time of life when words are not known, the feeling can still be translated into words.

When the infant is left alone over long periods, his feeling is one of deep emptiness and hopelessness. This is in contrast to the intrauterine state. A fetus in Mother's body is feeling and moving with her movement, with the function of her organs, her breathing and heartbeat. As the fetus develops hearing and sight, it senses the constant changes in the sound level and the light in the environment, including Mother's voice. All of this is filtered through Mother's body. Mother's thoughts and feelings are stimulating the fetus and being stored in the deep unconscious mind.

But after birth the infant exists only in relation to the action, the touching, the presence, the holding and caring of people around. Left alone while awake over a long period, the child feels a world that is cold, empty, and desolate. The only movement is the light that comes in the window. This changes as the sun moves across the sky, and finally it gets dark. The feeling is of nonexistence or death. Anaclitic depression, or infant depression, is usually caused by being left alone in a crib or playpen for long periods of time, and this isolation eventually feels like death to the infant. Babies actually die when left alone without being touched, even though they have the necessary physical care.

One of the concepts most damaging to infants is the cultural belief that they should be left alone to cry and should only be fed on schedule. Mothers who don't want to be bothered with their babies use this belief as justification for leaving their babies alone 24 hours a day with only an occasional diaper change and a bottle, and many infants live on the borderline between life and death during their early months. This can be the beginning of chronic, life-long depression for the individual and is a basis for autism (non-relating), schizophrenia, deep chronic depression, and other illnesses, both physical and emotional.

In addition to pervasive depression set up by acute deprivation and isolation in infancy, there are other sources of depression that may be initiated by more circumscribed events, such as grief following the death of a core person in the family. Because the impact is more limited, the experience can more be easily retrieved and dealt with than can unrelieved isolation and neglect. In such an experience the infant is impacted in two ways: it takes on the depressed feelings of the mother as its own and it suffers deprivation because the mother's grief diminishes her energy to deal with her baby. Here the goal of therapy is twofold: to release the patient from feelings that actually belonged to the mother and to recover and work through the infant's anger at the neglect.

In contrast to a depressed life climate, often with diminished stimuli, the baby's life may be haunted by inappropriate fear as the result of violent threats and turmoil in the childhood environment. The primary source of a chronic anxiety disorder lies in this violent daily living atmosphere of the family where the patient grew up. Later these words and feelings become a program for living. One can be certain that a particular event contributed to the disorder if the anxiety and pain diminish after the patient has re-lived the trauma. In general, in successful therapy feelings and behavior become more comfortable and appropriate, enabling the patient to live in a more satisfying way.

The following convictions guide my approach to the recovery of childhood memories:

1. Each child is an individual, unique being.

2. Children need to have the same respect as adults have of their persons, their space, and their possessions. Children are not simple. They are as complicated as adults.

3. Children have feelings that are just as painful and joyful as those of adults.

4. Events in the prenatal period, infancy, and childhood affect a person for life.

5. Every incident and event is preserved in the unconscious mind from conception forward.

6. Children need emotional nurturing as much as they need food and shelter.

7. Emotional abuse is just as damaging as physical abuse.

8. Children need to express their feelings and opinions.

9. Children need to have a family system that gives them a feeling of being safe, being loved, being cared for, being listened to, and in which the child is free to express, to create, and to grow into a unique being.

Case 1. Anaclitic Depression in Infancy

When David first came to me, his complaint was his pervasive sense of isolation and depression that had led to withdrawal from people at all times except at work. He barely got himself to work each day and had to lie down at lunch time because he was so exhausted. At the end of his work day he came home alone and never went anywhere. He had no social life. The feelings he described were lethargy, energy drain, powerlessness, hopelessness. To search for the origin of these feelings we went back to his infancy.

There is no set formula for my questions or directions. My interventions depend entirely upon the feeling and response of the patient. For instance, I might instruct him to "Be aware of your body. What position is it in?" If the patient is a tiny infant in the scene, the response can be "I'm lying on my back," or "I'm standing up holding onto something." With the latter response I know that the patient is an infant who is old enough to pull himself up and hang onto the side of the crib or playpen. David was able to sense his orientation in his crib at an early age.

    T: Do you feel like you are alone, David?
    P: Yes, I'm alone.
    T: Say it again: "I'm alone."

I had the patient repeat his words to intensify awareness of where he was and what was happening.

    T: Is it light or dark where you are? (This is something that even the tiniest
         infant knows.)
    P: It is light.
    T: Which direction is the light coming from? Left or right? Head or foot?

Infants do not know direction but they know where the light is coming from in relation to themselves and they unconsciously translate that knowing into present-day knowledge of direction. The light and its direction have no importance in therapy except to establish the patient in a past scene where the trauma can be expressed and the beginnings of resolution can take place. David tells me the direction of the light.

In David's case I have established that he is an infant in a crib and it is probably daytime. He is alone. Now we have a scene in which he is re-living an early experience. The aloneness and nothingness can be felt and any changes detected. Sometimes the only change is the variation in light as the sun goes down and it gets dark and he is wet and cold. The most important event is someone entering the room and doing something. He or she who enters can bring a bottle and change a diaper, or simply enter and look and depart. The person might enter and perhaps start screaming in anger, or a wonderful thing could occur—someone could enter, pick up the baby, and carry him out to a change in scenery. What a miracle this would be! This didn't happen to David.

Now that the scene had been clarified, the problem was to get David to express the feeling he had. He lay on my couch with a sad expression. I seized upon any expression of feeling or awareness, to clarify it and intensify it.

    T: Now you are a little baby lying in a crib on your back. You can see the
         light, you are all alone. (All of this is information that the patient has
         given me.) Say the words again, "I am alone." Let your feeling talk, even
         though you couldn't talk back there as that baby. You can talk now, so let
         your feeling say words.
    P: I'm all alone.
    T: And say the next words that come to mind.

At this point there was a strong reluctance to speak. The infant's consciousness, which David had entered, was sad and hopeless.

T: *Tell me, is your feeling happy and satisfied, or is it unhappy?*
P: *There's a sad feeling.*
T: *Say the words, "I'm sad."*
P: *I'm sad.*
T: *Say it again, "I'm alone and sad."*
P: *I'm alone and sad.*
T: *And the next words.*
P: *It is all hopeless.*

David had finally translated the infant feelings into words but only with urging and support. After each word or phrase I urged him to continue, and gradually he became able to express more and more feeling.

P: *It is all grey where I am...I'm suffocating...nobody ever comes. I can't move. The blankets are too tight. Please, somebody come and get me.... Never come...too tight...can't breathe.*

There were long periods of silence in which David would not speak. His expression was one of deep despair. It seemed that Mother had pinned his clothes and blankets down to the mattress and he could not move. He was left unable to kick or move his arms for long periods of time. His infancy was spent all alone. When Mother did enter the room, she was angry because she had to take care of him. David felt terrified and hopeless.

P: *I'm dying. I'm so tired. It's totally dark and I'm lost...just drifting around.... There is nobody there...dark and silent now...can't move...nobody is anywhere...there is nothing...can't get out...chest is heavy...can't cry anymore...no hope for me...no one will ever come...it is so heavy...they will never come.*

David became silent again, and there, clearly, were the origins of his deep depression and inability to relate. As an infant, his world was empty, with no movement and no one to touch or care. It was hopeless because no one ever came. If his mother did come, she was angry and terrifying. The sad thing is that David's infancy is not unusual. Many babies are left alone in a room nearly all the time.

For the purpose of therapy, it is necessary to find methods of getting clients who have regressed into infancy to express the feelings and beliefs that go with it. All of their words are expressing these beliefs:

They'll never come.
It will never end.
No one will ever help me.

It is all hopeless.
I'll die here all alone.
I'm dead.

It is not enough merely to go to a childhood trauma. That trauma must be *expressed* in order for a person to release the energy from it. Some scenes need to be repeated many times in order to release the feelings and beliefs. This is particularly true of an infant who was left alone.

To keep a human being trapped in a room alone where there is no action, no touching, and no caring for the first months and years of life is a hideous deprivation, worse than the suffering of children in so-called deprived areas. Children who grow up in poverty may not receive adequate food, clothing, and shelter; however, if they learn how to relate to another human being, they are better equipped than the child who stays in a room alone for the first year of life. Some mothers even keep the shades down in the infant's room, believing that the baby will sleep more and be less bother. When the infant cries, he is ignored. The early developmental period is spent in a tomblike environment. The most critical deprivation affecting mental and emotional health is lack of human contact.

An infancy spent alone results in a lifetime of feeling alone. The painful feeling of aloneness and abandonment is suffered throughout life, as was David's experience, even when he was later surrounded by people. We think of trauma as occurring in the course of actions and events. It is the fact that there are *no* events in the isolated child's room that makes the experience traumatic. The need for someone to come, the need to be touched and held, the need for the cessation of monotony, and finally, the feeling of utter hopelessness and despair, are all traumatic and painful. It is this painful feeling that the therapist must defuse.

From the beginning I knew that David's case would require years of therapy, but he has great courage and has been willing to continue to make small step after small step on his journey to become alive.

Case 2. Mirroring a Mother's Grief

Valerie came in with a chronic feeling of blackness and aloneness. She had had many kinds of therapy of all theoretical persuasions, but through it all she held onto her depression. When she was experiencing her deepest feelings of suffering her face looked dark, with red blotches, and she found it almost impossible to go out and be with other people. She could think of endless excuses to isolate herself at home, which was not difficult, since her husband had divorced her several years before and her children were grown up. She was the world's expert at analyzing her problems and knew all the correct ways of doing therapy, but none of it had done her any good.

At first Valerie was a little suspicious of my unorthodox approach—regressing her back to find the origin of her problems—and she felt it was strange that I did not use a hypnotic induction since I was sending her back to a time of which she had no conscious awareness. All she had told me about her history was that she had been born soon after World War I during the worldwide flu epidemic, but I trusted her unconscious mind to find the old pain.

I had her lie down and close her eyes and I directed her back to the time when she was inside her mother's body. I suggested that it be a time when Mother had the same black, painful, alone feeling that Valerie was suffering. She lay silently for a few moments and finally began to speak.

Prenatal

> P: *I've given up any hope.... Everything is just getting worse.*
> T: *Say the next words.*
> P: *I can't make it...it's too dark and there is too much pain.*

The tears were seeping out of her eyes and down her face. This was a hard session for her, so after each sentence or phrase I needed to encourage her to continue. It was obvious that after sampling Mother's feelings she would gladly have avoided the whole thing.

> P: *I feel like dying, too. Everyone is dying. I can't think about this baby. We were going to have our babies together, and now she's dead. How can I live? Her baby died with her. How can I live and have a healthy baby when both of them are dead?*

Valerie's mother and her sister (Valerie's aunt) had been expecting babies together, but the sister died in the flu epidemic with her child still unborn. Valerie's mother suffered heavy guilt feelings for being alive and having a live baby.

> P: *It isn't fair for me to have this baby...I didn't even get a chance to talk to her. She couldn't talk...I'll go to the cemetery and get her and bring her back...I can't have this baby.... What can I do?*

Valerie was crying but I kept encouraging her. Each word came out with difficulty.

> P: *I have to keep working.... She is dead. Why am I alive?...It's a dark time.... How can I live?*

Birth

The dark, grieved, alone feelings continued through the birth. At the birth the conversation was focused on sickness and death because Mother came down with the flu, too, and everyone was afraid she would die as her sister had a couple of months before. First, here are Mother's thoughts:

> P: *I'll die with this baby just like she did.... How can I live when she is dead?... The pain is too bad...it's all too hard...isn't fair for me to have this baby when she is dead.*

The thought of death and pain went over and over in her head like a record that is stuck. The conversation in the room about Mother during Valerie's birth was just as depressing as Mother's thoughts.

> P: *She has been weak since her sister's death.... Why did she get the flu now? One would think she wants to die.... Please, help yourself, help this baby to be born. It will die if we don't get it out of there.*

For several sessions we returned to the sister's death and went forward through the birth. Valerie began to lose her dark, splotched, depressed appearance and came in smiling. It was obvious that she had begun to release the prenatal and birth programming that had initiated her depression.

Childhood

I knew that a chronic, depressed feeling such as Valerie's had to be reinforced in childhood. Basic programming is recorded in the unconscious mind during the prenatal period but is locked into place by early childhood experiences and decisions. This was certain to be true with Valerie because Mother's depression and grieving continued after she gave birth. She held onto her weakness and misery for years, living out a deeply ingrained pattern.

Valerie reported that Mother had stayed isolated in her room and that during childhood she was kept alone in another room, always being told not to cry because it would disturb her mother or make her mother sick. So Valerie developed into a quiet, good child, alone in her room while the older children and Father went about their busy lives.

I used the prenatal time as a springboard into childhood.

> T: *Now we are going from this black, painful, alone feeling up into early childhood when you felt the same way. Your unconscious mind knows where it is. Say the first words that come to you.*
> P: *Hear me!... I'm here.... Come and get me...I'm the only one here.*

As always, when going through a painful, traumatic time she stopped between every phrase. The unconscious mind tries to protect the person from pain and so retains its secrets and gives them up with reluctance.

> T: *Feel your body. What position are you in?*
> P: *I'm standing up holding onto the side of the crib.*
> T: *If your thoughts and feelings were talking, what would they be saying?*
> P: *I'm afraid...I'm the only one here...I can't see them. I'm trying to climb out.... Come here.... They'll never come...I can't cry...they won't let me cry.*

We went through all the early years of her life, and it was always the same. She was alone in her room while her mother was alone in another room.

> P: *I'm afraid...I can't breathe...I'm so afraid.... They all went away and forgot I'm here. I don't want to live here in my room...I'm dead here. The life is out there with you.... Why was I born to be dead?*

It was clear that Valerie felt separated from the real world. She wasn't alive. The real world where people were living was out there in some other place where she could hear them but not see them.

> P: *I know you are there...I can hear you.... Come and get me.... You can't hear me.... You don't know I'm here...I'm not in your real world...I'm dead here.*

Valerie's feeling of being alone and isolated in her house became a familiar one. She recognized that it had been there all her life. She took it with her wherever she went because of her decision as a child that where she is is not the real world. Where she is, everything is dead, and life is out there where other people are talking and living.

She became aware that as an older child of eight or nine she had started to give up her sadness, but it came back. She was riding in the car with her parents and looking at houses as she passed them when the return of the symptoms began.

> P: *I can't breathe.... The houses will swallow me up.... The people there are in such pain...I'm afraid of seeing those houses...too many...I have pain.*

She felt the houses as sharing the desperate pain of her aloneness in her room as a small child and even further back the closed-in pain of being in her mother's body. Everything was grief and sorrow and darkness. To her, people who were closed in their houses must have the same feelings.

As she worked through this material Valerie gradually gave up her pain and sorrow and could be with people more. I never again saw her with the dark mottled-looking skin that she had had when in deep depression. Her pervasive feeling that life was only out there with other people changed, and she began to feel that she was really living when she was in her own house.

As with everyone, it was necessary for her to go back to the prenatal period and birth to find the template for the repetition of these feelings and problems in childhood. A chronic condition will be found in both periods. The death of a mother's loved one during the prenatal period can fill the beginning of life with sorrow and grieving and set the program for depression and preoccupation with hopelessness and death throughout her child's life.

Case 3. Chronic Fear Absorbed from Mother

Matt, a 30-year-old handsome and healthy-looking man, gave as his presenting complaint that at unpredictable times he went into extremely painful fear reactions. He was dogged by fear that overwhelmed him when he was in the car, at work, at home, in bed, anywhere. He trembled and perspired, and often he felt so dizzy that he could hardly work or drive. The worst affliction was a pain in his chest and accompanying difficulty in breathing. Other therapists who had worked with him with behavior modification techniques or medication had provided him no relief. I automatically requested a medical examination for a heart problem, but after a thorough examination his physicians pronounced him healthy.

Eventually we found several sources for Matt's panic attacks. The basic cause was his mother's constant fear, which Matt had experienced in the prenatal period and during his early childhood. The mother had come to New York from Italy and was terrified. She knew little English and was in constant dread of making a mistake, a dread that was reinforced by a husband who yelled and criticized her with every breath. Mother's fear during the prenatal period had been continuous. Father threatened every day to leave, and Mother was in a panic at the prospect of being deserted with one child and another on the way. She did not see that her husband's threats were a means of control and she was convinced that she and the children would die without him.

Prenatal

When Matt re-experienced the prenatal period he felt his mother's fear as though it were his own. Eventually he became able to find words for it.

P: I gotta make him happy.... He'll go...I don't want to be left.... Don't leave me now...I'm alone...I can't go back to Italy.... What did I do wrong?... He's always so mad...I'll be good so he won't leave me. I don't want to be left again. I can't make it alone.

Obviously Father had detected Mother's script, that she had been left alone before, probably in childhood, or had felt abandoned and feared that this might occur again, and he played on it. The core fear was confined in the words, "I don't want to be left alone again." Her husband's threats increased and perpetuated that fear. Nothing could be done perfectly enough to prevent his leaving. This tyranny of terror and rage extended throughout his children's lives.

Birth

We returned to the prenatal period many times before identification with Mother's fear began to diminish, and, as always, we worked through the birth process following the prenatal experience. It became clear after re-living the hours in the delivery room that, in addition to the mother's fear, there had been a crisis after Matt's birth. He had gone through the birth feeling Mother's fear but without any physical complications until he was out of his mother's body. It was then that his voice changed. A crisis was occurring for Mother. Something had happened, probably related to hemorrhaging.

The words Matt brought out were obviously related to his mother but were spoken by the medical personnel and reported by Matt as if they were his own:

P: Hurry up...hurry...get that over here...I'm not getting anything. Lift that thing up...we need more blood...I don't know if she'll make it.... We don't have enough time.

Matt internalized this panic and made it his own, though the panic was actually coming from the words and actions of the medical personnel.

Early Childhood

The feeling of panic in the delivery room sent Matt's mind forward to another scene of panic. The words "Hurry up—hurry up!" determined the choice of the scene. All this was done on an unconscious level, with Matt mystified about why his mind went from one scene to the other. However, the unconscious mind has an unerring awareness of related feelings and took him from this delivery room scene to a scene in the car with Father, Mother, and Brother. Everyone was terrified because Father was driving so fast.

Several of the many scenes of terror and panic in Matt's childhood occurred while he was riding in the car with Father, who appeared to become a maniac behind the wheel of a car. As is the case with many fearful and helpless men, he loved to show his power while driving. The automobile had become a symbol for the power he wanted and a tool for terrorizing his family and making them feel the terror he himself had probably felt as a child. He lived in a rage so that he wouldn't feel his own fear, and he made the childhood of Matt and his brother a reign of terror.

These experiences with Father underlay the shaking, sweating, and attacks of terror that Mike experienced many years later while driving. A parent can tyrannize without the use of physical force. Matt's father rarely hit anyone, but his words, voice, and demeanor were so threatening that everyone in the house lived in fear. In many of the most pathological families there is no physical or sexual abuse but the emotional abuse can be controlling and terrifying. By returning to the actual words, thoughts, and behavior in these homes, the abuse emerges clearly and the origin of fear and paranoia can be known and resolved.

Later Childhood Trauma

Re-living experiences lessened Matt's terror but did not release all of it. Soon after the regression to those first childhood memories we discovered a related source of panic. From the one hospital setting we went into another one. Matt was in an operating room and the lights were bright. He felt himself screaming and crying.

> P: *Let me go...let me go...don't kill me...Mommie, come and get me.... Where are you? Why did you leave me?*

Mother and Father had left him in the hospital because he was to have eye surgery the next morning. He was terrified and certain that his parents had left him there because he had done something wrong.

> P: *Why do I have to stay here? Why are you leaving me?...What have I done? What did I do wrong?... I don't wanna be here. I must be stupid.... You left me here for them to kill me...I can't do anything. It's my fault they left me here.*

Even in the most extreme trauma and abandonment, the child must protect his parents. No matter how cruel they are, without them he has nothing. They are his whole world. The younger the child, the more this is true. Without Mother and Father, there is non-existence or death. Infants and young children know no other life. Even when Matt felt he had been abandoned to die, he spared his parents from blame. "What did I do wrong?" he asked. "I must be stupid. It's my fault that they left me."

Paralyzed by terror, Matt was taken into the surgery. As the nurses pushed him along the corridor he kept looking for Mother.

> P: *Where are you? Why don't you come? I'm here all alone. What are they doing to me? What have I done? Come and get me!*

His fear was overwhelming and catastrophic. Going into the brightly lighted operating room increased his terror. He couldn't see the faces behind the white masks. He had entered a completely alien world, and Mother and Father had left him forever. This was the end.

> P: *Help!... Help!... Let me out of here! Come and get me!... Please let me go. I haven't done anything wrong.... Where am I? What's the matter with me?*

These and many more words were what Matt said when I told him to let his fear talk. His panic increased until he was screaming and crying, kicking and trying to get away. Voices around him said, "Shut up. Hold still. We won't hurt you. You're all right." Matt heard none of it. It was only later that we knew that these words were spoken, when his terror had diminished after we had gone through the scene for the third or fourth time.

During this scene Matt was flailing and fighting, turning his head to try to get away as he screamed. Two or three people tried to subdue and hold him. One man held both of Matt's hands and pressed them down on his chest, pinning him to the table. The hands pressed so hard on Matt's chest that he couldn't breathe. (Here we pinpointed the source of his chest pain.) Terror became desperation.

> P: *Help! Help! Help! Help!... Don't kill me! Let me go!... Help! Help! Help! I can't move. Come and get me.... Help! Help! I don't wanna die...I can't breathe...Mom! Mom!*

With the unbearable, hurting pressure on his chest, someone held his head and put the ether cone on his face. Now came real panic.

> P: *Get it off! Let me go! I can't breathe. I'm dying...choking.*

Then came the death of unconsciousness. In Matt's perception they had killed him. Mother and Father had left him there so that they could kill him. Nobody helped him and nobody protected him. In the surgery experience the world was a terrifying place. The first time that he re-lived that scene, he cried and screamed, and it was only in following sessions that we began to get the words that his terror said. The words were important because they contained the hypnotic beliefs that had to be released.

Medical personnel, in their ignorance about feelings, treat human beings, particularly children, as if they were machines and ignore their fear. Their reasoning is that children will get over it. "Having parents around just causes trouble. Tell them to stay home until the surgery is over. We'll anesthetize the child and he'll forget everything." But children, even the youngest infants, need to be talked to about everything that is happening. They understand, know, and feel a thousand times more than is believed.

Matt's fears were consequences of his internalization of Mother's fear, both when he was *en utero* and later as a child. Mother cried when Father raged and that made the children helpless. If Mother, who was a big person, was afraid, then there was no help in this terrifying world. Everyone was at the mercy of this raging, angry man, but without him they would die. The hospital experience intensified that feeling of desertion and helplessness.

As a grown-up person, Matt's unconscious mind did not perceive that conditions were different in his current life. Driving in any car felt for him like being in the car with Father, the raging maniac, forty years ago. Being in bed when he was 45 years old could be turned into panic because a noise out in the hall might mean that Father was coming. The memory of these old events was kept in the unconscious and out of awareness. So the inappropriate sweating, shaking, choking feeling that seemed a mystery to Matt actually did make sense because in the deep unconscious old conditions still prevailed.

After Matt had re-lived the experience and released the trauma, the quality of his day-to-day life steadily improved. He began to trust his feelings and became more relaxed in all areas of his life, and especially in driving!

Repetition of a Pattern of Fear in the Uterine Experience, Birth, and Childhood

by

Claire Etheridge, Ph.D.

Introduction

When there are indications that fear has started early in life, the patient and I initiate a search to find out where it began. I do not necessarily emphasize one period over another as a possible source but allow the patient to go to whatever level he wishes. Often he will skip from childhood to the prenatal state and then to birth, picking up different expressions of the same pattern. One of the levels will emerge as especially significant in the etiology of the problem and other levels will be brought in like harmonics.

The course of therapy seldom runs straight. The patient is not suddenly cured after one recall, whether of his prenatal experience, his birth, or his early childhood. When a patient comes back feeling distraught, it is apparent that not all of the story has been ferreted out. The therapist must ask, "Did I get it all out yet or is there more to come?" The patient's symptoms or behavior under stress will reveal the answer.

To induce trance I use standard hypnosis techniques, building on autogenic training and related methods of sensory awareness that encourage a state of relaxation and homeostasis. The body awareness approach enables the patient to tap into the data stream of the body's feelings and sensations and to become more aware of body systems and their free or blocked functioning. Following this, I check on the information yielded by body feelings with the objective of determining if the problem the patient has presented originated as a response to fear, and if so, under what circumstances.

Case: Layers of Ambivalence

The case of Matthew exemplifies the process of searching through levels of soul experience and finding on each of them significant dynamics. His experience could as well be put in the section on prenatal programming or in a chapter on birth, but the patterns revealed in the early experiences of this patient found their clearest manifestation in his early childhood. However, he needed to return repeatedly to the earlier experiences to clarify and deepen understanding of his childhood anxiety and confusion and the later feeling of helplessness that pervaded his life and made decisions difficult for him.

Matthew was just establishing himself in a promising career as a social worker in a large hospital. His presenting problem was a crippling ambivalence about marrying his girlfriend Kathy, with whom he had lived for five years. He loved her and felt ready to accept the responsibilities of marriage, but whenever he contemplated this he found himself moving away from her. In discussing his ambivalence and fears, his account was permeated with words such as "stuck," "closed in," and "smothered." This suggested that a very early trauma lay at the root of his anxieties. The first six sessions explored his ambivalence over the relationship. In the seventh session, in trance, he began to touch on the source of the problem. He began with a prenatal memory.

Prenatal

> P: *I hear my parents talking. They want me to be a boy. Dad wants me to be what he isn't, to lead a perfect life. They are saying that their children will live out what Dad preaches and the family will validate the ministry. They must raise the children right to prove that what they are teaching is the truth.*
>
> T: *What are you feeling when they say this?*
>
> P: *I feel closed in! (Spoken with great emotion.) Smothered. In order to get love I have to do and say the right things. I'm stuck. The way to get approval is to do what they want. But that's painful. I'm living my life for them. Oh, I feel bound, tight, gagged!*

Birth

> T: *And how do you feel about being born?*
>
> P: *Oppressed. It's performance time.*
>
> T: *Do you want to be born?*
>
> P: *No. It's too painful. I can't be myself with six brothers and sisters to always be policemen. So I decide to outperform everybody else. I forget my own feelings and perform. I am too afraid of making a mistake. I teach myself*

not to cry when I get a shot. I want to be different and I am the only one of my brothers and sisters who doesn't cry.

Childhood

In the following session he reported that he had looked for wedding rings but still had feelings of anxiety and his chest felt tight and smothered. I suggested that we explore the source of those tight feelings in his chest.

P: *I feel helpless. I get spankings. I'm aware of my Dad's voice: "Matthew, when are you going to grow up? Your mother wanted a big family." I tell him, "You take away my space." I hate my life. I'm being suffocated. I'm angry. "Be good. Be a model child. It will prove my preaching is right. You are supposed to live out my teaching."*

I'm tied to "shouldn'ts" and "oughts." My mother is saying, "Matthew, you are a validation of your father's ministry. Remember, everything you do reflects upon your father. You should do everything to the best of your ability. You should be a star...you should prove that God's way is the best way. Please me and fulfill my wishes all the time because my needs are important.... You should be in the ministry—it's God's highest calling.... You shouldn't be married. There's no one good enough for you...I want you all to myself.... Matthew, you should be what your father never was—successful. Own a home, money, be charismatic...I wanted your dad to be interesting, exciting, scintillating, life on a long parade."

T: *What do you do when you are told these things?*

P: *I throw a tantrum and withdraw.*

T: *Ask your mom to withdraw instead, taking her fears and injunctions with her.*

P: *Okay. (Pause.) She does. (Pause.) Wow! Do I feel better!*

Birth

In the next session we worked on his feelings of pressure and of being alone and isolated and again went into his birth.

P: *I'm being smothered. I feel like I want to curl up in a little ball. (Curling up)...I'm being smothered. I can't breathe. There is something on my chest...I feel like something is over my nose and mouth. I feel helpless...like I'm going to die. I feel trapped! I can't get out! I feel closed in. Everything is closing in! I can't breathe! (Breathes heavily.) I don't know if this is ever going to end...I've got to get out of here!... There is no one to help me.*

T: *What are you feeling?*

P: *It's painful. My chest and neck. I feel like I want to get out! I don't want to leave but I don't want to stay. I'm afraid I'll die if I leave...I want to curl up tighter so I won't leave...I'm afraid I'll suffocate going through the birth canal...and I'm going to be cut off from my mother. I'll be alone. (Moves around.)*

T: *What's happening?*

P: *Pushing and shoving. I feel like I'm being kneaded from side to side. I'm kicking. Trying to stay, but I can't. I'm being pulled out. More and more! I feel like I can't breathe.*

Now I'm in the canal...I don't think I'm going to make it out! I feel panicky...I can't go back. I'm stuck. I'm going to die!... I feel helpless. Don't know what to do. (Breathes heavily and closes eyes tightly.)... Somebody help me! I need to get out and I can't get out...I feel stuck. I feel locked in. I feel pushed and pulled....

I'm going to be torn apart.... My neck hurts and something is on my chest. Someone is pulling on me...on my feet! My head is last...I'm stuck in my chest. It feels like my head is going to stay inside the body...I don't know what to do.... Someone else is panicking, too! They don't know what to do, either.

My head pops out! (Body uncurls and relaxes. He collapses, exhausted.)

T: *You are alive. You are okay. You made it. Your whole body relaxes now and that baby goes deeply asleep with healing dreams for that memory. Now you are free. And you are going to be all right.*

P: *(Later) I was really afraid I wasn't going to make it. Wow!*

The next session he reported having a hard week with his girlfriend. He felt that the relationship was strained, labored, too much work and that he preferred to stay stuck. I put him into an altered state and in trance asked him to go to the event where he had preferred to stay stuck, half in and half out, uncommitted and depressed, and he returned to the birth process and the moments immediately following.

Birth

P: *I feel like I'm half in and half out...breathing hard—not enough air, feels like a lot of work...I don't want to leave and I don't want to stay. I'm pushing and something is pushing me. I feel it around my shoulders, somebody's pulling on my feet.... My whole body is tight. I'm cold...I feel alone. I don't know where I am.*

Then I hear voices..."It's a boy...he's small. I wonder if he's going to make it." I can't breathe! I can't breathe!... They are trying to get me started, get me going. I'm cold.... My dad's not there.

I feel like someone is pushing on my chest, trying to clear out my mouth. Someone has a finger inside of it. Oh, it's sharp. I want to gag...someone is hitting me on the bottom. I feel panic all around me! Something feels wrong..."We can't get him to cry! We can't get him to breathe! He's small! What are we going to do?"

Someone is running their finger around my mouth. I feel cold. They are trying to get me to breathe, get me started. I don't know if it's going to start—if I want to. I feel so different out here. My bottom. My mouth. My chest...I feel like I'm not going to make it! (He begins to shiver and his body is stretched out.) I start crying!

I feel warmer—someone is massaging me. I'm choking...there's something on my nose—it helps me breathe. Some of the pain is gone. I feel better, more relaxed. I still feel cold.

I haven't been with my mother yet. I don't know where my mother is. I'm alone and everything seems very bright. Feels cold!

T: *Go ahead in time now until you've just been fed and put down for a nap.*

Prenatal

In the next session he reported a low level of energy. Once in trance, he buried his face on the ottoman and again went back in time, this time further back to the prenatal.

P: *I want to strike out. I can't. I feel trapped. (His arms are flailing.) I can't touch anything. I feel frustrated and helpless. And I hear my dad saying, "I've gotta know what we are going to do. We don't have enough money. I don't know how you got pregnant."*

Then my mother says, "I don't want to say it, but I don't want this child." She's feeling oppressed. Depressed, restless, like she doesn't know if she wants this. This is more than she bargained for. I hear her saying, "Why did I do this?"

T: *Realize these were your mother's feelings, not yours. And you caught them. But now you can separate from them. Bring light around you like a cocoon, an insulatory barrier from your mother's fear. And let the light come into your thoughts and feelings, into every cell of your body, and let it heal your memories.*

Birth

The next session Matthew again reported a feeling of hopelessness, this time related to the birth trauma.

P: *I just want to get out. I feel like I'm being poisoned. Feels like I'm going to be destroyed if I stay inside. I can hear the voices. In the kitchen. My mom is sitting down in front of the sink. My father is pacing up and down. Blue tile on the counter top. My mom is sitting down in a chair and crying.*

Dad is upset, saying, "I don't know how we can afford this." He's talking about his church. That we'll have to move. He feels pressured. He's angry. "I don't know what we are going to do. I don't know how we can afford it. This isn't anything we planned."

My mom is crying. "It's not my fault! You are blaming me!"

And I feel like it's my fault.

Meanwhile his mood lightened. He had finished a large project and rewarded himself with a great vacation in the mountains. In spite of a few reservations he was talking to Kathy about marriage. In trance he returned to his infancy.

Infancy

> P: *I want something from my mother but if I get my needs met she becomes unhappy. I'm at her breast. She's angry. I am being nourished and comforted but I feel her anger. Her body is misshapen and she has low energy, like she doesn't have enough time and energy for me.*

Childhood

The following session he went ahead into his childhood.

> P: *There never was a time I didn't feel like a victim. I hear Mother talk about Satan going around like a roaring lion seeking whom he may devour. I feel anxious. I don't know where he is, like he can pop up anytime to get me. Mother is scary. When she cries I get afraid. I'm afraid of Dad coming home and Mom is crying and it's my fault. If I were acting right she wouldn't cry.*
> *My father isn't really there for her. He was beaten up emotionally by his own mother and never recovered. I feel discouraged. I'm afraid I won't get out of this pattern. It feels too strong, all black, everything is black. I feel like I'm fighting something off all the time, like I'm fighting Dad.*
> T: *Talk to your dad and give him his own light. Let Matt follow his own life and light. Let dad set Matt free.*

As time went on, Matt was able to break the pattern and live his own life. After gaining release from his mother's and father's crippling attitudes, he decided to get married and after that his depression lifted. He was no longer paralyzed by ambivalence, which had been a major problem for him.

Therapy had shown how, following his prenatal absorption of his parents' feelings of ambivalence regarding his birth, this ambivalence had been constellated in his birth trauma and then carried forward into childhood. Only as Matt understood how his present feelings were duplicating past fears and conflicts was he able to let go of the fears and get on with his life.

Childhood Memories Triggering Past-Life Traumas

by

Roger Woolger, Ph.D.

Introduction

Specific incidents in childhood reactivate or trigger a latent past-life story that belongs to the inherited or karmic level of the complex. These incidents carry a symbolic resonance with the specific past-life trauma that they trigger. Phobias and an exaggerated reaction to loss or separation often prove to have such past-life roots. The re-living of a past-life story may be even more painful and dramatic than the re-living of a current-life experience, but it has the potential of resolving and dissipating the energy that has been bound in the complex.

Case 1. Abandonment

Past-life experiences often interface with childhood abandonment stories. With loss comes grief and the necessary process of mourning. Past-life sessions give a person the opportunity to finish old pieces of unfinished grief, fragments of which have surfaced in childhood in the ending of love affairs or in the loss of loved ones.

Sol was an osteopath and healer in his late 50's who had always been conscious of his health. In spite of good self-care, however, he had suffered throughout his life from sinusitis, which had resisted every kind of conventional and alternative therapy.

During a recent tour of the Mediterranean he had gone to Jerusalem and at the famous Wailing Wall had found himself weeping uncontrollably. We thought that this experience might stem from a past-life memory, but we had no clue of what this memory might be.

I had Sol lie down with his eyes closed and focus on his breathing, particularly his nasal area, and suggested that he let himself go directly to the time when his sinusitis had originated. Instead of going to the scene at the Wailing Wall he went back into his current childhood and found himself in sandals and short corduroy pants, walking along a damp forest path.

Childhood

> P: *I am nine years old. It is a summer camp in Michigan. There's half a dozen of us walking along together. It's been raining. I fell in the creek and that makes me even wetter. I'm miserable. I'm so cold I'm shivering.*

Sol started to shiver, despite its being a hot summer day, and his eyes were tearing. Both the biographical and the somatic levels of his complex had been touched.

> T: *Stay with your feelings and just say whatever comes to you.*
> P: *I'll never see her again.*
> T: *Who won't you see again? (I hand him a box of tissues.)*
> P: *It's my mother. She's very sick, in the hospital. Dad put me here for the summer so he can look after her. She may die. I'll never see her again.*
> T: *Do you share this with anyone in the camp?*
> P: *No. I've got to be tough. I mustn't cry. But I feel so unhappy.*
> T: *Let yourself express what you couldn't let out then.*

As with re-living any story, present or past, it is important to express the buried affects. It was becoming clear that Sol's sinuses were where he had been holding all the feelings that his strong little nine-year-old self had egoistically refused to allow to surface. After he unburdened his tears for a while, we went on.

> T: *I want you to repeat, "I'll never see her again," and let the words take you to any other story they have meaning for.*
> P: *I'll never see him again! I'll never see him again!*

With the change in this one word a new paroxysm of sobbing burst out of Sol—deeper, older tears.

Past Life

> P: *They've taken him. I'll never see him again! What am I going to do? We could have done something. It's too late. We abandoned him. I'm standing behind a large crowd. It's Jerusalem. I'm a man in a long robe. They've taken Jesus, and I'll never see him again!*

Sol saw himself as a Roman who had come to Jerusalem on commercial business for the Roman imperial authorities. A chance hearing of Jesus' preaching had changed his life and he had exchanged his high rank for a local post that enabled him to live permanently near this remarkable teacher. He even married a Jewish woman and wanted to convert to the Jewish faith so as to be closer to Jesus. More than anything, seeing Jesus heal someone made a profound impression on him. He spoke almost ecstatically through his tears and then told of pieces of Jesus' message handed down to him.

P: *We can learn to heal if we have faith and love.... We are all one.... We must love one another....*

These were simple and familiar words but seemed to arise spontaneously from a deep place within Sol. The rest of his story was commonplace—no special revelations of how Jesus died and where his body was taken. With crowds of others he kept vigil until the body was taken down. He never saw his teacher again. Later he banded together with other followers of Jesus and they studied and worshipped together as a form of remembrance. Living as a merchant for many more years, the Roman convert finally died of natural causes at an old age.

Sol emerged from his story with great emotion. The experience produced a true catharsis for him, an emotional cleansing. He recognized the spiritual roots of his vocation as a healer and how this vocation is entangled with a penitent sense of responsibility toward his abandoned master. The memory from his current childhood, coupled with this life as a Roman merchant, showed him the two sides—being abandoned and abandoning someone dear to him—and brought with it a kind of completion.

Integration

When we talked afterward, Sol said he had been with mother again after that childhood incident, that she had not actually died in the hospital but had recovered. The thought of losing her had, however, brought up an unhealed karmic level of the complex that remained too severe to release fully at the time of his childhood and had remained buried with his tears in Sol's sinuses.

It is possible that his visit to the Wailing Wall had set off an unconscious fantasy, since the great archetypal dramas of history and literature can provide a focus with which to identify on many levels, and meditations on Jesus' passion and death abound in Christian devotional art, music, and literature. But there was an ingenuous simplicity and unaffectedness about

Sol's story that rang true. Be that as it may, it was his story, his drama, and not one that any culture or creed had forced upon him. Therefore it gave him a deeply meaningful personal myth. From the therapeutic viewpoint, Sol's story worked as a vehicle for the abreaction and release of a buried aspect of a deeply entrenched complex, and it gave a spiritual meaning to his vocation as a healer. It also had a profound psychological meaning for him and left him with much food for meditation. It enabled him to experience the archetypal or spiritual octave of abandonment that interfaces with the biographical and past-life experience of loss which, when traversed, can bring a deep sense of peace, trust, and what might even be called faith.

Case 2. Etiology of a Nightmare

There are many cases where a relatively innocuous stimulus, such as the sight of a military uniform or the sound of a scream, may trigger a past-life memory in the child's deep unconscious. The child's intense reaction may be suggestive of childhood abuse, but often there has been no abuse in this lifetime. What has been triggered is a past-life memory in the child's deep unconscious. Such residues often constitute the stuff of night terrors.

Cindy had been in therapy for quite a while, working on issues of deep emotional longing mixed with fear of rejection. She wanted dependable love so much, she said, that it was like "being eaten from the inside," and she indicated her belly. She was also tormented by a severe childhood nightmare of flashing eyes and teeth in a dark corner of her childhood bedroom. In her interview the two issues seemed unrelated, but they were equally troubling to her. One well-meaning therapist had urged her to imagine a monster in the dark and then to befriend it, but somehow this ploy had not lessened the residual terror.

Childhood Nightmare

Working on the assumption that the childhood night terror might well be a past-life flashback, I had her find herself back in bed as that terrified child.

> *P: I'm standing in my bed clinging to the railing. There are horrible yellow eyes in the corner and it looks like teeth. Mommy! Mommy! Help me! They're trying to tear me up! Help me! Help me!*

Her mother came and hugged her and told her it was only a dream and she should go back to sleep. She lay down, but the eyes were still there in the corner. There was still terror in her child's body, especially in her belly.

Past Life

I directed her to look closely at the eyes and teeth and to stay with her feelings of terror, reminding her that her body as Cindy was safe and sound there in my office. I had her repeat one phrase as she looked into the darkness.

> P: *They're going to tear me up! They're going to tear me up! Oh, help! I'm running. I'm in a forest. It's almost dark. They're coming after me! I'm a boy, about six years old. They've caught me—it's a pack of wolfhounds! Help! Help! Their teeth...." (Screams and writhes violently.) They're tearing me up.... Help me! Help me!*

After an agonizing five more minutes of screaming and writhing, Cindy suddenly went completely limp.

> P: *It's all over. I'm above the body. They (the wolfhounds) are all eating it. Ugh! They ripped out my guts, my neck, my chest. Oh, it's awful! But I'm dead now. I don't feel anything.*

Cindy wept for some time while I encouraged her to breathe and let go of as much of the trauma as possible, especially what was lodged in her belly. She realized that her belly was where she had always carried all the terror from this memory.

I guided her to look back on the young boy's life until then. He had been the son of a peasant woman who worked as a serving woman to a particularly brutal feudal lord. On a cruel impulse the lord and his cohorts had selected a human victim for their hunt one day and had driven the boy into the woods for sport. Although the mother had been helpless to prevent it, the boy felt deeply betrayed by her and by her master. The failure of Cindy's mother to rescue her from her night of terrors had unfortunately served only to reinforce the old deep wound of betrayal, a wound that had become increasingly generalized in adult life and had lodged itself symbolically in her stomach as a gnawing longing for trust and protection.

Age Regression in Childhood as a Bridge into Past Lives

by

Irene Hickman, D.O.

Introduction

In waking consciousness some subjects object to the idea of going back into other lives. Therefore I avoid suggesting that they go back to a particular point and ask only that they go to a time that will be effective in helping them understand themselves. This often turns out to be a childhood incident. When this incident has been explored, the subject often feels comfortable enough to go to intra-uterine and past-life experiences that underlie the childhood incident.

Case: Tracing the Source of a Physical Symptom

Justin Arnold, an intelligent professional person in his early thirties, felt lonely and depressed and suffered from stomach ulcers. He questioned my qualifications as a doctor because I was a woman, doubted the value of hypnosis, and did not think he could be hypnotized. Because he expected nothing and doubted there was anything about age regression that could help him, his resistance was minimal, and he quickly became a good hypnotic subject.

Childhood

In the second session, while searching through his childhood Justin told about Christmas when he was six years old. He was standing at the blackboard in his school room with his favorite girl friend.

T: *What is your girl friend's name?*
P: *Jean.*
T: *What's your name?*
P: *Justin.*

T: *I am going to count back one more year and you will be five. One, two, three, four, five. Now you are five years old. Find a happy time and tell me about it.*

P: *I'm with my grandma.*

T: *Tell me about your grandma.*

P: *She loves me, but I'm naughty.*

T: *Let's go back a little further and see what it is like when you were four years old. One, two, three, four, five. You are four. Tell me what you are doing now.*

P: *(Begins to cry.) Nobody wants me.*

T: *Why don't they want you? If you talk about it you will feel better.*

P: *(Sobs deeply.)*

T: *It's very hard for a little boy who's just four when he feels this way. But tell me about it and you will feel better. Where is your daddy?*

P: *Gone.*

Interrogation brought out that his grandmother and father were gone and his mother didn't want him.

T: *Whom are you living with?*

P: *Lots of places.*

T: *Are they good to you? (Justin continues to sob.) Well, we'll not talk about it now—some other time. Let's go to a time when you are three. Go back until you are three years old and tell me about it. Is it happier when you are three?*

P: *No.*

T: *Where are you living now?*

P: *New Mexico.*

T: *Whom are you living with in New Mexico?*

P: *Grandma. We go to church.*

T: *Now let's go back to the time when you were two years old. Now you are two. Look around you and tell me what is happening.*

P: *It's better.*

At two he was living with both grandparents. His grandfather sang to him and played the fiddle.

T: *That is pretty good, isn't it? So now we will go back to one year—to the time you are one year old. Tell me exactly how you feel and what's happening all around you. You will be able to speak about it as an adult, but you are actually living the experience as a one-year-old baby.*

P: *(Begins to cry, then to sob.) I'm all alone.*

T: *Where are you?*

P: *In a room. I'm locked in.*

T: *Who locked you in?*

P: *Mother.*

T: *Do you know where your mother went when she locked you in?*
P: *No. I'm hungry. I'm on the floor. I'm crying.*
T: *Have you been there long?*
P: *Uh huh.*
T: *Now let's go forward a little bit—until someone comes and unlocks the door. You will know who it is and what they do and say. (Pause.) Who is that coming in?*
P: *My daddy. He picks me up. He loves me. He's holding me.*

Birth

T: *Now you feel better. Now we're going back a little further to the time just before you were born. You are able to think about this as an adult, but you will be feeling everything just as you did when you originally went through it. As I count backward to zero you will be in the birth canal just about to be born. And you will know what it feels like. You will re-experience your birth, still thinking about it as an adult so that it does not upset you. One, zero. You are ready to be born. Tell me everything that is happening to you and whether you are being born head first or feet first.*
P: *Head.*
T: *Now at the count of three the head will have been born and you will feel a lot better. One, two, three. Now the head is born. The body is not yet born. Tell me how you are feeling.*
P: *Relaxed.*
T: *You are able to hear everything that is being said and to know everything that is going on in the room. As the birth progresses you will tell me everything that is happening and everything that is being said in the room.*
P: *They're talking, but I can't hear.*
T: *You're going to be able to hear it a little clearer with the count of three. One, two, three. You are hearing plainer now. What are they saying? Who is in the room besides you and your mother?*
P: *The doctor. He's young, blond. Mother's disappointed.*
T: *Why is mother disappointed?*
P: *I'm a boy.*
T: *Did you hear her say this?*
P: *Yes. She killed my brother.*
T: *Did she say that?*
P: *No.*
T: *How do you know it?*
P: *She didn't feed him.*

This would be knowing a fact that occurred before the present body was conceived, as well as knowing it at the time of birth.

T: *You know this even though you are just a newborn baby?*
P: *Yes.*

Interim State

At this point I wanted to explore why Justin chose this family and these parents. One might think that the soul would choose a pleasant and happy situation if it has a choice as to what body it will occupy. But apparently the soul does not operate on the pleasure-pain principle. It seeks to solve its karmic problems, to work out its own perfection.

> *T: Do you know why you came to this mother?*
> *P: No.*
> *T: Well, we can go back a little further—back to the time before birth, back to the time where you will know why you are coming to live this life. So go back in time until you have an awareness of the reason you are coming back into an earth experience again. You will know why you are coming back to this particular mother and father. You will know and you will be able to tell me. So go back through time on to the time of this decision. Now, you know why you came to these parents. Why did you come?*
> *P: For my daddy.*
> *T: Had you known him before?*
> *P: Yes.*

First Past Life

> *T: Let us now go back to the time when you knew your daddy before. Your subconscious knows and it can search through your memory until it finds a time when you and this daddy were together before. When I reach the count of seven you will have found that time. One, two, three, four, five, six, seven. Look around you and tell me what is happening.*
> *P: He's my brother.*

At this point all resistance to going back into past lifetimes was dispelled. The material from the age regression had constituted a bridge across which Justin passed easily into previous experiences.

Questioning elicited the information that he was living with his 17-year-old brother Jerry in a log cabin in the United States in the 17th century. He was seven and struggling with arithmetic. Jerry was the only one who was good to him.

Second Past Life

> *T: Let's go back through time and see if there was another time when you and Jerry were together. Was there another time?*
> *P: He's a grown man.*
> *T: And you?*

P: *I'm grown, too. He's in uniform, a soldier.*
T: *Do you know him well?*
P: *He's my sweetheart.*

It is commonly believed that each soul must experience life on earth in both male and female bodies.

T: *Would you like to marry him?*
P: *Oh, yes.*

The young woman, Kathleen Morris, did not realize her wish to marry. The lover went to war (the Civil War) and did not come back.

T: *Now we will go forward to the time when you have lived out that life as Kathleen and, just as in a dream, you will be able to know the cause of the death and how long the life lasted. Tell me what happens.*

Kathleen never married but died alone of old age.

T: *Now you are between lives. Tell me what is happening, how you feel, and what your thoughts are.*
P: *It's better. I saw him.*
T: *Your sweetheart?*
P: *(Joyfully.) Yes.*
T: *Now you are going forward to the time when you and Jerry were brothers, then into your present life when he is your father. As I count to ten you will come forward all the way to the present. One, two, three, four, five, six, seven, eight, nine, ten. You may wake up feeling very good. Wake up!... How do you feel?*
P: *Wonderful. I feel different. So that's why I have always felt so alone. I've been alone for many lives.*
T: *That was a long time ago. Now that you have reviewed this, you can let go of that pattern and enjoy your life now. You are not alone now.*

Justin's ulcers healed and did not recur. He was able to move out and become more sociable and within a year he was engaged to be married. Both his health and his mood have continued to improve.

Reframing a Parental Image

by

Winafred B. Lucas, Ph.D.

Introduction

Regression to childhood is not always for the purpose of uncovering hate; it can also uncover love in a healing way. Parents often turn out to be disappointing to their grown children but underneath the disappointment can be buried a perception of sincere caring by parents for the less complicated and demanding child that the adult once was. Not all parents batter, and they are sad and often puzzled when they have done their best and cared deeply and then as they get older are perceived in a negative way. Much of the anger toward parents could be lessened or dissolved if they could once again be perceived with a child's eyes in the framework of adult understanding.

To get to this place of understanding and reframing it is necessary for the adult to immerse himself in the feelings of the child, and this is possible in altered-state work, in contradistinction to the recital of sheer conscious memories, which are minimally transformative. In an altered state the feelings of childhood constantly become juxtaposed against the different feelings of the adult until the validity of both come to be recognized and balanced.

One block to an easy recognition and acceptance of former childhood feelings is the existence of sub-personalities, which usually emerge at the age of three or four. Such personalities are concerned with survival and are appropriate in childhood but later, when adult strength and competent functioning have developed, they continue on in spite of not being needed and thread adult functioning with unnecessary and inappropriate perceptions and behavior. The release of such sub-personalities allows the adult to function more harmoniously and also more rationally.

Forgiveness of anger, even when the adult is open to forgiving, is often made difficult or impossible by the continuing existence of such sub-personalities. Only when the childhood feelings can be re-lived and the nature and survival function of the sub-personalities be realized and resolved, can the true healing of forgiveness take place. Prior to such a resolution, the attempt to forgive often meets a stone wall: it is sabotaged by the patterns and fears that belong to the sub-personality.

The release of anger moves through several stages. The anger must first of all be felt—out to its furthest and deepest perimeters. Only then can the next steps of the forgiveness process take place and healing work be done, an important goal because the release of anger heals in an encompassing way, the body as well as the mind and the emotions. The second step is a search for the origin of the anger, for we are seldom angry at what we think we are. For instance, in the following case the patient was angry, not about the triggering incident about money, but about the violation of her childhood trust, for which anger turned out to be no longer appropriate. This misconception blocked her ability to love. Anger is almost always rooted in and implemented by a sub-personality, which needs to be uncovered, honored for its survival value (no matter how negative its manifestation in adult life), and resolved, integrated, or reduced in importance. Then, within the framework of this new perspective, anger can be released and forgiveness can take place.

The process cannot be hurried and small steps must often be repeated. The therapist needs to take an active role as a guide, suggesting new ways of perceiving old situations and having the patient try out expressions of these until they are genuinely comfortable. Attitudes that have become embedded and encrusted must be prodded free and released sensitively. New insights must constantly be reaffirmed or they will sink back into the unconscious and allow former ones to take over. The highest and most healing energy is love, and where appropriate, transpersonal techniques help in releasement and facilitate moving to a permanently different vantage point.

Case: Search for the Good Father of Childhood[2]

The patient, Carrie, a brilliant and successful physician, had worked with me in therapy on and off over the years. From the beginning of her therapy her relationship with her father had been like a thorn that festered a little but never made her really sick. Recognizing her father in other lifetimes and forgiving difficulties and character traits similar to what she had experienced in this life had made her finally ready for a resolution. In this session she dealt with her wish to love her father and her stuck position because she felt she could not risk doing this.

The dialogue tells the story. It is often repetitive, but it demonstrates the small steps, the gropings, the back-sliding, and the final breakthrough into resolution. It reveals in moving transparency the sincerity and the honest seeking, the courage, and the deep loving-kindness of a gifted professional in a world where such attributes are not to be met at every turn. I thank her for her willingness to share this experience. Her commitment to deep searching was the more moving because this regression was one in a series videotaped in a research project with the Mind Mirror to document levels of brain functioning during regression.

The process of Carrie's exploration and resolution followed a sequence of clear-cut steps:

The problem
The induction
The triggering incident
First attempt at forgiveness
The barrier to loving emerges
A sub-personality emerges
Search for the sub-personality
Return to childhood in the search for the sub-personality
First attempt at resolution
Transformation of the sub-personality
Tuning in to childhood love for Father
Restructuring of attitude toward the sub-personality
Beginning acceptance of Father's love in childhood
Deepening realization of love for Father
Further restructuring of attitude toward the sub-personality
Restructuring attitude toward Father
Final resolution
Closing meditation

The Problem

T: We've been talking about what we could focus on and we thought that perhaps we could focus on your feeling about your father. Why don't you tell me just where you are in your feelings about him and we'll go on from there.

P: I'm terribly angry with my father. I was close to him growing up, and throughout my adult life I felt he was extremely supportive in my career and in things I was doing. I also had a feeling of trust and when that feeling of trust was shattered I've never really been able to forgive him. I see now clearly that that's the way he has always been. In this particular case I gave him money, which he then just took. It's not the fact of the money. It's the fact that I trusted him. Also, I told him confidential things about the family that I wanted to keep secret, and he blabbed them all over the family.

T: He violated your image of him.

P: Yes, it was such a violation of my trust. His faults revolve around the fact that he's a very violent man. He was violent with Mother throughout our childhood and I always forgave him for that and kind of took his side, but I always thought the quid pro quo was that I was his special friend. I stood in a special relationship with him. He really preferred me over the other children. And then I came to find out that wasn't true. He just used this approach to manipulate me. It was such a consistent violation of the image. And I see that over my lifetime that's the way he's dealt with everyone. My brother told me that when he was in the army he regularly sent home all his payroll checks for three years, and when he got home he found that my father had appropriated all that money. He was totally shocked when he found out. I told my brother that I didn't know that—or else I had screened it out—that's what I'd done. And when it happened to me I was totally shocked. Even if I had thought he would have done that to my brother or sister, I would have been sure he would never have done it to me. I was his special person. And it's been such a violation that even though I can understand it intellectually, emotionally at a deep level I cannot forgive him, I just cannot forgive him.

The Induction

T: *Let's put you in a very relaxed state. And let's go back to early childhood and see some of the things that might have happened. Let's begin by having you relax totally into the cushions. You've had a pressured day and lots of responsibilities. Breathe deeply and let relaxation spread through your body. Image a ball of light over your head and break it and let it come flooding down around and through you, covering your face and eyes, your shoulders and arms, and flowing down through your body until you're all covered with a blanket of light. Breathe deeply and become relaxed.*

Let's ask your Inner Mind, that knows all the answers and has all the memories, to give us some memories to help us resolve the problem of holding anger about your father. So he's done a lot of things and it's easy to say, "Well, he deserves for people to be angry at him." But that doesn't help anybody. Even though it was miserable, he did the best he could, taking care of himself in his way. So let's ask your Higher Mind to give us some very clear memories so we can release some of the charge, some of the angry, negative feelings around it.

The Triggering Incident

T: *Let's start with the most recent thing he did that angered you. Where was it and what did he do?*

P: *Uhh...the most recent thing he did was—I handed him cash to pay the gardener with and he took the money.*

T: *How did he justify that?*

P: *He made up a story, like the gardener overcharged him or something like that.*

T: *Let's go into it as though it is happening right now. I give him this money and he takes it. This is what is happening. Describe it in the present.*

P: *I'm handing money to my father to pay a gardener who worked on one of my rental properties but who is also going to work on Dad's property today. So I'm handing my father the money and he says not to worry about it. He'll pay the gardener. So I get in my car and I drive home.*

T: *Now we go to another day.*

P: *I ask my father, "Did you pay the gardener?" He says, "Well, he didn't really want the money because he didn't finish the work he did, other work." What he's saying doesn't make any sense. It doesn't make any sense at all.*

T: *How are you feeling?*

P: *Confused. When I try to pin him down he's getting angry. When I ask him he goes through a litany of words that don't make any sense, that the gardener didn't finish the work or something. I get angrier and angrier because I know he's taken the money. I just feel it.*

T: *What happens?*

P: *He says he'll give it to him next time. So I demand the money back. I say, "Dad, I want $100 back. If you've lost or misplaced half of it, I want at least half of it back." So he gives me the $100 and I take it. And I'm angry.*

T: *Why did you ask for only half?*

P: *Because that is all he has.*

T: *How do you know?*

P: *Because he tells me this cock-and-bull story about how he had to pay these Mexican workers, other Mexican workers who came up and demanded the money for working on my property, so he didn't get to pay my gardener. He gave it all to these Mexican gardeners that were working with the gardener. And he didn't have their names or addresses or anything. And meanwhile my gardener didn't get paid because my father says he paid out a hundred dollars of the money but he'll give the other hundred dollars to the gardener later. It's just a bunch of bull!*

T: *So how do you solve it?*

P: *So I take my $100 back and I'm pissed!*

T: *Do you pay the gardener the $200?*

P: *Of course I pay him $200, but I'm pissed. Dad never paid him a penny.*

T: *And you're terribly angry about that.*

P: *Of course I'm angry! (Voice rises.)*

First Attempt at Forgiveness

T: *Let's take this instance of the gardener and your father taking the $100 of your money and trying apparently to get the whole thing. Can you say to him, "I'm really furious at you for treating me this way. It's wholly crooked and I'm really upset about it. I would have preferred you'd..." Tell him what you would have preferred.*

P: *I'm really terribly angry at you for treating me this way and giving me some half-baked excuse and expecting me to believe it. I really wish you had been honest with me and told me you were frightened about money now that Mom's gone, and you're really feeling insecure because the person you* *leaned on all this time is dead. If you'd been honest with me, I'd have said, "Just keep the whole $200." I'd have assured you I'd be here to help you if you needed anything. How can you expect me to be your friend when you lie to me and steal from me? You always told me I was your special person and that you cared about me and you'd always be straightforward and honest with me, that you may lie to other people but you'd never lie to me. And now you pull all this crummy stuff!*

T: Can you tell him what you would prefer?

P: I would prefer that you tell me the truth.

T: First of all, I'd prefer you not to take my money. If you do, I'd like to know it straight.

P: Yeah, first, I'd prefer you not to take my money at all. But second of all, if you do take it, I'd prefer you to tell why you took it honestly, without cooking up this cock-and-bull story that doesn't make any sense at all when you and I know you took it. And then you deny it *(voice rises)* forever and you make it impossible for us to have an honest relationship.

T: But you couldn't do this. You couldn't be straight and honest with me because you don't know how to do this.

P: That's right. You couldn't be straight and honest with me because you have no idea how to be straight and honest with people!

T: So I cancel my expectation that you should be any different and accept you the way you are.

P: So cancel my expectation that you should be any different and accept you the way you are.

T: How does that feel?

P: Better.

T: Can you say it and mean it a little bit?

P: I'm angry about the way you really are but I understand you don't know how to be any different.

T: So I cancel my expectations and accept you that way, even though it's crummy.

P: So I cancel my expectation and accept you that way even though it's crummy.

The Barrier to Loving Emerges

T: Let's see if we can raise it up to the heart level. Can you say, "And in this space I send out my love to you"? You may not be able to say it.

P: *(Long pause.)*

T: Does that feel too much?

P: In this space I send out my love to you. *(Hesitates.)*

T: How does that feel?

P: I do love him. But I'm angry with him.

T: Do you think anything will happen to you if you say, "In this space I send out my love to you?" Will it hurt you in any way?... You might feel that way. Just look around and see. Will it make you threatened or duped or...?

P: I feel that I want to punish him and hurt him the way he hurt me. So I don't want to send out my love to him. *(Angry.)*

A Sub-personality Emerges

T: *Yes, that's why I asked you. What would happen if you didn't punish him, if you just accepted him? What would happen? There's something you're afraid of, something... Do you feel like a fool?*

P: *I do feel like a fool. My God, for 48 years of my life, I was...felt close to my dad. I was his special friend. One of the biggest breaches he did was to blab all over the family. The fact that I couldn't trust him with money is just a small little part. It wasn't the money. It's the fact I couldn't trust him. He wasn't my friend. He isn't my friend. I can't have an honest relationship with him. And if I can't have an honest relationship with him I don't want a relationship with him.*

T: *Loving him is not necessarily making a relationship with him.*

P: *I do love him. I do love him. (Tears.)*

Search for the Sub-personality

T: *I think we have to search together to find out what would happen if you did accept him the way he is. Would you be in danger of being duped again? Or would it make you terribly vulnerable? What kind of thing would happen?*

P: *Well, I do definitely think I was duped and blind.*

T: *If you accepted him right now, what would happen to you?*

P: *I feel that when I was a child and growing up that I had blinders on. Everyone else could see his antisocial behavior but me. I just accepted him and felt I was his special friend and it made me blind (agitated) to other people and it put me in danger. It made me naive where people were concerned. I wasn't at all smooth in any kind of business or social setting. But one thing I profited from individually is that when my blinders came off in regard to my father, they also came off in regard to the world. And I saw people in a different light. I'm not vulnerable any more at all! (Defiant.)*

T: *If you did accept him the way he is it might mean you would become a sucker.*

P: *A sucker again. And I feel I was a sucker. In many ways I was terribly naive. As to people, if they told me something, I just believed it at face value and went on right on their word. I never saw ulterior motives in people.*

T: *So there's a part of you that you're keeping under firm control that's called "the Sucker."*

P: *Right!*

T: *It got taken advantage of a lot of times in your life. And now you're determined that you're going to turn the key in the door and not let the Sucker out anymore. If you accepted your father it would mean maybe the Sucker would get out.*

P: *That's true.*

T: *When we can't release our anger, it means that there's something we could call a sub-personality that's left over and it's that that's causing the trouble. And I think you really did feel he made you a sucker.*

P: *I know that.*

Return to Childhood in the Search for the Sub-personalilty

T: *Let's go back to when you were about three or four years old when you first felt you were a sucker, where being a sucker meant you would get along with your father and would get his appreciative affection. Can you remember a specific incident about that?...any one.*

P: *He let me do special things. I can't remember...the ways he treated me especially. Little things. Dumb things. He and Momma always had coffee in the morning and he let me dip my toast in his coffee, always, because I was special, and he wouldn't let any of the other children dip their toast in his coffee. He always told me I was special.*

T: *And all the time was he using you or were you really special?*

P: *No, I really wasn't. I was a sucker.*

T: *How was he using you?*

P: *He was using me as support for his violent personality against my mother.*

T: *So he really didn't care.... He was using you as a sucker.*

P: *I was a sucker. He loved us all equally. As much as he was capable of loving us, he loved all three of us equally. But I was the sucker.*

T: *I think the problem is...you're saying how hard it is to forgive him. The real problem seems to be that if you forgive him, you'll feel you're going to let the Sucker out.*

P: *Right.*

T: *You don't see how you can love him and not allow him to make you a sucker again. But you can. Let's have a little talk with the Sucker. You can image the Sucker. What would you like to say to the Sucker?*

P: *How could you be such a fool as to garble up that in front of the whole family, for Christ's sake?! They must have thought you were a stupid ass. Everyone knew he lied through his teeth, and you had to hang onto every word! What a jerk!*

First Attempt at Resolution

T: *Okay, now be the Sucker.*

P: *But I wanted him to love me.*

T: *Say that. I wanted him to love me and I have to buy this or he won't. Can you say that?*

P: *I want my father to love me, and if I don't do that, he won't.*

T: *If I don't buy into it, I won't be special and he won't love me.*

P: *If I don't buy into it, I won't be special and he won't love me.*

T: *What do you want to say to the Sucker about that?*

P: *You don't need him to love you.*

T: *Okay, go into that a little more. You might even say that you're not a little girl anymore.*

P: *I'm not a little girl anymore. Therefore, I'm not going to crumble and cease to exist if he doesn't love me.*

T: *And so I could forgive him and not be in danger.*

P: *I could forgive him and not be in danger. It's just that I feel such a fool.*

T: *You had better tell the Sucker that the little girl who wanted to be loved so much—that you will take care of her yourself. She only wants to be loved, you know. She's not a bad person, really.*

P: *(Crying.) May I have a Kleenex?... I'm a calm, capable individual and I am capable of taking care of my own emotional needs.*

T: *I'd like you to picture the Sucker.*

P: *(Violently.) I hate her!*

Transformation of the Sub-personality

T: *Well, we have to deal with that. She's a girl?*

P: *And she's needy.*

T: *Yes. All right. Is that a crime?*

P: *Yes. She shouldn't be needy.*

T: *Well, she won't be needy if you take care of her.*

P: *I didn't know how to then.*

T: *We're talking about now.*

P: *I can take care of the Sucker's needs...I can take care of you.*

T: *What does she look like? Can you see her, the Sucker?*

P: *Like me when I was young.*

T: *Your personality was taken over by her when you were a little girl?*

P: *My whole personality was the Sucker. That's how I interacted with my whole family. That was my role.*

T: *One of the things that is important is...I want you to talk to her and ask why she was a sucker, why she came into being. She helped out. She didn't come in for no reason. She helped you out.*

P: *Because I wanted my father to love me.*

T: *Say it more intensely. I want my father to love me.*

P: *I want my father to love me! I want to be loved!*

T: *And the only way I know to be loved...*

P: *Is to play the sucker. My mother was going to love me no matter what.*

T: *Did she? Did you have to play the sucker to her? You didn't.*

P: *No.*

Tuning in to Childhood Love for Father

T: *So what you're saying is, not that you totally wanted to be loved but that you wanted your father to love you.*

P: *Yes, I did.*

T: *He was very important to you.*

P: *He was very important. What he did for me when I was little was that he totally supported my personality. He always told me how great I was. He always told me what a success I was. He always told me how bright I was. He always told me that he loved me. And I needed that to grow. I needed to believe it. He's the one who made me believe in myself.*

T: *Yes.*

P: *He's the reason I'm such a success today. He believed in me and he made me believe. He was my greatest cheering section always. And that's what the Sucker gained.*

T: *Could you conceive of the fact that maybe you were special during those years. You know, it is as though you had to re-see the whole past because of things that have happened when you were a woman. Maybe he was sincere or maybe he wasn't, but I wonder if you haven't done a little transforming that wasn't necessary. Get into the person of the Sucker or the little girl. I want you to feel the yearning for your father, to realize that he did a lot of the things you wanted. I don't believe that if they had been so false they would have borne such good fruit...*
   Can you tell me what you are feeling?

P: *I know he did a lot of good things for me (tears). He took care of me when I was sick. He braided my hair.*

T: *It sounds...*

P: *He took me to dancing school. He took pictures of me when I was dancing. He told me I was the best dancer and he always said I could be anything I wanted, and I always believed him. (Deep sobbing.) And I wanted to love him.*

T: *But he did. People can change. Maybe he got a little frightened when you got so strong and brilliant.*

P: *He's proud of me today. He's always proud of me. He wanted me to be strong and brilliant.*

Restructuring Attitude toward the Sub-personality

T: *A part of him has been threatened by that, perhaps. So there really was a lot of love and the Sucker did get you some good things. Would you like to say to the Sucker, "Thank you for helping me get those good things, for believing what I was told, because maybe, as I now see, maybe they were true." You've hated the Sucker but maybe that has to be straightened out a little bit.*

P: *(Sobs.)*

T: *I'd like you to talk to the Sucker and then have the Sucker talk back to you just a little bit to see where we are.*

P: *I'm telling the Sucker that it did get me a lot of good things.*

T: *Why don't you talk to the Sucker? The Sucker is really a side of you, the little girl who wanted to believe what her father said. Have compassion for her and talk to her a little bit. She got a lot for you. It was her way of coping, wasn't it?*

P: *Yes, it was.*

T: *Let's not blame her for that. She was three or four years old. I'd like you to put your arms around her and say, "Thank you for trying so hard and for succeeding sometimes, too. That happened because I was little, but I don't have to do it still. And you don't have to be so afraid either, because I'm going to take care of you.*

P: *Thank you for trying so hard. And thank you for succeeding. You don't have to do that anymore because I'm going to take care of you.*

T: *Imagine taking her in your arms and holding her tight and letting her know she doesn't have to try that way anymore. It was appropriate and got some benefits when you were little. Now it's not appropriate. But you don't have to tear her apart because of it. That's a lost self of yourself. As long as you're afraid of it, it's going to keep you from lots of things. You don't have to be afraid of it. If anybody in the world won't get taken in, it's you.*

P: *(Laughing.) That's for sure!*

T: *You don't have to worry, so love her a little bit. I think it's not just that you can't forgive your father, but you can't forgive yourself for being a sucker. After all, it was a survival mechanism. It was a way of getting something important, and it worked to a certain extent.*

Beginning Acceptance of Father's Love

P: *You know, I do know Dad loves me. He used to work with me no matter what I was trying to achieve. He'd stand hour after hour watching me until I could actually turn flips. In those days we didn't have coaches and stuff but he would give me all kinds of suggestions and I learned—I learned (spoken with intensity)! He put a lot of energy into me. He always told me I could do it—no matter what it was. I could do it. And I did it.*

T: *Don't you think that was pretty valuable. How many people get that?*

P: *Right.*

T: *Would you like to speak to your father and say "Thank you for that." Leave the other things aside for a moment and just say thank you for that.*

P: *Dad, thank you for all the energy you put into me. (Crying.) And for believing in me.*

T: *And for giving me the script that I could do anything I want. That's a precious script. Very few children get that script.*

P: *(Weeping.) Thank you, Dad, for giving me the script that I could do anything I chose to do, anything I wanted.*

T: *See if you can look at your father and see that sometimes he was insincere and sometimes he meant what he said. Sometimes it seemed it had to be all one way or all another—either he was totally reliable and did everything right, or at other times he was a complete shmuck. But it really isn't like that, is it?*

P: *No.*

T: *Sometimes he really gave and sometimes he really cared, as much as he could. And some people can love children so much better. Once the children grow up and are their own bright selves, it's not so easy to be straight with them.*

P: *Yeah. (Tears.)*

T: *He couldn't get along with your mother. He's probably the kind of man who relates to children better.*

P: *Yeah, he does.*

Deepening Realization of Her Love for Father

T: *So what would you like to say to him about the whole subject, as a child and now?*

P: *Well (tears), I really don't want to be angry at you anymore because I really love you. (Sobbing.) You really helped me a lot.*

T: *He really did.*

P: *Just because you weren't always honest with me you still helped me a lot.*

T: *I'm not going to throw out all the good things and all the love I had because of things you've done lately. I need to love you.*

P: *(Sobbing.) I need to love you!*

Further Restructuring of Attitude toward the Sub-personality

T: *Let's go back. I'd like you just one more time to tell the Sucker she doesn't have to function anymore. Those days are over and it served a purpose. It probably helped a lot, even though it was kind of a crummy thing to do, but at least it got you some of the things you wanted. And maybe it wasn't so much a Sucker. Maybe your father did mean some of the things he said. And when you believed it, that was okay. But you don't have to be a sucker anymore just because you love someone. You do need to see that. So what would you like to say to the Sucker? I'd like you to put it in your own words now, to validate the effort of the Sucker to give you something you needed at that time and to say that now you are older you can take care of that little person in you and it doesn't have to cause all these problems.*

P: *Um. I do understand why I did what I did. And I want to tell the Sucker that.*

T: *Tell it.*

P: *I realize that you tried to give me something when I needed it, that you did give me something, but now I don't need it, and I can take care of you....*

Restructuring Her Attitude toward Father

T: *Now that you know you don't have to let the Sucker out, it doesn't have to take over for you anymore. There are certain people you can't trust.*

P: *No. I would never trust my father. But that doesn't mean I can't love him just because he took my money.*

T: *Exactly. And because you love him you don't have to be a sucker. You've just put it the other way. You used to say that because you were a sucker you couldn't love him. But it's really that you can love him as much as you want but still take care of yourself.*

P: *Exactly. One of the things that bothers me—I can handle the gardener but I can't trust him with my secrets because it goes all over the family.*

T: *So you can't trust him.*

P: *Then how can you have a real relationship with him if you can't trust him?*

T: *Maybe you can't, but you love him.*

P: *I do love him.*

T: *It looks as though you can't have a real relationship, but that's okay, too. He's given you a lot.*

P: *So what does that mean?*

T: *It means that you give out in your love for him and don't necessarily get anything back.*

P: *So what do you discuss when you go to lunch? (Sarcastic.) The weather? Like men. This is what men do all the time. They don't talk about anything that means anything.*

T: *Maybe you don't go to lunch with him. You have to decide what can be a valuable experience. Maybe nothing. But that doesn't mean you have to hate him or you can't love him.*

P: *(Hesitates.) I can do that.*

T: *Can you do that?*

P: *What I can't do is see him be phoney and talk about the weather. But if I tell him what's in my heart, that won't work, either.*

T: *Maybe that isn't appropriate.*

P: *But I need him to listen.*

T: *You have another little child that's connected to the Sucker and really wants to have somebody listen.*

P: *Yes, that's right!*

T: *You have your husband.*

P: *Yes, I do.*

T: *Your task is to separate the need to trust and share from your willingness to forget and to love him. You've got them hooked together.*

P: *Yes, I have.*

T: *You don't have to share anything. He gave you a lot as a little girl. It didn't have to last forever, but he gave you a lot as a child. It was trust then. It only turned into a sucker when you felt he changed and you couldn't trust him. Perhaps now you can't go to lunch with him and you can't confide in him but you can love him.*

P: *Thank you. I know I can do that.*

Final Resolution

T: *I know you can, too, if you just realize they don't have to be tied together.... Can you say, "I would have preferred you had remained the same wonderful father you were when I was a little girl and I could believe what you said, but for some reason you aren't trustworthy now. I cancel the expectations that you remain the father who would listen to me and be trusted."*

P: *I cancel my expectation of you, Dad, that you would continue to listen to me and be a friend. And I cancel my expectations that I can trust you with my money. And I accept you with all your limitations.*

T: *...which I'll be careful about.*

P: *...which I'll be careful about.*

T: *And I send out my love to you.*

P: *And I send out my love to you, which my heart really wants to do.*

T: How does that feel?

P: (Emphatic.) That feels right!

T: Does it feel right? You just have to remember to nourish that child. I don't believe that child was really always a sucker. She was a trusting and loving child and she only decided she was a sucker when her father changed. You have to be able to see that you can separate those things. To say that you have to be able to trust everybody you love is not a valid statement.

Closing Meditation

P: I never thought of that. I really didn't see. Everyone I've ever loved I've been totally open with. Can I do a meditation on this?

T: What kind would be most helpful?

P: I want to send my father love from my heart. I want to cancel my expectations of him. I want to thank him for all he gave me when I was a little girl.

T: Okay. Let's imagine him sitting there. Put some rose light all around him. Let's see him in a glow, almost like Buddha sitting there with rose light around him. Can you see that? Say, "Dad, thank you for what you gave me when I was a child. The fact that you couldn't give me that same thing later doesn't change that. It doesn't cancel the validity of what you gave me when I was a child. That's still very valid."

P: Dad, thank you for being a deep source of strength and energy when I was a child and for helping me believe in myself. The fact that later on it wasn't the same doesn't take away from what you gave me then. I'm not any longer going to feel I can't love you because I can't trust you.

T: I do love you and I put all this light around you.

P: I do love you and I put all this rose light around you and I'll put a little rose light around you every day and send you love which comes from the depth of my heart.

T: I cancel all my expectations.

P: I cancel all my expectations and recognize that you're on a different light path of growth than I am—we're all on different paths. And now maybe I can't trust you with my secrets and my money, but I love you and thank you for what you gave me.

T: I'm putting light over both of you and as you come back into this present time and space, bring joy and strength and beauty and peace and a great deal of love. You will increase this love every day for everyone you view, which probably isn't very easy in your profession.

P: Oh, I do love my patients! They are special to me.

From the time of that session Carrie has retained a comfortable and accepting attitude toward her father. She no longer is compelled to meet him for lunch, and she has no business dealings with him, but when she runs into him in family affairs, she is able to be truly loving toward him. Her warm feelings sparkle around her and light up her face. The good things he gave her when she was a little girl are now firmly in her hands.

Chapter III

Child Abuse

Even with the spotlight of publicity on child abuse today, confusion and misunderstanding reign regarding its occurrence. Hostility and even hatred of children exist in our culture and in other cultures as well, and the prevalence of abuse and the enormity of its effects are still not recognized. A large segment of the population still believes that child abuse is insignificant and members of this segment are convinced that children lie about and exaggerate such abuse.

Alice Givens

When the patient recovers such a memory, his first impulse is to feel that he made it up. Fear of the abuser, who has almost always instilled a program of silence about the abuse, causes the memory to be shrouded in guilt and fear. Sharing the incident with the therapist provides the first breakthrough in dissolving these attitudes. After that it becomes possible, though not easy, for the patient to share the memory with others until the charge of fear over betrayal of the secret is dissolved.... In situations of remembered abuse the therapist plays a significant role, both in supporting the intense suffering of returned feelings and in actively helping with reframing. One form of reframing is forgiveness, wherein the memory of hate and hurt are transformed into something easier on the heart.

Afton Blake

Bibliography

Givens, Alice. "The Child Is Innocent." *The Journal of Regression Therapy,* Vol. IV
    No. 1, 1989.
———. *The Process of Healing.* San Diego, CA: The Libra Press, 1990.
Hickman, Irene. *Mine Probe—Hypnosis.* Kirksville, MO: Hickman Systems, 1983.
Miller, Alice *For Your Own Good.* New York: Farrar, Strauss and Giroux, 1983.
——— *Thou Shalt Not Be Aware.* New York: Farrar, Strauss and Giroux, 1983.
Woolger, Roger. *Other Lives, Other Selves.* New York: Doubleday, 1987.

Child Abuse

Introduction

Discussions on child abuse often imply that it is a specific type of experience, reprehensible and often criminal, and usually done with deliberate intent by strangers. Abuse is presented as though it pertained to a small, clearly differentiated segment of the population, usually not us.

My own experience is different. Ninety percent of my patients have been abused in some way, physically, sexually, emotionally, or through neglect. Throughout history much of this abuse has been considered culturally appropriate and has been accepted as such, even by the recipient. Usually it has involved families or close friends. Most abuse has become pushed underground, where it has remained anything but quiescent, emerging through the surface of consciousness as fantasies, compulsions, obsessions, fears, phobias, intractable anger, depression, or a variety of other expressions, including the formation of multiple personalities. The abused person often later inflicts on others what he/she has suffered.

Child abuse is only slowly becoming unacceptable in Western cultures. It is more comfortably integrated into the lifestyles of those cultures where the adult, especially the male adult, is conceded absolute power over the child, in which case it is not considered abuse, but even in our own country our democratic leanings have not extended to children until the past century. Many cultures have not considered a child to be a person, and they have had minimal awareness of the effect of childhood abuse on the psyche and development of the individual. Freud's hint that extreme sexual abuse existed led to serious repercussions for him and set an unfortunate precedent. For decades afterwards a reactive and frightened public tried to fall back on the assumption that the traumatic incidents of sexual abuse were spun fairytales, and it is only in the past years that such an explanation has been exposed as invalid.

Currently we are becoming increasingly aware of feelings in general and of a child's feelings in particular. In the last half century we have begun to observe what experiences impact children as they grow, and this has made us aware that abuse of any kind and at any level is detrimental to growth and can even interfere with maturation. Why do we approach the area of child abuse with such skepticism? If we could see deep into our memory world, we have probably all been both abusers and abused and we cannot bear to look at what we have not yet faced. The deep hurts and fears that we have hidden from ourselves get reactivated when we hear about the abuse of others.

The spectrum of abuse is broad. Physical abuse, because it has so long been culturally sanctioned, even encouraged, often passes unnoticed unless it is extreme. But any insult to the body, and not just sexual abuse, wounds self-concept and shakes self-confidence because we are identified with our bodies, especially when we are children. Physical abuse is not the only form of damage to the body; neglect and failure to give food and warmth and protection are also damaging.

Emotional abuse is more subtle than physical abuse but it can be even more destructive. Demeaning, frightening, and threatening attacks on the child lead to withdrawal, depression, or rebellion. Emotional abuse often accompanies physical abuse, as with Matt, whose terror at the threats of Satan are described by Givens, and with Blake's patient, the aviator Dan, with whom demeaning emotional attacks accompanied traumatic sexual abuse. Just not giving any praise or positive reinforcement is a form of emotional abuse in this difficult world.

Sexual abuse is the current area of concern. It is as though we had just discovered that it exists. The memory of it is frequently repressed and can then only be recovered in an altered state, into which the person has been precipitated by some external situation, has been led into by a dream, or has experienced with the help of a therapist. We need to recognize indicators, such as a strong attraction-repulsion attitude of a child to a family member along with unpredictable spurts of anger, a damaged self-concept, and guilt. Often, a specific symptom will emerge, such as Dan's fear of flying; or physical symptoms will be evidenced in the body, such as the frantic gasping of C.K. that Hickman describes, or Melinda's frigidity in the regression done by Woolger.

Within the circle of family and friends, sexual abuse often begins as a loving action and proceeds to get out of control. The child becomes ambivalent, and in an altered state of high excitation his ambivalence combines with the abuser's threats or instructions for concealment to seal his lips. I once treated a 10-year-old girl who, along with a group of girls of the same age, had been seduced by the neighborhood Pied Piper. He took the group to Disneyland every Saturday morning, spent the afternoon in experiences that pleasured him and gave the children some pleasure, too, and then made them promise on their Brownie's honor that they would not tell. This went on for several years, with the tacit blessing of the parents, until one newcomer spilled the beans. When the Pied Piper went to Atascadero, a prison for sex offenders, my young patient shed tears for him. Even in the case of Dan, the original strong emotional bond between father and son initiated a situation that the little boy at first tried to like and only repudiated when his drunken father became sadistic.

We intensify the impact of sexual abuse by escalating it to the position of a disaster. The guilt that stems from the experience hangs like a pall over the abused and can disrupt an entire family system unless the situation is shared and reframed and no longer viewed as a catastrophe. Consternation over it tends to make the abused feel marked and lessens their ability to take responsibility for resolving the experience. It encourages the abused to self-label themselves as victims. This does not mean that the child is responsible for its abuse if one is taking this lifetime as the unit under observation. Within such a conventional one-life framework, patients can be helped to accept the abuse as a vicissitude of life and go on without feeling permanently sullied, once it has been remembered and worked through. But from the extended perspective of past lives, the experience is found to be appropriate and can be integrated as an experience chosen by the soul for its growth or for balancing karma.

Regression techniques make possible the recovery of memories that have been unavailable in normal states of conscious. The empathy and unconditional regard of the therapist encourage the unconscious of the abused patient to trust the safety of the therapeutic situation and to re-experience what has been taboo for a long time. Just the re-living reduces the impact of the situation. Often there is a significant lightening of the personality after such a discovery.

The uncovering of pattern repetition in past lives and in the prenatal state and birth, as well the experience of the reversal of roles (when the current abused experiences himself as the abuser) reduces the impact of the experience. In an altered state the abuse can also be reframed and positive affirmations can be put in to replace the old hurtful ones, as Alice Givens suggests.

Induction techniques to retrieve childhood abuse are similar to those used to recover childhood incidents in general. Age regression is a common approach that is used when there is no specific memory, but if patient and therapist are aware that there has been abuse, then either a statement of feelings about the abuse or focus on a part of the body that feels abused can function as a bridge to the memory. For this to occur the therapist must first have built up a situation of trust and security where the patient has *no doubt at all* that whatever he says will be accepted and never, *never* be judged. The unconscious will not open up and disclose its pain unless this condition is met. If the trust and a feeling of security are deep enough, either bridging through feelings or a step-by-step scan of childhood years can expose abuse that up to that time has not been remembered. The usual reaction of the patient is that he/she has made it up, but in my experience such memories are valid and must be protected and encouraged like a fragile plant.

When the regression is confined to this lifetime, the reframing and release are accomplished without benefit of an awareness of the repetition of patterns and of role reversals. In such a case, some of the healing is best accomplished by using some form of forgiveness when the patient is ready. Forgiveness is the salve that gives balm to the wounds of abuse after they have been thoroughly exposed and lived through. Without it the wound doesn't quite heal.

Therapists who have worked through their own abuse and can look with compassion and openness at whatever abuse they themselves have experienced can be maximally helpful to patients. If therapists can release such experiences and discuss them with compassion and without shame, patients come to feel they can do likewise.

The Child Is Innocent: Releasing the Effects of Child Abuse

by

Alice M. Givens, Ph.D.

Introduction

Even with the spotlight of publicity on child abuse today, confusion and misunderstanding reign regarding its occurrence. Hostility and even hatred of children exist in our culture and in other cultures as well, and the prevalence of abuse and the enormity of its effects are still not recognized. A large segment of the population still believes that child abuse is insignificant and members of this segment are convinced that children lie about and exaggerate such abuse.

When Freud first wrote about sexual abuse in 1896, his theory that neurosis was caused by sexual abuse in childhood drew a horrified reaction from medical and lay communities. He was forced to rescind his theory and shift the source of neurosis to the child's fantasies of abuse rather than to actual events. Today it is generally conceded that Freud changed his belief only because his body of work would not have been recognized and accepted if he had insisted that parents' abuse of children caused neurotic problems later in life.

Though we now live in a more enlightened age, information about child abuse remains sparse. Child-care personnel and child therapists tend to blame children for drawing abuse upon themselves, probably because such professionals have not released the energy that remains from similar events and feelings from their own childhood.

Past experience determines the course of our lives. Although most therapists are aware of this, they do not always know how to transform negative experience. Fortunately, the feelings and events that occurred during our earliest development can be re-lived and resolved. Knowledge about every detail of our past remains deep in our unconscious mind—our memory extends back to the earliest beginnings of life, through our past lives from incarnations as the most primitive humans, up to the present time. The uniting of sperm and ovum in our conception can be brought into our awareness, as can the cutting of the umbilical cord.

Messages, both verbal and non-verbal, given to us in childhood and sometimes later as adults, program us and control us for life. Messages transmitted to us during experiences that are fearful, humiliating, or painful are especially powerful. Particularly in the abusive family, the child spends a great deal of time in an altered state because fear and pain paralyze the critical factor in his conscious mind. Thus, words that are said during these periods are accepted and preserved in the unconscious mind. This principle is the basis for the belief that many people maintain about themselves—that they are worthless, wrong, lazy, or evil.

Words spoken to a person who is already in an altered state induced by fear or other strong feelings are the major reason that incest, molestation, and rape are so often kept secret. The hypnotic words tell a victim that the sexual abuse is his or her fault, that he wanted it, it felt good, that he had been asking for it, and that he shouldn't tell anybody or they would know it was his fault. The victim then forgets the pain and fear and believes that whatever the perpetrator said must be true.

However, simply to remove the hypnotic words that are programmed in is not enough. Each person needs messages that help develop compassion, love, and self-respect. The messages must be said in a child's words while the patient is in an altered state. This does not mean that a therapist needs to reprogram with words that have no truth. We state reality: "You are an innocent, good child." The therapist should give truisms that the child wants to hear and that unfortunately are seldom spoken: "You are trying your best to please Daddy. You are a good girl." This is true even though the child might have accidentally dropped a bowl of cereal and broken it.

The therapist should always defend the child in the memory, even though an adult patient may insist that in his current perception he or she was a bad child. Nearly all punishment of children is for normal child behavior: innocent, good children wet their clothes and beds, soil their pants or diapers, speak in a loud voice, slam doors, spill their milk, drop dishes, defend themselves verbally (talk back), stay out too long, are jealous of the baby, get hungry and cry. They cry because they want to be loved, touched and consoled. They cry because they don't want to be left alone. Children are cruelly punished for all of these behaviors and also because they are curious and sometimes look at their own or other people's genitals. If a therapist feels judgmental toward the child in the patient, then that therapist needs to deal with the hypnotic critical parent that has been programmed into his or her own unconscious mind.

For permanent change, the energy must be released from these past traumas, including fear, anger, humiliation, and hopelessness. Simply talking about the past is useless. Too often people merely repeat old myths and legends about their family and themselves. Merely knowing about the past is not enough; old fear and hopelessness must be relinquished. Regression therapy is a process of returning to the past, re-living the experience, and removing the energy from old feelings and beliefs. Re-living details of the experience leads to expression of the feelings and this in turn contributes to healing.

Child rearing is the most important task in the world and yet there is little preparation and education for it. The survival of the human species is dependent upon how children are treated while they are growing from infancy into adulthood. Too often their most impressionable years are lived in an atmosphere of heavy control, intolerance, violence, and anger, and they grow up to create the same kind of world. We can begin to solve the world's serious problems by helping children to grow up in an environment of love, respect, and tolerance.

This paper deals with child abuse that has occurred in this lifetime and with regression to the childhood of the current life in order to resolve the trauma. It may be helpful, or even necessary, to go back to past lives for full resolution of child abuse.

Types of Abuse

Sexual Abuse

The most dramatic type of abuse, and the one that receives the most attention is sexual abuse. Sexual abuse ranges from the subtle, such as rubbing breasts and legs, to the extreme, where the infant or child is raped anally, vaginally, or orally. In sexual torture the child is held or tied while foreign objects are forced into the orifices of the body. In all sexual abuse, even the most subtle, the child feels trapped, powerless, and humiliated.

Physical Abuse

Physical abuse takes many forms: twisting ears and arms; grabbing the upper arms and shaking until the infant or child is dizzy, unconscious, brain damaged, or dead; beating with switches, belts, boards, purses, ropes, or any other handy items; throwing the child into bed, against walls, down the stairs; tying the infant or young child by his hands and feet in his crib, in the closet, or to a tree. Many adults can think of ingenious methods of torture, such

as burning with cigarettes, holding hands over flame, or strangling to near death.

Neglect

Distress over being neglected emerges clearly in depressed infants who are left alone in their cribs. They never bond or learn to relate to another human being. Children of all ages are sometimes left for days or even weeks with little or no food and no sanitation. Later they learn to steal at the neighborhood store, or they collect bottles and sell them to buy food.

Emotional Abuse

Emotional abuse has not been understood or seriously considered in the past, and, to a large extent, today. However, damage to the emotions persists for a longer time than any other type of abuse. There are homes in which a blow is never struck and sexual molestation never occurs, yet the emotional climate is so pathological that the child is permanently maimed. In these homes children grow up exposed to deep depression, to continual screaming and criticism, to iron control, or to continual chaos and crisis.

Words spoken during this kind of abuse are just as damaging and hypnotic as they are in sexual abuse. In traumatic scenes the young person feels trapped, fearful and helpless. The same words are repeated over and over in scene after scene. One mother says, "What's the matter with you? Are you dumb?" Another favorite is, "You deserve what you get." One patient's mother told her at least once a day, "Just look at you. You're so dirty. Your hair is ugly and stringy. Your teeth are crooked and you're fat as a blimp. How did I ever get such a child?" This little girl, grown up, is attractive, slim, and has beautiful hair. But until recently she felt ugly, fat and worthless, no matter how slim and well groomed she was. Her mother's continuous criticism programmed her unconscious mind.

Diagnostic Indicators

Although most victims of abuse develop amnesia for the abusive situation, there are many states and symptoms that provide clues that abuse has taken place.

Chronic Depression

One of these, which is usually indicative of neglect, is chronic depression. This disorder originates in one or more of the following situations: when the mother is depressed during the prenatal period; when the infant is left alone in a room and comes to perceive life as hopeless because no one arrives to pick it up or hold it; when the caretaker during childhood is a depressed mother and/or father; when fear and anger are so great in early childhood that depression is used as an anesthetic to keep the pain from being felt.

Generalized Panic Disorder

Generalized panic disorder in which the person has panic attacks at unpredictable times, can indicate early abuse. As such persons grow up, small events or even thoughts can trigger in them a repetition of terrified feelings. Any and all kinds of abuse underlie episodes of panic. In the borderline personality disorder, the person is emotionally unstable and shifts from a happy mood to anger, fear, rage, or depression within a short period of time. This disorder, which is chronic, long-term, and extremely difficult to change, seems to originate in very early cruel and painful abuse. The infant internalizes its mother's rage and fear as well as its own rage and fear. Part of the personality splits off to avoid unbearable pain.

Fear of People and Work

Other indications include addictions, such as alcoholism and eating disorders, which anesthetize the pain from childhood. Fear of people, whether it is of men or women or both, stems from childhood. The more intense the fear, the greater the abuse that is found in the source experiences. Paralysis in work covers fear of doing anything. This fear can be manifested as anger; however it is basically fear, and the roots lie in childhood.

Sexual Disorders

In sexual disorders the most common complaint is inhibition in the sexual response cycle. There may be no interest, no excitement, no erection, no orgasm, or no resolution. Other sexual disorders include exhibitionism, fetishism, sexual masochism and sadism, pedophilia, and other sexual disorders. In my experience all originate in the prenatal experience or in childhood.

Chronic Emotional Disorders

Any serious chronic emotional disorder is usually an indication of child abuse, although occasionally the disorder originates in an event that occurred later in life, such as the Vietnam war or in the experience of being victimized by crime. Such post-traumatic stress disorders are related in aetiology to the terror and anger of early childhood experiences.

Induction

We are in alpha, an altered state, at least a third of our lives, just as we are in sleep almost a third of our lives. All that is required to induce an alpha state is to distract the critical factor of the mind so that messages to the unconscious are not blocked. The distraction can occur through fatigue, fear, awe, shock, anger, relaxation, intense interest, repetition, pain, and other conditions. When a client enters my office, I begin to center on feelings that he experiences at home, at work, while driving, or during any current experience. The objective of therapy is to erase the disturbing feeling that he has described and my induction centers on this feelings. It begins when the patient enters the door because from that moment on we are talking about feelings—the stress and trauma from the past and present. If the problem is fear, then he is already in fear, and his unconscious mind can quickly go back to an old and frightening experience.

Before the first induction and regression to the past I explain to each patient what regression therapy is and why I use it. This explanation is followed by an initial induction statement, such as:

> T: *We will return to your experiences of your childhood and your infancy, clear back through your birth, your prenatal experiences, and even back to your past lives. The memories are all in your unconscious mind and can be remembered as I direct you back to them. Each person has all the memories of the past in his own mind. All I have to do is help you reach the experience and re-live it.*

Most patients respond at first with skepticism about the possibility that they can retrieve such memories.

P: *I don't think I can do it. I can't remember anything except what I've told you.*

T: *I have no doubt that you can do it. Your unconscious mind knows everything.*

P: *You have more faith in me than I do.*

T: *I have faith in your ability to work through your problem.*

It is true that I have faith in the person with whom I am working. I trust his unconscious mind to return to the appropriate experience and work through it. I have found that the efficiency of our minds is miraculous.

With most people the induction is that simple, although the first experience may take a little longer. No formal hypnotic induction is necessary. I have the patient shut out the present time by closing his eyes. Then I keep the message of where he is to go both short and simple, and I trust the unconscious mind to select the appropriate incident. Even if the incident doesn't seem right, I simply trust the process.

A word of caution is in order. The induction begins when the patient walks in and begins to talk abut his old disturbance. If he deviates subsequently and spends some time talking about a more recent event, be sure to take him back to what he has first talked about. Otherwise the patient becomes confused when the recent event and the words in the induction, which refer to the original complaint, do not tally, and the process is slowed down. Explore the person's current stress and any other material, such as past-life memories, as far as is feasible, and before the actual induction direct him back to the childhood trauma and the scene from the past. The key to simple and quick induction is an understanding and trust of the unconscious mind.

Case 1. Mike—a Child Threatened with Satan: Physical and Emotional Abuse

In my first session with a patient named Mike I made the following notes: "Wakens suddenly in a panic—can't breathe, shakes, shivers, is deeply anxious, has shortness of breath and fears loss of control; fears that he is going crazy or that he won't do anything right. He often feels spaced-out, cut off, distant, and unreal. He is convinced he can't get anything done, and he wants to get away from having to try." This patient expressed enough feelings during this first session to produce induction material for months.

I suggest routinely that the patient sit up or lie down on the couch, according to his preference. In Mike's induction he chose to lie down.

> T: *You can close your eyes and we will go back into a childhood experience. We are going to the origin of the feeling that you are shaking and shivering and afraid. Your unconscious mind knows where to go. You are shaking and shivering. Be right in the scene and tell me the first thing that comes to mind.*
>
> P: *(After about 30 seconds) I see my grandmother's kitchen.*
>
> T: *Feel your body there. What are you doing?*
>
> P: *I'm standing around a corner. She's going to get a switch. Oh, no, here she comes...I don't wanna go through this!*

Usually the patient enters the scene either before or after the fearful trauma. If he enters after it takes place, it is best to direct him back to the beginning of the incident and then take it through to the end. Use a description of the scene to help take him back, such as, "Be back at the time when Father is beating you," or "Be back at a time when you are tied up." With Mike I repeated his own words: "Be right where you are, shaking and shivering. Your unconscious mind knows where to go." The unconscious mind is already there because the patient has just been talking about the situation.

Mike was a slim young man of about 35. His father had left before he was born, and Mike grew up with a stern and religious mother and with a grandmother who was a psychotic and sadistic religious fanatic. His therapy centered around terrifying fanaticism and physical abuse, such as the first regression where he was switched on his bare legs in his grandmother's kitchen.

In another session Mike described waking up from a sound sleep in a panic, shaking and shivering. As he talked his teeth chattered and the word Satan kept coming to mind. I told him to lie down and close his eyes.

> T: *Let your unconscious mind guide you back to a time when you are shaking and your teeth are chattering. The word "Satan" comes to mind. You are afraid of Satan.*
>
> P: *I'm in a shower. She's holding me there. It's cold water coming down on me.*

Mike's body began to shiver as he lay on the couch.

> P: *She's saying, "Satan, get out of him. You're bad. Get the demons out."*

Grandmother hit him all over his body and then pinched him. (From the time he was 18 months of age he was left every day with this sadistic grandmother.) He was in terror. All he could do was cry.

T: *Let your crying talk!*

P: *"I'll get the demons out of you. Out, Satan, out! I must beat the demons out of you. The devil must die. You're bad. You have to go to hell."*

T: *Recognize that you are not bad, Mike. You are an innocent baby.*

P: *I'm all alone. She'll hit me. I have to go to hell.*

T: *Those are grandmother's words and none of them are true. You are a good boy. You are not going to hell. Her words are not real or true. You are a good boy.*

I had to remove the hypnotic messages in Mike and replace them with affirmations of his own goodness and innocence. (Fanatical religious messages are hypnotic, both in childhood and in past lives where we often find Satanic cults and ancient religious rituals.) Grandmother took care of Mike until he was six years old, regularly beating Satan out of him and threatening him with poison. We worked on her cruel punishment for months.

On Sundays his mother took him to a fundamentalist church where the preaching was about hell and brimstone. As he grew up he was required to sit in the kitchen every night and listen to the radio evangelists. His mother chose the preachers who were the most fanatical in their beliefs. Mike was afraid to believe and afraid not to believe. We returned many times in regressions to the scenes in church and to listening to the kitchen radio, hearing the actual words because the unconscious is efficient and had recorded all the words Mike heard.

P: *"God is powerful. Repent or you'll burn. God kills people. God will crush me. Jesus shed blood for a perfect world. No way out. I'll go to hell."*

Obviously Mike was repeating the preacher's words combined with his own thoughts. Each time that we went back to the fanatical religious messages, I made statements to replace the damaging religious beliefs.

T: *Say all the preacher's words and recognize that he is wrong. God is a force of love. You can remember that now. Let the words go. God is the creative force in the universe.*

We kept returning to the origin of his cut-off, spaced-out feeling. He was constantly listening to frightening religious predictions about wars, famine, eternal damnation, doom, burning forever. His thinking was confused: he didn't know what was true.

Mike's case is an extreme example of hypnotic childhood programming by both words and physical abuse. I had him repeat all the words of the preacher each time he was in a childhood scene. Saying the words out loud helped him to release the power of those beliefs and the fear that they generated. Messages from me to him were given while he was in the alpha state. My objective was to replace the fanatical, terrifying religious programming with a belief in a loving God rather than in a punitive, tyrannical God. My affirmations to him when he was in the cut-off, spaced-out state were designed to give him faith in his own ability to think and choose his religious beliefs. I reminded him that he had a good brain, could think clearly, could know what was real, what was true and what was false.

Mike recovered from his panic attacks and ceased having periods of feeling cut-off and spaced-out. His was a difficult case because the long exposure to fanatical religion combined with physical abuse had thoroughly programmed his unconscious mind.

Case 2. A Victim of Hypnotic Programming: Physical and Emotional Abuse

Jeanie, 24, was referred because she frequently cried uncontrollably and was failing in her college classes. She had consulted psychiatrists and psychologists since she was 16 but had experienced only temporary help. Memories of her childhood included scenes of screaming, fighting, and terror. When she said, "I was the bad one," I knew that this statement was a hypnotic belief.

Jeanie was easy to regress back to childhood.

> T: *Close your eyes and be back in your childhood in the source of your feeling of crying.*
> P: *I hear his footsteps. I'm too scared. I hope he doesn't come in here. He'll hit me. I'm afraid of his eyes. I'm bad. There's something wrong with me.*
> T: *Jeanie, tell me the words that Father is saying that suggest you are bad, that there's something wrong with you.*
> P: *He's saying, "Stop crying. You're a bad girl. I don't know what's wrong with you."*
> T: *Know that you are a normal, good child, Jeanie. There is nothing wrong with you. You are a good girl.*
> P: *Could that be true?*
> T: *Yes, I know it's true.*

Jeanie cried through Father's whipping. Then she was alone. The sadness and hopelessness came after the terror, so the scene was not over when the violence and pain ended. Jeanie lay on her bed, afraid and depressed.

> P: *They'll always hurt me. I can't stand it. I want to die. I'm all alone and can't get away. Nobody wants me. Nobody will ever want me.*

Jeanie was three years old in this scene, and there were similar scenes all through her childhood. When she was 16 Father hit her in the face and knocked her down on the floor.

Through the first few months I saw Jeanie twice a week, then once a week. She re-lived the painful trauma that had later paralyzed her work and school. We removed the hypnotic words that had made her believe that she was "bad, wrong, never doing anything right, never doing what she was told." She released the notion that she was stupid and nobody could help her. The words had become powerful, programmed in because they were repeated over and over in scenes during her growing years.

It was a happy day when Jeanie came in to tell me that she had earned an "A" in a college course. She was no longer terrified of her teachers and other authority figures. She had not seen her father and mother for two years but felt that she could now visit them without panic.

Case 3. Rescripting an Untrue Message: Sexual Abuse

When Winnie was 12 years old an uncle took her to the store and on the way home stopped the car in an empty lot and raped her. Winnie cried and struggled to push him away, but he was brutal and insistent. As she grew up she remained ashamed of the experience and never mentioned it to anyone. Months after she began therapy she returned to the incident during regression and cried in pain as her uncle forced her.

P: *It was my fault because I liked him.*
T: *Let your unconscious mind take you to the words that tell you whether it is your fault.*
P: *I'm telling him that it hurts and I never want to see him again.*
T: *Say the next words that he is telling you.*
P: *Don't tell me that you don't wanna see me again. You know you loved it. And don't you dare tell anybody. Your dad will know you wanted it and it was your fault. You wanted it when you came with me.*
T: *Winnie, recognize that his words are not true. You didn't want it. It's not your fault.*
P: *I just feel confused.*
T: *Be back in the time when he first stopped in the empty lot and tell me how you feel.*
P: *I feel confused. I don't know why we're stopping.*

Winnie went through the experience again. At the height of her pain and fear, I helped her into a correcting statement.

> T: *Say to your uncle whether you want this, or not.*
> P: *Get off me! Quit holding me down. I hate you!*
> T: *Recognize what your real feelings are while he is raping you. You didn't want it. It is his fault, not yours.*

We completed the experience, repeating all of the uncle's words so that Winnie could recognize that his words were lies uttered to justify himself and assure her secrecy.

At the conclusion of the session Winnie was no longer confused. She had come to understand that her uncle's words—and not her own knowledge of herself—had been responsible for her feeling that she was the guilty one, the bad one. Returning to the scene where she could hear the words spoken and could be aware of her feelings and her body pain, made it possible for her to recognize the reality that the words that had hypnotized her all these years were not true.

Research tells us that messages heard during an altered state tend to be programmed in, just as in a computer. These messages must be deleted and reality recognized while one is in an altered state. The person must be taken back into the scene and the words that were said by the parent or other powerful person must be reheard, and the patient must recognize that the hypnotic words were not true. Infants and children see the adults around them as all powerful and all knowing—what big people say must be true. Words of parents and abusers are hypnotic and become the beliefs of the child. To wake from this state is to recognize reality and to feel one's own goodness and innocence.

The effect of childhood trauma is clearly revealed in regression therapy. We can see that behind later disorders are painful childhood experiences. We are shaped by our past but through the process of expressing old fears and grief we can begin a creative and loving way of living.

Phobias and Sexual Abuse

by

Afton Blake, Ph.D.

Introduction

In conventional psychotherapy there is little indication of the frequency of sexual abuse in childhood because such abuse is usually covered up by both victim and perpetrator. In altered states, however, many incidents of abuse become remembered, incidents of which the patient has had no conscious knowledge. In such patients memory has become replaced by vague fears, seemingly irrational spurts of anger, depression, and a derogatory evaluation of the self. Fear, especially, has lived on and has become transferred from one object and situation to another, often constellating in a phobia or in multiple personalities.

When the patient recovers such a memory, his first impulse is to feel that he made it up. Fear of the abuser, who has almost always instilled a program of silence about the abuse, causes the memory to be shrouded in guilt and fear. Sharing the incident with the therapist provides the first breakthrough in dissolving these attitudes. After that it becomes possible, though not easy, for the patient to share the memory with others until the charge of fear over betrayal of the secret is dissolved. In situations of remembered abuse the therapist plays a significant role, both in supporting the intense suffering of returned feelings and in actively helping with reframing. One form of reframing is forgiveness, wherein the memory of hate and hurt are transformed into something easier on the heart.

What is interesting in the following case is the linking of the father's sexual abuse with flying in such a way that a phobia developed. This could be relieved only when the original experience was recovered and released. The release was initiated by breaking the power of the father's command to secrecy, and it was then reinforced when the patient uncovered the connection between flying and his father. The final healing came from the attempt at forgiveness.

The subject himself brought up the question of why such extreme trauma did not leave him psychotic or with a multiple personality. What caused him to survive as a functional, although handicapped, human being? Perhaps the answer lies in the secure loving environment of his very early years that through adequate infant bonding gave him the ego strength to survive. Children who do not have such a sound beginning lack a core of resistance to fragmentation. In Dan's case his mother appears to have been relatively stable, if unperceptive, and she possessed enough strength to leave her untenable situation when he was six years old, once she realized that the father was being abusive. The reason for her sudden separation was not known to Dan at the time but became clear as he recovered the incidents in his childhood prior to the time his mother left his father.

Case: The Grounded Aviator

Until his early twenties Dan had managed to give the impression of normal development. He was an excellent student and eventually earned an M.A. in English, and his exceptional writing potential qualified him for teaching on a college level. This was a second-best option, however, for his first choice had been to be a pilot. At 17 he had begun work toward a commercial pilot's license and a few years later he was accepted for pilot training by the Air Force.

A series of increasingly intense experiences of fear eventually terminated his progress toward becoming a pilot. Very early, while Dan was on a solo training flight, an emergency developed and he came close to being killed. Though he landed safely and without apparent injury, on his next flight he developed a phobia of flying solo. The sensation "jumped" him unawares. His skin began to tingle, he went numb, and he felt himself leave his body.

In spite of this experience, he persisted in flying, but soon after this his training as a pilot came to a disastrous end following the day his instructor played for the trainees a tape of a civilian pilot who had become disoriented and suffered vertigo. As this pilot's plane spiraled down out of the sky he held the keyed microphone and screamed in a high pitched unearthly voice, "Help me! Help me! Oh, God, please help me, help me, oh God!" Finally the impact of the plane as it crashed silenced the voice. The desperation of this voice stirred a memory in Dan, though at the time he did not know what the memory was. Following this experience, he found himself unable to fly and left the Air Force.

When he was 23 he told a friend of a dream he had. In response, the friend asked him if his father had ever beaten him, and he found himself rolling on the floor and screaming, "Daddy, Daddy, please don't! Oh, God, don't touch me! No, no, stop, please!" This intense and seemingly exaggerated response puzzled both him and his friend, but since he had no context into which to fit it, he could do nothing to disentangle its meaning.

Until the age of six Dan's family had consisted of his mother and father, a sister and himself. At six his mother left his father abruptly and moved with the children to a Southern town to live with her family. There the two children grew up in a warm and protective atmosphere. However, Dan remained frozen and confused in his relationships, especially with women. From adolescence on he seemed to choose a series of women who ended up not caring about him, and his one attempt at marriage ended in divorce.

Because of the sudden early separation from his father, Dan's relationship with him had been ambivalent and ambiguous. Apparently the very early years had been ones of love and trust, for of that time he was later to write in his journal, "Your father was the angel of your life; your mother was the soil. The world was rich and filled with love, the atmosphere itself of blessed days and a four-year-old weaving light sublime." Something had interrupted this.

Much later, when Dan had finished his academic degree and knew that he still was not able to fly, he decided to renew contact with his father and try to clarify their relationship. His father was in California working as an actor, and Dan went there and acted with him in at least one movie, wrote a book of poems, and often supported himself with carpentry work. However, the longed-for relationship with his father did not materialize.

Dan originally sought therapy for three reasons: to deal with the problem in his relationship with his father, to understand his contribution to the breakup of his own marriage, and to work through his fear of flying. He had had earlier contacts with therapists, which he considered valuable although he had not been able either to work out his problems with his father or to find the source of his flying phobia. That these two problems were related was never suspected by any of his therapists, though his last therapist thought that there might have been sexual abuse in his childhood, which provided a valuable lead for us. With that therapist Dan could not remember anything, and there had seemed no way at the time to contact the memories of such a possible experience. Eventually Dan decided to seek another therapist to pursue this lead and he began to work with me in 1987. Through our work together, answers, sad and disturbing answers, began to emerge.

In the beginning we scanned other lifetimes for patterns of relationships and for a possible clue to his phobia around flying. In the process we learned a great deal that clarified his relationship problems. Then in his most recent lifetime he found himself as a B-17 Bomber pilot in World War II. He and his crew were killed on their ninth mission over Germany in 1943. Because their plane had lost power, they had to leave the formation. Fighters swarmed around them for 20 minutes and shot them to pieces. Dan's copilot had his head blown off, and over the intercom he heard the screams of boys crying for their mothers as they died. In the end they blew up and the big plane rolled to the left in a huge fireball. Dan's last thought was one of rage.

> P: *It is a lie, it is a lie, it is all a lie! There is no reason, no cause so great that one should kill another. None!*

Like many writers Dan kept a journal, and in early entries he tapped feelings of despair at not being able to understand what was crippling him. He felt like a man "who had been through an accident and had both his legs cut off and was trying to adjust to being a half person." "I am in such a state tonight," he wrote shortly after we began to work together, "I want to scream, just bellow into the night. What is it that has been so wounded and why haven't I healed? Why does a human rage? Is a baby born with such a hate?"

Regression to Childhood

After a year of therapeutic work we made the first regression back to the period of Dan's childhood. By this time a foundation of trust had been built and he felt comfortable in altered-state work. I suggested that he go wherever his Higher Self wanted to take him.

> P: *I'm at the Alexandria Street house. This is where it all happened. I'm standing on the front steps. I'm afraid to go in. It's very dangerous in there.*
> T: *Dan, know that you can watch the events, whatever is there, as if you were watching yourself in a movie.*
> P: *Okay, that's good. I can do that.*
> T: *Good.*
> P: *I'm on his lap. We have our clothes on. Now this is a memory. I've got this one. He's tickling me. I'm laughing and laughing. We're having fun. All of a sudden he flips me over his knee and spanks the tar out of me. I'm stunned, simply stunned. What did I do wrong? I don't feel any pain, just complete surprise.*
> T: *What happens next?*
> P: *I don't know. That's where the memory stops. It just stops. I've had that memory my whole life. Now my instincts say that it started that day, right after the spanking.*
> T: *Go ahead and see what happens next.*
> P: *Okay, but I think it's real bad.*
> T: *Remember, you can watch it all as a movie.*
> P: *Okay. He—the little boy—is lying on the bed naked with my father. They're laughing, playing with each other; my father's tickling me. He says, "Do you want to play a fun game?"*

When I say yes, my father says, "Okay, lick my pee-pee." That's a scary thought but the little boy does it though he doesn't want to. But he starts doing it, and then it's kind of fun. It's exciting, and the boy feels special. He likes all the attention. He's scared a little bit, but not too much.

My father says, "Oh, my little son, you smell so clean and fresh. I love you so much. I love you." There is whiskey by the bed—my father's drinking it. My father's moaning now, thrusting his hips, groaning with pleasure. He gets wilder and wilder. Suddenly he grabs the boy's head by the hair and shoves his penis into...it's violent, he really jabs him hard—in the mouth, into his mouth, yes, his throat.

The boy can't breathe. He's terrified. He's thinking, "What happened? It's all out of control!"

T: *Where are you now? Where do you, the observer, see yourself in the room?*

P: *I'm floating up by the ceiling. A whole part of me, most of me, has split off and left my body. It's too awful, too painful to stay. Part of me stayed though, in my body. It had to stay and keep my body alive.*

But it's enraged at my father and at me for leaving it alone. It's alone in hell. That's the problem, one of the problems, at least. I have to somehow put us back together. I'm in pieces. It is the same feeling I have when flying solo. The thing comes over me, and I can hardly stay in my body. Everything becomes dreamlike and my skin tingles and goes numb all over. Then another part of me comes out and is so enraged it wants to crash the airplane in this horrible fireball. It wants to mutilate me. That is the war in me.

As the regression continued, Dan experienced a series of tortures, the sexual acts being only one component of his father's sadism. We repeated the experience until he was able to stand apart and process it from broader perspective.

At the end of this regression Dan returned to his experience of hearing the voice of the disoriented pilot. The first time he had tried to take a plane up after that experience he remembered that he had heard a sweet voice "soft and alluring like the Sirens calling Ulysses to the rocks" that told him to kill himself, to let go of the stick on the final turn and "let the beast smash home to bits." Then another voice spoke up strong and clear and said not to. He followed the second voice and walked away from his jet, not to return. After that, different voices had come, "not voices really as you think of sound, but voices as you think of thoughts, voices distinct from each other, autonomous and individual, each with its own agenda." It took the utmost courage to go on living with all these voices competing.

He felt that he was in the middle of a perilous climb where attainment of the summit was by no means guaranteed. He was crying, full of cold and ache, with starving lungs. "Why did I come?" he wrote in his journal. "Where am I in this cloud on this rock; how am I here?" Memories of a warm life back home were merely dreams that never were, absurd and laughable. He felt "born out of rock, to suckle on a frozen granite tit, to hang until he could hang no longer and then fall, and die alone. He takes another step towards some imagined...maybe summit, the wind whips at him, and the temperature swallows him at twenty degrees below."

Even at this early time Dan began to connect this experience with his fear of flying, and in later sessions the connection would emerge even more clearly. He realized that the loss of oxygen he had experienced as his plane precipitated downward in that early flying accident had triggered a body memory of loss of oxygen. The memory was of oxygen loss from forced fellatio with his father that had led to feelings of dissociation. This dissociation occurred even more strongly when Dan's father held his head underwater, an incident remembered in the second regression.

Second Regression

The first regression had been understandably so disturbing that Dan considered further exploration of this period with reluctance. We worked a long time to help him become relaxed and comfortable enough to be ready to look again at those distressing events in his relationship with his father.

P: *God, I can't get it out. It's so awful. Like a great constipation. It's big and it's really bad.*

T: *Try to let yourself experience the feelings.*

P: *Jesus, I'm so afraid it will be too loud. I'm gonna' be screaming like a mad man. People will think I'm being murdered.*

T: *Don't worry about the noise. Just let yourself go with the feelings, and know that your Higher Self will not let you experience anything that you are not prepared to handle.*

P: *Okay. Here goes, if I can get it out. It feels lodged in my spine. If I could just break open my spine....*

T: *Well, imagine just that, that your spine breaks open.*

P: *That's a good idea. I can do that....God, oh God, my legs are tied up with sheets. I'm dragging myself across the floor. He says, "Why are you making me do this to you? Why, son, why? You little shit, you got a little bitty dick, not like mine. I'm a man. Mine's huge, see!"*

Bastard shoves it down my throat. I got to get out! I got to get out! He's dragging me by my legs across the floor. "No, no, please don't, Daddy. Daddy, please, oh please, oh please, don't!"

I'm in the tub. He's put me in the tub, taken the sheets off. He says, "Don't move, you little puke. Don't move one muscle."

I'm frozen, seems forever. I sniffle.

"You moved, son. You're not listening to me. So you know what I have to do?" God, no, no, no! He's shitting in my face. He's pissing on me....

> *Now the tub is full of water. Now he's drowning me, holding me under by my hair so as not to leave bruises. He's very good and meticulous about not marking me up. He raises me up, down under again, up, down, up. He'll kill me! He's going to kill me! He's greasing up his penis, laughing, just laughing so evil. He picks me up and sticks me down on it. My eyes are coming out of my head. The pressure, the pressure! He comes. He's done.*
>
> *He drops me like a rag doll and walks away.*
>
> *He's sitting on the sofa, staring at the wall in a stupor. I'm looking at him through the door. I start to vomit but I hold it in my mouth and swallow it in little gulps. If I let it out, he'll kill me.*
>
> *He turns to me and says, "Come here." I go. He grabs me by the throat and squeezes gently. "If you tell anyone about this, anyone at all...if you tell Mom, ever, I will kill you. I will come and find you, wherever you are, and I will kill you."*

It was during this time that Dan remembered an airshow he had attended with his father just before the abuse started. It was the first time he had seen a plane, and his father held him up so that he could get a good look at the cockpit. Of this memory he wrote in his journal:

> *All I ever wanted to do was fly, just fly. It was the dream I held first in my heart as a little boy, the day my father held me up to look inside an airplane, quiet on the ground, miraculous inside: the dials, all the switches magic-tucked, and the wide wings lightly rocking in the wind that gently swept our way with mint and fresh cut clover on the breath—serene. "Papa, hold me high, hold me tight to see," I said.*
>
> *Then a day came, another morning, and in that morning my father killed me under a great and tremendous pressure; within me, airplane and father fused into one, and from that addition a terrible summation had begun: "Flying is magic. It's also demonic; Evil must be destroyed." Flying is Daddy; Daddy must be destroyed. Now when I fly—my God!—I'm in his arms again, pinned and prodded.*
>
> *It comes to me again, and once again surprise to think, believe, that I endured horrendous devastation as a child, of which only a part of me survived while the other segments were blown to dust. And that at 35 I'm like a ghost of that one signalman who with a lantern in the night comes roaming around the tracks searching for his head.*

In his therapy Dan came to realize that in the incident of observing the plane, his father had somehow become identified with the plane. When he started to fly he had become increasingly afraid that his anger at his father/plane would cause him to crash.

It was an incident that occurred on the weekend before the third regression that pressed him to continue his exploration of those painful years. He had gone to an air show and as a result of attending this, he promised himself that whatever it took, whatever he must see, no matter how horrible, he would see it and go through it: he wanted to fly again. It was a consuming goal.

Third Regression

During this period of his therapy he had a dream about a mutilated animal, and, following that, several violent dreams whose imagery was of severed appendages and bloody parts. Also, he was awakened several times at night by a popping sound, a cracking noise, sharp and quick. It awakened him from sleep and left him disturbed and upset.

In order to deepen Dan and give him as much protection as possible for this regression, I began to work with light in the chakra centers, beginning with the crown chakra. I had just reached the throat chakra when he started screaming.

P: *He's putting it in my face. He's laughing. He's sitting on top of me, on a pillow. He has killed our pet cat Friday and cut him in pieces. The pieces are on a newspaper by my head. He picks up part of my cat—he's like a dentist picking up a tool. He runs it over my face. He's forcing it into my mouth.*

I don't scream. I'm not so afraid this time. Though it's happening again, I don't feel as betrayed. I know he's a sick fuck. The first time the terror and the betrayal overwhelmed me. This time it's a matter of survival. Just survive! How to endure these torture sessions. Figure it out. Figure it out.

I should have hit Friday, our cat, made him run away; then he would have lived. I knew my father might kill him, but I didn't think he really would. I should have been mean to Friday and thrown rocks, to make him run away, but I didn't, and my father killed him.

T: *It's been my experience, from what I know, that animals choose to stay with their masters as long as they can. They want to go through what their masters are going through, and they sacrifice themselves for their masters, usually much more easily than people do. I'm sure Friday knew, in his own way, that he probably would be killed and that he could have run away, but he chose instead to stay with you as long as he could.*

P: *I've always thought animals were little angels, silent little angels, watching over us, quietly helping, teaching where they can. Maybe my present cat is Friday, come back to me. I feel like he is. He and I have been through everything together for nine years.*

T: *Maybe he is, and I think he knows of your suffering.*

P: *It feels good to me, calming, to think that way.*

T: *What did your mother think about Friday's disappearance?*

P: She said he'll come home, tonight or in the morning. "Here, kitty, kitty, kitty! He'll come home."

T: But you knew differently.

P: Oh, yes. He won't be coming home, Mommy. Daddy killed him.

T: Did you tell her?

P: With my eyes and looks I tried, but she didn't see. She didn't want to see. God damn her, she just put blinders on.

T: Children always think their parents should be able to tell when something's wrong.

P: God, how stupid could she be, all this happening under her nose! No, no. That's not true. If she had known she would have gotten us out of there. I know she would. She is a good mother. She is. He picked up so good. She'd come home and there wasn't a trace of anything. That was part of his pleasure. How far could he go and not get caught.

T: Do you have a sense that this experience, the killing of Friday, comes after the other experience?

P: Oh, yes. He was expanding his repertoire. Feeling more confident.

T: Do you know if there are other times after this one?

P: Oh, yes, there's more, more, more.... I should have thrown rocks. Oh, I can't believe all this is coming out of me. How did I survive? I should be a multiple personality or a maniac. How did I keep it together so well? Seems worse than Sybil.

T: I think each spirit born into this life comes into the world with its own strengths and weaknesses. Your suffering made you stronger. Take this time, all the time you need to just feel how alone you were then and how you struggled so.

P: Oh, poor little boy! Poor, poor little boy. My little cat. Oh, it's all so sad! So sad. So so sad. I can't believe how I suffered then. My poor little boy!

You know, I think I made a conscious choice to forget. A part of me feels like an old, old man, ancient, and he would come out then, after the torture session was over. I'd try to tell my mom, and I knew it was hopeless. The old man would come out and say, "You must forget now. That is how you will survive. Forget." And so I'd take a deep breath, hold it, bear down, and force memories deep, deep into myself and out of sight. When I opened my eyes I had forgotten and was happy again. At least, I could play and have a sort of normal life until Mr. Hyde would come for me again.

T: Dan, see if you can be the old man now and with your little boy and Friday let a healing occur.

P: My left knee is Friday and my right knee is my little boy. I am the old man. I'm stroking them both. "The Peace of God. The Peace of God. The Peace of God." I'm saying it over and over. It feels good. Sad, so sad, but good.

T: Good. Take as long as you need with this.

P: My God, I can't believe all this is coming out of me. How have I lived with all of this in me? Unbelievable. Simply unbelievable. The one change

> *I can really feel is that I want to kill* him *now and not me. Up to now I've always wanted to kill myself.*
>
> T: *Now you're more valuable than your father.*
>
> P: *Yes, and that's good. That's really good. But I've just exchanged homicide for suicide. What I realize is that finally I must forgive him and let it go. The real healing is in forgiveness. So I see where my work is to be.*

Months of further processing followed this regression. Dan wrote about this:

> *My father lives in my body. I know he does, though he has moved from the hands and feet and eyes of me the fighter pilot, to the lower regions below my solar plexus and into my throat, which is my voice, and into my spine. He lives embedded in every muscle and the fiber of tissue in every nerve. How to release him? How to let him go?*

Sometimes Dan doubted that the whole thing had ever happened. Perhaps he had made it up. How could it have happened and been so totally forgotten? He vacillated between terrible anger at his father and reluctance to accept that a father whom he had loved so much had done such things to him. He lived in a world of such ambivalence that sometimes he could scarcely hold it together.

As an outer gesture toward freeing himself he visited his mother and sister. He kept hearing his father saying, "If you tell anyone, anyone at all, ever, I will come, and I will kill you." But he told his family, and they heard him with compassion, and this opened up a depth of relating with them that he had never had before. The birth of a niece at this time was like a new birth in himself, and this child became especially dear and meaningful. The power of the father's interdiction was broken, allowing healing to spread through him.

When he returned from his trip to visit his mother, he told of how, as the jetliner dodged through a towering line of late summer thunderstorms over Texas, he watched its wings flex in great arcs up and down and was amazed, even as a pilot, at those elastic and giving wings. He knew that if they were rigid they would snap, that for wings, to be flexible is to be strong and to be rigid is to break. He remembered that once he had wanted to be an oak, but now, he said, he was content to be a willow.

> *A tree who is easy moving with the wind, friend to the whippoorwill, a tree who cries for a sorrow that cannot in words be told, a tree who bends and bends and gives, and by yielding to the storm, survives to be the willow by the stream. Over it one night the butter moon rises and under it a boy throws a gossamer line for silver trout while his gentle father watches with a smile.*

His longing for the good and kind father he had once known remained, but he integrated this longing into himself and took over its functions for his own battered child self.

Processing and integration were made easier for Dan by the writing of his journal, where his intense feelings could burst into images of beauty. All the poet in him found scope, and in this period he prepared another volume of poetry for publication. One of his poems dealt with his traumatic abuse and his current healing through the exposure of the situation in spite of the ingrained command not to talk and through the process of forgiveness to which he had committed himself.

> *Forgiveness will reign as the clouds*
> *Will rain, and the tears of my sorrow will*
> *Water this patch of earth, and I shall play*
> *In the spray, in the deep muddy puddles play*
> *Laughing, crying from the sheer release.*
>
> *And the flash and crack kabooms of thunder*
> *Are the cries...are the cries of a child*
> *Who never made a sound, but shuddered,*
> *Shuddered, and now booms out: It Happened!*
> *Hear me, my world, I am an honest child,*
> *I do not lie. I do not lie. It happened.*

Our thrust during this period was to reach the state of forgiveness that he perceived he must find. We worked at this in many ways. After the retrieval of his experience with his father, he could not deal with actually seeing him, and I saw no reason for him to try. One idea Dan had was to write a hundred times every day, "I forgive you." We worked with meditation and sent light to his father. Using the psychosynthesis technique of forgiveness, Dan released his expectations of his father and became able to accept him as he was. He committed himself deeply to this inner work, and slowly the healing from it permeated him.

As he became whole again, he grew increasingly disenchanted with his outwardly unfruitful life. His identification with his actor father dissolved, and poetry did not seem enough to sustain him. Earning a living by carpentry was not what he wanted. He began to feel ready to fly again, and one day he went back to his home where lay opportunity to resume his life as a pilot.

Some months later a letter came from Dan.

Dear Afton,

I am flying again! Saturday I soloed in a Cessna 152. I passed my first flight review checkride so I'm a legal pilot again. But I soloed! And I was as okay and clear-headed as I've been in my life. I felt at home, as if I'd come home after a long, long absence.

I think this summer I'll attend a professional flight school in Florida. It will take five or six months to complete, but after that I'll be employable. Imagine that! Earning my own money at something I love....

I wish you peace, Afton, and can only say I will go on to help others in my way as you have helped me in yours. Our work together was extraordinary. I'm flying again! I'm writing! I knew that I had to come here to this—to fly.

I will keep you posted as events unfold.

Peace,

Dan

Childhood Sexual Trauma

by

Irene Hickman, D.O.

Introduction

Not all repressed feelings and thoughts originate in other lifetimes. The process of recall and healing is the same, however, whether the emotional stress occurred, as in this instance, in the current childhood or in another life. It is important to remember that regression to childhood can act both as a springboard to memories of similar traumas that occurred in other lifetimes or as a stage for healing in itself.

Case: Healing the Memory of a Repressed Childhood Incident

Ellen, a woman of 52, had had episodes of heavy gasping for breath over 45 years. This frantic gasping would recur several times a year and would persist day and night until she became totally exhausted. In order to control these episodes she would be heavily sedated, sometimes for several days and often in a hospital setting. Some episodes even required general anesthesia. Such sedation or anesthesia helped to stop individual episodes but did not affect the frequency or the severity of her attacks. Her frustrated physician sent her to me saying, "If you can do anything for this woman, I will be most grateful."

The history of the problem indicated that it had begun when she was seven years old. In that first interview her memory was that she had refused to go to school and had been constantly spanked until she thought of school as the lesser evil. Formerly she had taken a short cut through a gully but on her reluctant return to school she opted to take the long way around, though she could not say why. Neither could she recall any event related to school or the gully that would account for the long-continued physical problem.

She responded well to hypnosis, and after an initial hour of interview and training she returned for a single hypnotic experience. I moved her back to age seven, asking her to re-live any incident that might be connected with her symptom.

She described a morning when she and her best friend, Nancy, took the shortcut through the gully on their way to school. Suddenly from behind a large bush a 15-year-old feeble-minded fourth-grader named John leaped out and grabbed both girls. He nearly succeeded in raping Ellen but she escaped from him and ran until she droped in exhaustion, gasping for breath. She had blocked out conscious memory of this rape attempt but the emotion had remained and had been back of her unwillingness to go to school. It had also precipitated her gasping attacks over the many years.

During the first re-living of the near rape, which she described in the present tense, Ellen screamed, cried, and struggled. Afterward I asked her to go through the experience again from the beginning, and this time the emotional outbursts were less extreme. She went through the re-living of the attack a total of eight times. Each time she was able to add details that she had left out during the previous tellings. Each repetition expended more of the emotion until in the eighth re-experiencing she described the incident in a calm matter-of-fact manner.

After each re-living of the incident I asked her if the fear was gone, and only after the eighth telling did she respond with a "yes." I awakened her, telling her that she would remember all that she had related. She smiled broadly and said, "I really feel different. I feel so much better. This pressure is gone. And to think that I carried that for 45 years and at such a cost!" The severe gasping episodes left her and did not return.

Sexual Abuse Rooted in Another Lifetime

by

Roger Woolger, Ph.D.

Introduction

Past-life regression has been used effectively in working with victims of current-life child sexual abuse because it displaces the trauma into a totally different psychological frame in the imagined or remembered past. Where many patients may have difficulty recalling and releasing fears about an incident with a living parent or known abuser, past-life regression seems to free up the unconscious to release both physical details and emotional aspects of the abuse that have become blocked. Most of the time therapists find it unnecessary to raise the question of reincarnation but simply suggest something like, "Just let a story emerge from the unconscious that might be the origin of your feelings, as though it happened in another time and place." The effect of re-living the "past-life" abuse is that the patient—often in the same session—slips into the current-life abuse scenario to find himself spontaneously saying the very same words or manifesting similar emotional and bodily reactions, such as disgust, terror, and physical writhing.

For the most part memories remain dormant but because of the magnetic power of a complex, they will become either imaginarily or physically replayed when the patient attracts related situations. It often seems as if the current-life abuse is part of a deep repetition compulsion, to use Freud's term, or a condition that has fatalistic or even karmic resonances to it. Even though the therapist may meticulously avoid suggesting any identification between past-life personalities and current people, certain patients frequently report recognizing their abusers from previous lives, although they may see these people in other roles as children, or as members of the opposite sex, and they may see themselves as abuser rather than victim of abuse. It can be quite sobering to discover in these seeming past lives that both abuser and abused have been through it all before and often with the roles reversed! At such times the idea of karma, that past-life actions precondition the circumstances of the present and patterns, seems inescapable.

Freud was confused as to whether adult hysteria arose from actual childhood abuse or from infantile sexual fantasies of incest. From the perspective of our current knowledge of past-life regression, it seems possible that he was misled by his adult patients' garbled recall of a mixture of both current-life abuse and past-life residues of abuse that had become fused in their unconscious memory. Or there may have been no childhood abuse at all but a relatively innocuous stimulus, such as the sound of a scream, that might have triggered a past-life memory in the child's deep unconscious.

Case: A Toned-Down Repetition of Former Abuse

Melinda had consulted several therapists about her failure to form close relationships with men and her near frigidity when it came to sexual contact. For a period she had been in a lesbian relationship, which helped her somewhat because her lover wanted companionship more than physical contact. Yet the root issue remained untouched.

She reported a clear memory of sexual molestation at 11 years. A 12-year-old boy from the neighborhood had enticed her into a unused garage and had fondled her genitally, though he had not attempted penetration. Her retelling of the story was cold and detached and she held herself clenched as she related it. Apparently she had talked about this event many times with her previous therapists and, though in addition to verbally processing it she had beaten out her rage on pillows and mattresses, part of her was still holding unfinished anger.

When I invited her to lie down and re-live the event, her clenched physical stance became even more exaggerated.

P: *I don't want to do this (markedly more anger in her voice)!*

With her eyes closed, a monologue emerged with little prompting from me other than to direct her to repeat certain phrases and to exaggerate her bodily posture.

P: *I don't want to do this. I don't want to do this. Don't make me. Don't make me! No! No! No! You're hurting me. Get away!*

She started to kick, shake her head and writhe, saying over and over again, "Get away! Get away! No. Don't make me!" She continued this way for a while and her body became more and more tense, her outrage more pronounced. I imagined that she must be re-experiencing the incident from her childhood, but suddenly her words indicated another lifetime.

P: They're raping me. Help! Help! There are six or seven of them, soldiers. I'm in a barn with my arms tied. I'm a peasant girl of 11 or 12...in Russia. Stop! Leave me alone!... I'm not going to feel this. I won't feel this.

Her pelvic area became stiff, her legs were taut, and her head turned from side to side.

T: Let these parts of the body express what is going on with them.
P: I'm not going to feel this. I'll never show you that I like it. That's my genitals. My legs say, "Don't touch me! Get away! I'll kill you! I hate you! I'll kick you!" But my head says that it's not going to see this—it's not happening.
T: Let your legs kick. Let your genitals record exactly what they feel. Allow your head to see and understand all of it.

There were kicking and weeping and rage and terrible convulsions as her genitals registered both pleasure and pain. Gradually as these sensations and movements surged through her body, she seemed to experience a releasing and letting go of the earlier clenchings, and this culminated in a bout of intense sobbing and convulsive movement in her pelvis.

Suddenly she was no longer with the soldiers.

P: I'm in that garage. I don't want him to touch me. I don't want to do this. Don't make me! I just freeze up but he doesn't hurt me. He's quite gentle, but my thighs just go rigid and I'm not really there.
T: Breathe deeply and see the similarity to the other rape scene.
P: Oh, yes! My body was remembering something else. It was like a flashback, but I didn't want to see it.

As Melinda surveyed the two stories and gave herself permission to really see them now, she had all kinds of spontaneous recognitions: how just being touched always led to a kind of freezing, how she was always somehow not present in sex, how she had always had fantasies of wanting to kick men.

In a later session she reclaimed more of the Russian girl's story: how she had become pregnant, raised the child, a boy, alone, and had bitterly avoided contact with men from then onward, dying quite young from a wasting disease. The crucial events, however, were clearly locked into the rape scene at 11 or 12. Her unconscious compulsion laid down in the previous life had led her—unconsciously, of course—to repeat a similar but far less violent sexual trauma in this life. The contemporary trauma served to reawaken the latent past-life level of the complex, fraught as it was with terror, humiliation, and rage.

Karmic Roots of Childhood Abuse Underlying Schizophrenia

by

Ernest Pecci, M.D.

Introduction

Regression work can safely release old knots in borderlines and schizophrenics if enough preparatory work is done and if the bonding with the therapist is strong enough. In the end it may be necessary for the patient to go back to the karmic cause in order to release the pattern of being a victim. The current rational self must be brought in to reframe and restructure the energy that started in another lifetime and is responsible for current distress.

The following patient worked with me for four years before she felt strong enough to go back to the source of her distress, which in her case was physical abuse. Any assault on the body of a child, whether physical or sexual, threatens and often effects disintegration of the child's coping self, which may result in severing physical and/or emotional symptoms or in schizophrenia, as in this case, or multiple personalities. A long healing within the framework of an unconditionally accepting relationship is needed to restore the strength of the coping self so that recovery and reframing of the originating experience can be brought about.

This case suggests that patients may at times tune into energy patterns that fit them rather than into "factual" past lives. The patient saw herself briefly as Ann Boleyn, a person with whom many others have identified during regressions, but her inability to pick up any details suggests that this story was actually a prototype of something that happened to her. Since this experience turned out to be therapeutic, the question of authenticity was not important.

Case: Emerging from Schizophrenia

Mary had been a borderline schizophrenic for years. She had known a lifetime of physical abuse, first at the hands of her father and brother and later by her husband. When she came to me four years prior to this session, I worked to help her build up ego strength through both group experiences and individual sessions. Finally we came to a place where it appeared that she could handle a regression to see if we could dissolve the schizophrenia.

T: When you look back now, what do you think your problem was?
P: When I first came to see you I had lost a lot of weight. I didn't know whether I was coming or going. I thought my husband had complete power over me. I felt he had some kind of special knowledge and was using this as power. I felt paralyzed. That was the main problem.
T: This is the feeling you've had most of your life. You have always had difficulty functioning, but it was worse at that particular period. All your life you've had problems with thinking and withdrawing into yourself.
P: I was so fat at one year of age. Everything seems to go back to that time. Something happened then so that after that I couldn't keep any weight on.
T: We need to get in touch with the shock you felt then.
P: Now I feel I'm ready.
T: Is there a situation with your husband?
P: I see that it wasn't my husband really. It was my father.
T: Can you see how you have drawn people, including your brothers and sister, to misuse you? I think you are ready to see if there is a link to an earlier experience. Would you like to look at that?
P: Yes, I'm ready.

Childhood

I had Mary lie down and I relaxed her, testing the depth of trance by her image of the number in the circle and by continuing the relaxation until it came to a five.

T: Now you're ready to go back to the scene in early childhood when you are very little and you're with your father. I'll count from 10 to one, and you'll see yourself as very little and with your father when he was very frantic and abused you. You'll be able to tell me about it. You're a very little girl. Let yourself go slowly back into the past. What's happening?
P: I'm standing there and I'm crying.
T: Why?
P: I'm so lonely.
T: How old are you?
P: Eighteen months. I can't stop crying. (Sobs deeply.) He tells me to shut up, and I can't stop crying. He says he's going to get me. He's coming! I

> *know he's going to get me! Oh! (Screams and gasps. Then breathes
> heavily.) Momma! I feel like something's happened to me. He beat me so
> much! I'm so numb. (Deep and agonized sobbing.) I'm not going to feel
> anymore.*

We spent some time going over the feelings of this experience of
physical abuse.

> T: *I'd like you to go into that scene now and hold that little girl so she won't
> be so afraid. Let's help the little girl get over the shock. Tell her she doesn't
> have to stay in shock. You've got to convince her not to close off. She
> doesn't have to.*
>
> P: *(Continues to sob and gasp.)*
>
> T: *I'll count down from 10 to one. A scene will open up. You'll go into a past
> life that has some relationship to that incident when you heard your father
> say, "I'm going to get you!" These feelings are going to take you to a scene
> in the past. Go down your life span and find a lifetime that has some
> connection. When you get a scene, you'll be able to tell me about it. Let
> your emotions take you there. Let your feelings of being attacked by your
> father take you there, where your feeling of fear closed you off.*
>
> P: *(Deep sigh.)*
>
> T: *What are you feeling?*
>
> P: *I'm blank.*
>
> T: *Look at the blank. Look behind the blank. Let's dare to get a scene. Let's
> dare to look behind the blank. Something happened there. Something you
> blanked out.*

First Past Life

> P: *It's seeming like...I'm in a castle somewhere.*
>
> T: *It will become clearer and clearer.*

Mary wavered among several lifetimes, beginning with being a boy, then
she became an old hag, and finally Ann Boleyn. She was unable to name the
date or tell what castle she was in. This confusion among lifetimes is not
infrequent. Help is needed to focus on one and develop it.

> P: *There's a wall—very grey. I'm in a dungeon. I'm chained. I'm an old hag.
> I've grey hair. Yes, I look like a witch. There are other people here and
> they're laughing at me. (Much sighing.) It's dark in the dungeon. Oh, she's
> changing! (Deeply distressed breathing.) She's changing into a man. My
> God! They're going to chop my head off. And I haven't done anything
> wrong.*
>
> T: *What is your name?*

P: *(Shifting lifetimes again.) Ann...Ann Boleyn. I'm in the dungeon. I'm so afraid. They're going to come and get me! They're going to take me to the tower.*

Second Past Life

T: *I'll count from four to one and you will go to an earlier lifetime, something related to all of this. Go to the earlier lifetime. Why is all this happening to you? When you get it, tell me about it...the earlier lifetime.*

P: *I'm somewhere in the desert. Somewhere in the Holy Land.*

T: *It will become clearer and clearer.*

P: *I'm a boy. I'm barefooted. I'm dressed in a skin. It's drawn around my waist with a piece of rawhide. I'm about 15.*

T: *Follow the scene.*

Mary described how she was envious of her older brother because he always did things right so that the father approved of him. Overcome with anger over this, she trailed him through the fields one day and killed him with a slingshot.

P: *Oh, my God, I've killed my brother! I've killed my brother! What have I done? I killed him with my slingshot.*

T: *What are you feeling now?*

P: *I don't want to face it. I just want to run (increasing distress). I want to run away from it. I'm running and running and I'm blanking out. I don't want to think about it. I killed him! I was feeling jealous because he was always getting my father's attention.*

T: *Did you plot to kill him?*

P: *Yes. I was angry and I wanted to kill him. I followed him across the fields. (Changing into the present tense.) I'm going to get him! I'll kill him with my slingshot. I want my father to love me.*

T: *You want to kill him so your father will love you best. You decide to get him.*

P: *(Anguished words.) He was getting all the attention!*

T: *What should happen to you now?*

P: *I'm going to have to pay.... It's getting dark.*

T: *You're going to have to pay for this crime. Have the adult Mary appear on the scene with that boy. You appear like a fairy godmother. Tell him, "I saw what you've done and I've come to help you."*

P: *There's so much energy...all through my body. It's all through my hands.*

T: *Let's do a healing on this boy. We must put in the thought that he doesn't have to suffer forever. What does he understand? Is he repentant? Is he sorry?*

P: *Yes, he's repentant.*

T: *It's important for him to know he doesn't have to suffer lifetime after lifetime. It was enough to suffer as Ann Boleyn. You don't have to get*

*anybody to punish you anymore. When you awaken, I want you to know
that. Your body has paid its debt and is now free. You have suffered a
great deal. I want you to have a feeling of self-acceptance. You have paid
your debt and your body is now free. I want you to have a strong feeling
of self-acceptance. Do you feel it?*

P: *(Moments of silence.) Yes. (Deep clearing sigh.)*

T: *Find a piece of green grass where you can dance and be free. You are
deserving of love. You deserve to be real, to love and be loved. You don't
need to be hurt anymore. From now on you will have a fresh start. I'll
count to ten. You will remember everything. You will be filled with a
wonderful feeling of being free from all the guilt you have put upon
yourself.*

P: *(After a few moments of silence.) It's a different kind of peace. I feel good.
I feel like I really understand. I feel peace and harmony.*

T: *Write up this experience in detail to help you keep yourself free.*

The patient's use of the same phrase toward her brother in the earlier
lifetime that her father had used toward her in this lifetime—"I'm going to
get him!"—is interesting. Certainly in this regression Mary touched
something that enabled her to begin dissolving the knot that had caused the
schizophrenia, for from this time on she became increasingly stable and
competent.

She was married to a wealthy man and had never worked or even
applied for a job, but after the regression she found herself wanting to be
more productive. She and her husband moved to Indonesia, and here she
applied to work in the public relations department of the Hilton and was
accepted. During her work experience she became very outgoing. I talked
with her later and found that she had changed strikingly. Talking to her was
no longer like talking through a fog. The repressed anger that had
characterized her schizophrenic state was gone, and an eager woman had
emerged who wanted her whole life to change and grow.

A *Karmic Source of Childhood Trauma*

by

Hazel M. Denning, Ph.D.

Introduction

In many instances recovering and re-living incidents of abuse that occurred in this lifetime do not bring the release and healing that are needed, even if the individual believes that dealing with such incidents therapeutically *should* result in healing. Though belief plays a significant role in healing, many cases suggest that the subconscious (or soul) senses other pertinent events, perhaps from another lifetime, and until these are recalled and dealt with, the individual may continue to feel a need for punishment.

In the following case Laura believed that recovery of the memory of childhood abuse would heal her hands, but only when she went far back into the karmic origin of her symptoms did healing occur. This questions the common explanation that past-life therapy works because the individual believes his story and has adapted material from an old movie or a novel he has read or something he has heard. Success is not a matter of faith in an explanation one has conjured up. It eludes patient and therapist until the truly pertinent material has been unearthed.

Case: Pointing a Finger through the Centuries

Laura was talked into coming for regression work by her enthusiastic daughter, not a compelling motivation for therapy of any sort! She was willing to explore her current life, particularly her childhood, and was also willing to investigate her fear of heights, although she was without any firm conviction that regression would successfully deal with this. However, after six months of metaphysical discussions and growing involvement with her life story, this fear of heights diminished.

Following this experience Laura was more willing to trust the regression process and she revealed that she had suffered pain in her hands most of her life. Her hands hurt so intensely at times that she had to get up in the night and put them in hot and cold water. Because no doctor could find anything wrong, she had assumed that nothing could be done to reduce the pain and had not bothered to mention it. Now she thought she might look at this problem and was willing to allow herself to go into an altered state to explore it.

We first went back to her childhood, and she recalled an incident that had occurred when she was three years old. Her mother had left her with a babysitter. The woman tipped over an oil lamp, breaking it and spilling the coal oil on the child's hands. Not only were Laura's hands painfully burned, but in addition to the physical pain, she had the added pain of being defenseless when the babysitter told her mother that Laura had broken the lamp.

Though Laura and I both felt that the source of her pain had been discovered and she could let it go, her hands still hurt when she returned a week later. There was evidently something we had not understood, so in spite of her skepticism about past lives, Laura agreed to see what might be found there.

Once in an altered state, she began to moan and press her hands together, moving them in a circular motion as though they were bound at the wrists and she were trying to free them.

T: *What is happening to you?*
P: *They say I am a witch. I told them we should leave this place, but they won't believe me.*
T: *Who are you? Why did you tell them that they should leave?*
P: *I am a seeress. I know things that are going to happen. I was supposed to warn the people of an earthquake that is coming. We must take our tents and move to another place. But they won't listen. It was that woman who convinced them not to listen. She told them I was a witch and not to believe me.*
T: *What woman are you talking about?*
P: *The wife of our leader. She put him up to burning me. I could have made him listen, but she didn't want to move, so she said I was a witch and a liar.*

At this point Laura went out of that body and was free from the pain of being burned.

Again we were certain we had uncovered the cause of the current discomfort in her hands, but again at her next session her hands still hurt. I suspected that she must feel guilty about something, and when she next went into an altered state, I asked about this. She explained that God had told her to warn the people, but she had failed. This did not ring true, and I told Laura that if she had done her best, God would not punish her for failing. She held to her story for three months and then one day exclaimed in surprise:

> P: *I see it all now. I am guilty! When I was burning, I pointed my finger at that woman and vowed I would get even with her, no matter how many centuries it took. I knew I would come back again, and I was determined to come back with her so I could get even.*
>
> T: *Is that the reason you are holding the pain in your hands—because of your curse?*
>
> P: *Yes. I hated her and I wanted to get even. But I knew it was wrong so I had to punish myself.*

Within a few days the pain had left her hands. A follow-up 15 years later found this symptom still in remission. Laura's experience suggests that it is not only the belief of the individual that produces healing. Though belief plays a significant role, many cases, such as that of Laura, suggest that the subconscious (or soul) knows the facts, and until they are recalled and dealt with, the individual may continue to feel a need for punishment.

Sexual Abuse in a Dysfunctional Family

by

Winafred B. Lucas, Ph.D.

Introduction

Childhood abuse is frequent in dysfunctional families, especially where alcohol or drugs are used. Even without these the chaotic and insecure lifestyles of these families leave the door open for inappropriate behavior that would obviously be taboo in families who live by more conventional standards and have a more developed ethical sense. In the dysfunctional family sexual abuse from a family member often is initiated by an early affection for the child. Because the abuser's ego boundaries are weak, this affection develops later into an inappropriate and even destructive response. In spite of the abuser's original loving attention, the harm is done and the child grows up with a personality twisted by buried anger and guilt.

The abuse situation is complicated by the fact that, except in the most punitive instances, the child derives some pleasure from the experience, especially in the beginning, and this adds to the guilt. The child may feel special and perceive him/herself as especially loved. There may be some physical pleasuring, too, ranging from none, where the abuse is experienced as traumatic intrusion, to normal reactions at being pleasured. This physical reaction increases in puberty, often leaving the abused child conflicted about terminating the experience. Later he may perceive himself, if he can bring the experience to memory, as totally a victim, but this has not actually been the case.

Hesitance about revealing the experience is reinforced by the family system, which does not want to learn that the abuse exists and more often than not will deny the situation or simply pay no attention. One patient of mine remembered that as a six year old she told her mother that her grandfather was playing with her sexually and her mother's response was, "Well, you *know* that dear old man wouldn't do any such thing!" The family does not want to hear because if it does, its neurotic structure will be exposed, and unwelcome changes will have to take place.

The sort of abuse experienced by the patient in the following case is typical of dysfunctional families. Healing came with her realization of the inevitable progression of events, one leading to another, and with no one who had the power to intervene. Interestingly, this father *did* have the ego strength to perceive the parameters of the situation and stop on his own when the girl reached her menarche and could become pregnant. Even this modicum of ego strength is not always available.

Case: Father's Cute Little Girl Grows Up

During her childhood April's family functioned like a collection of unmatched wheels and bolts that were incapable of moving together. Her mother, deeply entrenched in a victim role, was not able to help April, even when she learned that the alcoholic father was abusing her sexually. The older brother was on drugs and the younger sister was bulemic, a situation that the family did not consider a problem.

As an adult, April had felt that her father was the most wonderful man in the world until half-memories of his abuse of her began to come back. Then she erupted into a volcano of rage that ripped apart her relationship with him. In an attempt to heal herself, she confronted her father, but he was indignant. It is possible that he, too, had repressed the memory. In this difficult time AA-related groups buoyed April up and helped her keep functioning.

April was a wiry redhead with a snub nose and a determined gait. When she came to me she had recovered only enough shreds of memory to feel tortured, and she alternated between rage and feeling that she had invented a fantasy, especially since her father had refused to validate her dim recollections. In between the times of rage and despair she struggled to be free of hate, to know that her father was sick, to try to forgive, but she never quite managed it. She had recently met him at a family wedding and had been too disturbed to talk with him or accept his current wife's invitation to visit. She felt violated and ashamed, like a rag doll that has been dragged through the mud.

In spite of her distress she was coping, drawing on some unguessed strength within herself and leaning on the help of her ACA and CODA groups and work with John Bradshaw in any form she could find it— workshops, tapes, books, TV appearances. She maintained her home well, struggled to help her husband, who had a carpet cleaning business, and dealt with his dysfunctional family. She chauffered her two little girls to a good playschool and spent time reading and playing with them. Reaching deep within herself she found not only strength but lovingness and courage. Best of all, she was moving beyond her need to please others, and into the more pertinent need to understand and be herself. In AA terms, she was growing beyond co-dependency. Currently she was enduring spells of weeping during lovemaking but knew that in time she would move beyond this, also.

Because April had made striking progress in her journey to find herself and because she was able to use the support of her CODA groups, we needed only a few sessions to fully expose the memory of the extended sexual abuse, and then to process and reframe it. I began with an exploration of prenatal memories because these were the most distant from the sexual abuse and would gently lead her into the more traumatic experiences. With a few moments of relaxation, deep breathing, and the use of light, she moved trustingly into an altered state and almost immediately tuned in to the feelings that her mother had had when pregnant.

Prenatal

> T: *Let us go back to the time when your mother discovers she is pregnant with you. How is she feeling?*
> P: *She's worried, because she doesn't have a good marriage and my father is out with other women. She's anxious, nervous.*
> T: *How are you feeling?*
> P: *I'm scared. I see darkness. It's cloudy. I'm scared.*
> T: *What else do you feel?*
> P: *I feel very little. I don't really feel wanted.*
> T: *Let's go back to the time when you were within your mother. Listen to your parents talking. What are they saying?*
> P: *My father isn't very happy. I hear him yelling, "How could you get pregnant!"*
> T: *How is your mother feeling?*
> P: *She's sad...frantic. He's saying she shouldn't have got pregnant. She already has a baby. She's frantic because she's afraid.*

In the prenatal state she absorbed her mother's feeling that she wasn't wanted and that her father was angry about her existence, which set the stage for her later desperate attempt to get her father to like her.

Birth

> T: *Let's go ahead to your birth. Who starts it?*
> P: *I do.*
> T: *What are you feeling?*
> P: *It feels pretty terrible—like I'm really closed in and I feel scared again.*
> T: *How does your mother feel?*
> P: *She's relieved I'm out.*

There was no joy in this birth, only relief on her mother's part that she was out. The "closed in" feeling probably became initially stamped in here.

Infancy

    T: Does she nurse you?

    P: No. I feel really alone. (Deep feeling.) I feel alone. It's frightening to be alive. It's scary. There's no one here. I have to be all by myself. I can't get anybody's attention. I just want somebody to touch and pick me up. Nobody does. I feel ugly.

    T: Can you tell me more about that?

    P: Because I wasn't really wanted. Later when I looked at pictures of when I was little, I felt really ugly. I felt I was undesirable.

In infancy the pattern of feeling not wanted was reinforced and with it came her conviction that she wasn't wanted because she was ugly.

First Years

    T: What is happening in your first year of life?

    P: I like to go places, and other people like me. I am in their arms a lot.

    T: What is going on between the time you are one and two?

    P: I think my father likes me when I am two...he has started to like me. He makes me feel cute so I have to be cute. I can't feel what I feel because I have to do things to please him...people...be cute.

    T: How are you feeling when you have to do this?

    P: I feel closed, shut off, like I always have to play a role.

Here we have the beginning of her close relationship with her father and insight into how she had given up her identity in order to become what would keep her close to him. This willingness to surrender her selfhood was motivated by a need to escape the painful loneliness she had experienced as an infant. She repeated the theme of being closed in.

Two to Three

    T: What is happening between two and three?

    P: There are a lot of dresses I have to put on. But I'm not cute so I have to do cute things. I just don't feel anything. I feel I'm by myself.

    T: What about your older brother?

    P: I feel that he hates me. Probably because I'm the new kid. He has a lot of hate.

    T: How does he show this?

    P: He hits me hard...all the time. On my arms. Pushing (gestures).

T: *Where's father?*
P: *He's on the phone.*
T: *How do you feel about that?*
P: *It's not doing anything to me. I kind of feel left out, but it's okay.*
T: *Where's mother?*
P: *I don't know where she is...she's walking all over. She goes to meetings and things.*
T: *How are you feeling?*
P: *I'm all alone and I feel I have to keep trying to be really cute to get their attention.*

The effort to be cute and attract was not yet successful, and loneliness still threaded her life, though not so pervasively as before.

Three to Five

T: *Go to the time between when you are three and when you are four.*
P: *I go places with my father a lot now because he likes me. We leave the house. He keeps telling me we're going to the hardware store. I sit really close to him. I don't think I like him but it feels really good that someone likes me a little.*
T: *Let's go to the time between four and five.*
P: *I still go places with my dad and I still have to act a certain way to get people's attention. He buys me things. I still feel ugly. All the things I have to do are to make people happy.*

In these years her ploy to be cute began to pay off. Her father paid her increasing attention. The loneliness diminished, but it was at the price of her own identity.

Five to Seven

T: *Let's go to the next year—from five to six.*
P: *I don't feel six. I don't see six. It's dark. I'm scared. (Crying.) It's like somebody's on top of me. On top of me really hard. My whole body feels terrible!*
T: *Who is it?*
P: *I don't know who it is. Now he's gone. I just see my father's face. But it isn't like it was him—it's really big.*
T: *How are you feeling about your father?*
P: *I don't think I like him now. I don't understand why he did that.*
T: *Can you say what is happening between six and seven?*
P: *I don't see that either. I feel that heavy feeling again. He's feeling my whole body...breasts, arms...really hard.*
T: *Does he touch your genital area?*

P: *It feels good but it doesn't feel like he should be doing it. I feel really confused. Why does he do that to me?*
T: *What do you say to him?*
P: *I don't say anything.*
T: *Does your father say anything?*
P: *He says, "It's okay. I love you. Don't tell your mother. She won't understand."*

In these years Father initiated his sexual seduction of her. She was on the edge of being frightened by it, but he moved so gradually that the fright never got entirely unbearable.

Seven to Eight

T: *What happens between seven and eight?*
P: *I feel the same thing. He's still on top.*
T: *Where does he touch you?*
P: *He touches my vagina. He puts his penis all over me.*
T: *How does that feel?*
P: *It feels disgusting. I like it because it's soft and all over. But it feels disgusting.*

Father expanded his repertoire rapidly during this year. April experienced his contact as at least partially loving and felt some pleasurable sensations, which left her conflicted.

Eight to Thirteen

T: *Now we're in the period between eight and nine.*
P: *It feels lighter...my body. I feel better. People like me a little.*
T: *And your father?*
P: *He likes me. He likes me to go everyplace with him. Only now sometimes he seems a little mean, a little stern. Maybe my mother thinks something. He's mad at me because I told her.*
T: *Did you tell her?*
P: *I try to tell her but she doesn't really hear me.*
T: *Do you continue with Father sexually?*
P: *I don't feel anything. He had sex with me.*
T: *Does he penetrate you?*
P: *It feels terrible. I want him to stop but it's just getting worse. It's killing me. I want to get away but I can't.*
T: *Do you try to push him off?*
P: *I'm scared to.*
T: *Does he ejaculate?*
P: *Yes.*

> T: *How does that feel?*
> P: *Feels part good and part bad.*
> T: *Does he say anything?*
> P: *He says, "I love you. Don't tell anybody. Your mother will get sick. I might leave."*
> T: *How are you feeling?*
> P: *I'm not feeling anymore. I feel sad. I don't understand anything. I feel really little. I think I'm little because I had to be cute all the time. My little dresses.*
> T: *How do you feel about yourself?*
> P: *I blame me. I shouldn't have done that.*
> T: *Does he do it again?*
> P: *Yes. Whenever he can.*
> T: *How long?*
> P: *Until I'm 13.*
> T: *Why does he stop then?*
> P: *I get my period. He does things but he doesn't do that.*

In the pre-pubertal years Father continued to increase his sexual pressure until he penetrated her. During this period she was especially conflicted because Father was giving her constant attention, which she liked, and there were also pleasurable feelings, but these were marred by the pain of the physical experience and by her uneasiness over the situation. To resolve the conflict she tried to tell her mother, but her mother refused to hear.

Her father manifested unexpected control as he expanded his sexual advances slowly over the years. Terminating the relationship with April at the time of her menarche, undoubtedly to avoid making her pregnant, also showed control and foresight. What was lacking was any sense of April's need or any compassion for her or an awareness of what was appropriate in a family. He exploited her loneliness for his self-interest. We can only speculate as to why he was so totally untouched by any awareness of the ages-long incest taboo in our culture.

> T: *When do you start to hate him?*
> P: *I feel like I've always hated him a little. I hated me.*
> T: *How are you feeling right now?*
> P: *I feel real peaceful. It really wasn't very much. (Said with relief.)*

The sudden resolution of this situation would have been surprising except for the effective work April had done on herself in her struggle to become a person. She had moved into a place where she wished to be able to forgive, and the gentle scanning of her life helped her to understand her motivations as a child, her ambivalence during those years, and the self-involvement of her father. She could then reframe the experience. She left the session feeling radiant and with a new love and protectiveness for herself and forgiveness for her father.

April felt that the healing would have been deepened if her father could have said he was sorry, but she realized that nothing would be accomplished by confronting him again. She opted not to have further personal contact with him or his wife except in family gatherings, and she was concerned about how to talk to him on even these limited occasions. I suggested that if she were inadvertently alone with him, she might ask him to tell her about his childhood and simply be a listener.

Some time later the family had a ski holiday and she and her father were left together while the children were sledding and the other adults were on the slopes. At this time she asked her father about his childhood, and for an hour he sat telling her of the abuse he had gone through, tears dripping down his face. She felt good about being able to be an acceptant listener and came to understand better why he had nothing to give her. Finally she could accept this and turn to the shining part of herself for nurturance. And her own children, so treasured and guarded, will not have to pass on the pattern of abuse. The buck stops here.

Chapter IV

Varieties of Interlife Experience

Life between life is not a fairy-tale world, nor is it an atmosphere of free-floating cottonwool emptiness. Those who have tasted its richness know that they have visited the ultimate reality, the plane of consciousness from which they embark on successive trials of incarnation and to which they return at the death of the body. The state of metaconsciousness that characterizes the interlife is one where the individual merges with the quintessence of existence; but, paradoxically, in surrendering his own identity he becomes at the same time more intensely self-aware.

Joel Witton

What happens when a soul is so filled with anger, hatred, and fear that it rushes through the interim state without being able to perceive the Light or observe the justice of the events that it has just passed through? Is it possible to rush through the Light and not see it, to be exposed to wiser beings or one's own former family and friends and not be able to consider what they are saying, or perhaps not even see them, as one struggles to incarnate in order to get revenge? Everything in the interlife is for the education of such a soul, but can the soul shrug off the classroom and its wisdom? And caught in the inevitable web of frustration and suffering that it has woven for itself, is it possible later for such a soul to return in an altered state to that interim life and learn slowly what it could have learned before and must learn sometime?

Winafred Lucas

Bibliography

Dethlefsen, Thorwald. *Voices from Other Lives*. New York: M. Evans and Co., 1978.
Evans-Wentz, W. *The Tibetan Book of the Dead*. New York: Oxford University Press, 1960.
Hickman, Irene. *Mind Probe—Hypnosis*. Kirksville, MO: Hickman Systems, 1983.
Loehr, Franklin. *Diary after Death*. Grand Island, FL: Religious Research Press, 198
Moody, Raymond. *Life after Life*. Covington, GE: Mockingbird Books, 1975.
Ring, Kenneth. *Life at Death*. New York: Coward McCann, and Geoghegan, 1980.
———. *Heading Toward Omega*. New York, William Morrow and Co., 1984.
Sabom, M. *Recollections of Death*. New York: Harper Row, 1982.
Weiss, Brian. *Many Lives, Many Masters*. New York: Simon and Schuster, 1988.
Whitton, Joel and Joe Fisher. *Life Between Life*. New York: Doubleday and Co., 1980.
Woolger, Roger. *Other Lives, Other Selves*. New York: Doubleday, 1987.

Varieties of Interlife Experience

Introduction

Events occurring immediately after death have been described in recent research into near-death experiences by Moody, Ring, Sabom, and others. These accounts can be summarized by saying that apparently never has a person been more alive. Near-death episodes describe the sequence of leaving one's body and floating over it and then proceeding, usually through a tunnel, to a place of light. But what happens afterward?

This experience is more vague and less documented. Two ancient books, *The Tibetan Book of the Dead* and *The Egyptian Book of the Dead* have presented theories about the process, and there have been some accounts in current regression work dealing with interim states. Whitton summarizes hypotheses and documents cases in his *Life Between Life*; and *Many Lives, Many Masters* by Brian Weiss (1988) provides an in-depth description of one patient's experience. Sandweiss reports one contemporary experience that moved considerably further into the interlife than is usual in documented near-death accounts.

Whitton's account points up several things. First, the impact of the interim state finds its source and meaning in the lives surrounding it. The preceding state provides material for the analysis and overview of patterns, and the lifetime following offers an opportunity to live out further what will be helpful for an individual's growth. The interlife cannot stand alone.

Second, the experience is of a transcendental nature, called metaconsciousness by Whitton, and because it goes beyond the scope of ordinary language, what the individual perceives can only be hinted at and expressed in metaphors and symbols. Not all patients are able to allow this spontaneous emergence of symbols from the unconscious to occur, even though they have readily recovered past lives. Many of Whitton's patients were able to report such interim experiences, but other therapists have treated only occasional patients who describe such journeys.

However, though many patients are unable as yet to uncover this sort of recollection, they can tap into surprising wisdom when with the therapist's help they review a past life immediately following their death in that lifetime. Such a review provides a truncated glimpse of the interlife with compressed kernels of its wisdom. As we develop resonance around the idea of the interlife, more and more people will undoubtedly become able to recall it, just as past-life recall is becoming an available option for increasing numbers of people, though a few years ago such recollection was rare.

Recovery of interlife experiences may become the spiritual thrust of the future. Like near-death experiences, they facilitate a transformation of consciousness and encourage an attitude of compassion, but unlike NDEs, they are under conscious control. Each traveler through the interlife can obtain exactly what is appropriate for his stage of growth. The wisdom and perception of love that he recovers are more tentative than in the near-death experience and work is required to integrate and retain what has been perceived, but the regression experience has the advantage of being universally available and of being able to be explored and processed.

Are all interim experiences positive? *The Tibetan Book of the Dead* and *The Egyptian Book of the Dead* suggest that although immediately after death everyone is able to perceive the Clear Light, following that, souls may be drawn because of anger or desire or misused lifetimes to less luminous states. My own patient Brad experienced nothing in his first interlife contacts and only gradually became able to perceive sources of wisdom and growth. For him it was as though a fog gradually lifted. The patients of both Weiss and Whitton experienced positive and stimulating interim states, possibly an artifact of their involvement with inner growth. They were open to the purpose of the interim experience, which is to perceive the pattern of the soul's journey so that a positive plan of procedure may be formed for traveling further. But other people, including some who appear in our offices, seem unaware that their souls are on a journey.

It is evident that the periods between lifetimes are uneven in length, varying from a brief interval, perhaps only a few days, to centuries. The meaning and source of this variation is not clear. Some souls may prefer a learning period in the interlife, while others are drawn to speedy reincarnation by desires and anger or by resentment about having the last lifetime cut short by sudden death. Other souls may be reluctant to leave the interim state because of the struggle involved in embodiment.

The existence of the interlife, and its potential for learning and for joy by those who are prepared, changes the complexion of death, according to the accounts of those who have gone through the near-death experience. Even the initial stages of the interlife so transform perception that almost without exception those who have had this experience lose further fear of dying.

In regression work, the process of dying and the interim period are experienced as an unbroken journey where each experience melds into the next, but *The Tibetan Book of the Dead* has charted the transition step-by-step. For those who take this treatise seriously, it reconstitutes thoughts of death. It describes the interlife, called the "Bardo," as divided into three stages.

The first stage consists of the perception of the light of higher consciousness. The Tibetan treatise, after describing the same blissful inner experience that those who have gone through the near-death experience report, states that if the dying person can recognize that this light is really his own essence, he will be absorbed into it and not have to reincarnate further. But since few can hold onto the light as the true reality, in the second stage the soul entity becomes caught in the thought forms that it has created during the lifetime just left behind. There ensues a fierce struggle between attachment to these forms and pure insight into the spiritual nature of being, a struggle that the involved soul seldom wins. This leads to the third stage, in which the individual, who has been unable to detach from his own thought forms, is sucked into the process of rebirth. The Tibetans taught that in the Bardo there is no divine intervention. The thought forms of deities projected upon the screen of the man's consciousness have no real existence but take the appearance of whatever the man has believed on earth. In the same manner evils and sins are nightmares that can dissolve like mist in the light of true existence.

This Tibetan description of the interlife differs in a number of ways from the findings of current regression therapists. It does not contain a panel of judges or a life review. The concept of judgment, however, is to be found in many religions, as for example in the Egyptian concept of balancing the heart in the scales of Maat and in the Christian idea of the last judgment. The Tibetan bardo experience of belabored souls, who have muffed their opportunities for growth because of attachments, corresponds to the concept of Hades in ancient Greek religious thinking and to purgatory and even hell in Christianity and other religions, but contemporary therapists only occasionally draw such material. The "valley" experience mentioned by Hickman and by my patient Brad is perhaps our modern equivalent.

What is missing in the older accounts but characterizes contemporary regression work is the element of conscious learning. Patients of the therapists represented in this section use the panel of judges and the life review to observe mistakes and consciously change. Hickman's patient Ann described with striking candor and insight her hard journey in the interlife back to a state of knowledge and power that she had formerly possessed but had misused. Woolger's patients Madeline and Roger healed current lifetime difficulties by returning to the interlife and making adequate restitution there. For each of Whitton's patients the interim period was, above everything else, a time of broadening concepts and learning. And Weiss's subject experienced waves of wisdom that healed her, even though they were beyond her current conscious understanding.

The interim is not just a period between lives but a permanent superconscious state able to be contacted in various ways: in near-death experiences, through the "cosmic consciousness" William James[1] describes, in profound states of meditation, in some psychedelic experiences, and through the holotropic breathing of Stanislav Grof,[2] to mention a few. Initiation into the Mysteries, the highpoint of spiritual training in Egypt, Greece, and other countries, may have constituted a direct experience of metaconsciousness.

How completely one can move into metaconsciousness and what sort of experience one has in psychedelic and interlife regression experiences depends, according to *The Tibetan Book of the Dead*, on the nature of one's attachments. The Tibetan mystics struggled to be free from attachments, from seeing the body and material world as realities instead of creations of their minds. In our current experience in regression therapy, probably because we find it difficult to consign all our material world to the fate of being mind creation, we are more modest. We seek to understand on a less drastic level that we have created our own destinies. In the interlife we struggle to create more felicitous patterns and to release the more destructive attachments, which can persist from lifetime to lifetime and impact our actions in our current life. In a lifetime in ancient Egypt my only friend was a Saluki dog belonging to my father, and for this dog I cheerfully flunked my temple initiation and died trying to find him in the interlife. Now, after breeding over three thousand Salukis and building the greatest Saluki kennel of all time, I finally understand the strength of that attachment and can release it! The Tibetans were right about attachments; they do compel action and choice. But if the purpose of living is to give experience to the soul, attachments may not be that bad—we just need to stand apart and observe them with a sense of humor. Perhaps the last attachment to which we must let go is attachment to non-attachment. When we are attached to being on our last incarnation, we have not yet made it!

Franklin Loehr's *Diary After Death* (1986) presents a whimsical and delightful low-key portrayal of the effect of attachments on the interlife experience. It follows its central character through his death, his reunion with his wife, who had made her transition several years earlier, and his continuation of their common thought forms about housing, eating, and socializing. Gradually, with the help of guides, they become willing to release these thought forms and attachments and open themselves to new ways of being, and their experience changes. They become able to create consciously through imaging and thinking. At the end of the book, they are preparing to leave their outward attachments behind and enter a more creative state.

The book prods the reader to consider the question: How do we release our thought forms? The Tibetan treatise exhorts one to do this and describes the results of not doing it, but it does not say exactly how to accomplish the release. Many forms of meditation are focused on such transformation, and the replay of past lifetimes, with their ups and downs, successes and failures, may help to unclutch our fingers. Loehr's portrayal suggests one possible process for those who have not made much progress in their lives on earth and a different process for those who may need only a few finishing touches.

If by moving into the interlife, which is ostensibly *between* lives but is actually *always there*, we can make effective therapeutic intervention, we open up a pristine thrust in therapy. Whether or not there is any "objective reality" corresponding to the interlife experience is unimportant if the symbol of it holds healing potential. It is a therapeutic plus to those who have been immersed in the material world and whose lives have been permeated by anger or violence at worst, or self-centeredness at best, if they can return to the interlife in therapy and take advantage of the insight that is offered. This is especially true for those who have rushed through their last interlife without learning anything. My patient Brad is making an attempt to do just that after other therapeutic approaches have failed. If the interlife is continuously available and the brief sampling of its wisdom that often comes at the time of a past-life death can be belatedly gained, for many patients this may be a path of growth.

Gaining Wisdom in the Life between Life

by

Joel L. Whitton, M.D., Ph.D.

Introduction

The life between life is our natural home from which we venture forth on arduous journeys of physical embodiment. Though we would prefer to remain in the lightness and love there, most of us choose to be born in order to go on with the journey of soul learning. We realize that enlightenment is a prize to be won only after a painfully slow journey of purification from body to body and that the price of advancement is always challenge and difficulty.

Life between life is not a fairy-tale world, nor is it an atmosphere of free-floating cottonwool emptiness. Those who have tasted its richness know that they have visited the ultimate reality, the plane of consciousness from which they embark on successive trials of incarnation and to which they return at the death of the body. The state of metaconsciousness that characterizes the interlife is one where the individual merges with the quintessence of existence; but, paradoxically, in surrendering his own identity he becomes at the same time more intensely self-aware.

The interlife, through self-revelation, places physical being in proper perspective. It shows that the spiritual in us—our essence—is beyond destruction, that at death we leave behind our chosen vehicle of flesh and bones so that another stage may begin. In the awakening and remembrance and the restoration of clarity within the interim world the individual gains expanded insight as to why he was embroiled in the circumstances of the incarnation just past and why he chose the setting and involvements of that life, including parents, careers, and major events contributing to both joys and sorrows. Seeing himself as he truly was, he is able to learn from his last expedition into earthly reality, assess his progress, and eventually plan the next incarnation according to his needs.

The qualities and events of past-life and interlife experiences bear heavily on the circumstances and relationships of following lifetimes, and, conversely, the current lifetime tends to be permeated with emotions that have their origin in thoughts, words, and deeds of the incarnations that have ended. Reincarnation history reveals to patients reasons for situational hardships and emotional difficulties, and the interlife experience puts them in touch with therapeutic guidance and provides enlightenment.[3]

Subjects who venture into the interlife in therapy originally do so on an experimental basis, but it is not long until their experiences are found to be of therapeutic value, deepening the healing obtained as the result of re-living terrifying and disturbing memories from past lives. In the life between life they are impacted by all manner of meaning and dreams that, if they are to communicate their experience, they must somehow decode and translate into language and images. Subjects vary in their ability to report this state. Those who can symbolize easily have most to say; those who have difficulty must remain relatively uncommunicative.

The experiences in the interlife fall into a number of stages.

Returning from the Earth Plane

Most journeys into the interlife commence with a death scene. Typically, this corresponds with the experiences of those who have had near-death episodes where, however traumatic the death may have been, all distress becomes drained away and the subject becomes captive to enthralling visions. In therapy, as the therapist observes this transformation occurring, he shifts from communicating with the personality before him to addressing the emerging eternal self that produces the temporary personality. The awakening to this disembodied experience is where the interlife begins. Subjects need to be given time to attune to this other reality before attempting to answer questions.

In contrast to near-death experiences, that provide only a taste of effulgence, subjects who explore the afterlife in an altered state, because they are freed by the death in the lifetime just viewed, experience no such limitation. However, they must become accustomed to the lack of temporal sequence and the absence of three dimensions that is characteristic of this new state, where, from the earthbound perspective, there is no logic and no order, no progression, everything happening at once. The therapist must ask his subject to isolate and describe specific events from this collage of simultaneity and to find symbols to express what is actually an abstract state.

The death experience varies from person to person. Personal attitudes, together with a person's quality of life and state of spiritual advancement, exert influences on how he experiences death. The smoothest transition from the incarnate to the discarnate state is accomplished by individuals who have spent their lives moulding an outer character in accordance with the soul's highest impulses—they are happy about leaving their bodies behind. Less developed personalities usually either struggle to remain in the body, or, particularly if they are in poor health, may wish to exchange their bodily vehicles as quickly as possible for a new body and re-enter rapidly into physical existence. If death has been violent or has happened suddenly, some disembodied souls may linger on the earthbound plane because of baffle- ment, hunger for continued physical embodiment, or their desire for revenge.[4]

Transition to the Interlife

The tube or tunnel serves as an image of conveyance to the afterworld. Most subjects tell of traveling alone and merging with a multitude of strangers at the end of the journey. As they enter the interlife, or Bardo, as the Tibetans called the state, a deceased relative or friend, a conductor, or a guide who has been watching over the individual during the last life, may welcome the new arrival. Such a guide is often seen to be carrying a torch to light the way. (This image of torch-bearing illustrates how nonmaterial impressions are translated into symbols. By its very nature the interlife cannot be a place and cannot have torches or any other earthly parapherna- lia. Thought alone exists, which the subconscious transforms into an object that can be described. If the interlife dimension is to be perceived, its abstract elements must be converted into imagery, using symbols either from the current life or from some other incarnation).

Although the experience of brilliant light greets the journeyer after each death, it never ceases to be a surprise. The nature of this profound experience of light and love varies from person to person and, like the details of the death experience, appears to be modulated by personal experience, consciousness, expectations, and preconceived ideas about the rest of the world. Subjects, for instance, may describe a wide variety of topography, giving settings they have imagined or wished for while on earth. Rudolph Steiner maintained that the thoughts and mental images of our inner realm appear to us after death as our external world. Settings may vary from splendid palaces and beautiful gardens to abstract settings or to nothingness. Accounts differ as to the degree of light or enlightenment at the threshold, whether there is a judgment board and what it is like, the extent to which the karmic script may be examined, and many other details. The type and amount of activity exhibited in the interlife also differ from person to person. Those who are keen to proceed with their spiritual development tend to be most consciously active between incarnations. Those who show little interest in the evolutionary process are inclined to sleep for the equivalent of huge periods of earthbound time.

No matter with what experience of brilliance the interlife begins, it soon becomes clouded over by the emotions of the most recent past-life personality, emotions that have had their origin in the thoughts, words, and deeds of the incarnation just past. The cognitive emotions of love, guilt, ecstasy, admiration, remorse, loss, and dread have been maintained in the shadow or astral body that has accompanied the soul into the interlife. So, though in entering metaconsciousness the individual first becomes one with the timeless oversoul that is his invisible cornerstone, the multiplicity of personalities that have materialized in previous existences emerge. The trance subject is able to scan the incarnate and the discarnate existence of these personalities in order to bring to consciousness past lessons that will hasten growth. In the review that is conducted following entry into the interlife he can gain greater self-awareness than he had on earth.

The Board of Judgement and the Life Review

Belief in judgment after death pervades every religious, philosophical, and mystical tradition, but the symbols and nature of the judgment drama differ from culture to culture. Many patients in an altered state confirm the existence of a board of judgment, often three in number, who can be of indeterminate identity or take on the appearance of mythological gods or religious masters. The members of this etheric tribunal are highly advanced spiritually. They know intuitively everything about the person who stands before them, and their role is to assist that individual in evaluating the life that has just passed and to make recommendations regarding the next incarnation. Subjects often perceive themselves as handicapped by their own wrongdoing and feel emotional suffering they have inflicted on others as keenly as though it were inflicted on themselves, but the judges radiate a restorative, healing energy that abolishes handicaps and assuages guilt. Rather than confirming the self-loathing of the contrite soul, they express encouragement, pointing out where the life has been positive and progressive.

For the purpose of self-assessment, the soul is confronted with an instantaneous panoramic flashback called the life review that contains every detail of the last incarnation. The soul absorbs every jot of meaning from his personalized videotape, which precipitates a rigorous exercise in self-analysis. During this the judges tend to remain in the background. Like loving teachers they initiate discussion of critical episodes in the last life and offer retrospective counsel and reassurance that each experience, no matter how unsavory, promotes personal development. They also assist the soul in an objective understanding of its actions within the larger context of its many lives. Only by observing karmic trends and patterns—always difficult to discern within a single life—can the soul gain some measure of its progress on the long journey of spiritual evolution.

Planning the Next Life

It is significant that many people plan their forthcoming lives while discarnate. The knowledge gleaned from the review process equips the soul to make vital decisions that will determine the form of its next incarnation, and these decisions are heavily influenced by the judgment board. Meta-consciousness shows, for instance, that the option of choosing one's parents is important in establishing and setting the direction of the lifetime to come. Planning for the next life is frequently undertaken with souls who have played a part, pleasantly or unpleasantly, in previous incarnations and who need to work on a mutual karmic pattern. The details of a life script may be more or less specific. Less developed souls seem to require a detailed blueprint of plans, while more evolved souls provide themselves with only a general outline so that they may act more creatively in challenging situations.

Souls who fail repeatedly to overcome major challenges in a succession of lives find that they are urged by the judgment board to place themselves in similar situations until these challenges are met successfully. People who commit suicide are frequently seized with feelings of dread in the interlife, and they are forced to return to cope with the level of difficulty that led to premature departure from the Earth plane.

While each person is at liberty to reject the judges' planning advice, this is ill-advised. Incarnation that takes place without a plan leads to a lifetime open to unproductive and unnecessary trial and hardship. With no script to follow, the soul becomes like a reed shaken in the wind. There is no penalty for failing to heed the judges, but at the end of that life about to be undertaken the individual will probably experience remorseful self-condemnation and a feeling that the lifetime has been wasted. The judges' recommendations are made according to what the soul needs, not what it wants—the price of advancement is always challenge and difficulty.

Activities in the Interlife

Acquisition of knowledge is another function of the interlife and follows the life review. Such learning prepares the soul for its next incarnation. Those who have made plans for several lives to come and are firmly committed to their evolutionary progress speak of spending most of their sojourn in the Bardo in study of some kind. They often find themselves hard at work in vast halls of learning equipped with libraries and seminar rooms (symbols for abstract states). Materialistic souls rush back into a body; while those without ambition, once they have appeared before the judgment board, fall asleep until they feel pressure to resume earthly embodiment.

Much of what will take place on earth later will have been rehearsed, to a greater or lesser degree, in the previous interim state. It is almost as though we are artists who in the interlife made a rough sketch of a fresco. Once incarnate, we set to work on our intended masterpiece. Eventually, through death or metaconsciousness, we are able to step back and view the work of art. Only on returning to life between life can we know how faithful we have been to our objectives. While incarnate, those who are living out their karmic scripts as they have planned them have an inner sense that life is unfolding as it should. Those who have strayed from their blueprint feel that their life course is haphazard.

Coming Back to Earth

Some souls look forward eagerly to the challenges of earthly existence, but most are reluctant to surrender the timeless, spaceless Bardo for the more limited material plane. The act of reincarnation can be resisted only so long, however; eventually there is an accumulation of cosmic pressure that coerces the soul to renew its development within the confines of a physical body. Just how much time is spent out of incarnation varies widely from person to person and from life to life. The average between-life stay—approximately 40 years—has been steadily declining, which may account for the significant rise in global population. Less developed souls who are eager for a new body do not spend long in the interlife, nor will those who see an early opportunity on the earthbound plane to make karmic compensation for actions in earlier lives. Extended stays in the interlife arise either from the desire to expend effort in preparation for the next earthly existence or, contrarily, from an apathetic attitude toward evolutionary progress.

Before entering the Earth plane in birth, the entity passes through an etheric barrier that lowers the vibrations of its consciousness. The memory of the Bardo, including its initial magnificence, if it has been perceived, dissolves. The amnesia allows the individual to embark on the new life unhindered by confusing echoes of past deeds and misdeeds. In souls who have experienced the light, it also prevents pining and homesickness for the grandeur that has been left behind.

First awareness of being in the new body may range from several months before birth to just after emerging from the womb. Many subjects mention hovering over the mother, encouraging her in choices of food and music, discouraging smoking and the use of alcohol, and generally directing behavior that will enhance their mutual welfare. The issue of when the soul enters the body and whether gradually or suddenly is difficult to access. The issue is confused by the presence of two types of memory, brain memory and soul memory. Because the brain is functioning within three months of conception it is difficult to know whether subjects in an altered state are relaying messages from the central nervous system or from the presence of the eternal "I."

As the new life progresses, the life between life may as well never have existed. The child develops a central identity that makes the assumption that it and the temporal environment comprise the only reality. Possible inklings of the original and more refined state of existence are dismissed as vague, abstract, and highly speculative. But in therapy or other, probably rare, perceptions of the interlife, a glimpse of the deeper reality brings the knowledge that the Bardo experience will reoccur, and this removes fear of death.

Nearly every traveller in the interlife retains a sense of a marvelous other world on awakening, but he has difficulty elucidating his memories because of the uniqueness of metaconsciouness. There is nothing on Earth that can compare with the interlife, and even symbols may fail to unfold the nature and meaning of the experience. Each person who returns has a different version to share. But in one fundamental respect all who have visited the interlife bring the same message: *We are thoroughly responsible for who we are and the circumstances in which we find ourselves. We are the ones who do the choosing.*

Case 1. The Cabbage with the Petals of Light

At the time of coming into therapy Linda was a petite, soft-spoken 30-year-old who had since high school set her intention on a career in healing. She had been graduated from the University of Toronto as an occupational therapist and since then had practiced in a hospital in the city's west end. But though her progress toward her vocational goal had been steady, all was not well in her relationship with herself and the world. Her complaint on entering therapy was of irregular, enervating depressions and a blocking of every attempt to realize her full potential.

Linda had had a difficult childhood. For as long as she could remember her father had been suicidal, and his desperation had frequently pushed her parents to the point of breakup. Linda, through strength and patience coupled with intuitive understanding, had been able to hold the family together. Though she could appreciate herself for having managed this difficult task successfully, in her mid-twenties she became subject to periodic depressions that she could not shake off. More and more she felt she was being blocked from experiencing who she really was. This formed an invisible barrier that curtailed her ability to be open and loving to others. In addition, she was afraid of speaking in public and was chronically afraid of making a mistake.

First Past Life

Linda's most recent past life found her in 1842 as Maria Tovar, the daughter of a wealthy merchant. She was in love with a young man named Carlos, with whom she experienced a lighthearted and pleasure-filled life. This changed drastically twelve years later when she found herself a stolid, grief-stricken widow whose husband (Carlos) 'had been killed during the Spanish revolution of 1854. She was left with twin sons of six and a three-year-old daughter Katarina. Her depression deepened as her life dragged on.

Fourteen years later, when Maria's twin sons marched off to fight and did not return and Katarina married and moved away, Maria withdrew into the home of her mother-in-law and nurtured her bitterness as though it were a rare and prized flower. At 45, while watching marching soldiers from a second-story window, she threw herself to her death in the street below.

Interlife

As Linda watched that body become pinned underneath wheel spokes, she became aware of a dazzling and lustrous light and sensed that she was being drawn through a cocoon or tunnel into a luminous environment. The blinding light forced her attention away from the street, and she entered a light more lustrous than the sun and more dazzling, yet devoid of any sensation of heat. This absorbing brightness exuded peace and serenity. Utterly relaxed, she bathed in its benevolence. Words were unequal to the task of describing the magnificent environment through which she was being drawn with incredible speed. She became increasingly aware that the body and life she had left behind were inconsequential.

At first she wasn't sure whether she was Maria or Linda, but neither name seemed particularly appropriate and all that mattered was the brightness and serenity. As she assimilated the wondrous atmosphere of the landscape-without-terrain, she could not talk at first. Finally she expressed intense sadness and insisted that Maria's suffering had been unfair. It was as though she had to defend and justify Maria and her suicide. But beneath this superficial layer of defense a deeper perception was beginning to emerge, and immersed in this she returned to the space-time world with reluctance when the therapeutic session came to an end.

During the next week she was without her usual alertness and was subject to long periods of deep sleep and low energy levels. During this passive period she had the opportunity to return many times to her experience of transcendence, and in these forays into the bright world she was able to do therapeutic work on her own. She thought of this world with longing, constantly returning to it in memory, and through these experiences of illumination she gradually became aware that Maria's despair, while flowing ostensibly from the death of Carlos, was not perhaps as unfair as she had thought. At the end of the week she wrote in her diary:

> *Looking at Maria from the vantage point of the interlife I see that she was selfish, caring only for her own welfare and her own need of love and companionship. I see also that she blocked herself from meeting these needs. She was not so much mourning the death of Carlos and her two sons as she was grieving at her own loss.*
>
> *After the death of Carlos she could have turned her grief to positive account by using it to deepen her empathy and strengthen the bonds with her children. But she refused to allow any light to enter her life and made only feeble efforts to overcome her grief and become a loving mother. The deaths of her two sons were less of a loss to her than a confirmation of the pain instigated by Carlos' death.*
>
> *By focusing ever more on that pain, she undermined her relationship with her daughter. Maria's selfishness is apparent in her reaction to Katarina's marriage—she felt no joy for her daughter, only more sadness and desolation for herself.*

As Linda worked to discern from the interlife how Maria's life and death had influenced her own incarnation, she had a vision of her oversoul as a cabbage of light with a dark mass of primeval sadness at its core. She saw that with each incarnation the cabbage unfolded a new leaf of light in order to release a few particles of darkness and shed some of its pain. After the growth of many leaves, or lives, the cabbage managed to expunge all pain and was suffused with effulgence. The cabbage was Linda's personal symbol for soul development. Her lives were seen to be endless as the leaves of a cabbage (in contrast to the rose, which dies soon after its petals open).

It became apparent then that Maria, by dwelling on her pain and grief to the exclusion of all else, had allowed her life to become stunted because she had blinded herself to her potential for growth. This failure, carried into the current lifetime, had provoked Linda's depressions and the block that stood in the way of personal development. As she recognized this, Linda felt the first ripples of liberation. Though her life had not been nearly so traumatic as Maria's, the similarity of her attitudes to those of her immediate past-life personality was shocking to behold. She, too, had allowed herself to be trapped in a self-defeating state of depression. This gloom, this block, was Maria's bequest to Linda, who, in becoming aware of the pattern, realized that she could throw off its inhibiting influence.

With understanding came freedom. Her first act was to call a boyfriend, over whom she had been pining since his marriage two years before, and let him know that her waiting days were over. She felt that just as Maria had waited for Carlos to return long after his death, her tendency had been similarly unrealistic—to hold on in spite of pain. Her visit to the interlife had helped her see that by staying attached to a man she couldn't have she was depriving herself of a rewarding relationship with someone else.

Over the next few weeks, bubbles of illumination arose from Linda's experiences in metaconsciousness and drifted at intervals into her waking mind. She came to understand that her extraordinary sympathy for her father and his suicidal tendencies stemmed from her incarnation as Maria. Most important of all, as she documented in her diary, she was beginning to enjoy herself. She felt that her energy was flowing much more freely and that the block was starting to dissolve. The intense depressions lifted. She was able to be more giving and receptive. The image of the shining cabbage reappeared over and over again, quietly exhorting her "to radiate as much light as possible."

But why had she lived so much of her life as Maria as though she were dead? And why did she still in this life become paralyzed by fear of making a terrible mistake? A particularly vivid dream hinted at resolution. In this dream a friend appeared and said, "I am going to show you something from a past life." At that point Linda felt herself turn over on her left side and become a man screaming from a sword wound that eventuated in his death. She concluded that this dream was a deliberate attempt of her subconscious mind to nudge into consciousness a significant past-life experience.

Second Past Life

When instructed under hypnosis to locate this key lifetime and explore its relevance, Linda returned to her dream where as a young man, Rudolph, she was experiencing the violent death that she knew was exactly what she deserved. To try to find context for this, she went farther back to Rudolph at twelve romping through a field of tall grass on a farm in Germany near the Swiss border as though he were enjoying his last moments of innocence.

Going ahead ten years, Rudolph at 22 was an aggressive cynical student at a Paris university, involved in social activism in pre-revolutionary France. The group to which he belonged didn't consider themselves to be the terrorists they actually were because, though their methods were not always acceptable, they were convinced their ends were good. Two years later members of the club began to disappear, and a club member's beautiful redheaded wife, who had been refused membership because she was a woman, gradually came under suspicion. Rudolph suspected that this Henriette was vengefully seducing and then killing each man, and when his best friend died, he became angry enough to plan Henriette's murder.

A powerful image of flames obstructed following regression sessions until at last Linda could see herself in Rudolph's body pushing a woman with long red hair into a fire. When asked, he said it was part of a plan but he couldn't talk about it—he must escape. As he had feared, he was captured and brought in chains to the concierge. Here day after day he met and watched the burning woman dance on the walls of his cell. Eventually, Henriette's brother took revenge and arranged Rudolph's murder. As he died he realized that though he had needed to stop Henriette from killing the men, he should have been able to do that without killing her, too.

Second Interlife Experience

It was then that Linda/Rudolph entered the interim state and the darkness became a sudden brightness as she was sucked through a pulsating, light-filled tunnel. All cares and fears were left behind. Space and time were no more than a memory. Linda became at peace with herself and at one with the engulfing beauty and serenity as she emerged from the tunnel into an ineffable light-filled vastness. She felt once again that she had come home.

As soon as she became acclimatized to these bright surroundings she found herself in a marble square that radiated the same intense brightness that had marked her journey. Three of the corners were occupied by beings she identified as judges. When she took her place in the remaining corner she was able to review with the utmost objectivity the life that had just ended. When the judges commanded her to speak, she said that she knew she had deserved to die violently. The judges agreed with this and said that her actions as Rudolph would mean prolonged suffering in her life to follow as Maria Tovar. However, in the life after that life Linda would "look at what went wrong and fix it."

In her current lifetime Linda had unconsciously become anxious because she carried the energy of Rudolph's tragic error in killing Henriette. She could now see that Rudolph's self-reproach had been brought forward into the life of today as fear of repeating such a mistake. Her understanding deepened following her experience of this interim state, and she wrote in her journal:

> *Ever since my life with Rudolph I have been punishing myself. As Maria I made myself suffer by living like a dead woman, and in this life, too, I was almost following in Maria's footsteps. Now I see that this is no longer necessary.*

Just as Rudolph appeared to be the source of many of Linda's problems, so processing the memory of him brought about their termination. Freed from the shackles of past-life wrongdoing, she has found herself more comfortable with this life at hand. The interlife imparted vital understanding that served to recharge her energies. At first she experienced her interlives as inexpressible abstractions, but with encouragement she was able first to give images to her sense of what was happening (such as the judges), and then to symbolize her soul as a cabbage with petals of light.

Linda was told in the interlife that in her current life she would "look at what went wrong and mend it," and she has accomplished this. Today in her work as an occupational therapist she is steadily accomplishing her between-life intentions, countering Rudolph's murderous urges by helping daily to mend the lives of others. The image of the shining cabbage remains in her consciousness, quietly exhorting her to "radiate as much light as possible." It has become the symbolic focus of her growth and provides energy for implementing changes and moving into continued insight.

Case 2. Recovering a Forsaken Path

When Heather came to see me her, immune system had broken down and her already broad range of allergic reactions was escalating. This acute allergic vulnerability and her low resistance to pneumonia and bronchitis, added to the periodic depressions that rolled like black waves over her, kept her from working and caused her to abandon a promising career as a jewelry designer. Extensive medical investigations had turned up neither cause nor cure.

First Past Life

Heather was a remarkably good trance subject and by copying hypnotic techniques she was able to hypnotize herself. Much of her regression work she conducted at home, using an account of it in her journal to save time in her therapy.

The first significant life she recovered was of Isobel, a concert pianist. This past-life personality was beautiful and gifted, but contact with her made Heather deeply unhappy. These strong feelings of unhappiness eventually inducted her into a memory of Isobel going over a cliff in a car driven by a young man named Robert. She was thrown from the car and terribly burned, and in the hypnotic state Heather coughed and sputtered as she experienced Isobel's lungs being seared by the hot black smoke. Then from out of her body she watched the rescue by the French ambulance and saw Isobel in a hospital room with the right side of her body burned. The recovery of this memory ended Heather's allergic reactions, but her depression continued.

Later she saw herself living alone in a cottage by the sea, her face scarred and her right hand useless so that she could no longer play. Pseudo-friends subtly taunted her with her plight until on a stormy night she walked out into the ocean to her death. Her black moods in the current life were linked directly to that grim night. After Heather re-experienced in trance her drowning in the English Channel, her rolling black waves of depression dissolved and did not return.

Second Past Life

Heather's sense of inadequacy remained, however, and we looked to other lifetimes for an explanation. One of these led to Spain where, as Evangeline, she fell in love with and later married a nobleman who when she met him was engaged to a woman she recognized as her current mother. The arch rivalry between the two culminated in a conspiracy against Evangeline that involved the feared Inquisition, and she was put in a dungeon and died as the result of torture. In the corner of the dungeon during her torture and death stood her dark-haired rival.

Childhood

Following this, we pressed for information on her relationship with her mother during this life. Materially, Heather had had everything but was starved of affection by a jealous mother who saw her daughter as competition, especially in the field of art. Heather reported that during the worst phase of her recent degenerative illness every discouraging word her mother had ever said came tumbling back. She felt she was unworthy and didn't deserve to be happy. It became evident that her last remaining problems, especially the feeling of inadequacy, stemmed from her childhood, rather than from past lives.

Interlife

We went back to the interlife in order to better understand the problems of her childhood. Less than ten months had separated her death as Isobel in the winter of '33 from her birth as Heather in the summer of '34, and we explored what happened in this hiatus, beginning with the scene of her death. In her journal she described drowning in the storm in the English Channel.

> *I could see Isobel's body floating in a dark, boiling sea. There was a massive storm raging. I knew that I had once been Isobel, but now I didn't have a body. I was floating in all-embracing golden light. I felt comfortable and warm and untouched by the elements. Even though I didn't have a body, I felt quite whole and at one with my surroundings. I realized I could see in all directions. Looking at Isobel's body, I felt no emotions. I felt no fear and no loneliness, although I seemed to be alone.*
> *Then the light spread and I appeared to be moving up. I felt tremendous warmth and love and happiness. All around me was golden light, as though I were basking in very bright sunshine. There was no division, no separateness. All was one. It was incredibly beautiful and peaceful. I saw flashes of pastel rainbow hues and heard hundreds of voices singing simple but beautiful*

melodies. I just floated there happily, feeling I was a part of it all, that I truly belonged.

Heather longed to remain adrift in this light-filled boundlessness, but as her soul script emerged it became clear that she had not prepared herself for or earned such a state and must leave it for the level that had been determined by her previous life. She found in the life review that in the interlife prior to her life as Isobel she had chosen a long and brilliant musical career, but she had not followed this path. Instead, she had plunged into a life of superficial sociality that contained no scope for her music. Wandering far from her interlife intentions she had opened doors to chaos and misery and had squandered all prospect of growth. Her current life had been hastily assembled as an emergency measure to cope with the karmic repercussions of Isobel's misspent and prematurely curtailed existence.

In the interlife immediately before this current life as Heather and following her life as Isobel, she learned that her allergies were more than a legacy of the unresolved trauma of the car accident. The karmic consequence of Isobel's action was her embodiment as Heather, who was to make reparation for Isobel's deficiencies. She wrote in her journal:

> *I also picked up from the interlife that Isobel would have died just recently as happy and successful and a great grandmother. If only she had been patient and persevering, she could have had it all!*

In that interlife experience following Isobel's death, Heather experienced an electrifying encounter with members of the judgment board as she attempted to clarify the major thrust for her current life. The judges stood at the end of a vast temple in the guise of the Egyptian deities of Ra, Osiris, and Isis. (It must be remembered that there is no specific content to interim experiences and the subject must cast them in some sort of symbolism in order to report them. This is apparently done automatically, drawing on the patient's belief system.)

> *As I entered the temple, I picked up the rattle of the sistrum, which became more and more persistent. Also there was the sound of flutes and hand cymbals...beautiful and elusive at the same time. I walked forward straight to Isis. She was incredibly tall and communicated without words. She told me I must pursue my artistic endeavors, that as I worked I would find my answers.*

Her soul's glimpse of her forthcoming incarnation as Heather was far from reassuring. All indications pointed to experiencing a dismal conglomeration of frustration, rejection and tears. Even more disturbing was the recommendation of the judges that she choose as her mother the woman who had been her rival in the Spanish life and who had been responsible then for her torture and death.

> *All of a sudden I felt horror and fear. I begged not to be born to my mother, but I received the impression that this was part of what I had to repay. I cannot describe my terror. Then I saw my grandmother, whom I recognized from a happier incarnation, and I started to feel a little better. I loved her and looked forward to seeing her again.*

As a result of Heather's anguish at what she had seen in the journey into the interim state, she experienced an acute attack of bronchial pneumonia that lasted several weeks. Once the illness ended, however, she felt clearer, calmer, and more optimistic, and her bronchial and pneumonic problems have never recurred. The account in her journal at the close of this illness gives an almost audible sigh of relief.

> *For the first time in a long time, I am actually starting to feel a little hope in this life. I feel that if I can ride out the storm, things will improve as I grow older. Already my life is slowly changing for the better, and I am starting to realize that people can like me. I even feel I might have a little artistic success if I can fight it through.*

Over the next three years Heather came to terms with the negative influences that had wrecked her childhood and crippled her adult life. By means of systematic orthodox therapy, without the aid of hypnosis, she came to realize at the deepest level of her being that she was worthy of affection and respect. She came to see that her previous feeling of insecurity stemmed, not from inherent inadequacy but from karmic demands that had brought about emotional repercussions with her mother when she was a child. Gradually she grew less insecure, and as her confidence grew, so did her ability to express herself.

Heather was able to channel her renewed energy into photography as well as jewelry design, and shortly after the close of her therapy she mounted her first show. She had been restored to a state of health and working capacity that she had only dreamed about. For many years she had felt that she had been wandering aimlessly through life without meaning or purpose, the result of the corrective process she had to go through, but her experience in metaconsciousness had helped her to complete this corrective process. She realizes now that she has finally worked through the karmic consequence of Isobel's errant life and is free to actualize her creative abilities. This she is doing, and her skills are increasingly attracting the interest of both art dealers and private collectors.

Case 3. Sharing a Karmic Ledger

Throughout his life, Harold, a 37-year-old behavioral scientist, had always had a close relationship with his sister Eileen. She had recently developed breast cancer that had progressed rapidly, and not only did she face a radical mastectomy but also possible death. Harold became distraught. Eileen had always been the strong one in the family, and he felt fragile at the thought of being without her. Also, he grieved for her husband and her two children.

In a restless night just preceding her surgery he found himself praying that somehow Eileen would survive the crisis and be restored to full health, and he offered his own life in exchange for his sister's. This was more than a gesture of brotherly love; it was an impassioned cry from his heart that came from a depth even he himself did not understand.

The next day, on the eve of the operation, in an effort to find emotional surcease, he made his way to an auditorium where a classical concert was being taped for the Canadian Broadcasting Corporation. During the performance of a program of Brahms, Harold went into an altered state. He felt light shining on him and then a rush of ecstasy that hit him like a tidal wave. He lost awareness of time and felt himself drawn up into brightness. (This was an experience of "cosmic consciousness" that William James has written about.) Tears streamed down his face. At the height of this awareness he knew that his sister would be all right.

The next day Harold returned to the hospital to await calmly the outcome of Eileen's surgery. The surgeon told him after the operation that the tumor was benign and had shrunk so dramatically that, by cutting away the non-malignant residue, the mastectomy had been averted. Eileen went on to make a complete recovery.

A year later Harold contracted hepatitis, which kept him from work for almost three months. For nine months after that he seemed in good health, but following that his ankles became swollen. Tests revealed that he had a potentially fatal kidney disease of unknown origin, and his chances of survival were rated between 10 and 20 percent. There was no known conventional treatment except cutting back on his salt intake. Certain innovative treatments were suggested, but Harold's attempt to implement them produced massive side effects so that he had to discontinue them. He was angry that conventional medicine not only could not help but made things worse. He realized that his only chance of healing now depended on taking responsibility for his own situation.

Prior to this time Harold had witnessed experiments in hypnotic regression and was acquainted with theories of reincarnation and karma. He began asking himself if there might be a karmic factor in his illness. This led him to treatment in order to seek an answer. When he first came, he was convinced that his offer to exchange his life for that of his sister meant that he would die. His subsequent experience in past lives and in the interlife, however, brought about a different understanding.

First Past Life

The lifetime pertinent to his search did not emerge immediately. It was only after seven months of regressions to various lifetimes that a past life as Edgar Courtney in Virginia at the time of the Civil War was recovered. This proved to be the life he needed to re-experience in order to understand and heal his illness.

Edgar, in that life, had a sister Sarah, whom Harold recognized to be Eileen in his present life. Their brief ill-fated and illicit relationship in the 19th century revealed the source of Harold's current repressed feeling of guilt toward his sister, guilt potent enough to lead to his offer of self-sacrifice so that Eileen might live.

Edgar and Sarah had grown up on a large rural estate hear Harrisburg, Virginia. Their special fondness for one another was self-evident as they grew up together. When Edgar was twelve years old and Sarah was sixteen, their mutual affection extended to a brief incestuous relationship. The episode took place when their father was away buying horses and they were picnicking in a wooded area some distance from their home. At that time Edgar promised Sarah that he would never mention their sexual indiscretion to anyone. But several years later, when Sarah became engaged to a suitor whom Edgar despised, he felt compelled to reveal their secret in order to drive the man away. The broken pact quickly became the gossip and scandal of the community.

In grave disgrace, Sarah was forced to leave home. Shame granted her no respite, and when she could endure the loneliness and self-torment no longer she committed suicide. Edgar's remorse was bitter and unrestrained. Having enlisted in a military academy, he threw himself gratefully into the fiercest of fighting on behalf of the Confederate army when the American Civil War was declared. In one of the earliest engagements of the war, Edgar was shot in the stomach and left shoulder. He died in agony on the battlefield.

In spite of the heat in my office, Harold was shivering when he regained consciousness after this session, and he clutched his stomach after the final traumatic scene of his death.

Second Past Life

Harold did not go immediately into the interlife following his experience as Edgar but touched first on his immediate past life as a child named Barrett, who died at the age of seven from chicken pox in a community called Quincy. By earthly reckoning Harold had spent 26 years in the interlife between this death as Barrett and his rebirth in 1937. It was in this interlife immediately following Barrett's death and preceding his incarnation as Harold that we hoped to learn more about his relationship with his sister from an extended perspective.

Interlife

Harold entered the interlife shortly after Barrett's death to find his discarnate self grieving over the boy. From out of his metaconsciousness he was able to report his initial experience of this period.

> P: *I'm looking down at Barrett, who is lying in bed in a white nightshirt. I know he's dead, but I don't want to leave him. But someone is calling me from far away, and I have to go...I find myself in a huge room without walls and without a ceiling. I am looking up as a child might do at many other personalities who are talking among themselves. They don't seem to have any interest in me. I'm just a kid, and they're busy chatting away to one another. It seems strange that I have the perspective of a child's consciousness while in other ways I feel quite old. There's no color in the scene. Its as though I were looking at a negative or a black and white photograph.*

In this experience we can see the individual awareness gradually fusing with the oversoul or eternal identity that has no time or substance or name and yet is more truly the individual than any of his incarnations. This gradually emerging oversoul then waited in the room without walls, sensing that it was actually a way station for those who have recently gone through a physical death, in order to give them time to move out of the identity of their last incarnation into their soul identity. He was approached by an elderly man who placed his hands on his shoulders.

> P: *That's funny, because I have no shoulders. But I'm not afraid anymore. Barrett's gone.... His body is no longer mine.*
> T: *So if you can't go back to Barrett, you can go forward.*
> P: *(Irritably) There is* just no time *in the place between lives!*

Harold then felt himself being led by the elderly man into a building like a church with a high, vaulted ceiling. His venerable escort departed, and three elderly beings dressed in white walked in and seated themselves behind a desk. The board of judgment had arrived. The thrust of this council was that Harold should study during the period between incarnations and make every effort not to waste the experience.

> T: *Perhaps you could search out plans for your forthcoming incarnation. How do you see the mother you choose?*
> P: *She looks just as if I were looking at a photograph of her as a young woman.*

> T: *And how do you see your father?*
> P: *Oh, I see that he is the affectionate, supportive uncle from my lifetime as Edgar, and the sister I am going to have was my sister Sarah in that life.*

Further exploration in the interlife confirmed that Harold had chosen to incarnate with the intent of rejoining his sister so that he could balance their shared karmic ledger. He learned that achievement of harmony with her and the healing of their relationship was the primary purpose of his current life and that it had been decided that he would move toward fulfillment of this purpose after he recovered memory of the specific nature of the karmic involvement. He could not in the interlife know exactly how this was to be brought about, but he could now see why he had prodded himself with various discomforts in order to be helped to move into memory of his life as Edgar.

> P: *I brought my illness about in order to propel myself toward this experience with you. It was not really in my karmic script—I didn't have to die because Eileen got well—but it was a tool to push me into a situation where I could understand. It was something I brought about in order to fulfill my plan.*

Harold saw that he had selected the broad plan of his life but that the details were woven in as he lived. He became aware of his reason for being. Now he lives like a man who has been raised from the dead, which is actually not far from the truth. His master plan had decreed that rather than die prematurely he must live and remember for the sake of reconciliation and harmony. In order to recover he needed to follow his intuition and become actively involved in his own healing process. He has done this, and self-responsibility has replaced his emotionally dependent and guilty attitude toward Eileen and led to harmony and balance between them.

The Interlife in a Current Death Experience

by

Samuel Sandweiss, M.D.

Editor's Note: The following account has been excerpted from *Sai Baba...The Holy Man and the Psychiatrist* by Samuel Sandweiss, M.D. with the permission of the author.[5] It is included, not because of the death experience, though this was validated by reliable professionals, but because it carries the interlife experience much further than has usually been reported in near-death accounts where the soul cannot return to the current body after it passes a certain point. Interlife experiences such as this one are commonly described following past-life experiences. As in other reports, it is necessary for the reader to understand that experiences that are not easily put into words have to be cast in the form of metaphors.

The following account was related by Dr. John Hislop, a former professor and corporate executive, then retired and living in Mexico, who witnessed the event. It concerns the reported resurrection of Walter Cowan, a long-time and valued friend of Sathya Sai Baba, who often spent time with Sai Baba in Bangalore and at the ashram in Puttaparti. The event took place on Christmas Day in 1971. The following is Dr. Hislop's account.

> Early Christmas morning news spread among devotees gathered about Baba that an elderly American had suffered a fatal heart attack. Upon hearing the rumor, my wife and I went at once to the Cowan's hotel, where Elsie confirmed that her husband Walter had died. She had prayed to Sai Baba for help and with great self-control and recollection of human mortality had ended the prayer with, "Let God's will be done."
>
> Walter's body was taken to the hospital by ambulance. Later that day, when Elsie and her friend Mrs. Ratan Lal went to the hospital, they found that Sai Baba had already been there as well. To their utter amazement they found Walter alive.

Recognizing the need for documentation of Walter's death in the form of medical reports and witnesses' testimony, Dr. Hislop investigated the matter fully. "At my request, Judge Damadar Rao of Madras interviewed the doctor who had attended Walter when he arrived at the hospital. The doctor's statement was that Walter was indeed dead when he examined him shortly after the ambulance arrived at the hospital. There was no sign of life.

He pronounced Walter dead, then stuffed his ears and nose with cotton. The body was covered with a sheet and moved to an empty room. The doctor then left the hospital and missed seeing Sai Baba while he was there. Upon returning to the hospital after Sai Baba had left, the doctor found Walter alive. He was unable to explain this.

Later that day Sai Baba informed his devotees that he had indeed brought Walter back to life. He did not disclose the reasons for doing so, however; this remains a mystery he has not yet chosen to explain.

When Walter had recovered sufficiently to be moved from Madras to Bangalore, he was described by Hislop as appearing extraordinarily well. "Dr. Gnaneswaran, with whom Hislop and his wife and I had been acquainted for several years, was the Cowans' attending physician in Bangalore. The physician had obtained Walter's medical history, with its specific laboratory tests showing severe diabetes of long standing and various other diseased conditions. He compared it with his own laboratory tests and could scarcely believe the results. Not only were the diabetic symptoms now completely absent, but the tests for other diseased conditions proved to be negative as well."

The following is an account by Walter Cowan himself of his apparent death and resurrection under the grace of Sai Baba:

> *While in the Connemara Hotel in Madras, two days after I arrived, I was taken very sick with pneumonia. As I gasped for breath, suddenly all the body struggle was over, and I died. I found myself very calm, in a state of wonderful bliss; and the Lord, Sai Baba, was by my side.*
>
> *Even though my body lay on the bed, dead, my mind kept working throughout the entire period of time until Baba brought me back. There was no anxiety or fear but a tremendous sense of well-being, for I had lost all fear of death.*
>
> *Then Baba took me to a very large hall where there were hundreds of people milling around. This was the hall where the records of all my previous lives were kept. Baba and I stood before the Court of Justice. The person in charge knew Baba very well, and he asked for the records of all my lives. He was very kind, and I had the feeling that whatever was decided would be the best for my soul.*
>
> *The records were brought into the hall: armloads of scrolls, all of which seemed to be in different languages. As they were read, Baba interpreted them. In the beginning they told of countries that have not existed for thousands of years, and I could not recall them. When they reached the time of King David, the reading of my lives became more exciting. I could hardly believe how great I apparently was in each life that followed.*

As the reading of my lives continued, it seemed that what really counted were my motives and character, as I had stood for outstanding peaceful, spiritual, and political activity. I do not remember all the names, but I am included in almost all of the history books of the world from the beginning of time. As I incarnated in the different countries, I carried out my mission, which was peace and spirituality.

After about two hours, they finished reading the scrolls, and the Lord, Sai Baba, said that I had not completed the work that I was born to do and asked the judge that I be turned over to him to complete my mission of spreading the truth. He requested that my soul be returned to my body under his grace. The judge said, "So be it."

The case was dismissed and I left with Baba to return to my body. I hesitated to leave this wonderful bliss. I looked at my body and thought that it would be like stepping into a cesspool to return to it, but I knew that it was best to complete my mission so that I could eventually merge with the Lord, Sai Baba. So I stepped back into my body...and that very instant it started all over again—trying to get my breath, being as sick as you could be and still be alive. I opened my eyes and looked at my wife and said, "You sure look beautiful in pink...."

After Hislop had heard Walter give this account, he asked Sai Baba whether Walter's experience was real or some sort of hallucination or illusion. Baba replied, "The experience was a real experience, not an illusion. It was an experience occurring within Mr. Cowan's mind, and I myself was there, directing and clarifying the thoughts." When asked if every person has similar experiences with death, Baba said, "It is not necessarily so; some may have similar experiences, some not."

Four months after his third trip to India, Dr. Sandweiss received word that Walter Cowan had passed away after having lived a year and a half following his apparent resurrection by Baba.

Learning in the Interim State

by

Roger Woolger, Ph.D.

Introduction

For many people the actual moment of death in another lifetime is experienced as a release, a peaceful separation from all the usual, as well as the exceptional, sufferings and conditions, and from old age, loneliness and illness. Most patients report floating above the body to some barely definable realm of peace and rest, and some see brief visions of light. Classical after-death images of hell have been quite rare in my practice, though they do occur.

Some patients report that following their deaths they see non-embodied spirit figures in the intermediary realm above or beyond the earth. These figures will frequently be the departed companions or family from the life just remembered, often a spouse or lover who died while the rememberer was on earth. Encounter with an enemy or enemies that have been killed happens only occasionally. More often some person or persons resembling the old adversaries will be encountered in the next life to be remembered, rather than between lives. A few of my sample met old teachers or gurus from the life just lived, or whom they knew in another lifetime. Some report returning to the same teacher, each time a different personality over a number of lifetimes. A common experience is that a discarnate personality meets some robed figure in white who radiates love and wisdom, and frequently several of these figures come in small groups, a kind of "karmic committee." These teachers forming the karmic committee help to review the life just past, advise the departed personality about the lessons of the life just lived, and work with him to plan the life ahead.

One woman reported being taken by such a luminous being to a celestial temple, where she was shown a huge book in which the life she had remembered and "many more" were clearly written. Another woman was similarly guided by a spirit figure and shown part of a huge tapestry that represented her many interwoven lives. Celestial gardens, mountains, and islands are sometimes glimpsed, as are "happy hunting grounds" following lives as tribal native Americans. Visions of Jesus will often occur following a devout Christian life, but these visions seem as much contingent upon the preceding life as do the images of celestial forests upon lives in a tribal hunting culture. There are also resonances with shamanism in meeting a sacred animal or bird.

Such visions usually come only after one has worked through many of the more painful lifetimes. These experiences seem to belong to a stage of integration that is reached when a large proportion of karma is about to be resolved. Encounters with spirit guides or a former teacher seem to be graces that are bestowed by the wisdom of the Greater Self only when and if a person is ready.

My experiences corroborate those of Dr. Raymond Moody and Dr. Kenneth Ring and others. The apparent resemblances persuade me personally that these are archetypal or universal experiences of death and transition that are recorded in the collective unconscious of the individual. The following cases are striking as archetypal visions that in one way or another integrate the sublime heights and barbaric depths that serve to make up the human comedy, in which it would seem that we have all played many parts.

Case 1. Madeleine's Ghost Life

Madeleine, a young teacher in her thirties, felt stuck to the point of despair in her life and was in a state of near suicidal depression when, after years in primal and other therapies, she sought out past-life work. We found a series of past lives in which violent deaths, torture, and rape came up one after another. It seemed that she was caught in a circle of karmic hell in which the dominant thought that kept repeating in life after life was, "It's all my fault. I am a wicked person and deserve to suffer."

Two crucial past-life stories stood behind the cycle of despair and punishment and the crippling negative thoughts that emerged. In the first one, in a life as a pirate Madeleine described in gory detail numerous executions, rapes, and mutilation, of which the following is a sample:

> P: *We're at sea. We've captured a ship. The first victim is a young officer. We behead him. His eyes are staring, the body crumbles.... Now another man. We shoot him in the face. Half his face is gone; there's an eye hanging down...*

This bloody life dragged on and on with more killings but no retribution. When the pirate was too old to go back to sea, he hung around in bars at port and eventually died of a fever, alone and destitute in the upper room of a tavern.

> P: *I am dying slowly. I'm cold. Now I'm hot, sweating...I'm no longer there...I don't understand where I am.... It seems to be a dark mist.... Oh, help, I'm seeing the faces of the people we killed. They're coming back to haunt me. I see their protruding eyes, the blood; there are so many of them, young and old, it's a kind of hell.*
>
>   *I'm a ghost, too. It seems like I have to walk the earth as a ghost for a long, long time. There's no place for me. I'm totally alone. No one is aware of me. This is my punishment. It's not on this earth but on some other desolate planet, dark and dull with cold mists. I remain here for a long, long time. It seems like an eternity.*
>
>   *I'm punishing myself. In this dimension a part knows that this is what I have to do to atone for what I have done to others; in order to be human again I have to feel what my victims must have felt before they died, desolate, alone, and without hope.*

Madeleine continued to traverse this awful psychic wilderness for a long time in this and other sessions, and it seemed that she recognized the faces of every man, woman, and child that she had brutalized in the pirate's life. She seemed driven to perform extraordinary acts of contrition, but eventually an amazing reversal occurred.

> P: *I'm walking from right to left. There's a light ahead of me; it's starting to get warm. I'm stepping onto the grass. There are people and voices ahead of me and I hear an authoritative voice which says: "Enough, enough. You have done enough..." I know now that my punishment is over.*

Shortly after this, the scene changed and Madeleine found herself briefly inside a mother's womb and was born as a baby boy. The following scenes revealed a simple but fulfilled life in which the boy came to maturity, worked as a carpenter, married the woman he loved, and experienced great happiness. When it was over, Madeleine asked herself how she could have deserved such a good life. A voice of wisdom within her replied, "You must learn through love, not just from suffering."

Madeleine had traversed a state not unlike that known to Buddhist teachings as the after-death realm of the *pretas* or hungry ghosts except that for her these ghosts were images of the happy life she had denied others and herself. Once she reowned her capacity for happiness, there was no need endlessly to repeat the cycle of self-punishment reflected both in the lives of violence she had remembered previously and in her current hellish state. She had descended into her own karmic hell and had returned ready to embrace life fully and joyfully.

Case 2. Reconciliation of Opposites in the Interlife

Milton was a middle-aged man who had recently separated from his wife, so our first task was to work extensively on lives that mirrored his patterns in relationships. At first we recovered lives where he had been betrayed or abandoned by women he loved. In search for the origins of the cycle of abandonment, the opposite picture began to emerge: lives of robbers, soldiers, slave owners, etc., that mirrored a cruel, callous, and abandoning side of Milton, what Jung calls the shadow side. He needed to look at the darkest impulses in his nature to become reconciled with himself at a deeper level. The culmination of this series of lives of power and cruelty was one where Milton found himself as a Moroccan bandit leader whose life consisted almost entirely of raiding, looting, and killing. Such an image of omnipotence was the reverse of the vulnerability that he had felt in earlier lives; the victim had now changed into the persecutor.

> P: *We're riding on horses, we're starting to cut them down. They're poorly armed. My men behead some of them. I cut down some women. They're herding others into houses and setting them on fire. Now I'm with this woman. I'm raping her. It's wonderful. Now I cut her throat. It makes me feel strong and masterful to have another's life and pleasure at my command.*

Having lived by the sword, this bandit died by the sword; he got a pike in his belly and his throat was cut in one misjudged raid. He floated out of his bleeding body, still stirred up by the fury of the battle. But as he went higher, a certain calm took place, and a spirit figure, some kind of guide, appeared to him quite spontaneously and began to speak.

> G: *You must meditate long on this life to look at what you have done. You must see the people you have killed, examine the deeds you have done, see if what you have done is good. You will have much time to examine these things—things you have not thought of much in that life, thoughts you had put aside. This task will take as long as you need to perform it.*

Milton then described his meditation in the following words:

> P: *I find myself in a great aloneness, alone but not alone. Nothing there, not even a sense of time. It seems to take forever, but somehow no time at all. No new thoughts come, all thoughts are known to me. I become aware of the souls of those I slayed, their presences, all equally strong because all equally important. I feel sorry for these souls, that I robbed them of their chance to grow further in that life—sorrow for myself that I did not grow close to the spiritual nature I feel about me. But at the same time I feel gladness that I removed these souls from the material realm at the*

appointed time and that I was thus removed. I feel happiness in the knowledge that those who lived, lived, and those who died, died.

I feel wonder at the glory of it all, at everything. I feel an awareness, almost of the whole universe and still the awareness of myself here. Such peace, such glory! And all creation, material, immaterial, animal, vegetable, and mineral—all this is a manifestation of Truth. Truth as it is. There is nothing else. I am aware that that life was a life of action, a life when I did things without concern for good or evil, but only for pleasure and pain. In that life I had power and used it without regard for right or wrong, or even awareness of right or wrong. I took no more than casual concern for Allah. I was a force in the world as I knew it but not a thinking force. Yet it was a life I had to go through. In that life I killed, raped, looted, without thought or concern for what I was doing, being an instrument only of the passion of the moment....

In this reflective state Milton had images of other lives to follow—a Spanish nobleman who killed for jealousy, a runaway who attained power among the Indians, a woman victimized during the Civil War, a lone cowboy who rejected power. He was shown a panorama of the entire spectrum of responses to power and passion in these various lives, ranging from utter powerlessness to the thoughtless abuse by the bandit. All extremes of the karmic complex were faced and in some sense known only to Milton, were reowned, accepted, and reconciled.

Learning in the Valley

by

Irene Hickman, D.O.

Introduction

The nature of the experience of souls between lives is only gradually emerging through observation of many individual instances. The following account suggests that after a soul experiences a life characterized by lack of compassion, or even by cruelty, it is offered an opportunity to grow and transform into a more compassionate and sensitive being. Various interim experiences reveal common themes, one of which is the choice given to souls to select parents who will best help them fulfill the goals that they and their advisors have set up for the life to come. The concept of "the valley" that appears in this account also appears in other interlife descriptions, though its actual significance is not clear. The appearance of the monsters is reminiscent of *The Tibetan Book of the Dead*, but this subject's awareness that she created them and that they could only be destroyed by a change of heart reveals unusual insight.

Case: Reschooling after a Life of Cruelty

Anne Armstrong had originally come to see me because of blinding headaches that made her feel that a spike was being driven through her head. Anne's work on her past lives extended over several years. Eventually she unearthed a lifetime where as a beautiful black priestess with extraordinary supernatural abilities she had misused her power by controlling others and wiping out her critics. One of her slaves showed contempt for this way of governing. Infuriated by his attitude the priestess had him brought to a banquet and drove a golden spike through his head.

Anne's headaches did not cease after this recall, but they did disappear after recovering her transformational work in the subsequent interlife. Here is her account of the experience:

P: I'm about to die. I have one of my slaves open my ring and pour poison into the cup. I raise it. It's very difficult to drink it.

T: Detach yourself and describe what's happening. Step aside and watch.

P: It's paralysis. It attacks the neck first, then the right arm. The muscles twitch and the stomach contracts. Then she slumps over. It is not a gruesome death. It is rather passive.

T: Then what happens to the body?

P: I had oil. I had given orders that the oil be spread all the way round my room and set on fire. This is what's happening now.

T: What are your thoughts and feelings now that you are out of your body?

P: Not good. I feel very sad. I can't quite understand it yet. I don't understand why I should feel this way. I don't feel a bit good about it.

T: Go on. Describe anything that you are experiencing after leaving the body.

P: I hung around there for quite a while. I couldn't get away. The attachment was too great. It was days before I could get away from there. The body was charred. There wasn't much left of it. I'm just looking and I feel sort of lost.

T: Go forward until a change has occurred in what you are experiencing. What happens next?

P: I ascended, but the door was locked. I recognized this path—I had been here before, but this time the door was locked and I couldn't get through.

T: What did you do? Where did you go?

P: They pointed down. I had to go down there. It's evil and dirty.

T: Did you recognize that you had brought yourself there? Were there regrets then for your evil life?

P: Terrible—terrible! I had to stay there for many years.

T: Tell me what it was like.

P: I knew there were others there. I could hear them moaning. I couldn't see them. All I could see were these monsters around me that I had created. I tried to abolish them with my magic but it didn't work. They just laughed at me. I tried calling up the flame to destroy them. It didn't work. There's one monster right in front of me. Hideous—it is one I created. I call him "the dweller." I call up the flame. He walks right through it. Nothing works here, I realize it now. I realize I will just have to stay here.

T: Are you aware of any change that has to occur before you can leave this place?

P: Something has to take place in my heart. A change has to take place within me.

T: Do you know what that change is?

P: It looks like the unfolding of a flower. It looks like petals that I have to open up.

T: As you look at this unopened flower, how does it appear to you?

P: It looks like a flower that has been very beautiful but has been neglected and no water given it. It is just limp and dry. But with proper care it would flower forth and be beautiful again.

T: Go forward in time to when the flower begins to be beautiful again.

P: *It's very slow—so slow. I feel as though I am lifted up and am dropping an outer body or skin that was very heavy and very coarse. Now it has been refined. The texture is different. There is an airy feeling as the flower opens up more and more.*

T: *Are you still surrounded by the evil beings?*

P: *Not so much. I know that they are there, but I realize that they can't hurt me now.*

T: *Describe any other changes that contribute to this greater feeling of purity and lightness.*

P: *I need to meditate and learn to pray.*

T: *Even though you have no physical body?*

P: *I just have awareness of my consciousness. I don't feel a body. Suddenly there is this ray of beautiful, beautiful sunlight. It touches me.*

T: *How does this affect you?*

P: *It attracts my attention and I look up—like a new day. I reach out and someone takes my hand. As they take my hand I float up out of the evil area and up into space.*

T: *What happens next?*

P: *I'm in the valley again. I look around. More meditation.*

T: *Is there any special meaning or significance to your valley?*

P: *The only thing I get is that this is the place where you learn to combine the physical with the spiritual.*

T: *You mentioned once before that when you entered the valley you felt very small and that you became larger and more complete as you progressed through the valley. Go on and describe any of the details of the valley experience that you may have omitted.*

P: *It seems as though I understand all nature here. It seems as though I can communicate with them—the trees, the flowers, the grass. I seem to be a part of them. I seem to be in this sphere that encompasses everything. I'm just one with them and they're one with me. As I move toward the far end of the valley, I understand these things more, and I feel more and more complete until I'm finally let out.*

T: *And when you are let out, what is that called?*

P: *Birth.*

I went over this and other interim states with Anne a number of times, and each time more details appeared and gaps became filled in. Metaphors, such as the valley, emerged and acquired deeper significance. It became increasingly clear that learning in the interim state influences the lifetime following.

Anne's life after that of the black priestess was as a Roman, Antonio, whose intention in that lifetime was to be of service—obviously Anne's soul self had benefited from that lifetime in the valley. Antonio resisted the pressure of those around him to murder Caesar, whose bodyguard he was, and as a result of his loyalty he died an excruciating death on the rack at the hands of a jealous competitor, whom Anne recognized as the slave she had killed in her lifetime as the black priestess.

Anne was a person of considerable soul development. During her lifetime as the priestess she had been deflected from her true soul path by misuse of her transpersonal powers, but after the relearning in the interim state, she continued on her path of growth. At the end of her current years in therapy experiencing her past lives, she emerged as a competent and loving psychic who has given abundantly to those whose lives have touched hers.

Between Physical Incarnations

by

Hazel M. Denning, Ph.D.

Introduction

What do we know about the interlife? As with everything else dealing with the spiritual dimension there can be no proof about life between physical incarnations. However we do have a significant amount of circumstantial evidence for making certain assumptions about what to expect when we find ourselves very much alive but without a physical body.

A strong case in point may be found in Sharifa Karagulla's book, *Breakthrough to Creativity*.[6] Karagulla did research with two remarkably gifted psychics, one of whom claimed to attend university classes at night in the spiritual dimension. This psychic reported details of the lectures she attended. One day she reported that she had "seen" a young acquaintance at the lecture and when she asked him later what he did at night, he smiled and said, "Yes, I attend night classes in the other dimension. I saw you there, too."

Many past-life therapists have listened to clients who, while in a state of hypnosis, report frequent details of their purported experiences in the spiritual dimension between their physical earth lives. Numerous books have been written by psychics describing interlife events.[7, 8]

In my own practice as clients recall past lives in the therapeutic process, incidents in the interlife often emerge as part of their recall. The following three case histories illustrate this phenomenon:

Case 1. Commitment from the Interlife

This professional woman was a friend as well as a client. We had never discussed her marriage but I knew it was not happy. Her husband was one of the most negative men I had ever known. He denied any belief in God and yet he blamed God for his many misfortunes. He was a truly sour man and his face showed his suffering, for around his mouth he had deep lines that turned down and made him look angry all of the time. His forehead, also, was deeply lined.

My client had been doing some work with me to develop her clairvoyance. She was a loving, gentle, compassionate individual. To know her was to love her, and her life was devoted to helping others. She had been married for 10 years and we had been friends for most of those years. I had never heard a word of complaint or irritation or an unkind remark from her about anyone. Her husband never abused her physically, but I had heard him rant and complain many times, always implying that she was responsible for whatever was not going the way he thought it should. Her response was always one of gentle concern for his discomfort.

One day when she was in an altered state something prompted me to ask her a very direct personal question, "Why did you marry your husband?" Her response surprised me. She said that when they had been in college she was often in the same classes with him and he pursued her for dates. She thought she had no interest in the relationship and often discouraged his advances, but he was persistent, and one evening when he again proposed to her, she heard herself accepting. She told me that she had never understood why she said "yes," and when she said it she had a sad, sinking feeling in her solar plexus. Through the intervening 10 years she had often wondered why she had been impelled to marry him and she wondered sometimes whether she could live her entire life with this negative man. She assured me, however, that she would never leave him, for she did not believe in divorce.

I then suggested that in this altered state she go into her interlife, the time between physical incarnations, and ask her higher mind to tell her why she had attracted this difficult experience. She was quite agreeable to this, and in a few seconds she began describing herself in the spirit world. She said she was very happy there and had no wish to come back to a human expression, but she met this unhappy soul who had lost contact with his spiritual source. He was frightened and seeking help. She had promised him that she would come back and be his wife and help him find God. She added that she had not realized how difficult it was going to be.

When she sat up following the session she stated simply, "It is not important whether I am happy in this marriage or not. I came in with a commitment to this person and I must keep that promise. I have stayed with him but I have not been the loving wife I should be, and he has felt my emotional withdrawal and so he feels unloved and abandoned."

The transformation in this man was quite remarkable. My own husband had no knowledge of the experience between my client and me, but he expressed surprise and wondered what had changed the man, who had bought a small powerful sports car and a sporty cap and drove around thoroughly enjoying himself. He invested in an expensive model train set, put it up in his living room and played with it by the hour. But the greatest change was in his attitude. He smiled often, displayed a delightful sense of humor, and one Sunday shortly afterward said, "Let's go to church today."

I have shared this case for one reason. It is a perfect illustration of the power of thoughts or attitudes. Regardless of what we say, our feelings speak louder than words. The wife never crossed him, was totally tolerant of his verbal abuse, but she could not love him and he felt that. After her insight she extended genuine compassionate love for the soul that was seeking help, and it transformed him as he responded to that unconditional love.

The couple have been married many years now and enjoy a rich life in their retirement. They travel extensively and pursue their individual hobbies and interests. That session has never been mentioned between us except on one occasion. We were having lunch about twenty years later and the subject of her marriage came up. My friend looked very pensive and said simply, "I have always been amazed that one simple insight could so totally change a person's life."

Case 2. A Cardinal's Assignment

When this client sat down in my lounge she banged the arms of the chair and screamed, "I can't stand it any longer. I can't go on living like this. There is no God, Jesus Christ is a fraud. I have prayed, I have studied the Bible, I have had private therapy, group therapy, I have meditated, and nothing does any good." She paused and stopped screaming and said, "You are my last hope."

I proceeded to listen to her history, which included a twenty-year marriage that she wanted to terminate but could not because she did not want to admit she had made a mistake. It seemed that everything in her life brought defeat. She had been successful three or four times in her business ventures, but just as they seemed to be going well something would occur and she would go broke and have to start all over again. She had three children who had given her considerable pain as they grew up, though at the present time only one was in trouble—with drugs.

She was well-educated, with a college degree which included a sizable number of units in psychology, so we could converse in the same language. I explained past-life therapy and how I thought it could help her. She said she thought she was a good hypnotic subject and she was quite willing to try anything that might get to the bottom of her problems.

Through the first three sessions we worked on her marriage and her relationship with her children. Past-life experiences uncovered her constant feeling that she could not be wrong—at least she could not admit being wrong. Her husband had tried to terminate the marriage for a number of years but she could not face having failed in the relationship. This insight gave her the strength to leave him. However, she realized that there was something she was still not facing, which manifested in a deep feeling of guilt.

When she arrived for the fourth session I suggested she face the original source of the guilt and assured her that whatever it was, she could handle it now. She was a good trance subject and almost immediately began describing a man in a beautiful and ornate garment with a tall headdress. She said he was a cardinal in the Catholic Church and she then began speaking in the first person. "I am that person." In considerable detail she described herself listening to complaints and accusations brought before her, and in a shocked voice she said she was sending many people to the rack. She identified the period as the Spanish Inquisition.

I asked her how she felt about torturing people, and she said she did not have to carry out the sentence. She never saw the individuals tortured. She admitted to a deep feeling of revulsion at times, but she explained that after all she was the voice of the church, and the church had ordered these punishments for anyone who defied the holy dictates. Had she refused to carry out these orders, she herself might have been killed, or at least excommunicated.

When she described her role she was very upset and said, "No wonder I am still feeling guilty about something. I was responsible for killing all those people. No wonder I am still feeling guilty. I *should* suffer for that!"

When clients have been perpetrators of pain on others in the past, it is not always easy to help them forgive themselves. In this case, where her past deeds had been so horrendous, I knew there had to be a different approach, so I explained that no human being has that much power over others unless there is a higher motive in progress. I asked her mind to tell her the purpose of the Inquisition.

She was silent for a moment and then she sounded very surprised as she reported that the Catholic Church was so corrupt at that time that the Inquisition was necessary to revolutionize the church. Then she said, "Now I understand how I could do that," and she described seeing herself in her spirit body meeting with a group of spirits in the interlife and discussing the situation and the condition of the church at that time. They all decided someone had to go back to an earth life and play that role. She was selected because they agreed that she was highly developed in spiritual understanding and she would be strong enough to carry out that assignment. The problem for her had been that she lost an awareness of her spiritual purpose, and in that personality she had carried a heavy burden of guilt which she had never been able to reconcile, even though she had been working on it through a number of lives.

She left the session expressing a tremendous sense of relief and two weeks later called me to report that the guilt feeling was gone and she was feeling like a whole person. In addition, her business had improved markedly and even her relationship with her children seemed to be working out well. A two-year follow-up found her a happy and successful woman.

Case 3. A Surprise Interlude

A teenage boy was brought to me by his mother in the hope that we could uncover the block he had to studying. He was an intelligent young man, but he could not seem to do well in school regardless of how hard he tried. He had some strange habits that she reported to me. From the time he had been a small boy he had collected bullets and had them in rows on shelves in his room. He insisted on wearing cowboy clothes and as a small boy carried toy guns in a holster. He was determined to study at the sheriffs' academy and as soon as he was old enough he was accepted there for training. When instructed in shooting at targets, he objected to holding the gun out in front of his body and said he could only shoot if he could pull guns from holsters at his side.

He was an excellent trance subject and on the first session saw himself standing at a bar with his friends. He reported that he had a reputation for being fast with a gun. As we explored that life he went back to his days in a country school under a harsh school master who whipped him if he did not have his work done properly and often told him how stupid he was. He was eventually kicked out of school and told he was too dumb to learn. Shortly after that expulsion his parents were killed by Indians and he was left on his own. He joined a band of gunfighters who robbed trains and banks and eventually, when he was only in his late teens, he became famous for his fast draw in a gunfight.

This experience explained his present problem with school, and his study habits did improve. In his second therapy session his first response to my questioning was, "I am dizzy, I am very dizzy." I asked a number of questions before he finally responded, "They are hanging me. I am hanging at the end of a rope."

I asked him to go to the moment of his death just before his spirit left his body and tell me his last dying thought. He said he realized he had not been a good person. Then I suggested he get out of his body and tell me what happened next. He said he was going to stay around for awhile to see what they did with his body. When he was satisfied that it was taken down and buried, he went on to describe, in much more detail than most people, what happened next.

He said three of his former gunslinging friends had appeared to meet him but he was surprised that the Virgin Mary had not come to welcome him. He had been under the impression that she greeted newly departed souls. He then told me that his friends said that was not the way it was, that the Virgin Mary did not greet newcomers. He then continued his conversation with me, saying that he saw a light out in the distance and he decided it was probably Jesus so he would go into that light and perhaps learn more about where he was and what he should do next. Again his friends told him he was wrong; it was not Jesus but it was someone who could help him, so he went toward the light.

There was a pause in his report to me and he made a clucking sound indicating that something was wrong. I asked him what was going on. He said that the person in this light told him that he had surely messed up his life this time. So he was promising that he would do better next time. In fact he promised that when he came back he would be on the side of the law and see how that worked out. He then told me that he was going with this person, who assured him he would have help in adjusting to his new condition.

It was interesting that he had no interest in the police department, or being a policeman. In this frontier life lawmen were sheriffs and that was the impression he had carried back with him so that even as a boy he talked about being a sheriff when he grew up.

He was very pleased with his altered-state experiences. They had been real to him and he felt considerable satisfaction in understanding his fascination with western things and his desire to be a sheriff. This insight satisfied that interest enough so that he soon lost his desire for a sheriff's role.

Returning to the Interlife
As a Source of Healing

by

Winafred B. Lucas, Ph.D.

Introduction

What happens when a soul is so filled with anger, hatred, and fear that it rushes through the interim state without being able to perceive the Light or observe the justice of the events that it has just passed through? Is it possible to rush through the Light and not see it, to be exposed to wiser beings or one's own former family and friends and not be able to consider what they are saying, or perhaps not even see them, as one struggles to incarnate in order to get revenge? Everything in the interlife is for the education of such a soul, but can the soul shrug off the classroom and its wisdom? And caught in the inevitable web of frustration and suffering that it has woven for itself, is it possible later for such a soul to return in an altered state to that interim life and learn slowly what it could have learned before and must learn sometime?

Case: Giving up a Script of Food and Revenge

When Brad was 20 years old he came for help in shedding a mantle of depression, loneliness, and frustration. He hated his family, had few friends, and struggled constantly against an overwhelming need to eat. In spite of his strong commitment to exercise, this failure to control his eating left him discouragingly overweight and pudgy. Although gifted with superior intelligence he had dropped out of college after minimal achievement because he could find nothing intellectual that held his interest.

Brad brought three assets into therapy. He was able to trust enough so that in spite of slow growth and deep discouragement he retained faith that he could be helped. Also, he had perseverance, the ability to hang on and keep trying for over ten years. The third asset was his ability to go with almost no induction into an altered state of unusual depth. At such times he sensed the intricate details of past lives and lived them out with an emotionality that was surprising, emerging as it did out of a stolid, stubborn, seemingly unemotional personality. He was also able to go into the interlife, and with each return he gained additional insight.

Brad was born into an orthodox Jewish family. His father had not been happy about his prospective birth, and while *en utero* Brad heard his father constantly complaining about the economic pressure of a fourth child. The only consolation the father voiced was that since his own father had died two months before, a new son could be considered a replacement. The mother had been more ambitious. She had wanted as many children as possible to help replace people lost in the concentration camps, but she agreed that Brad was to be her last child. The father, who was economically insecure throughout Brad's early childhood, founded a food supply business and steadily prospered, so that by the time Brad came into therapy his father was already a millionaire and his net worth seemed to be escalating.

On a trip to Germany in his teens Brad had become briefly psychotic after visiting Dachau and because of his disorientation had to be taken to a police station. From the beginning of his therapy he constantly returned to his previous lifetime in that concentration camp. So immediate were his memories and so strong was his anger at what had happened to him there that it was almost as though he had rushed into this lifetime dripping with the dregs of his experience in the camps. The process of death and rebirth had contained no hiatus in which he could refresh himself—his anger over the camp experience was as immediate as though it had happened a few hours ago. He remembered every nuance and accompanied his narration with wild crying and rages. Many re-livings did nothing to relieve the stress.

Over the years his story remained consistent, and each repetition recovered new details. He remembered that in the late 30's he had been discriminated against at school as a young boy because he was Jewish and that when he was eleven he had finally been pushed onto a train to Dachau. His mother followed shortly afterward, and the rest of his family were eventually taken. Because the officers at Dachau were amused at the young boy's desperate claim that he could entertain, they kept him from the extermination showers and used him as a sexual pawn and plaything. At first he allowed this because it meant he would have food and live, but he became an object of contempt to the other Jewish prisoners. Finally, after several years his mother was killed as a result of an intervention on his part to try to make life easier for her. He was forced to retrieve her body from the gas chamber and put it in an oven for burning. He rebelled and as a punishment was deprived of food. He had no support system from either Jews or Nazis, and emaciated with hunger he was thrown on a pile of corpses in a ditch to die. His last thoughts were of vengeance and food.

As many times as we went over his last thoughts, it was always the same.

P: *I'll never trust anybody again. I'll never let anybody get close to me again. And food. I want food. Food and revenge. You took my mother away—made me disentangle her and put her in the oven and then look at her. You ground your cigarette butts into me. You made a monkey out of me. I'll get you, you bastards! (Violent sobbing and tears.)*

On his first visit to the interlife Brad was aware of nothing except his choice of a father. He rushed through (actually the interval was about nine years) and chose a father who was going to become a food wholesaler so that he would never be hungry again. He saw no teachers there and did not reflect or learn. In an earlier past life in the 12th century as Rolf he had been unbearably cruel, and for moments in the interim state he sensed a connection, a balancing, but easily lost this insight and returned to rage at what he had gone through.

The one area where he became increasingly softer was his concern for his mother in that life. She was a different soul from his current mother, who is narcissistic and habitually depressed, caught in a marriage that gives little to nourish her. The mother in that life was wise and loving. Gradually feelings came through for her, though with them also came intense guilt for what he assumed was his part in her death. Returns to the interlife began regularly to include her, and Brad could hear but not heed her advice.

T: *See if you can recover more impressions about the interlife. Do you see anyone you know?*

P: *I go to join other souls floating around. I ask them about their experiences. I circle around checking out the camp. Then I go to meet my mother. I apologize for what I did.*

T: *Does she say anything to you?*

P: *She holds me close in her arms and hugs me and says, "It wasn't your fault. It's good to be with you again."*

T: *Do you believe her?*

P: *I guess I'm kind of confused. She's holding my head real tight to her breast. I told her that I felt if I hadn't said anything, maybe she would have made it.*

T: *What does she say to that?*

P: *She says that it wasn't in the cards anyway. I say she had a good position in the sewing room and maybe she would have made it.*

T: *What is her answer to that?*

P: *She says, "Now go and find the rest of your family and speak to them." I go off to find the rest of my family. My sister—they turned her into a field whore and a soldier wanted to have intercourse with her and she slapped him across the face and he shot her. She was 14.*

T: *What happens next?*

P: I take a little time out to regroup myself and analyze things. I want to go back to my mother but she suggests that I try to work things out by myself. I ask her if she is rejecting me because of what happened in the camp, but she says it is only that I won't listen to her advice. I find Boris. He was on the same train with me to the camp. He says I need to forgive for my spiritual growth so I can move on and grow. Those aren't the answers I want to hear. I want to hold onto my hate. I just rebel against everyone.

T: What lesson did you choose for this lifetime?

P: I didn't choose a lesson. I wanted to strike back and eat.

T: Why do you suppose you chose these parents?

P: I chose my father because he had the food business. And my mother seemed to be a caring person.

The concepts of forgiveness and lessons that Brad talked about in the interlife were not concepts he thought of or would have considered in his conscious state. They were not included in his philosophy of the space-time world. He struggled with them in the interlife experience but would not address them when he had left the altered state.

In the following interim experiences the judges appeared. He projected onto them his own current conceptions and at first gave them short shrift. We entered the interlife by first returning to his death in the camp.

T: What is your last thought and feeling?

P: I will get even somehow. I will never trust anybody again. I'll never let anybody get close again for two reasons. People I trusted let me down, and being close physically is like being on this heap of corpses—it's insufferable. I'll always be on guard. I will have the bread I want. I will come back and haunt these people.... It's awfully cold out here.

T: Where are you?

P: Floating around. I'm going to the heavens and I'm going to give whoever is in charge of this bullshit experience a piece of my mind. I'm going to take someone apart piece by piece.

T: Do you find anyone to say this to?

P: There's a jury of old men, a panel. These are the guys I want. I tell these guys I resent the whole thing.

T: What do they say to that?

P: They tell me that I dished out things in this life and in other lives and they've decided to give some back to me.

T: Is it true that you did some things yourself?

P: Yeah (dismissing the confrontation lightly). Then I say, "What's my next assignment? What do I do now? You've devastated my spirit." They say, "Maybe you need some food. If you're interested, we have this lifetime coming up. But perhaps you should have a breather." But I'm impatient. I don't want to hang around with these old guys. I'm young.

T: What happens?

P: We work out a compromise. I wait ten years. I eat some food, try to regroup. I think they come from the old school—an eye for an eye and a tooth for a tooth. They say they let me off easier than I had let others off—I didn't get hung or cut the way I made others suffer. I just sort of petered out.

T: *What do you do during this time?*

P: *I just hang out pissing and cussing. They don't let me into this lifetime for a while. I get tired of horseshitting around. I know it's all tests and games anyhow, so why should I trust anybody?*

In one interlife experience Brad met a crowd of people who had died in the camps because he had informed on them in order to find favor with his captors and get something to eat.

T: *What do they say?*

P: *They call me the camp spy and say I ratted on them. I wish I hadn't been so quick to sell out. (Deep sobbing.) I didn't give much thought. I messed up a lot of other people's lives and their families. I didn't give much thought to how much havoc I could create. Their lives and their families were worth something, too. I wasn't the only one who counted. Other people counted.*

T: *Could you tell them that?*

P: *I want to say I'm sorry. I wish I could have thought ahead (constant crying). I tried to sacrifice your lives for me and it didn't work, anyhow. I caused all of you to lose your lives and your loved ones. Please don't judge me and make me an outcast. I'm sorry. I truly am. I wish I wouldn't have done it. I was just a dumb little 11-year-old. I couldn't think of you people.*

What do you want from me? What can I give you? It's awfully scary when you're an 11-year-old with bayonets pointed right at me and German Shepherd dogs and all sorts of scary stuff. Please don't condemn me. I know that because your mother died and your father died, I guess that makes me responsible for their deaths. I'm not a murderer. Please don't call me a murderer. Maybe it would have been better for me to die back there than to go through this living hell. If I had known, I would have given up my life back then.

T: *How do they respond to what you are saying?*

P: *They're spitting on me and throwing rocks on me and judging me— because I'm a murderer and a traitor. I sold out. I sold out for some bread. I traded human lives for some goddam bread (deep wild crying.) I'm a traitor. They've turned their backs on me. They don't want anything to do with me. They want me to be outcast and alone. They've walked away....*

I'm to be alone. I'm to be in solitary confinement for the rest of my life. (Deep uncontrolled sobbing.) I'm to be disconnected and disassociated.

T: *Is that the way you feel in this life?*

P: *This solitary confinement is killing me. There's no parole. No time off. No time off for good behavior. Your sins are unpardonable. Mother was right in this lifetime when she called me a Nazi-Jew killer. I didn't stand up in 1979 in the temple because my back hurt. And I broke fast on top of it.*

T: *How do you feel about where you are now?*

P: *Nobody you approach will be there for long. If for some reason somebody likes you, they'll die or move away. Nobody's there. How does it feel, Buddy? Get used to the feeling!*

T: *Where are you now?*

P: *I am alone, sitting on the dirt of the camp, with my head between my knees. I'm desolate, with nothing around. I've always wondered why in this lifetime in a similar situation it feels so natural and at other times it feels so hellish. And sometimes it vacillates.*

T: *Is there anything more you want to say to yourself?*

P: *You want to eat, huh? You want food? You are sentenced to be a prisoner of food as well. You'll have all the food you want. In order to help you with the isolation process you will make yourself grotesque from fat. You will begin to self-destruct your body. If the isolation doesn't do it, the food will. It will make it impossible for people to like you. They'll never get to know you. They'll never get to know the selfish you that thinks only about himself.*

Are you feeling a little depressed by now? You should be. Don't worry about dying young. You won't. That would take away our pleasure of getting back at you. We want you around for a long time. If you step in front of a Mac truck, it won't kill you!

Brad and I spent a long time processing this session, many months, in fact. We worked toward the realization that the purpose of the experience had been realized because he was gaining compassion. He had been punished enough. He could now release his guilt and get on with his life. He did not need to overeat to punish himself for taking Nazi bread or because he had starved in that lifetime. I helped him make affirmations about a truer state of being, but he was as yet uncomfortable with these and continued to run himself down. I tried to help him reverse this by taking time while bringing him back at the end of an altered state to put in suggestions for serenity and joy, but he could not accept them at that time or connect with them as something he could have, and he remained isolated and deeply lonely.

In the intervening years I had him work with a male therapist who was successful in assisting patients to organize their lives and work toward a goal, and during this time Brad finished college with credible scholarship but not much involvement. Meanwhile, he had been a salesman for his father's company, something at which he was gifted, but he continued a bitter feud with his father, who met his scathing verbal attacks by retiring under a shell, although allowing the paychecks to continue. Once Brad tried leaving his father's company and starting out on his own, but his easily triggered anger and his inability to get along with anyone quickly sabotaged this, and if subsistence paychecks had not been coming his way, he would have had a hard time. Eventually he returned to his father's business, where he was made a vice-president but given little responsibility or power. In retaliation he continued to treat his father with the anger he had turned on the judges in the interim state. His frustration at work was intensified by a dramatic creative flair set in the matrix of his basically gifted intellectual endowment, and when his company refused to honor his innovative ideas, his anger escalated.

Brad was particularly depressed by his inability to get a girl friend. He did not connect this with his failure to trust or care or be willing to be close, and though we often explored this intellectually, any beginning insight melted into thin air. But surprisingly, while in a restaurant in New York, he met a beautiful Parisian girl Suzette, who became drawn to him for his wit and energy. Many trans-Atlantic calls later and after a number of visits back and forth from Paris and the United States and even to Brazil, where Suzette's father lived, the two became engaged. Brad's anger had become muted enough to allow this but not muted enough to keep him from putting rocks in the path of the relationship. Brad complained that Suzette vacillated between enjoyment of being with him and a judgmental and critical attitude, which was exactly the way he treated her.

Following this we went into an interim state where Brad spent most of his time with his mother of that life. The sobbing that flooded out whenever he talked about her was unusually racking and desolate.

P: *I guess for so long I've felt bad for what I thought I did to you. And I felt I didn't deserve love or support. I've felt lonely for so long. It comes up in my dreams. I've tried to cure my loneliness by substituting food, by running from one group to another, by collecting phone numbers, by books and tapes, by being and doing and having. I'm trying to turn everybody into my parents. I was kind of hoping maybe you could help me out with some advice or some words of wisdom. I've been chasing after whatever for so long that I don't know what I'm chasing. I'm like the Coyote always chasing the Road Runner. He didn't know why he was chasing.*

T: *Does your mother say anything?*

P: *"I'm with you all the time and I love you and the first thing you need to understand is that you need to love yourself before anything good can happen to you. In the camps it was a losing situation."*

T: *What does your mother say about her death?*

P: *"Naturally I would have liked to have continued my family life and raised you up. The whole thing was a disappointment but sometimes things don't work out the way you want. I think both of us learned a tremendous lot in this experience. We learned compassion and humility."*

T: *What does she think would help you?*

P: *I need trust and discipline, follow-through, consistency, structure, commitment, persistence, balance, assertiveness, motivation.*

T: *Ask your mother if she has thoughts about Suzette.*

P: *She says that I have to reassure her about my caring because some of the criticism comes because she's not secure. I need to keep my weight down and keep physically fit. I must clean up my place for her, become more proficient in French and Portuguese, try to honor her point of view while holding onto mine. I need to set a model of being honest.*

Meanwhile, though in his outer life Brad remained belligerent in his father's plant and suspicious of Suzette and her motives, something in him was softening. Although he started out in our next foray into the interlife with the same pugnacious attitude he had shown before, he now exposed himself to more interactions with others and listened to what was told him, though usually not agreeing. To induct him into the interlife I always used regression to his death in the camp, and each recalling brought out new details.

> P: *I really loved Mummy. (Deep sobbing.) I remember being on the outside of the shower banging on the walls, knowing what was going on inside. They made me put her body in the ovens. It was then I turned on them and the system. I refused to be an entertainer. I refused to retrieve bodies. I became an outcast. I was no longer in their favor. The Jews in camp wanted nothing to do with me—they said I was on my own. The officers did, too. They made me look at her ashes. The morning had started out so nice. We had seen each other and she had kissed me. It turned out so horrible. It wasn't supposed to happen. (Wild crying.) They wouldn't feed me any more. As I got too weak and was just laying down, they took me and threw me in this pit on top of the skeletons.*
>
> T: *What were your last thoughts?*
>
> P: *(Repeats almost exactly his feelings of wild rebellion and intention to eat.) Let nobody or anything approach you. Be a total rebel. The system let you down once. Don't trust it. I float off and leave my body and I go and see Mummy and Boris, the magician who was on the train with me.*
>
> T: *What do you experience?*
>
> P: *I don't trust so I don't experience much. I find Boris over in the valley. He chose to go there. It's peaceful.*
>
> T: *Could you talk with him?*
>
> P: *I tell him I'll never trust again and my mission is to eat and take revenge. He tries to talk to me and say this isn't spiritually appropriate. He says, "I've never let you down. I must tell you you're on the wrong track and you can't do this." It wasn't what I wanted to hear. I wanted encouragement to go forward with my plan. He pleads with me, "Please put your sword down now." I say some horrible things I should never have said—I accuse him of being weak. I insult him horribly (wild crying). I shouldn't have said that.*
>
> *But I think Boris was wise enough and solid enough in himself to not get affected by the horrible things I said. Then I go to seek out Mummy. I tell her of my encounter with Boris. She says Boris was right—I should listen to him. I tell her they must pay for the horrible things and I am the one to administer the retribution. My mother says, "You're very stubborn!" I tell my mother it's up to me to enforce retribution. My mother says to me,*

"Don't do these horrible things!" I say I must take revenge for what they did to her.

T: *What do you do then?*

P: I decide to take a few years out to plan just what I want—ten years of plotting and scheming. I must choose—I choose a mother who loves me and I love her—a different mother but they do look alike.

T: *How does it work out?*

P: I knew she would help indulge me in my food. All I wanted was food and revenge.

T: *How did it work out with your father?*

P: There were problems. I guess in my anxiety to be sure I had food, I overlooked the treatment I would receive. Both of my parents had strong roots in Judaism, so I knew I would be coming into a religion where I could better take revenge. I thought that was a unique combination—heavy Jewish background and food. In my opinion this was the best combination. But I don't think my father ever wanted me. My mother did.

T: *Were there any people in that interim experience from whom you could learn things?*

P: I wasn't open to any learning. That wasn't part of my game plan. There was a rabbi who tried to talk to me, but I fluffed him off. I felt not wanted.

T: *Did anyone help you think about your relationship with women?*

P: I didn't think about marrying. I don't want any goddam corpses hanging around me. Who wants to get married! That's a booby trap. Who's going to get trapped with a corpse?

T: *What about body contact when you were an infant? Did you nurse?*

P: No body contact with corpses! Strictly business. I had a nurse I liked because she brought in the food. Everything was planned...I made sure I got pneumonia. They wouldn't let me be—tried to cramp my style. This was a part I didn't plan, that every time I tried to assert myself I would be knocked down.

T: *How has this attitude worked?*

P: I don't think it's got me very far. But it has protected me.

T: *How can you relate to Suzette if you don't want to be close?*

P: My mission was to be angry and criticize her and she has a lot of anger, too, and criticizes. Part of me wants to cling for safety to people. And other times people are corpses and I have no time for corpses. But I can't stay this way or things won't work out.

T: *Can you ask you Higher Self how to change?*

P: One can change. I don't know how to let anyone help me, though.

The images of the judges became clearer as Brad returned again and again to the interlife, and his interaction with them became more involved and softer. He began to listen and grudgingly even to respect them, though he found them tough and crusty. One of them he described as resembling Gavin McCloud.

P: *These judges see me as having a chip on my shoulder. But maybe they have more wisdom than I think. This one is old and hardened, but he's interested in my best interest. He tells me, "I've been that route, kid—I know all about getting even, but I know it's a spiritual cul-de-sac. Take advantage of all your gifts. Remember the old adage, Good living is the best revenge."*

T: *What do you think about that?*

P: *It looks like what he says is true, but I don't know how to relate to his world. I have an idea, but I'm afraid of what's out there. I don't feel secure.*

T: *Does your mother have anything to say today?*

P: *She says, "You should drop all you anger. You're throwing your life away."*

T: *Let yourself feel all the goodness and wisdom in you mother.*

P: *She says I could do whatever I want if I could focus, and I can't focus because I'm angry.*

T: *Can you find an image of yourself?*

P: *I feel I'm a baseball diamond, all of it, the grass on the infield. Once out there you're everything, the pitcher, the field, the roar of the crowd, the wooden bat, the umpire, the glove with its smell of leather, the ball with its smell of horsehide. It's a total experience. The image seems so ingrained in me. I met Suzette because I went to see the Yankee stadium.*

At the same time that Brad was able to interact in more depth in the interlife, he recovered more and more details about his death in the camp, but the recovery of details and the re-enacting of intense feelings of distress that always accompanied them, for some reason did not mitigate the situation for him. In a regression some months later he became devastated again by the horror of his mother's death. He had been forced to push her body into the oven after her death in the gas chamber.

P: *The guards stand there. I want to die. I want to leave. I don't want to be conscious.*

T: *And then?...*

P: *Then I see one of them push the button. I open the door to try to get to her. They say, "Take a look inside!"*

T: *What do you see?*

P: *I see mostly ashes—and a few bones. Mommy is gone. (Deep keening.) I'm feeling a big mess-up.*

T: *What do you do next?*

P: *I throw up. I lie down in depression on my back. I stare into the sky.*

T: *How long does this last?*

P: *Several hours. I'm thinking how stupid I am, how everything I do is stupid. It's all my fault. I never know when to keep my mouth shut.*

T: *What happens next?*

P: *A guard finds me and kicks me in the ribs and asks what I'm doing lying down. I don't know if he knows what happened to my mother. I'm in a daze. I stumble around in a daze. They're looking for me because I was supposed to take the bodies out of the gas chambers, but I've wandered off. I'm supposed to go back to the gas chambers, but I'm feeling ill. I think I need to go to the infirmary. They tell me to go lie down on my bunk. I just lie there. Maybe because I am a child. Maybe they let me get away with lying there.*

T: *What happens next?*

P: *Eventually, after several days, I force myself to go back and do little odd jobs. I make up little odd jobs—wash the windows. I can't cope. I can't go on. I'm so empty, so lonely, so much of a failure and a fuck-up. I feel I must get back at these people. When I can, I commit little acts of vandalism, like breaking a window. I'm not getting too much food, and I just kind of fade away. Once in a while I try to dig around in the garbage cans. I'm so hungry. I want to eat.*

T: *How does it end?*

P: *I'm too weak to move and I wake up one morning in my bunk and I can't get up. So the guards come and they throw me down this long slide—horrible nightmare with all these naked bodies. I vow I'll never trust again, never. I'll never let myself get close to people, emotionally or physically. I'll get revenge. Anger is my motivator. Righteousness is my friend.*

Each time Brad went into the interlife he was without perception of the Light that so many dying experience. But he began to pause for more extended interchange with the judges and experienced an intensification of his feelings about his mother.

T: *Where are you now?*

P: *I'm in front of the supreme court justices in the sky.*

T: *What do they look like?*

P: *Old, wise, a little hard and toughened from life. They look at me like—"Did you learn the lesson, boy?" I ask them what lesson they are talking about. "The lesson about what it feels like to have pain inflicted on you?" I know they must be referring to when I was Rolf in the 12th century. I tell them this is a harsh and unfair way, and they answer, "Life is not always fair." I ask if they can help me find my mother and Boris, the magician.*

T: *What do they say?*

P: *They say they don't know if I'm ready to see my mother or Boris. I should spend more time reflecting. I tell them I must see my mother, so they summon my mother and Boris.*

T: *Do they come?*

P: *Yes. I tell my mother how sorry I am for what happened. My mother is wonderful. She holds no malice in her heart—she is so understanding. She's so pretty—wearing a crown and long auburn hair and a long white dress—and a scepter in her hand.*

T: *Is she ruling something?*

P: *(Ignoring the question.) She's angelic, very heavenly. She says, "Listen, my son, you must understand that I love you very much. You mustn't hold this against yourself. It was a learning experience."* She hugs me and embraces me and pulls my heart against her breast, a feeling I would gladly die for. She tells me that I should not be so embittered toward the Nazis—they were just accessory to the lesson and they will face a panel of judges. It is not for me to be the vigilante. It is enough for me to learn my lesson. I tell her that isn't good enough for what they did to her. She answers that I mustn't waste my time and my life—I must go on.

T: Does she convince you?

P: Not particularly. Next I go on to Boris. But first I ask Mommy if I can see her again. She says, "Anytime you want. You can always summon me." She gives me a kiss before she sends me on my way. She gives me a neck chain with Chi on it, which is Jewish for light. It's just like the neck chain my mother in this life gave me. I promise to keep it for all time.

T: Do you talk with Boris?

P: Boris tells me the same thing—I should let it go. These are not the answers I want to hear. I want to hear the people support me in taking revenge. I'm feeling like maybe Mommy and Boris have a lot of wisdom, but I'm having trouble seeing it.

　　A couple of judges on the board talk to me in a blend of compassion and sternness. "Take it from us—we've been around since the beginning—we know the principles. It's not for you to rewrite the principles. Things do not change."

T: What principles are they talking about?

P: In the end light and love prevail. Those that do evil are repaid— you can be sure of that.

T: How do you respond?

P: I'd like to leave the jail cell but it's scary.

T: Do you think you can?

P: I can try. I don't know if I have the strength but I can try.

T: Do you say anything to the judges?

P: I tell them, "I have decided to abandon my need for revenge and being a vigilante. I've decided to forgo all that and go on with my life." They all sort of nod their heads and hit the gavel. Case closed. They nod at each other in agreement.

T: What happens next?

P: If I'd only done that, I'd have chosen different parents. I chose a father who had lots of food, but my parents are not nurturing.

For a week Brad felt better, but then his depression began to return, and we went back to the interlife. Even here he had backslid slightly and had to recover himself. The session was initiated by a dream in which he was being thrown into a pit with skeletal-like things. Many of the limbs were truncated and came to a point, and the bodies festered with growths that resembled fungus balls. We used the dream as an induction.

T: Go into the feeling in the pit.

P: I'm feeling grossed out by this. I don't understand these disgusting growths. I don't want to be in the pit. I hate being in the pit. I feel trapped by this flesh and growths and truncated limbs. What am I doing here? I want to get out of here...I'm so hungry. I'm hungry and I'm angry. Very disappointed. How could I be stupid enough to let this happen to me? I should go get something to eat. I must go into the next dimension. I must have nourishment. I must prepare myself to come back and take revenge. And I must recruit others. It will be a great effort.

T: Is one of the corpses you?

P: Not the truncated ones but I think one of the others.

T: What do you do in the next dimension?

P: There's Mommy and there's Boris.

T: Are they coming to meet you?

P: I think they're coming to meet me because they know what I have on my mind. Both have grabbed me by the arm and they say, "Stop! We know what you have on your mind. Stop! Release it. It isn't worth it. We can see it in your eyes. It isn't worth it." But I know I want to take revenge and seek out as many Nazis as I can and destroy them.

T: Do you listen to them?

P: No. Unfortunately I'm very pigheaded. They tell me to release my anger, and I ask, "Do you mean when they sexually abused me, hung me upside down, killed my mother, made me put her in the oven?" I ask them if they want me to drop this, turn the other cheek. I tell them I don't find these acts pardonable. I lay there on a pile of corpses rotting with someone's feet in my face. Cold. Hungry. I tried to be nice to these people. I tried to do the right thing. (Violent crying.) They separated me from my family. They made me untangle corpses in the oven. They beat and tortured people in front of me. I'm going to get them for this—nobody's going to stop me!

T: What do your mother and Boris say?

P: They're trying to implore me, beg me not to do it. I hug them both and tell them to get out of my way. I have a mission. Anger is my motivator. They laughed when they told me to put my mother in the oven—those fuckers! (Violent sobbing.) We'll see who laughs last!... First thing—I make up my mind I will never be hungry again. First order of business is eating. I eat everything.

T: Even here in the interlife?

P: Yes. I have prime ribs of beef, duck l'Orange, all kinds of breads—rye bread with lox and cream cheese, all kinds of cheeses, omelettes, toast and butter and lots of jam. (Sobs.) I'm trying to fill myself. I've eaten everything. I'm out of control. I can't stop eating. Help me! (Wild sobbing.) Get away (gesture)—I don't want to see food again.

T: What's happening?

P: I'm throwing up. I ate too much. I'm lying down. I'm lying in bed. I'm staring upwards.... Now I recuperate and I feel...I feel...I'm afraid of food. I don't know how to put it in proper perspective. I see the effects of sugar. Come and get me! Come here! You can have donuts, ice-cream, apricot

> *pastries. You always love the Jewish bakeries—cherry pies, lemon pies, maybe fried chicken. I always love breaded things....*

For several pages Brad dictated a list of foods. Since his father's company carries over 4000 items and he had sold them all, he had a good resource. When he stopped to take a breath, new ideas would come and he would start out again.

P: *I love food. I can hardly wait for my next meal. Wouldn't it be nice if life were one continuous meal? Wake up in the morning and just eat. Cupcakes. How could I forget garlic bread? Eating and throwing up. And I'm trying to check out books on the art of war. Ice cream—how did I forget ice cream? (Names 41-plus flavors.) Right now I'm eating a turkey drumstick. Eat and plan my strategy. I have to come back in this world. I've got to choose parents who are appropriate so I can have food and a means to attack and be aggressive....*

I go around and try to do a little rabble rousing, but I don't seem to have much success. Perhaps I should take that as a hint.

T: *What about your committee?*

P: *I've already dealt with them. Kind of a huge panel there. It appears there are nine men and four women—total 13. I tell them what my plans are and why I'm doing them. They say the reasons why I went through such things are karmic—because of Rolf. My taking revenge is a total tangent from what I have to learn.*

T: *Do you listen?*

P: *No. It is more important to me to get even for the oven.*

T: *What about the fact that the judges say there will be karmic consequences?*

P: *I didn't think about this. I thought I had to stick to what I had determined. I'm still trying to think how I could get even and still avoid karma. They explain to me that all those people in the camp will get their own karma, and taking care of it is not my role. They're trying to make it very clear to me that it's not up to me to play the role of judge and executioner.*

T: *What happens?*

P: *My new decision or the old one?*

T: *The new one is the only one that counts.*

P: *If I give up my old goal I have nothing. I will die. I will cease to be.*

T: *Ask the judges if this is true.*

P: *They say no. I could become very successful, which terrifies me. I don't know how to relate to success. To be successful would equal death.*

T: *What about the wife and children you were thinking about?*

P: *I tell them that a wife and children is a dead weight, is a ball and chain.*

T: *You don't want a wife and children?*

P: *No. They say it depends on how you see it. But it doesn't feel right. But I don't want to be alone.*

T: *It sounds as though you don't want to marry Suzette, so don't put the blame on her. What do you decide?*

P: *The jail cell is safe. And not being successful.*

T: *What about the revenge motif?*

P: *I don't know if I could live life another way, built around love and success and being close to people, having a wife and children. Relating.*

T: *Do you have the will to let go of the revenge motif?*

P: *Yes. If I could have a wife and child and not do evil onto them, I could feel better. I'm afraid to open myself.*

T: *How do you feel about food now?*

P: *Does that mean that my project at the plant wouldn't go? No more prime rib?*

P: *It means being willing to allow what is appropriate to come about.*

Shortly after this session we went to Brad's prenatal period, where he entered into his mother's thoughts. Not surprisingly, she was occupied with thoughts of food (in reality she is considerably overweight). She felt empty and was trying to fill herself with food and her pregnancy, but she dreaded the arrival of this fourth child when she could hardly cope with the first three. She felt especially handicapped by a husband "who wasn't worth a shit."

Brad tried out a bit of vengeance at the time of his birth.

P: *I am one day from being four weeks late. I'm very angry about things. I'm feeling—this is one way I'm getting even. You didn't want me so I'll show you—being around me with chocolate and prunes and cigarettes! Now it's my turn. See how you like it!*

T: *What were mother's thoughts while eating while she is carrying you?*

P: *"I hate myself for doing these things to my body and my unborn child but I'm out of control."*

T: *How do you feel in the birth?*

P: *I feel trapped. It's a familiar pattern. I feel like I'm back in the pits, back in the Iron Mary (refers to another lifetime). I'm not sure I want to come out. I sure as hell don't trust anybody out there. My birth is slow, but eventually I come out. The doctor says it's about time. My mother is perspiring very heavily. My mother holds me. I didn't think she was that interested to have me, but I guess she had mixed emotions.*

Brad's perception of his mother's thought, "I'm out of control," mirrored his own feeling of helplessness in dealing with food, and we spent time helping him to see that these were his mother's thoughts and he did not need to take them over. He remained unconvinced, since the program for food that he had put in at the time of his camp death was so strong.

In our last session to date Brad came in with the same negative attitude toward his father and his father's henchman Dennis. Still there was something different about him. The 35-year-old little boy seemed to be disappearing and in his place was emerging faintly a strong and balanced adult. It was hard to see how this could be when Brad still complained about his loneliness, his problem with food, and the crookedness of Dennis. But his tone about Suzette was different. He had stood up to her for his right to be himself, and she had accepted this and apparently even respected him for it, as she was contemplating coming over to try out a living arrangement with him. It was clear that he had begun to take to heart the insistence of the interim judges that her behavior was largely motivated by her insecurity, and there were glimmers of protectiveness as he talked about her.

Both Brad and I sensed that he should return to the interlife. Since he had never perceived the light that is so characteristic of most reports of entering this state, I made an especial effort to see if by any chance I might be omitting something that would help him see it, but he paid no attention to my questions and instead went immediately to the valley he had touched on several times.

> T: *What is the first thing you see in the interlife?*
>
> P: *Well, I had a dream. There was a special place like a purple valley. That's where I am now. Oriental women dressed in red are suspended under tree limbs by gravity—face down. It's a special place—music, singing, different. Just special. It seems like a valley. That's where you go (Violent sobbing.) when you go to try to heal yourself. (Deep crying continues.)*
>
> T: *(Gently.) Could you share your experience with me?*
>
> P: *I feel funny in my stomach. It is a place where all of the energy is an energy of love. It's a curtain of love and something spiritual that fills the air. It's very enveloping. It's song and music and light. It's very energetic here. There are many more souls and spirits. (Crying.) It's timeless. It's ageless. It's very spiritual. It has beautiful gardens.*
>
> T: *How are you feeling about it?*
>
> P: *Shall I trust it? Or is it very safe? It's very special. I start to go down a path and there is a sanctuary there and I walk through, and as I walk through, the Oriental women in red under the tree limbs bless me and welcome me. There is a kind of flutish music and the birds are chirping and singing.... I continue to walk down the path. It's a nice garden and yet simple, very well taken care of. I remember this in the dream. I don't remember how the dream ended. I think I was very impressed with the beauty of the whole thing.*
>
> T: *How are you feeling?*
>
> P: *I'm kind of afraid to expose myself and be open.*
>
> T: *It seems to require an act of will.*
>
> P: *How do I know they won't attack me?*
>
> T: *Perhaps you have to take a chance.*
>
> P: *I will to be open. (Long pause.)*
>
> T: *What is happening?*
>
> P: *(Sobbing.) Now all the spirits and souls have come toward me to...(Wild crying)...come rushing forward to me to embrace me. (Sobbing.)*
>
> T: *Do you feel they embrace because they care? Do you feel they love you?*
>
> P: *(Crying.) It seems as though they were waiting all along. It was up to me to see them and they would come.*
>
> T: *What happens now?*

P: *They have a blessing for me. They are being...appear to be doing something...I don't know.... It's just a dance, swirling around in a circular clockwise motion.*

T: *How do you feel as they do this?*

P: *Safe and protected.... I'm thinking about food and if I could release my love affair with food. It would be nice if I could put food in a proper perspective.*

T: *Perhaps you could ask them to help you.*

P: *They will help me. Perhaps they could help me enough to start a trend in the other direction.... It came to me in a dream I had about Satan. He was sitting in my car. The car began to shake violently even though the motor wasn't on. Something about Satan.*

T: *Ask the people in the Valley about it.*

P: *One of the guys on the committee—he came to the Valley. He says, "It's a lot of the bad or negative energy that has carried over from the camps." They are a lot of my fears. Some anger, repressed anger.*

T: *What does he suggest?*

P: *I should be—I have good reason to be secure about the future. I should focus more on the desired results, not on worrying about failing. I should forget about my father and Dennis. They do not figure in the future. I shouldn't any longer worry about my powers. I have always been afraid of my own self and my powers. I have worried about whether I would do any harm with them, but I shouldn't worry. It is not in me to do that. It's time to stop worrying. It is time to accept my talents and start being the marvelous person I was meant to be.*

He says, "You have our blessing. The world has been waiting patiently. All you have to do is just be yourself. The world is waiting with open arms and you will be successful at anything you put your mind to. You have to focus. You have so many talents it is hard for you to focus. We will help. The going has been rough. We had to pick somebody tough like you who could go through this. The rewards are around the corner. There will be dividends for your tenacity. Times are turning. People will be appreciating your ideas more. It would be easy for you to throw in the towel but we know you won't."

T: *Would you like to ask him about Suzette?*

P: *He says, "Suzette has been scarred by the separation of her parents. As you have done in your life, she seeks much approval. Give it freely and openly to her. She needs it. In time it will help your development and her approach toward you.... I wonder if I could ask them for some help with my father. (To Guides) Would you help him see the light?... They say that he is a typical man but they will speak to him. I tell them I want him to respect me more. They say, "Don't worry about him. You are in the flow. Can't you feel it? You're developing a new product. Be careful not to become too obsessed with the project. Try to keep it in proper perspective. Whether or not your father chooses to support you emotionally won't ultimately affect your destiny. You can feel people warming up to your ideas."*

T: *How is the Valley appearing now?*

P: *It's purple with streaks of white mist.*
T: *Let us come back now into the space-time world, but as you come, bring the healing power of the Valley back with you. Bring balance, joy, and forgiveness.*

In this session Brad moved to a new level, and the change was so sudden after years of moving slowly, that I was taken by surprise. Evidently the last session had been a final stand to stay stuck, and having made the stand, he was able to let it go. The brightness that he had seemed not to see was finally perceived in the Valley. He defined this Valley as a place of healing, and certainly it was for him. For the first time he could let in love and simply and directly ask for help. Also for the first time, he could listen to positive things about himself, which for eleven years he had felt compelled to shut out.

When he left my office he seemed a new person, quiet and direct and confident. The innovative approach to representing merchandise that he was developing had taken on the quality of a vision. For the first time since I had known him he felt the strength to become independent of his father and move out on his own as a unique adult.

Following this session Brad's life moved into a time of challenge. Totally unexpectedly his father's business crashed into bankruptcy, apparently the combined result of the long-standing covert dishonesty of the Arab, who was second in command, and his father's resistance to updating his business practices. Equally precipitously Suzette married an Italian. Brad has faced these losses with surprising strength, almost as though he was relieved that life moved in to help him release the attachments he had outgrown. In spite of the pressures of the time he has been able to bring his weight under control and he is now seeking a new position with relative maturity and confidence. Some of the wisdom he contacted in the interlife has slipped but now there remains something radiant and healing to return to, a direct experience of wisdom and love to retrieve.

Chapter V

Conversations with the Unborn

If we look at life as a continuum, which the concept of reincarnation enables us to do, then a soul is not destroyed when an abortion is performed. A soul entering into the earth plane at this time is a being that has had prior existence and will have existence after this. This is not the only life, and if an abortion is performed, this is not the end for an entity, and it will not result in its losing a chance to express itself.

Gladys McGarey

The ability of the mother to communicate directly with her unborn child and the corresponding ability of that child to respond in a way that the mother can understand offer a powerful agent for the resolution of ambivalence regarding pregnancy and provide healing if the pregnancy is terminated. Dialogue with the unborn child, whether in thoughts, words, or images, allows the needs of both mother and child to be explored. Spontaneous miscarriages often follow upon such a dialogue where a decision has been reached mutually by neonate and mother that this is not an appropriate time for a child to be born.

Claire Etheridge

Bibliography

Chamberlain, David. *Babies Remember Birth*. Los Angeles, CA: Jeremy Tarcher, 1986.

Cheek, David. "Techniques for Eliciting Information Concerning Fetal Experience." Paper presented at the meeting of the Society for Clinical and Experimental Hypnosis, Los Angeles, California, 1977.

Findeisen, Barbara. "Rescripting in Pre- and Perinatal and Early Childhood Regression Work." *The Journal of Regression Therapy*, Vol. II, No. 1, 1988.

McGarey, Gladys. *Born to Live*. Phoenix, AR: The Gabriel Press, 1980.

————. "Let the Baby Decide," in *Venture Inward*, 1990.

Riley, Clara (Claire Etheridge). "Transuterine Communication in Problem Pregnancies" *The Journal of Pre- and Perinatal Psychology*, Human Sciences Press, Vol. 2;, Spring 1987.

Verney, Thomas. *The Secret Life of the Unborn Child*. New York: Delta Publ. Co. 1981.

Conversations with the Unborn

Introduction

The deadlock between pro-life and pro-abortion advocates places a premium upon finding an alternative viewpoint. A good place to start might be to question whether murder really takes place in an abortion, whether a soul can, in fact, be murdered. That seems a strange concept, but it is the implication in the argument of the pro-lifers. And if the soul cannot be murdered but what is destroyed is only the physical sheath that is being prepared for it, what happens to the soul? A hypothesis that the soul can choose another sheath would considerably modify the arguments of the pro-lifers.

My own induction into a new way of considering abortion began when my daughter broke her engagement, after discovering that her fiance was alcoholic, and then found that she was pregnant. She was not near enough to completion of her doctorate to be able to support a child or give it the necessary attention without sacrificing the years of study that she had already put in, so an abortion seemed to be the only alternative. At the time this occurred I took time off from my practice, went into an altered state, and addressed the child. I told it I was sorry that my daughter couldn't have it at this time, and I explained why she couldn't.

I had expected this to be a one-way conversation, but to my surprise I heard a peal of laughter and saw a little boy, who spoke to me joyously. "Don't worry! I intend to have Afton for a mother. I'll be back in two years!" I told my daughter about this, and when she became pregnant two years later with a sperm-bank baby, she confidentially announced that it would be a boy. At the end of her pregnancy, the radiant little boy I had seen two years before appeared.

This gave me the idea that perhaps it would be possible to dialogue with a soul before any abortion attempt and discuss the circumstances. At that time I felt that if the soul was insistent on being born, that should be enough to convince the prospective mother, but later I saw that the needs of the mother have to be weighed against those of the baby. The unborn child does not have all the choices, as pro-lifers of today might believe.

Later, in my practice I found that a prospective mother who has gone through an abortion and is grieving can dialogue with the soul whose body she has aborted and that healing can take place for both mother and aborted baby. Someday we may also routinely dialogue with unborn children who are wanted, in order to find out what they are like and to plan more adequately to be of help to them. This process, as it has been presented by Claire Etheridge, is simple. Following the lead of David Cheek,[1] David Chamberlain,[2] and Thomas Verney,[3] she introduced the idea of a dialogue process between the mother and an unborn child who is wanted, in order to initiate an early bonding.

As a result of my experiences, I felt that I had discovered a unique approach to resolving problems around abortion, but actually it was a discovery that had also been made by others. In the early 80's a scattering of therapists had had experiences similar to mine. Each of us had independently made the discovery that dialogue is possible with the unborn child and that such dialogue is healing to both mother and child. It was as though the consciousness of our time had become ready for this understanding to emerge.

One of the first therapists to initiate such a dialogue was Gladys McGarey of the A.R.E. Foundation in Phoenix. As early as 1980 she encouraged patients to engage in inner meditation on proposed abortions, and later suggested an active dialogue with the unborn child. She was the first to document that when inner resolution takes place, a spontaneous miscarriage often follows.[4]

Such an approach was developed independently by Barbara Findeisen, whose concern about the scars of abortion on adult patients led her to work on preventive measures.[5] About the same time, Helen Watkins became concerned because she found that ego-state development was impaired by attempted abortion, and she, also independently, wanted to take a preventive measure for the sake of the patient. Louise Ireland-Frey found evidence that aborted souls often hung around their mothers or other adults as obsessing entities, and she worked on a way to prevent this.[6] Claire Etheridge, as others had done earlier, sought an effective method of helping pregnant women come to an appropriate decision about abortion, and she encouraged dialogue with the unborn child and deepened the communication between mother and child.[7] All of these therapists found that when a satisfactory dialogue was made with the unborn soul, mother and unborn child were brought into harmony. In the case of a decision to have an abortion, often a spontaneous miscarriage followed.

We are only beginning to understand this experience. The idea of including an unborn child in the decision about abortion is still inconceivable to most people. One stumbling block is that therapists lack confidence that the unborn soul is available for dialogue. In actuality, it is not even necessary to go into a deep altered state in order to undertake such a dialogue—probably it could take place in a journal dialogue process such as that developed by Ira Progoff.[8] Most experiences suggest that the unborn soul is only too willing to be taken into consideration and will eagerly respond to questions and comments. Experience shows, also, that unborn souls are usually amenable to reason and are willing to leave if approached with love and clear statements of the situation that show that their birth is inappropriate at the time. One of the keys to resolution seems to be a loving but firm attitude on the part of the mother. Hugh Harmon reports on just such a situation in his article.

The next step may consist of developing techniques for helping the unborn soul back to the Light in cases of abortion. To date the focus has been largely on helping the mother by persuading the unborn soul to commit to leaving, but this approach may turn out to reveal a limited perception of what is needed for the good of both mother and child.

New Light on Abortion

by

Gladys McGarey, M.D.

Introduction

The important key to understanding abortion experiences lies in awareness of the spiritual and volitional factors involved. If there is communication, if there is a sought understanding of a life purpose, or at least the direction toward a life purpose, and if there is the awareness of the continuity of life and that the choices each person makes are either constructive or destructive, then when the choice is made, it will be right for that time and place.

If we look at life as a continuum, which the concept of reincarnation enables us to do, then a soul is not destroyed when an abortion is performed. A soul entering into the earth plane at this time is a being that has had prior existence and will have existence after this. This is not the only life, and if an abortion is performed, this is not the end for an entity, and it will not result in its losing a chance to express itself. With that in mind, the idea of having an abortion, though I would not personally choose it, is something that can be incorporated into one's concept of life so that abortion does not make a murderer out of the mother. This is a saner, more sensitive way to respond to the strongly polarized abortion issue.

The development of my current attitude toward abortion has been the result of sharing many experiences of those who have become aware of the consciousness of the fetus through personal experience. One early thrust in this direction was a mother's story about her four-year-old daughter, who not only recalled a previous lifetime but told her mother that there had been another time when she was "four inches long and in your tummy, but Daddy wasn't ready to marry you yet, so I went away. But then I came back." This referred to an aborted pregnancy that the mother had had before her marriage that only she and her husband and the doctor knew about. When the two parents did get married and were ready to have their first child, the same entity made its appearance. The child was saying, in effect, "I don't hold any resentments toward you for having had the abortion. I understood.

I knew why it was done, and that's okay. So here I am again. It was an experience. I learned from it, and you learned from it; so now, let's get on with the business of life." Though the child didn't have that kind of vocabulary, that was in essence what was being related by the mother.

There is an interesting follow-up to this account that I heard from the mother when her daughter, then 16, had become pregnant and decided to have an abortion. Previously the mother told her daughter that she would be willing to take the baby in her home. Then surprisingly, after the daughter's abortion, in spite of the fact that the mother had had a tubal ligation performed, she became pregnant. Her interpretation of what happened was that when her daughter had the abortion done, this same entity came into her in spite of her having had the tubal ligation. What this says to me is that if we're dealing with the continuity of life and real consciousness, a child like that could have understood the circumstances and realized that though the first option was not feasible, there was another option.

The experiences of the women with whom I have worked convince me that if the circumstances are such that it is really best not to continue the pregnancy, the soul is willing to go away and wait until things get better, in much the same way that a host may say to a guest who proposes a visit that it isn't the right time but six months later everything will be all right. The person can then agree to come back in six months or perhaps give up the idea of the visit. As conscious beings if we communicate with the baby we can tell it the circumstances and the baby can choose. I have come to see that abortion is frequently reasonable, understandable, and the "right" thing to do. If the entity really understands what is happening, and if the decision to have an abortion is made in an understanding, thoughtful manner, then the outcome is bound to be a constructive learning event.

Not only does approaching abortion in this way reduce guilt, but it has another positive outcome. When the nature of consciousness is understood, women are much less apt to use abortion as birth control because they are aware that they are dealing with a profound and significant event. Abortion is not something they can any longer undertake easily, so they are more careful that an unwanted pregnancy doesn't happen. And when having a baby would be destructive to everyone concerned, this approach offers an option that is not condemning. The process of abortion becomes in a sense a spiritual act, one coming from love, not just a mechanical thing.

Originally, in order to help patients tune into the consciousness of the fetus, I asked them to take time to write down all of their reasons and feelings for having an abortion and the reasons and feelings against it. I suggested that after that they should make the best decision possible for all concerned. Then they should go thoughtfully about the business of life, either after an abortion or without having had one.

I came to see that they could do even more; they could talk to the baby or write a letter or a song or do something to communicate. They could say something like, "Look, this is a lousy time. It'll be terrible for me; it'll be awful for you. Why don't we take a raincheck and see what will happen in the future?" What has sometimes happened is that when a mother has done this, she has aborted spontaneously.

I think communicating with the baby's father is often an important step because if he's going to be involved in the decision, then he needs to communicate with the baby, too. If the father is not a part of the situation, then the baby needs to know that, also. The mother could say something like, "Your Daddy is not going to be a part of this picture and it would be hard for us." Be truthful about what's happening and what the options are. Talk to the doctor about it, talk to the family, pray about it, contact a worthy counselor on it. But most importantly, communicate with the entity who is hovering, waiting to be born. Telling that individual what is happening and why it is happening moves the situation into accord with the life patterns and needs for all involved.

Case 1. Spontaneous Abortion

The following case helped me to develop a counseling approach to patients who come to me conflicted about whether or not to have an abortion. A 15-year-old girl came to the clinic one day, pregnant and distraught. She was still a child really, not ready to have a baby. This pregnant girl and her family were confused about what should be done. I suggested to them that they meditate on it, ask for dreams, and then let me see them again after they had come to a firm conclusion.

The return visit revealed that they had all come to the same decision— there should be an abortion; they all felt that was the best thing to do. I began the arrangements to have it done, but the next morning I got a call from the family telling me that the girl had aborted spontaneously. I checked her in the office and all was well.

Did the entity that was scheduled to come in get in on those plans and considerations that the family was making? One never knows in a drama such as this, but it makes one wonder. Perhaps that entity is in a holding pattern until the girl gets married and is ready to have her first child. Perhaps, on the other hand, the experience was what was needed, and that particular entity will find what is appropriate elsewhere. The story has fascinating implications. Perhaps there is a spontaneous release mechanism that comes into operation when all the questions are faced with depth of insight, with meditation and communication with the Divine within, and induced abortion is then not necessary.

I've known several other girls who had the same type of life-changing experience in the years since this first event came about. When the lesson is learned, when the person understands what needs to be done, then life itself—we call it nature—takes over and changes the course of events, and a spontaneous abortion may be the result.

The January/February 1990 issue of *Venture Inward* contained an interview titled "Abortion: Let the Baby Decide," in which I discussed the concept of dialoguing with the unborn soul and making a mutual decision. At the close of the article I invited other women who have had such experiences to write me about them, and I have received over a hundred letters. The experience is clearly not an unusual one, but like other types of transpersonal experiences, those who have these experiences lack confidence that they will be understood. I share two of the many heart-warming and much appreciated letters that I have received. (Names have been changed for confidentiality.)

Case 2. Asking a Baby to Wait

Dear Dr. McGarey:

I was very interested in the article on abortion in the last issue of Venture Inward because I had an interesting experience concerning my second child.

In July of 1984, when my son was a little over a year old, my period was late. This was hard to tell, for I'm quite irregular, but I knew something was up. Sure enough, I was dizzy and nauseous for days, and I knew I was pregnant again. I also felt sure that the entity was a daughter, which distressed me deeply.

Not only had I had an unexpected Cesarean section with my one child, which had upset me greatly, but I was going through a period of extreme anger towards my mother for problems we had had in the past (and I was also taking it out on my son, unfortunately). The last thing I wanted to be was pregnant with a daughter. Without really thinking about it, I pleaded with the incoming soul to wait for a while until I was ready to have a daughter. I asked her not to take it personally, for I felt she was a lovely person, and I would love to have her back, if only she could wait a few months. A few days later, I had an unusually heavy period. When I went to the doctor I was sure I had miscarried, though he said there was no way to tell.

In March of 1985, my husband and I decided to try for a second child. In May, we took a vacation to Scottsdale, Arizona (my favorite place on earth!), and it was just the right week. We made love several times, and I remember on one occasion inviting the entity back, saying that I was ready now to have her.

And she came back! During my pregnancy with Jenny, I felt sure it was a girl, the same soul who had left the previous July. My husband, who is quite leery of this "psychic stuff," even went out and bought a baby girl dress! We never even settled on a boy's name. When the baby was born, also by Cesarean, the doctor said, "It's a girl." It was no surprise to me!

I also had a wonderful religious experience during this pregnancy, when I was agonizing over how angry I was with my son, who really didn't deserve it. I knew that I wouldn't treat this second child that way, and I knew it wasn't fair that David bore the brunt of my problems. A glowing entity said to me, "Okay, so you've been lousy to him. I forgive you. So now what are you going to do about it?"

Jenny is an unusually empathetic and intuitive child. If it is true that the eyes are the window to the soul, then she has the clearest soul imaginable. One day, when she was about three, she said to me, "You love me more than David." I told her that was nonsense, and asked her why she would say that. She looked at me and said, "You invited me and he wasn't invited." Well, you could have knocked me over with a feather! Although it was true that David was a surprise pregnancy, there was no way she could know that. Naturally, I dispelled her feelings as best I could, but her insight then and at other times has truly amazed me—we call her "earth baby." She reflects my moods and emotions and even "mothers" me when I'm down, which embarrasses the hell out of me.

She is also a little mother to her cute baby sister, and a wise helper. I am glad she waited and gave me a chance to mature a little, and I am thrilled to have her for a daughter. By the time her sister Emily was born, I was thrilled to have not one, but two daughters. And my relationship with my son has improved tremendously. I make it a point to tell each one of them how much I love and value them and how glad I am to have them in the family!

What a wonderful idea if everyone would speak to their babies and miscarry naturally, instead of having to go through the pain and trauma of an abortion. I hope your viewpoint gets more and more exposure in the future; this issue has become monstrous in this country. Good luck!

Sincerely,

Marguerite Parker

Case 3. Convincing a Soul to Seek Other Parents

Dear Dr. McGarey:

I read your article in the January 1990 issue of Venture Inward with great interest. I regrettably had an abortion when I was 19 because of social pressures. I believe I also had a spontaneous abortion at the age of 33 when I used a communication technique such as you suggested in the article. I wish I had known about that approach when I was 19, for I certainly would have preferred having that as one of my alternatives.

My circumstances at 33 were as follows: I was quite excited the year my second child started school full time because it enabled me to regain some personal freedom. I believe I became pregnant a few months later. I did not confirm this with a doctor but had physical symptoms that were identical to those I had experienced with my first two children—nausea, breasts swelling and extreme tenderness. I was also late for my period. I was quite distressed at the idea of starting to raise a baby all over, so I began "talking" to the being within me. My philosophical studies included a belief in other lives and the instant presence of a being at, if not before, conception. Anyway, I started communicating how very flattered I was that this being had chosen me for his mother but I was quite happy with only two children and was making plans to restart my career. I reminded the being how there were many women who would love to be pregnant and were having problems. One of those women would be a much better choice for all concerned. I repeatedly gave positive strokes to the being, trying to avoid hurting its feelings. I communicated on and off very strongly for about a week and the physical symptoms began to subside. I then had a seemingly normal period. I have never missed a period before or since that time, so I really believe the being was persuaded to find another mother.

I wish the whole concept of other lives and the power of communication with spiritual beings was more widely accepted so your approach to abortion would become commonplace. It must produce insecurity to have a mother abort you with little explanation as to the reasons. I'll certainly spread the word. Keep up the good work.

Sincerely,

Laurel de Bona

Dialogues with the Unborn in Other Cultures

by

Anne Hubbell Maiden, Ph.D.

Introduction

One of the strongest contributions to my growth as a psychotherapist has come through the inner deepening and expanded perception called forth by research in other cultures. So I begin with three examples of traditional dialogues with the unborn, one each from Bali, the Basque country, and Tibet. Then four cases illustrate how these methods from other cultures work in group, couple, and individual psychotherapy with mothers-and fathers-to-be in my urban professional San Francisco office.

Dialogues with the Unborn in Traditional Cultures

Stories from other cultures provide a comfortable way to introduce clients to new experiences in consciousness. Simultaneously, a story of a birth dialogue gently invites a listener into an expanded state of awareness and offers affirmation that dialogue with the unborn is a simple and natural process, familiar and useful to others. Here I have selected three different approaches to dialogue.

Case 1. Bali

Wayan, in Bali, told me her story. "I married when I was pregnant, as we do. Then I went to the dukun in our village, a wise healing man who helped me talk with the baby inside me, to find out who she was and what she needed for her purpose in life this time." Balinese believe that if the mother knows who her child is and what purpose the child has in life, then she and her family can better prepare for it in the time before it is born and better guide its growth after birth.

In the guided dialogue Wayan learned that she was carrying her own mother, who had died the year before and was almost ready to come back to Bali. (A major cultural value in Bali is to return to life there as soon as possible.) Wayan also learned that certain things needed to be done to complete her mother's ceremony of cremation, believed to free the soul of the body and past karma so it can be born anew.

"A great deal was required to complete the elaborate ceremony, more than I thought was possible," Wayan reported, "but she told me a lot about how to prepare for it, and what she needed to be free. I put those conversations all on tape so I could remember, and all she said worked out. Brothers and sisters, friends, and village groups, we all got together, and we worked hard, and we had the cremation.

"And then the talks were about what she needed to learn for her new life. Her purpose this time was to create dance and art for her people. So I did what she said—sometimes the dukun helped me understand what she meant. I listened to a lot of music and sang more and learned some new dances. Sometimes she wanted special things to eat and my husband and I got those. I noticed how beautiful things around me are, flowers and rice fields and mountains and Bali. My husband painted beautiful things for her. We made the offerings she suggested."

"And then," Wayan said, "there is always a special sign, like a mark on the skin, or a shape of the chin, or a way of walking, that reminds us who our daughter is."

"Does it make a difference," I wanted to hear, "in how you are with your daughter now that she has been born, if she does something that irritates you, or if you have a strong disagreement?"

"Oh, yes. I see how that's like what I know from her when she was inside me, or I look at what she needs in her life. I remember. And then I can decide better what to do now. I'm glad for that!" We laughed together.[9]

Case 2. Basque Country of the Pyrenees

In the Basque country birth is highly valued as a practice for facing what is new, including the ultimate new experience, which is death. Children are treasured. Conception is a sacred act, considered only within marriage, and Basque men and women wait to marry until they have come to maturity in their thirties or forties.

Angeles Arrien, cultural anthropologist with a Basque folklore specialty, told me about pre-Christian birth customs still practiced by those in the Basque mystical tradition, a minority of 15% or less in modern times.

When conception has occurred, the mother- and father-to-be begin to tell each other stories about the baby and their new life, for the baby to hear, another variation of the dialogues with the unborn. They also sing songs that will be repeated during and after the birth. At conception the mother begins to commit to memory her dreams of the child, along with impressions, stories, and events, all seen as part of a dialogue within the family, to be passed on in the oral tradition. Years later, usually after puberty, in young adulthood, or before the child's marriage, the mother finds the right time to share the dreams and story that began at the child's conception.

I have found this exercise in listening, attending, and sharing invaluable for parents and children of all ages. It can offer a rare perspective in our fast-paced "now" culture. Some of my clients have chosen to create a journal. I have watched a brash, rebellious teenager who, as she read what her mother wrote of her conception, early life, and observations of growth, soften, become reflective, reach for her mother's arms, and sob in reconciliation and reconnection with her mother and herself.

Case 3. Tibet

With Lobsang Rapgay, a Tibetan monk trained in Tibetan medicine, I pored over an eleventh century Tibetan medical text that illustrated the development of embryo and fetus and described its experience during each of the 39 weeks of pregnancy. "In the 26th week in the womb," he translated for me, "the child's awareness becomes very clear and it can see its former lives. It can see if it was a pure being or if it was an ordinary being, and what type of birth it had before it took this birth. And then from the 27th to 30th week, gradually all the different sense organs, which are already functioning, develop further and ripen. The mind begins to function and the baby can sense and interpret things to some degree."

Tibetan mothers attend to their dreams during pregnancy and may consult a lama (a spiritual teacher) about the meaning of a dream and what to do about it, another form of dialogue with the unborn. It was an American mother who told me that during the weeks of her pregnancy she had strong, powerful dreams of a nature quite different from any she had recalled earlier. "I knew they were not my dreams," she said, "and this Tibetan belief helps me understand what was happening."

In the dreams of Tibetan mothers, the consciousness of the child can be perceived as communicating with the consciousness of the mother through the language of symbols. Dreams of fruit, eggs, of a white conch shell, of sunrise or a dawning day or playing musical instruments, or of a spiritual teacher are symbols of good fortune that Tibetans learn from poems, stories, songs, parents, and teachers.

Other dreams hold less auspicious symbols, like falling off a cliff, sunset, darkness, wandering without ornaments or jewelry on an empty, deserted plain. These, along with dreams of arguing with others, of crying or being carried by water, may be the occasion of a consultation with the family lama. For healing the difficulty the lama may give blessed herb and mineral pills, prescribe special cleansing rituals and mantras or healing prayers, or suggest actions such as alms-giving through feeding birds, animals, and children.

Dialogues with the unborn may occur in a variety of languages, and when they begin to be understood, such dialogues prepare parents and newborn for more sensitive contact throughout infancy and life. The language of movement is another mode of communication for the unborn. Tibetans have long understood that alcohol and heavy or too sweet foods are not good for a baby in the womb and say that when a mother drinks or eats food inappropriate to its state of development, the baby will struggle by kicking and vigorous movements to let her know its displeasure and aversion.[10] An additional benefit of attention to the language of the unborn is that parents who open their impressions in these ways to their unborn child are likely to listen to new levels within themselves as well as to each other and to their other children.

Dialogues with the Unborn in an Urban Professional Practice

In my San Francisco psychotherapy practice, based in a training center for psychologists and Marriage, Family, and Child Counselors, I have found that dialogues with the unborn make readily available to parents-to-be a sense of connection with their child and their own inner resources. Simply introduced, dialogues provide a direct, clear experience of contact, communication, bonding, and reassurance that can be re-established whenever it is relevant. In my experience, the process is empowering to the mother carrying the child and develops trust between partners when it is shared.

Instead of walking toward Bali's sacred Mount Agung, or high in the Pyrenees of the Basque country, or up the foothills of the Himalayas, the people who come to me climb to the second floor of a redwood and glass office building in the Marina area below the hills of San Francisco. They come because they have acknowledged that they want their lives to be different in some way. Often they seek deeper family connections, more profound relationships, healing of wounds, resolution of conflict, and more creative involvement in their work. Some come to take part in groups, some as individuals, and some in couples.

Case 4. Dialogue in a Group Setting

One of the groups is a birthing circle, which includes those preparing for conception, pregnant women, their partners, children, sometimes extended family and friends, and birth attendants. Two couples in their thirties came to the circle. Each wanted to become pregnant. Each had a history of early miscarriages. We addressed a variety of fears each prospective mother and father held, and we celebrated when each announced a pregnancy. Then one of the mothers came one evening agitated, fearful through a dream of miscarriage, which indeed happened the next day. Within the week her friend also miscarried.

At our next meeting they and their partners shared their grieving and dialogued with the spirits of their little ones. Each found there was another step to take in their lives before they were fully ready to parent. One heard, "I need you to give more attention to your body and your health, to live in your own rhythm with yourself." The message for the other couple was different, "I need your relationship to be more committed, in accord, and joyful. Then I'll come back."

After one woman found a less stressful job and completed graduate school and the other couple had made time for travel, hiking, and deepening their love together, each became pregnant again. This time each carried to term, with ongoing dialogue and bonding through pregnancy. For these parents, miscarriage, like fertility issues or planned abortion, stimulated acute awareness of intense feeling and openness to new learning.

Now their daughters are reaching, crawling, and laughing in their play with each other. And the parents, as they watch their fast-growing offspring and remember their messages from the womb, are each planning conception of a second child.

Case 5. A Dialogue with the Unborn in Individual Therapy

Often a dialogue with a planned child or a fetus clarifies issues of individual lives. Here I want to give an example of another kind of dialogue with the unborn. A highly creative, successful, isolated young woman who had become pregnant had worked through many issues of severe physical and sexual abuse by her father. Ready for a next step in her life and our work, she spontaneously gave voice to a deep inner experience, which she later identified as her own knowing from before she was born. She spoke clearly.

The purpose of my life now is to serve the people on this earth. There is a lot of suffering on this earth, that I have seen from previous lives and struggles to sustain life. As I have failed to reach my goal, and have learned lessons, I have become more determined to live with compassion, love, and caring. No matter how many lessons I learn, I continue to learn every day. As I give love, compassion, and care, my capacity to compost anger and hatred grows, and I am building a better world. The purpose of my life is to teach compassion, love, and caring until we can all live in peaceful community with each other, with animals, and with the vegetation on earth. Earth was here before we came. We are only a small part of this universe of life. I am thankful for earth and life and land. I feel very grateful and thankful I'm a part of it.

Having made contact with this ongoing "original self," as she called it, she continued the dialogue through writing in her journal. In this writing she was able to integrate the imperative expression of her strong feelings with the thoughtful perspective she needed to give direction to her life from day to day.

In a later inner dialogue with her unborn child she discovered views akin to those of the traditional Balinese, Basque, and Tibetan cultures. As her inner identity grew stronger, her understandable fears of those around her lessened, and she began to extend her earlier abstract compassion, love, and caring to relationships with friends, colleagues, and a new profession.

Case 6. Dialogue with a Couple

In my practice I see more and more couples who want to conceive and who have experienced intense feelings of impatience, failure, frustration, and heartbreak through repeated anticipation and disappointment. An example is a professional couple I saw some time ago. After many years of a marriage that they both described was loving and good, they experienced a fervent desire to parent a child together. They were considering the long-term implications of in-vitro fertilization, donor insemination, adoption, zonal drilling, and what might be invented if they waited a few more months.

I saw them both together and alone. In one of my meetings with the woman, who had no prior experience with meditation, I led her into a guided dialogue between what could be called her core, seed, or original self and the seed self of her unconceived child. She let me know when she had established connection from the bottom of her spine to the core of the earth, then up through her own spinal column, and then from the top of her head to link with her original self. I did not know whether it would work, but she lifted her thumb to signal she was connected, and then that she had connected with the original self of the not-yet-conceived child. When she asked what the child needed, my client reported that she heard, with clarity,

"I need you to make more space for receptivity and love in your being and your life."

Another time when we were meeting together and her husband expressed concern about how a child would feel to know that it was conceived by a donor insemination, we established again, for both of them together, their connection to earth, and to original self, and then to the original self of their unconceived child.

All three of us were moved when each in turn gave an identical report of the experience in dialogue. From their child's original self, each received the clear message that love was the most important element in the formation of their family, and that the particular physical and material means of their coming together was unimportant compared to the quality of their relationship with one another.[11]

Conclusion

Therapists who introduce dialogues with the unborn can give courage, recognition and acceptance to an ongoing experience of self and inner knowing in parents. Through giving support to dialogue between parents and unborn child, we can encourage parents to develop flexible hypotheses about what life with their child may be like and thus bring to light underlying parental projections or expectations that could become hindrances to their relationship with each other and with their child. Exploration of such anticipations can invite an open readiness for the presence of the unborn to be a guide. In providing the opportunity for parents to create what was not created for them, they call forth healing of early wounds and generate awareness of a larger framework of life. Dialogues with the unborn bring us naturally into contact with the numinous, an inner experience of ongoing and connected consciousness. Do we, as professionals, give permission to our clients to touch this connection, so often forbidden in our culture? Do we welcome our responsibility to help clients listen on many levels? Do we support their experience and so become co-creators of an invaluable gift?

All the methods illustrated—dialogues guided by a healer, carried on through storytelling and song, by writing and drawing in a journal, in dreams, or through movement—indicate the power of these gifts. And these are only a sampling; therapist and client together can invent what is needed as they prepare coming generations to meet new life callings on this swiftly changing planet. From such dialogues grow indelible bonds that strengthen the capacity of a parent-child relationship to weather the buffeting winds and raging challenges of changes so speeded up and vast that we have few ways to anticipate them. Through such dialogues both therapist and client learn to provide a core of understanding, offer abiding connections, and present each child with a responsive environment as he or she enters the world. They give courage, recognition, and acceptance to an ongoing experience of self and an inner knowing that heartens the identity of those with whom they work.

Communication with the Fetus

by

Claire Etheridge, Ph.D.

Introduction

The ability of the mother to communicate directly with her unborn child and the corresponding ability of that child to respond in a way that the mother can understand offer a powerful agent for the resolution of ambivalence regarding pregnancy and provide healing if the pregnancy is terminated. Dialogue with the unborn child, whether in thoughts, words, or images, allows the needs of both mother and child to be explored. This sort of dialogue also enables a mother to better understand and prepare for a child to whom she intends to give birth. Such communication is not difficult in an altered state with the help of a skilled professional.

The dialogue between mother and child is built on the assumption that life continues, whether in or out of a physical structure. If the pregnancy is terminated, the life of the fetus is seen as returning to its source, i.e., "the Light," where it will continue in some form. If it is decided that the pregnancy is to continue, life is respected and affirmed in its physical form. In cases where abortion is being considered, one decision is not necessarily seen as preferable to the other by the therapist: the mother is helped to consider all ramifications and make a decision taking *all* factors into account. When this is done, the affirmation of the fetus in the decision is clearly felt, even when the mother's decision is to terminate the pregnancy. The mother's values and belief systems permeate the content of such a dialogue, while the therapist functions as a guide to facilitate communication within the mother's value system and frame of reference.

Spontaneous miscarriages often follow upon such a dialogue where a decision has been reached mutually by neonate and mother that this is not an appropriate time for a child to be born. The mother can move out of her conflicted state into peace of mind about her decision and is free to go on with her life without the encumbrance of conscious or unconscious guilt.

Case 1. Spontaneous Abortion Following Conversation with an Unborn Child

In my initial interview with this young woman I suggested that she dialogue at home with her unborn child. During the following session she reported that she had conversed with the spirit of the unborn child but wanted to talk to it again in the office with me. She went into self-induced hypnosis and spoke aloud:

> P: *I feel that this isn't the right time for you to be there, growing. I don't know why you are there. But it's not the time for you to be there. The attention...everything a baby needs...I couldn't give you what you want. The love wouldn't be there. There would be tension and stress. You should have warmth and love surrounded with happiness, and I can't give you that.*
>
> *I want you to go away. Possibly another lifetime. But I can't think of one good reason to bring you into this world. It would be unhappy for you. You wouldn't want that.... So please, I ask that you go away. I do love the spirit of the baby, and even though I don't know why you are there, I'm sure there is a reason. But I want what is best for you, so please go away. There's no other way.*
>
> *I don't want to have to do what I have to do tomorrow. Please go away on your own. Please hear me, as I'm as close to you now as I'll ever be. And I'm sorry. I really am sorry.*

The following day the patient miscarried. When I saw her two weeks later, she reported that she felt calm and positive about the resolution of the problem pregnancy.

Case 2. Resolving the Emotional and Spiritual Aspects of an Abortion

In the second case the mother and I discussed the unplanned pregnancy in great detail in the office, and I suggested she dialogue at home. She came in two days later with this report:

> P: *It was very vivid to me when I was talking with it. I said I did not want to hurt the person's spirit and it would be so much better for it to leave than to be pulled out artificially.*

She then went into trance to talk further to the baby.

> P: *Dear baby, I hope you had a chance to think about what we talked about yesterday night. (Cries.) It makes me sad...to have to...go through this...and tell you this...and do what has to be done. (Cries.)*

> But I believe that you are a very wise spirit and can understand what I am saying and thinking and feeling. I do love you and don't want you to suffer. Right now I cannot give to you what you deserve. Right now, I'm like a baby myself in a lot of ways. I need time...and for that reason I'm not ready to bring you into this world as my child.
>
> You've had a purpose already in my life in teaching me things I don't understand as yet. And I thank you for that.
>
> And I ask you to decide at this time to go back to wherever you've come from and come back to the earth at a different time, whether to me or someone else, I don't know. Whatever is best for you.

A week later the patient reported that she and the fetus had taken care of the spiritual and emotional aspects, and the clinic took care of the physical remains. She expressed a sense of sadness coupled with a feeling of relief, alleviation of guilt, and, eventually, positive resolution.

Case 3. Emotional Closure around an Abortion

In the third case the mother explained to the unborn child the difficulties associated with the pregnancy. Then she paused and repeated:

> P: I ask if there is anything you want to be able to say to me, or anyone else, that you speak to me, that I might be able to hear what you have to say....
>
> I feel that he came back to teach me love and understanding. And forgiveness...I ask God's blessing be upon this spirit, this baby, this life, no matter where he is or what he chooses to do.... Baby, it's safe for you to leave to go into the Light. You are free to go back into the Light. Don't be afraid. It's safe there...I'm sorry. (Cries.)

After a while she opened her eyes, and spoke to me.

> P: I'm really glad you are here with me.
> T: How do you feel?
> P: I feel a sense of release and safety and security of that spirit going back into the Light or where it was before it left. I somehow feel a sense of departure.

Shortly after this session the patient miscarried. (The fetus was malformed.)

Follow-up over the past three years with each of the women indicated that each was satisfied with her experience, felt a sense of closure, and reported a deeper appreciation for life.

Case 4. Dialogue with Unborn Twins Leading to Their Birth

Some years previously I had treated a fourth woman for depression and life adjustment problems. At the time she returned she was 43 years old and pregnant with twins. Her stated purpose in coming was to have help in weighing the pros and cons of keeping her babies. The pregnancy had been a surprise to both her husband and herself, as both of them had been diagnosed as sterile. They had adopted and reared two children, now in their late teens, but this was the patient's first pregnancy.

All seemed to be going well physically. In her sixth week of pregnancy her physician had found her in general good health and told her that she was carrying twins. She had concern over giving birth for the first time at 44. Her husband was anxious about the situation, and their financial state was uncertain.

Several other considerations arose as we talked about conflicts that had to do with the babies themselves. The mother, who was deeply religious, sought meaning in the unexpected event. At the same time she was expressing natural concern over the babies' physical condition, and she wondered why she would get pregnant at this stage of her life.

Using her concerns as a guide, we formulated questions for me to ask her while she was in an altered state. Based on the mother's agenda, the dialogue went as follows:

T: *What is the plan or purpose of this pregnancy?*
P: *It is God's will. They are God's will. I keep hearing, "Thy will is done."*
T: *How does the life within feel about it?*
P: *They want to live. I can see little babies wrapped up in a blanket. I can feel them. So warm. I'm just holding them. I don't want to put them down.*
T: *Are there physical problems?*
P: *There's nothing wrong. No problem.*

After this dialogue the patient reported that she was still undecided, especially since her husband was insistent on terminating the pregnancy. Three days later both parents came in and went into trance together with the objective of continuing the dialogue with the "life within." The same format applied of my asking in trance the questions the parents had posited. In this dialogue the mother and father spoke not only *to*, but *for* the babies.

T: *How are you doing?*
E: *It's okay. The other one is so little...so sleepy. It's terribly hard to breathe. My heart is going crazy.*
T: *Are you from the same egg or different eggs?*
E: *I see an egg breaking in half.*
T: *Do you want to be born?*

E: I don't know yet. Not enough information to decide...if you want us...

T: Do we get to know if you are boys or girls?

E: I don't want to tell you.

T: Why did you pick these people as parents?

E: They picked me. I want to be born if they want us.

T: Why do you want to be born?

E: I want to do things. I want to be loved. I want to do lots of things.

T: Do you know your mother is 43 years old?

E: I know. My friends will think I have an old mom and dad, but it doesn't matter. They don't act old. I think they are better. They're not so dumb as some of my friends' moms and dads. I could make them real happy. But I don't want to come unless they want me.

T: How do you feel about their being undecided?

E: It's all right. It was a big surprise. They have to change plans.

T: What about the other one in there?

E: He's just sleepy or lazy right now.

T: Does he feel the same as you?

E: I don't know.

T: Is there anything special you want to say to your daddy?

E: No. Mom and Dad are just like one right now. They both know what I'm saying.

T: How do you feel about talking to us right now?

E: *This has been fun. It gets boring in here. I'd like for them to talk to me more, ask me how I am, tell me what they are thinking. Ask me what I think.*

T: Can you remember anything before you came into this body?

E: I was just tumbling around...like washed down a drain or slipping through some place.

T: Can you remember coming out of the Light?

E: No. I feel God all the time. I feel this light around me. Makes me warm.

T: Would you like them to read you stories?

E: Um hum, I'm getting tired. I'd like to take a little rest.

T: Baby Two, do you want to wake up and talk to me?

E: I'm waking up. I've had a long nap.

T: Are you okay?

E: Um hum. I need to grow a little more. That's why I'm sleeping. I have to catch up. I think I'm doing okay. I really need to sleep. If I don't, I won't catch up.

T: Is it okay to call you Baby Two?

E: Yes.

T: Baby One, is there anything else you want to say?

E: I'm smart. I already know how to read. I'll do really well if they let me be born, but if they don't, it's okay.

At the end of the dialogue both parents felt relaxed, but they reported that they could not remember everything that had transpired. The father was still reluctant to have the twins, and the mother wasn't sure.

> P: *Right now all that feels real good, but I still have this nagging voice within me that says, "Be logical."*

The mother considered the material of the dialogue for a week and then decided to continue the pregnancy, even though it was against her husband's wishes and could lead to the break-up of the marriage. She reported that the deciding factor in her mind was the sense of reality she had felt after the experience of the dialogue with her unborn children.

The twins, identical girls now 13 years old, have presented no particular problems, although one was initially much stronger than the other. The marriage did break up, but both parents enjoy the children and find them smart, inquisitive, and a joy to know.

Case 5. Prenatal Communication to Promote Mother-Child Bonding

As in so much of science or medicine, we first discover or study the pathological and then ascertain if these findings are applicable to a normal population to enhance health or the quality of life. I decided to investigate the possibility of conscious enhancement of the fetal environment through positive prenatal communication.

A patient, Mary, was six months pregnant and happy at the prospect. She was a perceptive woman of 27 who was herself a wanted, cherished child. She and her husband had planned this, their third child, and were eagerly looking forward to the birth. She was enrolled in Lamaze childbirth classes. So far her pregnancy had been uneventful.

Mary agreed to come to my office weekly and in between to keep a daily journal of her communications with her unborn child. A summary of our weekly sessions and excerpts from her journal follow.

Week 1 (At the beginning of the sixth month of pregnancy)

During this first session I used a standard Ericksonian induction to hypnosis, which is primarily talking, and asked Mary to imagine herself in a safe place so that she could get in touch with her own inner wisdom and tune in to her baby. I shared with her the Chinese conviction that there is consciousness before birth. I explained that just as she would want to make the baby comfortable in its crib after birth, she might talk to it and ask how she could make it comfortable now.

> T: *I don't know precisely how this communication will take place, whether with images, words, thoughts, impressions, or just a sense of knowing. But give yourself the opportunity to tune in.*
> P: *It's saying something like, "Mother, you get really hassled sometimes and just need to quiet down. This (self-hypnosis) is really good for you." (Pause.) It likes this. Now I'm thinking of alcohol. The baby doesn't like it. (Long pause.) It doesn't like alcohol at all.*
> T: *How is the baby communicating this?*
> P: *Just with thoughts, but it was very real. I felt I really was tuned in to it.*

Weeks 2 and 3

Mary reported delightedly that she was able to communicate with the baby even while not in trance.

> P: *Now when I feel him bouncing around, I stop and think what he's saying to me. Once I started being aware while in trance, I was even more aware when not in trance.*

Her journal reported that she was beginning to relax and meditate more and to be more generally aware of the baby.

> P: *He gave me a kick when I was too busy and overdoing it and wasn't aware of him. He kicked up a storm as if to say, "Here I am! Consider me!"*

During the trance session she reported visual images of the baby inside the womb.

> P: *It's really weird. It's hard to distinguish my own thought processes from those of the baby, but I'm aware of every drink I have. It's like he's saying, "I'm down here—don't take that drink!"*

She then went into trance and reported the following dialogue.

> P: *How are you today, baby?*
> E: *Oh, very fine.*
> P: *I love you baby.*
> E: *Yes, I know. (Very calm and secure.)*
> P: *What can I do to make you more comfortable?... He wants me to lie back farther in the recliner chair. I felt him pushing me back, but I say, "I'm comfortable the way I am. You'll just have to adjust."*

Mary and I then began a dialogue to ascertain if the baby was a boy or a girl.

> P: *The baby was real quiet, then, like rocking, like it was playing with me, moving but not kicking. Then it got still and didn't do anything, like teasing me.*

Her doctor said the baby's heartbeat was like that of a girl and at first she thought it might be a girl, but she really wanted to be surprised with the sex at birth and never felt she received a clear message. The following week the ambiguity with sexual identity continued.

> P: *I'm thinking of her as a person rather than a being. So when I think of her, I think, Kimberly. Wouldn't it be a joke if it were a boy!*

During this session she once again explored the effect of alcohol and of her tennis playing upon the baby and asked its taste in music.

> P: *The baby was real quiet, wallowing in the fact I was tuned into it. It didn't want me to come out of trance.*

Week 4

Mary reported that she was very conscious of the baby's movement and wondered if this were in some way a reflection of herself. She was aware that the baby was growing and not having so much room.

One night she had gone to the house of a friend who played loud rock music that was disruptive.

> P: *The baby was very quiet during the music and afterwards began hopping all around. It was almost overwhelming. I felt that I should leave but I didn't.*

When she finally did go home, she developed a severe gastrointestinal upset that she felt was directly related to the loud music.

Weeks 4 and 5

Mary was developing a strong sense of mothering and was feeling much more peaceful at home. Outside activities were losing their appeal. She was trying to communicate with the baby, who was in the breech position, and tell it to get itself in the right position.

During the trance session she explored further the effects of diet and music.

P: *How are you today?*
E: *Fine. Peaceful and quiet.*
P: *How's the nutrition?*
E: *Too much sugar!*

Mary added that this really was apparent—the baby became "too hyped" when she ate ice cream, sweet rolls, M&M's, and other sweet things.

We then played several types of music. The baby was edgy with Eastern music with no beat, "went bonkers" during rock music, but was relaxed and peaceful with classical music.

T: *Can the baby give you a general message?*
P: *Relax. Quiet. Calm yourself. Quiet.*

Mary reported the following week that when she had become upset at a school board meeting, the baby was "going bananas, like a ship inside" so that it was difficult for her to get to sleep that night. She wrote about this incident in her journal.

She apologized to the baby for being so upset and the baby advised her to follow her father's advice to disengage herself from the situation that had upset her. She found it hard to let go, but the baby became very active as if to insist that she must. It also told her it wanted softer names than the ones she was considering. She resolved to spend more quiet time with her family and work on releasing her anxiety so that she and the baby could relax.

Week 7

At her childbirth class Mary was enthusiastically teaching other mothers to communicate with their babies and found out that many of the parents were already doing this. One mother was instructing her breech-positioned baby to turn for a normal birth. Mary reported that she felt more calm and serene with self-hypnosis and was increasingly able to tune out external problems.

During trance we agreed on several stimulus words with which to test the baby. Its responses to "alcohol" and "sugar" were "terrible." To M&M's it responded that it was good while you eat them but later there was a terrible reaction! It called the brother's tantrum "silly" and said it felt "impatient" at the father's yelling.

In her journal the mother had written that the baby somehow accepted the fact that she had commitments to fulfill to the Children's Home Society. It understood *her* need. Then she visualized her baby at birth and wrote:

> P: *(In journal) I'm holding my child rather than having my body carry it. We're looking into each other's eyes. It's a feeling of "Hello, friend! So glad you've finally arrived." I can't wait, but my baby is saying I should be patient. It needs time to prepare for the journey. Okay, I'll wait...patiently, I think.*

Weeks 8 and 9

Mary reported that though this was a very active baby it became quiet whenever she did self-hypnosis.

> P: *It's getting real snug in there, as if to say, "You be quiet, too. We've got to get ready for this trip we are going to take—birth."*
> *Three more weeks until the delivery date! When it kicks I can tell it wants to stretch—frustration—like it's too tight.*
> *I'm very confused on its sex again but have settled on a boy's name. If it's a girl, I'm not sure.*
> *I'm eating really well. No sugar. Lots of chicken and fish. Baby likes that.*

During the hypnosis session she felt as if the baby were asleep and she received no particular impressions. After the session we discussed the results of her cytotoxic test, a test that determines allergy to various foods. She had decided to have this test after realizing the effect of various foods on herself and the baby. As a result she was planning her meals differently.

The next week she reported feeling much more calm since eliminating cow's milk and grains with gluten, which were contraindicated by the cytotoxic test.

> P: *I'm nesting! I'm tuning into myself more and have open communication with the baby. I know it's in there doing fine, getting fat, moving into position for birth.*
> *I'm increasingly aware of the baby's schedule. It's really active in the evening when I'm quiet. Eleven a.m. is its time, also mid-afternoon and 9 p.m. It will be interesting to note if it keeps the same schedule after it's born.*

Later she wrote in her journal:

> P: *Knowing this baby will probably be my last, I feel a sense of extra anticipation. The first child has a special place, of course, and the second child, being the first son, offers the mother/son relationship, which is so dear. The third baby is a bonus. I have a sense "she?" or "he?" will be an open person, likeable, creative in a worldly way, an explorer of possibilities. Possibly this will frustrate his father, as I do at times, but will grasp his heart. It is certainly a plus to explore all this. Reflection enhances it all.*

Week 10

Mary's doctor reported that the cervix was starting to soften and the baby was in place.

> P: *All is ready! I have a visual image of the baby and know where the head is—down. I've been watching my diet and have had no heartburn for three weeks. I've eliminated coffee altogether and have minimal milk. Baby likes the new diet, too. I don't feel so bloated.*
>
> *The self-hypnosis is going fine. Baby acknowledges I go into trance and we just "be." I wonder if I will have a closer insight into baby's needs due to all my focusing and attention to communications with him or her. I have the feeling the baby will come in about ten days—close to Easter— rebirth. Thanks!*

Week 11

From Mary's journal reports it was apparent that the baby was changing its pattern of activity. She perceived less motion, more of a settling. The baby was sleeping soundly and gave her little feedback. She felt that it had centered itself on getting ready for the trip through the birth passage. After the hypnosis session she wrote:

> P: *I found myself focusing on baby's health and had a feeling of "more protein." I shall get some fish tonight.*
>
> *Baby was calm and quiet. I need to calm down, too. Relax and enjoy my time of peace now. Peaceful expectations of becoming a mother once again. A mother...such responsibility and yet such a sense of belonging. A new step and chapter of my life. My husband is gearing up, too. This baby will hold a special place in his heart.*

On the morning after Easter I received a telephone call from a euphoric Mary from the hospital. About an hour after arriving at the hospital she had delivered naturally in the "birthing chair" with no anesthetic. The father was present the entire time and was helpful throughout the birthing process. Mary had already nursed her baby and greeted him.

T: *What did he say?*

P: *Hello! I'm glad to meet you! He is strong and alert. He held his head up and looked around right away. I feel closer to him than I did to the other two at birth. He is already a friend.*

So we came full circle in our realization that communication with the unborn child is happening all the time. Whether it will be a two-way communication is dependent on the openness of the parents. In this particular case, Mary was able to adjust her attitude, life style, activity level, and dietary habits in a way that would enhance her life and that of the baby. The ongoing communication led to an intuitive grasp of the baby's personality and even to some understanding of what to expect in terms of accomplishments and interpersonal relationships within the family. A groundwork was laid for communication with the child and formed a basis for the enhancement of family relationships.

The Therapeutic Value of
Talking with Aborting Fetuses

by

Barbara P. Lamb, M.S., M.F.C.C.

The highly controversial legal/moral battle about abortion raging in the United States overlooks or fails to mention a metaphysical perspective. This different perspective can be profoundly helpful to pregnant women (and their partners) who are struggling with the dilemma of whether to continue their unwanted pregnancies to full term and birth or terminate the pregnancies through abortion.

The assumption seems to be, according to advocates of both sides of the question, that the choice is made *only* by the expectant mother (enabled or constrained by the legal system in her state), and *not* by the unborn fetus. The pro-choice advocates insist that the mother has the right to bring the embryo/fetus into life or to eliminate the possibility of its being born and living a lifetime. The anti-abortion advocates believe that upon becoming pregnant the mother is automatically under moral and legal obligations to continue the pregnancy, to give birth and to be responsible for the child. This may involve arranging for adoption. She must carry her child through to birth regardless of the circumstances of the conception, her ability to raise the child, and her true feelings and needs.

Nowhere have I seen published any consideration of the thoughts and wishes and intentions of the unborn child. Yet psychotherapists and hypnotherapists who use hypnotic regression techniques with our clients have learned that a person is conscious and aware, while in the womb, of the emotional/psychological state of the mother and that he registers in his unconscious mind the statements and feelings of the mother. He also has awareness of and feelings about the situation into which he will be born. As we see through hypnosis, he is often profoundly affected by these factors, sometimes to the degree of being traumatized for his entire lifetime. Through hypnotic regression we can communicate effectively with the unborn child. We can discover the beliefs, conclusions, and decisions he has been forming while in the womb (or even at the moment of conception) that have influenced him during the present lifetime. We can also regress a person to the period when he chose the parents and circumstances into which to be born.

We sometimes learn that a soul realizes that it made a mistake by coming into conception with its perspective parents at that time and that it became afraid to come fully into this life. Sometimes, on the other hand, we learn that the soul has chosen to be conceived by and live with a mother for a specific purpose, which includes the *brevity* of the experience.

We can relate significantly to a fetus *currently* gestating in the womb through altered-state work with the pregnant mother, through hypnosis, or through guiding her into a relaxed state and asking her to tune in to the fetus and dialogue with it. Since a fetus's vocal chords, speech apparatus, and mental development are not developed enough to accomplish this, we direct the mother's communication to the *consciousness* or *soul* of the fetus who is developing in the womb.

Even though there are different understandings and opinions about when the soul enters the developing embryo/fetus/baby, the soul that is choosing to experience this manifestation into physical incarnation is present and conscious and able to be contacted. In a relaxed, receptive state of consciousness, while focusing all her attention and intention upon the soul of the fetus, the mother can experience a profound sense of connecting with this soul, imparting her sincere thoughts, feelings, intentions and considerations, as well as *hearing* important thoughts from the soul. She can experience a resolution and completion about the decision to abort the embryo/fetus, and she can lovingly release the soul into the Light, where it will be cared for and safe, and from where it can choose to incarnate with her later on or with another mother.

A key element in this work is the understanding that in any pregnancy termination, whether by spontaneous miscarriage or by chosen abortion, the *physical body* of the embryo/fetus dies, but the *soul* continues on. A mother can make it impossible for a soul to incarnate through her body at a given time, but *she can never kill the soul*. I liken this to an analogy of a person wanting to buy a certain house at a particular time for a variety of reasons, putting a deposit on the house, going through the escrow procedure, becoming increasingly prepared for and expectant about living in this house, and eventually realizing that the transaction cannot be completed at this time. This realization may be surprising and disappointing, even startling, but the person eventually lets go of the idea of living in this house and goes on to live somewhere else, preferably in a house that is fully available and appropriate. Although the opportunity to live in that first house was eliminated, the *person himself* was not eliminated. This is a hopeful viewpoint for the pro-choice/pro-life debate and the idea of abortion being thought of as "murder."

Inasmuch as the developing embryo/fetus has a continuing conscious soul that has chosen (at least temporarily) to develop into physical manifestation in the body of the mother at this time, it is important to talk to this soul and hear *its* thoughts and feelings, too, about an impending termination of the physical body. In my experience in working with women who are considering abortion, and in facilitating their dialogue with their fetuses, the souls of the fetuses have had surprising things to say. Often the soul shares its purpose for coming to this mother, this family, these circumstances, etc., for many reasons, including coming into physical form for only a *brief* period. In these dialogues the mothers often feel convinced they are making agreements with the soul and are obtaining the consent of the soul to have the abortion. When this happens, the mother feels a significant relief from conflict and guilt and an overwhelming sense of love and admiration for this soul.

Case 1. Gaining a Soul's Consent to Abortion

I became involved with the process of talking to fetuses in the mid-1970's when a young woman colleague shared with me her struggle over her decision to have an abortion. She knew inwardly that her existing marriage was over, though she still lived with her husband and had not told him of her decision. She had become pregnant "by mistake" and could not tolerate the prospect of raising this second child as a divorced parent. It was going to be difficult enough to raise and support herself and the son she already had. She cared about this child *en utero* and was concerned about its feeling shocked and rejected by being aborted. She wished that she could talk to it and explain why she could not have it. She wanted to hear *its* feelings, too. Neither of us knew whether such a process was possible, but we ventured forth.

I guided her into a state of deep relaxation with her eyes closed. I suggested that she imagine, sense, or feel the presence of this soul in any way she could and begin to speak to it as if it were really present, saying anything she felt like expressing.

> P: *I feel terrible about this, but I really can't have you come into my life at this time. Your dad and I won't be together to raise you. I'm scared of doing it on my own. Besides, I'll have a lot of trouble separating from your dad. He'll resist our living apart and he'll be very angry and difficult to deal with. It will be painful and hard for a long time. And it would be very hard on you. I wouldn't want all that strife for you. I need to finish my education and become licensed and develop my practice as a therapist so that I can support your brother and myself. I know your dad will help as little as possible, if at all. Please understand. I'm so sorry. It's nothing*

against you personally. It's just that our circumstances are so bad. *I love you and wish you well.*

When she finished, I suggested she remain seated quietly, receptively, and sense how the soul was receiving what she had said. After a minute or so she felt a "warm sense of presence," and she seemed to listen attentively.

> F: *Thank you for telling me. I didn't know it would be so hard! You seemed like such a nice mother to come to. I would love to be with you but not if it's so difficult. I'm wanting a nice, secure family, with a mother and father and brother, and it looked like this was it. But I guess it's not. Too bad. Maybe this wouldn't work out so well...not what I really want or need. I should go somewhere else, where it'll be better for my growing up. I'm sorry too.*
>
> P: *Oh, I'm so glad we're talking about this together! I really think you understand. And I want you to have the kind of family you want, and to grow up with security and love from both parents together. Thank you for wanting me to be your mother but it wouldn't be a good deal for you. If you can, please choose someone better to be born to. And I send you off with love...greatest love. And I hope you won't be too hurt with the abortion procedure.*

With tears streaming down her face, this mother expressed a strong sense of mutual loving and caring. She talked further with the soul of the fetus and eventually felt completely relieved. She went ahead and had the abortion, without telling her husband. She reasoned that it was her own personal decision. Soon afterward she initiated the marital separation, went through the difficult divorce and property settlement, and continued with her education and professional career. She has not yet remarried or had any other children. She recently told me she thinks lovingly of the soul whom she released many years ago and feels completely resolved with her decision. She believes she is very special friends with this soul, somehow, somewhere.

Case 2. Asking a Wanted Baby to Wait

The second pregnant mother I encountered who was considering abortion was a dear friend in the late 1970's. She had two young children by her first marriage. She was engaged to a man who needed to get his business started and help his recently immigrated parents become established and self-supporting before taking on the responsibilities of marriage and raising her children. She was supporting herself and her two children and building up her career as a dance teacher. Although deeply in love with and committed to this man and longing to have his child, she knew the timing was very bad for bringing a new baby into their lives. The pregnancy had not been planned, and together they struggled with the decision about abortion. They were spiritually-oriented people and had a strong reverence for life.

I guided her in a meditation in which she explained their situation to the soul of the fetus.

> P: *Dear precious little Being, we want you so badly and know you are a beautiful expression of our love. We wish the timing was right for us to have you, but it isn't. Please wait and come to us again when we are more settled and married and can give you a better life. We'll welcome you fully when we can concentrate on raising you and loving you. Please know that we'll always be wanting you and trying to get our lives together and ready for you. We're so honored that you chose us for your parents, and please choose us again in a few years. We truly want you but just can't have you now.*

She sat silently in tears and "saw" a little male Being dancing around, smiling, nodding, and radiant.

> F: *You are my true mother and father, and I will be with you. I'll wait and I'll come to you when you invite me, when you're ready for me. In the meantime, I'm your special "guardian angel," and I'll be with you in spirit. I'll help get things going well in your lives.*

This mother had the abortion, with her fiance attentively present. They both meditated together before the surgical procedure and sent abundant love to this soul. A few years later they married and prospered and were buying their own home. They chose to get pregnant and consciously invited the same soul to them. Sitting together in deep meditation they called out to this Being and affirmed their love for him and their desire to have him be their child. They both felt a sense of radiant presence and warmth. The mother "saw" him dancing around them, smiling joyfully. *"Okay, I'm ready! I've been waiting! Here I come...get busy!"* Soon they conceived and had a strong conviction that this baby was the same "guardian angel" who had waited for them. They did indeed give birth to a fine baby boy.

Case 3. A Soul with a Short-term Purpose

I worked with another young couple to help them dialogue with the soul of the fetus during an unwanted pregnancy. The two were drifting apart, each busily immersed in his separate career, and were afraid that raising a child would separate them even further—they hardly had time for each other as it was.

In our session I directed the couple to close their eyes, breathe deeply, relax, and invite the soul of the fetus to come to them. I suggested that they sit and wait for a sensation of "change" or "presence" and then speak about their situation and their need to release the soul. They "heard" it say cheerfully,

> F: *It's okay. You can let me go. I understand. The real purpose for my coming to you and causing this deep concern was to give you the impetus to come closer together, to deliberate, to commiserate, and to communicate about whether to keep me or to abort me. I've served my purpose, and it's okay.*

This couple had the abortion, feeling close and mutually supportive. They felt resolved about their decision and were happy to feel closer than they had for a long time. Both believed that this generous, conscious soul had served them well and that it was managing well and without any hurt or bitterness.

Case 4. A Determined Soul

A single young pregnant woman came to me for therapy, feeling conflicted in her deliberations about having an abortion. She had no intention of marrying the father or of being a single parent, yet she did not want to reject or harm this tender life. She resisted the idea of talking with the soul of the fetus, assuming she would feel silly and fail to accomplish the task. However, she did agree to try hypnosis for this purpose. After guiding her in deep relaxation techniques and with suggestions that her higher consciousness would be able to recognize and communicate with the soul, she seemed filled with wonder at a sense of presence and then totally focused on her conversation. She explained why she needed to release the soul of the fetus at this time.

The soul, who seemed clearly to be a girl, said in a cheerful, spritely tone:

> F: *If you abort me now, I'll come back to you eventually anyway. You are going to be my mother sooner or later! I was just eager to get on with it, but I can wait!*

The young woman felt relieved and confident about her decision to have the abortion. She knew the baby's soul understood the timing was not right. She felt deeply complimented that the soul had chosen her for a mother and would choose to come back to her under better circumstances. She no longer worried about the abortion being taken as a drastic rejection.

Before the scheduled abortion could take place, a spontaneous miscarriage took place. The young woman believed it was an enactment of the soul's agreement to leave. For several years this woman carried the sense of a "special presence" waiting to be conceived by her and born to her. Whenever she thought of eventually having a child, she remembered the plucky spirit and the determined attitude of this particular soul. When she married and gave birth to a girl, she felt convinced that this was the same soul keeping its promise to have her as its mother.

Case 5. Delayed Conversation with an Aborted Child

An interesting and complex situation occurred in connection with a very close relative and myself. This young woman in her early twenties, without intending to, became pregnant. Lacking a strong commitment to the father and needing to complete her graduate school education and launch her career, she decided to have an abortion. She felt loving toward the fetus and highly conflicted about going against the strong maternal feelings in her. She worried about killing a life. I suggested that she talk to the fetus, but she thought that was a strange idea and felt unable to do so. She urged me to accompany her to the hospital for the surgical procedure.

During the abortion I meditated in the nearby waiting room and focused my attention completely on the soul being released from her body. I mentally explained what was happening and the reasons for this decision. Above all, I projected green unconditional love from my heart chakra to the heart of the fetus. I surrounded the fetus with white light from the highest source. I kept sending love, wishing the soul well and affirming our caring. It was an intense, moving experience. My heart felt completely open to this young mother and to this soul who was being released from her body.

Three years later I had a private spirit releasement session with Bill and Judith Baldwin in which we discovered the spirit of a baby girl living in the area of my heart. She told me:

> F: *When I was made to leave your relative, you were nearby, talking to me, reassuring me, loving me, and making me feel safe and welcomed. I came right over to you and have been with you ever since. And this way I've been close to both of you. I know that you still care about me.*

I felt surprised and deeply moved that she had come to me immediately after the abortion, and yet it all made sense. With the assistance of Bill and Judith I lovingly sent her all the way into the Light:

T: Look up and see those in spirit waiting to receive you and help you. Reach up and join hands with them, and let them guide you to your true home where you will be cared for and guided. Going into the Light now you will be able to return to the woman who conceived you or to anyone else you choose, when the time is right. If you come to our family again, you will be wholeheartedly received with love. In the meantime I send you abundant good wishes and love.

We completed the release, trusting that this was the finest gift we could give this soul.

A year later the same relative discovered she had a large fibroid tumor in her uterus that needed to be removed surgically. During her recuperation from the operation I asked her if she had any thoughts about why this tumor had grown in her uterus. She cried and said she thought it was somehow due to her bad feeling about the abortion. She sobbed with grief and guilt about having "killed" that baby while feeling so close to it emotionally and while feeling such strong maternal urges.

I shared my understanding about the impossibility of killing the soul and about the soul continuing "alive and well" and being available to talk with. I guided her into a dialogue with this soul:

T: Turn you attention inward and call forth this soul from the Light. Ask her to come and be with you for a few minutes. You have some important things to say.

She poured out her sorrow and her guilt and her caring for this soul. She heard the soul answer:

F: That's okay. I hadn't been really sure about living a physical life. I hadn't done that for a long time. I wanted to be with you, but coming to you when I did meant I would try being physical for only a very brief time. That was all I was ready for...just to get used to it a little bit. That's why I chose you then. I knew you wouldn't be able to keep me. I still want to be with you, but I'll wait until it's a good time for you when there will also be a father who wants me. Thank you for letting me be in your physical body for a while. It helped me get ready for when I'll make the "big plunge." I really felt your conflict and your intense love.

After further dialogue and a release of deeply buried emotions, the young woman felt complete. "Now I won't have to grow any more tumors!" She has shared that many times since then she has happily sensed a "special little soul hovering around, waiting for a good time to fully come to me."

In conclusion, each of these women later expressed having felt profoundly moved by these guided altered-state experiences of talking with their aborted children. They mentioned having experienced a sense of relief from grief, from conflict, and from guilt. They felt release, completion and an ongoing sense of being specially connected to a precious soul, an endearment, a thankfulness for the largesse, understanding, and forgiveness on the part of the soul. They experienced occasional sadness about the unwanted pregnancies and the abortions but recognized a special growth and perspective that came from their experiences.

Helping Women Make a Choice Regarding Abortion

by

Barbara Findeisen, M.F.C.C.

Introduction

Increasing research indicates that the fetus is a conscious, aware, learning being and that communication with it is possible and effective. We are learning among other things, that it is possible to dialogue with a fetus about a proposed abortion.

I see my role in this process as assisting my client to clear away the rubble in her psyche so that she can see what is the best possible decision for her and the baby at this point in their lives. I may support her decision to keep the child, adopt it out, or terminate the pregnancy, but whatever the decision, it is important that the child be considered, talked to, and treated respectfully as the spirit it truly is. I attempt to help to heal the situation in any way possible. A growing network of professionals work with women in open adoptions, and others lovingly assist women to end pregnancies; my task is to help women choose which route to go. The women's decisions are not always, nor should they be, in alignment with the way I might choose. Discrimination, honesty, and acceptance of differences replace my personal judgment as a therapist.

The process I use for women who come to me with an unplanned pregnancy is one of non-interference, since my position is that only the soul of this woman knows that is the right thing for her to do. Sometimes having the baby is completely right for her and sometimes it is not right. I help her to clear away the barriers of the ego-self so that she is able to make that decision clearly and feel in her heart that it is the right one. My task is to enable and empower the woman to find out what path holds the deepest meaning and the most learning for her. A decision made under force or obligation results in negative repercussions in the life of the baby as well as in the life of the mother.

In helping the woman communicate with the spirit of the unborn child, I put her into a light trance and ask her to invite the soul of the child to the present. This initiates a dialogue. I suggest to the woman that she speak the truth from her heart to the soul of the unborn child and that she listen to the communication that comes from this child to her. This is not difficult. After the woman has shared what is her reality with the soul of the unborn child and listened to any communication, the woman can then invite the child to leave, explaining to it why this is not the right time for her to have a baby and why she cannot care for it. I try to help the woman move into a sense of acceptance and peace. This is made easier because, almost without exception, the spirit of the child comes from a position of love and support for the mother. Often the child will communicate that what the mother has said is acceptable to it and it will wait for a time that is better for her if it wants her for a mother. As a result of these conversations with the soul of the unborn child, often the woman will report a spontaneous miscarriage before the scheduled abortion. The soul of the child is no longer energizing and empowering the baby—the woman feels that it simply leaves.

Past-life work indicates that the soul chooses the mother and father, the circumstances of the life, and the time that will best enable it to learn and to progress and to experience its own unique spirit while in form. At what point does the spirit incarnate in this body it has chosen? In many cases people regressing to the prenatal months see themselves as not being a part of their body for some time. They feel they are observing their growing body as if from the perspective of their soul self. A few people seem to enter the body sheath at the very beginning, but most enter late in the pregnancy and sometimes not until birth, or even a little afterward. There is also a variation in attitude about becoming physical. Some anticipate this experience eagerly but others are reluctant and resist incarnating in a body, as if they realize there are going to be sad and disturbing experiences to work through.

In my work in pre- and perinatal psychology I have also seen a need to expand our consciousness to include the healing of wounds over loss of previous pregnancies. Women who have had miscarriages, stillborn babies, and natal losses of any kind need counseling before they become pregnant again or adopt a child. The psychic womb needs to be cleansed. If feelings are repressed, old fears will cloud further pregnancies. When a lost pregnancy has not been grieved over, a new fetus may think it is conceived in order to replace a lost child and not feel accepted for itself. A baby who has died remains a part of a family, and this needs to be acknowledged and accepted and experienced. Denial and repression insure that the problem does not go away but instead lies in our subconscious mind, collecting interest and exacting its toll in our lives, even if we do not consciously remember.

For example, one of my clients insisted that she had had four abortions but no feelings about them. In order to check this out, I took her back in an altered state to the first time she knew she was pregnant. Much to her surprise, she was elated. She had wanted a baby! There had been no one to support her in having the child, so she repressed her wish and had the first abortion with no feeling. In the session she felt the grief and loss of that child and of what she had really wanted. Subsequent abortions were a repeat of the first one, mechanical, robot-like. Following the therapeutic work on her abortions she expressed a new desire to have a child, a buried wish that she had finally allowed to come to consciousness.

Dialoguing with the soul is also helpful when a baby has died at birth or shortly after birth. Grief over such a loss can be devastating and can affect future pregnancies, as well as other aspects of the woman's life. Unresolved grief takes a toll in our lives; people stay stuck in the past, not just in the past of this lifetime but in that of previous lifetimes. Unresolved grief, like unresolved hatred and anger, clouds our ability to see clearly and to follow our spiritual path. We constantly seek for someone to fill the niche of the lost child, or we may feel we can never risk loving again because the pain of that loss was so great—opening one's heart to another child seems too dangerous.

The procedure is simple. As with women contemplating abortions, I put the mother into a light trance and ask her to invite the spirit of the lost child to be with her and to communicate with her. I have the woman share her feelings and thoughts about her loss of that soul and be open to communication from the spirit of the lost child. The dialogue, which often brings up deep emotions, can be highly cathartic.

I believe it is important to release the spirit of the deceased child in order to allow it to move on freely. The transition from the physical to the spiritual realm can be difficult if there is a strong pull drawing the soul to stay on this level. Often coming to a place of peace with the lost child acts as a simple releasement for both child and mother.

Case 1. Spontaneous Abortion Following Dialogue with a Fetus

A client, Betty, came into my office in an agitated state after discovering that she was pregnant from a casual affair. Marriage was out of the question and she felt conflicted as to whether to terminate the pregnancy. She became calmer as we talked, and we explored a number of possibilities, but none of them felt right to her.

I asked Betty to lie down and breathe deeply for a few minutes. As she sank into a peaceful and relaxed state, I gave quieting suggestions. Finally I asked her to invite the spirit of the child to be with us. (I assume that the soul is always conscious, perhaps even more spiritually conscious when not yet identified with a body and ego.)

In a brief time Betty felt that there was another presence in the room, that of the child. I requested her to explain in detail all her feelings and thoughts about being pregnant at that time and then to dialogue with the consciousness of the child. This was done in silence. I give clients the option of working within in quietness, or verbally. Since the purpose is for them to find healing, it is not necessary that this work be done so that I can hear it. It is enough that it is communicated to me later.

In the altered state Betty struggled, with tears running down her cheeks. Gradually her face cleared, her breathing slowed, and there was a sense of peace about her. Later she told me that the child had communicated its love to her and desired to cause her no pain. Betty said that she firmly believed the incoming child was to be a girl. When she left my office she was still not clear as to exactly what she was going to do but she knew that the situation would resolve itself and that she and the child would be all right.

Two days later Betty called to inform me that she had had a spontaneous miscarriage. She believed that the soul had left the physical level and had returned home to spirit, perhaps to come again at a later time. The healing was complete. As I write, Betty is pregnant again, and this time happily so.

Case 2. A Difficult Decision

A woman came to me in turmoil. She already had two children and had become pregnant with a third when her husband walked out on her for another woman. It was a traumatic time; she had reluctantly accepted that she was going to have to return to work to support her children and then discovered she was pregnant. Her husband didn't want her to keep the child, and her anger at him made her oppositional so that it became difficult for her to sort out what she should do. Because she didn't want to have an abortion to please him she found it difficult to tune into what she herself wanted.

We had to separate the issue of a possible abortion from that of going along with her husband's wishes. In addition, we had to address her Christian beliefs that were against abortion, making the decision especially difficult. After much prayer she was ready for a dialogue with the unborn child. Though she was deeply conflicted herself, she felt that the message that came from the baby communicated acceptance of her decision and showed no judgment about it, though the child was very sad. Soul consciousness seems to be able to accept just what is without judgment. As a rule it shows acceptance, not resistance. Judgment may be a quality of the ego mind, not of the spiritual mind.

After this dialogue my client felt that the most loving thing she could do for her other two children and herself was to have an abortion. She did not have a spontaneous miscarriage, but after the abortion she felt that the spirit of this child stayed with her for some time, and she felt comforted by that. Some months later she felt the spirit of this child depart, leaving her in a healing peace. She felt content that she had prayed deeply for her own spiritual guidance, had dialogued with the unborn child, and had had the blessing of the soul for some time afterwards.

Her social world did not go along with her decision about the abortion. When she told some of her friends at church, they shunned her and in a sense branded her with an "A," not for adultery, but for abortion. Just when she most needed the support of the people that she loved and cared about, they turned against her so that she had to find another church. It took her several years to get back on her feet after the trauma of the divorce and the abortion, but she kept the feeling of peacefulness and the sense of having done the right thing that she had gained from the conversation with the unborn child. Eventually she remarried.

It is to be hoped that people will become able to respect the mutual decision of a mother and of a child whom she cannot care for and support. For both mother and child the abortion can be a deepening and spiritual process, and this needs to be respected and supported without judgment.

Communication with Life En Utero

By

Hugh Harmon, Ph.D.

The body of evidence of both memories of life within the womb and communication with a life *en utero* suggests that spirit/intelligence is present from conception on. If this is so, what are the implications regarding terminating pregnancies, as by abortion? What are the rights of this unborn soul, and also, what are the rights of the mother? In most pro-life discussions, it is assumed that all the rights are on the side of the unborn soul.

While it is true that a spirit/intelligence is indeed present within or about the developing embryo, it is also true that a spirit/intelligence is present in the woman whose womb that embryo, or spirit/intelligence wishes to use for its development. And it is generally recognized by those of even the strongest moral objections to abortion that each spirit/intelligence, or soul if you will, has been given a will and a right to exercise that will as long as it does not interfere with the will of another. When a soul enters the egg and/or the embryo, it seeks to further its will, its desires, its aims, but in doing so, it has no more right to interfere with the will, the aims, or the desires of another than if it were outside the womb. Therefore, the will of the one in whom that soul wishes to grow must be considered and respected.

Spirit/intelligence cannot be destroyed. When the vehicle for a soul is destroyed, the soul returns to its true spirit state. In the case of miscarriage, abortion, or other termination of pregnancy, the soul that has associated itself with the fertilized egg in the womb, if one has indeed done so, which is not always the case, will return to the state of spirit and await another time or other parents. The choice, therefore, belongs with both the soul (the spirit/intelligence) and the woman in whose womb the embryo wishes to grow. Any decision needs to be mediated between the two.

This can be done, far more easily than is usually postulated, by a dialogue between the two and an exchange of views. When this takes place, a mutual decision acceptable to both can be reached, and the woman is left without any guilt and the soul without any anger or resentment. Often the soul produces a spontaneous miscarriage and is spared trauma from a surgical procedure.

Case 1. Convincing a Persistent Soul

A woman came to see me who was continually getting pregnant, even though she was consistently using normally reliable contraceptive measures. She had already had five abortions and was pregnant for the sixth time. She came to me to ask what I thought might be going on and what she could do about it. She was unwilling to have her tubes tied but she did not want any more children, as she felt it was all she could do, given her circumstances, to raise the two she had already.

I suggested we try to contact the embryo. She was willing but expressed doubts about the possibility of there being a communicating intelligence to contact. In hypnosis, I had her ask if she could talk to the spirit or intelligence of the embryo. "Yes," was the given response. Through the altered state of the mother, the embryo spirit announced it was a male and that he had tried many times to have her for a mother, feeling rejected every time she'd had an abortion. He was determined to try again.

She responded that she would not allow this, as she simply could not have another baby. He insisted that she must be his mother, to which, she answered, "Maybe in another lifetime, but not in this one." (This was an answer that surprised me, as I was aware she did not consciously believe in past or future lives.) She further stated that she would indeed terminate this pregnancy and would keep terminating future pregnancies and asked if he would please cease trying to make her his mother. He agreed to "think about it." Within two days she spontaneously aborted and, in the 15 years since, with sex on a regular basis and the same contraceptive measures, she has not had another pregnancy.

Case 2. Confirming Pregnancy

An OB nurse, a client of mine, arrived for her appointment one day and said that she felt she might be pregnant. She'd been an OB nurse for 15 years and had seven children of her own, so she knew the signs of pregnancy well, but she still wished to confirm if she was indeed pregnant, as it was in the very earliest stage. She wondered if we might be able to tell with hypnosis. I suggested we use kinesiology testing to ask her body. The response was that yes, she was pregnant. We further asked if it was a girl or a boy. A girl, we discovered.

Sure enough, about eight and a half months later she delivered, at home with all her children and her husband in attendance, a beautiful, healthy, baby girl. Over the months of her pregnancy I'd trained the mother in hypnosis for the birth, and during the sessions we had even talked to the developing embryo and fetus. When it was time to push the baby out, the mother, who had been lying on the bed, decided it would be easier to squat, and she got up and squatted on the floor, pushing the baby out easily and comfortably into the father's waiting hands. She then immediately took the baby to bed to nurse her and called me to announce the birth to and invite me to come and hold the baby myself.

I was there in less than an hour, holding that baby girl on my lap and looking into her eyes. As soon as I spoke, that child's eyes locked on mine and she smiled with a wonderful glowing, vital energy. The baby is now a small child and is extremely bright, totally secure, and very comfortable with herself and her surroundings. I am waiting for her to be able to speak a little more clearly and lucidly so I can ask her about her experiences in Mommy and coming out of Mommy.

Case 3. Convincing the Unborn to Change Birth Position

A woman called me to say she that had started labor pains but the doctors had told her the baby was in breech position and they felt they would have to do a Cesarean section. I asked her to take time to talk to the baby, to reassure it and tell it what it had to do to turn around. She did so, telling the baby it was loved, wanted, and welcomed in every way. Within ten minutes, the baby had repositioned itself in the perfect position for birth. I had previously coached this mother on hypnosis for birth and she experienced a completely pain-free labor and delivery.

Many people will insist that this incident was a lucky coincidence, that it is impossible to communicate with a baby before delivery and convince it to change its position. We need to be open to this possibility, however, and gather more evidence as to what the unborn child can understand and carry out. The universe is a marvelous, vast, and unknown place. Many of its laws and truths are scarcely known to us as we dwell within our physical realm. Of all we have been taught, perhaps two of the most helpful tenets in approaching situations beyond our usual awareness are "Judge not," and "Love one another," messages of all major religions. Both of these thoughts can be helpful in approaching such a controversial subject as abortion.

Releasing the Attachment of an Aborted Entity

by

Louise Ireland-Frey, M.D.

Introduction

Each individual case of prospective abortion needs to be considered on its own merits and demerits, and the decision as to the rightness of the abortion should be the outcome of such a weighed consideration. No decision, whether to abort or to bear the child, no matter how carefully considered, can always please the unborn soul. Many abused or neglected children who were *not* aborted later sob despairingly, wishing they had never been born, and some child-entities whose bodies were aborted say that they were glad they didn't have to live. On the other hand, there are many entities of aborted infants who are frightened and feel rejected and worthless, or who are maddened by the pain of the abortion procedure and become enraged and vengeful, who wanted to live but were cut off by abortion. To avoid this, careful evaluation of the situation is needed to avoid unnecessary suffering on the part of either the baby or the mother, either before the child is born or after its birth or the abortion.

Although the various physical factors carry weight in such an evaluation, the psychological factors are fully as important. In addition, there are karmic and spiritual factors, such as a past-life connection between the soul of the baby and its parents, or karma that needs to be balanced by this particular situation or educational opportunities for the psyche of the child or its parents. All of these need to be considered by the persons involved, preferably before a contemplated abortion is performed.

If the mother is young and unmarried, her emotions are likely to be full of feelings of fear, embarrassment, guilt, and probably anger, shame, and defiance. She may also feel betrayed and deserted by others. The feelings of the child's father and of her own parents may well add to the intensity of her own feelings, whether or not these are expressed verbally. All of these, after all, "mark the baby," as the old midwives used to say. If she decides to have the baby, her ambivalence imprints itself upon the child's psyche, along with deep feelings of self-blame. It is as if the emotions and words of the mother and people associated with her become obsessing thought forms within the unborn infant's psyche, coloring and molding it deep in its subconscious, to appear later as a profound lack of self-confidence in later years. Or it may emerge as a phobia for dark holes and sharp points (in the case of a failed abortion), or as rage or fear in situations of helplessness or frustration.

If the child's psyche already has a history of strong negativity through many lifetimes, the addition of pain and rejection from its parents during the contemplated abortion and after it is born only increases its own unpleasant nature and predisposes it to a life of hate, anger, and vengefulness. In such a case it might be a blessing to allow the entity a longer period between earth lives so that it can soften and grow a little more spiritually. We consider an abortion justified or indicated when the physical body is defective, but perhaps this should be equally true when emotional and spiritual development is inadequate.

The karmic necessities of the fetus make up an area of exploration in which most prospective mothers have little experience, but this area, as well as other considerations, both from the side of the mother and from that of the fetus, can easily be explored in an altered state using the prospective mother to channel the thoughts of her fetus. The client allows the psyche of the infant to place its own thoughts and feelings into her mind and then speaks them aloud, guided by the questions of the therapist. In this way there is direct conversation with the psyche of the fetus and the differing viewpoints of fetus and mother can be weighed and a mutual decision reached. If the soul of the fetus comes to understand that the parents do not want any child at this time and that the reasons for this stand are viable, it usually will agree. Sometimes it will even abort spontaneously. But whether the abortion is spontaneous or induced, such a conversation will enable the soul to continue on its journey and not become an obsessing entity to the mother or to some other person who promises a warm haven from its wanderings.

When the therapist speaks to the psyche of an embryo or infant, it should not be with condescension but with respect and consideration, keeping in mind that this infant is a feeling, understanding individual, alive in the present, not a "thing" or a concept. Gentleness and compassion are necessary for a successful conversation with the aborted soul, and for assisting it to find ease, safety, and peace is of paramount importance.

As with any altered-state work, the wordings of the therapist are important in eliciting a specific type of awareness and level of response. If the therapist asks questions about physical feelings and processes of the body, the answer is likely to come from the cellular level of awareness. If the questions concern spiritual cause or choices made by the entity, the answers will come from the superconscious level. Answers from this level include awareness of higher entities and plans to which the soul has made a commitment and from which it has accepted a task to perform. In between these extremes is a wide spread of altered consciousness that includes a broad exterior awareness of the environment, such as past events about the mother and father; causal events, such as "it is a time of famine"; and the mother's feelings and thoughts before and during the delivery. Sometimes it is valuable to explore on all levels. Other times, such as in the case of the twin fetuses (Case 4) this is not necessary.

Case 1. A Compatible Abortion in Another Lifetime

The following case demonstrates the ability of a fetus to evaluate its potentials for a productive life. It concerns a fetus that was aborted in another lifetime and combines prenatal, birth, and death experiences as seen from both exterior and interior viewpoints of the entity's mind. The dialogue and procedure are similar to conversation with a fetus in a current lifetime where abortion is being considered.

The client, a retired army nurse, was asked in a demonstration to go back in an altered state to a brief, pleasant birth experience. She found herself in rural Hungary. From an exterior position she saw a young woman hunching under a tree, looking uphill at a shack and wishing she could get there but knowing there was no time. With minimal discomfort her baby was born. Focus was then shifted to the consciousness of the baby.

> E: *I'm looking up at my mother. She's pretty. What a big thick braid.... Oh, she's a gypsy!... She's thin—and she's thinking about all the other children, seven or eight of them. All she has to feed them is water that she heats, and she puts dirt in it to fill their stomachs.... Everybody is starving. It's a time of famine. My father is gone somewhere—off to war, I guess. He was told he had to go. He didn't want to go and leave my mother alone.*

All this came spontaneously, with numerous pauses, or else in response to questions from the therapist. The dialogue continued:

> T: *Are you a big baby?*
> E: *Oh, no, I'm real little! I'm looking down at my body...*
> T: *Looking down? Are you dead and looking down at your body?*
> E: *My mother put her finger over my mouth.*
> T: *Do you mean your mother killed you?*
> E: *She didn't kill me. She just put her finger over my mouth.*
> T: *How do you feel emotionally about that?*
> E: *Oh, it's a relief. It was a relief to come out and it's a relief to be free.*
> T: *I asked your mind to bring us a pleasant experience. Was that it?*

> E: *Well, I took on a task, a duty, and I did it. I feel real good about that. And I was glad I didn't have to live. It really wasn't unpleasant, except the starving before I was born. That was awful!*

Subsequent re-living in an altered state brought out that the mother, finding herself pregnant, had wondered what to do about another mouth to feed. Finally she asked a neighbor to show her where some "baby leaves" grew in the forest. The bitter leaves were an abortifacient, and when she ate some of them, contractions began a short time later, increasing so suddenly that she was not able to get back to her shack. The delivery of what seemed to be a six-month fetus was quick and easy.

After coming out of the baby's body at its death, the mind of the entity looked down and evaluated it.

> E: *Its head looks funny—different. It has no forehead. It has no top to its head, no brain. There is just skin straight back from the eyebrows.*
> T: *Why were you chosen to be the soul of this child?*
> E: *I was among those available to take on this task, and I volunteered, I guess. I was told (by spiritual sources) that it would be for only a short time and then I could come back (to the spiritual world). I was glad I didn't have to live.*

This entity moved from exterior descriptions, including awareness of its environment and of causal events such as the famine, to a spiritual awareness of its choice for that kind of experience. This spread of awareness is characteristic of fetal consciousness and is often more easily retrieved than awareness of similar areas in early childhood. It makes possible a profound resolution of the dilemma over abortion.

Case 2. Contacting the Psyche of an Aborted Infant

Expulsion of an entity by induced abortion of the fetal body, unless an understanding has previously been reached with the mother, can lead to karmic and emotional repercussions. One outcome is that the psyche of the fetus may flee the abortion scene and wander, frightened, in the earth-bound state for an indefinite period. Or it may seek warmth and refuge in some hiding place, such as the body of a living person, especially its mother, obsessing that person and bringing into that person all the fear, loneliness, and feelings of rejection and abandonment, the pain and anger, that the entity felt before and during the abortion procedure. Releasement not only frees the client from the obsessing infant-entity but also frees the frightened astral consciousness of the aborted infant from its fears and pains and assists it to go to the warmth and safety of a higher astral condition (sometimes called *The Summerland*), a garden-like state for children whose bodies have died.

When the soul or psyche of an aborted infant is discovered obsessing a client, the therapist talks to it as to any other obsessing entity, using the client to channel the aborted infant's thoughts and assuring the infant that it can understand the questions and can put its thoughts and feelings into the mind of the client, who will then speak them aloud. Such thoughts are transferred either by telepathy or by direct mind contact, and the unborn entity (its body now dead) can still hear, understand, and respond, even if its brain is not yet formed or has never developed. It is the individual being, the conscious self, that responds, guided by the wordings of the therapist.

A woman who has had an abortion can talk to the infant's psyche, explaining why she felt it wise to end the pregnancy and assuring the entity of the child that it was not a personal rejection of this particular soul but just a reluctance to have *any* child at this time. She may wish to add that at some later time she would welcome the entity as her child. This may be all that is necessary to alleviate the loneliness and sadness of the aborted psyche, whether or not it has been obsessing the mother in the literal sense.

The process of working with the aborted psyche's consciousness begins by raising its consciousness to a higher level by suggesting that its mind let go of all personalities and go to the High Place from which it can see clearly back into the past, down into the present, and forward into the future. The therapist then asks that the entity focus on the planning stage, in which it made decisions regarding the coming incarnation into physical life. Some helpful questions from the therapist are:

Did you choose your mother? Your father? Did they want to have a baby, or not? Did they plan this pregnancy? How did they feel when the pregnancy became known? What did they say, and what were their exact tones of voice? What was your reaction to their reactions? Have you been with either of your parents in past lives? What karma did you hope to balance by belonging to this couple? Or did you hope to help *them* in some way? Was there any change in your feelings and expectations before the abortion? What were your feelings regarding the decision to abort your body? Who made that decision, you or someone else? For what reason?

Each aborted entity can describe the method used for the abortion, even in detail if encouraged by the facilitator, though this is not necessary, for with hypnosis the amount of pain, revulsion, and fear originally experienced can carefully be controlled and softened, and should be. It is not necessary for all the original suffering to be re-experienced in order to gain complete relief for the psyche of the child. Questions regarding the abortion process might include:

If the abortion was originally your own decision, did you change your mind at any time during the process? What was your way of reacting to your helplessness? Anger? Hate? Grief? Hear clearly any words spoken by the persons performing the operation or by your mother. Tell us those words in the exact tone of voice. Now hear clearly any words spoken and contact any strong emotions of the persons after they have finished performing the abortion, in their tones of voice.

When cold, insensitive words are spoken or similarly rejecting unspoken emotions are present, verbal cancellations of these rejecting feelings are of great benefit therapeutically.

Next, the psyche may be questioned about actions following disembodiment, because these may lead to the releasement.

What is your feeling just after you are out of the body: Relief? Rage? Peace? Desire for revenge? Desire to escape, to hide? What do you do: stay there for a while near your mother? Stay in the place where the abortion took place? Wander off? Or seek a place of safety? Do you find a place of warmth and safety? If so, where is it and how does it feel? (Find out clearly if it is in the body of a living person.) How are you feeling right now, as you talk to me? You know by now that I am your friend and want to help you, and you are helping me by answering all these questions. I appreciate your help. Thank you for talking with me. It has not been easy for you. You have been very brave.

The therapist needs to take over at this point and release the child's psyche from its own fears and other negative feelings, canceling out all remaining pain and adverse imprinted words spoken and all feelings of inferiority and other negative attitudes of its own self as well as those of others involved.

In closing, the therapist needs to guide the child's psyche toward a warm stream of love, substituting words like "liquid" and "water" and "fluid" for the word "light," since the safety of a fetus is in the warm amniotic fluid of the womb. A spiritual helper may be invited to come and carry the little one to its own warm, safe place. The helper may be visualized as a motherly or angelic being who holds and cuddles the infant. The client who is doing the channeling may see such a helper, and it is wise to accept as true all such visualized phenomena, since whether these are symbols or images produced by the therapist's suggestions or actual astral beings makes no difference therapeutically.

One such release was a brief contact at the end of a lengthy session with a young woman who was in therapy for other reasons. In these few minutes the two infant-psyches of her two abortions were released and the client was free from their influence on her emotions. Whether the two babies she had aborted were actually *obsessing* (residing within her body) or were merely *oppressing* her (by clinging to her aura or shadowing her emotionally) was not determined. Both infant psyches came when called and replied to the therapist's questions by finger movements and by the client channeling what they were feeling. The following is a brief account of the release of the second baby following the successful release of the first baby.

T: *Now I am calling the entity of the second baby whose body was aborted. Are you the same soul as the first one?*

E: *(Indicates "no" with finger movement.)*

T: *You heard my conversation with the other baby's soul, didn't you?*

E: *(Indicates "yes" with finger movement.)*

T: *I ask you, too, to put out of you all the fear and pain and the anger and frowning and resentment and jealousy. Just urinate them out of you, just breathe them out with little chest motions.*

E: *(Frowns and scowls.)*

T: *And the next thing is to feel the opposites, the positives, coming into you to take the place of all those bad old things, so you will feel good, feel happy and safe.*

E: *(Continues to scowl and grimace.)*

T: *Honey, you do understand that your mama wasn't rejecting you yourself, don't you? She just didn't want to have any child at this time.*

E: *(Still scowling) I don't like it! I understand but I don't like it!*

T: *Yes, the abortion spoiled your plans?*

E: *Yes!*

T: *Well, little one, be quiet now and let all the pain and the bad memories fade away and go out of you. If you chose this lady to be your mama, you didn't choose the right time to come to her. Maybe at some other time she may be able to welcome you and you can come to her then as her baby. Now let all the frowning go away.*

E: *All right. (Face smooths out.)*

T: *I ask someone to come as a gentle, mother-type guardian angel to take this baby safely home. Be patient, honey. Now be carried to the Garden, to the beautiful warm pool, if you wish. Or you can grow, if you wish. Do you want to grow?*

E: *Yes.*

T: *Are you ready to go now?*

E: *Yes. (Smiling. Deep sigh.)*

T: *Then bye-bye, Honey.*

E: *(Whisper) Bye-bye.*

The client, on returning to waking consciousness, had to urinate. The unconscious mind, like a child, takes words with *exact* literalness: the baby's psyche used the client's kidneys to urinate the bad things out!

A Therapist Learns about Abortion

by

Winafred B. Lucas, Ph.D.

Introduction

Dialoguing with an unborn soul is easier than it seems. I have begun to see that we do not have to guess at what the unborn soul wants or what it has suffered—we just have to communicate. I have learned also that both mother and fetus have needs, and the needs of either one do not necessarily take precedence; there must be a balancing. As therapists we can provide healing for the unborn soul, and we can facilitate healing for the mother. Numerous possibilities open up to assist in working out problems with the unborn child and its mother, and most of these involve direct communication.

Case 1. Balancing the Needs of Mother and Child

Allison was a young actress who had spent time in therapy learning to find out who she was and how to make wise and self-protective decisions about a career that had many ups and downs. During our previous year together she had carried the lead in a long-running play in the Los Angeles area that had brought her favorable notices and positive attention. Following this, she was offered her first starring role in a movie in which she felt she could be competent and creative. At the same time, she discovered she was pregnant. She was not deeply involved with the father-to-be and could get no help from him, but she had a loving and supportive family who offered to take the baby for her until she was through the movie. The complication that she kept coming back to was that the movie role was such that it could not possibly weather the changes in physical appearance that pregnancy brings. She came back to therapy to try to resolve the dilemma.

I felt that the soul she was carrying might be able to communicate with her about the situation, so I took Allison into an altered state and had her summon the child. Almost immediately a little girl appeared.

T: *You might ask her why she chose you as her mother at this time.*
P: *She tells me that we have known each other before and she wants the things I can give to her as her mother.*
T: *What, for instance?*
P: *She says I am creative and free and she wants to share the experiences with me.*
T: *You could tell her that it is not a good time.*
P: *She says she wants to be with me now, that she doesn't want to wait until I am older.*

This strong wish on the child's part seemed to me to be the deciding factor, and I had Allison assure the child of her love and say goodbye. I assumed that the desire of the child took precedence, and I completely overlooked Allison's struggle to become an actress of stature. A pregnancy at the time would seriously interfere with Allison's efforts to establish herself. I did not take account of the fact that in the uncertain milieu of the motion picture world she might not get another chance to do so and that she might, perhaps unconsciously, feel a lifelong resentment toward a child who had caused her career to end abruptly. My most regrettable omission was that I did not encourage the interchange to continue so that Allison could state her feelings and needs and so that a compromise could be worked out.

Allison left my office ambivalent, but I assumed that the idea of an abortion had been dismissed. I did not hear from her directly again. Later I learned that she had had the abortion and following it had successfully completed her acting role. She never came to see me again.

The experience with her became my teacher. I realized that I was right when I thought a dialogue was possible between a prospective mother and the soul whose new body she was carrying. What I had not realized was that the mother has rights and needs and these must be negotiated and balanced with the needs of the prospective child. The mother's situation must be honored or the new soul may be born into an inhospitable world. It is a two-way street!

Case 2. Resolution with an Aborted Soul

Melissa was a high school senior when at 17 her inconsistent birth-control approach failed. She was a beautiful girl, blonde and statuesque and artistically gifted, but volatile. Several years of drug exploration and casual relationships with boys had interfered with the development of her talent. Her parents—her father a minister in a small church and her mother a legal secretary—had despaired over their daughter's deviant behavior. The mother alternated between pretending Melissa did not exist and berating her to the point of shaking her.

When Melissa became pregnant she appealed to her boyfriend and his family for support, but they felt frightened and impotent in a situation they could not accept, so she finally had to tell her mother. The mother's response was to order her to get an abortion the next day or leave the house. Melissa, seeing no source of help and feeling unable to cope on her own, complied, but she was angry at having been given no choice and remorseful over the loss of a child that she felt, even if she had released it in an open adoption, would have been something of her own. So intense was her distress that she became unable to achieve academically, and she stopped her art work altogether, though in former stressful situations her art had given her emotional release. She became depressed and moved without energy in a dark cloud of confusion. The parents, who had become increasingly frustrated and knew of no way to pressure her into conformity, with reluctance referred her for therapy.

When Melissa first came, the dark cloud that her mother had told me about was obvious. Melissa moved slowly and her eyes looked haunted. I wondered if perhaps the baby, so suddenly wrenched from its secure home, might be unsure of what had happened to it and could be shadowing her. All I said, however, was that it was possible to talk with the baby and perhaps later we could do so. I did not pursue this because I needed to see if Melissa could accept this process as a valid one.

We spent most of the early sessions in psychological testing and talking about her life. I attempted to raise her level of involvement in her artistic work and in her preparation for college entrance exams, using every legitimate evaluation I could extract from her testing, which showed her to be in the superior range intellectually, as well as creative and surprisingly integrated. With Melissa's blessing I also fed back some of this positive evaluation to the mother in order to help restore what I could of the mother-daughter relationship.

As Melissa's relationship with her parents became to some extent repaired and she began to study and paint again, she became more confident, and it was at this point that she reminded me that we had not talked to the baby. Following this lead I took her into a garden meditation in order to provide a structure for meeting the baby. She saw a gate into her garden made of green lattice work. Within was a spread of orange lilies. Yellow roses appeared and purple and red peonies and hibiscus. There was a fish pond set smoothly in the grass with a bench nearby, and she could hear birds and see flashes of color as the birds flew through the garden. Her artist's sensitivity was evident.

When I asked whether she had wanted a boy or a girl, she said that she had wanted a little girl and would have named her Cybelle. I then had her ask the soul of the aborted child to come and talk with her. Almost immediately a sturdy blonde boy appeared who greeted her with, "Hi!"

At my suggestion she asked the child why he had chosen her for his mother.

P: *He says it's because I'm an artist and he wants that kind of mother, but I'm telling him that it wouldn't have helped anyway because he would have had to have been adopted by someone else were—my parents wouldn't have let me keep him.*

T: *Does he have a response to that?*

P: *He says that he wouldn't have wanted that. He's disappointed but it's okay about the abortion. He says that maybe he'll come back later. But he understands.*

T: *Is it all right that he comes back? For you?*

P: *That's fine. I thought I wanted a girl, but I like this little boy.*

T: *What does he want in a mother other than someone who loves beauty and is an artist?*

P: *He wants to be happy and safe, and that's what I couldn't have given him this time.*

T: *Can you see what he's like as a soul?*

P: *He's sensitive. Very understanding. Loving. Sincere. Fun...I just want to listen to him for a moment.*

T: *(Remaining quiet for several minutes) How does he feel now about not having you?*

P: *He says he's just letting go.*

T: *Perhaps you could think of a gift to give him.*

P: *I have a pine cone in my hand that came from a tree on the edge of the garden and I give it to him.*

T: *What does he do with it?*

P: *He's holding it close and his eyes are happy.*

T: *Does he have a gift for you?*

P: *He is giving me a shining blue stone, just like his eyes.*

Following this session Melissa was at peace about her baby, and shortly afterward she terminated her therapy. Her mother told me later that she had passed her SAT's and entered an eastern women's college prepared to take an art major. She had a new boyfriend from a neighboring men's college. The wound of the forced abortion appeared to have been healed enough for her to go on with her life. If the baby had been shadowing her earlier, she had released it to go on its own path.

Chapter VI

Contemporary Approaches to Releasement

The conviction that spirits possess living people is based on the premise that life does continue after death. Earthbound entities are simply those who did not make the natural transition to higher planes of existence. Possession reinforces the evidence suggesting that only the physical body dies and that personality survives, that we are immortal beings.

Edith Fiore

It is usually necessary to do therapy with the possessor before he can move on. Full dissolution of the possession involves a resolution of the relationship between possessed and possessor. That resolution can be attained only when the possessor has come to terms with his unhealthy attachment to the host.

Adam Crabtree

Bibliography

Baldwin, William. *Regression Therapy: Spirit Releasement Therapy.* Enterprise, FL: Bethel Publications, 1992.

Chaplin, Annabel. *The Bright Light of Death.* Marina del Rey, CA: DeVorss and Co., 1977.

Crabtree, Adam. *Multiple Man: Explorations in Possession and Multiple Personality.* New York: Prager Publishers, 1985. (To be re-released in 1993 by Harper-Collins)

Fiore, Edith. *The Unquiet Dead.* New York: Doubleday, 1987.

————. "Freeing Statements in Relationships by Resolution of Entity Attachments." *The Journal of Regression Therapy,* Vol. III, No. 1, 1988.

Ireland-Frey, Louise. "Clinical Depossession: Releasement of Attached Entities from Unsuspecting Hosts." *The Journal of Regression Therapy,* Vol. I, No. 2, 1986.

Kapferer, Bruce. *A Celebration of Demons: Exorcism and Aesthetics of Healing in Sri Lanka.* IN: Bloomington University Press, 1983.

Lucas, Winafred. "Spontaneous Remissions." *The Journal of Regression Therapy,* Vol. II, No. 2, 1987.

————. "The Weighing of the Heart and Other Hells." *The Journal of Regression Therapy,* Vol. III, No. 2, 1988.

————. "Releasement in Sri Lanka." *Newsletter—The Association for Past-Life Research and Therapies,* Vol. 12, No. 2, Summer 1992.

Motoyama, Hiroshi. "A Case of Possession in a Past Life Resulting in Physical Problems." *The Journal of Regression Therapy,* Vol. II, No. 2, 1987.

Naegeli-Osjord, Hans. *Possession and Exorcism.* Great Britain: Colin Smith, 1988.

Wickland, Carl. *Thirty Years Among the Dead.* Newcastle, England: Newcastle Publ. Co., 1974.

Contemporary Approaches to Releasement

Introduction

There is no altered-state work into which I go more reluctantly than into that of attachment and releasement, not because these are difficult, either conceptually or therapeutically, but because they constitute an area of treatment that is not as yet adequately grounded or documented. However, I have felt compelled to consider in depth my own experiential data and that of others, no matter in what strange and untenable directions they lead. The other contributors in this section have had similar experiences themselves or have been confronted with them in their therapeutic work and also have been compelled to take some position regarding the phenomena, uncomfortable through it has been to do this. It is not possible for us to put our heads in the sand and pretend that we have observed nothing. Nor is it helpful to describe our experiences as vagaries of the imagination. The experiences are too graphic and the resolution of them too healing to be dismissed in such a way.

My personal experience began when I was having lunch with a close and long-time friend, Iona Kaplan, whose famous philosopher husband had succored and supported me when he was a member of my doctoral committee. Iona and I chatted for a while, and then she pulled out a small book, handling it as though it would burn her fingers. She told me that an old friend of hers, Annabelle Chaplin,[1] had written it and she didn't know what to think. Would I give her my opinion?

I took the book home and through it moved into a startling new understanding of areas of therapy where no current technique seemed to give explanation or healing. It was an area dealing with the release of souls who have not gone into the Light. Of this I knew nothing, but Chaplin's writing was simple, obviously sincere, and clearly the observation of a sound, loving, and careful therapist. There was no way that I could summarily dismiss the experiences it described. When I told Iona that I had taken the book seriously and felt that it might touch on something significant, she accepted this reluctantly. It was obviously difficult for her to understand how a woman she had known well and cherished could have moved so far in a non-traditional direction.

A year or so later I had occasion to test out Chaplin's hypothesis. My former husband, whom I had not seen for many years, after a lifetime of alternating frustration and depression, hung himself. It had been difficult for me as a therapist, while we had been together, to find my profession and myself impotent to help him in spite of his struggle to be helped, and that he had finally given up brought sadness. My grown children and I went to Seattle for a memorial service. He had loved poetry, and whenever he could emerge from the dark pall that chilled his life, he had loved people. Each of us chose a favorite poem to read. All of his family said goodbye to him with caring.

The day I returned home, I found myself overwhelmed with such a dark oppressive mood that I could not get up until noon, and from then on this shadowing began each of my days. I had to force myself out of bed to meet my obligations, but about noon the shadowing would dissolve, and then for the rest of the day I functioned well. This inevitable morning darkness never lessened, and I began to wonder if I had some sort of serious illness.

The following December I spent several weeks in the high desert with Brugh Joy. At the close of the first week the group entered a 60-hour fast and silence. When this was nearly over I wandered into the desert and slipped into an altered state in which it occurred to me that the type of attachment Annabelle Chaplin had talked about in her book might explain my shadowing. Since I had nothing except my memory of the book to guide me, I simply called to my former husband and asked if he were still hovering around me. He was there immediately and answered that he didn't know where he was. Remembering the instructions in the book, I told him carefully how he had hung himself from a tree above a beautiful lake that he had loved, and about the note that he had written saying that psychiatry had failed him. I said that he needed to go to the Light, that staying around and bothering me did neither of us any good. He agreed to leave, and I never experienced the morning shadowing again. It was only years later that it occurred to me that he himself had been heavily shadowed and that was why he had been so unresponsive to conventional psychotherapy.

This experience encouraged me a year later to re-examine the situation with my son, who had been in a similar shadowed place for 16 years. He had grown up joyous and warm as a child, and as an adolescent he had had many friends. From the age of six he had been involved in writing plays and was considered by his teachers to be highly gifted, but a month after graduation from a small private school, a pall came over him. He started to smoke, he was unable to complete any writing, his personal relationships constantly disintegrated, and physically he appeared sallow and without energy. I did my best to understand, and I found for my son the most competent therapists in our area, but nothing changed. It was humbling that once again my profession and I had failed.

At the end of a workshop given in my home by Robert Waterman, I asked Robert, who was a psychic as well as president of a small alternative college, if he could help me determine whether my son was shadowed. It was Christmas Eve and the workshop members had gone. Robert said that we could try. We went into the meditation room and lit a candle and I brought out my son's picture. Using a pendulum, Robert asked if there was an entity shadowing my son, and the answer was yes. I asked it if was his father, and the answer was no. (His father had died only a year before so it seemed unlikely.) Robert asked if the entity was friendly, then if it would like to go to the Light, and both answers were affirmative. He then did a releasement and finally asked how long before my son would feel freed. The answer was four hours. We blew out the candle.

I felt that I must have known the person who was shadowing my son, and during the following week, using Kahuna techniques[2] that I was trying out at the time, I recovered the memory that one of his classmates, who had been his devoted follower but had few other friends, had been killed on a motorcycle a month after that high school graduation. That was also the month my son began to smoke, though at the time I did not see a connection because I was under the impression that the student involved had not smoked.

My son had been in Seattle with his grandmother for the holidays and did not call me until several weeks later. At that time he reported with enthusiasm that his life had completely changed. He had quit his "lousy job," he had sold a script for $2,000, and he had met a wonderful girl. It was a new life! When I asked him when the change had taken place, he said things had begun to change the day before Christmas. He thought it might have come about because of visiting his relatives.

His life continued to become freer and happier and more successful. For several years I said nothing about the releasement work. Then one day I remarked carelessly that there had been a reason why he had had such a hard time for so long, and he insisted that I tell him. When I finally discussed the experience he was quiet for a moment and then said that if he hadn't had psychosynthesis work, he would think I was crazy, but as it was, he wasn't sure. I let it go at that, and my impression is that he currently thinks the account is a fantasy. However, when he finally stopped smoking a few years ago, I remarked that I would have understood his starting to smoke when he did if his friend had smoked. It was then that he told me that his friend had "smoked like a chimney."

How much should these experiences impact me? Certainly it is necessary to consider other explanations. For instance, perhaps the deep and moving work with Brugh Joy during that retreat changed some perspective in me, shifted some energy field so that I was able to move out of the cloud. But the situation with my son could not be explained by any sort of suggestion because he was not with me at the time and did not know about the releasement until years later. Calling such experiences spontaneous remissions or coincidences does not provide any real explanation.

Work with entities currently is fighting an uphill battle for acceptance and respectability. The metaphysical framework of the contemporary Western world automatically dismisses releasement as a viable option in psychotherapy, and only recently is the possibility opening up that an aspect of the human being—soul/spirit/core personality—does not cease to exist because the body dies. Religions have always postulated such a continuation, but cognitive scientific thinking has been sure that the idea of persistence of a core personality is an illusion devised by people who are afraid of death, and experiential data refuting this have been brushed aside.

Recently, however, the pioneer work of Raymond Moody (1975),[3] and the data of Ring (1980),[4] Sabom (1982),[5] and others, have documented near-death experiences over an extensive population sample. Many of those who reported these experiences had previously held no concept of any ongoing aspect of themselves. Their experiences have been surprisingly consistent and have duplicated, not current Christian beliefs, but ancient Eastern concepts, such as those outlined in *The Tibetan Book of the Dead*. Current research into near-death experiences has finally opened up the possibility that the materialistic view of death as a final ending may not be correct. The research of Ring, Sabom, and others suggests that there may even be a fairly routine mode of transition into another state. This involves the assumption of an ongoing core self, a concept necessary to ground the existence of entities who have not properly completed their transition from space-time life to the next stage. Until this phenomenon was conceptualized the question of entity influence made little sense and therefore was unacceptable to the professional community.

The second difficulty in accepting entity influence lies in its history. Not just the Christian church but other religions as well have postulated demonic entities that have to be "exorcised"—thrown out (goodness knows where) without any semblance of the love that those religions preach. Such entities have generally been considered to be non-human. This hypothesis has little in common with the current understanding that entities are lost souls, usually family members, needing therapy and rescuing; but since similar terminology is used, the fear and negative feelings involved in the old concepts spill over into the new ones and interfere with objective scrutiny of what is happening. Archaic terminology, such as "possession," could more profitably be replaced with terms such as "attachment" or "shadowing," which are more accurate. Ireland-Frey has written an excellent discussion of appropriate terminology. Perhaps a standard terminology will emerge as we recognize the different intensities of attachment.

One of the earliest modern commentaries on releasement work was written by Karl Wickland in 1926.[6] Much of what he found has been confirmed by later therapists. However, he depended on his wife to channel the entities, and today we reject such an approach, finding that our patients/clients are able to channel their own entities. We are in a do-it-yourself phase, which allows the subject to take part in the therapeutic process of both himself and the entity.

The great pioneer work on releasement of entities as it is currently carried out was that small book by Annabelle Chaplin, *The Bright Light of Death*, that introduced me to the area. With little pertinent theoretical material to help her, Chaplin was able experientially to determine effective techniques. An impression of possible obsessing entities appeared in therapeutic work with her clients, and from this, often with the client, she was able to address the entities and release them. She did not use her clients as channels for the entities themselves, a characteristic of techniques of releasement that have been developed subsequently. However, she was aware of other significant factors that have been increasingly confirmed since her book was released: that releasement needs to occur in an extended therapeutic relationship, that attachments are usually formed by family members, and that the objective of the releasement is to benefit the entity as much as, if not more than, the client. She introduced an exceptional compassion into her work, and it may be that releasement work can be done successfully only by compassionate people.

Fiore's book *The Unquiet Dead* (1987) made a major contribution in detoxifying the subject of entity releasement. She presented the process as a simple and understandable technique following easily-understood rules of procedure, sort of in the category of "how to wash dishes." The field will probably turn out to be not quite so simple, but Fiore must be appreciated because she presented a formerly shadowed and esoteric field in a matter-of-fact and non-threatening way.

Crabtree in *Multiple Man: Explorations in Possession and Multiple Personality* (1985) had a scientific and cautious approach. A significant new thrust is his extension of the area to attachment by living people (limited as a rule to parents). This possibility must be seriously considered and opens up a modification of the way we view cases where patients seem stuck in some sort of family matrix. My own impression is that he is right and that we need to extend our therapeutic approach in this direction, which will undoubtedly be uncomfortable. As we come to understand more about energy fields, the possibility that energy systems of living people can take over and influence others may not seem so incredible, especially as we do experience this in many ways to a lesser extent and on more obvious levels.

It is necessary to read Crabtree's book in order to appreciate the amount of careful observation that underlies his theoretical position.

The most dramatic changes in the current attitude toward possession/obsession/shadowing is the attitude toward the entity. As all our contributors point out, releasement is for the entity as much as, if not more than, for the subject. The new techniques that are currently being developed are concerned with helping the entity make its necessary transition, and often extensive therapy for the entity is indicated. Crabtree points out in *Multiple Man*, that this is may be simpler than therapy for the subject because the problem is clearer and more focused.

The principles of therapeutic healing for the entity are similar to those used in work with past lives. First, there is work with the entity's etheric-physical body. Often just bringing it through its physical trauma, especially its death, will release the patient/client from a similar condition, as in my case of the mother who was shadowed by her two children who were killed in a former lifetime. We may come to find that it is helpful to do healing routinely on a traumatized entity body in order to release the etheric patterns, both of the entity and of the patient.

The bulk of therapeutic work with entities seems to occur on the emotional level, predominantly around anger. Perpetual, unresolved anger at *any* level exacts a toll. Denning, Motoyama, Fiore, Ireland-Frey, and I have all dealt with anger in entities. Anger must be resolved in the subject as well, because otherwise the subject's anger continues to act as a hook for the entity. Both subject and entity must release expectations of each other and each must accept the other as he is in order that healing take place.

Therapy, whether for entity or patient, usually involves some sort of reframing. Crabtree's work with Susan's father involved helping him to look clearly at his relationship with his daughter and change his perception of it. My Egyptian entity had to reframe his ideas of "the weighing of the heart" in order to complete his transition.

It is becoming increasingly apparent that every attachment is facilitated by the subject. Entities do not just float around zapping people with whom they have no connection. Chaplin and Crabtree hypothesized that nearly all entities are family connections with whom there have been unresolved interactions of some sort. There may be other facilitating conditions, such as addiction and anger, that are sometimes obvious but often obscure. Attachments may take place in previous lifetimes or be the result of a temporary weakening of the subject's aura in this life, but there is always a reason, some sort of hook for the attachment. In order for the therapeutic process to be complete, it is important to expose and deal with this vulnerable area in the subject. In the case of influence by a family member, family dynamics need to be explored and healed through conventional therapeutic techniques. Coaxing the entity to leave while allowing the subject to retain his neurotic inducement for attachment accomplishes little, and the entity often returns, especially if it, too, has not been sufficiently helped. These two processes, therapy for the entity and healing for the subject, take time. The healing cannot be rushed.

Releasement is not the equivalent of exorcism, where a raging demon is extricated by force from a helpless, innocent victim. We must let go of this outgrown and inaccurate concept and move into a more therapeutic stance. Even if non-human entities turn out to exist (which seems to have been documented by the Catholic Church and by other religions but which most of us have not experienced), they can be treated with loving consideration. The hypothesis that there is a core of potential good in all entities, human and non-human, may well turn out to be true, and it must be remembered that entities, as well as living persons, have the power of choice, and often viable choices cannot be made until therapeutic work is done.

Fiore's and Ireland-Frey's implication that states of entity influence, called variously attachment/obsession/shadowing, are common and perhaps almost normal, will provoke skepticism. Only careful research and observation with a strict definition of the attached state will give a credible answer. At the present time we have only the spectrum of impressions of various therapists. If it is found that attachments are common and frequent, we need to consider how to help patients, children, and others be less open. As in areas such as drug abuse, to which attachment is loosely related, prevention is of equal or greater importance than treatment. Crabtree's caution about patients inventing entities because the possibility has been suggested to them, causing them to leap in the direction of a magical cure, will have to be checked out.

Harold Saxon Burr[7] and Edward Russell (1976)[8] and Motoyama,[9] along with the former research studies at UCLA by Valerie Hunt[10] and Thelma Moss,[11] are approaching a breakthrough in understanding the energy fields of the human body. When that happens, the process and nature of entity attachments will be better understood and may confirm Chaplin's hypothesis that entities become enmeshed in a human aura and remain magnetically bound there until released.

It is possible for the field of depossession/releasement to be explored with conventional research techniques. Although many experiences currently described as releasement of entities are subject to alternative hypotheses, often these hypotheses do not explain the actual happening. In the end, as Ireland-Frey points out, simply taking the entities at face value is the most parsimonious approach. Good research is needed to throw the balance of credibility one way or another. Such research is hard to get funded and is handicapped by lack of therapists competent to do effective releasement work.

One excellent design was reported in *The Journal of Regression Therapies*.[12] This study, worked out at Colorado State College, was a response to the failure of psychotherapy in the treatment of thousands of Vietnam veterans. Its hypothesis was that soldiers killed in the field, because of the suddenness of their deaths, did not make their transition but attached to their fellow soldiers, later resulting in the Post Traumatic Stress Disorder in those soldiers. Conventional therapy has had little impact on this condition in these veterans. The weakness of the design of this study, as I see it, is the minimal amount of time allowed for the releasement work—one session with some follow-ups. No other type of therapy would expect results in one session. It is to be regretted that this study could not find funding. It would have shed light on the subject of entities and it might possibly have opened up an effective form of therapy for a large suffering population. If no improvement took place, that would be a finding, too, which would require us to re-examine our hypotheses.

Those of us who deal with entities, reluctantly because we are only too aware of the storm of controversy the concept stirs up, often do so because of experiences of healing in ourselves and others. This is a difficult field, impossible to conceptualize if death is considered a termination, and hard to defend. In a sense we put ourselves on the line when we attempt to describe it. I thank all the contributors who so willingly allowed their material to be used.

Therapy for Posession

by

Adam Crabtree, M.A.

Introduction

My experience with possession involves attachments by human beings, usually those related to the victim by blood, and possession by family group minds. In the course of my therapeutic work with this type of problem, I have discovered certain basic elements that have proven cohesive enough to justify speaking of a "therapy for possession." The following discussion concerns attachments by human spirits only, living and discarnate.

The Process of Exploration

Exploration of the possibility of possession involves four important steps:

Exhaustion of Conventional Therapeutic Possibilities

Possessed individuals frequently come to the therapist complaining of certain specific symptoms. Most frequent are hearing voices, a sense of something residing in a specific location within the body, or a feeling of regularly not being oneself. When symptoms such as these are spoken of, the therapist needs to undertake a period of exploration with the client to discover precisely where the work needs to be done. Symptoms such as these are not unfamiliar to the psychological worker and do not of themselves indicate a possession experience. For that reason, the first line of approach for the therapist must be to see if such symptoms are manifestations of well-known syndromes of mental disturbance. In these cases such symptoms will yield to conventional psychological approaches. In cases where clients have already spent time in some more conventional form of therapy without result this step does not take as long as in the case of those who start without such background.

Alteration of the Therapeutic Expectation-Framework

When a conventional therapeutic approach is insufficient and despite the most assiduous application of the best techniques the voices persist, the alien mass remains, or the sense of not being oneself lingers, one should consider altering the framework of expectation within which the therapeutic work is taking place. Every therapist has a certain theoretical/practical framework within which he approaches his cases. That framework will have been built up from a combination of factors, not the least of which is the original training he received. It consists of a set of expectations about the type of material that the client will produce and the nature of the underlying causes that will be discovered. These expectations are influential in determining the way the therapist speaks to the client and the techniques he uses to elicit material from him. The expectation-framework serves a useful purpose in the therapeutic process, but it limits the imagination of both therapist and client in the therapeutic encounter.

When the client walks into the therapist's office and sits down, the expectation-framework of the therapist immediately comes into play. It may never be explicitly spelled out, but the client soon senses what it is. He comes to recognize what the therapist is looking for, what type of material he believes important, and what is irrelevant. The client automatically starts responding to that expectation-framework and often becomes so immersed in the therapist's way of seeing things that it is virtually impossible for him to speak about matters that do not fit into that framework. He may retain a consciousness of the material, but that consciousness will only come into play in other contexts. He can respond to signals concerning inhibiting messages that escape even the therapist's detection. One must never underestimate the power of the therapist's expectation-framework to censor the client's thoughts.

It must be emphasized that in the case of influence by the therapeutic expectation-framework, such influence takes place outside the awareness of both client and therapist. The client does not intend to withhold important information, nor does the therapist intend to suppress the client's thoughts. But if the therapist is getting nowhere with his usual approach, he may find that by deliberately altering his normal therapeutic expectation-framework, new material will surface. He must find a way to make the client become aware of those thoughts, feelings, or attitudes that have generally been dismissed because of the framework. Once that difficult task has been accomplished and the client has allowed his own peculiar way of experiencing things to come forward, the therapist may make some surprising discoveries.

Whatever is true of negative or inhibiting suggestions is equally true of positive or eliciting suggestions. For that reason the therapist must guard against subtly suggesting to the client that he has possessing entities within him and in that way inducing the client's subconscious to create them. When I am working with a client who exhibits symptoms that are often associated with possession, I endeavor to carry on the exploration process in such a way that there is as little chance of suggestion from myself or the situation as possible. When the client already has a feeling of inner presences, the problem is greatly lessened. It is then simply a matter of exploring what he already feels. However, where the symptoms are more vague, such as the experience of an inner voice, the presence of some alien "thing in the body," or the feeling at times of not being "oneself," greater caution is required.

At times the therapist encounters cases in which the client already is aware of inner presences before he comes for help. This may have been produced through suggestion received from elsewhere in the client's environment. One would hope that if this were the case, that fact would be discovered in the process of applying conventional therapeutic approaches to the client's condition. The problem of suggestion-pollution from the client's environment is a real one and must be given serious consideration. It is particularly difficult to avoid when clients come to know each other, as they do in a group-therapy situation. When this happens, they can easily influence each other's expectations and create powerful suggestions in the subconscious mind.

Amplification of Weak Signals

The therapist may have to help the client make the internal experience strong and clear enough to work with. Sometimes the client's relevant inner sensations are feeble or indistinct. The inner voice may be shaky, the feeling of an alien substance vague, or the sense of not being oneself confused. These weak signals need to be amplified. Often the client will recognize that he has "always" or "for a long time" been aware of the symptoms, and he reveals that he has tried to ignore them or has even carried on a continual battle to suppress them. The therapist must now help the client to approach the symptoms in an entirely new way. Instead of trying to dismiss them or fight against them, the client must actually give them *more* energy.

The therapist can allow his client to do this only if he has judged that the client is strong enough to take it, that his ego is strong enough to remain intact while allowing other ego-like elements to express themselves. If the therapist judges the client capable, he will reassure him that it is beneficial to let it all happen, that he can safely let those weak, nagging impulses grow strong and clear. The client will also need to know that the therapist will stay with him and see him through the process. As the therapist assists the client in making the inner signals stronger and clearer, there may be a breakthrough of new material. The client may suddenly be flooded by a host of vivid impressions. He will need to speak about them and allow them to take him where they will. He may discover from those impressions that he is undergoing an experience of an unusual kind.

When the expectation-framework has been altered and an attempt is being made to amplify weak signals, it is essential to let the phenomenon manifest *in its own terms* and not subtly steer it toward some predetermined outcome. The therapist must not hint that he expects to discover other presences within the client, for if he does, he is sure to "find" them, whether they were there originally, or not.

Discovery of the Elusive Element

Discovery is the simplest step. If the therapist has succeeded in altering his expectation-framework and has worked to help the client amplify weak signals, he will be ready to pay attention to whatever the client brings forth. Discovery is simply recognizing the nature of the client's experience as he is experiencing it.

The client may be having any of a number of different types of experience. He may feel he is being controlled or influenced by an inner presence, an entity other than himself: in other words, he feels possessed. Or he may be flooded by "memories" of another time and place. Such reincarnation-type experiences are not rare. Or he may turn out to be having some unusual inner experience of a kind not treated here. It is important that no matter what experience is described, no matter how unconventional it may seem, it be allowed to manifest fully and be recognized on its own terms. Only then can the full extent of the client's experience be appreciated. And only then will the therapist be in a position to gain new information about the nature of inner human experience.

Neither therapist nor client need be convinced that the experience is in reality what it seems at first glance. All that is necessary is that they be willing to allow the experience to evolve completely and become clearly defined. This will permit a suitable therapeutic approach to be developed.

When the possession experience is treated *as if* it were exactly what it appears to be—invasion and control of the client by another human spirit—the condition can almost always be cleared up. Success does not depend upon my conviction or my client's that the experience corresponds to a metaphysical reality; it is necessary only for us to accept the *experience itself* as valid and worthy of serious attention.

The Therapeutic Process

Making Contact

Once a possessing entity has been discovered through the exploration process, it is necessary to make effective contact with it. That may not always be easy. Sometimes the entity will be reluctant to talk to the therapist, or if he does talk a bit, he may refuse to cooperate. The therapist must find out how to "hook" the entity. He must discover a way to get his attention and eventually, his willing participation in a solution. He must, in other words, draw the entity into the therapeutic process. There are no general rules to guide the therapist in this matter; it is almost entirely a matter of intuition and ingenuity.

Every case of possession in my experience has had the possessor speaking through the possessed. The vocal apparatus used was that of the client. There is often a pronounced alteration in vocal quality and sometimes a dramatic change in facial features, but it is not necessary to move beyond ordinary explanations to account for them.

Exploring the Possession Relationship

Once the therapist has an exchange going with the possessing entity, he can start to gather information about the possession state. He will attempt to discover whether the possessor knows where he is and what he is doing, the time and circumstances that led to possession, why it happened in the first place, and the reason for its continuing.

Answers to these questions vary greatly. Sometimes the entity does not know where he is. More frequently, he knows that he is somehow involved with the client but does not at first recognize that he is exercising control over him and interfering with his life. There are cases, however, in which the possessing entity knows exactly where he is and what he is doing. As to the time and circumstances of the original entry, there are as many answers as there are individual cases. As a rule, this information is useful but not crucial. Of great importance is information about the *reason* possession originally took place and the *purpose* it continues to serve for the possessor. This knowledge will provide the key for the therapy work that follows.

Most possession cases in my experience have involved invasion and control by the spirit of someone related by blood to the host. In such situations it will be necessary to explore the basic dynamics of the client's family constellation in order to reach resolution of the possession. The power of the family influence in these cases is hard to overestimate. Often it is felt that the rights of the individual member are subordinate to those of the family as a whole. In these cases the "good of the family," the "way of the family," the "custom of the family," the "reputation of the family," are of supreme importance, and the individual family member must be sacrificed to preserve them. The family operates like a unified living organism that survives from generation to generation. The organism has a mental and emotional life, imbued with certain attitudes and a character that has been formed through untold generations of family experience. The individual members exist to perpetuate the family ideals. They must not defy those ideals, nor even change them in a substantial way. The individual members are, therefore, subservient to the good of the whole and considered the possessions of the family organism.

Special consideration must be given to those cases in which the possessing entity is someone upon whom the host had a great dependency in life. In these instances it is often easy to trace a progression from possessiveness to possession. The most common example of such an evolution is that of possession by a parent. The child is naturally open to the parent in every way, and if the parent exercises too great a possessiveness, there is little that the child can do to resist. It is sometimes difficult to determine at what point the parent's possessive invasion becomes possession. However, if it has not happened before, it may well occur upon the death of the parent.

Therapy for possession by family members must deal head-on with the issues that have traditionally been considered parental or family preroga-tives. It will have to indicate where these prerogatives are the enshrinement of family structures designed to control individual members rather than free them. Both possessor and possessed will benefit from such an analysis.

Therapy for the Possessor

In the course of my work I discovered it was seldom a good idea to try to be rid of the possessing entity quickly. It is usually better for both possessor and host that the entity be helped as much as possible to understand the possession situation and eventually leave it for something better.

Sometimes the possessing entity does not have any special purpose in being there. He is simply confused and has entered into the host almost accidentally. Usually in these cases the therapy for the entity is brief: it amounts to enlightening him about his condition, much as Karl Wickland did,[13] and helping him to move on. Occasionally, however, once the confused entity does discover where he is, he realizes that he has an unhealthy attachment to the host. Therapy is necessary to free him from that neurotic bond.

In other cases, the possessor is present in the host to assist him in some way. Although the motive may be basically positive, the method is not. Instead of helping the host, the entity causes confusion and distress. In contrast, sometimes the purpose of the possession is basically selfish and in this case, a great deal of therapy needs to be done with the possessing entity.

When therapy is undertaken with the possessing entity, the therapist works as he would with any flesh-and-blood person. This proves to be surprisingly easy once things get started. The possessor responds as a person quite independent of the host. He speaks of the host in the third person and is capable of a range of emotion towards him. He has his own personality with its unique characterological traits, his own set of memories. Through the therapeutic process he will uncover his own neurotic life patterns based upon his personal life history. He will eventually come to his own therapeutic resolution of those problems, often after recovering painful, repressed memories. In dealing with cases of discarnate possessing entities, the therapist will generally find that this work proceeds more swiftly than does therapy for the living. Relevant repressed material is recovered more quickly, and progress toward resolution is more rapid.

Therapy with living possessing entities is more slowly paced. In that respect it is similar to working with a normal client. A peculiar thing about working with living possessing entities is that the therapist often has the impression that he is not dealing with the entity's complete personality. Instead, it is as though a fragment of the person, while remaining connected to the whole, has split off to be with the host.

Resolution

It is usually necessary to do therapy with the possessor before he can move on. Full dissolution of the possession involves a *resolution* of the relationship between possessed and possessor. That resolution can be attained only when the possessor has come to terms with his unhealthy attachment to the host. Resolution between possessor and possessed is the same as resolution between any two individuals in a relationship. Both must take part in the resolution process. Each must come to terms with the other. They must learn to see each other realistically and come to a mutual agreement as to how they want to be involved with each other.

As the possessor gains understanding of the neurotic nature of his tie to the host, he will desire to end his unfair usage of him. He will give up his possessive attitude towards the host and allow a relationship of independence and equality to develop. As he relinquishes his possessive *attitude*, he will also be ready to leave behind the *state* of possession itself.

It is important to note that in the kinds of cases I have encountered, the possessed often—almost always—has a hidden attachment to being possessed. This hidden attachment must be uncovered and openly recognized by the possessed. Otherwise he will unconsciously hinder the resolution process and not allow the possessor to go.

Moving On

When resolution between possessed and possessor has been reached, the possessing entity will naturally desire to move on. For the living possessor, "moving on" is simply a matter of becoming wholly present to himself. He realizes that much of his energy has been siphoned off into preoccupation with the host. Now this is about to cease and he looks forward to having all of his resources available to do whatever he wants to do with his life. This will happen when the split-off fragment of his personality, which has possessed the host, returns home. The discarnate possessor, on the other hand, experiences moving on in quite a different way. He realizes that he has been living a limited existence and is interested in having a fuller life. He feels ready to enter into the next phase of existence.

Failure in the treatment process can happen at two stages—failure to discover or failure to resolve. Sometimes, even though exploration procedures are carried out, no new material or new view of what is happening emerges. In failure at resolution, there is an exchange with an entity or a recovery of reincarnational material that is inconclusive and eventually fizzles out, leaving the client no better than when he came. Failure in which there is no conclusive resolution is more likely to happen when the possessing entity is still living. Sometimes the living possessor just does not want to give up his hold on the host—the only spice in his life seems to be derived from vicarious living through his victim. In every case of this sort I have found the possessor to be a parent.

I consider successes to be those cases in which there is some change for the better. That change may vary from slight improvement to a radical, positive alteration in the personality. For some clients there are striking positive changes. It is my estimation that approximately two-thirds of the fifty cases of possession by human entities with which I have worked fall into this category.

Positive results are tricky things to evaluate, particularly in the realm of therapy, and when working with possession cases one is tempted to think that positive results indicate that possession is an objective reality. This conclusion is not justified. It has been shown again and again that, when it comes to healing emotional ills, widely differing techniques based on radically opposed metaphysical systems can produce equally good results. The positive outcomes, therefore, are obviously due to some factor other than the philosophical belief of the therapist. The most one can say is that the *as if* approach is fruitful. If the therapist accepts the client's experience on its own terms and proceeds *as if* it describes an objective reality, he is likely to meet with success. As a worker interested in relieving emotional ills, the therapist can rest content with that.

Case 1. The Confused Father

Susan was a successful professional counselor who inspired confidence in both colleagues and clients. Her personal relationships, however, were unfortunate. A marriage in her early twenties had ended in divorce, and shortly before the work described here, she had broken a relationship with a young man so harshly that it could not be repaired. In the dissolution she had become cold and closed and had felt such a strong feeling of vengeance that she realized she must do something about this.

She had become convinced that the vengefulness originated in her feelings toward her father, and she felt that her father, now dead for many years, was actually with her in some way and that his presence was helping to keep her vindictive feelings alive.

Susan, her therapist, and I met for the first session in his office. Susan was nervous and had to be given time to release the agitation she was experiencing. I asked her to put aside any expectations of what "should" happen and let things develop on their own.

> T: *What are you experiencing?*
> P: *He is here. My father.*
> T: *Does he feel close?*
> P: *Yes, and I want him to communicate with me.*
> T: *You will find that he can speak through you if you want that.*

Susan relaxed further, and I noticed the subtle shift in facial expression that often takes place. Her words were in a lower pitched voice, delivered slowly.

> E: *What do you want?*
> T: *To talk to you.*
> E: *Leave me alone. I don't want to talk. (The delivery was sluggish, as though thoughts were being gathered with great difficulty.)*
> T: *Why don't you want to talk?*
> E: *I am tired. I need to rest.*
> T: *Who are you?*
> E: *John.*
> T: *John who?*
> E: *John Driscoll.*
> T: *Susan's father?*
> E: *Yes. I am tired. Why are you bothering me?*
> T: *We have been asked to. Do you know where you are?*
> E: *(Long pause.) I don't know.*
> T: *Do you know who I am?*
> E: *No. I am too tired. Let me rest.*

> T: *Now look, John, I know you want us to leave you alone. I know you feel*
> *too tired to be bothered, but we have a problem here. You don't know*
> *where you are or who we are. Wouldn't you say that is peculiar?*
> E: *Yes. It seems so.*
> T: *Why do you suppose things are so unclear to you?*
> E: *It's the fog. There is a fog all around. I can't see anything clearly.*

It was like talking to a man who was asleep and who was speaking from
a dream. He did not wonder about things that were strange but accepted
everything as given, in the same way that in a dream even the most bizarre
circumstances go unquestioned. There was no spontaneity and his mind was
sluggish, nearly to the point of paralysis.

I knew that Susan's father had died from injuries sustained in an auto
accident. Those who write about human survival of death believe that the
way one dies affects one's state immediately afterward. Where there is
gradual progression toward death, as in disease or aging, the individual has
a clearer consciousness of his condition, but with sudden death there is often
great confusion. The person does not realize he is dead; rather, he
experiences a period of fogginess that gradually clears as his true state
dawns upon him.

If one accepts the possibility that John was still around after his death,
he was a classic example of the latter state of consciousness. The passage of
years had not helped him clarify things, and I speculated as to whether this
might be because he had remained attached to his daughter, insulated from
other influences. It seemed important that he get a clearer picture of where
he was.

> T: *Do you know where your daughter Susan is?*
> E: *At home, I suppose.*
> T: *No, she is here.*
> E: *Oh. (He was seemingly indifferent to the information.)*
> T: *Now, John, would you like to find out what is going on?*
> E: *I guess so.*
> T: *Well we can help you do that if you will allow it. Would you like that?*
> E: *I guess so.*
> T: *All right. We are going to end this session now but we'll be getting together*
> *to try to see more about this. Are you agreeable?*
> E: *Yes.*

I asked John to "move back," and called Susan "forward." She remembered everything that had taken place in the session, felt relieved that the
process had started, and was amazed at the state her father was in.

The next few times we got together were spent in trying to get John to
at least question where he was and what condition he was in, but his
confusion was so great that we did not make much headway. When we told
him that he was with Susan—that he was in fact in her—he could not

believe it. So I asked him to become aware of his body, and he was astonished to find that it was female. When we told him it was his daughter's, he accepted this, though with surprise. This realization seemed to shock him into greater alertness so that he even began to question things for himself. This was the breakthrough we needed. Now we could do some real work.

In this case the real work had to do with John's recalling to his consciousness certain unfortunate things he had done, looking squarely at their consequences and experiencing the guilt he had so long avoided. Susan had known before we began this work that her father had interfered with her sexually when she was very young. Therapeutic work two years earlier had uncovered memories of her father putting his penis in her mouth when she was a baby. This had happened periodically until she was three years old. In that earlier work Susan had not only recalled the incidents but re-experienced them emotionally, realizing why up to that point in her life, sex had always involved fellatio. After the work with these early memories, Susan lost all interest in oral sex—a fairly good indication that the work we had done was on target.

But there was more to the story. As the fog lifted and John's thinking became more focused, he began to face other disturbing memories. He was shocked when he remembered the early fellatio incidents and realized that he was accountable for the way this had affected his daughter's life. But John's next set of disturbing memories surprised everyone, for he recalled that when Susan was in grade school he would go into her bedroom at night after she had fallen asleep and fondle her genitals. Susan did not appear to awaken and he would leave after a few minutes. He apparently did this frequently over the years until Susan was 16. Then he had suddenly perceived her as a fully developed woman, had become frightened about what he was doing, and stopped.

At the end of this session with John we spent some time talking with Susan about it. In her adult life she had no conscious memories of these incidents, which meant that if she was aware of her father's action when they occurred—which seems likely—she had immediately repressed that awareness. Also, throughout the whole period of these events, Susan's mother seems to have been oblivious to what was taking place. Susan told us that all through her adult life she had difficulty getting to sleep. She had always felt as though someone were watching her as she was falling asleep. Now, after this session with John, this particular problem disappeared, not to return.

As the work with John progressed, it became clearer to Susan that she must come to terms with her own role in the neurotic tie between herself and her father. From the time of her adolescence she had felt an irritation with him, bordering on contempt. While not consciously aware of the sexual incidents at night, she sensed her father's attraction to her as she matured and sometimes took the opportunity to behave in a provocative way, driven to make him suffer for his sexual feelings towards her.

Susan's contempt for her father spread to her relationships with young men as they began to enter her life as a teenager and an adult. She would feel very interested in her boyfriends and responsive to them at first but before long grow unaccountably impatient and angry with them. This became a pattern, with disastrous results for her love life as the unresolved sexual tie between Susan and her father was played out time and time again.

At this point in the work Susan had to come to terms with her desire for vengeance against her father, for only then would she be able to let him go. And only if she could accept him as a human being, flawed as he was, would her love relationships have a chance. As her father confessed his actions, Susan began to mellow toward him. He had been a tortured man long before he mistreated her, himself a victim of sexual mistreatment early in life. Susan appreciated his courage in speaking so candidly and soon felt compassion for him. It was a short step to complete forgiveness and acceptance.

Once John had reached sufficient clarity of mind to realize where he was, we periodically spent time reconstructing the events around his death and developing a clear picture of his present state of existence. He recalled the drive that ended in the fatal crash and began to realize that when he died he had been afraid to go on and had been drawn to Susan as a place of refuge. She was vulnerable to this invasion because of his previous sexual interference. Once he had taken possession of her, he had remained in a kind of foggy sleep, his thoughts and feelings subliminally impinging on Susan's, causing her much confusion.

Now that he recognized clearly that he had died, he became curious about the next phase of existence. We periodically asked him to become aware of that next phase through a process of mental visualization. We suggested he consider that up to now he had been looking "down" at Susan and the events of this world, completely preoccupied with earthly concerns. He would now find that he could look "up," and if he did, he would see new things.

John followed our suggestions and soon began to see a "light." Eventually he recognized human presences in that "light": his aunt and his mother, both long deceased. John realized that he would have to leave Susan, now that he had reached the point of resolution, yet he said he was still afraid to go on, even though he wanted to. Then one day, after about six weeks of sessions, we called upon John and he was not there. He had taken that final step on his own, and Susan was free of the possession.

Susan experienced a palpable change in her state of being after the work. She had always felt as though there was a shroud over her, as though she lived behind a veil, slightly separated from people. That feeling disappeared completely with John's departure.

Her attitude toward men also altered radically and a few months after the completion of this work Susan fell in love with a bright and successful young man. Her feelings for him were free of the ambivalence of her previous love relationships. They were soon married, and their life together since has been a witness to the permanence of the changes within Susan.

One further interesting point about this case is that shortly after her father's death, Susan had developed a severe phobia for birds. She could not understand this since she had had a pet budgie for years and loved to let it fly around her room and land on her shoulder. She had suddenly become terrified of any bird that flew near her. After the completion of our work with John, Susan lost that phobia. She believed that to her unconscious, any bird represented her father's spirit which had entered her at the time of his death. But now the possession was over and she no longer responded to birds symbolically.

Case 2. A Living Family Member: The Complaining Mother

This case involves control by a living blood relative, the host's mother. Every instance of control by a living family member within my experience to date has involved the intrusion of a parent.

Art was a successful professor in a small university, a sophisticated man of the world, well-traveled. He had married at thirty, had two children, followed by the eroding of his marriage to his wife Elaine and his divorce. Currently he was contemplating marriage to a young woman he had met at the university, but he had become increasingly uneasy and neglectful of his fiance as the time of the new marriage approached. A part of his mind and attention seemed engaged elsewhere, involved in some peculiar inner dialogue which distressed him so much that he sought help.

Art had been experiencing this inner dialogue for years and in going back over notes in a journal he had begun before his marriage, he found clear references to a kind of "inner storm" that would last four or five days. During this time he felt that he was not himself and that he was under pressure from some inner source that he could not control but only endure. While the storm was raging he would hear a censorious voice speaking inside that would criticize him and anyone who was important to him. Elaine had received the most criticism—from the first days of their courtship the voice had found fault with her. Currently it was Melanie, a business colleague with whom he had a social friendship, who came in for the heaviest attack. While the voice held sway, Art would fight with all his strength to push it aside or block it from his consciousness, but he was not successful, for it always came back, hounding him and robbing his life of pleasure.

Now that he was approaching his second marriage the voice was becoming even more obnoxious. Art had been involved in therapy for some time and had often spoken of this inner influence, but therapeutic work had not made a difference. He was determined to do something now, once and for all.

In looking back over his journals Art developed a different view of what was happening to him. He had always thought of the voice as an unacceptable negative aspect of his personality that would speak the nasty thoughts that he could not himself own up to. Though he had long ago associated the critical attitude of the voice with his mother's personality, he believed he had incorporated this aspect of her into his unconscious mind. Now, as he reread his journals, he found references to his mother's "long arm" reaching over the miles from her home in Detroit to maintain her hold upon him, and to feeling that he was literally "possessed" by her, that she was an entity in him, exercising a direct influence upon his thoughts.

Art wanted to find out if his mother was literally with him—if she was somehow residing in his body even though she was living in another city. He proposed to me that we explore the possibility.

I asked him to become relaxed and then inquired if he could there and then become aware of the voice within and allow himself to enter into its thoughts and feelings. After a brief pause Art said he believed he could.

T: *Can you hear the voice?*
P: *Yes, I can.*
T: *Is it familiar?*
P: *Oh, yes. It's my mother's.*
T: *Stay with this. Can you actually experience the way she is seeing things and the emotions she is feeling?*
P: *Yes.*
T: *Do you suppose you could let her speak now?*
P: *Yes, I think so.*
T: *What is your mother's name?*
P: *Veronica.*

At this point I began speaking to the "voice" as if it really were Veronica. I talked about Art's coming marriage and the importance of his making a good start. I said that I was sure that as his mother she wished him all the best. After going on in this vein for some time, I asked her to respond.

T: *Can you speak, Veronica?*
E: *Yes, I think so.*
T: *What do you think about what I was saying?*
E: *Art is mine and his life is mine. That's not going to change. I have to make sure Art knows how kooky all these friends of his are, especially that Melanie. I don't let anything about her go by.*

T: *What do you mean?*

E: *Well, she proposed that Art and their friends fix up this cabin to use as a ski lodge on weekends. She got it all organized and they spent three days working on it. Art thought she did such a great job and worked so hard on it. But I told him she couldn't have done all that. She was just making it look like she was working hard.*

T: *You want Art to think badly of her?*

E: *That's right. And it works. Oh, he thinks he likes her. He admires her professional ability. But then I throw these thoughts in, and before you know it he is doubting himself and his feelings toward her. Also, once he starts listening to me, there is no more fun for him anymore. That is what happened at the ski cabin.*

T: *Why shouldn't he have fun?*

E: *When you have too much fun, you forget what life is really about. It's a burden. Sooner or later everybody has to see that. I helped Art see that sooner. Besides, when he has fun he forgets about me.*

Veronica came across as blatantly, almost naively, self-centered, but she was not hostile. She agreed to take up the dialogue at our next session. When she moved back and Art came forward, he remembered everything that had happened during the session.

When we next got together, Art and I talked for a while about his relationship with his mother as he was growing up. She had always been heavily possessive and when he entered puberty she became even more watchful, pointing out the dangers of liking girls too much. They were living in a small town then, so Veronica easily kept her finger on every aspect of Art's social life.

At the same time she tied Art to her with the double bond of closeness and conflict. Even into his teen years, Veronica would call him into her bed after her husband had left for work. There she would stroke and tease him, creating a high pitch of sexual agitation. Later in the day, however, she would often yell at him about some mishap or other and hit him with kitchen utensils as she chased him around the house.

At the very time when Art should have become more independent of his family, Veronica's tactics helped maintain her position as the central figure in his life. It was with great relief that he finally left home to study in a boarding high school, a step which seemed to Art to be his first chance to develop a mind of his own. Unfortunately, by now the inner possessive bond with his mother was so powerful that it severely limited any independence. This became clear in Art's first serious love relationship—that with Elaine. While courting her, he became consciously aware of an inner voice that spoke distinctly and forcefully, addressing its comments directly to him. It operated most powerfully during the periods of "inner storm."

Elaine was given special attention. Hardly anything she did escaped comment from the voice. As the couple had moved toward marriage, the inner complaints grew. After they were wed, the complaints continued, contributing significantly to the trouble that developed between them. As Art reflected upon things now, he was convinced that the inner voice was indeed his possessive mother at work in him. He was now more determined than ever to bring the matter to a complete resolution.

From the beginning Veronica admitted that in fact she possessed Art. She thought that was the way things should be between a mother and son. Now I asked her in session if she thought such a state of affairs could really be good for either Art or herself. Incredible as it seemed, she had never really considered that question before, but as she reflected upon it, her attitude began to change.

She had to admit that it might not be so good for Art after all. Taking the fun out of his life and blocking him from any significant relationship—even friendships—did not, upon consideration, seem like something he would appreciate her for. She had done these things "automatically," thinking they were "for his own good." In this she had simply been doing what was traditional in her own family. But in thinking about it now she admitted the approach might be wrong.

Veronica also started to recognize the effect that the possession of Art was having on her own life, tying up as it did a whole large block of her personal energy. She began speaking of a "Veronica here" with Art and a "Veronica in Detroit," the latter leading quite a drab and boring life. It now dawned on "Veronica here" that perhaps if she paid less attention to Art and more to "Veronica in Detroit" things would be different. This came to her as a revelation and she immediately wanted to see if her hunch was true. So we set up an experiment in which she would start spending more and more time with "Veronica in Detroit" and less and less with Art.

Once this point had been reached in the therapy, things moved steadily toward a resolution. Art noticed that he was hearing less from the inner voice. And even when it was there, he said, it seemed to have lost most of its punch. To all appearances, Veronica seemed to be withdrawing her energy from Art.

As this happened, Art was surprised to find that he missed the voice, even the carping and the inner arguments where he would oppose reality and reason to the voice's pettiness and irrationality. He now came to realize what his own important part had been in preserving his neurotic state of possession:

I saw why I allowed those thoughts to go on. They served as a buffer, a way of removing myself from people and from the challenges of life. Those thoughts produced a kind of narcissism in which I became so involved with the action inside of me that I could hardly become engaged in life. It was a way to elude pain and upset and to avoid taking chances. Also it was a way of my not having to admit my own feelings about things, a way of avoiding facing my own irrationality. Really my mother served as a very convenient buffer against life.

While we were doing the work, Art's mother in Detroit had an operation to remove a cancerous growth of a serious type. I asked "Veronica here" about this and she realized that through her concentration on Art, she had robbed "Veronica in Detroit" of essential vitality. She thought refocusing her attention on her own life might help that.

Here the therapeutic work with Veronica ended. There had not been a dramatic departure of the possessing entity, simply the gradual shifting of the center of gravity from host to self. And the inner voice that had plagued Art for more than ten years had ceased.

I then did a short piece of intensive therapy with Art himself, after which his life began to change dramatically. He now felt ready to enter into the marriage he had been contemplating. In addition, he found his professional life taking a new creative turn as he embarked on some original research that would bring him broad recognition in his field.

Art also changed in the way he related to his peers. Those who had known him up to this point generally considered him a charming but non-challenging kind of individual. Now he became much more questioning of people and situations, a transformation which affected both his professional and his personal life. Some who had felt comfortable with the old Art became uneasy with the new one. But on the whole, Art's friends soon welcomed his new assertiveness and found him a much more interesting person for it.

There was also a remarkable change in Art's mother. Up to the time of the sessions she had been deteriorating physically and emotionally, apparently withdrawing from life. It even seemed that the discovery of cancer might signal the end for her. But after the work with "Veronica here," she started to come into her own, gradually gathering strength and vitality to the point of being more engaged with people and life than Art ever remembered. She seemed to have gained the proverbial "new lease" on life.

Art had given this piece of therapeutic work its direction. After more than ten years of hearing the inner voice he had decided that something had to be done and he had a clear idea of how to do it. For the most part, I simply followed his lead. The resulting changes in Art seem to amply justify the tack taken.

As for Veronica, the improvements in her life started around the time the work with her was completed. Such an alteration could also be attributed to a spontaneous transformation in the face of a life-threatening crisis—the cancer. It is impossible to know for certain. But the possibility of a direct link between the therapeutic work and her improvement is an intriguing one.

Release of Entities

by

Edith Fiore, Ph.D.

Introduction

The conviction that spirits possess living people is based on the premise that *life does continue after death*. Earthbound entities are simply those who did not make the natural transition to higher planes of existence. Possession reinforces the evidence suggesting that only the physical body dies and that personality survives, that we are immortal beings.

The majority of my patients who have recalled previous incarnations under hypnosis related death experiences that were remarkably similar to those documented by Dr. Raymond Moody.[15] For them death involved a smooth, natural transition to a spirit realm with no loss of consciousness. They noticed an immediate feeling of relief from the pains, discomforts, or fears that they had been experiencing just before they left their bodies. Almost all reported a feeling of lifting up and floating. They could clearly see their bodies below and observe whatever was happening around them. Often they tried to reassure their families that they were fine and alive. With a wonderful sense of freedom they continued to rise and were drawn to a bright white light. They were joined by loved ones who had already died and often by a wise and comforting highly evolved spirit guide. They found themselves in perfect bodies; any defect had been corrected. Amazingly, their spirit bodies seemed just as real and solid as their physical bodies had once been.

If the regression continued, many reported experiences of a rich, full existence in another world. At one point, they reviewed with wise counselors the life they had left, and saw it as though watching a film. It was clear to them that the purpose of this review was to enable them to see where they had passed key challenges and failed others. Spirit counselors pointed out what they still had to learn in order to make the necessary spiritual progress. The planning of the next incarnation was based on this knowledge.

Occasionally, however, experiences were quite different. Instead of a smooth transition from one world to the other, some remembered actually fleeing from the Light in terror or turning away from their departed relatives (in spirit) or guides. Many were unaware of their deaths and felt that they were still alive, becoming totally confused and frightened when they could not make impact on their survivors. These individuals remained earthbound —tied to the physical plane despite the fact that their bodies had died. Some of these spirits seemed to merge with or attach to living people. I have found that many victims of suicide, especially, remain as discarnates, feeling just as depressed as they were before their deaths. Some of these are rescued by spirit helpers, but many attach to unsuspecting living people.

Sudden, unexpected death often results in confusion and in souls becoming earthbound and staying where they die for days, months, in some cases even years. This state is especially characteristic of suicides, who wander about without direction making futile attempts to communicate with the living and often attaching to them. Suicides only postpone the working out of their lessons and retard their spiritual progress, for in some future life they will find themselves in another test situation with suicide as a strong option.

Why do many spirits resist the experience of the Light and remain in the physical world without bodies of their own and, in their ignorance, condemn themselves to a miserable earthbound existence? There are a number of reasons. The most usual are ignorance, confusion, fear (especially of going to hell); obsessive attachments to living persons or places; or addiction to drugs, alcohol, smoking, food, or sex. Also, a misguided sense of unfinished business often compels spirits to stay in the physical world. Some remain because they are determined to get revenge.

Other reasons are given by entities who remain earthbound. One is that they are ashamed of their former deeds and don't want to see their spirit loved ones. Obsessive attachment to the living is another compelling reason why some entities remain earthbound. But no matter how well-meaning the motives, the attachment of spirits always causes serious problems: overprotective parents retard their children's growth and development because they infuse these children with their own fears; loving spouses become upset when widowed survivors remarry, and they often deliberately create havoc with the new marriages.

The motives of possessing entities are not always benign—they can be malicious, even vengeful. Several of my patients were plagued by the spirits of people who had been hostile to them while alive, and others were besieged by vicious entities whom they had not known. Just as there are individuals whose lives revolve around getting revenge, there are similarly-minded spirits. If they were murdered or felt they had been wronged, they might remain after death to deliberately hurt their malefactors.

However, by far the strongest tie that binds spirits to the physical world is addiction—to alcohol, drugs, sex, smoking, even food. If a person dies while in the grips of such an addiction, he feels overwhelming need for the addictive substance or sensation immediately after death. The spirit is resistant to leaving and seeks only to fulfill the compulsion. Spirit guides and relatives are ignored; the Bright Light goes unnoticed. Spirit addicts tend to cluster around living addicts and the places they frequent, attempting to experience again what was once the dominant theme of their lives, and they actually *do* experience this again after possessing the individual. From this time on they can exercise control and have what they want when they want it. Patients who are addicted to drugs, including alcohol, usually open the door to possession by indulging in the drugs and thus attracting the addicted spirits. But in some cases the person is simply in the wrong place at the wrong time, at a bar or party that by its nature has already attracted spirits waiting to indulge.

No matter what needs such earthbound spirits are seeking to fulfill, they are frustrated, confused, and unhappy; they can find no peace or lasting satisfaction while inhabiting other people's bodies. They are truly *lost souls* who do not know that they are hurting themselves. Their influence on their unknowing hosts' lives and behavior is *always* negative, sometimes fatal!

Once addicted spirits gain entrance, they literally have a stranglehold on their victims. Their hosts then interpret impulses to use drugs, for instance, as entirely their own. Under the influence of the substance, they abdicate even more control over their lives. This permits the spirits—usually there are multiple possessions—to indulge to their hearts' content. *They* don't have to pay the price in broken relationships, destroyed health, lost jobs, and even greater lowering of self-esteem and respect. The aura becomes weakened from continued drug use, allowing easy possession by still others. This type of possession can be life-threatening, sometimes provoking a fatal accident or overdose.

Earthbound entities seem to remain exactly as they were moments before their deaths. It is as though they have been "freeze-framed." Throughout their stay in the physical world they do not change or profit from anything they experience. They have all their previous attitudes, prejudices, addictions, skills, interests, fears, and hang-ups. If their deaths involved physical pain, this continues unabated, even for decades. If they were anesthetized, or drugged by alcohol, prescription drugs, or illicit substances before they died, they feel "spacey" and "out of it" for as long as they are earthbound. Possessing entities who committed suicide continue to feel desolate, regardless of their hosts' experience.

The possession itself can range from being nearly total, in which case the original inhabitant is almost completely replaced, to a very minor influence. Some of the factors that determine the extent of the possession are the intrinsic strength of the individual compared to that of the possessing spirits, and conditions that weaken the possessee, such as stress, drug abuse, illness, etc. The more that the afflicted persons abdicate control of their consciousness, the greater the influence of their possessors. If the possessed drink, especially if they get drunk, they are unwittingly giving control to the entities. Blackouts are examples of total, though temporary, surrender of consciousness. That is why others say, "He's a completely different person when he's drunk." He is! His role has been reduced to zero during that time.

One of the most important factors in possession is the time when it occurs, though the onset of the possession may be only vaguely perceived, if at all. A great many people are possessed as young children, especially following hospitalization for such surgeries as tonsillectomies, or during severe illnesses. Picking up a spirit at that tender age and growing up with it on board makes it nearly impossible for the people possessed to differentiate the boundaries of their own personalities from those of their possessors. The possession weakens the child's aura and creates a vulnerability to further possession. On the other hand, if the possession happens when the individuals are older, the "before and after" differences are more clearly apparent, though in the majority of cases there is a blending of personalities.

Sometimes spirits seem to bring an imprint of their physical bodies exactly as they were at death. This affects the living organism of the possessees and can result in physical symptoms of all kinds, among them pains, most frequently headaches, including migraines, PMS with edema, cramping, insomnia, obesity with the resultant hypertension, asthma and allergies, lack of energy or exhaustion. Often when elderly spirits possess younger people, the possessee begins to feel old, sick, and even develop symptoms, such as extreme fatigue, weakness, aches and pains, blurred vision and arthritis.

Many mental problems result from intervention by spirits. The most prevalent are lack of concentration and memory problems. Sometimes there is a loss of an aptitude that was formerly available.

Emotions are usually affected when there is possession. Anxiety, fears, and phobias are traceable in many cases to possessors. Phobias frequently are related to the circumstances of the entity's death experiences, which it vividly remembers. When the people the entities are possessing are in similar situations, all the original fears come back and the possessees feel them and assume that it is they themselves reacting, not realizing that they are possessed. Depressions are often traced to despondent spirits who usually don't realize they are dead. Because many people who commit suicide are still suicidal, they pose real threats to the lives of the possessed and regressing to past lives shows that at times these distraught entities have driven their hosts to suicide.

We seem to be protected from possession by the strength of our auras. When they are vibrating at high frequencies, they cannot be entered by spirits vibrating at lower ones. The aura is to the emotional-mental-spiritual dimension of a person as the immune system is to the physical body. Just as a weakened immune system leaves the individual susceptible to diseases and infections, so a diminished aura creates a vulnerability to spirit intrusion. Excessive negative emotions such as anger, depression, and grief all lower the frequency of the aura and diminish its protection temporarily. Fatigue, especially exhaustion, and illness also weaken the aura's protective capacity. If there are spirits nearby waiting for bodies to enter, they slip right in. Behaviors that put people in jeopardy, such as drug and alcohol abuse and even innocent experimentation with "recreational" drugs, can result in years of possession. Every one of the hundreds of patients I have treated who had abused drugs and alcohol was possessed.

There are two major categories of conditions or behaviors that result in possession: those in which people actually invite spirits to enter and those in which they are not only unaware of the possession but, at least on a conscious level, are completely unwilling for it to happen. In this second category are many instances of attachments made in hospitals. People die, often drugged or in a state of confusion and fear, and may remain there, earthbound. These spirits roam around in hospitals and easily latch onto people whose auras are open. Severe illness greatly impairs the aura, so most hospitalized patients are vulnerable. This is especially the case with young children, who can be readily dominated by adult entities. However, many times their possessors are seen as comforting persons and are welcomed. Once they are possessed, their auras are weakened even more, for they blend with the auras of their possessors, which are generally negative because of their fears and confusion. With diminished protection, children then become open prey for still other entities desiring physical bodies. The more spirits, the lower the vibrations of the possessee's aura.

The deaths of loved ones or close friends create vulnerability because of the physical and emotional upheaval the survivors feel. To add to the problem, the survivors usually have exposure to three places in which there are the greatest concentration and number of spirits: hospitals (including nursing homes and convalescent hospitals), funeral homes, and cemeteries. In addition, ties of love and affection sometimes create binding attractions when the loved ones die. Often the deceased are prevented from going on and are pulled magnetically back into their survivors' auras. But though in many cases the victims are both unwilling to be possessed and are unaware that it is happening, in other situations people deliberately ask to be possessed, without realizing the consequences. These include people who dabble with the Ouija board, try automatic writing, or expose themselves to seances. Imaginary playmates, a childhood phenomenon often encouraged by parents, may in reality be entities.

Do people ever just "pick up" spirits? Or does the explanation lie in past lives? Is the possession an aspect of karma? It could be that there were bonds formed between the possessees and the possessors during former lifetimes. In the many complicated cases of possession that I've investigated in depth, I have found that there were usually past-life connections and motivations for the possession.

Case: Triangle from Another Lifetime

First Session

Anne was an attractive young businesswoman in her mid-thirties who was on the verge of sacrificing twelve years of business gains because she found herself in a personality conflict with her boss. She felt he wanted power over her, and she refused to allow this. At the beginning of their association two years before, she had felt that they were friends, but since then their relationship had gone steadily downhill. "I have even had a dream that Bill was trying to kill me," she reported in her first session.

I explored several areas to try to determine what was involved.

T: *How do your co-workers see the relationship, Anne?*
P: *They talk about him all the time and tell me that I'm right, that he harasses me. He's taken away most of my responsibilities. He's turned me into a secretary—just tells me to put memos on the PC without even asking for feedback. Little by little he's chipped away at my self-esteem.*

She reported that her husband was totally supportive of her and was even ready to sell their house in order for her not to work for a while if she needed to leave her position. She was close to her father and reported a good relationship with him. The situation with Bill seemed unlike her relationship with other men. Anne herself brought up the possibility that she had known him in a past life.

P: *I've been doing a lot of soul-searching for the past six months and wondered if we knew each other before—you know, in an earlier life? Do you think it's possible that Bill and I have been together before?*
T: *Anne, whenever we have a relationship with someone, we have been with them many times before, especially if it's intense. You've been with your husband maybe hundreds of times, in many roles, even as a male. You may have been his father, and he your daughter. You can tell a lot about what you've worked out before by the quality of the relationship now. If it's harmonious you can be pretty sure that, at least in the last few times together, you've had good relationships. If there's a conflict, as there is with Bill, then you've had problems, maybe much worse. You and Bill have tangled before. We'll have to get back to that time to help you get rid of the charge with him; then you won't have any buttons for him to push.*

Since Anne's inability to cope with her relationship with Bill didn't fit with her obvious competence and achievements, I considered the possibility of possession, but first I went over my mental checklist. I found that her memory and concentration had deteriorated significantly in the past year. When I asked about hospitalizations, surgical operations, or accidents, she told me that she had been hit by a car when she was almost three while she had been running across the street to join her mother. She had been taken to the hospital and remained in a coma for several months and was not expected to live. Her parents were told that if she survived, she would never be normal or able to communicate, but she recovered. Four years before I saw her she had been injured in another automobile accident and was still in therapy for that.

When I eased into the topic of spirit possession, I noticed that her chin was quivering and she confessed that she could hear her heart pounding, and tears began to run down her face. An entity was upset! I told her a little about hypnosis and had her put her chair in a reclining position, close her eyes, and concentrate on her breathing. Then I gave her soothing and positive hypnotic suggestions, which I recorded for her to listen to later as she drifted off to sleep at night.

Meanwhile, she had become deeply relaxed, and turning the tape over I recorded a depossession. As soon as I addressed any spirits that might be with her, she shifted from a blissful expression to one of total agitation and began to sob. As I routinely do, I invited in the spirit's loved ones and witnessed the entity calming down, and the tension in her body was abruptly released. I ended the depossession and brought her out of the trance.

P: *He didn't want to go (crying). I don't know why, but I feel sad.*
T: *What else are you aware of?*
P: *I can feel a fluttering here (pointing to her chest). When he doesn't feel threatened, everything calms down.*
T: *Could you tell me who it is?*
P: *A man. For some reason, I feel sure it's a man. I don't know who, though.*

Since he probably had not left, I asked Anne to close her eyes again and to monitor the reactions she felt as I talked directly to that spirit. Tears streamed down her face as I pointed out how hard it was for a man to be trapped in a female body. Then I invited him to go with his loved one, perhaps his mother, to the spirit world where he would be in his own strong, healthy, male body. Seeing that Anne had relaxed again, I brought the depossession to a close.

T: *Could you feel him go this time?*
P: *I think he went with his mother. When you mentioned that maybe his mother was here for him, I could feel a change. My body felt suddenly calm.*

I told Anne that if he had not left then, perhaps he would when she played the depossession tape, which I told her to do daily when she was alert. The other side of the tape could be played as she drifted off to sleep and she would absorb the suggestions, even if she weren't awake.

Since we still had time left, I suggested a regression to find out if she'd been with Bill before.

> T: *If you have, we'll see if you can remember the event that is causing the tension between the two of you. The remarkable thing is that if you do, he may have a change of heart. There must be a telepathic link between people that causes a reaction automatically. When you experience the past life, it not only heals you, but maybe him, too, even without his knowing anything about the regression.*
> P: *That would be great. Do you think I can recall a previous incarnation?*
> T: *It's not hard—if you don't try. Trying gets in the way. Just know that it's as easy as remembering something that happened yesterday.*

We talked about what a regression was like and I gave her suggestions to regress to the particular time when she and Bill had been together before that was having the greatest effect on her now.

She saw herself as a girl walking with her boyfriend in the early 1900's. When I moved her ahead she said without any feeling that the relationship had ended. I assumed that there was something traumatic she didn't want to remember and gave her some suggestions to overcome the resistance.

> P: *They're having an argument...hands lashing out...beating on her.*
> T: *Tell me more about it.*
> P: *It's pretty violent. She's screaming. He's throwing her to the ground. She's crying. (Long pause.) My mind is blank. They're gone!*

At this point I decided to try another tack.

> T: *Tell me your dream again, the one of Bill killing you that you mentioned when you first came in.*
> P: *There are some trees and a library in a small town...and a couple. (Pause.) The same couple!... He killed me!* He killed me *(covering her face with her hands and sobbing loudly)* with his bare hands. Oh, my God! I don't want to know any more!*

I appealed to the part of her that wanted to be healed and helped her to overcome her fears with reassuring suggestions. She went on with the story.

> P: *They're fighting with him, trying to stop him. Now he has something in his hand...and he's beating me with it*—over and over! *(shaking violently as she remembers her death). It's over. (Long pause.) I feel very light...and now I feel like I'm floating up.*

I asked her to look down. She saw herself lying on the ground, and the man, who seemed almost happy, just standing nearby as some women rushed to help her. Then, realizing that she must remember the reason for the argument, I regressed her to the beginning of the fight.

> P: *He's accusing me of something...of being with another man. (Long pause.) This* other *man! The one in my body! (Opening her eyes and bringing herself abruptly out of trance) That's what it is...I feel different! Strong!*

A beautiful smile lit up her face. We had recovered a triangle from another lifetime.

Second Session

Anne was stylishly dressed and moved confidently into my office for her second session. She said that she felt much better and that even her driving was different. Because of an intervening holiday she had seen her boss for only half a day, but she felt her approach to him was entirely different and that he was much more friendly. She felt different toward herself, had more energy, and was putting more effort into herself. She thought the spirit had left, but as she told me this she was aware of a surge of heat, though it was not hot in the office.

I sensed that her reaction was probably the entity partially manifesting because of my question and I wondered if he was re-living his death, which might have involved fire. I decided to check this out and under hypnosis suggested to Anne that she explore their relationship in the same past life we had tapped into last time.

She tuned into a tragic story. She and the man had been in love and had decided to run away together. In that life Bill was an older friend who had taken care of her and trusted her, treating her like a sister. After she and her friend had planned their "escape," they decided to rob Bill's safe and steal his money. Her boy friend went into the building to light a stick of dynamite while she hid in the bushes. Something went wrong and the dynamite misfired and her friend was killed in the explosion. The building caught on fire and everyone came running to put it out.

I continued the regression a few more moments to a time when she wasn't upset, and then I had her speak out loud to the spirit and tell him in her own words that she wanted him to leave now.

Anne did this and then confessed that the spirit had stayed because she wanted him to. He left, telling her that he felt it was time for him to go. When I asked her how she felt, she said she missed him, making clear that the attraction had been from both sides.

> P: *How could he be a spirit now? It was a long time ago. Do spirits stay here that long?*
> T: *Only he can answer that question. He may have reincarnated and then after his last death, he remained earthbound and was attracted to you because of your past-life bonds.*

We set up another appointment in two days, and she left saying that she felt much better.

Third Session

When I saw Anne for the third time it was apparent that there were still problems. Everything had been going well with Bill, but that morning she had become dizzy and was close to vomiting and passing out. When she tried to work at the office later she couldn't concentrate and had to go home; then as she was driving to my office she became dizzy again. When I asked about previous experiences of dizziness she said that eight and 11 years before she had had two migraines and these had been accompanied by severe head pains.

After she was in hypnosis I suggested that she go back to the event that was responsible for her dizziness. She found herself as a high-ranking officer in the Spanish military who was overthrown in an upheaval and had to flee to a remote island. Here his enemies caught up with him and demanded that he give them certain information. When he refused, the commanding officer of his enemies ordered him to be killed, and he was hit violently on the back of the head and lost consciousness and died.

When Anne had told me at the beginning of the session about being dizzy as she drove to my office, she had used the pronoun "we," though it turned out she had been alone. Now that she had dealt with the event that probably had caused the prior migraine problem and associated dizziness, I decided to find out who the "we" were—a slip of the tongue had been a giveaway that she had someone else with her.

I knew that it was also possible that the entity that we had worked with during the past two sessions had not left. She was still deeply hypnotized and enjoying being in the Light following the death she had re-lived. I intruded into her mood and asked her what she meant by "we."

> P: *There are others with me. They control me. They are very concerned that you might try to make them leave. They are very strong and are angry with you now that I know about them being with me.*

I regressed her to the moment they joined her. She re-lived being on the operating table when she was a child, after being hit by the car.

> P: *Something sharp, metal, has cut me. The back of my head hurts. The doctors are panicky. I'm hardly breathing. This goes on for quite a while. I'm going deeper and deeper. My arms hurt. It's hard to breathe...my chest is very heavy and my leg hurts...I'm going deeper. I'm having trouble breathing. I feel like I'm barely alive.... That's when another person comes with an old dark, wrinkled face. There are three of them. They take over. I feel real warm when they take over. They make my body feel better. They make the pain go away.*
> T: *Did you agree that they could take over?*
> P: *No, they just came. Two women and one man. The man is very old and very tired.*

I then spoke directly to these entities, telling them that their work was over. They had saved the life of the little girl 31 years ago, but she was well now. They needed to think of their own welfare and go with the loved ones who had come for them. All three left within seconds.

Once out of hypnosis Anne talked further about her accident when she was three with its grim prognosis that she would never be normal again.

> P: *Maybe they not only pulled me through but helped me to develop normally. They meant well.*

Fourth Session

Five days later Anne looked radiant. At work her boss had gone out of his way to explain things and was much more flexible, and she found that she had stopped criticizing him behind his back. All of the depression, the thoughts of leaving and selling the house, were gone now. Her energy had heightened.

I suggested that it would be helpful to explore her relationship with Bill, since we really didn't know much about him other than that he had killed her. She agreed with a guilty smile.

> P: *I'm really curious how he found out about the other man.*

I regressed her to the moment Bill discovered her involvement with her lover.

P: *The night of the explosion...some horses are coming up with a wagon. It's Bill. He asks me what happened. The house is burning. People are running around trying to put the fire out, and he's running around giving orders to people. I'm feeling real bad.*

> *I think they found the body...yes, we all did. I'm looking at it also. Bill's looking at the safe. It's open and he's finding out what's missing. He looks at everyone. He notices me. He's always trusted me. (Long pause.) I was like a sister to him—we grew up in the same family. (Cries.) That's why he trusted me so much—we were raised together. He's looking at me suspiciously. He finds it hard to believe, but there's too much evidence for him to doubt.*

T: *What are you feeling?*

P: *I never should have betrayed him. He trusted me.*

She was crying hard, but she managed to continue the regression, describing how he had taken care of and protected her, smothering her with devotion. After the fire she wanted to move to another town, but he refused to give his permission. Sometime later she confronted him as they were coming out of church one Sunday and told him that she was definitely leaving. He argued with her about it but when she remained adamant, he became irrational, to the point of going crazy and finally attacking her. She re-lived her death again, adding that she realized she didn't want to live. By slipping out of her body she escaped from her guilt and the trap she felt she was in.

P: *Bill is going to be gone for three months to set up another sales office in Japan, and now I wonder why I didn't wait it out instead of going through this.*

T: *It seems that everyone seeks help at the time that is best. There are no accidents. If you had waited, four lost souls would still be imprisoned here on the earth plane, and you and Bill would not have made your peace, which is probably one of your purposes in this lifetime. You've healed yourself spiritually and you've helped him. I wonder if there weren't highly evolved beings, your guides, who inspired you to give yourself a chance to be freed, not only from the possession but also from the negative memories of the past.*

We agreed that would be our last time together unless something else came up. Apparently all has gone well and the releasement of the entities has held.

In Anne's story we see how her personal attachment to a man in another lifetime, because it was rudely interrupted by a violent death, drew him to attach to her in this lifetime, both because of his probable confusion resulting from such a death and because her yearning drew him to her. Intermingled with the situation in that lifetime was her connection with the second man. Because Anne's relationship with this man (Bill in this lifetime) was disastrously concluded by murder, it had reappeared in this life to be dealt with more wisely. Though in the old lifetime the two connections formed a triangle with Anne, in the current life this was not a pertinent consideration unless one hypothesizes that the possessing relationship was interfering with a harmonious relationship with Bill.

The other past life where Anne, as a man, was murdered by being hit in the head, set the pattern for painful migraines in this one, and the accident when she was three, when she was run over by a car and struck in the head, reinforced this physical template. Following this accident, three additional entities, uninvited, entered Anne's consciousness as a result of her weakened condition. They apparently saved her life, but though their helpful intervention was long over, they had stayed trapped in her consciousness until the therapeutic release.

Clinical Depossession

by

Louise Ireland-Frey, M.D.

Introduction

In modern times more and more therapists are returning to the once-common assumption that discarnate entities can and often do invade living persons. This change in therapists' attitudes is due to the spontaneous complaints presented by clients that lead the therapist to suspect the presence of an invading entity, of which the clients themselves may be entirely unsuspecting.

Process of Attachment

Research in near-death experiences suggests that as souls are freed from their bodies they look for a light, which may seem to be at the end of a tunnel or over the top of a hill or temple, and then go toward this light. Entities who remain "earthbound" have for some reason not followed this procedure. When entities are asked why they entered a client after the death of their body, they usually say that it is because they didn't know where to go. They see their bodies down below, inert and lifeless, if they look; sometimes they do not look and may be unaware that they have "died." They feel a difference that bewilders them because they know something has changed, but they don't know what. Thus they wander lost in a dimension in which space and time are non-existent in the sense that we know them; they wander in the "outer darkness" of which religions have spoken. They are not spiritually lost or condemned, but certainly they have missed the rightful path into the next stage of life.

For a time immediately after death the entities can see and hear living persons clearly, but persons in living bodies are unable to see or hear the disembodied souls. Many entities go back to their former homes after the death experience and try to contact family members, only to find themselves totally ignored. This creates pathetic frustration and loneliness for the newly dead. Eventually they wander away (they are not sure where) and for a timeless period (they are not sure how long). They may be drawn to a lighter or warmer area, which turns out to be the energy of a living human body. Seeking comfort and safety, they enter.

Often an entity will say that he entered a living body to comfort or help the person. Further questioning usually brings out that the entity was also seeking benefit for himself, unaware that his parasitic presence in the host would be detrimental to both. When this is explained to him, he is usually sorry and asks forgiveness before he leaves. While in the host, however, he seems to be unable to leave, trapped in a strong magnetic force until released by a therapeutic experience with a therapist or priest. A small number are able to come and go, or to leave one host for another one.

There are several degrees of closeness of attachment between entity and host:

> 1. Sometimes the term *shadowing* is used for the loose relationship where the entity is outside the host's body but staying nearby, influencing the host intermittently or mildly.

> 2. *Oppression* is the term used when the entity is inside the aura of the host or affecting the host emotionally somewhat more perceptibly.

> 3. *Obsession* is the condition of invasion of the physical body by the entity, who brings with it all its own personality traits and habits, including some that are far from desirable, often perplexing the host.

> 4. *Possession* is what occurs when the invader completely pushes out the resident person's psyche and takes over the physical body, through which it exhibits its own behaviors and speaks its own words. There may be alternations between possession and partial possession (obsession).

Most cases of true possession are confined to mental institutions or jails because the changes in personality and behavior are so dramatically conspicuous. Obsessions, on the other hand, are far more common. They usually affect the physical body, causing symptoms such as headaches, respiratory problems, obesity, compulsions, phobias, suicidal urges, or emotional excesses, such as sudden rages.

Entities can come from any period of history or even pre-history. In the extended dimension of existence, time does not have the same linear meaning that it has here. The entity, when asked how long it has been wandering, only knows it as "a long time" and has little ability to estimate. It may be astonished to learn that the "present" is in the 1900's. It is not only stopped at the date of its death, but it has also been halted in its spiritual progress until it can move on.

Occasionally a client who has suspected the presence of an entity or energy has been able to expel the invader without assistance, either by meditation or religious means. But in some such instances the invader only goes as far as the outside parameters of the person's aura and remains "plastered" there, so to speak, sometimes causing a condition of oppression. The energy and words of one or more living persons are usually necessary for the complete releasement of the trapped invader and its safe direction into the light. I like the word *releasement* for this work because it implies release not only for the client but also for the entrapped entities.

The distinction between invading entities and multiple personalities is still being argued. Many of the so-called multiple personalities in a client may turn out to be entities who can be released with relative ease in one or two hypnotic sessions, leaving only the true multiple personalities to be dealt with.

Among healthy persons the condition of obsession appears to be surprisingly frequent, so common that one can wonder if it is "normal." However, it is never entirely beneficial for either the client or the trapped entity to be in this relationship, unlike the situation of contact with high entities. (It should be remembered that high entities do not invade: only confused and earthly or evil types, and occasionally well-meaning but intrusive ones, invade.)

It is possible to determine the presence and number of entities by finger signals that tap into the client's Higher Mind. Specific fingers are selected as "yes" and "no" fingers. Later on in treatment work, finger signals can also be asked to give information that is being produced reluctantly.

Method of Releasement

Preliminary conversation is usually necessary unless the client is already acquainted with the concept of obsession. This talk should be tailored to the client's personal attitudes of mind and religious beliefs. Mention of the frequency of obsession helps. Speaking of deceased family members who have been found to be entrapped is understandable and even comforting to most clients. Concern about spirits being evil can be dealt with by explaining that these are only occasionally encountered, and they too, can be released. It is reassuring to explain that most entities that invade people are simply wandering and lost.

An important distinguishing characteristic of current releasement techniques is that the channel for the disembodied entity is the client, who speaks the entity's words. The client's own mind is still present, aware of all that is being said, but he feels the entity's emotions and receives many other impressions that may not be expressed until after the altered state is lifted. Formerly, entities were contacted through deep trance channeling by someone else, and the channel was usually so removed from the process that no memory remained of what had been said. In contrast, the client, as channel, has full memory of what has been said and done.

Usually there is little difficulty in establishing contact with disembodied entities. Most of them appear to be glad to converse with someone. By questioning such an entity we acquire a sketch of its sex, personal traits, last death experience, age, present state, and its influence on the living person with whom it is in contact. As therapists, we then help it to move into its rightful pathway out of the earthbound state in a forward progression in its own journey to the Light. Earthbound spirits manifest a range of feelings and attitudes. Many are full of strong negative emotions, such as guilt, fear, anger, or depression. Some are lost and totally ignorant of where to go. Others are simply very tired and weak, having carried these feelings over from the last days of life.

Releasement appears to require an altered state that is not as deep as is required by many regressions, and such deepening as is necessary can be obtained by various methods in general use. It is not necessary to utilize hypnosis as such, for there are numerous other methods that lead a client into the altered state. So far as I have been able to tell from personal experience as a subject, the altered state is similar, if not identical, when induced by any of the various methods, and all seem to be equally effective.

Often I begin the actual releasement by using the finger technique to find out how many entities we have to deal with, if any. Then, if an entity is indicated, I ask it to come out.

> T: *Thank you for letting me know you are here. Please come out and tell me your name. Put the thought of your name into John's mind and he will speak it for you. John, when a name comes into your mind, just say it.*

In most cases there is little or no delay in getting a name. Some entities say they have no name or are ashamed of it or are reluctant to comply. In such cases I tell them there is no need to tell their real name, and I assign a name and ask their permission to use it. Sometimes entities agree with this, and sometimes they prefer to choose a name themselves or even to reveal their true name.

In the initial interview with the entity, via the client, I ask how old it is (it stops aging at death), when and why it entered the client, what happened on the last day it was in its own body. In a few minutes a distinct impression of the entity, the circumstances of its death, and its personality traits and needs are revealed. These are valuable to know in order to help the entity by verbal therapy of the directive type before it progresses "into the Light."

It is important always to remember that therapy for the entity is as important as therapy for the client. To completely defuse the death experience and other traumatic experiences for each entity encountered and released may require more time than is available, but much can be accomplished simply by directive neutralization and cancellations.

Techniques for the releasement of the obsessing consciousness, and therefore the releasement of the living client from the invader, are in general the same techniques as for regression therapy. In these cases the therapy is first for the invading entity and secondarily for the client who has been parasitized. If the client's symptom has been due to the problem of the (deceased) invader, it automatically disappears after releasement, usually within a few hours, days, or weeks, leaving only the client's own problems to be dealt with.

It is to be noted that obsessing entities are not multiple personalities; each has its own life story and death experience, complete with names and dates. Nor are the conversations obtained during releasements, past-life experiences, and mind-contacts the same as Gestalt conversations, the "as if" role-playing conversations that have helped many persons. To the contrary, in such cases as the ones under discussion, it appears that these are simply and literally what they purport to be: experiences of disembodied minds able to report their past and present thoughts, feelings, and livingness through the client's vocal apparatus as s/he channels for them in "blended conscious-ness," his/her own consciousness remaining aware of all that is being said and felt.

When finger signals indicate that there are several entities, I ask for the strongest entity to come out first and set about freeing him and helping him to enter the Light. Sometimes, though rarely in my experience, the strongest entity is a being of the demonic type. When dealing with such dark forces it is imperative to call, either mentally or aloud, for assistance from Beings of Light. With the back-up of such Beings there will be no fear in the therapist and through him the White Forces will be in control of the situation.

Three techniques help in releasing these dark entities. First, they must be reminded that they do have free will and can make choices and decisions of their own. They can choose whether to go back to the Darkness or turn toward the Light and begin to "unlearn a lot of old things and learn many wonderful new things." This choice should be made with a friendly eagerness and for the entity's own sake. The second technique is to ask the entity if it has ever been happy and if it wouldn't like to be happy now, giving it illustrations of what happiness is like. Then I suggest it turn from the darkness and face the Beings of Light and feel warmth on its face. A third technique, (introduced by Baldwin, 1992)[15] is to have the entity search within itself for a core of non-darkness, like a tiny light or a softly glowing pearl, and watch this grow in strength. Having the client take a deep breath, or asking the entity to do so, seems to increase the brightness of the interior light. When this inner light is found, the therapist can point out that its presence proves that the entity was originally a child of light, not darkness.

In dealing with a stubborn entity that has been human and is unwilling to leave the client, this use of the dim pearl is again helpful. Also, asking the entity to recall someone or some animal it has loved and see it as welcoming, is particularly effective. If an entity willing to leave cannot see a light anywhere to indicate the direction it should go, I suggest that it rid itself of any dark heavy things, such as fear, anger, hate, loneliness, confusion, or feelings of unworthiness or inferiority. Different metaphors can be used for this, such as seeing light transforming a pile of black things into clear, pure water, or sitting down in a beautiful river and letting the water softly dissolve all the negative things and float them away downstream. The next step is to see the good things remaining—courage, gentleness, friendliness, etc.—until the entity can finally perceive the Light.

People who die suddenly from any cause tend to become earthbound. For instance, persons who kill their bodies seldom find their rightful soul path in the way that normally dying persons do. Instead, they tend to remain earthbound or to advance to only lower desolate astral regions because of their heavy weight of desperation, fear, sorrow, and guilt. Death from a murder, which is usually sudden, almost invariably causes its victim to become earthbound. The psyche of a victim of murder leaves the body with intense emotions of various kinds. Fear is often paramount; rage or vengefulness are frequent. Whatever the manner in which the victim was killed or whatever the emotions of the psyche when contacted, the therapy consists of allaying fears, quieting rage, and persuading the entity to cast away all dark, heavy feelings that keep him from going to the Light. Psyches of children who are murdered seem to seek refuge and a hiding place in the body of a living person, and many psyches of infants whose bodies have been aborted, either spontaneously or by intent, have become obsessing entities in either the mother's body or someone else's, bringing deep, irrational feelings of fear, sadness, and rejection.

Victims of mass accidents or natural disasters present a special challenge. For them death comes suddenly or fairly rapidly and without previous mental preparation. The psyches crossing over feel confused when such an incident happens and helpers should visualize in meditation a safe road or highway and call souls to get on the highway. Helpers from the other side will be there and receive those who are to come over.

Since therapy in all cases of releasement is for the attached entities as well as for the host, work must be done until the entities have been safely directed toward and escorted into the Light. For most of them it is possible to find a family member or someone they loved who will act as a guide.

Sometimes in guiding the entity into the Light the therapist must be innovative. Persons and contacts and concepts that are meaningful to the entity, as gleaned from its history, may provide the helpers needed. This is especially true in cases of sudden death where the entity is in shock and, feeling its experience as alien, needs something familiar to console and assist it.

One entity I helped was a lone man with no relatives and no friends except his horse. The horse had stumbled on a loose stone and thrown him, and his head had struck a rock, resulting in his death.

E: *Brownie wouldn't leave. She stayed there by my body for two weeks and nearly starved before someone found us. They shot Brownie and took my body away.*
T: *Have you seen her waiting for you on the other side?*
E: *I don't see her.*
T: *Have you searched for her? Why don't you look around?*
E: *There she is! She's coming. (Ducks head to hide tears.)*
T: *What is happening?*
E: *She has her head down...on my shoulder...my arm is around her neck....*
T: *Horses have keen intelligence. Brownie knows the way to go. She will take you home.*

In this case neither friend nor guides came, but I am sure the love between the entity and the horse was entirely adequate as compass and escort. The light was "all around."

In another case a male entity said that he had died in a great fire in Boston Harbor. He presented blocking and resistance until questions gently led him to express extreme anguish and guilt because many people had died in the fire, including his brother.

E: *I caused it. I was careless...and the fire spread.... It spread even to oil spilled on the water.*

He and another man escaped the flames in a small boat, but in his desperate guilt and grief he jumped back into the burning water. Because his name was Italian, I thought he might be Catholic, and he confirmed this.

T: *Mother Mary, please come to this soul so full of despair. (To entity) Look into her face and tell me what you see there.*
E: *Compassion—forgiveness (choking back tears).*
T: *Give your hand to her and let her take you Home.*

No human absolution could have helped him as well. Besides seeing the Virgin he also saw his brother coming, with forgiveness in his eyes. The vision of the Virgin was probably a thought form, but it was ensouled with her life and with the compassion that is attributed to her. Those who have left their bodies in death do not immediately shed the emotional ties and religious perceptions with which they have grown up. Familiar concepts and loved people can help them to feel their situation as less alien and facilitate their journey into the Light.

Following the releasement of the entity, the client is the sole recipient of any further therapy. His mind, habits, and problems are all his own now, and he is ready for past-life or prenatal or other work. I complete each releasement session with guided meditation, putting a protective bubble or capsule around the client, and I suggest that the client meditate upon this protective bubble several times a day for a week or two. After releasement the usual reaction of a client is a joyous exclamation: "Oh, how light I feel! I didn't know I was carrying such a burden."

As for theories, I've come through the stages of cautious doubt, incredulity, and then amazement, to a casual, almost a shoulder-shrugging acceptance of these entities as being just what they say they are. Another indication is the astonishment of the clients: "Where did all that come from? Why did I say that name? I don't know anyone by that name! Did I make all that up?" The efforts of psychology and psychiatry to explain the experiences in other ways seem far more complicated and tortuous than simply accepting what the entities themselves say they are—not multiple personalities but obsessing minds or souls.

Case: Insomnia Resulting from Entity Attachment

When a therapist begins regression work or releasement work, it is truly a case of a double-blind operation, for neither the client nor the therapist knows what may be brought up from the client's subconscious mind or what obsessing entities or energies may be uncovered. This makes it all the more remarkable that a client, speaking for the entity, routinely brings forth a complete, coherent, believable story, often quite ordinary, such as Harry's being killed by a car in the following account. Only a few are "romantic," like Robert's tale of heisting a sailing ship long ago.

As is illustrated in the following case, it isn't easy for the therapist to know whether it is the client himself speaking or an entity who is being channeled through the client. Only the client can tell us (and of course the entity, too). At times it seems as if the two blend, as in the following case where there is discussion of spaceships and rock 'n' roll music. Harry, the entity, would be aware of both, since he is in Jim in the *present*. Perhaps some entities keep up with current events, though most claim their age to be what it was at their death.

First Session

A large number of attachments begin in this lifetime, as was true in the case of Jim, a reputable lawyer in his early fifties who listed his problems as insomnia, lack of energy, and stress. Because standard medical treatment had not helped, he had started herbal therapy with a local therapist and was referred to me for hypnotherapy. He reported that he fell asleep in a normal way but then awakened at 3:36 a.m. and was unable to return to sleep for several hours. He would then sleep late the following morning and in mid-afternoon struggle against sleep at a time when in his occupation he still needed to be mentally alert.

When Jim's subconscious mind was asked in hypnosis to go back to the cause of the sleep problem, it first took him back to the fourth grade when a teacher, a man young Jim respected and considered fair, accepted the falsehood told by another student that Jim had taken a small article, a protractor. The teacher accused Jim of the theft and shook him by the shoulders. Jim was deeply hurt that the teacher did not believe his denial and was not "fair."

T: *What is he thinking and feeling about you?*

C: *He genuinely believes I took it. He doesn't look down on me. He doesn't hate me...it's a lesson. He shakes me because he believes I took it, but...he thinks those things just happen. He says he shakes me to teach me to tell the truth.*

    The truth is very important to me. There are so many things in this world that aren't the truth. Truth is like a core, a shining sphere—no, not like a sphere. It has the dimensions of a corn cob, bright, light, but shrouded. It's my job, always has been my job, to peel away the shroud and release Truth. You have to peel it away so people can see what the truth is.... I didn't do it! It hurts when people can't see it, can't see the truth.

T: *Jim, as your grown-up self, go and put your arm around young Jim's shoulder and tell him you believe him. Tell him you understand. Comfort him.*

C: *What?*

T: *Put your arm around young Jim's shoulder and tell him that you believe him and understand. Past and future don't make much difference in hypnosis, you remember. They don't matter much. Go and put your arms around him.*

C: *(Speaking to his child self) You're okay, Bud.*

T: *Is young Jim all right now?*

C: *He understands. He got it. It really doesn't matter. (The attitude of, "It doesn't matter" is a sign that the emotion of a painful experience has been neutralized.)*

T: Now, as I count from one to four, let your mind rise to the super-conscious dimension. Let your Higher Mind search back all through your life, clear back into infancy and even before birth, and find the cause of the sleeping problem. One...two...three...four.

C: It's just...I'm searching...I'm looking up, and it's like a computer search. I go from grade school, then I'm searching in high school and college... through experiences in the years, not just places. Oh, boy, what a ride! The sleep problem is a problem with my job. Another problem is that I'm allergic to alcohol. If I drink more than two beers, I won't sleep. Maybe that's in my head, too. I don't know if I'm making this up or just remembering it. I don't know if I'm "under" or "frauding" you. I don't want to 'fraud you. But something is different. From my shoulders to my feet it's like when you're frozen in the dentist's chair.... There's no feeling...I'm paralyzed. No, it's not unpleasant. When you ask questions and talk, I have trouble concentrating. I'm workin'. I'm workin'! But seems like there's a devil in me that keeps me from thinking clearly.

T: (Taking advantage of the remark to sidestep into a releasement) Is there any soul or entity in Jim who is not Jim himself? Let the fingers answer.

C: ("Yes" finger moves reluctantly.)

T: More than one entity in Jim?

C: ("Yes" finger twitches slightly. Jim laughs.)

T: I'm asking the strongest entity to come out and tell me your name. Jim, say aloud the first name that comes into your mind.

C: Well, when you started asking, the name "Harry" seemed to come, but then "Robert," so I don't know which.

T: When the subconscious mind answers, it is the first flash that counts. So, Harry, I thank you for letting me know you are here. How old are you?

C: Well, I got 43 and 26. But he's not going to tell the truth!

T: I'll ask the fingers. Is Harry the one who is 43 years old?

C: ("Yes" finger lifts.)

T: Is there another entity in Jim who is 26?

C: ("Yes" finger lifts.)

T: Is it Robert?

C: (Slight twitch of the "yes" finger.)

T: Are there still other entities, some who don't want to be found?

C: ("Yes" finger moves.)

T: Well, don't be afraid of me. I'll talk to you later, but first I'll talk to Harry. Harry, how old was Jim when you found him and went into him?

E1:   Fourteen.

T: How did you manage to enter him? Was he more open then?

E1:   Yes.

T: Why? Was he sick or under stress?

C: I'm having trouble finding answers. I'm trying.

T: You are doing fine. Just let the impressions come into your mind and then speak them aloud. This is not memory, and don't try. Don't try to figure *it out. (To E1) Now, Harry, did you choose Jim because he is similar to you in some way?*

E1: Yes.

T: *Describe yourself, Harry.*

C: I perceive...(E1 taking over) I'm red-headed, no part in my hair—it's smoothed back. I have a round nose. I'm rugged, somewhat overweight....

T: *What is your personality like? Can you describe yourself that way?*

E1: Oh, I have...I'm engaging—I like to jest and laugh—heartily! And I like whiskey! I appreciate Irish bars.

T: *Harry, go to the last day you were in your own body. You know you are in Jim's body now. Without fear or pain, see what happened to your body and tell me.*

E1: The last...is being...in an auto accident. I was coming around a corner, walking. It was a 1919 Studebaker that got me in the leg.

C: I don't know if I'm making this up, or not.

T: *It's all right. Just keep going. You're doing fine. Harry, what year was it when you had the accident? Say whatever comes to mind.*

E1: 1927.

T: *And what country is it?*

E1: Ireland.

T: *What is your last name, Harry?*

C: Harry...Menushaw?... (Seems to switch to Jim.) That's not right. I want to tell the truth. (It is not clear whether Harry or Jim is speaking.)

T: *What are your last thoughts?*

E1: Oh! Well, the bumper got me in the left leg! It was above the knee. It caught the leg underneath. I don't remember dying.... Whoo!... I was making a right turn around the corner and the car came along and the bumper hit me. Goddam, I got in an accident, didn't I?

T *Go to the last moment you are in your body.*

E1: I see it.

T: *Are you in a hospital?*

E1: No, no, no—it's right there in the street, on the cobblestones. That bumper got me, it flattened me to the ground. I hit the right side of my head. I got knocked down in the brain...and I come up...and I can see me lying there, and my left leg is killing me...and I'm out of my body...I'm flying...I'm flying. Woo-woo, what a ride! Rock 'n' roll!

C: But people don't know about rock 'n' roll yet! (Harry does know because he contacts Jim's knowledge.)

T: *In the state you are in, Harry, past and future and present don't make much difference. Now I need to explain something to you. Jim has a right to his own body without anyone else being in it. You have been using his energy and he feels tired without knowing why. And you have been trapped inside of him and haven't been progressing on your own spiritual path. You have had fun with him and have enjoyed the sense of humor together....*

E1: (Interrupting) We've been buddies for years. We've had good times.

T: Yes, and that has been good for you both, and when you go, you can leave him some of your good humor. But it is time for you to leave. You heard me telling Jim how to use that little magic whisk broom to brush out of himself everything he wants to get rid of, didn't you?

E1: Yes.

T: Well, you use it, too, and brush out sadness and sorrow.

E1: Well, I tell you what. I'm not too proud of my life. I drank a hell of a lot of whiskey. I didn't apply myself to anything. But I'm not a bad guy. Old Jimmy here, he's a go-getter.... That's why I got into him! He'd do okay on the work, and I could just ride along...I'm tired.

T: Harry, finish with the whisk broom. Brush out the alcohol addiction. You'll be given another chance to do better. Now look for a light.

E1: That car knocked that outa me!... Oh, yeah, let me tell you how it is. When you come out of your body, they raise ya, and ya see your body... and the.... Have you ever...? No, I don't suppose you have.... Ya kinda hover like a...like a space ship over your body...and it lifts ya, and you can fly, and soar...! And the light ye're talking about is the Truth, and the shroud is around it, and when it's off, you can fly to the truth.... We'll go. We'll go. But flyin' may get boring after a while.

T: Oh, you won't fly forever! Someone is coming to escort you to your own right place, much better than this down here on the earth plane. And you'll keep the friendship with Jim. Leave him some of your jesting, too. He needs a little bit.

E1: Where did you get "wise"?

T: I've been learning lots in these past years. Do you know, Harry, that this is the year 1990 now? And you have been stuck down here since 1927!

E1: I won't argue with you. You want me to go so you can help Jim. You're helping him.

T: And help you, too, just as much as Jim. It will be much better for you, too. See or feel someone coming for you.

E1: Well, but you see, the thing is...it's my mother, I think! She has that blue dress on again!

T: I think she's wearing it on purpose because you would recognize her in it better. Thoughts are very strong where you are. You can even change your age. Do you want to be younger?

E1: I kinda like this age.... And my mother has her hair all fixed up, and the blue dress on. I kind of took care of her.

T: Do you see some of your old buddies? Do you want to tell them to go with you?

E1: Oh, no, oh, no! They drank too much. Just good old boys. Just because they drank, they aren't all bad. But I'll go just with my mother now.

T: Thank you for coming for Harry, Mother.

E1: She wants to thank you, Ma'am, for finding me.

T: And what about Robert? Does he want to go with you?

E1: You better take care of him another time.

T: *Then have a happy little journey with your mom, Harry. Goodbye....*
Robert, I'm speaking to you now.

C: *(Seeing Robert and describing him) You're going to love him. I see a ship.*
It's a fourmaster. Robert sails. He is in 17th Century clothes. He's 26, a
real handsome fellow...ruddy...white skin, black hair pulled back in a bun,
sharp features, bold. He's the captain, English...he's English all right, a
damn pirate!

T: *Robert, it is time for me to stop now, so I ask you to remain quiet in Jim*
until I can talk to you next time he comes. Just round up your personality
into a comfortable little ball and stay quiet within him.

E2: *Oh, Madam, you ask a difficult task! When a ship is sighted I might go*
off on my own. You wait until my heist is over, there's no time then.
We're too busy! We'll go now.

T: *All right, Robert, but I ask that you promise not to hurt or kill anyone*
while you are out of Jim. I'll call you when Jim comes again and tell you
some things you need to know for your own sake. I'll call you, and you
will hear my voice no matter where you are. Do you promise not to bother
any living creature, human or non-human, while you are out of Jim?

E2: *Very well.*

Following this I did a routine closing.

T: *Just imagine that a light is starting to shine in you, maybe in the heart*
region, maybe in the solar plexus. It is your light. It grows and spreads
throughout your entire body and limbs, then radiates out around you
about a yard on all sides, over your head and under your feet as a
protective capsule of light. And in it are circulating streams of energy,
sparkles of green for healing and rose-pink for love. Just visualize this
protective capsule several times a day for a couple of weeks. We call it
"changing the spiritual dressing." And now I'll count from one to ten. Let
yourself come up lighter with each number, and on number ten you are
wide awake, feeling grand in every way, happy and smiling. (Upcount to
ten with interspersed short programmings.)

After this I reminded Jim that this was called "spiritual surgery," and
since he was in a "post-operative state" he should treat himself well. I
reminded him that the "openings" where Harry had come out had already
been cleansed by use of the whisk broom. Then I used a variation of
Therapeutic Touch to close the openings, passing my hand a few inches
above his body and smoothing out his aura.

Second Session

Jim had been amazed at the material in the first session. When we discussed Harry, he felt that Harry was familiar in some way and that he, Jim, would miss him. Then I reminded Jim that I had made a promise to Robert and would need to see him again in order to keep that promise.

This time I inducted Jim by words I had programmed in during the previous session, "Rest now!" I deepened his level of trance in three countdowns from six to one, chiefly because Jim's conscious mind felt that he was not deep enough, even though his "Yes" finger said he was.

T: *Robert I'm calling you now. Are you here?*

E2: *("Yes" finger rises.)*

T: *Are any of your men with you?*

C: *I'm not down deep enough.*

T: *(Second count down) Now I ask the fingers: Are you relaxed enough now?*

C: *I'll try.*

T: *It isn't a matter of trying. I'll count down again (Down count with interspersed programming of colors and symbols.) Now let the finger answer. Is Jim deep enough?*

C: *(Finger answers "yes".)*

T: *Robert are you waiting?*

C: *(Finger says "yes".) I cannot see or hear him. There is a handicap.*

T: *(Ignoring Jim's remark) Robert, think back to the last hours you were in your own body. Just see as an observer and without fear or pain tell about it. Think way back, Robert, a long way back.*

E2: *Galley. I was in the galley...*

T: *(Mistaking the term galley to be a galley ship) Was it your ship?*

E2: *It came to be my ship.*

T: *Do you mean you got it by one of your heists?*

E2: *Yes. It was out of Plymouth.*

T: *Plymouth in the New World or Plymouth in the Old World?*

E2: *The Old World. It was in 1614.*

T: *Are you a pirate?*

E2: *(After a pause) Yes, but I am better than an ordinary pirate. I have more discrimination. I never attack just any ship but only those with treasure. And I have a sense of humor.*

T: *Are you one of the oarsmen of the galley?*

E2: *The galley was in the stern. It was my ship.*

T: *When you heist the ship, do you split your crew up so some of them are on each ship?*

E2: *No, we boarded in Plymouth.*

T: *You mean right in port? You took her right in port?*

E2: *Yes.*

T: *Was there any trouble?*

E2: No. No one was on board.

T: Robert, go to the last hour you were in your body and tell me about that.

E2: We're in the galley. There's a storm. Water comes in through the back. The water catches me...forces...forces...The force of the water...

T: Go to the moment you leave your body. Let it come clearly to mind and tell me.

E2: It is like it just burst me out of my heart, the water-force bursts my body out into the ocean...and down, sucking it down. It catches me in the right side and forces me up to a corner of the ceiling and pushes me through my body, through my heart...I am free of the ship. I rise out of the water and up...

T: And then where do you go?... Do you find and enter any other living person before Jim?

E2: (Shakes head.)

T: Do you just wander?

E2: It is dark. (Shudders.)

T: Is it cold and dark?

E2: Not so much cold as just dark. (Body jerks.)

T: What year is this, Robert?

E2: 1617. In the ocean, south and west, southwest of the British Isles.

T: Robert, you have been wandering a long time, over 300 years, in the dark. Then you find Jim. How old was Jim when you found and entered him?

E2: Seven.

T: Why did you choose him to enter?

E2: He needed...he needed a father.

T: You felt you could be a father to him?

E2: No, just a...a friend (suddenly sobs).

T: (Not knowing whether the emotion is Robert's or seven-year-old Jim's) What are you feeling, Robert?

E2: Nothing.

T: Tell me about it Robert. That little kid "needs a father" and...?

E2: He's okay. I don't know whether...he's just...I can share adventures with him and teach him independence.

T: Those are good things. But you didn't know that you were all these years using some of his physical energy and making him tired and that you have been trapped in his body and not progressing on your own path. Is any one of your crew with you?

E2: None.

T: Then, Robert, just shove all the dark heavy things out of you, things like anger, hate, jealousy...regrets, remorse, selfishness, greed, egotism. Just pretend that all of these are like a heavy old filthy overcoat and just shed it from you and throw it away! You keep the wisdom you have learned from all of these experiences but just get rid of that heavy dark overcoat. Are you doing this?

E2: ("Yes" finger.)

T: Good! And remember, Robert, that gentleness and humility can be strengths. Look inside yourself now and see the bright things there: courage, independence, and wisdom. Did you throw away that overcoat?

E2: (Finger says "Yes.")

T: And now think, Robert, did you ever love anyone? Or any cat or dog?

E2: Spirit!

T: Did anyone ever love you? A parent? A dog? A cabin-boy? A woman?

E2: Yes...a woman...Rachel.

T: Did you love her?

E2: Yes.

T: Then I think now you can see the light, the light that came when you left your body.

E2: It's to the west...like the light from the sun in the clouds when the sun is setting. It's off to the west. The sun is in the clear.

T: Let the light shine into your heart and melt away any darkness remaining.

E2: I'm going off the ship...to the right, to starboard...into the Light! Yes...

T: Do you see anyone in the Light or near it?

E2: Anna! My little daughter. She looks at me and takes my left hand.

T: Anna, thank you for coming. Robert, I ask one last favor of you. How many others are in Jim?

E2: I see....(Long pause.)

T: Well, I won't hold you back any longer. Happy journey with Anna, Robert.

C: They flew...blue...blue...the light's gone. Blue takes its place.

T: Now I'm calling the next entity in Jim. Will you tell me your name?

C: (After a long pause) Nothing.

T: There used to be others, or another in Jim. I am speaking to these entities now. Are all of you willing to leave Jim and go into the Light?

C: ("No"...then "yes")

T: Are one or more of you ready to go into the Light?

C: ("Yes")

T: Are all you willing to go into the Light?

C: ("Yes")

T: I'm glad.... What do you see, Jim?

C: I see a woman...in a carriage. She's in a black dress. Pretty. Dark circles around her eyes...angelic look. She's looking out...

T: Lady, Jim sees you. Why don't you change the color of your dress to a beautiful light blue? And change your face, make your eyes clear and bright, and smile? Look for the light, Lady. That's the right direction.

C: She's changing. Her eyes are bright. The horse and carriage are moving into the clouds.

T: Are they dark clouds or light ones?

C: Silvery lined, beautiful clouds. The horse's color has changed from grey to a dappled white.... She goes with majesty.

T: Is she safe now? Is there any other entity in Jim?

   ("No" finger moves.)

T: *Subconscious mind, is there any other basic cause for Jim's insomnia that we should get at this morning?*

C: *("No" finger lifts.)*

T: *Jim, do you feel any other entities near you, even if not inside?*

C: *No. (Long pause.) I don't know whether my thoughts of being conscious were a handicap. I tried to go deep.*

T: *(Chuckling) You went so deep that often I could scarcely hear you. And now, I'll count from one to ten. Let yourself come closer to normal waking consciousness with every number, and when I get to ten you'll be wide awake and feeling fine in every way. (Slow upcount, interspersed with the same procedure as before.)*

Follow-up after the Session

Immediately after returning to full awareness, Jim relapsed into an altered state and with eyes open began to add details about Robert's heist of the ship in Plymouth of that time. He related both physical features and psychological states of the persons involved.

C: *The crew of that ship in Plymouth harbor was not aboard. They were all in the town...up here. The town is up here. And the pilot, or the owner... it's the owner of the ship...he's in a house right here (gesturing). And he's upset about something. He's middle aged, has white knee-high stockings and knee-length pants, and he's rounded...(Gestures with both hands showing a round belly) He's really upset. Something about the barrels isn't right. The barrels contain white powder...sugar? No, I don't know what it is.*

Robert knows where the crew is, and he knows where the owner is. He and his crew just board the ship in mid-afternoon. Only two men are on board as guards. One has a black tri-colored hat. He's the foreman, I guess. He doesn't get much pay, so when Robert comes aboard he just shrugs and thinks, "Why should I fight and die for what I get?" He tells the other guard, "Come on, let's go." So they just leave. Robert has to get the ship out of harbor in daylight while the wind is right. If they left after dark, there wouldn't be the wind. They just sail off, tacking back and forth.

Jim was sitting up by this time, eyes half open, staring across the room with a calm, almost blank expression as he talked and gestured. "I just tell what I see," he explained to me very simply. To him it was so simple that he was rather amused by my interest in such deep channeling, as he had previously been a down-to-earth type with an analytical mind and without awareness of this psychic potential.

At this time it would have been appropriate to ask Jim to tune in to the tie-up between the entity experiences and his awakening at a specific time each morning. Since his subconscious mind had said in the first session that his sleeping problem had to do with his job and later he felt that this early morning wakefulness was probably from Robert's influence, it might have been that as captain Robert had a habit of waking to check the ship. However, I was so involved in the material that Jim was producing that I did not ask. If a question is not asked, the client seldom offers information voluntarily because of the drowsiness of the altered state. Jim would have known the answer, but this was not important in terms of his general release from his sleep problem and the return of his energy.

When I called his home a month later to see how he was faring, his wife reported that he was definitely sleeping better than before and was a lot more relaxed. Both of them still had restless periods in the early morning (not unusual these days) and still had strange dreams, but not nightmares. She reported that Jim felt a sense of relief and was without anxiety—the pressure was off. She had always enjoyed being with him but felt that he was much easier to live with now. "I don't know how much more of this I can stand," she laughed.

Differentiating Past Lives from Entity Attachment

by

Chet B. Snow, Ph.D.

Introduction

This case points out what I see to be a growing trend of already vulnerable people risking further ego-destabilization at the hands of psychics and mediums. It demonstrates that even accurate clairvoyant readings of a person's psychic background can be misinterpreted and require corrective therapeutic intervention. The psychic who had advised my patient had correctly picked up the lifetime of a French courtesan but incorrectly assumed it was a past life of the patient when it was actually the lifetime of a possessing entity.

The case shows also the complex etiology of some disturbances. The attachment of the entity came about because of a childhood vulnerability in the patient in her current lifetime resulting from irresponsible actions in a previous lifetime. The healing therefore occurred in two phases: first, the release and healing of the entity, and second, the healing of the past-life incident and the understanding of its connection to this life.

Case: Clarifying the Roots of Emotional Distress

Francine, a 26-year-old French national of Flemish origins, currently lived in a Mediterranean city where she had an excellent job assisting the chairman of a new marketing firm. Her position required a variety of public relations and administrative skills. She was an exceptionally attractive and vivacious woman. A divorced mother, when she came to me she had been involved with a new man for about four months, though she continued to live alone with her young daughter.

Her problem was two-fold. Although externally she seemed successful and happy, she described her life as one of inner torment, with violent, irrational jealousy and frequent mood shifts. She confessed a deep fear of abandonment (seemingly confirmed when her husband left her for another woman) and a persistent feeling of failure, both in romantic relationships and in her chosen career. Second, although she was skeptical of reincarnation, she had recently consulted a professional medium when problems had arisen in her new romance. This woman had severely frightened Francine with a tale of her having once been a famous royal courtesan whose cavalier treatment of men was now being repaid. She predicted that the young woman would continue to "suffer at the hands of men" until the scales were balanced.

First Entity

Because Francine had clearly been upset by this psychic prediction, at our second meeting I moved her rapidly into a light trance through my usual technique of controlled breathing and chakra visualization, followed by descending a stairway and opening the door that her subconscious felt would best answer her current needs. Although quite tense at first, within a few moments Francine began describing the feelings of a pretty 30-year-old woman dressed in rich 18th century brocades. Her name, she said, was Therese.

However, something appeared to be wrong because, as I asked for details of her surroundings so as to deepen the past-life identification, Therese described herself as standing in a dingy modern hotel room. This was hardly the court at Versailles! Immediately I suspected the presence of a separate entity's energy, somehow tied to Francine's own vibrational wave pattern. This was not Francine's own past life but that of a confused spirit, apparently still wandering the earth, attaching from one incarnate individual to another. My tactics shifted to helping Therese accept her discarnate status and move beyond this intermediate "attached" state to a higher spiritual realm where she could continue her own destiny.

I began by instructing the entity, Therese, to return to an earlier time when she had had her last memory of personal sensory perception such as "touching your gown" or "feeling the cool breeze against your cheek." This technique moved her back first to the court at Versailles at the time of Marie Antoinette and then, following my gentle but insistent requests to come to the "last clear memory," to a street scene in Paris, apparently after the Revolution. There, dressed in modest clothes, she experienced being run over by a runaway horse-drawn wagon. She was shocked and surprised to discover that she didn't feel dead, and she soon integrated herself into a passing pedestrian, "because it feels warmer that way." A few additional questions determined that, left destitute by political events, she had been living as the mistress of a rather miserly married bourgeois man and had supplemented this income with occasional prostitution.

Not wishing to take the time to investigate all her intervening adventures, I then asked Therese to move forward into the 20th century and describe the person to whom she was attached in the dingy Parisian hotel room. As I suspected, it was a rather seedy prostitute who died there, apparently from alcoholism and possibly drugs. But Therese didn't die; again she went out in the street, this time in Francine's native Dunkerque, and attached herself to a sad little 10-year-old girl, Francine, my client.

> T: *(To Therese): What attracted you to that particular little girl?*
> E: *I felt a loneliness in her and the same kind of lost feeling I had. There was just something about her.*

At this point I realized that I had little more to learn from Therese. As she had already acknowledged her death and attached status, it was relatively easy to persuade her that she could leave this lost feeling behind by looking for a Bright Light and moving toward it. My own experience and that of other therapists is that moving into this Bright Light signals an energy shift from a shadow-like existence still tied to earthly events into complete spiritual status. Reports of near-death survivors seem to confirm this. As I helped Therese to make the transition, I asked Francine to monitor Therese's departure and signal me when it was complete, which she did shortly thereafter.

Second Entity

By now I felt that I had answered the question of what the medium had picked up, but I wasn't satisfied with Therese's answer as to why she had tied herself to the 10-year-old Francine. I then asked Francine, still in trance, first to return to the age of 10 in her current lifetime and then to regress further until she found a time when she didn't feel sad or lost. Soon I found I was dealing with a very small baby who was delightedly bouncing around in her crib. The entire room seemed to brighten as Francine recalled those happy moments. This mood lasted while I slowly brought her forward until she reached the age of five. There suddenly it shifted and she began to cry.

> T: *What's happening now? What's making you so sad?*
> P: *Oh my God, it's Pierre, my brother Pierre. But he's dead!... He died before I was born but he's here crying. (Shift in voice.) Oh, I feel so lost and alone!*
> T: *Pierre, is that you? Can you talk to me? I'd like to be your friend.*
> E: *Yes, I'm here. I didn't know anyone could hear me; Mommy never could. All she did was cry and hold me.*

T: *How old are you, Pierre?*
E: *I'm five.*

Subsequent dialogue confirmed that Pierre's spirit had apparently become confused after his death in his mother's arms from a sudden illness. When his younger sister had reached his age, the similarity in energies had attracted him away from their still-grieving mother and into the younger sibling, bringing with him the lost and confused emotional patterns that had later attracted the entity Therese and that doubtless contributed to the intense mood swings still felt by the adult Francine. His presence also seemed responsible for some of her child-like jealousy. As the family's only son, and apparently an often sickly one, he had been very spoiled.

As with Therese, it was time to help Pierre recognize his true discarnate existence and finally pass over into the Bright Light. This was accomplished as I cajoled him with promises of lots of toys and a fine, healthy body that could run and skip and jump as much as he pleased, and also by using the help of his guardian angel.

Before bringing Francine back to normal consciousness, however, I had her first call on her own Higher Self to assist her in checking her total energy pattern to make sure that there were no other shadowing or attached spiritual entities. She reported finding no further shadows, dark spots, or outside energies. Satisfied that her field was now cleared, I moved her back to happy times as a small baby and let her re-experience the freedom she had felt then. Suggesting she could bring that positive energy forward now, I helped her complete the session with a healing visualization of pure white light flooding throughout her entire being, cleansing and filling in any perceived cracks or empty spaces left behind after the removal of Pierre's and Therese's energies. When that was done, I brought her back to the room for a short post-regression discussion.

Obviously, much of that discussion revolved around Francine's shock at finding herself host to two foreign energy personalities for much of her current lifetime. She rapidly acknowledged that indeed she had had a deceased older brother named Pierre, who had died at age five a few years before her own birth.

P: *My mother still keeps his photo on the mantelpiece, with fresh flowers, after 30 years, like a shrine. If she only knew!*

I reassured her that there were many ways to interpret her experience and that the essential thing was that she understand now that these influences need no longer trouble her, that she could let go of them if she chose to. I also pointed out that the issues raised within the regression session might have some connection to her own previous life experiences, that it was unlikely that all of the symptoms she described in the initial interview had resulted solely from the spirit attachments. I also requested that she make a conscious effort daily for the next several weeks to revisualize herself bathed in the white light. This would help protect her until any possible scars left in her energy field had completely healed. She agreed to this and left telling me she felt much "lighter and freer."

Foundations for the Attachments

I did have one further session with Francine about a month later. If anything, she looked more beautiful than ever. She reported continuing the meditations, although irregularly. Her self-confidence at work had risen considerably and she no longer experienced wide mood shifts, even in the face of occasional disappointments. She was still, however, subject to fits of jealousy when she caught her attractive boyfriend looking at other women.

I requested that she return to the most recent past life connected to her current jealousy feelings and she shifted smoothly into a 1920's setting. Again an attractive woman in her thirties called Janice, she described a "Great Gatsby" kind of lifestyle of free-flowing liquor, money, music, and fun. She felt completely free of social conventions and responsibilities and apparently enjoyed numerous love affairs with both men and women. This had led her into a violently passionate triangular relationship with a man named Robert and a woman called Anne. The climactic scene came one afternoon when Robert, a more serious type who did not suspect her infidelity, surprised the two women together.

> T: *Move forward, now, to the most important, the most emotional moment in that relationship with Robert. What's happening?*
>
> P: *It's a warm afternoon; I'm at the beach house, in bed with Anne. We're making love.... Oh, my God, it's Robert! He came home early without calling. Oh, the look on his face; he can't believe it.... It's too funny for words. I can't help it and I laugh out loud!*
>
> T: *Now, move ahead in that same lifetime and find another moment, one that comes in direct consequence to what you just experienced, to that laughter....*
>
> P: *(Somber, shocked tone.) He's dead; he shot himself! I can't believe that he'd really do it just because I laughed when he told me he loved me. Why did it have to come to this?*

Apparently furious with Janice's betrayal, Robert had told her to choose, and again she'd only laughed at him. So in a jealous rage, amplified by liquor, he'd killed himself. Janice lived with that memory for the rest of her life, although it seemed to have no relationship to her own death in an automobile accident several years later.

The story wasn't yet over, however.

> T: *Now, you've left that physical body behind. Move forward in time until just before you're to be reborn as Francine L. Look ahead in that lifetime to come. What seems to be the most important purpose behind this new life?*
>
> P: *I need to reintegrate my life, to bring my physical, emotional and spiritual selves back together. It's going to be difficult, I can see that. I can see that I want my mother to love me more than my sister.*
>
> T: *Is there anyone, any human energy pattern, that you see in this upcoming, life who was with you as Janice?*
>
> P: *(Hesitates.) Yes, oh, God, yes, there's Robert and Anne again, only this time, she's my sister and he's Pierre, my older brother. (Sobbing.) I'm going to have to live with him dead!*

After helping Francine work through the emotional impact of this revelation, I again contacted her Higher Self to assist her in achieving mutual pardon for what Janice had unwittingly caused and finding some reconciliation between her and Robert or, more recently, Pierre. During our post-regression discussion, she told me that she felt "cleansed." Although I have not seen her in therapy since, mutual acquaintances have reported that she is much less tense at parties, and they have seen no jealous scenes, such as had been frequent in occurrence before this time.

Karmic Consequences Activated by Possession

by

Hiroshi Motoyama, Ph.D.

Introduction

The necessary steps in transcending karma, as I have come to understand them from study and experience, are three:

1. **To realize the karmic situation.** For the ordinary person this requires consultation with someone who has the ability to help the patient go beyond time and ego to understand what connections exist. With appropriate help the ordinary man or woman can begin to see the patterns, the seeds that have been sown in past lives. These seeds are latent energy patterns in the astral dimension. With the proper conditions in the present life, they sprout and grow, but if we are able to transcend our past karmic conditions, these seeds will not sprout and their energy will be exhausted before they become manifested in this life.

2. **To accept the reality of our present situation as part of our karma.** Our present situation in this life—where we are born, our physical constitution, our character, talents or lacks, our family and circumstances—all are decided by our past lives. This does not mean that we cannot change in this world, but our present situation and condition must be understood and accepted for us to go on to the third step.

3. **To perform our best in this lifetime without expecting good or bad results from our actions.** Perhaps this is the most difficult to understand and to accomplish. We must become detached in order to transcend our karma. Detachment means freedom from desiring good results or dreading bad results. They seem very different but they are the same thing in different forms. If we have any kind of attachment to future results, the ego continues, which contains and creates these seeds of karma. The seeds or latent energy patterns from past lives need to be diminished and to manifest themselves in a less difficult fashion. Only an absence of attachment (desire for a good or fear for a bad result), can truly help us transcend our karma.

Conditions such as physical or mental illness, divorce or family pain, or even ambition (as with the feudal lord mentioned below) are karmic problems that will take place again and again until we resolve them. We must learn to detach ourselves from our lives, to do our best in this life without thought of our own welfare and without judgment.

Case: Bodily Healing through Releasement

I will describe a case in which I was asked to intercede that is a clear example of a serious ailment caused by a past karmic action or event. In November of 1982 I was telephoned in Tokyo by a Mrs. Y, who was at a hospital in Akashi City, 380 miles away. Mrs. Y's husband had just undergone his sixth abdominal operation for twists and consequent blockage of his small intestine. He could not pass the contents of his intestines, and his abdomen was swollen like a pregnant woman's. After the operation his condition was critical and he seemed to be dying. Mrs. Y was in great distress and asked me to help her husband.

I immediately changed my clothing and went to the Shinto shrine, where I am the head priest. After five minutes or so of meditation I entered into a deep trance, and though I knew nothing about the Akashi area of Japan or Mr. Y's history, I was able to see the past circumstances of the situation and examine his physical condition. The upper part of the small intestine running horizontal to the large intestine was twisted, causing blockage and great pain. I tried to send healing power to this part of his body but for a time I had difficulty penetrating there. After ten or fifteen minutes I succeeded in making the connection and correcting his condition in the astral dimension.

Then I saw a feudal lord who had been the head of the Akashi clan some 250 years before. I realized it was one of Mr. Y's past lives; he had been the court physician to this lord. The lord had no children and when one of his wives became pregnant, Mr. Y (in his past life) had delivered a stillborn baby; thus, there had been no heir to the lord's clan. Because of the failure to produce a living heir, the lord's clan was rejected by the Shogun and his reign collapsed. The lord and his followers had remained in great pain and suffering in the astral dimension for the past 250 years, and they blamed the court physician for their downfall. The lord was now possessing Mr. Y's body and causing his abdominal condition.

I advised Mrs. Y to begin a 100-day regimen of prayer: first, for the feudal lord and his followers' pain in the spiritual world and for the soul of the dead infant, and, second, for the release of her husband from his condition. I directed Mr. and Mrs. Y to pray for the entities to accept their apologies and to ask them for forgiveness. On the third day of these prayers, the spirit of the feudal lord was able to understand that the stillbirth of his child had been due to a deep karmic cause of his own. The lord forgave Mr. Y and ceased possessing his body. The prayers were continued for 200 days, after which Mr. and Mrs. Y and their son came to our shrine to hold a ceremony for the souls of this lord, his child, and his followers.

At that time Mr. Y informed me that his family had indeed been court physicians for generations to the clan in Akashi. Mr. Y himself had wished to enter medical school, but due to the early death of his parents he had been unable to carry out his plan.

Releasement of Entities Resulting in Physical Healing

by

Winafred B. Lucas, Ph.D.

Introduction

In the dozen or so experiences of shadowing with which I have been involved over the past ten years, most have been associated with severe energy drain. Physical concerns were usually non-specific and involved chronic fatigue. It was not my impression that physical problems of any severity could be released through working with shadowing, so the three experiences in my practice in which such a reversal occurred were unexpected and led to reflection on what had happened.

Case 1. Attachment through Anger

The first experience concerned a sculptress who in the midst of an apparently successful career gradually developed such extreme enervation that it was considered by her physician to be a serious illness. It had accelerated until she could not sculpt or drive and had to spend most of her time immobile in her house. At this time, because the escalation of symptoms could not be stopped, it was labeled "probably terminal." Her husband attended one of my workshops, and when I mentioned shadowing he came up and asked me to see his wife. I felt reluctant because I do releasement work only occasionally and then with patients I know well, but he was not willing to hear me say "no."

When I first saw Ursula she had been brought to the office by her husband against her wishes, as she had lost hope that there would be any solution to the continuing deterioration. I spent the first session getting background and trying to find an entering point. Her marriage seemed sound and supportive and she had made steady progress in her sculpting career with several shows to her credit. When I asked about the onset of the enervation and pain, she said that it had started just after her return from

Kashmir three years before. The trip had been delightful, a good sharing with her husband, and she had enjoyed their houseboat on the Dal Lake.

Knowing that shadowing often begins with a sudden death of someone the patient knows, I asked if anyone close to her had died at that time. She said that her sister had been killed in an auto accident while she was in Kashmir. She told me about her sister, who, according to her, had become very angry when Ursula had been able to break out of a suffocating home and go to Chicago to begin her career as a sculptress. Ursula portrayed it as a one-way anger, her sister's bitter resentment against her.

On her second and last session I took Ursula into a meditation garden, entrance into which effects a deep altered state, and had her call her sister to come. The speed with which entities appear, whether they represent real energy fields or metaphoric representations (which may be the same thing), is surprising, and my patient reported immediately that her sister was there. When asked if she was shadowing my patient, the sister confirmed immediately that she was, at which point Ursula broke out in a tirade against her. The angry dialogue that followed, both sides of which were reported by Ursula, progressed from anger at the sister for bothering her, to a series of recriminations from both that went back to their earliest childhood. It became apparent that they were tied to each other through pervasive and long-standing anger.

I allowed the exchange to go on for some time, exploring incidents and feelings by asking questions and making comments to facilitate expression. Eventually the anger thinned until neither sister had anything further to say. It was then apparent that some sort of forgiveness of each other was necessary in order to release the two from the anger that bound them. I asked Ursula if she could let go of her expectation that her sister should have been different, but Ursula felt unwilling to do this. Her sister proved to be equally uncooperative. I told them both that it was their choice—they could go on carrying the burden of anger: the sister could stay bound to the earth plane and not go on with her soul journey, and Ursula could keep the shadowing going and eventually die from it. No one could make them give up their anger. It was totally up to them.

There was silence for a while, a silence that I did not break. Finally the sister said she would release her expectation that Ursula should have cherished her, and would accept Ursula the way she was, and Ursula decided to let her hostility, apparently triggered by her sister's dependent and demanding attitude, be diffused in some understanding of how it must have been to grow up in a family where another child attracted all the attention and approbation. We worked on the process a long time, testing every assertion to see that it was congruent, until the anger transformed into the beginning of caring for each other. Finally, I had the sister look around for her Guides, and I called my own to help, and Ursula and I walked a little way with her to the Light and then let her go on her journey.

When we left the garden and came back into the room, Ursula's face was serene. I had no idea what ongoing effect this imaging would have, and, not wanting the experience to be negated by her skeptical social world, suggested that it might be better if she didn't mention it to her husband or friends until we saw how things worked out for her. She called me several days later and said that all the symptoms were gone and she had begun sculpting again. It was apparent that she had told everyone in sight, including some psychologists who were mutual acquaintances. I had no doubt that my reputation was in tatters!

Ursula kept in touch with me for some time and maintained her good health. Her doctor, though surprised, considered her physical recovery to be a spontaneous remission. When she tried to explain what she thought had happened, he attributed what she said to the general instability of the artistic temperament. Finally Ursula sent me a flowing statuette of a young woman leaning slightly backward to catch a feather, and this closed our interaction.

Case 2. Children Attaching from a Former Lifetime

It is uncomfortable enough to work with shadowing that starts in this lifetime, but when it originates in another lifetime it makes serious inroads into our comfortable space-time paradigm. My first experience with this occurred with Philene, a woman in her late twenties whom I had seen for extended therapy until the previous year. Originally she had come to see if we could find emotional blocks to her becoming pregnant, since doctors could find no physical ones.

We spent several years exploring her current lifetime without finding an answer. Philene, who had wanted to be an artist and had never done anything about it, felt so unfulfilled as she went from one doctor to another trying to get pregnant, that therapy seemed to have sufficient scope in helping her develop a sense of identity and competence. While in therapy she attended a good art school for training in commercial art, graduated, and found a position on a magazine, at which point we discontinued her therapy.

A year later she called, saying that her arms and legs had gradually become full of pain and she had had to quit her job. The doctors did not know what the trouble was but suggested bone cancer and were going to do more scans, and there was the possibility of amputation. Naturally Philene was frightened, and after the heavy slugging through therapy to an apparently successful end, I felt discouraged. I wondered what I could do for her that her doctors had not been able to do.

Philene had always been physically fragile, in spite of careful attention to diet and exercise and the practice of various healing meditations. When she arrived for this new try at therapy she appeared to be even more fragile, and her fright over her condition was not helping. During the first session I explored what had been going on in her life.

Work, before she terminated, had had its frustrations, but they seemed more the result than the cause of the problem. Her marriage to a young professor was stable. He gave her as much support as he could, but he was frightened, too. Her most obvious frustration was that not only had she not been able to become pregnant but no baby had become available for adoption until a few days before, when a child in another part of the country that was about to be born three months prematurely had been offered to her and her husband. The decision as to whether to accept this child accentuated her distress.

During the second session I used what I considered to be a safe and effective imaging technique. Without taking Philene into an altered state through any particular relaxation process I told her simply to become her arms and have them talk and say why they were in such pain. Another approach would have been to ask her to go back where the pain started, but she looked so fragile that I wanted to avoid regression work for the time being. My caution was to no avail, for she became agitated and began crying out and sobbing.

> P: *There's a lot of red and they're gone! There's blood everywhere, a field of blood. I see the back-end of horses and men with metal on them. Everything's gone. (Screaming, her body rigid.) ...Joyce cried and said her arms are gone! (Waving her own arms up and down.) Mary's going up and down—her legs are gone!*

I sat quietly in the face of this agitation, glad there was no one else in the office that early in the morning, and suggested to Philene that this was another lifetime: it was not taking place now and she could step outside it and become an observer. At this, Philene began to speak more quietly and described the situation. She lived with her two daughters, nine and twelve, in a village in a very early time. While her husband was away with the other men of the village pillaging, marauding soldiers swept down on her village and started killing everyone. They tied Joyce, one of her daughters, by her arms to the back of a horse and dragged her until her arms were pulled out of the sockets. They cut Mary's legs off above the knees and carried her along on horseback so that she appeared to be bobbing. Both girls died. We explored the situation until Philene became able to move from the role of observer back to that of participant and work through the devastating experience.

> T: *Both your daughters have been killed. Let's meet them and see how they're getting along. Do you see them?*
> P: *Yes, they're here.*
> T: *Ask them if they have clung to you through lifetimes since then.*
> P: *They say they don't know where they are. They miss me and want to be with me and don't know why I never hear them.*

We told the girls that they were dead, explained how they died, and told them that it wasn't helpful, either for them or for Philene, to keep trying to stay with her. They seemed relieved when we said we would help them to the Light. I had Philene work with me to image healing their physical bodies, just in case that might make a difference for them in future lifetimes, or to my patient who was suffering in similar parts of her body. Then we called their Guides and I called my own to help, and we said goodbye and watched them go to the Light.

Philene emerged from this experience calm and radiant. We talked briefly about the baby offered to her for adoption, and I suggested that she did not have to choose a child with problems now—she finally really did have a choice, though I would support her in whatever decision she made.

She called me a few days later to say that she and her husband had decided against the adoption. Meanwhile, the pains in her arms and legs had disappeared. Her physician decided that she had experienced a spontaneous remission from severe bursitis.

Synchronistically, the next week she was offered another baby by a mother of several healthy children, who had become pregnant from a one-night experience. The baby, a boy, turned out to be healthy and attractive, and the adoption went smoothly. I have kept in touch with Philene for two years, and the pains in her arms and legs have not returned. Her chief problem now is the pressure many young mothers feel when they have underestimated the amount of work involved in caring for an infant.

Several other possible healing agents must be considered. In the case of Ursula, the resolution of anger, which often causes illness by release of lipid fatty acids, may very well have been healing to her body, though the speed of the remission was surprising. Also, transpersonal concepts postulate that we exist in an energy field that includes the past as well as the present. Healing is a transformation of this field, effected through various modalities. Reynolds (1986)[17] and Mehl (1986)[18] suggest that in therapy the healing takes place in the energy field between the patient and the therapist, and what is said and done is adjunctive. The therapist's ability to change the state of energy with the assistance of powerful metaphors must be considered a viable if not well understood hypothesis.

Related to this is the concept of synchronicity, described by Jue.[19] When the field of energy that encompasses a patient is transformed, broader fields become opened up, and appropriate experiences can come through that were shut out before. According to Jue, it is experiences of synchronicity that validate or manifest transformation in the personality. If this is a valid hypothesis, we could understand Philene's almost immediate opportunity to adopt an appropriate baby as a resultant of the opening up of her field to this possibility by the release of the shadowing.

Case 3. The Weighing of the Heart

First Attachment in the Cairo Museum

In a recent stay in Egypt I deepened my understanding of the nature of entity attachments. Our group of 23, under the leadership of Dr. Brugh Joy, spent a week riding camels across the Sinai and climbing mountains there. During a particularly steep climb, in which a fixed rope was used to assist the ascent, the rope broke and the person on it, John, fell some distance, scraping rocks on the way down and landing on his left ankle in a shallow pool. Several of the men carried him back to where the camels had been left, where the group, many of whom were healers, succeeded in reducing the inflammation. However, the possibility of a ruptured Achilles tendon led Brugh to decide that John should return on the most dependable camel, along with a companion and two guides, to the Gulf of Akaba where he could hitch a ride over the border to Israel, which was not far away, and seek medical evaluation in a hospital there. (On the almost deserted Akaba road, John and his companion did find a ride—with a physician from Brooklyn!)

Several days later John rejoined our group in Nuweiba on the Akaba Gulf. When we embarked on our Nile cruise boat, the Noor II, at Aswan, he was able, though on crutches, to take part in sightseeing activities. Just after we sailed toward Luxor, however, he became ill. His intestinal distress, which was extreme, escalated, no matter what treatment was attempted, and he became severely dehydrated. Within a day he could scarcely speak and seemed to be fading away. At this point Brugh held a meeting on deck and said that he felt John had contacted an entity during our two days in Cairo at the beginning of the trip. He asked what could be done.

Releasement

I suggested a releasement, and Brugh responded, "Exactly," and told me to take over. John was carried up to the deck and laid on a reclining deck chair. He was so weak that even though I sat almost over him I could scarcely hear him. However, I inducted him into a garden meditation to accustom him to imaging and then asked the entity to appear. He came, and I asked where he had made the attachment. He responded through John that he had attached on the first day of our trip, when we were exploring the second floor of the Cairo Museum. He shared that his name was Horeb and that he needed to "piggyback" into the Light. Since it was his impression that John was having longings to "return home," he had taken advantage of this to get a ride with someone who was sure to go to the Light.

Because I could scarcely hear John, who was growing increasingly weaker, I cut short the usual conversation with the entity that I would have liked to have had and simply explained that John did not mean to "go home," and the entity would do better to go to the Light on his own. I asked him to speak through John to say if he was willing to go, and if he was, I would find helpful guides for him. Under my persistence the entity finally agreed to leave, and I sent him on his way but didn't check to see if he actually went.

I protected John with light and brought him back into his body. Almost immediately he started getting well and by the next day was hobbling along on his crutches for our explorations of the temples. He continued to improve to where he could manage without crutches, but upon his return home, X-rays showed that the Achilles tendon had been severed. The hands-on healing had acted as an aspirin to relieve some of the symptoms while obscuring the true situation. Norman Shealy, in *The Creation of Health*,[20] claims that this is often the case.

Later in the trip John had a dream in which he was struggling literally to go home, and with this wish made conscious he could work on the underlying depression. The dream and its symbolism became an extended focus for the group, enabling John to do the therapeutic work that would allow permanent healing to occur.

Second Attachment in the Temple of Karnac

Much of my interest in visiting Egypt was due to regressions I had made to an Egyptian life where I had my first Saluki (an Egyptian dog which in this lifetime my daughter and I bred and showed). I had recovered specific images and memories of this dog, set in the time of Ramses II, and the evening after the releasement I spent some hours with Ashrod, a Cairo tour leader who was managing our trip. He enjoyed a broad-spectrum background of Egypt, and I asked him about the Salukis of the Pharaohs. He replied that the Pharaohs didn't have Salukis; the one in the Cairo Museum belonged to a desert tribe.

This information negated all my memories, which up until that moment I had considered informative and authentic and which had always checked out with archaeological evidence. It meant that I would have to start over to develop a sound world view, and with my 77th birthday coming up in a few days, I wasn't sure if I had the energy to do that. The next morning I joined the others in the horse and buggy procession to the Temple of Karnac, but the shock and depression of the night before muted my interest. I walked through the extensive courts, the broken temples, hypostyle halls, transverse halls, obelisks, and sanctuaries of what seemed to me, in that mood, a wasteland charged with negative energy. I began to think about having to start over again, about the contraindications to further living, and I found myself beginning to consider the merit of "going home." By the time I got to the shabby Sacred Lake I felt desolate.

Almost immediately I became ill. That isn't unusual in third-world countries, so I found a bathroom and made my way out of the jungle of broken columns and took the next carriage back to our boat.

Second Releasement

In my tiny stateroom I began hours of continuous heaving, which Lomotil and all other medications failed to stop. I felt as though I were being compelled to heave out my entire insides, and I found the pain and distress overwhelming. Then it occurred to me that this was exactly what John had gone through, and I called the entity Horeb and asked if he had not gone to the Light but instead was still hanging around. The answer was immediate: he had to find a way to piggyback—he could not go on his own. In the Temple of Karnac he had been drawn by my thoughts of "going home." Rudely I told him to "get lost," a sad injunction to an entity who was already hopelessly lost! I sensed that he left, and immediately I stopped vomiting. In a few hours I felt better, though I declined to join the group that night for the Sound and Light Show at the Karnac Temple.

Later, while going through the tombs at Beni Hassan, I found inscribed on the walls scenes of Salukis that exactly resembled those in my regression memories. I realized that my host was uninformed in this area, and that my suffering had been unnecessary. However, I felt glad that I had been willing to release a conceptualization when it seemed to be without foundation, even if it meant starting over in my attempt to understand the nature of things.

Therapy for the Entity

I found myself in an introverted mood when I returned home, and I spent the first weeks thinking about the events of my Egyptian sojourn. Early in this meditation I realized that I had never understood what the Egyptian entity Horeb had meant by piggybacking, and in the pressure first of John's escalating weakness and then of my physical distress I had not asked. I called Horeb and found, as I had expected, that he had not gone toward the Light but was still hanging around. When I asked him why he hadn't gone and what it meant to piggyback, he explained that he was afraid of the "weighing of the heart." He told me that he had been an overseer in the time of Ramses III and in a dispute over land had killed a man. He was sure that his heart, put in balance against the feather of Maat, would sink down and he would be thrown to the crocodile-headed Ammit, who was waiting in the dark Netherworld to devour those who did not pass the test.

The Weighing of the Heart

Meskhenet. Ani's The Anubis. The feather Thoth. The "Eater of the Dead."
Renenet. heart. Luck. of Maat.

I told him that the true situation was different, and I offered to take him to the Light. I hadn't been able to do this sort of guiding before, but now it was possible, and once in the Light, I told Horeb that between lifetimes he would always have a similar glimpse so that he would know where he was headed, though each time he would be pulled back to the soul level of the preceding lifetime. No one was ever lost to the Netherworld forever. For a long time after that, whenever I remembered the joy and relief that this guilty and frightened soul experienced when he realized that he wasn't condemned forever, tears came to my eyes.

This Egyptian experience and its aftermath convinced me that when we work with releasement we need to do careful therapy with the entity; this is just as important as doing careful therapy with a patient. We need to know why the entity has not gone to the Light. It can be attachment or anger, but it can also be guilt over misdeeds and a fear of punishment, the result of that lifetime's conceptualization about sin and punishment. As in any false conceptualization, reframing is necessary, and this must be handled patiently and gently. Blasting an entity into the Light or giving it a hard sell for the sake of a patient is not enough.

Finally, attachment experiences exhibit pulls from both sides. One aspect of the releasement is the unearthing of whatever pull the patient, often unconsciously, has exerted on the entity, as with John's and my tentative thoughts about "going home." Attention to these factors is needed if releasement is to result in a permanent resolution of the patient's difficulty.

Attachment by Living Parents

by

Rob Bontenbal and Tineke Noordegraaf

Introduction

The therapist confronts a variety of kinds of attachments in his practice. Besides the categories defined by Louise Ireland-Frey to differentiate the intensity of an attachment (attachment, oppression, obsession, and possession), we distinguish between passive and active spirits and between spirit attachments and those by living people. With active spirits there are usually karmic interactions and transactions involved, often revenge, hate, anger, possessive love, and the need to feed an addiction, and/or guilt. Active spirits usually are aware of the fact that they are dead, but their feelings and needs keep them earthbound. Passive spirits often are unaware that they have died and have a hard time accepting this. They can attach to those whose state of mental, emotional, and/or physical health has weakened the aura. As with active spirits, most of their attachments are the result of addictive behavior and traumas with severe shock.

Attachments by living people have a similar etiology. For instance, friendships are attachments that give positive feelings, but they can turn sour and in some relationships result in a flow of negativity. This negative energy can attach itself to the person who was formerly a friend, causing mental, emotional, and physical problems. However, attachments here, as with discarnate spirits, can only occur when the client is vulnerable in one way or another, in a state of shock resulting from unresolved trauma, or when not on guard because of having no awareness that an attachment can take place.

When any sort of attachment is suspected, whether by a spirit or living person, it is important to find the reason that it attached. Essentially the therapist has two clients. In most cases the spirit of a person who has died is released rapidly by being sent to the light or to some other positive afterlife projection. Following this, the therapist helps the client to process the events that caused the attachment. Without processing and integrating these events, the patient can easily draw the attachments of new spirits.

The same approach is appropriate for attachments by living persons. They must be worked with and helped to release the client, and the client must become aware of how he drew the attachment from such persons (usually a parent). Attachments by the energy of living persons can cause severe problems, and later awareness of them makes it possible for therapist and client to understand the often strange patterns that show themselves in therapy. The following case describes the effect of an over-possessive living mother.

Case: Attachment by a Clinging Mother

Peter, a 40-year-old man, had already had considerable therapy with one of us. All his life he had been his parents' "problem child," the youngest of three brothers. His birth had been long and painful and had caused Minimal Brain Damage. He had attended a normal elementary school but the MBD had made it difficult for him to meet the requirements of such a school.

He then moved to a special school, where he felt much more at ease and even enjoyed going to class, but at the age of 15 his parents decided to find him a job in a grocery store, which he hated because of the humiliating way he was treated by the owner. After changing jobs several times he found a position in the production department of a large newspaper publisher, where he still works.

His chief problem was that of his relationships. He was not married and had never had an intimate relationship with a woman. He had visited a gay sauna several times to find out if he might be homosexual but decided he wasn't. He often had problems at work because he couldn't handle the humiliating jokes of his co-workers. The MBD gave him less control over his body and he sometimes panicked when there were problems with the machines of the production line at which he worked. His colleagues made fun of what he himself called his clumsiness. But his chief problem was his relationship with his parents. He couldn't stand his mother's protectiveness or his father's lack of respect for him because of his difference from his brothers.

He consulted a hypnotherapist who helped him to re-establish some of his self-confidence. Later he switched to reincarnation therapy because he felt that there were deeper causes for his problems. Though he had started life with a handicap and had left school at the age of 15, he nevertheless proved to be a good subject for reincarnation therapy, showing a more than average intelligence and admirable courage and introspection.

During the first couple of sessions it became obvious that he had a strong symbiotic relationship with his mother. He worked slowly backward, processing the many humiliations of his first job after he had left school too soon, the problems with learning in elementary school, the protectiveness of his mother, especially in his early childhood and infancy, and his father's lack of respect. Then he was able to move into various past lives. In one of these he was the mean foreman of a lumber factory, coercing the workers he was in charge of until they caused an accident and left him to die in great pain, after which they left the factory to enjoy a free Sunday. This polar life explained a lot to him about his neglect, punishment, etc., which emerged as a clear pattern.

Next came the important prenatal and perinatal areas. A number of sessions were dedicated to the long, painful, and complicated birth-experience that brought the relief of expressing much anger, sadness, fear, and guilt, both his mother's and his own.

While processing all this, his way of communicating with parents, co-workers, and friends slowly but steadily improved. Once in a while he experienced a humiliating confrontation with his father, mother, or a particularly disagreeable co-worker. At such times he experienced strong feelings of aggression that he did not know how to express in a constructive way. Because of these reactions we agreed to do a few sessions with the two of us working as a team.

During the second of these sessions we went back to his feelings of guilt toward his parents, which he expressed in the following phrases:

They are getting older. I can't drop them now.
You have to show respect for your parents.
They are still your parents.

Taking "You have to show respect for your parents" as an entrance, we had begun building the MES bridge when the client made grimaces.

T: *What are you feeling?*
C: *Something blocks me, moves in front of my own feelings.*
T: *Can you get an impression of what moves in front of you?*
C: *No, but I feel attached to it...I don't like it.... It doesn't feel right.*
T: *We ask what—or whoever it is that you feel attached to, to come forward and speak directly to us.... You can speak through Peter's voice.*

There was a dramatic change in the client's voice when he answered.

C: *Why don't you leave my boy alone? He's mine!*
T: *Excuse us, but who are you?*
C: *His mother, of course!*

We knew that his mother was still alive, which meant that either we were dealing with the spirit of a mother from a previous life or with the attachment of the energy of a living person. Soon it became quite clear that we were talking to Peter's mother in this life.

It was scary to witness how his mother took over his personality, explaining again and again to us why it was impossible for her to let go of her son. He was her baby, different from the others, and therefore needing her protection. After a time we addressed Peter again, but he could scarcely come through. His voice sounded thin and weak, much different from the nagging but clear voice of his mother.

In Dutch, as in many other languages, there are two words for the pronoun "you"—a formal one, "U," and an informal one, "jij." The generation of Peter's mother prefers being addressed by the word "U," certainly by people they don't know well and often also by younger relatives, even their own children. Because we had been addressing Peter, as we did all clients, with "jij," Rob continued to do so when the mother came through. When the mother became quiet after a few questions, Tineke said dryly, "I think Peter's mother does not like to be addressed with "jij." After we corrected our mode of address, the mother was willing to talk to us again.

And she knew how to talk—or better, how to defend herself. Whatever we tried, it seemed impossible to break through her armor of the loving, protecting mother. We used different techniques from different sub-personality models, telling her that we were convinced of her good intentions but that the means she used no longer were acceptable to Peter. She hardly seemed to listen. Often she sounded like a scratched record, repeating herself time after time, presenting one cliche after the other. Whenever we were close to cutting through or moving around her paradoxal postulates, irrational arguments, or double binds, she hid behind her husband, telling us what he thought Peter needed.

We came the closest to detaching her when we asked her to move back in time and tell us what kind of relationship she had had with her mother. It became obvious that the attachment was one in a line of very protective mothers—her mother, her mother's mother, etc.

When pregnant for the third time, Peter's mother prayed with all her heart that it would be a girl. Her disappointment in another boy and her feelings of guilt about the complicated birth resulted in Peter's MBD and actualized his feelings of disappointing others and of guilt stemming from other lifetimes. Both Peter's feelings and those of his mother made a co-dependent attachment inevitable.

Even processing some part of her own youth and the experience of giving birth to Peter did not convince this mother to leave her son alone. We were forced to use our last resource.

> *T: Okay. Because you obviously don't want to listen, we have no choice but to force you to let go of Peter. We will count from one to five and at five we will forcefully detach you from Peter.*

We concentrated deeply, asked Peter to count with us, started counting in loud voice and at five said:

> *T: Let go! Out! You leave now! Now!*

Peter, who had counted with us, and sounded stronger with every count, told us that he felt something leaving him. He was very emotional about what happened because he had never known that his mother had been such a powerful part of his being. It was good that instead of guilt about the forceful departure, he felt relief.

We were quite amazed, working with another male client the next day, to encounter an almost identical "mother-part." There was a difference though. This mother attachment soon understood that the means she used to reach her intentions were contrary to the will of the total personality of the client. This insight transformed her during the session from a possessive party into a creative, sensitive part willing to help the client by establishing a new relationship.

With Peter we did two more sessions. During one of these we came across a father attachment that was also very strong. Although armed with even more arguments, the father part, a very unpleasant personality, transformed in no time into a pathetic old man. Peter, using one of the strongest expressions of anger we have ever encountered, was able to rid himself of all the negative father energy in his system and again felt relieved.

By the time the three of us decided that he was ready to terminate the therapy, Peter felt good about himself and independent of his parents. At work he showed much more confidence and this put an end to his colleagues' tendency to ridicule him. Just recently we heard that for the first time in his life he was in an affair with a girlfriend.

Good for you, Peter!

Possession by the Living

by

Kenneth J. Naysmith, Ph.D.

Introduction

There is a continuum of pathological closeness that can be developed between people during their past lives that may lead to involvements when these people are born together later. Both intense, misguided love and strong hatred can lead to such entanglement. Parent-child and sibling relationships seem to be the most frequent vehicles for expression of this problem of obsessive attachment that may lead to possession by the living.

One example of what this continuum of inappropriate closeness can lead to is exemplified by a case in which identical twin sisters grew up experiencing each others' emotions and sometimes each others' thoughts. When their lives were going in the same direction, this psychic openness to each other was acceptable and even titillating. But eventually one twin entered a spiritual life of discipline and profoundly resented the feelings of the other when that other was getting ready for, or experiencing, a sexual "date," which she did nightly while the first twin was trying to meditate and pray in her own home miles away. The religious counselor they went to knew nothing of possession and could not help them. Was this a case of some kind of biologically-based, involuntary psychic openness or a treatable case of mutual possession?

Case: A Father's Obsession with His Daughter

A typical incident of possession by someone still living (which, as in this case, often does not end with the physical death of the possessor) concerns a woman called Annabelle, whom I treated in Toronto, Canada. She had been born of immigrant German-Dutch parents and was raised until her mid-teens in St. Louis, Missouri. Her mother, Gretchen, died when Annabelle was six years old. Her father, Hans, a taxi driver in St. Louis, raised Annabelle and her brother. Hans was intensely attached to Annabelle.

With the death of his wife he became more doting and controlling than ever. He wanted to live in and through his daughter, though he did not physically or sexually abuse her.

The father died in 1951. Twelve years later Annabelle came to me for therapy and in the first session made this complaint.

> P: *I'm a lesbian and I don't like it but fooling around with men makes me sick. I'm really lonely. There seems to be something in my aura that repels people. It happens each time I meet new people.*

In the second session she said that she always had feelings of futility, and she felt her father had given her these feelings.

> P: *I dream over and over about my father, year after year. He invades my dreams of the past and he is there in my dreams of the present.*
> T: *How long has this been true?*
> P: *Well, since I was a kid, since a couple of years after Mama died, I guess. I've always had trouble with him being in my dreams. He gives me a yuck feeling. I left home and moved to Canada in my twenties to get away from him. He followed me to Toronto. I moved to British Columbia. He followed me to British Columbia. I moved to Edmonton, then back to Toronto. He went back to St. Louis for periods of time, but wrote and phoned regularly. Once when he had saved $15,000 he flew to Canada and gave me $10,000 of it.*

We did a number of sessions on past-life therapy but these were not fruitful, so I explained to her the phenomenon of possession and she agreed to try it. First, I elicited a firm pledge from her to release her father and not call him back or allow him back once he was gone, even if she got very lonely in her daily life and decided that bad company was preferable to no company at all.

I put her into a deeply relaxed, interiorized state and proceeded:

> T: *Annabelle, I want you to recall to memory a clear picture of your father's face, a clear memory-picture of your father that you see now, right here in front of you. It doesn't matter what age he was....*
> P: *I can only see him as a young man.*
> T: *That's fine. Now I want you to recall his voice. Remember that voice, just what your father sounded like when he spoke with you.*
> P: *Okay.*
> T: *Now, I want you to continue visualizing him as I ask you some questions. I want you to just relax your mind completely and simply allow your father to answer my questions through your voice—or if you hear his answers to my questions you may speak them for him. Do you understand what I'm asking.*

P: *Yes. All right.*
T: *Good. I just want you to be fully relaxed and at ease, to allow your father who you are now inwardly perceiving to speak through you without your censoring anything or thinking about what is coming through you.*

Annabelle shifted uncomfortably.

T: *Have you ever been hypnotized or worked in an altered state or consciousness before?*
P: *Hypnotized. I couldn't remember later.*
T: *Would you like for me to tape-record this session and give you the tape after it's over so you know exactly what went on?*
P: *Yes. Please. I'd like that.*
T: *Okay, you just relax and concentrate on your father's presence while I put this tape in. In a totally focused, relaxed way see if you can hear what he's saying as I turn this tape on.*

At this point I set up the tape. I contacted her father and she relayed the answers for him. Then I addressed her father directly, and her voice and manner changed. Her voice was lower and her manner less sure and with a confused air about it.

F: *Well, uh, no, I'm not alone here. I broke the ground with Annie when she was a little girl. She didn't know it. Three others joined me since then. I can't remember when the others came. It was easier after me, somehow. It gets lonely, you know.*

I talked to Hans, through Annabelle, about how much less happy he is than he should be, how his loneliness would have ended long ago if he had gone on to the other world at his own physical death as he should have.

T: *Why didn't you go?*
F: *Well, I'd already been with her before that. You know, I spent every free minute with her as she grew up. Not just physically. Mentally. I visualized where she was, what she was doing. I went to bed thinking of her. Driving my cab around St. Louis I would be with her with part of my attention. I woke up thinking of her. I went to bed thinking of her. I'm not hurting her. I'm not doing anything wrong. I saw the big light there when I died, but I glanced at Annie and I was just in her all of a sudden. It's what I wanted, anyway.*

I did a spirit releasement for the four possessors, first concentrating on convincing the other three of what they had missed out on by getting hung up with Hans and his daughter.

Then I brought Annabelle out of the altered state. She told me she remembered being vaguely aware of three voices inside her over the years, talking to a fourth. One was her father's. The other three she saw at the end of the releasement as outlines of light, surrounded by light, which rose up from her and were taken away by light.

In the next session I contacted Hans easily after relaxing Annabelle and counting her down to a deeply interiorized state. I spent time trying to reassure Hans regarding his fears of death, assuring him that he would have to deal with moving on when Annabelle's body died, and trying to explain that punishment for past wrongs exists largely here on this physical plane and the plane between earth lives is for learning wisdom, for peace, for rejuvenating the energy spent on earth, for tasting true spiritual freedom. He was missing out on all that, as well as missing out on renewing old friendships of long-departed friends who could end his loneliness. Then I called on the light and old friends to lead Hans away and into a happier land than he would ever know with Annabelle on earth.

As I was sending her father away, Annabelle felt a pain in the back of her head on the left side (a common, but not invariable, occurrence). The pain ended completely and suddenly, as Annabelle inwardly saw her father go into the light and out of her aura for good (we thought!).

The following week she came in depressed and said that one evening during the previous week her father had seemed to return suddenly, and with his return she felt a sharp pain in the back left of her head. And he was back in her dreams.

I guided Annabelle within, then had a half-hour argument-conversation-exhortation with Hans. At first he was his ambivalent self, agreeing with me one minute and disagreeing on the same issue the next. I increased the strength of my voice and told him to pull himself together, that he was not aware, not fully aware, of what he was doing to someone he *claimed* to love, nor was he aware of the happiness he was denying himself.

F: *You don't understand.*

T: *Then* help *me understand!*

F: *It's lonely. I'm scared. The light and warmth around my Annabelle are greater than that around the old friends you have called to come here to walk with me to the other side. So why should I stay with them?*

T: *I see. Thank you for helping me, Hans, because I only want to help you, to be your friend. Please think for a moment. Is there anyone, a spiritual leader, for example, who has more warmth and beautiful feelings for you than Annabelle?*

F: *All I can think of is that once in Toronto—I don't know, maybe Vancouver—Annie was going to this Buddha-place trying to learn to meditate. But she couldn't. The other three inside kind of laughed at her, and most of the time I was bored and wanted her to leave and she felt it and couldn't*

*meditate. But I remember one time this perfect person whom she couldn't
see came and tried to tell her to be patient. He was so beautiful.*

T: *Hans, something really wonderful is happening right now. Look around
you at the light that is increasing. He is coming. The perfect one you met
is coming back, and this time he is coming, not for Annie, but for you.
This is your time, Hans. He is here; do you see him?*

F: *Oh yes. Oh yes. He has brought me a beautiful red robe. It is beautiful. It
is perfect like him. It...it holds something of his warmth and love. And it
is mine; it is for me....*

Hans departed. Annabelle stirred.

P: *He is gone. They walked off together into the light. He is gone for good.*

The conversation with Hans had revealed his dynamics. With his wife's
death the morose, lonely, dependent man had begun to obsess over being
with his daughter constantly, first in daydreams, then half in reality as his
consciousness began to be attuned to being in her aura. Obsessed with living
through his daughter's comforting vibration, he did not think of death or
prepare to cross over the river to the next world as he became older.

And so, at death, he became one of the "lost ones," one of the "unclean
spirits" mentioned in the Christian Bible's dozens of references to possession, one of the "multitude of tramp souls" the Hindu scriptures say do not
get off the earth when they leave their bodies because the only commitment
they could ever make in their earth lives was to things of this earth. His
strong attachment to Annabelle made his releasement difficult, but the
helpful figure of light made it possible. As is usual in cases of attachment,
the therapy was even more important for him, the obsessor, than for
Annabelle, the identified patient.

Drawing Entities through Anger

by

Hazel M. Denning, Ph.D.

Introduction

My initial interest in possession involved the investigation of haunted houses. During the 1970's I investigated many houses that were believed by the owners to be haunted. At that time I was active in the Parapsychology Association of Riverside, and many people called us to report strange and often frightening phenomena in their homes. In the beginning, because it seemed difficult for people to channel an entity, I worked with a psychic who was able to perceive any energies that were present. My involvement was for one purpose only, to relieve the distress of the people who were calling for help when they found themselves subjected to an experience they could not understand and that was causing them fear and pain. We were not paid for this service, and often we traveled many miles to help those in distress, but the appreciation from the people was more than adequate compensation for our time.

Many of the discarnates with whom we worked were trapped in an interim space from which they could not escape. Some did not realize that they were "dead." Many were afraid to leave the safety of their physical environment because they believed they would go to a place of punishment for their misdeeds. Others wanted to make various requests from the new tenants of the houses if only they could get these new owners to hear them. In almost all cases we were able to liberate these entities from their earthly entrapment.

My first personal encounter with a haunted house occurred in my own home, and it was a terrifying experience. I was in my twenties, and my explorations into the paranormal were only beginning. My husband had gone to a bankers' convention and I was alone with our baby son for a week. On the third night I awoke about three in the morning and knew without a shadow of a doubt that I was not alone. I immediately thought of a burglar and very cautiously opened my eyes. The room was light enough from the street lamps to allow me to see objects with a fair amount of clarity. I saw nothing unusual and slowly turned my head to take in all of the room. Nothing was there except the furniture, but that feeling of a presence was very real and "heavy." I vividly recall feeling the hair rise on my scalp and goose bumps erupt on my arms. In sheer terror and total helplessness I pulled the covers over my head. Since nothing happened, my shaking gradually subsided and I fell asleep.

I reacted similarly, though not so intensely, when the same experience occurred the next night. When I described the happenings of the two nights to a friend who had had more experience than I in the parapsychological field, she told me that someone had probably died traumatically in that house and did not know how to leave or where to go and so had remained earthbound. She assured me that I was in no danger, but she suggested that I demand that the entity leave the house.

I inquired about the previous occupants of the house and discovered that a woman suffering from pneumonia had died of strangulation in the front bedroom. The possibility that it was the presence of this woman that I had sensed provided an explanation for other happenings that had seemed inexplicable: on a number of occasions I had heard the clunking of the heavy Yale lock on our front door when no one had been near it; articles had fallen off shelves for no apparent reason, as had my husband's tennis racket, which had been leaning against the wall at the very back of the shelf on which it had been placed. I had wondered how it could have fallen to the floor but at the time I let the matter go. Then I began to question if the night visitor could have had anything to do with these occurrences.

Two nights later I was awakened a third time by an overwhelming sense of a presence. I sat bolt upright in bed and in as firm a voice as I could manage said, *"This is my house. You have no right to be here, so get the hell out, now! And don't come back!"* I sat there in the bed, waiting for something to happen. It could have been my imagination, but my strong impression was that the atmosphere in my room changed and the oppressive feeling left. I would explain it now as a negative energy leaving the room, but at that time I did not know about energies and had no knowledge of how to help souls who were caught in their last environment. Now I know that the release of such souls is, if anything, more important than clearing a house for the benefit of new tenants.

Following this incident I learned how to help trapped souls and was often called by people who sensed presences in their homes, often old houses with a history of unusual events. If those cases were isolated experiences, they could be dismissed, but there are many such happenings. The only evidence for their reality lies in the total recovery of the subjects from their symptoms.

Could there be other explanations for this recovery? The most obvious one and the one most accepted by the scientific community postulates that the recovery is the result of belief. This explanation would suggest that a dehaunting experience instills in clients a new belief system that totally replaces their fears. This explanation has considerable merit, for we do indeed create a new belief system when we release entities, but it is based on more than a fanciful fabrication. In many of our cases the individuals under attack have previously called in other specialists, including psychologists, ministers, exorcists, priests, and psychics, with no positive results. The psychologists used reconditioning measures and logic and at times committed the "possessed" person to a mental institution. Ministers were for the most part limited to prayers and exhortations that generally proved ineffective. Exorcists approached most cases with the premise that the offending spirit was the Devil or his henchmen and must be forced out in the name of God or Jesus Christ. As a rule, such exorcists were the primary resource of priests. The success of psychics was limited by their skill, but even those who were skillful were often frightened by the manifestations they encountered. Since none of these approaches worked, even though the victims believed they were calling on people who were skilled in solving such problems, it seems logical to assume that belief alone is not powerful enough to free victims of psychic harassment.

As the result of our cultural non-belief, even those who have understood how to be effective in this field have been the objects of harassment by the scientific community and have had to work incognito, and many gifted people have been pronounced mentally ill. Even our psychological personality profiles measure a person's sanity by a response to such questions as, "Do you ever hear voices?" with the judgment that the subject is not in touch with reality if he answers affirmatively. Most regrettable is the fact that many clients who have had such experiences do not dare to disclose them to traditional therapists for fear of being diagnosed as abnormal. I believe we would find that such experiences are even more common than we have thought if people were not so afraid to reveal them. Fortunately, that kind of fear is gradually being dispelled by an escalating interest in paranormal events.

Although my own initial interest had revealed evidence that many people suffer from harassment of entities who remain attached either to the people or to their dwelling places, for 20 years I reacted to the judgment of my professional community that this was not a respectable area of inquiry, by turning to other subjects. I kept an open mind about entities but by the time interest in possession became renewed in the past decade, I had moved in other directions and was no longer drawing clients who manifested symptoms of possession or psychic attack.

Recently, however, I have had several clients who have encouraged me to renew my search for explanations in non-physical areas. It was because these clients had developed serious physical problems that had not yielded to medical treatment that I felt compelled to move in a different direction and explore the possible impact of entities. What especially suggested to me the possibility of psychic attachment was that each of these clients had recently experienced rage that was ego-dystonic and alien and did not fit with their habitual calm approach to life. In each of these cases the client was able to channel entities who had stimulated the rage, and releasement of these entities freed the client. Since other approaches had been ineffective, the use of releasement in these cases seemed both justified and valid.

I will present a sampling of cases in the chronological order in which they occurred. It will be observed that I have developed increasing confidence in the ability of clients to act as channels for the entities interfering with their lives. At this time it is not possible to say if this is always possible in cases of haunted houses.

Entities Attached to Houses

Case 1. A Murdered Soul Requests His Burial

One of my earliest exposures to the occupation of a house by its departed owner came to me second-hand from an elderly physician who had a wealth of knowledge about life and the paranormal field. He was psychic, though he did not claim that ability. For instance, this doctor explained to me that the phenomenon of the phantom limb occurs because after any amputation the energy or life force of the lost body part remains with the body and must be drawn up or back into the remaining part of the body in order for the individual to be comfortable, a simple process accomplished by the mind visualizing this energy and ordering it to return to the body.

When this doctor learned that I was interested in haunted houses, he offered to share with me his most frightening experience. In a friend's house everyone who slept in a certain room had been awakened at midnight by a terrifying apparition in the form of a large angry-looking man who stood over the bed and held his hands over their faces in a threatening manner. Because the story was passed from one to another who had slept in the room, they felt that the experience might have been triggered by fear and an expectation prompted by the stories. Did the fear create the experience and was it purely subjective?

To decide whether this was so they placed in the room a three-year-old child who knew nothing of the apparent hauntings. Promptly at midnight the child screamed in terror. Everyone came running and found her sitting on the bed, shaking and crying as between sobs she stammered, *"A terrible man tried to get me!"*

When my doctor friend heard the story he volunteered to be the next one to sleep in that room, feeling sure that ghosts would not bother him. He was sleeping soundly when he awoke with a feeling that he was not alone. Startled, he opened his eyes and watched a large man approach his bed and stand over him with huge hands stretched out threateningly toward his face. With as much bravado as he could manage he said, *"What do you mean by scaring everyone like this? What the hell do you want, anyway? If there is something I can do for you, just say so."*

The spirit apologized and explained that he had been murdered in this house and was buried in the basement. He described the exact spot in which his body had been buried and begged the doctor to help him find peace of mind. He believed his soul could not find rest until he had been given a proper Christian internment.

When the family who currently owned the house agreed to the digging in their cellar, the bones of a grown man were unearthed in the exact location the spirit had described. Everyone cooperated in giving him a Christian burial, and from then on no one who slept in that room was disturbed.

Case 2. Two Levels of Anger

My experience has been that where there are negative manifestations, the object of the harassment harbors emotional negativity in the form of anger or resentment, fear, and frequently guilt. In our investigations of haunted houses, the physical and non-physical worlds interacted continuously in accordance with spiritual law. Powerful negative energy continues to hold two personalities locked into a painful relationship until the problem between them is resolved in a way that dispels that negative energy. Such an unpleasant relationship may be expressed on two levels—in the personal relationship or in the negative energy that acts as a magnet for a similar energy in a house haunted by a negative entity. No one is annoyed by entities unless some attitude or emotional state attracts this phenomenon.

When I met Ann I thought I had found the exception to my belief. She was a beautiful woman in her late thirties, well-educated, the mother of two grown children, and apparently quite successful in a joint business with her husband. Her attitude toward her husband and children indicated a deep love and pride in them, and there was nothing that gave any hint of friction between her and her husband. We talked about her haunted house as calmly as one would discuss the weather.

The house she and her husband had purchased was attractive, with a high and thick stone wall enclosing the entire front. It was landscaped with shrubs and beds of flowers, including a rose garden of unusual beauty. Ann reported that both she and her husband felt that the thick wall gave their house the impression of a fortress, and they decided to remove it and share the garden with neighbors and passers-by. They hired a crew of workmen to remove the wall.

Almost immediately strange things began to happen. The men would find their tools apparently moved from one place to another, and one of the workmen insisted he had been pushed from behind and knocked to the ground, but there was no one there when he looked around. A number of injuries occurred, and two of the workmen quit.

In addition, Ann was uncomfortably aware of a presence that she could not see or identify but that caused her to be afraid. She also believed that objects were moved in the house, and unidentifiable noises could be heard almost daily. She related these things to me objectively, explaining that she did not believe in ghosts but felt these experiences were certainly not normal. She was determined to find some explanation. She questioned her own memory, but the feeling of a presence could not be rationalized. It was the "feeling" that bothered her the most, since she felt she had lost control and was not comfortable with the thought that something outside of her had that much power.

At that time I was using a psychic to contact the entity attached to a building, and as Ann and I were talking, my colleague walked through the house. Returning, she reported that she had contacted a spirit who was angry with Ann. This spirit and her husband had built the house to fulfill a lifelong dream. They liked being by themselves and had built the wall to keep everyone out except those specifically invited. She especially disliked children and wanted to make certain that they did not come on the property.

This entity had spent months planning and working in her yard to create the beautiful garden she wanted, but she and her husband had had only a few months to enjoy their dream house before they were both killed in an accident. She had put so much into the house that she could not leave it. When the strangers, Ann and her husband, took over the property and began tearing down her beloved wall, she was furious and determined to make them as uncomfortable as possible. She had tried to stop the workmen from tearing down the wall but did not have enough power to do this and had to stand by and see it demolished. She followed Ann around the house, sending her anger and wishing she were dead. It was not surprising that Ann, even though she had never considered herself psychic, reacted to this negative energy.

Ann was visibly relieved by this explanation and said she could understand the entity's feelings. She apologized to the former owner and said she was sorry she had hurt her but insisted that the house was no longer the entity's property and she must relinquish it.

At this point it was our responsibility to help the disturbed entity. I explained that she was "dead," which at first she vehemently denied but finally had to acknowledge, since she could not refute the evidence we gave her that she no longer had a physical body. We explained that she could be happy by moving into her new dimension and building another house there that could be an exact replica of her earthly one.[16] She soon agreed to leave and departed willingly with a spirit helper whom we had requested to come and help her.

Two weeks later, when I visited Ann to follow up on the releasement of the entity, I found that all was well on that score but that underneath the haunting of the house lay another level of anger and struggle. This involved Ann's relationship with her husband. In contrast to her earlier portrayal of accord between them, it turned out that they had sharply disagreed on the remodeling, especially on the destruction of the wall. The husband had thought the wall might give them a privacy that would be rather pleasant, and he could see no reason to go to all the expense of tearing it down. This disagreement was only the most recent expression of a long-standing conflict between them. He had nearly always disagreed with what she wanted, and in their business, if she did not go along with his decisions he made her feel inadequate and stupid. The remodeling of the house was her project away from their business and was one in which she could express her own creative ideas. This was the arrangement they had made when they bought the house, but he had changed his mind when it came to the actual labor and what he considered an unnecessary expense.

On the whole, Ann was not unhappy with her life and acknowledged that her husband provided well, never abused her physically, and could at times be pleasant, so that their marriage was considered by their friends to be a good one. It seemed to me that though she was well-educated and knew how to put on a good front, underneath she was emotionally crippled by feelings of inadequacy. I suggested that she might benefit from therapy to help her have a better image of herself, and we parted on a positive note.

Later on, as I considered her anger and resentment, I realized that though in the beginning she seemed to have done nothing to attract the entity, in reality she was no exception to my earlier conclusions. Where there are negative manifestations the object of the harassment invariably harbors emotional negativity in the form of anger or resentment, sometimes fear, and frequently guilt. It is this negative energy field that makes possible—or even draws—the manifestations of the entity. Often, to effect permanent release of the entity, the client's field must also be changed.

Evidence seems to point to love as the ultimate solution to man's conflicts. In working with a client, whether individually in a regression or in a context with an entity, after the problem has been identified and analyzed it seems necessary to go through an integration process. The most important question to ask the client is, "Whom do you have to forgive?" Since anger at others is almost always a projection of some darkness in ourselves, the answer is almost always the same—"myself."

All of our experiences are lessons, challenges, opportunities for learning. What is important is not what happens to us but the manner in which we react to the experience. When we react with anger, resentment, jealousy, or any other negative emotion, we set in motion a pattern of negative energies that are like a boomerang. They bounce right back on the originator of the negative energy. Reacting to the vicissitudes in our experience with anger, resentment, fear, or guilt creates blueprints for pain and illness in the future. The only real freedom any of us has is the freedom to choose the way we react to every given situation that life presents to us. Ann needed to re-evaluate her feelings about her husband and bring balance and love into her field, both so that her outer relationship would be more comfortable and fulfilling and so that she would not generate a negative field that would draw entities with a similar field.

Case 3. Releasing the Victim of an Accident

In another case, an entity attached itself to a young professional woman and also haunted her house. The woman had moved into a new home and had not been able to unpack some of the boxes that were in the garage and on the floor of the house because she felt that something was in the house, though she saw nothing. She had also heard a few strange noises that she could not identify or trace to anything human or physical. Moreover, she felt as if her head were full of fragments of thoughts, so that it was impossible for her to hold onto an idea and carry it to completion. She felt at times as though she were literally flung apart.

Fortunately, she was an excellent hypnotic subject who could channel the entity herself.

T: *Is there anyone in you or with you who can speak to me?*

E: *Oh, yes, yes, help me, please help me! I don't know where I am or what happened to me. I am so frightened and I can't find anyone to help me. No one will listen.*

T: *Can you go back before you became so frightened and tell me what happened to you?.*

E: *While I was walking along a dark street alone, something hit me from behind. That's the last thing I remember clearly. Since then there has been nothing but confusion. I don't know where I am and I can't figure out where I am going. When I saw this lady she looked kind and I thought she might be able to help me. But she doesn't answer me when I try to talk to her.*

My subject was a loving and kind person, but she had been having personal problems with some members of her family. These problems had kept her in a state of emotional confusion for some months. A young male spirit apparently gravitated to both her nurturing self and her confused mental state. Until the entity invaded her energy field in his mental turmoil she had been able to handle her emotional state fairly well; afterwards in her vulnerable state she took on his feelings, and her confusion escalated.

For a half hour I conversed with this confused spirit, explaining to him what had happened and what he could do about it now.

> *T: So you can walk ahead now into the light and go on your way.*
> *E: I'd like to do that but I don't think I can. I'm not good enough to go into the light.*
> *T: Open your eyes and look at the light. Anyone can do that.*
> *E: (Still hesitates.)*
> *T: I'd like you to imagine a path with flowers on both sides and a light at the end of the path.*
> *E: It's beautiful. I think I can walk into it. (After a few moments he seems willing to go.) Thank you, oh, thank you so much, both of you! Here, I would like to give you a flower to show my thanks. (Subject's hand comes up off the chair and extends toward me as if handing me something.)*
> *T: (With a gesture of reaching out.) Thank you.*
> *E: Thank you! Thank you both again for helping me. Goodbye.*

It was as touching an experience as I have ever had with a spirit.

> *P: Oh, my what a relief! I feel so good, and I am happy for him. He was so relieved. (Coming out of trance) I feel wonderful—I can't find the words to describe the difference. I feel as if all the fragments have come together again and I can think clearly.*

Follow-up a year later confirmed that her improved mental functioning had held.

Entities Originating in Other Lifetimes

Case 4. You Can't Kill a Soul with a Knife

Jackie reported that all through her present life she had been plagued by the feeling that something bad in her background was "doing her in." She was afraid other people would recognize that. They would look into her eyes and see something evil, something that was not her. Recently she had felt swells of rage breaking through her that she could not identify or recognize as appropriate for her current life.

Jackie's chin often quivered slightly when she talked, and she cried easily —recognizable indications of her repressed tensions. She was an excellent subject and entered an altered state in seconds. I asked her if there was someone with her, and she gave an immediate reply:

E: I am the other side of her (Jackie) that she hates.

T: Who are you?

E: I am...(pause). No, she doesn't hate me. She's scared to death of me. If she didn't have me she wouldn't be here; she wouldn't even have a life.

T: Is there another energy in Jackie besides anger?

E: She wears a very good mask to hide it all. There's a light in the dark. That one has the power. The other has the anger.

Jackie is a healer, and I believe the "power" referred to that aspect of her.

T: Can I talk with the one who has the anger?

E: Oh, yes.

T: What is your name?

E: Ish—Ishl—Ishmal.

T: When did you join forces with Jackie?

E: (Deep sigh) In 1863.

T: Tell me about it. What were the circumstances?

E: She is standing over me with a knife in her hand. Stupid bitch!

T: Are you a man?

E: I am a man. She is a woman. She is my whore. She's supposed to be mine, but she says she's not. I'll knock her around a couple of times and she'll be where she's supposed to be....But she says, "You are not coming near me!"

> *I tell her, "You'll do what I say!"*
> *She replies, "Never!"*
> *I insist, "Oh, yes, you are, and you will like it!"*
> *She says again, "No, I'm not, and if you come near me, I will show you!"*
> *"Ah, you stupid bitch, give me that knife!"*
> *She yells, "I will! I will! If you come near me, I'll kill you."*
> *I taunt her, "Oh, no, you won't!"*
> *The last thing I hear her saying is, "Okay, Okay. There! You have fixed it so I have nowhere to go, no one to take care of me. You have ruined everything for me. And—now you are stopped."*

T: Is she standing over you with the knife?

E: She killed me with it, stupid bitch! And now she thinks she's done with me. She's not. Not yet!

T: Have you been with her ever since?

E: Yes—most of the time. Except lately. She's getting harder to come to.

T: Why is that?

E: She thinks that she's—she's getting stronger. Well, she is getting stronger.

This could have been the result of Jackie's therapy sessions where she had been working on her spiritual growth.

T: So you can't control her as you used to?

E: That's true. But there are moments when she's vulnerable, and I can get to her and get back at her.

T: *Have you been happy all this time getting back at her? Wouldn't you like to move on to a happier place?*

E: *I always thought I cared so much for her, that I loved her, that I was supposed to take care of her.*

T: *Did you know that you could be free and go wherever you wish?*

E: *Yeah, but not without her.*

T: *Do you love her or hate her?*

E: *Both.*

At this point I suggested that Ishmal call on someone to help him—perhaps his mother from that life. He did, and his mother came, expressing joy over their meeting. He went with her with little hesitation, saying he was ready for a change.

I asked Jackie, while she was still in an altered state, if the rage in her was hers against the entity or whether it was his rage against her. She said she felt it was her own rage carried over, apparently from the brutal treatment.

She reported that all through her present life she had been plagued by the feeling that something bad was in the background "doing her in." She was afraid other people would recognize this, but now she felt that she could finally let go of her rage and say, "That is enough." When she returned to her normal state of consciousness, she sat up and remarked, "Geeze! I feel ten pounds lighter!"

A three-week follow-up found her still free from a weight of anger she had come to take for granted.

Case 5. Who Was Responsible for the Bridge?

In Marie's case, also, I felt hesitant about bringing up the idea that she might be possessed, but usual therapeutic techniques had brought no relief from her problems. Since adulthood she had become perfectionistic to an inhibiting degree, especially in her work, where she seemed terrified of making a mistake. In recent months, surges of rage had interfered with her usual composed approach to her life, and her body was beginning to suffer as a result, especially her neck and back, where at intervals she felt intense pain. Her symptoms suggested that there might be entity interference. She was distressed by the idea of possession but saw no other way to go. In an altered state she came almost immediately upon the entity who had been bothering her.

T: *Is there anyone with you having an influence on you?*

P: *Well, the first thought was, "Try it and see."*

T: *All right. I am asking again: Is there someone with you?*

P: *Wow! The thought is, "Marie is getting in the way. She doesn't want to admit it, and so she's getting in the way." There's another thought wave of some kind. A lot of times when she's thinking optimistically, there's a thought wave that can come in and says, "I wish I were dead." She doesn't know where it comes from. And every so often there's a behavior pattern that's not like her, particularly when it's anger. And sometimes she's just not in a good mood.*

I asked this entity, whose name I learned later was Dick, to tell me what made him so angry.

E: *Unfairness, and the ability to not seem right when I know that I am right.*
T: *Can you describe this a little more?*
E: *It comes up when I can't explain something, and I know I'm right, and I can't make them understand. That really makes me angry.*
T: *When did this happen to you?*
E: *Seems like it's in a court room. I feel like my wrists are manacled and I'm in England and I'm in a dock. It's like two posts with rings and I'm—it's '73, I think. (Century is not mentioned.)*
T: *Are you a man or a woman?*
E: *I am a man and I am telling the truth, and they won't believe me. I'm being accused of many deaths. I am not responsible, but they think I am. And it's so frustrating because I know I'm going to be hanged if I can't convince them. And I can't.... I'm an architect, I think. And it was a bridge, I think. And they're blaming me. But it wasn't me—it was the people who constructed the bridge. I have the proof, but they won't believe me. I am really, really angry. Those judges—they're so ignorant!*
T: *So what happens?*
E: *They're taking me out, and I'm furious. I tell them that they're killing the wrong person, that it was not my fault. I would like to curse them—all of them—for being so ignorant. They aren't punishing the people who did it. And they'll build more bridges, and more people will be killed.*
  We're all going to be dead by morning. Yes, there are others being killed. And hanging is the worst kind of death. You hang there for a long, long time. Being beheaded is a noble way.
  I can't stand it! My parents sacrificed to put me through school to be an architect so I would take care of them in their old age—and I am innocent!

He was hung, and his last thought was a curse. He saw his body hanging there and people spitting on it. Later his head was put on a spike and hung there until the crows devoured it.

E: *I was innocent, and they wouldn't listen. I would like to put a curse on those accusers—and on those builders, those construction builders. They were the ones who put the blame on me. They knew they used inferior materials. I really would like to curse all of them. And I do. I would like to haunt them.*

T: *Why did you decide to express your anger through Marie?*

E: *Well, the Carters (Marie's married name) were some of the people who built the bridges, and I've haunted the members of that family for generations.*

T: *Are you happy living this way?*

E: *I don't think these people deserve it, but I'm used to doing it. This is my job.*

T: *Have you ever contacted your parents? You can now, you know.*

E: *They were devastated. No, I haven't ever seen them.*

T: *Would you like to see them?*

E: *I'd be ashamed. I didn't live up to their hopes. They were so proud of me. I didn't do anything wrong, but how would they believe that?*

T: *They would understand now. If you will ask them to come, I believe they will. Tell me when you see them.*

E: *They're here. They're holding out their hands to me (deep emotion.) It's pretty hard.*

T: *What are they saying to you?*

E: *Come, son. We know. We know it was not your fault.*

T: *How do you feel about that?*

E: *Bad. It makes me feel sad.*

T: *Why do you feel sad?*

E: *(No answer.)*

T: *You can now be free and go into the light.*

E: *I feel that Marie is holding me.*

T: *What do you feel from her that is holding you?*

E: *Well, she needs my righteous anger sometimes.*

T: *Don't you think she can generate her own anger?*

E: *Maybe she can. But I'm used to her. I feel a painful tug in my heart. It hurts to break away like this. It's been such a long time.*

T: *Ask your mother to help you. She can explain the situation.*

E: *"Well, Son, if you will come with me, you will lose all that hatred and frustration and anger. And you will not be punished for all those curses. You were right, and whatever reason you had for choosing that death, you have paid for it. As for us, we were always proud of you. So you can come with us, and things will be better. You do not need to hang on to the pain and the shame anymore. You can leave them behind."*

T: *You can express your feelings on your own, and Marie can express hers on her own. You will both be better that way.*

Marie announced that Dick was gone. She added that she felt a pain in her back and chest and a feeling of emptiness.

T: *Do you like the idea of someone else controlling your emotions?*

P: *No. No, I don't. It's always been a handicap. But I've been better about that. I've been working at staying apart from other people's emotions.*

T: *Is there any connection between that and your compulsion to do everything exactly right?*

P: *I still want things to be right.*

T: It's not that, it's the pressure you feel to be perfect.

We discussed that for a while, and presently Marie said she realized that getting things done perfectly was not a life-and-death matter.

P: If he is gone after all these generations, it will be a wonderful thing. But I guess that for a long time I've felt dependent on Dick as a back-up for verbal fights, for anger, for feelings of being right in some situations, even for a good curse now and then. Now I won't have to be so pushy about getting my points across.

Marie was still feeling the pain in her neck and back, which she related to being hanged and placed on that hook. But talking about it further brought rapid relief. A few days later Marie reported that the relief had lasted. At this point she left the city for an extended absence, so further follow-up has so far not been possible.

Releasement in Sri Lanka

by

Winafred B. Lucas, Ph.D.

Recently I stayed for a month with a friend in a large hillside property in the mountains east of Kande, in Sri Lanka. The goal of the visit was to make a video about a cottage industry: spinning and weaving silk into exquisite wall hangings and carpets. My hostess, Magda, in addition to her weaving enterprise, also bred dogs, and at the time of my visit she had about 50 in her kennel. Magda had a Cuban mother and a Hungarian-Jewish father and was married to a native of Sri Lanka, Ranjith, who, in addition to being handsome and an extremely kind person, was also a business man with legal training. Two Nordic-looking teenage boys from a former marriage of Magda's guarded with devotion a pixyish and delightful five-year-old girl from the current marriage. In most third-world houses conveniences that Americans take for granted are missing, even when the owners are in the upper stratum of the economic ladder, as my friends are. Electricity had been brought to Ranjith's and Magda's house only months before, and there was still no telephone. Water was hauled up daily in large trucks. There was a complicated melding of native and more modern approaches to living.

When I arrived I found a pall over the house. From the beginning of the kennel five years before there had been accidents and deaths among the dogs beyond normal expectation. Then, in spite of their earning what was for Sri Lanka a good salary, more and more women were not coming back to the weaving sheds. Over the entire property there hung a pall of shadowing and depression.

The rumor was that a man who had owned the property many years before had killed a number of people and buried them there and was still attached to the land, especially now that so many young women were coming. Magda was skeptical of such a story and remained on the sidelines when Ranjith, not usually interested in religious things, found a young priestess to do a depossession. Following this, the main houses and yards seemed much lighter but the atmosphere of depression continued in the hillside dog runs and in the weaving sheds.

In gratitude for what the young priestess Asanka had accomplished, Ranjith had arranged a year before for a small temple to be built (perhaps nine feet square). Magda was confused about the situation, resisting being gullible about native magic but realizing that it was imperative that something be done. Intuitively she liked Asanka.

I walked around the property, through the dog runs and the weaving sheds, sensing the areas that seemed most saturated with a heavy darkness, which felt like thick, sooty fog. Things had not been going well. A dog had just broken a leg and several dogs had suddenly died from no apparent cause. Meanwhile, the weavers had shrunk in number to under 200, and looms were idle; something seemed to be scaring them away.

Shortly after our arrival, Asanka had a day of celebration for the first anniversary of her little temple, and Ranjith and my companion Lorraine and I joined the hundreds who were honoring the day. The country road to the temple was clogged with celebrants. Lorraine and I left the car and followed the dancers and floats, while Ranjith went ahead to help with last minute details.

Sri Lanka's religious practices are charismatic, a blending of Hinduism and Buddhism, not unlike the charismatic Christian church or the Quakers. While in an altered state many Sri Lanka worshippers become possessed by an exuberant contact with what they believe to be their deities, especially Siva. Some embrace masochistic experiences, the most unusual of which is putting needles through their tongues and lips or hooks through their backs. One man in our procession was even suspended by hooks from a pole above the truck in which he was being carried. Throughout the process the celebrants are entirely joyous, and when the needles and hooks are taken out and a dab of some sort of powder is sprinkled on the holes, within a few minutes there is no evidence that anything had ever happened. It reminded me of the firewalking in which I took part a few years ago, and, in fact, fire-walking is often included in these celebrations, especially at Kataragama, the southern precinct that is sacred to Siva.

Asanka led the procession over the several miles to her temple, dancing and chanting in a totally altered state, and behind her people danced and sang joyously. When she arrived at her small temple, which had been swept clean and decorated with flowers and coconuts, she stood in the doorway chanting a rapid invocation to Siva and broke a coconut on the ground in his honor. To our surprise, Lorraine and I were the guests of honor and we were led to the front row of the privileged group that had managed to stand within the small area in front of the temple. Asanka's expression and voice were loving, and as she invoked Siva a radiant yellow butterfly circled around her head.

Asanka began to give darshan (a blessing) and almost immediately called Lorraine and me. As I knelt before her I felt enveloped in a powerful love energy. Then I stood up and we put our arms around each other as though we were old friends come together. Later I realized that we had been sisters in an ancient lifetime, but at that time all I sensed was an overwhelming flow of love between us.

The celebration went on all night. Lorraine and I stayed through the bathing with holy water of the image of Kataragama (Siva), which had been brought out from the inner part of the temple. Asanka danced with garlands and flowers and a torch, and offerings of food, pineapple and papayas and bananas and coconuts, were made to Siva by many of the celebrants. At midnight Ranjith, sensing that we were tired, took us home, where a curious Magda waited to hear our reactions.

After that it was apparent that any releasement work on the property of Ranjith and Magda must be a joint effort between Asanka and me. Asanka readily agreed and we set a night that she felt was auspicious. I found a gong and some rosemary and benzoin and Magda came up with an incense burner with a long handle. On the night agreed on, Asanka and all Ranjith's family and Lorraine and I walked in the dusk through the kennel runs and the five weavers' sheds. Magda's older son carried the burning herbs. Regularly we talked to the souls of those buried on the property and to the soul of the man who had killed them, invoking him to leave and sending him our love, spreading light everywhere. Always at my side walked Asanka, merging into this different form of releasement with no effort. Toward the end I became aware that the entity was leaving. Peace and quietness began to fill the grounds, especially the weaving sheds.

Asanka had brought helpers with her and after our walk through the property they spent several hours making little cages from coconut fronds into which they put carefully prepared pieces of papayas, pineapples, and the little Sri Lankan bananas. Garlands of flowers, especially jasmine, were everywhere. At nine o'clock Asanka began the ceremony with the breaking of a coconut and a lengthy and rapid invocation to Siva. As she whirled and chanted holding an oil lamp, she addressed Siva and exhorted him to bring the soul of the entity into his light. Then the offerings of fruit were made to him. Later she told me that she was aware he had already gone but she had sent a wave of love after him and exhorted him not to return. She then spent several hours in a trance state giving darshan to everyone present individually and channeling for some of those around her, telling them what their lives had been and foretelling the future. Ranjith said she had been surprisingly accurate about his past, concerning which she had little knowledge. Lorraine and I stood on the sidelines for this part of the ceremony. Once again, Asanka went on all night but we became tired and went to bed. Toward morning the fruit offerings were taken out of the grounds to a nearby temple.

Later I discussed concepts of releasement with Asanka. Our cultural props differed from each other but our understanding of what happened was remarkably similar. Both of us saw the soul going into the light. Asanka saw it as the light of Siva and felt that all souls needed to go to the abode of Siva.[21] She felt they should be helped to go with love and offerings, such as the fruit. She, too, perceived that their continuous sojourn following death in an earthly place, such as this hillside property, promoted a dark energy and negativity. Neither of us felt we needed to make any judgment, even in the case of multiple murder, such as had evidently happened here. As adjunct to the releasement I used a gong and herbs. She used herbs, also, an oil lamp, coconuts, fruits and flowers, all to invoke Siva, and gave the cages of fruit as gifts to the entity. She saw herself as calling Siva, who in turn called the soul and took it to his abode of light.

When I asked Asanka questions about herself, she told me she had had several lifetimes as a priestess. She told me about her calling to be a priestess in this life and about her training at Kataragama, the extensive temple complex dedicated to Siva. Most of her work involves healing (where she uses an Ayurvedic approach), some releasement, psychic readings, and general counseling. She does all these things in trance. She seems to put herself into an immediate trance state by knocking her head hard over the third eye with her fist. I suggested she might try to retain awareness of what she said and did while in trance, since I feel that that is what the consciousness of the planet is moving into. She was interested in the possibility of this, which she had not considered before.

We saw each other several other times, including on an expedition higher up in the mountains for my eightieth birthday. When we parted she said she would get an oil lamp and burn it for me every day, and I told her I would think of her and send her energy and love while I burned a rose candle. Currently I feel the vibrations she sends to me, and I trust she feels those I send to her.

Later I went back over the kennel runs where the murdered victims had been buried and cleared up the remaining pall. The proof of the effectiveness of these rituals will be an improved state of health in the kennel population and a return of the weavers to the loom. By the time I left, a number of women had already come back.

Chapter VII

Death, Dying, and the Dead

It is at the junction of the two major transition points in human existence, birth and death, that there is a heightened intensity of consciousness that makes it possible to perceive the programs or samskaras that determine the course of the lives to come... In working through past-life deaths a beginning is made in releasing old and unproductive patterns, and practice is initiated in consciously working through the death process. Therefore, attention to the death experience is of optimum importance in past-life recall. Taking a patient to the point of death and beyond brings a sense of completion, detachment, and often, though by no means always, resolution. It is to be hoped that it will also help to release negative samskaras so that the same disastrous experiences will not have to be re-lived.

Roger Woolger

Death appears to those who have approached it in the near-death experience to be a transition, not an ending. The essence of us remains, along with such learning as has been gleaned in the preceding lifetime. Gradually the concept that we are the victims of death, laid low by the "grim reaper," is becoming seen as invalid and inaccurate. The new conceptualization also outmodes our current cultural behavior that fights desperately to keep those we love from dying. We are moving into a time when we can help each other make our transitions joyously and with awareness, rather than as passive victims.

Winafred Lucas

Bibliography

Evans-Wentz, W. *The Tibetan Book of the Dead*. New York: Oxford Press, 1960.

Kübler-Ross, Elizabeth. *Death: The Final Stage of Growth*. New Jersey: Prentice-Hall Inc., 1973.

———. *On Death and Dying*. New York: McMillan, 1965.

Loehr, Franklin. *Death with Understanding*. Grand Island, FL: Religious Research Press, 1987.

Moody, Raymond. *Life After Life*. Covington, GE: Mockingbird Books, 1975.

Ring, Kenneth. *Life at Death*. New York: Coward, McCann and Geoghegan, 1980.

———. *Heading Toward Omega*. New York, William Morrow and Co., 1984.

Sabom, M. *Recollections of Death*. New York: Harper Row, 1982.

Snow, Chet. "Death Comes to Marie France." *The Journal of Regression Therapy,* Vol. II, No. 1, 1987.

Death, Dying, and the Dead

Introduction

Attitudes and beliefs about death and dying are passed from one generation to another and result in stereotyped concepts and behavior. They resist modification, but the growing number of self-reports by those who have had near-death experiences have made the concept of death that has dominated the idealogy of the past decades appear inappropriate. The extensive documentation of near-death experiences by Moody, Ring, Sabom,[1] and others has brought a reluctant concession of authenticity to a new and more comfortable concept of death.

Death appears to those who have approached it in the near-death experience to be a transition, not an ending. The essence of us remains, along with such learning as has been gleaned in lifetime just over. Gradually the concept that we are the victims of death, laid low by the "grim reaper," is becoming seen as invalid and inaccurate. The new conceptualization also outmodes our current cultural behavior that fights desperately to keep those we love from dying. We are moving into a time when we can help each other make our transitions joyously and with awareness, rather than as passive victims.

Research also brings into question our belief that we are cut off from a soul by death and suggests that this may be our experience only because we believe it to be true. There seems no reason for communication to be broken just because death has occurred. Those of us who work with entities who have not completed their transition know how easy it is for our patients to channel them. If such entities can be contacted, those who have gone to the Light may be equally available, and we might extend our contact if we could believe this to be possible. A conspiracy of silence about communication with the dead has evolved so that, though many people have such experiences, they are considered to be hallucinations. Lamb documents the experiences of souls who were open to such communication.

My own approach to death has been formed by personal experiences, beginning when my mother died suddenly of a stroke when I was 22. Her face appeared to me that afternoon, luminous, at peace, letting me know that she was all right, and the memory of that serenity has never left me. Many other contacts with the dead have come since then, and in spite of the fact that they were not generally acceptable to my professional world, I chose to acknowledge them. We can easily fail to validate our experiences because of scientific skepticism.

Not only are we currently becoming more comfortable with the concept of death, but data from a variety of sources suggest that we are moving into a new paradigm of dying in which we will be able to determine the time and method of our transition. Many of those who have been progressed into future lives experience themselves as determining their own deaths. They see themselves deciding the time and leaving, either while lying on a table under certain colors of lights or in a bed surrounded by friends or special people trained to help in transitions. This type of experience has been documented in our present era, though it is so difficult to understand in terms of our old concept of death that it is conveniently dismissed with a shrug.

My first experience of this was during graduate school at the time of the transition of Senzaki, the first Zen Master to come to California. During the 50's I often spent Friday evenings sitting in meditation with him and his group, mostly Japanese, in his humble home. One night in February he announced that several months later he would make his transition. He named the day and promised he would dictate a tape to be read at his memorial service. Caught in the web of the cultural concepts of that time, I was shocked and frightened that anyone could not only talk about his death with cheerfulness but even predict when it would take place. Senzaki made his transition exactly as he had foretold, and his wise and hopeful message was read at the service for him in the old church at the end of Alvero Street. Many years later when I was at the Frey Luis Center in Rio de Janeiro I found that its great mediums routinely choose their deaths and are lifted out of their bodies by the other mediums. Photographs on the walls of the center document such occurrences.

Probably often, if not always, on an unconscious level we choose our deaths—cancer is considered one way of doing this. Because of the unconscious nature of the choice it is helpful if the therapist in a gentle way can assist the patient to make it overt, as I did with Rhoda. Many times the awareness that one has made such a choice is resisted because of fear of what might come or because of guilt over giving up.

Sudden deaths through war or accidents often leave the dead confused and even unable to move toward the Light, so sometimes groups or individuals work to help those who have been killed to orient themselves. When I come upon a fatal accident or hear about a disaster where lives are lost, I try to take time to meet the souls and help with the transition. There is no way of objectively knowing that such intervention actually has an effect, but it takes little time and if it can help, that makes the effort worthwhile. Just the attempt to gain contact makes one feel more bonded with all of life.

When the Challenger exploded, I went immediately within and met the crew in an effort to be helpful, but to my surprise I found that instead of being lost and devastated they were confident and joyous. They assured me that they had chosen the experience in an effort to deepen the consciousness of our country, which at that time was rather superficial. Later that day I was talking with Hazel Denning and shared this experience. I told her I had been so surprised that I considered I must have invented what I perceived. Hazel reported that she had had exactly the same experience earlier in the day when she had contacted these souls in a similar effort to help them become oriented toward the Light, and she also had been surprised that they had planned their deaths and were radiant in their experience. Needless to say, it was with joy and relief that we learned that this death had been planned and totally accepted.

Certain rituals of passage encourage an easy and peaceful transition. Many years ago I worked out such a ritual for the occasional patient who suffered a terminal illness or for patients who had relatives in such a state. I modified suggestions from *The Tibetan Book of the Dead* and added details appropriate for our culture. At this time a client became impatient with her brother who was dying of ALS in a hospice. His dying had dragged on, and his sister resented the hours she had to spend with him and the drain on family funds. I suggested that on her next visit she dismiss the nurse and take time to share with her brother the good times they had had together and remind him of the qualities in him she most appreciated. Then she should put light around him and tell him that she loved him. My patient wasn't sure about the light, but she did follow the procedure, and an hour after she left the hospice her brother died peacefully. I thought I had discovered a unique approach, but I found that this ritual of helping people die was being used by others. In *A Way of Being* Carl Rogers[2] described an identical experience with his wife when she was dying. Snow documents such an experience in his article "Death Come to Marie-France."

An effective technique for helping patients become comfortable with death is the process of going through past-life deaths. Besides the comfort factor, there is an additional motivation for including the death experience in a regression. At the time of death physical conditions, emotional patterns, and cognitive programming that are in the forefront of the dying consciousness seem stamped into the soul configuration. Last thoughts and feelings apparently form a computer program that strongly influences the life, or even lives, to come. Woolger, both in his section in Volume I and in his article here, describes the nature and programming of the ongoing samskaras (soul patterns) and discusses how they become constellated at death.

Individual therapists use various approaches to explore past-life death experiences. Fiore and Hickman explore the death process thoroughly, even repeating it in the same session or returning to it in subsequent sessions to recover further details. Hickman had her patient who had a phobia of cats repeat the episode eight times to experience totally being killed by a lion so that she could release the death trauma. Fiore pressed a patient, who was killed by falling from a cathedral roof that he was repairing, to find each detail of his death. Remission of symptoms followed for both these patients. Deaths often take place in frightening situations and frequently involve bodily damage, as they did in these instances. Such phobias, allergies, and psychosomatic symptoms as are tied in with the body and the autonomic nervous system appear to be held in the energy body and can be released simply by intensive exploration. Woolger would say that damage has been done to the etheric body, and that recall alone is sufficient to bring healing to this body.

Many therapists follow in-depth memory recovery of a death with cognitive and emotional exploration and with a search for patterns. In this process, not only are phobias or physical symptoms corrected, but an attempt is made to release the karmic patterns as they manifest themselves in the death process. Usually the patient is encouraged to identify patterns that were similar in that past and in the current lifetime, and is asked his last thought or feeling to see how this has influenced his current behavior. Woolger considers such resolution of the karmic patterns in which symptoms are embedded to be the pertinent objective rather than the remission of the specific symptoms.

Some therapists feel that emotional sets of past-life death, especially anger and guilt, must be recovered and their effect on the current life recognized and modified: by catharsis, by working in the interim state, by forgiveness of self and others, or by reframing the situation. Denning pays particular attention to feelings of guilt that are stamped in during the death experience. She points out how readily the individual can take on the accusation of those bringing about the death and suggests how such programming can be reframed and released. Pecci explores the programming of guilt in an effort to deepen the patient's spiritual perspective.

Emotional attachments and relationships often emerge at the time of death, and their compulsive and addictive characteristics can be modified. Jue is particularly aware of this therapeutic potential and made use of it in helping Dawn understand her bonding to her son.[3] My own case of Rosemary traced dynamics of a mother-daughter relationship to another lifetime where the emotional set of victimization had been stamped in at the time of that earlier death.[4] Snow is particularly involved in working through relationship patterns, whether or not the specific individuals are brought forward from another lifetime to this one or only the pattern is repeated. In the case of Anne-Marie he modified the death pattern, which had stamped in a pattern of failure, both in relationships and as a person, by rescripting.[5] Findeisen prefers to work with similar sets and patterns that emerge at the time of birth. It seems to be therapeutically unimportant where the patient retrieves patterns, whether in birth or death—they are the same.

Pathways and realizations of the soul often emerge clearly at the time of death, which Woolger and Jue and Pecci consider a spiritual focus of work. In general, the goals of therapy at any point of entrance into the patient's material are forgiveness of others, acceptance of oneself, and realization of one's soul path, along with patterns that constitute stumbling blocks to following it. These broad-spectrum concerns are especially visible at the time of the various past-life deaths.

When a terminal patient in the current lifetime is open to deep exploration, there are a variety of transpersonal and altered-state techniques available that focus on helping him/her shift to a heightened state. Culturally induced fear of death can be modified by working through past-life deaths and then progressing to death in the current lifetime. In this way death becomes comforting and reassuring, and this opens up an increased perspective on the nature of that person's soul journey. In Chapter IX of this volume Pecci and Loehr provide examples of such progression.

I believe that those dying will increasingly desire such a heightening. My experience with Rhoda was profound for me as well as for her. In about eight months and in fewer than a dozen sessions she underwent a transformation that changed her death from a disaster into a joyous and fulfilling experience. We used regression, progression, imaging, and dialogue, especially with her body. Our profession needs to come to the place where we are more effective in helping people die. When we help such a heightening to take place, the experience of death will change and anxiety over it will dissolve in the light of increased perception of who we are.

The Transformation of Negative Patterns in Past-Life Death Experiences

by

Roger J. Woolger, Ph.D.

Introduction

Working through the death experience in a past life has two therapeutic aims. First, death, whether traumatic or peaceful, is frequently the locus or point of accumulation of all the negative thoughts, feelings, and sensations of a particular past life. Work needs to be done to express, release, and, it is to be hoped, reverse these psychic residues. This can be done with psychodrama, dialogue, affirmations, or meditation.

Second, when properly handled, the death experience can provide a valuable ritual for psychodramatic healing by virtue of its archetypal structure. Undergoing a visionary death in all its terror and sublimity creates a psychic event of such intensity that it allows an individual to detach consciously from the highly charged programs or samskaras that have accumulated in that or many lifetimes. We undergo a kind of cathartic ego death by virtue of our separation from an intense identification with the secondary personality or other self that has unconsciously been dominating our thoughts and behavior.

The classic Buddhist scripture, the *Dhammapada* expresses the concept that our psychic residues or samskaras determine our lives:

> All that we are is the result of what we have thought: it is founded on our thoughts, it is made up of our thoughts. If a man speaks or acts with an evil thought, pain follows him as the wheels follow the foot of the ox that draws the carriage.... If a man speaks or acts with a pure thought, happiness follows him, like a shadow that never leaves him.[6]

This is the doctrine of karma in its purest form. And it is at the junction of the two major transition points in human existence, birth and death, that there is a heightened intensity of consciousness that makes it possible to perceive the programs or samskaras that determine the course of the lives to come.

The heightened consciousness that occurs at death imprints with exaggerated intensity the dying thoughts, feelings, or sensations on whatever we call the vehicle that transfers our essence from one lifetime to another—soul, spirit, subtle body, or akasha. Frequently these programs will be reactivated during the birth trauma as well, but whether this happens or not, the dying state of awareness will inevitably "fix" the samskara or karmic complex in some form of the transmigrating psyche. Common past-life death scenarios that may become imprinted concern losing parents as a young child, dying from a sudden accident or surprise attack, being betrayed by a lover, or suffering physical accidents or torture. There are numerous variations on these as well as hundreds of other themes. Powerful karma, according to ancient insights, may either be created or relinquished at the moment of death.

Bardo Thodol or *The Tibetan Book of the Dead* is a collection of ritual prayers for the dying, prayers that concern themselves with the possibility of dying consciously.[7] These texts are actually meditations to be made prior to and in preparation for death. A student learns that by meditating on all aspects of death, both before and after, even though he/she is not actually dying, he/she will be fully prepared to undergo eventual death in full consciousness—and possibly will be able to avoid being sucked down by negative programs or samskaras. For most people who do not know how to meditate or who have not learned to remember past lives, moments of understanding in the death process are extremely rare, and because of ignorance and the reactive fears to which the mind is prone, the moment of death is more likely to be one of confusion or panic. Rather than reprogramming the samskaras at the time of death, most people are helplessly drawn once more to imprint old patterns drawn by the compulsive power of karma, and particularly by the thoughts that have again been crystallized at death.

Past-life work provides an alternative. In working through past-life deaths a beginning is made in releasing old and unproductive patterns, and practice is initiated in consciously working through the death process. Therefore, attention to the death experience is of optimum importance in past-life recall. Taking a patient to the point of death and beyond brings a sense of completion, detachment, and often, though by no means always, resolution. It is to be hoped that it will also help to release negative samskaras so that the same disastrous experiences will not have to be re-lived.

Case: The Death and Transformation of Michael

Struggle with negative samskaras is well illustrated in the case of Michael, a man in his thirties who tended to keep his feelings well hidden. Michael remembered life as a woman in New York City in the early part of this century. Unable to find work in the 1920's, the woman ended up as a high-class prostitute, selling her favors to rich business men out of better-class bars. Singlemindedly she hooked a man who fell in love with her, made her his mistress, and married her after he had become divorced. Since she was only out for herself, she finally found that all her material gain counted for very little, a perception that became especially clear when she was dying.

> P: *I'm quite sick and old now. It's pneumonia. I know I am going to die. So does my family. They're all here—my husband and my grown children, Fred, Angela and Minny.... They don't give a damn. They're just going through the motions. Making nice noises. They can't wait for me to go.... Oh, my chest. I can't breathe.... It hurts...I'm very weak. I'm going now.*

Michael evidenced convulsions, coughing, and then went quite limp on the couch.

> T: *What is happening?*
> P: *I'm not there anymore. I seem to have floated above my body. I'm not in it now; no more breathing. Thank God, that's over! My, how they hated me. And I gave them good cause. I manipulated all of them, especially my husband. There, Minny's crying, but she was always sentimental. She didn't care about me any more than the rest. Well, I'm leaving now. It's beginning to seem very far away. I'm floating off somewhere else. Oh, my chest hurts!*
> T: *Look back over your whole life and see how your selfishness arose.*
> P: *Oh, I see myself as a little girl in a tenement in Brooklyn, playing. Mother was bitter. She never had much after Father left. I learned to grab, that you didn't get anything unless you grabbed.*
> T: *Do you blame that little girl?*
> P: *No, I don't blame her. She closed up, like Mother.*
> T: *Is there anything you might say to her now, looking back?*
> P: *Yes, don't close up. Life is hard, but you don't have to become hard-hearted.*

Michael touched his chest, quite unaware of the body symbol, and a new burst of sobbing started.

P: I want to tell them I'm sorry.

T: Good. See your husband and family now. Tell them you are sorry.

P: Please forgive me, Fred, Angela, Minny. And you, Henry, how I used and bullied you! You were really a dear, simple man. I never thanked you for anything. How can you forgive?

T: Ask them.

P: Can you forgive me?... They're smiling. They just couldn't get through to me. Yes, they forgive me. They do.

T: What happens now?

P: I'm in some kind of simple room. It's not on the earth. I've been sent here. I just have to sit and think about my selfishness. How it's still in me.... I'm here for a long time before I come back again.

In past-life therapy this is called the review stage of the life. The separation from his past life that Michael has just experienced is a typical death transition in past-life work. I use this state of detachment to help the departing past-life personality evaluate him/herself within the context of that life. In this case I had Michael take that woman, the woman he had been, back to her childhood defeat in life and have her express the thoughts and feelings unsaid in that life as a whole.

These after-death dialogues are a sort of a psychodrama created by deliberate intervention on the part of the therapist. Sometimes an exchange of recriminations will occur and lead to further conflict in yet other past lives. But when, as with this woman, there is genuine remorse, there can also be genuine forgiveness and repentance. Frequently, when karma releases in this way, there is a remission of physical symptoms associated with blocked emotions. Certainly this man's chest had carried a "frozen heart" memory that was here opening and unburdening.

Communication from the Dead

by

Hazel M. Denning, Ph.D.

Introduction[8]

Contact with the dead is quite common. In all probability such visitations would be perceived more often if people were not so frightened of them. If these experiences were not taboo, the reassurance and information they can give could be accepted readily. Following my lectures I have often had individuals share long-kept family secrets about such visitations, incidents that could have comforted family members when they occurred if the significance of these events could have been recognized as a normal part of human relationships.

These returns from former earth residents serve a variety of purposes. Most commonly the entities want to give reassurance that they are all right, that the state of being beyond death is a good one. They come to comfort a grieving friend or relative. Sometimes they return for the purpose of delivering a last message, or they may return periodically to check on former loved ones. At other times they provide information that they feel is of benefit to those left on earth.

Many people have the potential for this kind of support following the loss of a loved one, but since our Western belief system denies the possibility of such contact, millions of individuals are robbed of the solace it could bring. In all the cases I have known, the visiting spirit withdrew immediately when the person visited became frightened. Spirits do not wish to harm or cause distress when they come in response to the suffering of someone they care about. When the one visited shows fear, they immediately withdraw, disappointed that they are not able to give the comfort or help they are capable of sharing.

Evidence seems to indicate that such entities are spiritually knowledgeable and have the freedom to come and go at will, from one energy level to another. These are not entities who have failed to make their transition to the next soul phase but instead are those who have completed the transition and return of their free will to perform some service or reassurance to those left behind. Usually they make a single appearance or stay only a limited time.

How do discarnates feel and think? We do not know, but their common intervention suggests that there is no such thing as death as it is commonly accepted. Life in that non-physical dimension is very real, very human. The traditional scientific community is still discrediting all evidence of any reality beyond physical concrete phenomena as they are measured by current standards. However, the evidence of another dimension of consciousness beyond the physical is so overwhelming that I am encouraged to share my experiences with the many who are ready to listen. Perhaps it will help them to be less fearful and more understanding of the paranormal manifestations so prevalent in our society today.

My philosophy was tested when my mother, my son, and my husband made their transitions within a few years of one another. All were dear to me, yet I felt no grief, only a joy for them and a feeling of missing them, as one feels when loved ones move far away. They are still out there though one can't feel or talk with them. My husband's death illustrated a loved one's concern and ability to help when there is sensitivity to communication. Even though there was no doubt in my mind about the continuance of life, it was a source of comfort to me when my husband contacted me an hour after his heart attack on the tennis court and very clearly said, "Honey, I did it, I did it just the way I wanted to." Since tennis was his favorite recreation, it was a perfect way for him to go, for he had always said he did not want to die in bed with tubes in his nose. That contact was a joyous experience for me because it was so real and I felt his happiness at being free.

As I review the years I have spent in investigating this field, I am impressed with the vast scope of knowledge contained in such experiences and with the life-changing effect of this knowledge. Given the possibility that these experiences are valid evidence of another dimension, the information that can be gleaned from them is exciting and challenging. The other dimension has taken on a reality for me that is as valid and normal as the physical world in which we all live. I no longer have any fear of death, and the loss of loved ones means only that they have "graduated" to a freer and happier experience. Missing them is normal, of course, but grieving for them is not possible, for if I love them I am happy for their new-found freedom.

Dramatic changes have occurred in the last few years, and at the present time I know many traditional psychotherapists who have accepted the validity of humanity's spiritual nature and our capacity to move into an exciting new dimension of reality. With this greater understanding and acceptance, many of our current personal and social problems can be resolved. Especially can the comfort and help of departed loved ones be accepted.

The following cases illustrate some purposes of the visitations by those who have died. In all cases the communications were intended to be helpful or reassuring. Often they seemed frightening, but with reassurance those perceiving their spirit visitors were able to take comfort from their appearance. Usually it takes only minimum reassurance to shatter outgrown concepts and allow the experience to be perceived as the gift it really is.

Case 1. Comforting a Grieving Mother

A nine-year-old girl, a second child, sensitive and beautiful, contracted spinal meningitis. The disease paralyzed her digestive tract, and though she was fed intravenously for three months, she slowly starved and wasted away. Her family was devastated and her mother could not control her grief when the child died.

On the third night after the funeral the mother was lying on her bed weeping when she became aware of a presence standing at the foot of her bed. She watched in amazement as the misty form took shape, and there stood her little daughter as real as she had been when alive and wearing what had been her favorite dress. Around her was a bright light, almost like a halo, in which the mother could see other vague figures. The girl spoke in a gentle, loving, but pleading voice. "Mother, please do not grieve for me. I am very happy here. Please let me go." Gradually the vision faded away and the room appeared dark except for some light that came through the window from the street lamp.

The mother felt a profound sense of peace pervade her body like a benediction. She began to ask why this lovely child with such a sweet nature had been cut off from life so young. But as she traced the little girl's life she became aware of the pain the child had endured. When she had been three years of age the family had moved to an undeveloped isolated wilderness area in Michigan and the child had been afraid of animals and of the harshness of their life there, and most of all she feared her father, who as an authoritarian man demanded instant obedience from his children. This little girl had suffered harsh physical punishment on numerous occasions. As the mother recalled this and other incidents, she felt a deep sadness and guilt for not having intervened. Both her other two children had seemed to be stronger and more able to cope. For a period of time the mother felt mesmerized, as though she could see the whole scenario, how the little girl could not handle the pain in her life. One particular beating had seemed to break the child's spirit and she had never been the same following it. The powerful images concluded with a feeling that her daughter had wanted to leave her harsh earth life and be free, and this perception reduced the pain of her grief. After that the mother made a real effort to be happy for her daughter.

When questioned, the mother could recall no other time when she had manifested any kind of extrasensory experience. Years after this event she reported that it was still very clear and she was certain her daughter's spirit had communicated an explanation for her departure in order to relieve her mother's pain. Fortunately, this mother did not react to her visitation with fear, as so many others do, and she was able to receive the insight and comfort that her child brought her.

Cases 2 and 3. Visitations to Provide Reassurance

The first of these two cases concerns a young woman to whom her father appeared. She was one of those who felt that such a visitation implied mental derangement. She became terrified and sent her husband to get me. I found her in her car, crying hysterically. She told me she had been at home, sitting on the sofa crying because she and her husband had quarreled and she was afraid their marriage was not going to work. Suddenly she felt a presence and looking up saw her father standing a few feet from her. He looked perfectly normal and as real as if he were a physical body. He smiled at her and said, "It's all right, dear, don't cry. It is going to be all right." She had screamed in terror and he had instantly disappeared.

From her point of view there could be no explanation other than that she was losing her mind. I assured her that this wasn't so and told her that I knew many people who meditated, attended classes, and tried very hard to have the kind of experience that she had had naturally. I emphasized the fact that many people experience such encounters, and I described how some people are more sensitive than others. She knew me and had confidence in what I said and very quickly became calm. We talked for an hour about her fears regarding her marriage and about death and survival. She let go of her fear and was comforted that her father still cared for her and had appeared in order to alleviate her fears. This experience opened new doors for her and her husband, and they both accepted that life was more than a physical dimensional world. As far as I know, she had no more encounters with a spirit, but many years later I found her to be still interested in transpersonal subjects.

The second case concerns a young woman who was not afraid when she experienced a similar visitation. She was enrolled in one of my para-psychology classes and had attended two sessions when her father became ill and died. A major purpose of my classes has been to acquaint students with the life-death process and help them understand the cyclical nature of life. Birth on earth is death in the spiritual dimension, and death on earth is birth in that other realm. The idea that life ends with death is a tragic myth to which many people have adhered for centuries. It probably causes more anguish than any other belief.

When my young friend attended my class for the third session, she asked to speak with me alone. She was smiling and announced that she wanted to thank me for those first two sessions. They had given her a new view of death, and when the doctor told her that her father was dying, she had sat by his bed in the hospital, held his hand, and lovingly told him it was okay for him to go and she would be all right. She assured him of her love and thanked him for being such a wonderful father to her. He had died happily, holding her hand.

The day after his death she was working in her kitchen when she sensed a presence. Turning around she saw her father a few feet from her. Only his torso and head were materialized as though he had no lower body, but the upper part was as real as a person in the flesh. She had started toward him to embrace him, but he smiled and vanished. She had the feeling that he simply wanted to assure her of his after-death reality. She said that prior to attending the class she had been afraid of death and would have been emotionally upset when her father died. She was convinced that she had been prompted to take the class so that she would be better prepared for his departure.

Case 4. Communicating Information about One's Identity

A client who attended my class once shared with me a strange psychic experience that her husband had concealed for years because at the time he had suffered ridicule and rejection by peers and reprimands from his parents and did not want anyone to consider him "different." However, he felt a need to share it and felt I would understand.

When he was fourteen he lived in a small rural town and worked in a mortuary, running errands, sweeping, and doing odd jobs for the mortician. One day a car accident took the lives of an entire family of seven, and within hours a man died of a heart attack in a local hotel room. The mortuary was not staffed to handle so many people so the mortician instructed the boy to put the body of the man in the refrigerator. As he wheeled the body he could not resist the temptation to look at the man, so he lifted the cover and stared at the dead face. He had never seen a dead person before, and this direct contact made him uncomfortable.

That night when he was in his room preparing for bed a figure materialized before him, and he recognized the man he had seen in the mortuary. The appearance was so terrifying that he could not move. The first words the spirit uttered were reassuring. He begged the boy not to be afraid but to listen. He proceeded to explain that his identification had been stolen with his wallet and he was distressed that his family would not know what had happened to him. He explained that he was a traveling salesman and lived in another state, and he gave the boy his family's name and address, begging him to notify his family of what had happened. As the spirit explained his distressing situation, the boy's fears diminished and he agreed to try to contact the man's family.

When the visitor disappeared the boy tried to sleep but the thought of telling his parents made him afraid. They would certainly accuse him of lying or would pronounce him crazy. In the morning he decided to tell them after all, feeling that he had important evidence in the address and name unless this proved to be false information. He did tell his parents and after much discussion they decided to tell the mortician, who was skeptical but took the name and address and successfully located the man's family.

If the situation had ended there, all would have been well, but the story got out and for months the family was persecuted. The boy was shunned and made fun of at school and rocks were thrown at his home. Obscenities were painted on the fence, and the townspeople avoided the family. When the incident reached the psi researchers at Duke University and a representative was sent to interview the family, they had grown weary of the harassment and they refused to talk. The incident was eventually forgotten and life returned to normal—as normal as life can be when one feels "different."

Case 5. Legal Help from the Grave

Numerous stories have come to my attention about husbands who have returned to assist their wives with the legal and financial problems that frequently follow the death of a family provider. One that I encountered in my own investigations involved a gentle lady, the epitome of the helpless female, who knew nothing about business. Her husband treated her as if she were his most cherished possession and provided her with a housekeeper. She had many friends and enjoyed a busy social life, with no real responsibility, including no children to occupy her time. She was unprepared to take the responsibility of her own affairs when her husband died of a heart attack.

Shortly after the funeral she lay in her bed weeping, feeling abandoned, when she felt a presence in the room. At first she was frightened, since the housekeeper was out of the house and she was alone. Then she saw her husband standing at the side of her bed. He looked at her sadly and assured her that she had nothing to fear—he had come to help her. She wondered if she were going crazy, but his presence carried a powerful energy of love and support, and her panic subsided as she listened to him explaining to her in a practical way where she would find his will, what lawyer to call, and where the key to their safe deposit box was kept. He went on to explain that his business had suffered some reverses in recent months and she would have to give up their large home and live in smaller quarters. Her income would no longer support a maid and he was sorry but she would have to learn to cook for herself. He promised to stay with her until everything was settled and she was knowledgeable about her affairs and could manage alone.

She discovered resources within herself that she had not known she possessed, and to her surprise she found it challenging and satisfying to be doing something that had significance. She faced her situation courageously, salvaged what she could from the business, and invested enough to give her a small regular income. She had never worked for a salary and had no marketable skills, so she sold her home and rented a small house, furnishing it with her most cherished possessions and selling the rest.

For a number of weeks when new decisions had to be made, she would sit down and ask her husband for help. He would generally appear, but at times she felt his presence and with her eyes closed could hear his voice as though he spoke to her mind. Then one day he told her that she no longer needed his help. She was doing well and knew everything about their business that she needed to know to handle her life alone. He said goodbye and reassured her of his love. She felt his energy leave her. For a moment the room felt empty and she was afraid, but the panic reaction left when she told herself that she was all right and she could take care of herself.

My church was close to where she had moved, and she came there because she did not drive. When I met her she was involved in making new friends and creating meaningful activities to occupy her time. Most of her old friends were no longer interested in her now that she was "poor." She laughed as she said this, adding that she was really richer, for she had now found people who really cared about her. She had decided that losing her money was the best thing that had happened to her because she had found things that money could not buy. "The people in this church opened their hearts to me when I came with my pain," she said. "They have given my life new meaning, and I have never been so happy."

She continued to be active in that church and was much involved in its program and had many friends there. I never saw her when she was not smiling and expressing a contagious enthusiasm for whatever she was doing. In cases such as this where the spirit returns and makes a specific contact with the loved one, the grieving period is often considerably reduced.

Spirit Visitations

by

Barbara P. Lamb, M.S., M.F.C.C.

Introduction

Spirit visitations do happen. They are experienced by countless numbers of people: by those acquainted with the possibility and even wishing for the occurrence, by those who have never believed in such a possibility, and by those who continue to consider any visitation they have had "anomalous" and not worthy of mention. Douglas Richard, Ph.D, professor and researcher of anomalous phenomena at Atlantic University, Virginia Beach, Va., states that according to a 1990 Gallop poll of the general United States population, twenty percent have experienced communicating with the dead.[9] In an Association for Research and Enlightenment conference survey, fifty percent of the group had seen an apparition.

A spirit visitation is defined, for our purpose, as "being approached and contacted, in some noticeable and definitive way, by the ongoing spirit of a person who has died." The person being approached, the recipient, feels impacted, impressed by the experience, and has little or no doubt about the reality of its having happened, regardless of his belief system or openness to this type of occurrence. The visit seems to serve a purpose and usually makes a difference to the recipient. It may even change the recipient's perspective on life and death. It often helps the grief process of the recipient and instills hope (sometimes reassurance) of his own continuance after death.

Spirit visitations are usually quite brief, at least in our awareness. They seem to come and go suddenly. Sometimes they happen without our being aware of them until we notice some physical evidence that the deceased person must have been there. Visitations are usually made by someone known to the recipient and usually are characterized by a sense of good will and good intent.

This discussion does not include the phenomenon of ghosts or apparitions, who after death seem to reside in the same location for long periods of time, sometimes even for centuries. These beings may be "stuck" in a certain place, having died and having failed to go into the appropriate next dimension. This discussion also does not include entities, earthbound souls who attach to people after dying, often for many years or the rest of the host's lifetime, instead of going "into the light" (into the next dimension).

We become aware of spirit visitations through our various senses. We may see a vivid image of the deceased person with our eyes closed or see the deceased person with our eyes open. Several people may independently see the spirit person in different locations, shortly after the person has died or they may hear the voice of the deceased inside their heads (telepathic hearing) or in the room. They may hear sounds in the immediate environment (tinkling bells, footsteps, knocking, rapping, clicking of a telephone, a child's laughter, a baby's cry). They may smell a scent associated with the deceased person (flowers, perfume, tobacco, aftershave lotion, cooking smells, etc.) or kinesthetically become aware of the deceased, feeling unusual body sensations—the "presence" of the deceased (unusual vibrational sensations, changes in warmth and coolness in the immediate environment, or being physically touched).

We can notice physical evidence of the deceased being present or of having recently been present. For example, without any visible cause, things may get moved, even broken, in front of us or when we are not present. We sometimes perceive with a combination of our senses. With some people there is an intuitive knowing that the deceased person is present, visiting in the form of a live bird or animal who carries the distinct sense of the presence of the person.

Spirit visitations happen in a variety of situations and states of consciousness. Sometimes they occur during sleep. The recipient has a vivid dream of the deceased person being strongly present or having a clear encounter. The recipient may hear a clear message from the deceased. He may feel a strong sense of presence of the deceased, even to the extent that he is awakened. He may have a strong visual image of the deceased or may even be transported mentally or astrally to other planes where the spirits are. Visitations may happen when a person is sitting quietly alone thinking, reading, listening to music, writing a letter, or simply musing. They can happen when doing "mindless activities" such as driving, washing dishes, vacuuming, or working in the garden. They can happen when not even thinking about the deceased person. Or, on the contrary, they can be invited, invoked by directing full attention to the deceased, holding an image of him, calling his name, and urging him to come. Visitations sometimes happen to the family and friends of a person suffering deep grief, instead of being noticed by the grieving person himself. Visitations can be facilitated by competent psychic mediums, who pass on to the recipient what they hear and sometimes see of the spirit person.

Usually a visitation happens after we know the person has died. However, sometimes it occurs before the recipient knows about the person's death. It can also happen before the death has taken place, perhaps as a foreshadowing or preparation about the impending death. A visitation can emerge spontaneously when the recipient is lost, when lonely, when feeling needy, and especially when asking for help.

I became interested in spirit visitations in 1968 when to my great astonishment I was visited by my favorite aunt, who had died three years earlier. Late one evening, while reading alone in my house, I felt a strong sense of the presence of someone in the room. I looked across the room and saw my aunt sitting in an easy chair and looking at me with a kindly expression on her face. Never having known that such a thing could happen, I was startled, shocked, frightened, and yet delighted and thrilled. The clear and distinct visual image of my aunt appeared to be physically real. All of the details of her clothes, hair, jewelry, and expression were exactly as I had remembered her. At the time I had no cognitive framework for thinking about or talking about this experience and kept it to myself for a few years. Eventually I attended a seminar on "The Naturalness of the Supernatural," in which my experience was validated by Diane Kennedy Pike and others present.

Since that time I have heard testimonies regarding spirit visitations from numerous people: friends, acquaintances, family members, and clients in my psychotherapy practice. Each person seems to appreciate having his experience acknowledged and accepted and knowing that there are countless others who have similar experiences.

I, too, have continued to have spirit visitation experiences. The image of my father's face appeared to me vividly, happily, radiantly, during a group meditation five weeks after he had died. I could telepathically hear him declare, "This is absolutely great!" A year later he surrounded me with a strong presence and enthusiastic words while I sat in meditation on the top of the Great Pyramid in Giza, Egypt. With my eyes closed I did not see him, but I joyously felt him and heard him. My mother telepathically spoke to me while I was packing up her belongings a few days after she had died. Seven weeks later she spoke to me for twelve minutes straight through a psychic medium. She gave evidence of having visited me at least several times since her death, unbeknown to me, by mentioning specific details of the home I had found and bought and redecorated since she had died.

The following true experiences will illustrate some of the purposes for which spirit visitations seem to happen:

Case 1.   Saying Goodbye and Giving Reassurance

During World War II a couple sent their young son off to war. They received letters from him regularly and knew he was far away. Suddenly one evening he appeared in his parents' bedroom, looking physically solid and real. He said, "I just came to tell you and Dad goodbye and I love you." His mother asked how long he could stay, assuming he was on furlough, and he answered, "Not long. I don't have much time." She begged him to wait for his father to come out of the shower and see him, but he insisted, "I have to go now. I can't wait. I just came to say I love you both very much." Then he disappeared as suddenly as he had appeared. Two days later the parents received official notice that he had died on Iwo Jima two hours before his visit.

Case 2.   Giving Warning or Preview of a Coming Death

A young woman washing dishes in her kitchen suddenly saw and heard the father of her best friend who lived two thousand miles away. The father emphatically urged her to call his daughter right away. "She'll be really needing you now!" He disappeared and the young woman called her friend. Her friend received her call with surprise and with great appreciation, for she had just learned that her dear father had suddenly died.

Case 3.   Reassurance about Continuation of the Soul

My daughter's best friend died of leukemia when they were age fourteen. A year later the friend appeared vividly and impactfully in my daughter's dream, looking healthy and radiant. She told my daughter, "I know you all think I died, but I really *didn't* die. There is *no* such thing as death." She smiled broadly and disappeared.

Another teenage girl lost her mother to cancer. A week or so after the death she saw her mother floating across the ceiling, in a beautiful long, flowing dress, smiling happily, looking radiant, and throwing a loving kiss.

Case 4.   Physical Evidence of Survival

A friend's husband died and later indicated his presence by leaving a wet, crumpled-up washcloth on the bathroom sink, behavior about which she had chided him many times during their 35 years of marriage. No one else was in the house, and she knew it had been left by her husband.

In another case an older man visited his family's gathering on the night of his funeral. He pushed over a standing lamp and lifted his favorite picture of a tiger off the hook on the wall and dropped it on the floor. A year later, during his widow's session with a psychic medium, the deceased husband confirmed that he himself had moved those objects, in order to get the family's attention and impress upon them his presence.

Case 5. Helping Loved Ones through Grieving

A 68-year-old woman remained inconsolable for more than a year over the loss of her husband. Through a psychic medium the deceased husband reassured her of his survival and complete well-being. He encouraged her to "live again." "Buy the beautiful flowers which you love, and plant the whole back yard the way we had planned to do. Enjoy the beauty." He told her to "contact our old friend Andy. He'll be a good companion for you. He'll take you out and around and help you to enjoy life again." He reassured her of his love and comfort. "Just know that I come and kiss your cheek every night when you get into bed, and I am loving you all through the night."

Case 6. Warning about Danger

A young woman sound asleep in a hotel room was awakened by the sensation of a hand gently brushing her cheek. It felt like the kind of touch her deceased father used to give her, and she awoke with a strong sense of her father's presence. In a moment she noticed that her room was on fire. She felt convinced that her father in spirit form had awakened her so that she could protect herself and escape from the fire.

Case 7. Bringing Important Messages

A woman in her mid-40's was visited by her 22-year-old son who had languished in a complete coma for two years before dying. During those two years he had shown no signs of awareness of her presence, yet she had continued to visit him every day. In his visitation he assured her that he had been aware of every one of her visits to him in the hospital and that each visit had meant a great deal to him, even though he had not shown any signs of recognition. This information was important for her and might be of assistance to other people visiting loved ones in comas.

Case 8. Keeping a Previous Agreement

A female psychologist had a male client who told her that he had been diagnosed as having a terminal disease that would end his life within three months. She asked him to let her know when he had made his transition to spirit life, and he agreed. A month or so later, while visiting her sister's home in another part of the country, she "felt someone step into the kitchen." She turned around quickly and "saw a flash of someone." She had strong thoughts of her client and noticed the clock on the wall was registering 9:30 a.m. Days later, back at home, she called his family and learned that he had died at exactly 9:30 a.m. on the day she had seen him.

Case 9. Anticipating the Future

A young married woman in the Midwest was visited by her deceased father, who told her emphatically, "It's time for you to have another baby, this time a girl. Don't waste any time!" Soon thereafter she did conceive and eventually gave birth to a baby girl. During the pregnancy her husband was killed in an accident.

A middle-aged woman going through a difficult divorce property settlement was strongly urged by her deceased father to open her husband's briefcase. She resisted, on the principle of never having snooped into his private affairs. Her father kept insisting, and "*made* me open the briefcase." Therein she found important papers proving he was withholding significant hidden financial assets.

Case 10. Completing Unfinished Business

A blizzard raged during the few days of my mother's funeral and family gathering, and we were unable to drive three hours to the family plot for her burial. We left her ashes sitting on the mantel in her empty home while I returned to my children and work in California for several weeks. Wishing to explain to her abut her ashes remaining in the unattended house, I set aside time to deliberately invoke her presence in a quiet, private place. I closed my eyes, called each of her names, visualized her face, and invited and urged her to come to me. After concentrating in these ways for several minutes, I experienced a strong sense of being with her and of our talking together and completing our unfinished business about the ashes and about other items. It was also a joyous, loving encounter, which helped my grieving.

My deceased mother knew, in her spirit state, that my brother and I were confused about which one of us should keep her lovely engagement ring and other pieces of jewelry. In a visitation through a medium she told me to find a little yellow note in her safe deposit box in a particular bank. When we followed her directions, we found the note and her instructions for the distribution of her jewelry, which cleared up our confusion safely and surely.

Case 11. Explanations

An elderly man who had promised his grown daughter that he would visit her after dying did not appear until two years after his death. When he finally made the contact he apologized, "I'm sorry I took so long to get back to you.... I was having such a great time that I just didn't get to it."

A deceased mother-in-law visited the wife of her son and apologized for having treated her so shabbily during her life. She explained that the reason she had been so negative and full of suffering was that a karmic situation stood between them from the previous lifetime. This mother-in-law has continued, after that visitation, to be a helpful guide to the daughter-in-law, especially in regard to setting up and running a business.

Conclusions

These cases suggest that for a variety of purposes spirits visit people they have left behind. They seem to want to be seen, heard, recognized, and accepted for who they are. They want to reassure us about their continuance after death and give us hope about ours. They seem eager to let us know that the love relationship and caring continue, even after death. They want to complete unfinished business. They want to be remembered. They want to help us, guide us.

The fact that some people are not aware of experiencing visits from deceased loved ones may be due either to the variance in people's receptivity to the phenomenon or to the variance in the "sending power" of the deceased. It takes intense concentration and energy for a deceased person to show himself through sight, sound, or kinesthetic means, and the energy lasts only a brief time. If this effort does not coincide with quiet receptivity on the part of the recipient, the visitation will not be registered.

The lack of appearances by the deceased should not be interpreted as a lack of caring. Many factors may intervene, and the spirit, who most likely is going back and forth between his spirit dimension and our physical dimension with some frequency, may care sincerely about the recipient. For anyone who wishes to have contact with someone who has died, it seems helpful to cultivate quiet, private time, focus on the person, and remain in a state of receptivity.

Death Comes to Marie-France

by

Chet B. Snow, Ph. D.

Introduction

During the years I have been commuting between the United States and France I have made friends and lost track of many Parisians, but an exception was Marie-France, who remained a valued friend for over twenty years. As a well-known jazz pianist she followed the vagaries of my changing career, from graduate student at the Sorbonne to researcher for the U.S. Air Force, and finally to regression therapist and researcher into past-life experiences.

Marie-France had undergone a lengthy psychoanalysis and from her long experience in introspection became interested in the idea of other lifetimes and the survival of the soul beyond physical death. This interest led her to do a session with me in which she discovered a recent past existence as a black New Orleans prostitute who had been a mistress to one of that city's noted Dixieland musicians, a brief liaison that ended tragically when she, as that girl, committed suicide following the break-up experience. Haunting fears of self-inflicted violence, along with a lifelong adulation of New Orleans and its "pure" jazz style, had dominated her current French life.

Back in Paris, I spent time this year with Marie-France, though not as much as before, for she had suffered a stroke two years before and lived in semi-retirement, leaving her apartment only for occasional musical appearances. Nonetheless, we spoke often by telephone and had occasional visits, and upon my return to France after a month's research foray to the United States in May, I was taken aback when I was not able to reach her by phone. After a few attempts I sent her a post card telling her to call me when available, but in my busy schedule I forgot about my request.

A week later I received a letter from Roland, Marie-France's nephew, containing the sad news that a new stroke had put her back in a Paris hospital, where she lay in a coma and paralyzed. At first there had been a few moments of lucidity when she had shown recognition of her family and friends by eye movements, but in recent weeks she had been inert, kept going by various respiration machines and supported by a strong heart, a condition which, Roland explained, could possibly go on for months. I wanted to see Marie-France, even in her comatose state, and phoned at once for the hospital address and visiting hours.

I had just come from a seminar where methods of contacting the soul entities of those who have died had been outlined, and I felt it should be even easier to get in touch with the spirit or mind of my dear friend whose body, aided by medical science, was still functioning. Also, as a trained hypnotherapist and regular meditator, I knew that in an altered state wider ranges of communication are possible than are recognized by "ordinary" consciousness. This seemed an opportunity, not only to test what I had learned but also to help my friend alleviate what must be an unbearable condition—trapped in an inert body kept alive by machines, an often-stated fear after her first stroke.

Several days later on a June afternoon I was at the Labosiere Hospital in her private room at the start of afternoon visiting hours. The nurse told me that it would be possible only to sit with her, as she could not communicate.

Alone with Marie-France I drew up my chair to the side of her bed. She was propped on pillows with tubes sticking in her arms and an oxygen bottle blowing air through a tube into her nose and down her throat. A heartbeat machine measured her pulse. Although her eyes were taped shut, the eyelids fluttered as I approached and the machine recorded several fluctuations in her brain and pulse activity, as if she recognized that someone was there. I stroked her hand and spoke in a soft voice, telling her who was there and adding that I was going to talk with her. When the machine quieted down, I slipped into a trance state and used a favorite "mantra," the Lord's Prayer, spoken in French. (Although I am sure that subconscious communication is possible without a common language, it seemed easier to use French, our normal mode of conscious communication.) Then I just sent her love, all the love I was capable of, for about 10 minutes. Love, Love, amour, amour...

After a time I felt a kind of mental tugging at the corners of my concentration. I felt she was listening. I repeated what I'd said earlier, who I was, that I was sorry not to have known earlier of her stroke and hospitalization and that I was there to help her. First, I asked her to allow her spirit to come out of that inert, useless body so that we could "talk." She seemed surprised but I felt her coming in stronger and I talked on to her real "soul" entity.

As she began to recognize this "soul" entity, her ability to communicate grew. Then I asked her to look over her body and become aware of what was wrong with it, to get in touch with her physical condition and to realize whether or not that body in its current state was repairable or whether she should leave it behind and go on to another state of being. As I let her do this I reminisced with her about the important and positive events of her life as Marie-France. I remembered our first meeting, the first piano piece I'd heard her play at that party and how much it had meant to me and how much I'd enjoyed all the other times we had been together. I reminded her of earlier periods of her life before I'd known her, information gleaned from previous discussions. I talked of her family, friends, and fellow musicians, and of all the love surrounding her here on the earth. Being realistic and honest also meant going over some of the difficult times, and I asked her forgiveness for a couple of our own personal differences from times past. In time I felt her returning love and knew that she had got her spirit up out of the body at last.

Again I asked her to check on the body's condition and to become aware of her options, either to return fully and help her body heal itself or else gradually to detach herself from what was a no longer useful shell. At this point I felt a surge of fear and realized that she was in terror of dying, for somehow, somewhere, her mind clung to the thought that to leave her body in this way would be the equivalent of suicide. Her past-life memory of that previous New Orleans suicide and all the resulting trauma and remorse still clung to her and was keeping her trapped in this comatose form. If she "died" in this way, she felt she would be cut off from all those she knew and loved and would again find herself alone at the end, just as she had been in that past life.

Once I understood that her fear was that to leave her damaged body now would be tantamount to another suicide, it was not difficult to talk it over with her. Her soul was palpably close and eager for help. I explained the difference, to my mind at least, between actively killing a body before its time, i.e., suicide, and freeing oneself from what had become a useless vehicle in order to find new life in other realms. This latter was the normal path, I assured her, and in no way would it "cut her off" from her soul self. Further, I knew that her mother and other deceased loved ones would be there to help her as she made the transition, and I explained what I knew of this passage, using images from the testimony of those who had returned from a "near-death" experience.

At one point I "heard" her ask me to inform a couple of our mutual American friends of her condition, as they would not know otherwise. I promised this. Then I pointed out the strain on her Parisian family and friends of having her hover between life and death in this comatose state, possibly for months. Again and again during this process, which took nearly two hours, I kept sending her reassurance and love that whatever her choice, it would not be "suicide." Eventually I felt Marie-France's mind-spirit calming and fading, as if tired from this new type of exertion. Visiting hours were over. I promised to be in contact very soon and left the hospital after a short closing meditation.

The next few days were busy ones for me as I prepared for an out-of-town lecture trip. I added Marie-France to my evening meditation and tuned in, feeling her still at the hospital and not yet decided, but much more comfortable and no longer in frustration and terror over her condition. A couple of days later I had some time in the afternoon, and although I couldn't go to the hospital I realized that I now could contact Marie-France from anywhere just by going within and calling her.

I did this and again we had a wonderful and warm contact. Although her fears of renewed suicide seemed gone, I felt that she was waiting for something or someone before making her final decision as to whether or not she should detach herself from that tired body. I respected her right to make her own decision and did not press when no further insight came. I did, however, get the distinct impression that she had inspected her brain's damage from the stroke and knew that her passing was just a matter of time. She was preparing for the final push.

The next day I had to leave Paris for another lecture trip. I was absent several days, and although I kept Marie-France in my meditation each night, I didn't tune in again during my absence. Perhaps my own conscious mind somehow was having trouble holding to the belief that such communication was possible in spite of the miles between our bodies. And, as so often happens, other current events replaced my concern over Marie-France.

When I returned to Paris, however, one of my first thoughts was to go back to the hospital. It was a Saturday and I remember that as I considered making the trip there, a nagging feeling came over me that I should call Roland first. But my conscious mind overrode this impulse and so I just showed up at Marie-France's room at the start of visiting hours. The bed was empty and the room silent, all the complex machinery removed. A chat with the floor nurse confirmed my intuition. Two days earlier, while I was out of town, Marie-France had died peacefully, apparently of a sudden heart attack. I felt glad that Marie-France had made her choice so rapidly. I felt sure she had now rejoined her mother and sister. In my meditation that evening I felt her presence close to me but as if in a deep, restful, unaware sleep.

About a week later I had occasion to contact Roland about another matter. He apologized for not calling me but said he had been extremely busy on a film he was producing and never seemed to be at home when he could phone. I told him I knew of Marie-France's passing and asked him exactly when it had happened. He filled in the final details.

Because of the pressures of his work schedule, he had been unable to visit Marie-France for a couple of weeks after his original letter to me and had been unaware of my visit. Finally, one afternoon he found a moment and had made a quick dash to the hospital. He said that when he went into her room it was as if she were waiting for him. Immediately the heart monitor began to fluctuate wildly and her body twitched and shook, but no sooner had he sat down next to her than suddenly everything stopped. The machines went silent and her chest stopped moving. Roland guessed she had had a sudden heart attack, for within a moment she was gone, despite the efforts of the nurses he alerted.

I had my answer. Marie-France had been waiting for Roland and as soon as this last good-bye had been made, she had felt free to leave and begin the passage to a new and, I know, richer, fuller life. I am confident she is even now preparing for her next appearance on earth's schoolroom stage.

Gentle Birthing into Death

by

Winafred B. Lucas, Ph.D.

Introduction

This account documents how a frantic clutching to life can gradually be transformed into a welcoming of death. In the process the patient, Rhoda, came to understand that on all but the most superficial levels of her consciousness she wanted to die and that this was all right. She came to see that she had done her best in this life and that though she did not feel she had been entirely successful, she had learned what she could learn and was ready to leave.

In the process of coming to this realization Rhoda explored in many modalities. She reviewed this lifetime—her prenatal experiences and birth, her early childhood, and all the losses she had suffered along the way—and she recovered a number of previous lifetimes. The interlives following these lifetimes were experienced not as a time segment following each lifetime, but as an experience of basic wisdom and love to which she could return after each life recall. She was able to review each life from her current soul perspective rather than from her stage of soul development at the time. These deaths and re-evaluations made possible a profound spiritual understanding of her current lifetime so that she came to see it as one meaningful segment in her extended soul's journey.

Her therapeutic process reached a deep level early because in altered states imaging came to her readily. Her vision of the drooping daisy, one that could be revived only by a love she did not have and could not get, was a salient statement that she was not going to recover. Dialogues with her body, with her wish to live and her wish to die, and her inability to find true images of recovery confirmed this.

As we worked together we came to see clearly the aura of uninvolvement and mild depression that had characterized her life and had also shadowed her parents' lives. The relationship with her twin sister held an unstable chameleon quality, as though Rhoda vacillated between resentment of her and indifference. Nor did she express any close bonding with either of her children, though she had provided intermittent support for them when they needed it. Her craving for a father/partner remained so unrealistic that no actual relationship sufficed. But though she achieved no bonding with a core person in this life, she had many stable and supportive long-term professional relationships.

At the end she gained the spiritual insight that a relationship with her Higher Self was what she really wanted, and this perception transformed her and made her able to go ahead to her death, which she entered without reserve. At that time, because the spiritual level of perception she had reached encouraged a new awareness of love and forgiveness, she called her daughter home and died in her arms.

Background

Rhoda was a trim, energetic woman in her mid-fifties, a longtime elementary school teacher on extended sick leave who invited interest and compassion by her courageous presentation of herself. By the time she came to me she had had two surgeries for breast cancer and was running from one alternative treatment to another at the same time that she was undergoing chemotherapy. Her hope in coming to me was that through the use of imaging techniques and past-life work, her body would be induced to give up the cancer.

Her determination to stay alive was apparently the first strong motivation she had experienced in her life. Throughout her childhood, adolescence, and college years she had drifted along without much enthusiasm, giving thought to becoming a psychologist but settling for a teaching credential, dreaming of advanced degrees but contenting herself with the knowledge that she was the only one in her family who had gone to college at all.

Rhoda's lukewarm involvement with life continued the limited motivation evident in the lives of her parents, especially of her father. He had retired from a job that he had always hated and that had led him to become a closet alcoholic, and almost immediately after his retirement he died of a heart attack. Rhoda's comment about this was that he had had "one foot in the grave for 15 years, anyway." In addition to her parents' lack of involvement with life in general, Rhoda perceived them to have had no involvement with their children. She felt that as a child she had been lonely, unloved, and constantly subjected to judgments. She saw her mother as a perfectionist, skilled in producing guilt trips. Negative occurrences, Rhoda had assumed at the time, were her fault. Her twin sister eloped after high school to marry a Pentecostal minister, leaving Rhoda, according to her initial report (which she later changed) "half a person." She appeared to have little warmth for anyone in her family, though toward the end of her therapy she became aware of how as a little girl she had yearned for her father's arms around her.

Rhoda's social life outside her family also had been a desert in the first part of her life. In her teens she had felt shy and unattractive and considered herself lucky if a boy looked at her. In her mid-20's she married a man on whom she had had a crush in high school. Earlier this man had married someone else and then had come to Rhoda after his marriage failed. He had had dreams of becoming an architect but settled for being first a cook and then a successful owner of several restaurants. In his pursuit of success he immersed himself for many years in a frenetic work schedule, which kept him away from home for many hours, especially in the evenings when Rhoda was free from teaching, so that she constantly felt alone. They had a son and daughter, but because Rhoda's need for attention from her husband had escalated as the result of his constant absences, she began to accompany him when he traveled, often leaving her children behind. At her husband's suggestion she attempted to save her marriage by agreeing to a four-way ménage, which backfired when her husband began an exclusive affair with the other woman, who had been her best friend. Rhoda became acutely distressed and left the marriage, though until her death she continued to socialize with her former husband and her friend, who eventually married.

Understandably, during this time the children felt neglected and developed severe behavior problems, including the use of drugs, and left the house when they were in their teens. Rhoda felt alienated from them, but later when they needed money or a place to stay or the use of her house for skiing parties, she always made herself available. However, though she could not establish stable core relationships, during her entire teaching career she easily made and held friends, especially among her colleagues. These friendships provided some nurturing, though never enough.

About three years before our contact, her boy friend, a married man who she hoped would leave his wife and marry her but who never did, discovered a lump in her breast. She took time having this checked, and when the physician suggested a biopsy, she announced she was about to go bird-watching in Alaska and would come in later. On returning, she had the biopsy, which indicated that the lump was cancerous. A surgeon suggested immediate surgery but Rhoda took her time and went to Australia first. Following the surgery, which disclosed that the cancer had spread, she had extensive chemotherapy and attended imaging workshops that she assumed would reverse the cancer. She was surprised and jarred when they did not. A second surgery, followed by extensive chemotherapy, relieved the symptoms temporarily, especially the fluid in her lungs, but it was evident that the cancer was spreading. Determined to become well, she began a series of pilgrimages to every healer whose name she came across.

Initial Exploration

As I listened to Rhoda's account, it seemed clear that on one level she had not wanted to live, but her insistence on her wish to recover was so strong that I could only gradually help her uncover this deeper attitude. Since two years of holistic workshops had made her knowledgeable about imaging and dialogue techniques, I suggested that she dialogue with her body and see what it had to say. In the dialogue her focus on health resulted in many parts of her body claiming to be in good shape: her feet reported that they were okay, her legs complained that they wanted to be walking more out in nature, her stomach appreciated her effort at good nutrition, and her arms had no complaints. However, other areas gave hints that turned out to be connected with her cancer.

> T: *What is your sexual area telling you?*
> P: *It feels deprived. It feels like I need a partner.*
> T: *And does your heart have a message?*
> P: *It feels like it wants to cry.*
> T: *Perhaps you could ask it a little more about that.*
> P: *Partly I want a male partner, somebody to share with. There's a little girl in there and she's sad. She needs more love. (This was the first clue that linked father and partner.)*
> T: *Do the lungs have a message?*
> P: *They're real tight. Real, real tight. They are saying to my legs that I can't walk very much right now. My legs are real tight.*
> T: *What about your jaw?*
> P: *I think I've been gritting my teeth: "I'm going to beat this!" I've never been a fighter, but now I am.*

Images of Cancer

Rhoda had been using the Simonton method of imaging for healing cancer,[10] and at our next session we explored in an altered state her images for the cancer, for her immune cells, and for chemotherapy. I took her into a deepened state by way of her first experience of an inner garden. She easily imaged a colorful garden with a profligate spread of wildflowers of all colors and defined beds of red and yellow roses. There were trees and grass and a deep pool, and she saw and heard a gushing fountain. In this deeply relaxed setting she shared with me her image of the cancer cells.

> P: *They're insects, maybe ants. Not very strong. Weak—they're weak.*
> T: *And what image do you find for your immune cells?*
> P: *Knights with lances.*

T: *How would the knights deal with the ants?*

P: *Clean them up and carry them out...or maybe step on them.*

T: *Have you an image for chemotherapy?*

P: *Might be like a spray of light. Ants are dark. Dark ants. Ants like the aphids on roses, so we have to get rid of the aphids.*

T: *What do aphids suggest to you?*

P: *Not knowing my direction. Not knowing how to play. Wanting a partner (escalating anger in her voice)! I'm angry about that. And I'm worried about health and wealth...and I need to be strong.*

T: *Perhaps being too strong, like the knights, isn't exactly what you need now.*

P: *(Tears.) I need to be a gardener. My dad was a gardener.*

T: *Can you call your father and ask him for some advice?*

P: *He says I should spray the aphids with something appropriate.*

T: *Can he suggest anything?*

P: *He gives me some candy and it turns golden. I put it in a bubble and it floats up. The color of the ants is gold now. The bubble goes out over the forest and settles down in a wild natural setting.*

Rhoda's images did not fit together and could not act as an effective tool against the cancer. Knights with lances can scarcely kill ants, and the use of light is not much more appropriate. The symbolism of the aphids and the golden candy and associations to them are confusing. "Knights with lances" is an image found in the literature, suggesting the possibility that Rhoda had borrowed it and therefore it was not specific enough to her situation to be effective. Her complaints about not knowing her direction and not knowing how to play are also common in the literature about cancer. The images reflected Rhoda's confusion in dealing with the disease process. The expression of anger, though not tied into the images, seemed the most charged with meaning for her.

In order to move her out of her confusion I suggested that she return to the garden and kneel beside her pool and look into it and report what she saw. She went unprompted into a past life.

First Regression

P: *Darkness, nighttime. A small boy, rough. It's like an alley, a curved kind of opening, like the Kasbah. A beggar boy, dark, barefoot, dirty. His clothes are ragged and kind of homespun. He's hiding from someone. He's afraid. He doesn't have a home.*

T: *When did you become a beggar boy?*

P: *I was cast out, not wanted. My mother was very young, not married. Her parents beat her. They didn't want me or want anybody to know about me. They mistreated my mother—they beat her and she died and they put me over a wall. And an old lady picked me up and raised me for a while, but she died when I was five and I've been alone ever since.*

T: *How do you manage?*

P: *I steal food and I'm hungry a lot. I sleep on the street wherever I can sleep. I'm hiding in this alley because somebody on horseback...the police...they want to get rid of me.*

T: *Do they catch you?*

P: *No—I'm too smart for that.*

I took her ahead to the next important incident in that lifetime and she related how the beggar boy, in order to keep away from the guards, eventually went out in the country and while passing through a village was offered the chance to work in the fields. The family he worked for gave him a home and gradually accepted him as one of them. He and the daughter of the family fell in love and were married and had two children. The parents had at first disapproved, but their animosity dwindled as their son-in-law began to provide well for them.

T: *When do you die? Go to that time.*

P: *Feels like it's old age—my wife is younger and sits by my bed. The children are grown and are away.*

T: *What is your last thought?*

P: *My wife is sorry to see me go. I'm leaving. It's exciting to go on.*

T: *You are leaving your body now.*

P: *Goodbye. I'm glad to leave you. You've held me down. It feels better to be up here in the Light.*

T: *From this perspective can you notice patterns that were the same or different from those in your current lifetime.*

P: *It's different because his marriage worked. He had companionship and I don't. It's the same because we're both strong. He was able to take care of himself, and so am I. I wasn't thrown out as a child, but my father didn't give me anything emotionally, and my husband didn't give me support when I was married. The men in my life have not given me what I want. (Her voice quavers.)*

It seemed strange that if that former lifetime had turned out as well as Rhoda reported it to have done, she should have been happy to leave it and that remembering it triggered her anger over lack of male support in this lifetime.

Second Phase of Exploration: the Theme of Loss

Image for Her Current Life

In the next session we explored the period of her life lived since she discovered her cancer. We began by seeking for an image of that time.

P: *I see a wilted flower. It droops. The leaves and petals are withering. It's bent over, limp. The colors are faded. It's a daisy—white with a yellow center. The yellow is mustardy.*

T: *What was the daisy like before the cancer?*

P: *Real perky.*

T: *What happened?*

P: *It didn't get water.*

T: *Is it dead?*

P: *Not dead yet. It needs water.*

T: *Will it get water.*

P: *Not unless someone gives it some.*

T: *Can you image that?*

P: *Yes. It's coming up straight. I don't know if the water will bring back the color of the center.*

T: *Look and see if it does.*

P: *It looks yellow right now. Its leaves are spurting upwards. The petals are straightening out—pointing outward.*

T: *What is the water in your life?*

P: *Love. But I don't have any.*

Rhoda then retraced the events of this period, focusing on her return for the biopsy and discovery of the cancer. She had put off surgery, taking the trip to Australia first, and finally had a mastectomy and reconstructive surgery. Two weeks after the operation she had returned to her teaching.

Dialogue with the Body about Cancer

During our next session she had her first dialogue with her body specifically about the cancer, leading into it by a review of her body's history.[11] The most striking experience, in the usual welter of childhood diseases and occasional accidents, was the breach birth of her son, who arrived five weeks early. At this time her husband left and she felt abandoned. Her summing up of her attitude toward her body was ambivalent.

P: *I feel I like my body—like it's good but it's letting me down. I kind of like my body. Most of life I've been judgmental about it. We're not getting along too well right now.*

T: *Perhaps you could ask your body why it got breast cancer.*

P: *It says I let people suck off me.*

T: *What could you learn from this?*

P: *I need to be my own person, stand up for myself.*

Second Regression

Following sessions explored other past lifetimes, all characterized by loss. In the first of these she was a successful merchant-craftsman whose wife was killed by robbers while returning from a visit to a neighboring village. He held onto his grief for the remainder of his life and died from malnutrition as the result of a drought that made his clientele unable to buy from him.

P: *I'm tired, glad to be dying. I'll get to see my wife, be with her.*

T: *You had a lot of sorrow but you lived a good life. What was the lesson of that lifetime?*

P: *To learn to love someone.*

T: *What do that lifetime and this have in common?*

P: *I want to love someone, too. I want to love someone now. And there's something about food and malnourishment and deprivation. I don't have a problem with food, but somehow I feel deprived.*

T: *Are there differences?*

P: *He worked with his hands. His life was simple and mine is kind of complicated.... I have a deep sadness and feeling of deprivation.*

Current Life Exploration

After this, we reviewed the losses of her life, beginning with the period following the breakup of her marriage 14 years before. After 20 years of marriage her husband had become restless, then pressured her to accept the two-couple arrangement and followed this with the affair with her best friend. She tried to adjust but could not and moved in with another friend. In the divorce process she lost her home, which devastated her. Though she bought another house, she never felt rooted again. By her own choice her relationship with her children was tenuous. She felt she had no family at a time when she most needed one.

Moving backward, an earlier significant loss was that of her twin sister during junior college. In spite of difficulties with this sister, when the twin eloped suddenly, Rhoda felt that she had lost half of herself. Her twin sister became immersed in a different lifestyle, had three children, and made no effort to heal the breach.

Childhood losses included constant moving and the absence of close personal affection from her father, especially during adolescence, a period when her father was absent in the service during the war. Talking about this stimulated Rhoda to return to consideration of her husband, who for most of their marriage had worked nights, so that they seldom spent time with each other.

Gradually we deepened Rhoda's perception of events and feelings that she had experienced around the time that the cancer began. She had felt bereft of substantive human caring and at the same time had begun to resent her job, complaining that there wasn't enough time to work with her pupils. She tried to reduce her discontent by taking a sabbatical and traveling to exotic places, by trying out other jobs, by reading extensively, and by developing a new hobby of collecting and selling semi-precious gemstones. During this period, as the result of the many workshops she attended, she began to give Turning Point seminars for teachers and also other workshops in transpersonal areas, and this had become the one area of her life where she felt she really "got high."

Further Regressions: Love and Loss

Third Regression

In order to uncover and deepen Rhoda's understanding of her basic patterns we opened up several further past lives. One of these took her into a lifetime in the early 17th century in France where she was a lonely farm child exploited by three older brothers as a household drudge and farm slave, constantly at their beck and call. She escaped by marrying a gentle man, with whom she had two children. The village was devastated a few years later by an epidemic that caused the death of all her family and finally of herself. Her last thought was that her husband and children would meet her and she wouldn't be alone.

Initial Interlife Experience

Following this, Rhoda made her first excursion into the interlife, which she entered and explored easily. Subsequent interim experiences were similar.

T: *After your family meets, tell me about your next experience.*

P: *There's a really bright personage of some sort and he guides me. He says, "Come with me." I go with him to this big building that looks like a temple, and I look at my life.*

T: *What do you see?*

P: *That I'm strong, that I can overcome difficulties, that life was good.... I'm going to school. It's in a building. There are a lot of us. It's like Plato and Greece—we're gathered around discussing.*

T: *What are you learning?*

P: *About love—it's all around.*

T: *Do you believe that?*

P: *It's always there.*

T: *Is your guide with you?*

P: *Yes—his name is Peter. I knew him in Biblical times. I was a man, too, and we worked together. We fish. My name is John but we're not the ones in the Bible. He owns the boat. I work for him—he's older than I. He's like a big brother. He teaches me about fishing. I look up to him. He's very wise, very practical, just but firm.*

T: *Have you ever seen Jesus?*

P: *He was supposed to be where we were but he didn't come. People expected him.*

This is the first appearance of the concept that "love is all around," a lesson that Rhoda needed to learn in order to deal with her persistent feeling of rejection and loss.

Fourth Regression and Interlife

In her next regression Rhoda delved deeper into the nature of loss, which had begun to emerge clearly as her core issue. When he was a trapper befriended by the Cheyenne Indians, Jacques Duval fell in love with the chief's daughter, whom he had met picking berries. The tribe objected to the marriage and Jacques had to fight the girl's brother.

P: *He's very strong, but so am I. A lot of people are there. I have to be careful because if I hurt her brother, that's bad, but if I lose, that's bad, too.*

Jacques got a winning hold on the brother, shaming him, and then took the girl to a hut in the forest, but several nights later the brother sneaked up on him with a knife and killed him.

T: *What is your last thought about that life?*
P: *I'm thinking about wife, losing her. I really loved her and I didn't want to lose her.*
T: *Go through your death.*
P: *I'm looking down on our small hut and on my grieving wife. She's very sad, distraught. She goes back to her tribe—not right away but when the baby is due—a boy.*
T: *Do you sense the lesson in this life?*
P: *To love other people. To open to others' personalities, people with different belief systems.*
T: *How was that life like this one or different from it?*
P: *I was loving with people with a different set of beliefs—probably not so much now. He was alone a lot, and I'm alone a lot. He was able to get along with everyone and so am I.*
T: *Does this have anything to do with your cancer?*
P: *It's the loss of a loved one.*
T: *How might one heal loss?*
P: *I need to change my mind about it. Loss is a part of living.*
T: *If you ask your Higher Self about it, what does it say?*
P: *It tells me loss is not real. I need to accept loss as a part of living.*
T: *How does that feel at a gut level?*
P: *It hurts.*
T: *Can you say anything to help Jacques?*
P: *It's okay, Jacques. You'll meet her again in another life.*
T: *Was there a lifetime before that had to do with your life as Jacques?*
P: *Yes...it's Greece. I see a short white tunic. I'm a young boy about 12. I see a beautiful woman, tall and regal. My mother. She's very kind and gentle and intelligent.... Oh, something terrible is happening to her. They're stoning her!*
T: *Why?*
P: *For adultery. She was in love with someone who wasn't available to her. It's terrible! My father threw the first stone. I love my mother!*

The mother was buried in a cemetery for paupers and her son grew up angry at the townspeople and alienated, shutting off all his feelings. He lived a long life as an apothecary and died alone after taking poison.

T: *What was your last thought?*
P: *I'm leaving this life because I don't want to be here anymore. I'm going to meet my mother. I love you. I've never loved anyone but you.*
T: *What might your Higher Self say?*
P: *It was too bad you couldn't overcome your grief and enjoy the rest of your life. You shut off all your feelings for other people.*
T: *Would you be willing to talk to that father?*
P: *My father in that Greek life was my father now. I would have preferred both of them have shown me more love.... I would have preferred that you*

had held me and given me more attention, but you couldn't, so I have to give up that expectation. I have to accept him. It's hard.

T: *Is there a Being of Light who could give you some help?*

P: *He's saying, "You're a worthy person. You need to be more detached, to love with compassion and detachment and be aware that you must love yourself wholeheartedly." ...I see two lines of light. One helps me with the anger and the cancer and one fills me with love.... Oh, I see that my mother in that lifetime was the girl I loved when I was a trapper.*

Fifth Regression and Interlife

Another lifetime again dealt with loss, Rhoda's constant theme, and again she easily retrieved the interlife and its evaluations. The past life recovered began by the imaging of a sunrise, and this gradually led to her awareness of being a girl of 18 watching cattle over a Swiss mountainside. Her mother had died in childbirth and she had had the care of a younger sister for eight years. Her father was a blacksmith, a stern man who became more and more quiet after his wife's death.

Shortly after the scene in the meadow she married and had a baby girl. She hadn't wanted the child so early and had taken something to induce abortion, which led, she believed, to the child being retarded. Guilt led to despondency and to her husband's infidelity. She didn't want more children, but her husband raped her, and eventually she had three normal and healthy children. Her older son was killed falling off a cliff while trying to rescue a cow, and she felt this was somehow her fault. Finally her husband drank himself to death. By this time the other children were gone—the normal ones had married and the retarded girl lived with her brother.

P: *I'm ready to leave. I wanted to learn compassion with my older daughter but I didn't do too well.... Oh, my loved ones are here to meet me—my husband, my son, and my father. They show me around—it's beautiful! Beautiful color, shiny bright light. A temple—or big square building with stairs leading up.*

T: *Can you see what you're doing?*

P: *You meet your teachers. You look through your lifetime to see how you did. I could have been more compassionate to my daughter and my husband.*

T: *Does your teacher say anything?*

P: *He tells me that I did the best I could. I need to enjoy the moment. I go to this temple every day for school. In my next lifetime I need to nurture myself. I'm getting ready to come back. Probably I'll be a man.*

Exploring the Dynamics of Her Current Life

Prenatal Period

Being in the timeless zone of the interim state made it easy to move ahead to the time preceding Rhoda's current life and tap into her decisions and motivations.

> T: *Let us go to the state before this lifetime and see how you planned for it.*
> P: *There are four teachers now. I need to work on compassion again. I choose a mother and father I knew before.*
> T: *Why do you select this mother?*
> P: *She kind of enjoys her life—at least, she helped me to enjoy the out-of-doors.*
> T: *And your father?*
> P: *He's real responsible. I think it was time for me to grow up and learn to be who I am instead of what somebody else wants me to be.*
> T: *Let's go ahead to when your mother discovers she is pregnant.*
> P: *At first she's kind of sick so she's not too excited about it. But she wants me. My father does too. It's been five years since my older sister was born and they want another child. It's crowded in here. Someone's pushing. It's crowded tight. (This refers to her twin sister.)*
> T: *What do your parents say to each other while your mother is carrying you?*
> P: *They never had an argument.*

Birth

From there we progressed through her birth experience. Her twin was mentioned only by inference.

> T: *You're about to be born. Can you describe it?*
> P: *I want out! It's real tight! It hurts. It squeezes my head. I really want out!*
> T: *Now you're out.*
> P: *That's a relief! Now I can breathe and move.*
> T: *How do you feel about the world?*
> P: *It's strange and bright and it hurts your eyes, and the doctors's mean to you.*
> T: *Now you're a few months old.*
> P: *It's hard to get enough food or attention. My mother's harassed. She's working as hard as she can but she's overwhelmed.*
> T: *How are you feeling?*
> P: *Kind of like a burden. I feel compassion for my mother—she's having a hard time of it.*

Following this, we progressed in a forward direction through her current life, increasing the scope of old memories and opening up new ones. Early years focused on her feeling of inferiority to her twin, which persisted in spite of evidence to the contrary. She changed one observation she had originally made concerning her twin's elopement. Formerly she had said it had left her "half a person." This time she reported that, "Now I was a whole person, not half a whole." Adult years were fleshed out by more information on her divorce and details of her long-time affairs that had left her feeling deserted and devastated, in spite of the fact that the first man had bought a house with her and had wanted to marry her. She had left him for a second man and bought out the share of the house. The sequence of trips and surgeries and subsequent retirement was reported somewhat differently in this session.

Progress toward Death

Rhoda was by this time in a deep altered state and we proceeded from her current situation to her death in this life.

T: *Let's go ahead to your death. Can you see where you will be?*

P: *It isn't clear but I suppose it will be in a hospice. That seems inevitable. It's not my preference but I'm accepting it.*

T: *Have your Higher Self speak to the Rhoda who is dying.*

P: *It's okay. You've had a full life.*

T: *Who is with you?*

P: *Friends—and I see my daughter is with me.*

T: *How do you feel?*

P: *Relief. I'm glad I'm going. It's a relief to leave my body behind. But it feels real sad to leave my friends.*

T: *What do you see?*

P: *A bright light. And I see my father. He's pleased to see me. I'm pleased to see him because he didn't believe there was an afterlife.*

T: *Where are you? What does it look like?*

P: *It looks like where I was before. I go to a beautiful house. It's wonderful light. There's a temple.*

T: *Are your teachers there?*

P: *Yes—four of them. There's Peter. And John from the Pleiades. There's an American Indian—he's a medicine man. And there's a woman—Miriam or Mary Ann.*

T: *Ask them why you got cancer.*

P: *Peter says nothing, but John says it's what I chose. It was to teach me to love myself and be more compassionate to people who are different. It made me aware that I am different. The American Indian says I was to learn to use natural things to heal. And Miriam says it was to make me aware of the beauty around me and to enjoy what I have.*

Evaluation of the Role of Cancer

Cancer as a Teacher

In the next session we pursued the function of her cancer as a teacher.

P: *I had to learn to express myself. I often hid my feelings rather than be forthright. I took a back seat to other people in expressing emotions. Cancer made me be more upfront, made me express myself more clearly.*

T: *Had you been aware before the cancer that you needed to do this?*

P: *I always knew. I was especially aware with my husband. When we were splitting up, I could write how I felt but I couldn't express myself to him. He could always best me verbally.*

T: *Could you express your feelings with your children?*

P: *I think I showed excitement with them.*

T: *Love?*

P: *I had trouble. I didn't know how to praise them and force their good points. Nobody had done that with me. My parents were critical. I was trying so hard to be a perfect parent that I didn't do much on the positive side.*

T: *Other lessons from cancer?*

P: *To enjoy life moment by moment—and something about trust. Trust that I'm on the right path and what will be will be.*

Comparative Valences of the Wish to Live and the Wish to Die

Because of the depth of perception Rhoda had reached in this dialogue, we moved into the ultimate question about the relative strengths of her wish to live and her wish to die. On a superficial level this choice can be rationalized, so it is important that answers come from a deep source of self-wisdom.

T: *Let us explore your reasons for wanting to live.*

P: *I don't want to leave the people who love me. And the unknown is scary. And I still want to do things, but sometimes that's not real strong.*

T: *And your reasons for wanting to die?*

P: *Why not? You can start over with a new life?*

T: *Have there been too many losses?*

P: *Sometimes it feels like it.*

T: *Can you give voice to that feeling?*

P: *You've suffered a lot of loss. You have joy, too, but the loss is heavy. You wanted to be a partner with someone (tears). I thought I was ready to be a partner. It doesn't feel okay. It feels like a hole—something I've wanted. I had the chance to do it.... It feels like I should want to do something more with my life, be more productive.*

T: *Longing for a partner is a very deep hurt.*

P: *Yes. It just comes up over and over. I really feel my marriage didn't work out. I worked so hard to change who I am. I felt I was ready to share with someone. It feels like it's kind of impossible in the situation I'm in now. Maybe I need to learn that I'm whole and complete in myself and don't need a partner. If I could do that, maybe the cancer would go away. And maybe I would find a partner. I don't know.*

T: *Can your Higher Self talk to you about this?*

P: *It's towering over me. And it seems androgynous. It's saying, "Even if you don't have a partner, go and be joyous."*

T: *Can your Higher Self take you in its arms?*

P: *Yes. That's the partner I've needed. My cancer came to teach me that.*

T: *Love is for one's soul.*

P: *Yes. "You are whole and complete. And I love your unconditionally." If only I could keep in contact with knowing this!*

Fifth Regression and Interlife

We deepened and grounded these perceptions in further imaging.

T: *Let us take a walk around a lake.*

P: *Yes. I'm walking along. I see trees. There are some wildflowers—orange and purple.*

T: *You might see a cave.*

P: *I'm looking. Oh, a light is starting to shine. It's getting brighter and brighter. It seems to be leading me. There's a bell. The bell is large, hanging on wooden supports. It's just there for me to ring.*

T: *Can you hear it?*

P: *Yes, it's beautiful. It's up to me to do it. There are lots of bells, and I can ring them all. I'm dancing while the bells ring.*

T: *Was there another lifetime with bells?*

P: *I think I've been there before. It's a church with bells. I think I'm an Armenian woman, 32, named Marcia. I wanted to dedicate myself to the church and to God.*

T: *When did you do that?*

P: *When I was 17 my father died and I became religious. I wanted God to take care of me and protect me because my father had died. The nuns told me my Heavenly Father would take care of me. I went into the nunnery and worked very diligently.*

T: *Were you happy?*

P: *Somewhat. But I couldn't find what I wanted. I kept searching and I couldn't find it. I wanted to have a close communion with God. It never seemed like it worked.*

T: *Go ahead five years.*

P: *It's about the same.*

T: *Can you go to your death?*

P: *I'm in my cubicle room—sick. I'm 63. I'm sick of trying. Some sisters are with me.*

T: *What is your last thought?*

P: *It didn't work. I'll try something different.... Maybe that's when I decided I wanted a partnership with a human. Oh, there's a beautiful light!*

T: *Can you put your finger on what were the similarities and differences between that life and this one?*

P: *They were alike in that I tried to do good things both times. Both times I was searching for something. Then I was alone, and this time I had a family. I was always a good person. She meant well.*

T: *Tell me about the Light.*

P: *I'm being met. By radiant beings. They surround me and love me and take me on. I feel totally loved.*

T: *Can you see what happens next?*

P: *We go to school to learn what we didn't do and need to do in our next lifetime. I learn that my partnership is with my Higher Self. I talk with my Guides about my next lifetime.*

T: *What year do you die?*

P: *1708.*

In this session Rhoda reached a deepened level of understanding of her problem of loneliness and its connection with her cancer, and following this, she interrupted her therapy to process it. She was often away for workshops (both taken and given by her) and for short hospitalizations. However, she was experiencing increasing distress from her disease and came for a session before returning to the hospital for extensive chemotherapy.

Final Synthesis

Entity Releasement

It was apparent both to me and, I think, to Rhoda, that she was dying, but she could not seem to complete her death. To my surprise, in this last session the possibility of entity interference came up. We dealt with this briefly.

P: *The wish to die is the reason why this cancer is still growing. But there's a real block to feeling that there's something out there I want to go for.*

T: *Does it feel like something is interfering?*

P: *There may be.*

T: *Go into the Garden and ask if anyone is hindering you from dying.*

P: *(After a few moments of going into an altered state) My father's here.*

T: *Ask if he's attached to you.*

P: *Yes. He feels sorry he hasn't been closer to me. He wants to stay here and care for me—make up for what he didn't do.*

T: *(To entity) You're not helping either yourself or Rhoda. You need to go on your own path—you can only hold her back. She must be free to choose her way. You make it difficult for her when you draw her toward death and then won't let her through. Are you willing to release her and go on your own journey to the Light?*

P: *He says that he is.*

T: *Let us call helpers for him and loved ones who have gone on ahead and start him on his way.*

With this, Rhoda and I walked her father a little way and then she came back into her body.

The releasement opened questions. Was this the same father she had earlier seen meeting her at the time of her death in the future? Had she in that imaging foreseen that she would release him and he would be able to meet her? Whatever occurred, it freed Rhoda for her final breakthrough to death.

P: *Now the block is gone.*

T: *Is there anything holding you back now from your leaving?*

P: *Only that I have always learned that it isn't okay to give up. One has to keep trying.*

T: *You have completed your work and have understood your lessons in it, and it is really all right to leave. You don't have to keep trying.*

P: *I don't? It won't be quitting?*

T: *No, it won't be quitting. It's okay to go.*

P: *(Showing relief) Then I'll leave.*

She went home, canceled her hospital appointment for further chemotherapy, arranged for nursing help, and called her children and friends. She was joyous and upbeat. Her son, who did not realize how close to death she was, had left for work and skiing in another state, but her daughter returned and was with her during her last few weeks. Friends, of whom she had many, came frequently for visits now that they did not have to be drawn into the futile struggle to prolong her life, and they brought thoughtful tokens of their caring. On my one visit I found Rhoda joyfully supervising the decoration of a Christmas tree.

There was one event that she was determined to live to celebrate. At the time that she was first separated from her husband and was especially lonely, she and a group of women friends who were also divorced or separated formed a support group, and each year just before Christmas they met for a day of sharing and mutual caring. Usually this had taken place in Rhoda's home, and she had set her goal for living to reach this special day. Two days before Christmas the reunion took place, this year attended not only by her women friends but by the men friends and colleagues who had known and cared about her. Her former husband and his wife who had been her best friend came during the last week to help out. She moved in and out of awareness during the festivities and occasionally greeted those who came to sit with her.

Those words of greeting at the gathering she had determined she would live for were the last words that she spoke. Christmas was quiet and present were only her closest friends, her daughter, and her former husband and his wife. The morning after Christmas, having accomplished her goal of living until the reunion, Rhoda died in her daughter's arms.

A week later her friends and family held a memorial celebration at her home. The house was full of people who had taught with her or been taught by her and by a spectrum of friends whose paths had crossed hers in her many endeavors. One after another those who cared about her talked of their feelings and experiences. I am sure that on her journey to the Light, which she had tasted so many times after so many lives, she was nourished by the love reaching out to her. As she had perceived, "love is everywhere."

The Transition of Animals

by

Winafred Lucas, Ph. D.

Note: Readers who have not experienced bonding with animals may wish to skip this section.

Introduction

Not everyone feels a bond with animals, but those who can relate to them are saddened by the prevailing insensitive attitude toward the deaths of animals. We need to work out a better way to support our animals' dying, both for their sakes and for ourselves. Leaving them to be euthanized by a veterinarian crumples our hearts.

The metaphysics of an animal's path are obscure and are seldom discussed. One of the few serious reflections on the nature of animal consciousness was made by Larry Dossey in his discussion of the interaction of human and animal consciousness in his book on the non-local mind, *Recovering the Soul* (1989).[12] Dossey feels there is good evidence, from both a historical and a modern scientific perspective, that something resembling mental communication goes on between humans and animals, something that is profound and that cannot be explained by known physical interrelationships. He mentions J. Allen Boone, a movie producer and former head of RKA Studios, who owned the great movie dog Strongheart. Boone in his book *Kinship with All Life*,[13] tells of the extraordinary ability of Strongheart to understand his thoughts and feelings and communicate back to him. Boone believes that we live in a totality that includes all life and that we share a common consciousness.

An ancient hypothesis suggested that the majority of animal species form group souls. Each group soul is represented by a deva, a form of consciousness that acts as a guide for the species and with whom it is possible to communicate. The theory further postulated that when individual animals are evolved enough to begin to develop attributes generally considered human, they choose a life situation where they will have maximum reinforcement of their thrust for soul growth. Such development makes possible their quantum leap into a human incarnation. This is not a popular doctrine. For some reason we guard jealously our special status as humans, in very much the same way that whites used to protect their special white status from infringement by blacks.

The hypothesis of a deva is especially jarring to scientific prejudices. Though I could not accept the current understanding of animals as sub-human, neither was I comfortable with the concept of a group soul with what seemed to me to be an intangible form of life representing it. It strained my credibility.

I realized how thoroughly I had been contaminated by modern thinking the morning I was confronted with the possibility of talking with a deva, which was so far beyond even my rather flexible and open metaphysics that I went through hours of being stunned. The triggering incident was an influx of dozens of tree rats into my canyon home after a time of flooding. The presence of my dogs contraindicated poison, and traps did little to reduce the escalating numbers. Eventually the rats found entry into the house, crawled along the wide beams of the ceiling, and letting themselves down the ropes of my hanging plants, proceeded to sheer them off.

One Sunday morning while I was having breakfast in the garden with a colleague from northern California, I shared with her my frustration. She suggested in a matter-of-fact way that I call the deva of the rats and ask her to take the rats away. I couldn't believe my ears and asked her if she were crazy. She smiled patronizingly.

I thought little about her off-the-wall suggestion until several days later when I found the great fronds from my favorite fern neatly cut off at the base and lying on the floor. Desperate enough to do anything, I went into my meditation room, lit a purple candle, and called the deva of the rats. My sense was that she came immediately. I told her in no uncertain terms to take her little rats away or I would have to exterminate them. Then softening a little toward the end, because I realized it wasn't the deva's fault that I was so skeptical, and remembering that my friend said I should be courteous, I concluded with a somewhat lame "thank you." The next morning the rats were entirely gone and did not return. I regret to say that a part of me was shocked and disbelieving. However, over the years I have had other similar experiences, and I am now sure that on some level there is truth in the theory.

The concept of being a helpmate for an animal's progression to a human incarnation is less difficult to accept. Those of us who have bonded with animals would like that to be true, even if from a scientific point of view we have no way of knowing that it is. If the theory holds, it puts on those of us who have highly developed animal companions an obligation to assist their soul development.

One instance where the concept of an animal preparing for a human incarnation is entertained is in Sai Baba's expectations for his beautiful elephant companion Sai Gita, now 40 years old. My conservative English roommates at the ashram were visiting Sai Gita one day in her enclosure a short distance out in the country from Puttaparthi when Sai Baba arrived to spend some time with her. According to them, she hurried out to meet him and encircled him with her trunk. He fed her fruit and when he was ready to go, she walked ahead of him and cleared a way through the gathering crowd so that he could get back in his car. As he drove away, they reported that great tears ran down her face. Some people asked Sai Baba if it is true that Gita is an Indian princess who incarnated as an elephant to be near him. He denied this, stating that Sai Gita has not as yet had a human incarnation but that this will be her last lifetime as an elephant.

It has been my privilege to live for over 30 years with many great dogs—Salukis, an ancient and highly developed breed. In the process of helping them I have also learned from them, especially in the experience of their transition. There is slight tradition in our culture for helping human beings through their death, and for animals there is nothing, but I have learned that it is helpful to support animals in their dying, just as it is helpful to support human beings, first by sharing the animal's lifetime, and, following this, by making an invocation that the animal retain such transpersonal qualities as it has manifested in that lifetime.

I share several of these deaths in the hope that my experience will help others to make the transitions of their animal companions positive events. All death can be perceived as radiant birth. This is true with people, and in my experience it is also true with animals.

American Mexican Champion Rama of Srinagar

Companion Dog, Perro Companiero, Coursing Champion
July 29, 1963—May 8, 1979

Rama is dead. For a long time he has been increasingly fragile, though his personality remained vibrant and enthusiastic. There was no evidence as to why his physical self was fading, even in an extensive examination that showed heart and lungs and kidneys and liver to be functioning as though he were much younger. Sometimes he would seem to be in pain and would cry out, but these times were infrequent. For the most part he continued to love living, roamed the garden slowly, and enjoyed lying on the carved cashew wood couch on Oriental rugs, surrounded by his famous grandson Brahma II and his first wife Taruna and his favorite wife Devi and closest friend Krisna. He moved slowly because small strokes had slightly crippled him. His feathering grew increasingly sparser, and his beautiful face became more silver than red. In spite of daily portions of chicken he grew razor thin.

How dear he was! How mellow was this great older dog! The scepter of authority had passed from him to Krisna, but Rama was still the quiet center of all activities. The younger dogs respected his rights and accepted that he should be fed first and have his favorite spot on the bed at night. When I took time to sit beside him and stroke his face, he responded in his throat with little grunts of pleasure, pushing against my hand with his head to let me know he was noticing and appreciating my caring. At night he lay very close, and it seemed that his aging and fragile body drew energy from me. When I had to be away for even a few days he was always weaker by the time I returned and would only slowly build back to where he had been.

Just before I left for Egypt in April he had several bouts of deep pain, and his feebleness increased so that getting up and down off the bed became almost impossible and even going out into the garden was difficult. I left with the knowledge that I might not see him alive again and I held him to me in sadness, for I did not know how to say a goodbye that would help both our hearts. I left a list of instructions for my niece Julie to cover every emergency, and I went away with the awareness that nothing was really finished between us.

Nearly every day on the ship I sat alone for a time and thought of Rama, imaging him in a body of light and allowing a flood of energy to come through me to him, the same energy he had depended on when he slept close to me at home. As I perceived him and filled him with healing, my love for him bonded us deeply so that sometimes in the intensity of this caring we seemed to overlap. And I sent a request to him, transmitted by image, to wait for my return if he could.

At the home airport my first question was about Rama, and I found he had held on feebly but stubbornly, drawing on his great pool of vitality. When I came into the house he moved feebly toward me and I lifted his dying body onto the bed and held him close, pouring love and energy around him that at this time could only comfort and not heal. At four he awakened in pain and I gave him a small amount of tranquilizer so that he could sleep.

During the long morning he lay on a blanket on the soft carpet and I sat beside him, knowing that now that I had come home he would die and I should help him. How does one help a great dog die? I truly did not know but opened myself to perceiving a way. I observed him on a deep level and saw that with so much strength in his physical body with its strong heart and lungs, his light body was having trouble leaving, but I also perceived it was time for this to take place.

"My Rama, let go of this outworn body which you do not need any more," I urged. "Leave it behind and move onward into a new form." I stroked his head tenderly and he moved against my hand to acknowledge my caress and gave a small feeble sound of affection in his throat. I saw that he was still having trouble dying and his light body did not know how to leave.

Then I looked inside to where he and I shared a common screen, and before us passed a panorama of pictures of his life. I saw him as a beautiful puppy with liquid dark eyes, long black whiskers that fluttered like butterfly antennae, luxurious feathering—a gleaming copper-red, exuberant, charismatic youngster. "You were most delightful," I told him. "All the great handlers picked you as the puppy most likely to succeed."

More pictures flashed by and we shared them together. "You were a gangly puppy and skinny for a long time, but you never were without mellowness and charm. You always cared to try to be what we hoped you would be." I remembered the Group I he took at a match when he was nine months old and how willingly he had moved out, scintillating delight at this first show...and never so enthusiastic again!

Exciting pictures came next of Rama coursing in the open field, often running with Taruna, the two of them working together and trotting back across the fields with their rabbit between them. Taruna was Rama's first wife, his running companion, his show partner, and they grew old together. "How you loved the coursing, Rama," I told him. "When the rabbit jumped, almost no one could hold you." And I remembered when he and Siva had pulled me along on my face after the Jack, with my movie camera bumping along behind me. So steady, so persistent, so powerful a courser was Rama that when he ran, the gallery stood still and watched. He climaxed his coursing career with the great Coursing Shield, seen as an accomplishment by me only, since for Rama nothing existed except the running Jack!

Then came a flash of a high moment at the Santa Barbara show in the days when lure coursing was getting started and jumps were a part of the day. Discussion had been hot and heavy all day about the relative virtues of Greyhounds and Salukis as runners, and after all the courses had been run, Rama was chosen to run against the winning Greyhound to determine this. Rama started out behind the fast sprinting Greyhound and comfortably trailed him around half the course, but on the final run the length of the field over two jumps he turned on all his speed, running with great heart and single determination, and soared like a flying red bird over the high jumps to establish for all the Saluki people who were watching, the clear superiority of our breed!

For a moment, then, I heard laughter and on the screen appeared Rama chasing a ram. I was startled and then remembered that our sweet singer Lee had taken him to Pearce College to represent the Saluki breed in a class presentation. Rama had seen the ram, slipped his leash from Lee's hand and taken off through the campus. I saw the crowds sitting laughing on top of the fence of the corral where he was finally stopped and Rama standing there with a delighted and satisfied look at the exciting ending to what had been a boring day. Did you remember that, my Rama, and feel your heart sparkle again at the good joke?

When the pictures of Rama's obedience career appeared, I smiled again, and I think he probably must have, too, for he accomplished his CD out of a wish to please but totally without enthusiasm. "Rama," I told him, "you lagged so and with such dejection that I am sure people must have thought I beat you! However," I added, "I do thank you for trying, especially when you found the obedience work so distasteful. It was good of you to cater to my whims. It probably saved your life when you wandered away from Emmy at the Renaissance Faire and she had the presence of mind to bellow out a for you to come as you were about to take off through the crowds. Nobody was more amazed than I when I heard you had simply turned around and come back and sat in front of her while she put your leash more tightly around her wrist. When your degree was firmly in American Kennel Club archives, we called it a day and let this activity drop!"

Pictures of Rama's show career started out with a little enthusiasm, but this, also, gradually petered out. His greatest fan from the beginning was the great Afghan breeder Kay Finch, and she chose a red and white son of Rama to sire a litter to her favorite bitch. Rama's career in the Midwest, while he stayed with breeders who wanted to special him, went better and he made nine or ten group placings to rank as Number Six Saluki in the country that year. "You didn't like to be away from us," I told him, "but you always adjusted. Even during these long separations you made the best of it, and when you came home it was without rancor. You simply moved in as though you had never been away, deeply loving to everyone and always special in everyone's heart." Then there were a few pictures of Mexico and the white shabby little town of Ensenada and Rama dramatic and sparkling in his prime and easily finishing his Mexican championship.

For a long time after this I sat there with Rama in a patch of sunlight, caught in an energy field of remembering, and I urged Rama to recall what he had done and been so that he would take with him the knowledge of what he was. And I saw him as a great producer, with nearly forty champion sons and daughters and behind them proceeding steadily a line of grandchildren and great grandchildren and all their descendants behind them, a column of great dogs with Rama's beauty and his balance and his speed and temperament...red and particolor and black and cream and grizzle, a spectrum of beauty. Four sons and daughters walked by with Best In Show rosettes, and behind them were other sons and daughters with lure coursing titles. Grandchildren with Best in Shows and Best in Specialty ribbons and lure coursing titles followed. Then came the champions from overseas, from Canada and Brazil and France and Finland. There were a few great obedience dogs, like Ramachandra. All this long winding line carried Rama's blood and quality.

And back of Rama by eight thousand years I saw again the Saluki, red like him and with the same balanced angulation and deep chest, before whose intact mummy I had stood in Cairo. Something of the mysterious and ongoing perfection of the breed stirred me, as though perhaps experiencing a Saluki lifetime was the last step before human experience and that was an explanation for the special quality in our dogs.

The pictures shifted to the forest above Arrowhead, and I saw Rama running with delight among the trees and along the lake with Siva and Taruna and snow-white Parvati and Suvarna, the beautiful one. How he loved that forest! The door of the mountain house would open and he would run swiftly over the rocks, his shining red coat dappled by the shadows under the trees. I reminded him how he used to go to find the dogs that would not come back. He always found them, chasing deer or playing with wolves or just enjoying running or whatever it was they did, and he enticed them home. "One time," I shared with him, as though he could not remember for himself, "a Siva grandchild was lost far up in the forest and you went out and were gone for a long time and when you came back you had him in tow, a very tired and scared little dog. I was appreciative, Rama," I said. "You always knew what to do and you could be counted on. How loyal and mellow you were!"

Pictures of Rama at the Topanga kennel flickered by, Rama talking to the coyotes through the fence, Rama leaping over the Dutch door to mate in one competent movement with a bitch brought in for him, Srinagar's most direct and effective stud. At the beginning Rama was second to Siva but as Siva began to die, Rama emerged as ruler at Srinagar. He had loved Siva and they were always together, and Siva's death left an empty spot for Rama, too. All of us mourned for a long time. And then Krisna came and he followed Rama, as Rama had followed Siva. And Rama carried his seniority with authority but never with aggressiveness.

The pictures were slowing. We were nearly through. I saw that his light body was still having difficulty. "Do not be afraid to leave this outworn shell," I told him again. "Behold the clear light. I am sure it is there for you as it is for people." And I shifted to another level and saw that Rama had already in his canine form worked through many of the tasks of consciousness and that he would indeed incarnate next in human form, carrying on the wisdom and balance of what he had achieved as a dog. "Reach toward the light," I implored him, seeing him in his final struggle to leave his body. "Choose wisdom and creativity and love and strength, all of which you have already begun to know. Move forward with surety. Choose according to the options you have already earned. Look ahead and have no regrets."

Wave after wave of love passed from me to him and I wrapped him in light. "I send you joy and love and light for your journey," I told him. As I looked down at the lovely face with the life ebbing out of it, I put my hands out, palms forward, and sent him energy for the difficult transition. I stroked his head lightly and the movement in response was only a feeble flicker, like the flutter of a butterfly emerging tiredly from its cocoon.

It was time for me to go to fulfill my own rhythm of work. I knew I would not see Rama alive again. I knew we were bonded with love and nothing in even a timeless universe would ever break this. I had shared with him all that it was possible to share and I was at peace. Observing him I saw that he, too, was at peace and wrapped in the light that I had channeled to him. So I kissed lightly in farewell the dear face with only a little life left in it. As I stood at the door before leaving him finally, I again put out my hands and sent him light.

Julie came quietly in to sit with Rama. A few hours later she called to say that she had been singing to him and while she was singing he slipped away. The room, she reported, was now charged with a high and unique energy. I did not really know what she meant by that, but I knew all was well with Rama. He had made his transition.

When I went into the room later that night I sat down beside the beautiful shell that was now utterly still and without pain. It had changed dramatically from the body of the living Rama. His face was relaxed and at peace and he looked much younger. His ears, which had lately almost always drooped, were set high, his throat muscles were firm and his eyes were open and dark and lustrous as they had been in life when he was a younger dog. A few tears came because there was such an empty place in our household now, but they were not 'for Rama, for I sensed he walked on a path of power and joy and he had heard my words. It was true that there was a strange and high energy in the room so that my hands tingled. At the same time there was an intense calm which reminded me of the energy and calm that I had recently experienced in the King's Chamber in the Great Pyramid at Gizeh.

We miss him in his physical body, which we found so beautiful. Krisna, who came into the room after he died seeking him, knows that Rama will not be back, and is preparing to join him—they were deep friends. The vet says that something is now wrong with Krisna's heart, and I am sure in a real sense he has been stricken by the loss of his friend.

So the earth turns, and one by one the dogs that were welcomed so joyously into the panorama of our life fade and slip out. Sometimes it seems like a dream, or Plato's shadow play on the walls of a cave. But the essence of our love endures. Rama has been a part of the skein of my life for nearly sixteen years and the pattern that he has woven into it will remain.

Nothing of him that doth fade
But doth suffer a sea change
Into something rich and strange.

Invocation to Zanande on Her Dying

June 24, 1969   Nordic Champion Zanande   May 13, 1981

The flame of this single lifetime
Is about to be snuffed out in you.
The air is still in your dying.
Your eyes seek mine with both a question and an answer.
Slowly I stroke your face
With fingers from which love drips
In a splintered silver stream.

Now for a moment merge with me
In a penetration that shall endure beyond this lifetime
And by its luminous loveliness
Transform my quiet tears
And soothe your passing.

I invoke you to remember,
To choose a further path enmeshed with mine
So that the radiant flow of my caring
Can torch your way.

Behold the light!
Behold the light that glows beyond your dying.

Chapter VIII

Progression to the Future

As human beings we live and move through a space-time universe whose primary function apparently is providing opportunities for choice. The concept of alternate futures implies free will and conscious choice for humanity and places the necessity of choosing wisely squarely on our shoulders as to which of potential future realities we will create. In effect, the choice between a holistic vision of a New Age of cooperation and harmony with nature and the competitive Brave New World of technocratic survivalists is ours to make today.

Chet Snow

Forward movement is valuable for those approaching death through a terminal illness, especially when the process of dying stirs up ambivalence and doubt.... *When patients are progressed to their death they have the experience of misty white light, an expansive place of existence in which they feel totally complete, whole, needing nothing, surrounded by life. From this place they ask questions regarding the purpose of this life, just as people examining past lives search for the nature and purpose of those lifetimes. Have they fulfilled their soul's purpose for this creation? Understanding this purpose reduces the fear of leaving.*

Ernest Pecci

Bibliography

Loehr, Franklin. "Death Preview: A New Direction in Psychography." *The Journal of Regression Therapy,* Vol. II, No. 1, 1987.

Pecci, Ernest. "Exploring One's Death." *The Journal of Regression Therapy,* Vol. II, No. 1, 1986.

Snow, Chet. "Beyond the Millenium—New Age or Brave New World." *The Journal of Regression Therapy,* Vol. 1, No. 1, 1986.

———. *Mass Dreams of the Future.* New York: McGraw Hill, 1989.

Progression to the Future

Introduction

In the past, and to a large extent in the present, progression into the future has been the province of soothsayers and psychics. Future forays were not for the ordinary, rational person. And because some soothsayers and psychics molded material to please clients and because their predictions were often inaccurate, they were not taken seriously by the more thoughtful public. The few predictions that foretold accurately—and some have, such as the assassination of President Kennedy that was predicted by Jeanne Dixon—were not heeded because of the poor batting average of psychics in general. There is no doubt that prescience does exist but is unreliable.

Going ahead in one's own psyche to span the future is another matter. Subjects, whether patients or research subjects, are chary of these personal trips, partly because they do not trust their capacity to tune in to them and partly because individuals are concerned that, if they make an accurate prediction, they are programming their future, possibly in a disastrous way. Even those skilled in going into the future and interested in doing so hesitate to lose the power of choice by pinning themselves down to a future scenario.

As therapists, it is not necessary to answer whether it is possible accurately to perceive what is to come in our lives. Techniques of tapping the future, like return to past lives and other altered-state work, have just one therapeutic focus: are such forays helpful and healing to the patient?

To date there are three areas in which the therapist attempts progression to the future. The first of these is a projective technique that surfaced in the 50's called the Future Biography. In it the subject is asked to describe a typical day five years from now. This is not taken as a reading of the future but as a method of tapping levels of motivation that are not consciously apparent. The most that can be said for the authenticity of the predictions is that the use of deep unconscious motivations is more likely to extract a valid future biography than are more conscious superficial wishes. Some examples of this projective technique follow.

Another form of tapping the future is progression to one's death, but most people are resistant to looking at their death. If the death is to be painful or premature, they do not want to know it. But for those with terminal illness who have had experience in recovering past-life deaths, the opposite is true; going ahead to the death experience can be comforting. Pecci, Loehr, and I have all taken terminal patients ahead to their deaths and found that the experience was healing and reassuring to them.

Whether it is appropriate or helpful for non-terminal patients to experience their future death, given that they have the courage and desire to do so, has not been determined. We do not even know to what extent people can predict their deaths, but we are aware that short life spans and accidental death, or long suffering from disease, can appear traumatic unless the person observing such a death realizes that what he has seen is the end result of how he is living now. A different script may be possible if we commit ourselves to making *current* changes, or to a deeper search into the understanding of our karmic path. My experiencing of my own death was profound, and I have written it down so that it can be checked.

The area of future progression that is in the forefront today takes place in specific time frames in the future, such as research into 2100 A.D. and 2300 A.D. that Wambach and Snow carried out. Snow's excellent summary in this section should whet interest in reading his book *Mass Dreams of the Future*.

How my planet and I function today will undoubtedly determine our future. Just as there are discrete types of current functioning, some more materialistic and characterized by environmental and social disaster, and others struggling for a more spiritual and loving perspective, so also there are alternative future scenarios. Versions of the future are also a projective technique. Which version each person sees as being the future is not a matter of chance: it is determined by who the person is and the present quality of his life. Future scenarios are not usually considered from such a perspective, but further study of connections between such scenarios and personality structures may encourage individuals to scrutinize where they are now in order to avoid being where they do not want to be in the future.

Some surprising general trends are noted in accounts of the future. One is a de-emphasis on food. My 2100 A.D. scenario showed us eating once a day—a small slice of melon; and in a progression to 2300 A.D. with Helen Wambach I found myself walking with others to a warehouse where I obtained a packet of powder that, when mixed with water into a sort of Nutri-Shake, constituted that time's version of dining. I complained to Helen that I certainly was making everything up—nobody would treat eating that way, but Helen assured me that nearly everyone who had progressed to 2300 reported such an approach. Gone were the dinners, the cocktail parties, the gourmet restaurants that had given color to our culture, especially in the 60's and 70's; other things were considered more important. It is interesting that currently in the early 90's the approach to food, influenced by our growing concern about nutrition, is becoming increasingly simplified. The sort of feasts that we used to compete with each other to produce are currently viewed as a physical disaster, and many of the great gourmet restaurants, helped along by the economic slump, are closing.

Another interesting perception of our future civilization deals with the use of time. In the future we manifest a pervasive concern with energy in one form or another, including computer types of energy manipulation and tapping into personal energy to provide transportation and influence our health. Many who have progressed several centuries ahead are concerned with creative energy, also, but not for reasons of financial return, fame, or adulation. Exhibits and screenings and reviews have yielded to the intrinsic value of just being creative.

Even in the mid-70's when a pervasive anxiety over nuclear bombing created the Cold War, almost no one saw any nuclear devastation in the future, but nearly all sensed a massive environmental catastrophe resulting in a decimation of the population of the earth. Such perception of the possibility of planetary destruction more nearly matches our current concern. At the time that Helen Wambach carried out her research, environmental concern was only beginning to emerge and it is only now in our escalating interest in the ozone layer that future scenarios seen 15 years ago in her workshops suddenly make sense. At that time almost no one was seen in the future as being directly exposed to sunlight; instead, all were living underground, under bubbles of glass, or in space stations.

Beyond the personal factor is the warning for our planet. Awareness of a painful future resulting from ecological imbalance may help precipitate a massive energy shift toward a more caring and nurturing attitude. In this way we may be able to avoid scenarios of pollution and destruction and move in the direction of a holistic New Age of cooperation and environmental concern. The World Environmental Conference in Rio, sadly unassisted by the United States, strove to initiate a reversal of what is already in the collective unconscious (Sheldrake's mind field) and will be actualized if we persist in avoiding perception of the negative future we are programming. A ray of hope is offered by the fact that Senator Al Gore, author of the spiritually profound and concerned account of the environment, *Earth in the Balance,* has become available to take over the neglected reins of our planetary destiny.

The Future Biography

by

Winafred B. Lucas, Ph.D.

Introduction

In the 50's there was an enthusiastic reaction to the idea that unconscious attitudes could be projected onto written and graphic material, and this spawned a number of projective techniques. Most of these flourished for a few years and then gradually disappeared, leaving only the Rorschach and Thematic Apperception Test in general use. One of the innovative techniques that had only a brief moment in the sun was the Future Biography. In this the patient was asked to make up a "typical day five years from now." It could be what he thought would happen or what he wished would happen. It was to include mundane events of the day—work, relationships, physical state, and recreation. Though the Future Biography does not use verbal or graphic stimuli, it must be considered a projective technique because it depends on projection for its findings, this time an imagined projection of a future state.

Those proposing the Future Biography never postulated that projecting a typical day five years ahead would in any sense foretell the future. Instead, it was assumed—and hoped—that the technique would tap unconscious motivations and goals that were not emerging clearly because of the obscuring programs of everyday life. In all probability it did not survive as a technique because its focus was much more limited than that of the TAT or Rorschach. However, there were times when it could clarify in ten minutes an obscure motivation or reveal what the dominant valence was when a polarity of equal values obscured the hidden direction.

The Future Biography was predictive because it revealed the deeper motivation determining the individual's process. It was as though it revealed a future that the individual was in the process of actualizing. No psychic prognostic ability was required, though this may have been present part of the time. Some individuals may have been able to "see" their futures as well as disclose motivations that would lead to such a future.

The following are examples of situations in which this brief projective technique clarified particular questions in a patient's therapy. An altered state is needed if a patient is to expose dynamics below the surface of consciousness and it facilitates disclosures of new and healing experiences. Simple relaxation usually induces sufficient depth to produce a revealing story.

In its brief and focused approach the Future Biography contributes insights in three areas. It clarifies obscure issues. It explores the relative values of polarities in a life situation. And it highlights a core pattern. If it predicts the future accurately, this is because the roots of the future are in the present.

Case 1. Exposing a Hidden Motivation

Richard, whose prenatal, birth, and early childhood experiences were described in Chapter I, continued to experience frequent criticism and confrontation from his wife, who demanded that he confess his sins (lying) and show remorse. Meanwhile his blood pressure escalated and it seemed that the scenes with Martha were becoming increasingly injurious to him physically. Unconsciously his body seemed to be finding its own way out of an intolerable situation through illness. Also, he was able more easily to handle Martha's attacks by withdrawal. They still enjoyed traveling together, but he often wondered if the relationship was worth it.

Thinking that his unconscious projection of the future might help to clarify the situation I suggested he relax and make up a story about his life five years in the future.

> T: *Start by saying, "I get up in the morning..." and then describe the details of your day.*
> P: *When I get up I'm far away—I'm in Australia.*
> T: *What are you doing there?*
> P: *Traveling?*
> T: *Are you alone?*
> P: *No, Martha's with me. We're at the Barrier Reef and we're going to spend months there.*
> T: *Where are you staying?*
> P: *At a motel. When we get up in the morning we go and have breakfast on an outdoor patio. We have some weird food.*
> T: *What do you talk about?*
> P: *About our plans for the day. We're going to go snorkeling. I want to get a boat and go out over the Barrier Reef. Martha doesn't want to go because she's afraid of getting seasick. So I go anyway. It's a little rough but I enjoy that very much. We get to an island beyond the barrier reef. The island has*

*some wildlife on it and we examine it. We get back in the late afternoon.
It's cocktail time. We find a quaint little place for dinner....*

*We're not in a motel—we're in a Bed and Board place. We're talking
with the owners and plan to go to a cattle place the next morning. It takes
four hours to get there.*

T: *Are you still working or are you retired?*

P: *I'm 65 and I'm retired. I don't think I give up working completely.*

T: *What do you and Martha talk about?*

P: *About what we're doing, not about gut issues. I see myself still having
ownership of my house (a mountain cabin he had in his own name),
someplace to escape to, but it doesn't matter. I have great remorse about
the way I treated her but I can't tell her or she'd want me to show it and
I can't, but I do have a good time traveling with her. I still see her in the
picture.*

T: *You used to talk about seeing yourself when you were older in some village
in the Caribbean helping the people to start a fish processing plant.*

P: *I don't want to be alone when I'm older.*

T: *That's why you keep on with Martha.*

P: *Yes. I can't face being alone.*

Richard had never before expressed concern for being alone in his older
years. It seemed as though this might be an explanation for his reluctance
to give up his marriage. We talked about the possibility of engaging in
altruistic work at home where Martha could be with him, even though she
refused to have anything to do with such activities.

I hoped that the exposure of this hidden motivation would make it
possible for Richard to deal with conflicting valences and shift his energy to
the side of health and serenity. Something did shift but in a way that
surprised me. Richard was caught red-handed lying to Martha about the
time it would take to get to a new office he had set up. He was so distressed
to have lied again, and this time so needlessly, that he broke down and
cried, admitting for the first time that he *had* lied and sharing his distress
over it. Martha was taken aback and responded gently, saying that all she
had wanted was for him to show remorse. The incident brought them the
closest they had ever been. There is still a long way to go, but this seems to
be a significant breakthrough.

Case 2. Exploring the Permanence of Interlife Changes

Prior to Brad's breakthrough session in the interlife (see Chapter IV),
his general mood had been one of discouragement and negativity. He had
constantly downplayed himself, feeling that he would never get anywhere in
a business way and that he was a failure in relationships. In spite of the

positive and comforting message from his Guides in the interlife sessions he remained shadowed by years of negative programming, though not as deeply as before. Still, I wondered how much the positive evaluations had permeated his perspective on life in general and on himself. One way to determine this was to take him into the future to see how he conceptualized it. A major areas to be looked at was that of relationships. Previously he had sabotaged any closeness because of his programming that being close to anyone was like being close to a corpse. Had this changed? And could he see himself as successful and happy?

T: *Go ahead five years and tell me about your day. Where do you wake up?*

P: *I see myself waking up with Suzette in a brass bed.*

T: *Where is this?*

P: *Here. We kiss and make love.*

T: *Do you feel close to her?*

P: *Yes.*

T: *Do you have any children?*

P: *Two.*

T: *What does Suzette do?*

P: *She pretty much stays home. She always wanted to live the life of Riley. She has a baby-sitter and once in a while she goes shopping and runs around with her friends.*

T: *Do you have your business?*

P: *Yes, and I'm also a consultant for food things. I seem to be doing creative things. Even though those advertising classes I took didn't work out, I've made it in assembling food brochures.*

T: *What do you see next?*

P: *I see myself standing at an easel sort of thing—no painting. I see photography.*

T: *Where are the children?*

P: *They're up playing with toys and making a lot of noise.*

T: *What do you see for breakfast?*

P: *Suzette gets out the cereal—she likes her European breakfasts. I get ready for work. I'm trying to see if there's an easel in the house or if it's somewhere else. No, I see it in the house.*

T: *Is your father alive?*

P: *I don't see him in the picture.*

T: *What happened to the business?*

P: *I think it was sold. I got a sum of money.*

T: *What about your mother?*

P: *My mother's alive. She has a housekeeper.*

T: *Are you earning good money with your food ideas?*

P: *It's pretty good. I think I've drawn a little from what I got. Suzette is pretty happy, but her father thinks I should be further along. Suzette purported to be ambitious because her father wanted that, but she's really doing what*

> *she wants to do. I keep seeing this easel thing. I'm doing what is right for*
> *me creativity-wise. My heart is to be thinking of creative stuff.*
>
> T: *Tell me about dinner.*
> P: *Suzette isn't into cooking that much but we have a Latino housekeeper*
>   *and she's cooking some stuff. The kids are little but they're at the table.*
> T: *What do you do in the evening?*
> P: *I watch TV or video. I hold Suzette. She likes to be held a lot.*
> T: *Would you say you're happy?*
> P: *I have a restless side. I wonder if I'm actually involved because even in*
>   *relationships I have a tendency to isolate.*

This future projection suggests that Brad's basic negativity has been modified. He can relate, at least superficially, though he still has a way to go to achieve deep commitment and intimacy. He sees himself as having mellowed, able to accept another person without judgment. He lacks enthusiasm for children but he can accept them. Most of all, he sees himself as successful in a creative endeavor. He does not project an extremely successful life nor does he see himself as completely happy but there is only the slightest trace of the negativity that permeated his existence for so many years. The "hangover" from his painful loneliness and death in the concentration camp is clearing.

Awareness that the positive restructuring of his perception of himself is infiltrating his life will make it easier to help him weather the dark and discouraged times that are bound to come. Whether the relationship that he foresees for himself will be with Suzette is unimportant. In his life he now feels comfortable with a relationship, and this will help him stabilize.

Case 3. Projecting a Unique Harmony into the Older Years

The nurse who had the breakthrough session with Rob Bontenbal and Tineke Noordegraaf (Chapter I) consented to write the following Future Biography. It reflects her new feeling of peacefulness and suggests that this is deep-rooted and permanent. After her divorce several decades earlier she had spent four years wandering around the Far East. She had lingered for a year in Sri Lanka and felt in some way bonded to this island, possibly because of previous lifetimes there.

> *I see myself sitting on the porch of a white bungalow, looking out over the*
> *ocean. I'm on an island and it seems like the southwest coast of Sri Lanka.*
> *I have a loose, lightweight cotton dress on and bare feet. I'm sitting with the*
> *man who lives with me.*
>
> *I'm telling the man that I have two clients to see. We then start an intense*
> *conversation about work with these clients and the work I do with the children*

who live in a nearby village. It seems that I'm about to make some decision about whom to work with, and the children seem more important.

Life here is different since something happened not so long ago. There are fewer people and life is slow and casual. The island is beautiful and peaceful. The people are more respectful of each other and life is more harmonious.

There is a large garden behind my house where I spend lots of time alone. I grow much of our food. The man I live with is intense but easy to talk to and discuss matters with. He has his own work that keeps him busy. Our lives are busy but peaceful, too, with time to sit and reflect.

Our food is very simple but tasteful. Our house is comfortable but also very casual and simple.

The subject's commitment to a peaceful and simple life emerges in this story, the antithesis of what she experienced in her marriage to a successful and ambitious physician. Her six children also interfered with such a life. Evidently her deep unconscious goal has been a simple life of reflection and service, a goal much more suited to Eastern countries than to current America. The confusion over her mother and father images in some way interfered with her actualizing of this goal. Rebalancing the parental images and releasing tapes that were really her mother's have freed her to move in a direction that is more valid for her.

Case 4. Candice's Inner Choice to be Herself

A couple in their 50's came to me for help with their relationship. Both were professional people and both were in the process of dissolving long-standing marriages that had become dry and unnourishing. Aaron was a successful and popular attorney who gave much of his time to charitable causes. As long as he and his former wife had focused on their four children, they were able to overlook their basic incompatibility, but as the last child left for graduate school in the East, his wife moved out of the marriage and did not look back. Aaron was taken by surprise and floundered inwardly. His new woman friend, Candice, with two adolescent sons, had given up trying to rescue her sociopathic and dependent husband and had struck out on her own, finding freedom and creative scope as a writer at a movie studio. But after years of intense commitment in her marriage, even though there had been little return, she, too, felt lonely.

Their relationship at first seemed what each had longed for, but soon snags arose. Aaron pressed for a permanent commitment, and when Candice would not make this, claiming that she wanted to explore being herself, Aaron was both irritated and disbelieving, convinced that she was deceiving herself, especially as when he retreated from her to give her the space she said she wanted, she invariably called him for time together.

Candice was not able to see clearly where the difficulty lay. She obviously did not want to lose the relationship, and each possibility that she might lose it caused her to snatch at it. It was difficult to determine what the problem was. Were there stumbling blocks in her ability to relate that caused her to vacillate between attraction and withdrawal? What did she mean when she said she wanted to be herself? She seemed to feel that Aaron was her ideal man, so why did she hesitate?

T: *Let us see what a typical day five years from now looks like. Perhaps it will help us understand the problem between you and Aaron.*

P: *Well, I'm waking up with the alarm clock. Outside the sun is shining, and birds are singing in my garden. I call to my sons, who are both in high school now, and fix some breakfast for the three of us. They go off to school, and I watch the news and drink some coffee and then drive to the studio. I love my work. I am collaborating on a screen play with a historical background. My collaborator is another woman, and we have a good time together. I have some definite ideas about living, and I slip some of my ideas into the mouths of my characters. I'm also a part of an environmental group to save our forests, and I'm working on a fund-raiser.*

T: *Is there a man in your life?*

P: *I hope so. I need someone who is strong but will respect me as an individual, not need me, just enjoy sharing with me. I need someone who will honor my ideas and not talk down to me. And I need a playmate, someone who will run along the ocean with me in the mist and just take off for some interesting place, someone reliable, but not too tied to his work.*

T: *Could you look back and see what happened to Aaron.*

P: *I lost track of him. I hope he was able to get the camp program for children started. He was so involved with it when I knew him. I hope he trusted that he was able to do it.*

T: *What do you do for lunch when you're at the studio?*

P: *Some of us on the staff get together and talk about the films that are being made. I keep wanting to write something better, something that will move people.*

T: *How are your boys doing?*

P: *They are in a magnet high school and they find their work exciting. I give them lots of loose rein. Sometimes they seem impossible, but I just hold my nose. I wish we didn't have to live in the city, but we make the best of it. They go up to a camp near Redding in the mountains during the summer. At least they can get away for a while.*

T: *Do you ever get away?*

P: *Just now I only go where they can go with me. We go camping and skiing together and they like jazz so we go to jazz concerts. They have a lot of good friends in their magnet school. Jay wants to be a physicist.*

T: *Tell me about dinner.*

P: *I try to cook what they like for supper. It changes from year to year. We have a lot of their friends over.*

T: *There doesn't seem to be a man in your life.*

P: *I would like to have a partner, someone to share things with.*

T: *How do you feel about yourself?*

P: *Each year I like myself a little better. I like my life. I feel good about everything—my writing and my children.*

T: *What happens in the evening?*

P: *Well, I don't have to help my sons. They already know more than I do about lots of things, and the kids in the magnet school seem excited about their work. But they have to study, so I read and do some writing. I think I'm learning a language—Japanese. I have a video cassette and I play it and work on the pronunciation. Finally I go to bed. I fall asleep quickly. Sometimes I think I'd like to make love and then fall asleep, but I realize that actually I don't have much time for a man. I'm not willing to give up what I have in order to have a relationship. I look back on all those years I tried to make a relationship in my marriage, and this is better. Men want too much. One learns a lot from trying to relate to them, but I feel I've paid my dues.*

After this progression I realized that the relationship was going nowhere. Aaron wanted a commitment and the sort of deferent accommodating behavior that his former wife had tried to provide and eventually had renounced. Candice wanted friendship, equality, and a guarantee of emotional freedom for each party. She wanted to be herself in every facet of her being and she saw no reason not to do this. When she completed the Future Biography I think she realized this clearly. Very gently I moved out of a therapeutic effort for the relationship and let it come to its natural end.

Case 5. Projecting the Fruit of Years of Therapy

Carrie was the gifted physician whose regression work is described in Volume I, Chapter XXI. Here she laid the groundwork for the later resolution of her conflict with her father that is documented in the section on "Childhood" in this volume in Chapter II. Her therapy over the years has not been continuous—she had returned when she moved into new stages of personality growth that needed clarification. Steadily her energy field has become balanced and serene and she is able to work with high effectiveness. Her marriage, always good, has deepened and matured as she and her husband have become increasingly acceptant of their differences and appreciative of what they can give each other. As she has moved into the final richly productive period of her professional life, all the threads of the years of struggle are resolving into a rich tapestry.

P: *I see myself as healthy. I get up in the morning...I'm putting on my sweat suit and my running shoes. Jogging.*

T: *Are you alone?*

P: *I'm alone.... Now I'm finished with my workout. I'm showering. I'm more relaxed. I don't feel such a push. I'm scheduling my day's work, writing out the list of priorities, but I feel more relaxed. I have a feeling of peacefulness about my life and my work. I'm in the desert. I'm sharing lunch with Brian (her husband). I'm off to some kind of an appointment—I'm not sure what. I'm playing golf in the afternoon and looking forward to it. I'm sharing dinner with Brian. I'm relaxed during the evening, reading. I'm happy. I'm deeply happy. I no longer feel that push. I think Brian is in the office—I don't know where he was in the morning.*

T: *Where is your office?*

P: *It's not too far.*

T: *What is your relationship with your children?*

P: *They're in their thirties. They don't have much to do with my life. My son is active, associating with a lot of people. I'm not sure he became a doctor. He's still manipulating, and I try not to be too close because I don't want to be manipulated. My daughter's still dependent. She's trying to break away. She's aware of the problem.*

T: *Do you still help her?*

P: *No. She's managing on her own. I have some rest in my life. My practice is on a much more manageable level and I'm feeling good about it. I'm also reaching a deeper level with Brian. A deeper relationship has become important. We've learned from each other. He doesn't have to see me as manipulating because he's done some therapeutic work with his mother and has learned to say no. We can relate to each other instead of being parents for each other.*

T: *Tell me about your work.*

P: *My work is peaceful and centered and creative. I feel really good about it. I've been able to move to another level. It's much more satisfying. It's a positive feeling. With my work I'm doing good things for my fellow men, but it's not frantic anymore. My life is richer, deeper, more satisfying. I feel as though I've accomplished what I set out to do and learned what I needed to.*

Carrie still has an awareness of problem areas, such as being comfortable with her husband's projection of his dominating mother onto her and the tendency of her children to perpetuate dependence on a strong mother. But the frantic driven quality that took her to the top medically but possessed her in the process, has diminished or is gone. Her healing work can now flow through her. All that she sees in the future is a natural outgrowth of what she is currently working to become. Carrie is an example of how a life through constant work toward balance and serenity can anticipate a rich fulfillment in the older years.

Exploring One's Death

by

Ernest F. Pecci, M.D.

Introduction

It is important that we learn not to fear death. One way of accomplishing this lack of fear is to explore the various realms of consciousness between the waking dream of earth-plane existence and consciousness after death. In recent years a number of books by Moody[1] and Ring[2] and others regarding near-death experiences have helped to focus my interest on the possible reproduction of the death experience in a clinical setting by using direct suggestion.

In dealing with past lives it is important for therapists to help their patients complete the lessons of given lifetimes by taking them through the death experience up to higher planes of learning, where they can review those lifetimes and their lessons. Patients can then make more positive and constructive ego decisions regarding attitudes to take with them into their next lifetime. This is one of the most important aspects of past-life work.

It seemed to me that forward movement would be equally valuable for those approaching death through a terminal illness, especially when the process of dying stirs up ambivalence and doubt. My subsequent exploration of future progression with such people has shown the process to be both feasible and helpful.

In this process I begin by reaching as deep a state of hypnosis as possible by having the patient write numbers on a silvery, shining, deeply fogged mirror, the mirror of the inner world. Only those who are able to reach a high number are able to dematerialize their bodies, become ethereal, and pass through the mirror through time and dimensions to the soul's true home. I protect the work I do by helping each of my patients make contact with the presence, the energy of a very high Christ-like spiritual teacher, who assists in the process. Absence of such a teacher contraindicates this type of exploration.

When patients are progressed to their death they have the experience of misty white light, an expansive place of existence in which they feel totally complete, whole, needing nothing, surrounded by life. From this place they ask questions regarding the purpose of this life, just as people examining past lives search for the nature and purpose of those lifetimes. Have they fulfilled their soul's purpose for this creation? Understanding this purpose reduces the fear of leaving. Sometimes this perspective enables the dying person to realize he has completed his life purpose. He then can let go of this lifetime and move easily into the transition to the next plane. At other times a patient realizes that he has not fulfilled his goals. Then his illness may remit and give him scope to accomplish these.

Case 1. A Man Who Had Not Earned His Death

An example of the latter situation was a psychologist who had been a close friend for a long time. He had been successful in his career and had attained a number of prominent positions in his field and yet, like many people who work compulsively, he judged his life to have been mostly a waste. He had had a difficult experience in terms of physical illnesses, including recovering from cancer, then developed a weight problem that not long before our contact had been compounded by a heart attack. His health was deteriorating rapidly, probably because of chronic depression and loss of interest in the world. He was married to a much younger woman to whom he felt he was a burden. Though she did not complain, he felt it would be a blessing to her if he were to go. He was also a person with resentments and anger because of the way the field of psychology had developed and because he had not attained the satisfactions, financial and otherwise, that he felt he deserved. He felt bitterness and resentment that led to giving up on himself and wanting to end it all.

With this set, in a sense working to kill himself, he developed severe pneumonia, which he thought of as a terminal illness. He could hardly breathe and was hospitalized. Because of his weight, his poor heart condition, and his resistance to recovery, he thought he would not survive, but he did get somewhat better and came home with an oxygen tent. After that he needed considerable help to move about and to get away from using the oxygen. He managed to make a slight recovery, though remaining largely incapacitated, a common experience in those who as the result of ambivalence and fear get to the threshold of death and linger there, dragging on for some time before they can move on.

I readily agreed to visit him. Because of his closeness to me he was open, and this openness was reinforced by his basic outlook, which was not that of a conservative psychologist closed to the concept of past lives. He had never talked frankly about himself, but now he opened his heart regarding his past, and I knew that he was ready. (I must emphasize here that readiness, as in all other regression work, is an important factor.) He agreed to try to live his death because he felt that he had nothing to lose in the process, and he was able to go to such depth that I felt he was a very old soul. He was a student of the Cabala and was able to feel and come to tears when he sensed the presence of his spiritual loving teacher.

I took him up into the white light where he was free from a contextual past. Here he experienced a relative lack of feeling of guilt and could see his essence, his core, which gave him an immediate dramatic sense of self-acceptance that he had not had at any time in his life. He saw himself at his radiant best. Then he began to ask questions about what he was supposed to learn in this lifetime. There is usually one word that encapsulates the learning and his word was "tolerance," but he also needed to learn how to receive. He saw that his wife had a karmic task to take care of him and did not resent it. He also saw that he still had something to offer, that he still had sufficient knowledge to do good work. He got in touch with a number of things that might yet be accomplished in this lifetime.

Most important was the fact that he had not really earned his death. I emphasize this last concept, that one of the most agonizing sources of pain people have on leaving this earth plane is that somehow they have not fulfilled their soul's purpose on a deep level. This agony is due mostly to sins of omission. Past-life therapy often focuses on dramatic acts of selfishness and violence where karmic guilt is developed, and lifetimes of retribution follow that often compel punishment out of proportion to the crime. I'm finding more and more, however, that the most severe agony is due to the sins of omission, that we have not taken the opportunities to learn, to grow, and to live. Re-living our life looking backward often brings deep regret.

This man returned from the experience of living through his death with his entire demeanor changed. His pneumonia went into remission and his health improved. With his wife he has developed a rehabilitation clinic to work with people who are severely disabled and need an advocate to work with attorneys, such as psychologists who can verify mental status in order to justify claims. He is developing a team and an excellent and needed clinic. I have become a member of it and am pleased with the kind of work he has been doing.

Case 2. A Woman Who Had Earned Her Death

An example of a dying patient who came to see death as a positive experience was a woman who had been the director of a mental health establishment. She was dying from cancer and was in chronic pain but because she was strong and did not like to show weakness it was difficult for her to accept her helplessness or express any kind of fear, and she denied that she was dying. I took her up to the misty white light where she felt a sense of completeness and total peace. She learned there that to a great extent she had fulfilled her purpose and had overcome selfishness through her work. She felt peace in terms of her children because from this high place she was able to look at them and get a sense of their direction and know that she had given them what they needed.

After this experience she was able to rest free from fear and pain and to sleep comfortably, and medication became unnecessary. We explored the dimension of dying on several occasions, during which she became increasingly at peace with herself, and one evening she made the transition very simply to the other plane.

Case 3. Helen Wambach

I would like to share the experiences that I had with Helen Wambach, whom I had the privilege of seeing near the end. She made a desperate call, saying, "Ernie, stop those doctors from trying to save my life. They keep me alive." She had been going in and out of the hospital with a number of severe medical problems. She would get better for a while and then would be taken back to the hospital. She wanted me to explain to the doctors that she didn't want that to continue. I could not do that, but I began to work with her on her ambivalence about leaving. Certainly no one deserved to be brought to a future life more than Helen, who had brought thousands to future lifetime existences while she was doing research. With her vivacious and loving nature she had personified life itself to me and to many others. However, she felt ambivalent regarding the continuation of her work.

She went easily into the white light and was able to call to her the soul of a previous lover for whom she had longed for many years and who had already made the transition. This soul was able to come to her and she had a conversation with him. As she reviewed her life she appreciated more fully the hours of shared love she had had with him and which, by their absence, had made her last years lonely. She had stayed on because she felt committed to her research, but from her increased perspective she now saw that she had found the right person to interpret and carry on the work that she had started. As a result, she experienced a feeling of completeness regarding this lifetime and was able to release her ambivalence and shortly afterward made her transition.

In regression work we are becoming increasingly skillful in integrating the lessons of past lifetimes and releasing the soul entity from ambivalence and regret. We need to move into greater understanding of this for the benefit of the terminally ill.

Healing the Dying

by

Franklin Loehr, D.D.

Introduction

The usefulness of past-life recall has already been strikingly demon-strated in the results of those counselors who have used it in their psycho-therapy with clients. It is a technique that is growing rapidly, as the recognition spreads that this is a method for attaining vastly deeper and more life-transforming results in strikingly less time. On the other hand, the element of cosmic purpose, that is, looking into the future to understand the present, has so far been less conceptualized and explored. In all these areas there is a common denominator in the recognition that the client's own decisions are decisive in his life.

In working with past lives a life review at the end of each lifetime is the basis for significant change. Then, when the working relationship of subconscious and conscious levels of mind in this sort of exploration has been well established, it is possible to go into an altered state of conscious-ness and review the current life to date. Researchers in the near-death experience, Moody, Ring and Sabom, report that a life review often takes place in such a state. In regression work, whether in the past or present, we ask the client to do essentially the same thing that occurs in the near-death experience: to look at the persons and experiences that were or are significant and to consider why they hold significance.

Following the recall of past lives and considerations of the current life to date, the patient can be moved into a scan of future events in this lifetime and eventually into a review of this life from the perspective of his future death. Clinicians report apparent good results in taking clients forward to observe future events, though things seen and reported in such sessions are more difficult to judge objectively than is past-life recall. A future projection inadequately handled can lead to fanciful or misleading results that only glorify the ego, but that is true of all subconscious work and merely underlines the need for professional competence in the counselor.

An especially valuable use of this forward projection is the Death Preview. This yields a great deal of information about the cosmic purpose of the individual's life. It can also uncover hidden death wishes and forces which, raised to consciousness, can be the subject of further work. When used with persons who face imminent death it produces a clarity and enlightenment that can change their attitude toward the death they face.

Case: A Courageous Embracing of Death

A revealing experience that illustrates the power of this technique in a person facing death occurred with Susan, a young woman in her mid-thirties with terminal cancer. Her cancer, when discovered, was inoperable, and this courageous woman chose not to undergo the painful and uncertain route of chemotherapy, radiation, etc. She came to me when it seemed she had only a half year or so to live, and I arranged for one of our most skilled researcher-clinicians to take her first into a number of a past-life recalls. Each time, the clinician lovingly and skillfully took her through the death experience of that past life. At first Susan was apprehensive of this, but in cautious steps and gradual increments she became able to go fully into the past-death recalls and reported after several sessions that remembering and re-experiencing the death experiences of those past lives had reduced her apprehension and fear of her approaching death in this life.

Following this preparation I took her into several experiences of a Death Preview of the death now approaching. Here she contacted the strong masculine side of her personality but also showed that she had gained a new appreciation of the feminine in this lifetime, "rounded and mounded" as she put it, and a greater initial receptivity to feminine lives, which had been difficult for her this time around. She gained early information about the astral post-death state that she would enter and became joyous at the cosmic learning she saw she would experience. It was a glorious experience for both of us! I learned through Susan a great deal of what death and life after death can be like. And Susan, after several Death Previews, came to a happy, even eager anticipation of the time when she would cross over the invisible line "for keeps." Visitors who did not know what preparation she had made remarked on how she had changed, not recovering physically but, after her preview of the coming state, characterized by a new attitude of happiness and sureness about herself.

I feel that human beings eventually will be able and allowed to choose their time of death. It would have been a much more satisfying and fulfilling experience for Susan if she could have made her preparations, seen her friends one last time, and said goodbye. Then in a setting of beauty and love and peace, with the closest of her friends and advisors around her, she could have reached out in full consciousness to her council of Guides and Teachers and others awaiting her across the line and could have gone over at that time to be with them. She knew them from the experiences of her death that she had previewed. She had tasted the love and growth and learning and adventures awaiting her. She could count on these experiences when she died but it might have been a more joyous experience if she could have chosen her own timing.

New Age or Brave New World?

by

Chet B. Snow, Ph. D.

Introduction

Today, as humanity struggles to avoid self-destruction, either through nuclear war or by environmental strangulation, speculation about the future is rampant. Many popular predictions from such diverse sources as fundamentalist Christians and New Age "channels" forecast some kind of impending apocalyptic doom. In addition, many respected scientists agree that even a limited nuclear exchange could trigger a "nuclear winter" with the potential to extinguish human civilization and most of the physical species living on the planet. Moreover, even without this violent scenario, the subtle pressures of unchecked population growth, burning fossil fuels, and continuing pollution of earth's air and water, all spell major problems ahead. Persisting world tensions, especially in the volatile Middle East, the specter of mass starvation and epidemics in Africa, and increasingly unpredictable weather make us stop and think as we approach the turn of the Millennium.

These considerations moved Dr. Helen Wambach, who was already noted for her pioneering research into past lives, to look at the mechanics of future prediction. Her earlier work had shown that when taken into a slightly altered state of consciousness or "waking trance," about 90 percent of ordinary, average Americans were able to tune into a past-life period and answer questions about sex, clothing, food, and money or medium of exchange. She found that her subjects' answers related to known historical facts such as population curves, gender ratios, and nutrition sources.[3]

The fact that many people reported that they had anticipated her questions during their past-life "trips" encouraged Dr. Wambach to explore whether altered-state capabilities could be tapped for exploration of the future. Thus, beginning in 1980, she offered the subjects in her research workshops the option of progressing into one of two future time periods: around 2100 A.D. or 2300 A.D. As before, her technique consisted of asking routine, statistically comparable questions. The results were startling.[4]

The first unusual finding was that only a minimal number of her subjects found themselves returning to physical incarnations in those two time periods—only 5 to 6 percent in 2100 A.D. and about double that for 2300 A.D. Their replies suggested that for some unknown reason the earth will undergo a steep population drop before 2100 A.D. and only gradually begin to rebound to more population in 2300 A.D. The gender ratio remains constant at around 50:50 but a few future-life subjects reported having androgynous bodies, neither clearly male nor female. This anomaly had never happened during trips to past-life periods.

The second surprising finding was that the lifetimes recovered from the future showed four consistent patterns or models. In 2100 A.D. these were: life in a space colony or space station off of the earth; budding New Age-style communities with increased consciousness potentials; technocratic and survivalist societies existing either underground (and underwater) or inside huge domes who found contact with the outside environment noxious; and finally, rural and urban dwellers sharing a primitive, nontechnical, or post-disaster setting. Later analysis of reports from 2300 A.D. turned up similar groupings but with more variations among each of the major types.

However, the data in general remained consistent. Helen Wambach realized that these reports could be the result of fantasy or projection, but she felt that they had deeper implications. They could be considered real, if incomplete, sketches of the world about a century from now, similar to past-life reports, which depict actual events but with lapses and inaccuracies. Evidently our linear time and space models of reality do not apply to the subconscious mind, which lives beyond such boundaries and is able under the right conditions to view the future simultaneously with the past and present in one coexisting whole.

Though it is possible that some of these future scenarios could exist together, it remains true that the four basic lifestyle types suggest that the futures depicted by the progressed subjects represent alternative models of potential future realities. Such alternatives might be expressed differently in different people, thereby coexisting within the same space-time framework, or, more gravely, they may represent planet-wide archetypes whose realization is dependent on the impact of a dominant majority.

This concept of alternate futures implies free will and conscious choice for humanity, and places the necessity of choosing wisely squarely on our shoulders as to which of these potential future realities we will create. In effect, the choice between a holistic vision of New Age of cooperation and harmony with nature, and the competitive Brave New World of technocratic survivalists is ours to make today.

As human beings we live and move through a space-time universe whose primary function apparently is providing opportunities for choice. The new physics of Quantum Mechanics demonstrates that the aspect of the material world that we choose to observe actually influences the basic nature of the reality we experience. Modern psychology teaches that conscious choice, as opposed to instinct, is a uniquely human characteristic and is a function of what we call the will or willpower. Learning to choose wisely among competing alternatives forms the basis for education in human systems as long as they exist within the bounds of linear time. Regardless of whether we believe in a prehistoric "fall from grace," or in our current material space-time state as a self-imposed experiment, it is clear that making choices and learning from their results is critical to our development, both as individuals and as a species.[5]

The philosophy commonly known as "Ageless Wisdom" and attributed to such venerable sources as the ancient gods Hermes or Ra, tells us that we incarnate on earth because we need linear time's educational qualities. We are here to learn from experiences that are designed to make us better co-creators of new and exciting realities within the overall divine framework or "All That Is." But though we must live with the consequences of our actions across linear time while in human form, we nonetheless *need* linear time's buffer between what our ever-active minds conceive and the experience of the results of our mental desires. Life would be chaotic if our every waking thought produced an immediate physical response.

According to ancient teachings and traditions from around the globe, we are now approaching a special time of critical choices whose consequences will have widespread and lasting influence on human history. Conditions within our linear time line must and will change soon. The collective psychic energies pushing for change have already become irresistible, but, as does a fetus nearing its term, we still cling to our warm, dark, and familiar womb until forcibly ejected into a new, at first hardly pleasant, reality. Whether we ascribe the coming widely-predicted changes to ecological imbalances, socioeconomic inequities, astrological cycles, UFO's, or the divine will of God matters less than our recognition that the first contractions of a new birth have already begun.

Some kind of change seems both inevitable and ultimately desirable. What remains to be seen, however, is how this dynamic for change will manifest and just how drastic events must become in order to produce the necessary global transformation. The future-life progressions begun by Helen Wambach and carried forward by Dr. Leo Sprinkle and myself provide a glimpse of some of the prevailing archetypes of our futures, at least for contemporary Americans. These stories, coming largely from the subconscious mind during dreamlike reveries, illustrate a framework of common expectations already deeply embedded in the collective subconscious of today's world. They confirm our inner conviction that significant events are about to occur. In large measure they also reaffirm both ancient and modern prophecies that widespread natural and man-made catastrophes are just around the corner.[6]

The two distinct and fundamental models of the upcoming changes—the New Age script and the scenario of the Apocalypse, have been so widely foreseen that they already possess tremendous psychic energy within the human subconscious. Our individual and collective choices over the next several years will influence the nature of the coming birth of the next World Age. The Apocalyptic model follows humanity's traditional archetype of revolution and resistance and has been widely predicted for the end of this 20th century. Depending on whether one adopts a Western or Eastern view of the nature of time, this model foresees either a once-only "Big Bang" end to human civilization as we know it or a periodic and renewable, if violent, cleansing of spaceship earth and its human passengers.

The arrival of the alternative New Age archetype has not been so explicitly prophesied across the ages, but it is nonetheless growing as a model in human consciousness today: it is humanity's ancient dream of mass cooperation, initiation, and rebirth. In this dream of global harmony the earth itself takes on a unified planetary identity (Gaia). Spiritual sources throughout history have reminded us time and again that despite our seeming separateness, all beings stem from a single common source. Our physical existence within the space-time universe has as its ultimate goal a complete and perfect self-reunion within that source, enhanced and glorified by what we have experienced here. The eternal promise of the Ageless Wisdom philosophy is that this reunion *must and will occur,* for, at some level of reality beyond that of physical time-space, it already exists. Nonetheless, as loved co-creators of All That Is, we retain the individual free will to advance or retard this reunion across linear time with our awareness. Thus, although Unity's ultimate realization is already set, the type and quality of the process used to make it happen depends on our individual and collective human choices.

The primary barrier blocking those choices that favor the birth of a harmonious new world is selfishness—choosing to follow the ego or lower-self's limiting time-bound desires instead of extending our awareness beyond immediate self-gratification and seeing our true multidimensional role within the greater Whole or All That Is reality. Attuning our will to that Higher Power brings us the ability and joy of unconditional love. If we want world cooperation and peace instead of competition and war, we must internalize these virtues in ourselves and act accordingly in our current relationships, right where we are now. As we move beyond egoistic pride and desire, we become ready and able to cooperate with others to find mutually acceptable solutions to today's problems.

Beliefs are a product of the interplay of both subconscious habit patterns, developed from many life experiences, and the conscious decisions of our will or willpower. Looked at dispassionately, it is not hard to realize that our culture's current habits and beliefs are steering us toward an Apocalyptic solution to the world's grave problems. Therefore only a sustained effort of collective willpower and individual self-transformation is going to stem that tide and turn us toward a harmonious global awakening to the reality of planetary oneness.

But the conscious mind, which controls the will, cannot bear the burden alone; it simply is not strong enough. This is the grave problem faced by the those psychological methods that rely solely on behavioral stimuli and conscious-level analysis to effect lasting change. To succeed in shifting humanity's energies from the Apocalyptic archetype to one of a New Age of initiation and rebirth we must also tap the limitless potential of the subconscious, acknowledging our negative hidden agendas stemming from fear and unavowable selfish desires. We must get in touch with our inner past, both its bright spots and its shadows, if we wish to change our outer future.

It is at this level of understanding that future-life progression therapy can benefit both individual and general processes of transformation. Projecting into a future incarnation allows us to preview some of the major consequences of the thoughts and actions we are currently setting up. If, as I believe Helen Wambach's and my research demonstrates, the subconscious "dreaming" mind has access to reality states beyond the normal confines of linear time and three-dimensional space, then as we access information about a perceived "future life," what are we experiencing? Are these eternally-fixed, predestined situations that we may merely observe and over which we have no control? I don't believe so, for then our experiences during incarnations within linear time would merely be a collection of predetermined happenings without purpose or choice. Such a belief system denies the patently instructional nature of living time after time in a world of cause and effect.

Instead, it seems more logical to assume that the future lives we access during altered-state work represent those actions and attitudes that best reflect the reality toward which we are heading *based on the sum total of our experience until now.* As such they reflect our true future down what I call the path of least resistance or destiny line. These are at least partial glimpses of the actual situations we will indeed face tomorrow unless we harness both willpower and the subconscious to change fundamental habit patterns and reactions, thereby learning the lessons of the past and making further similar events and sufferings unnecessary. Thus, altered-state progressions into future lives complement and complete the results of past-life and childhood or perinatal age regression work. All of these techniques provide us with tools for bringing about lasting personality improvements, both individual and collective.

Many different paths lead inward toward this cleansing and internal awakening. It is the sum of all the individual strivings for self-knowledge and acceptance that will make the difference globally. Furthermore, once we have begun to look within, we must then replace our outmoded egotistical programming with the most positive universal spiritual ideal that we can conceive and hold to it despite the resistance that we will inevitably meet. Persistence in our intent to break established habit patterns that no longer serve us assures us of final triumph. Ultimately our true inner awakening will always prove far more powerful than the resistances we'll encounter both within and in the world around us, if we retain our resolve to change.[7]

There will be a slow but sure altering of reactions to problems, emotional attitudes, and even physical cravings as our bodies and minds adjust to the spiritual growth we have set in motion. Consistency and persistence in whatever spiritual practice meets one's needs will bring us closer to the ultimate self-reunion that is our birthright and life's final goal.

Case 1. Future Assistance for Earth Restoration
(Model of Life in a Space Colony off the Earth)

As mentioned above, one of the benefits of future-life progression is that in projecting ahead into a future life not only can we receive information about those trends that currently exist in humanity's collective unconscious but we can also access the direction in which our own path, the sum total of what we have become at this time, is leading. The following case reflects both these aspects, as it is typical of what I call the Type I (Space) environment in my book, *Mass Dreams of the Future*, and it also reveals personal progress in several key therapy issues for the client.

In my earlier section on past-life therapy, I described a dramatic session with an attractive southern California housewife I called Bea. During that session she discovered how unresolved conflicts and emotional attachments from an earlier life in Scotland had erupted into her current life, threatening her marriage through a passionate affair with a younger man, an affair that she felt helpless to stop. Re-living those events helped Bea to sort out her true current feelings and assisted her in regaining control over her emotional life.

About a year later, after reading my book, Bea expressed an interest in undergoing a future-life progression. A good subject, she experienced no difficulty in relaxing her body, allowing her mind to reach that level where it could receive information without regard for the rules of linear time or three-dimensional space. In response to my suggestions that she would progress into her next incarnation, she soon found herself in a slender, very fair-skinned body of a twenty-year-old woman named Rhea.

Looking down, Rhea discovered she had on a form-fitting one-piece jumpsuit of "pastel blue," including matching soft cloth boots. Apparently some kind of research scientist, she was working in a laboratory with 14 others of her "unit." Although not able to see outside, she intuitively felt that they were in a space station orbiting high above the earth. It felt a somewhat "sterile" environment to her. She was particularly drawn to one fellow unit member, Randol, whom she later described as "my partner." This seemed her only close emotional tie.

P: *I don't feel close to anyone in the unit but Randol. Somehow I know he and I agree on the ultimate purpose of our work but the others have different plans. It's a bit tense for us at times because we know that dissent is not really tolerated. So we have to keep our opinions to ourselves.*

T: *What is your "unit" working on?*

P: *Our project has to do with reforestation of the earth below. We are supposed to develop ways for accelerating the growth cycle of certain trees so that they will be able to restore the planet's atmosphere as quickly as possible. I don't know what happened that upset the balance previously; I'm not sure anyone does, but apparently there were only a few trees left and that upset the balance of nature.*

T: *That sounds like a worthwhile goal. Why do you and Randol disagree with the others?*

P: *Most of them don't think that it will work and they're preparing to give the project up. It's like they're just working on it as routine and aren't putting their hearts into it. No one wants to get involved; everything seems cold and emotionless except where one's immediate personal wants are concerned. Randol and I—there may be more of us but I'm not aware of it—think differently. I want to help restore the old beauty of earth as well as its functional qualities.*

T: *I understand. Is there anything in that life that you are able to do to persuade your colleagues to change their point of view? Or are you basically helpless to change things there? (Note: A feeling of personal "helplessness" to alter dysfunctional life circumstances had characterized Bea's past-life sessions and had carried over into her current feelings when we'd begun therapy.)*

P: *Randol and I have a small sitting room, our private quarters, I think. I'm finally talking over my feelings with him and I find that he agrees with me. It's wonderful; we totally understand each other. Now that I see that he, too, feels the same way, I know we will have an impact on the unit.*

T: *Very good. Now I want you to go to the most significant direct consequence of your sharing your concerns with Randol. What happens as a result of that?*

P: *I'm older now, in my mid-forties, I think [Bea's current age]. And it's wonderful! I see that we succeeded in persuading several of our colleagues in the laboratory because people are much closer now and there's an atmosphere of hope. Apparently the trees are regenerating things in those sections of earth faster than anyone had predicted.*

And I seem to remember another occasion where I was able to assume responsibility for what was happening all by myself, when even Randol didn't think it would work. That's all come together now and I realize that I can take charge when I have to.

T: *That's excellent. Now, I want you to move forward to the last day that you spend in that lifetime in that body as Rhea. You'll have no physical pain and no fear but will be able to review your conscious thoughts and actions at that time.... Now, it's the last day you spend as Rhea. What's going on?*

P: *(With a note of awe in her voice.) I think I'm down on the earth's surface now and we're actually going "Outside." It feels very special to be going Outside somehow. Part of me doesn't want to leave the project just yet but I know that it is time and that I have chosen this day and this place to depart. Those close to me in that life are gathered around. I see Randol there.... Oh, he's the same one as George in Scotland and John today, no wonder we've been so close! And there's my [current-life] son, who's a close and respected colleague then. It's beautiful.*

(Sighing.) I know I must go now and it's not really sad, something like when you send a friend off on a long journey and you know you won't see them for a while.... I'm ready now.... And I sit down and just go....

(Strong emotion in voice.) Oh, now I'm able to float up above and look down on the earth below. The earth is coming back to life; the forests are starting to expand and there are fewer dry, brown spots below. My gift was to leave a better earth behind than when I entered that lifetime.... It was a good life and I'm glad I came back for it.

Bea's progression experience was positive for her in several respects. First, her peaceable reunion with John, the lover who had caused so much trouble as George in Scotland and who nearly broke up her marriage in her current life, seemed to indicate that she was now resolving that karmic pattern. Finding her son as a respected colleague was also reassuring. Most important, however, was finding that her current struggle to build self-confidence and gain control over her personal life would bear fruit in the future as she used authority responsibly to help restore the planet she so loves today.

Case 2. A French View of Future Life on Earth
(Model of a Technocratic and Survivalist Society and of a Primitive Post-Disaster Setting)

Jean-Claude is a young Frenchman who, at 22 years old, sought me out, not so much for intensive therapy as for counseling about alternative spiritual paths and advice about discovering his life's purpose. Although presently employed as a night hotel clerk in Paris, his true passion is painting. Despite little formal training, his work reveals the sensitivity of the true artist and, having already put together two successful shows in the French capital during the two and a half years I've known him, he is well on his way to making art his livelihood.

After three or four sessions in which he remembered past lives ranging from an aborigine in the Australian outback before the first European explorers, to an "empty life" as an early-19th century French provincial housewife, to a frustrated art dealer who dabbled in the Impressionist movement during the "Belle Epoque," Jean-Clause asked me about progressing to the future. As he was a good hypnotic subject and I felt that such a progression might reveal more about his personal search, I agreed.

Within just a few moments of my initial suggestions to "breathe deeply and relax," Jean-Claude found himself in the body of a "slender, very white-skinned" man.

> P: *(Even, flat tone.) It's night and I'm outside, which seems strange, unfamiliar to me. The air is very warm and although my chest is bare and I'm only wearing white shorts and soft-soled shoes, my face is entirely covered with a breathing mask.... (Pause.)*
>
> T: *What are you doing there outside?*
>
> P: *I can see better now and realize that there are several of us out there and we're using some kind of chemicals to fight a fire, apparently caused by a lightning strike. But somehow I know that even without the fire, I cannot survive long out here away from the domed-over city behind me. Just looking back at it gives me a good, protected feeling.*
>
> T: *All right, now I want you to go back in that lifetime to a time when you are inside your domed city, when you are with your family there.*
>
> P: *Yes, I'm only eight now but still dressed in similar white shorts, a tee shirt, and soft shoes. I'm in a rather small interior room with my parents. They're tall and thin and both dressed in one-piece white suits. My mother's complexion is much lighter than my dad's although both have pale skin. Although no one expresses any outward emotions, I know they're concerned over something. It's about me, that I have some kind of examination to pass soon and they wonder how I will succeed.*
>
> T: *Good, let yourself go forward now to that time and become aware of what happens there.*
>
> P: *Did I say that everything is painted in shades of white or very pale pastels here? Even the living quarters. Now I'm in a larger but still off-white room with several other children. We're all about 10 years old and dressed in white jumpsuits. A large round crystal ball is on a raised dias in the center.*
>
> T: *What's happening with the crystal, or is it just decoration?*
>
> P: *No, it's the focus of everything. One by one we are guided up to the crystal ball and we stare into it. It's as if it, or some force coming from it, knows everything about us. Is this what my parents were concerned about?*

T: *What happens next?*

P: *I feel no fear when it's my turn. In fact it's very peaceful; I feel it instills total peace within me and I give over my mind and my emotions to it gladly. Now that I think about it, I realize that there are similar, smaller crystals both at home and in the classroom I was in earlier. It is all so quiet and peaceful.*

T: *All right, you've passed your examination by the crystal and now you're going forward to a time when you are doing whatever occupation or job you perform in that lifetime. Where are you now?*

P: *I'm 21 years old and in an ultra-modern office complex. There are around 15 of us in my "team unit." Each of us is working at a different task, mostly using computer screens with very complex graphic designs. Maybe we're developing models of some kind of space craft. I'm using a light-tipped pen to create graphics on the screen. You can draw and draw but the images erase themselves until you enter them by code into the computer.*

T: *Very good, now, I want you to go to a particularly important event from that life, something that stands out from the rest for you, that influenced your life there.*

P: *I'm back at the time of that fire that I saw earlier. There's a big electrical storm outside the dome, much bigger than usual. It's almost strange because no one seems upset or afraid even though I know none of us has seen anything like it before.*

T: *Does the lightning strike the dome?*

P: *Oh no, it's protected. It strikes some trees outside; there aren't many out there and these catch fire.... (Pause...for the first time his voice assumes a more emotion-filled quality.) Oh, There are some people out there taking shelter under the trees. I think some of them may be injured. So that's why we're going outside, not just to fight the fire but to take medicine to them.*

T: *Move forward now. Do you get near these people? What do they look like?*

P: *They're human beings just like us but they're wearing dark clothing and look awfully dirty. They even smell funny. There aren't a lot of them and they're huddled together and act very suspicious of us, like they're afraid. I've never seen people like them before but I know they exist.*

T: *What do you do next?*

P: *I'm carrying some packages of medicine forward and putting them down on the ground. Another person is checking over one man who seems burned. He's the only one whom they pushed forward for treatment. Soon we must return back inside the dome.... We go down a deep elevator shaft so I guess most of our living space is underground. Before we can go back we must strip off our clothing and shower off the dirt and soot from the fire.*

T: *What happens then?*

P: *(His voice regains its flat, emotionless quality.) I'm going into a large amphitheater space where people meet and socialize. It's very quiet, since we don't have to talk but communicate telepathically. It's peaceful and pleasant again.*

T: *Did you ever see any of those people again?*

P: *No, although I know they come around the city's perimeter sometimes, but it isn't my team unit's job to interact with them so I'm not involved. The fire was the first time I really saw them up close and realized they were human beings like us.*

T: *All right, now let yourself move forward until you get to the last day you spend in that body, in that lifetime. You have no pain and no fear. Now, where are you? What are you doing?*

P: *I'm in a hospital or clinic room, lying under a white sheet in a kind of elongated box. Artificial life support systems are keeping my body alive until the time I've chosen to leave it. I feel it is my choice when I want to go although I know that my life here is finished.*

(Pause.) Now, I'm ready and I just release my thoughts from the body and float up and up and up. I see the earth from up in the sky for the first time and realize I chose this lifetime in order to be a part of a project to advance the human race. We were helping earth and humanity recover from some past calamity, I feel. It was a good life if a bit sterile. Everything was in shades of white it seemed. I think that city was near what is now called the Dalmatian coast and the time is around 2100 A.D.

(After his return to full waking consciousness.) Well, it certainly was different from what I'd expected I'd find in my next incarnation but I kind of enjoyed the peace and serenity we had there.

Jean-Claude's progression was typical of the future civilization I dubbed Type III or "Hi-Tech" in *Mass Dreams of the Future*. It provides an interesting and rare glimpse of what may be the limited interaction between that group, which always lives underground or under artificial domes that keeps the outside environment out, and those primitive "Rustic" people whom I call Type IV in my book. The most striking characteristics of this underground civilization were their lack of emotions, their almost sterile or monochrome environment, their high level of technology, and their artificial climate. Jean Claude's group's involvement with the large crystal ball and the project to restore the earth's environment, as well as his feelings that the overall atmosphere was peaceful and serene, were more positive than many other reports from this group.

In discussing his experience afterward, Jean-Claude decided that after thinking it over he was not terribly surprised to find himself in that kind of setting for a future life. He was particularly intrigued with the light-tipped pen and vivid graphics he found himself working on, feeling it was like an extension of one of the art styles he was currently developing. Since that progression he told me he has become more interested in both space travel themes and in how the earth's ecological balance may be restored.

Case 3. Arcadia Ahead (Model of a Harmonious New Age)

Important personal benefits can also be derived from undergoing a positive future-life progression. After attending one of my recent day-long workshops in the Washington D.C. area, a 40-year-old computer programmer I'll call Greta arranged for a private, individual appointment. She had been intrigued by the future life, apparently in 23rd century Greece, that she'd experienced during the group session and she wanted to explore it further.

"I was especially interested by the combination of advanced scientific research going on and the high-spirited atmosphere of the community I found myself living in," she commented in her pre-session interview. "It said something to me about the seemingly mutually-exclusive goals I've been striving for in my current life with some success but much less than I'd like."

An attractive brunette, in her current life the divorced mother of a teenage daughter, Greta proved an excellent subject, slipping easily back into her clearly-male lifetime about 200 years "ahead" across linear time. Once again she found herself standing in the doorway of a large, round room.

T: *Now describe yourself as you stand there in that circular room. What do you look like?*

P: *I'm a young man, around 25 years old. I've a trim, very fit body, with short dark hair and a medium build. The skin tone is strikingly white and I appear to be a picture of glowing health. It feels good in this body.*

T: *Look down at your feet and slowly scan up your body; what kind of clothes are you wearing?*

P: *I've sandals on, they could be synthetic or perhaps made of bleached leather. I'm wearing a kind of long ivory-colored tunic or robe that is soft and comfortable. It's belted with a golden cord at the waist. Short, fitted sleeves that seem more decorative than functional complete the outfit. It has an open collar with some kind of gold embroidery around the neckline. It's quite attractive and seems suited to the comfortably warm room I'm in.*

T: *All right. Now, look up and take stock of your surroundings. You've said you're indoors; is this where you live or does this place have some other function?*

P: *Everything here is exceptionally clean, almost sterile. The walls are a pleasant pale blue and there's definitely scientific equipment, like a computer control panel and an examination screen off to one side. It seems to be a medical laboratory. I don't feel exactly as if I live here, but I know I spend a lot of time in this room. It's a very comfortable feeling.*

T: *Okay. Now move yourself forward a short while until you find yourself performing whatever duties or job you have to do in that lifetime at that place. You'll remain at about the same age.*

P: *I'm walking across the room to the control panel. Even though it's not like anything I'd recognize today, I know it's familiar to me there. I think I designed it. Yes, that's it; I helped design this new, more efficient scanning and analysis system and today is its final test. I feel excited, confident but just a bit nervous, nonetheless.*

T: *Continue forward until the test is in progress. What's happening, now?*

P: *A young woman volunteer is standing in front of the examination panel. She's quite beautiful with shoulder-length auburn hair. She's clothed only in a thin gauze-like garment. Five of the community "elders" are present. I call them "elders" out of respect but one looks only about 20 years old. They're here to witness the test and decide if the device will benefit our community.*

T: *Let yourself go ahead a few moments more.*

P: *Now the panel is moving; it glides completely around her like a curtain and although it never touches her directly I know it is measuring activity levels in every cell of her body. Plus it can somehow "see" her surrounding electromagnetic energy field as well. Any hint of disharmony in that field will be detected long before it reaches the cellular level. Any patterns of discrepancies will be noted and appropriate remedies applied.*

T: *Move forward until the test is over. What are the results?*

P: *We're in a different place now, a large rectangular room with bay windows and a wide balcony terrace at one end. I'm standing outside, in a similar long robe, only this one's light green. I'm elated, as I know the test went very well. But most of all I'm in love with the view from this balcony. It's set on the crest of a pointed ridge overlooking a calm, turquoise sea. It's the Aegean Sea. There are groves of fruit trees off to one side and I can see other smaller white buildings dotting the hillside. Our whole community is like this, nestled above that beautiful shimmering sea. I feel we're both a scientific research group and spiritual center.*

T: *Are you in your home for this celebration or somewhere else?*

P: *No, it's the community building, set at the loveliest spot of the settlement. We share it both for daily meals and community events. Right now there must be 100 people, practically the entire adult population, gathered here to give thanks for the success of the new medical equipment. But it's more like a party or elegant communal dance than a religious service. I feel such an equality, a oneness of purpose among everyone here. Still, the same "elders" do seem to be leading things and the atmosphere is highly spiritual as well as festive. I think it's the most deeply-moving moment in my life. I'm especially proud to share it with my new bride. I realize now that she was the volunteer tested earlier.*

T: *That must be very rewarding for you, to know that your design was successful. Can you move forward again, now, until a moment when you're a little older, and this time, back in your home?*

P: *(Pauses.) I guess I'm at home for it feels homelike to me, but in fact I'm now standing outside in a kind of cloister, only it's also an impressive garden with flowers, vegetables, and a border of olive trees. I think several families share this two-story building set around the garden compound, which has a fountain in the center as well as the plants. There's an older woman who I think is one of my neighbors sitting in the shade of the olive trees at the far corner.*

T: Can you go inside?

P: *Oh yes, but it's so pretty out here just as evening falls. Somehow I get the impression we enjoy being outside mostly at dusk and dawn; it may be too hot or too sunny in the middle of the day. No one I've seen looks tanned by the sun, although some have naturally darker skin than mine.*

After ascertaining that prolonged exposure to the direct rays of the sun at midday wasn't considered healthy (possibly due to increased ultraviolet rays—several future-life workshop participants also had noted having pale skin), I took Greta forward to a moment when her future-life male *persona* was at home sharing a special moment with her family.

P: *I'm in my late thirties now and it's my daughter's sixth birthday, a time of celebration for it marks her entry into the community as an independent person. Although she'll still live with us, most of her time will be spent at the community learning center now, discovering and developing her special talents. We've just returned from a formal initiation ceremony at the center. Now each of the family is offering her a gift, something they've created just for her. My gift is a hologram that creates different images in response to directed energy visualization. I also see my wife present and two older boys. They look about 10 and 13. All the children are very handsome and healthy looking.*

T: Are there any older people present?

P: *Yes, my wife's parents. They live nearby. But except for their clothing, which is beige and somehow denotes their age or status, they look almost as young as we do. I recognize my mother-in-law as one of the "elders" who inspected my invention earlier. I think my own parents have already made their transitions. It seems to be more a matter of personal choice then anything else here.*

T: How do you feel about that? That they chose to leave?

P: *Quite accepting and at peace. The important thing seems to be your quality of life and fulfilling whatever contribution you've chosen to make. Everyone knows the truth of spiritual immortality and therefore feels free to come and go as they please. I feel everyone cares deeply about everyone else and respects and honors their decision.*

T: It sounds idyllic. I'd like you to move ahead of yourself now, to that time when you are about to make your own transition. To the day you will leave that physical body. You'll feel no pain and have no fear.

P: *(After a pause.) Yes, I've made my decision. It's time to go. I'm at home and see my daughter, now a grown woman, standing beside me. I think my wife has already gone. My work is over and I'm feeling tired within, even though I don't look over 40.*

T: *Move forward to the moment when you separate from that body. Where are you now?*

P: *There's a special spot overlooking the sea on the opposite side of the ridge from the community center. You can see the sunset from there across the sea and other inlets. I've chosen to leave my body there after witnessing one last display of Earth's lovely pastel colors. Two or three others are with me and we're in silent communion. I watch the sun go down and feel my breathing get shallower and shallower. It's time to go. I sense a lightness of being....*

  Now I'm looking down on the scene from above. It's an incredibly beautiful feeling. I consciously send love to those who remain below and know they sense it. My daughter looks up and smiles and points upward; I know the Path. A Light beckons and I feel a warm, loving Presence reach out for me. "Good-bye, old man," I whisper.

Both Greta and I were profoundly moved by the experience of calm and beauty we'd felt in the room as she described those last earthly moments of the medical researcher in that future Grecian Arcadia.

"What a send-off," she remarked at the end of the session. "I guess with that to look forward to, it's worth the occasional pain and frustration I feel today in trying to integrate my left-brain logic and research interests with the spiritual certainty of rebirth and eternal life that I feel so deeply."

In a later follow-up conversation, Greta expressed a continuing sense of harmony and oneness in her life since the future-life session. Its positive message had reinforced her innate spiritual convictions while at the same time reaffirming others in both her current and potential future lifetimes. She concluded:

I know that even then the whole Earth won't have become a new "Garden of Eden." We're a long way from that now and it'll take a lot of hard work just to undo the environmental damage we've already caused. But it's important for me to know that even if such communities are small and separated from each other to start, they can and will exist as models for the regenerated Earth and liberated humanity I believe in.

Chapter IX

Synthesis

The events of one's lifetime often appear to be accidental happenings, disconnected footprints on the sands of our experience. But if one looks beneath the surface, connections appear, singly at first and then in a tangle that, as it becomes sorted out, makes clear that everything is interconnected. These interlocking events gradually reveal a pattern, not exactly a cause and effect connection but an interrelationship, so that early events time-wise become hooked into later events and vice versa.

Winafred Lucas

Return to Berlin

by

Winafred B. Lucas, Ph.D.

The events of one's lifetime often appear to be accidental happenings, disconnected footprints on the sands of our experience. But if one looks beneath the surface, connections appear, singly at first and then in a tangle that, as it becomes sorted out, makes clear that everything is interconnected. These interlocking events gradually reveal a pattern, not exactly a cause and effect connection but an interrelationship, so that early events time-wise become hooked into later events and vice versa.

Out of these many patterns and interconnections that eventually turn out to be related to each other, occasionally a single tangle of threads makes a discrete pattern that often can be exposed by exploring a few recent lifetimes and early childhood experiences. Undoubtedly, further probing of even earlier lives might expose deeper roots and more interconnections, but enough of the pattern emerges so that events occurring in this lifetime come to be seen in a different perspective.

The first inkling of one such pattern in my life occurred during the three years I lived in Germany during the mid-30's. A friend and I had entered the country through Hamburg, where we bought bicycles and cycled down the Rhine. Though near Berlin at the beginning of our journey, I had no inclination to visit it. That in itself was not particularly strange, but as the years went by and I cycled up and down Germany, testing every sub-culture and trying out every accent, I did occasionally wonder why I avoided the great capital city. In my mind I saw it as dark and full of shadows, a sad city filled with tears and soot. I could not blame my distaste on the Nazis, since Hitler considered Munich, where I lived, as his headquarters and was frequently there, and I didn't mind that. Three years later I made my way to Paris and sailed home, still without visiting this frozen, dismal, and shadowy city.

Another thread in the pattern, indirectly related to my distaste for Berlin, emerged during those Munich days, but all the connecting links that might have opened up my understanding of it were covered over. The thread was the material that emerged during my first analysis, an experience initiated through friendship with a girl who had just completed her doctorate in Sanskrit, then my major, whom I met in the Sanskrit library at the university. To my shocked astonishment she was living with a Munich analyst. In those days people in the United States did not live together casually, so I was unprepared for this different lifestyle.

Also, I had never heard of analysis. In 1934 I did not know of the existence of Jung and I had only heard Freud mentioned once, rather disparagingly, in the University of Washington. However, I allowed myself to be talked into a deep analysis, seven days a week, for which I was charged nothing because I had little money. The analysis was ostensibly to deal with my inability to finish what I started to write. What emerged instead was my flaring anger at my father, to avoid whom I had propelled myself a third of the way around the world. Coupled with this anger, to my unutterable shame, was so intense a fear of the penis that at first I could not even say the word. I avoided the subject for two weeks by concentrating on the Jungian approach to dreams and writing a scholarly paper on the subject. Then I got to work.

Over the year of intense analytic work, my father transference emerged with a strong sexual flavor. My analyst first corrected any misconceptions of his generosity by charging me two and a half dollars a week, which set off a wild anger against him. This he handled with discretion, sensitivity, and impersonal caring, skimming off gently and with exquisite skill my wild tantrums against him. But neither he nor I suspected that this anger was linked to an experience of early sexual abuse, although now I see that it was staring us in the face. Freud suggested that such a childhood experience leads to an interminable analysis, that the transference becomes so sexualized that it is unanalyzable; but, fortunately, we didn't know this. Slowly, persistently, my analyst reduced the anger at my father and desensitized my fear of the penis. This analyst never became involved in my problem or in any way exploited the situation. I remember him saying once very tenderly, when I was stuttering especially badly trying to talk about my fear of the penis, "You have to become friends with that little animal." Slowly and gently he helped me accept the penis as a penis, a potentially friendly part of man's body, and my anger at my father thinned and at times almost disappeared. To this great and good man I owe not only the dissolution of a distorting neurosis but also a valuable model of good psychotherapy.

This therapeutic work made possible for me later a healing physical experience with a man, a German boy my age who was just as frightened of sexuality as I was. He found an upper story apartment for us in a village high in the Alps, and in the early spring we spent a month there pleasuring each other's bodies, skiing over the surrounding mountains, and listening to the music in the little church. We weren't in love with each other and we never attempted a complete sexual experience, but we did become comfortable with our bodies and we learned many ways to enjoy them. Later he escaped to the United States and married a loving girl, and I am sure our experience shortened his road to complete sexual enjoyment. For him, also, I feel gratitude.

When, under the pressure of an emerging war, I finally left Europe, I did not go back to Seattle to a father to whom I had not written for several years but instead settled down to write in a cabin in upper New York State. The anger at my father seemed gone, but a discomfort remained so intense that I could not bring myself to contact him. The memory of the abuse had not been retrieved, and I never dreamed there was anything to remember, but I felt compelled to avoid my father as I had avoided Berlin. This was sad because he had lived for his children and we had all left home, not to return. He had encouraged us to hold both hands out to life and to move with courage, and we had taken him at his word. But he had not anticipated the great empty house and sparse letters from my brothers—and none from me—to be his only recompense.

He had lived for his family. To him this was the great good in life, and with the loss of family contact his courage, which had burned high for 75 years, flickered and went out. The news of his death came to me as I was absorbed with cutting wood for the old stove in my mountain cabin and pumping water at the well, activities that wiped out any literary production. My father had died from pneumonia only a few months before antibiotics were discovered. Without money, abandoned in the lonely house and living on sourdough flapjacks that he had learned to make in the Yukon, he had walked across the great white bridge and hitchhiked to town in a storm to eat his Thanksgiving dinner in a restaurant where no one had the time to talk to him. While walking back through a high wind he felt a chill that he did not bother to fight. At least, that was what I saw when, in a rush of guilt and remorse, I tuned into his last days and tried to heal myself by writing thirteen drafts of a short story about his death.

At the end of the story I perceived him moving toward a fire, and since he had always seen his task as "keeping the home fires burning," I assumed that it was toward those home fires, a symbol for the Light, that he was moving. So I released him and finally felt safe in a world where I had never felt safe before. The shreds of my remaining anger were pushed down, and over them I spread a layer of compassion for all that he had tried to do and a beginning appreciation for the father who had been a great adventurer and a lover of people and who had taught me to hold out both my hands.

Then a strange thing happened. I changed direction. My intention was to fill my life with writing and seeking. I had never had as a goal marriage or children or a doctorate or any profession other than writing. But within a year and a half I was married, within another year I bore my first child, then another child, then divorce, and after that I finally finished what seemed a necessary doctorate. Against my intention, I found myself committed to a different identity. I had taken over my father's goal of "keeping the home fires burning." Why?

Fifteen years later, with two adolescent children, the unwanted doctorate, and an involved professional life gathering momentum, I had my next clue to the mystery of my repudiation of Berlin. In 1957 I was asked to be a control in an LSD research project under Sidney Cohn at UCLA. No one knew much about LSD in those early days, so I had no expectations: my intention was only to be helpful. At that time I had not thought seriously about past lives. They seemed part of the Vedic baggage that I had chosen to carry with me from my childhood, but I hadn't considered them in relationship to myself because I assumed they couldn't be remembered except after years of training in concentration. However, among many jewels of perception in that LSD experience were included five memories of past lives. Four of them were full of poetry and sadness, but the final one was gloomy and almost ugly. I found myself walking the streets of Berlin in the early part of the 19th century. I was a young woman of seventeen, dressed in a dark skirt and coat and with a shawl over my head. I felt that I was a fallen woman, and though I did not know what had happened, my 20th century self decided that I must have been a prostitute. How else could I be a fallen woman? I understood then why I had seen Berlin as full of despair and shadows.

I was in psychoanalysis at the time and with the compulsion on me to say whatever occurred to me, I had a bad time of it trying to report these past lives. I finally described them as images, which my analyst accepted, and he suggested that the centuries in which the imaged lives took place corresponded to the ages in my current life. He made a good case for the correspondences, which I find an imaginative person can do, and perhaps there was actually some synchronicity. At any rate, I was grateful that he let me off the hook. Privately, I was sure they were actual past lives, but since that was my only experience of LSD, I didn't get to explore them further at that time.

Years passed, including journeys with four American analysts, sometimes stormy, sometimes fruitful. My Munich analyst, who had been influenced by both Freud and Jung, had released me from my deepest fears and tempered my anger. With analyst number two, a Jungian, I learned in an overpowering series of images that the only good mother I would ever know was within me and that was enough. Analyst number three, also Jungian, suggested pathways through the blooming and thorny thicket of my unconscious. Although his paths turned out not to fit me well, I became more at home and focused as I roamed through the twilight world, shaping stories and tuning into inner poetry. (This analyst was often ill and lay on his couch while I sat in the chair.) Analyst number four, a Freudian at the peak of his fame, taught me primarily what not to do and what doesn't work, a major contribution. When I had hepatitis he did encourage me to be more patient with my body, but he missed completely a clear dream that stated that a cancer was forming and, more significantly, that the cancer was connected with my last lifetime with my father. Unable to understand the clear and wise admonition of this dream, this analyst retreated into psychoanalytic mumbo-jumbo and of course was impervious to the dream's implication of a past life, which I myself did not at that time recognize. His callousness forced me eventually to take back my own power, for better or for worse, and I never again committed my life to any therapist or guru. For this I thank him. Analyst number five, whom I respected but to whom I did not commit myself, showed me that my anger was not lethal, especially to him, and could be dealt with and transformed. These analytic experiences helped me realize how continuous and complicated is the reweaving of a life. My energy field grew more balanced over the years, but underneath this increasing serenity I sensed a volcanic wasteland of forgotten material waiting to erupt.

Whether the spade work had been deep enough to bring me close to memories of other lifetimes or whether a change in the consciousness of the planet as a whole made such remembrances easier, I do not know, but about the mid-70's past-life memories began to break through. The first one was a spontaneous return to the experience of being guillotined in the French Revolution, which left me like an empty bag of skin for several days afterward but helped me understand my resistance to seeing anything good about Paris. Following that, I recalled nearly 30 past lives, some emerging spontaneously, some self-induced in meditation, some birthed by good friends and fellow therapists. I returned to languages that I had learned easily in this lifetime, scenes that explained preferences, prejudices, and aptitudes, as well as emotions with which I am still dealing.

Most of my mentors and family were met in these lifetime recalls, but not my father; he did not appear in any of them. Missing, also, were memories of the last two lifetimes. I vaguely sensed that I had known my father in the Klondike gold rush in my last lifetime, but I took it for granted that I was a woman, probably a prostitute, since that was about all women were equipped to do in the Klondike at that time, and this assumption acted as a gigantic boulder blocking any recall. The lifetime in Berlin I simply avoided.

Are things synchronistic or happenchance? In the early 80's in order to renew my psychologist's license I had to take a workshop in child abuse, the focus for clinicians at that time. (Poor Freud! He finally was justified in his initial brilliant discernment.) I drew an unusually gifted workshop leader, and sometime in the middle of the afternoon of our final day, I went into an altered state and the doors of memory opened, not to past lives but to my childhood. I remembered, with a clarity that made the repression of the years hard to believe, that my father had molested me when I was three. Never had this occurred to me, nor to my analysts. And yet, as often happens, I could not believe I hadn't remembered, because the sequence of events was so inevitable and fitted into such a clear pattern.

The opening memory was a few months after the birth of my second brother. My father was tortured by his love for my mother, who seemed to become pregnant whenever he looked at her. She had conceived me on her wedding night, my first brother when she was nursing me, and she became pregnant again when nursing my first brother. With no contraceptives available at that time, my father had been forced into abstinence and in his frustration had come to me, who was the apple of his eye. It was loving oral sex which made me feel special, though at the time I found his erect penis frightening. I am sure that he rationalized, as most men do, that a child does not remember things, and undoubtedly there were weaknesses in his ego boundaries.

I realized as I thought about it later that the devastating thing was not the sexual experience but what my father did afterward. He was a highly moral man and guilt ran through him as if he had swallowed flagrantly colored dye. So he turned against me. I did not understand how anyone who had seemed to care so much and had initiated warm and sensuous feelings could suddenly not only withdraw but treat me cruelly. Whenever I did anything he considered inappropriate, such as helping my brothers dump 50 pounds of grain for a lost chicken, he pulled my pants down and beat me with a shingle or ruler on my bare bottom and on my genitals. The only explanation that I could come up with was that I had done something wrong, that I was bad, and it was this feeling of being a bad person that went with me through my life, no matter how hard I tried to prove that it wasn't so.

Also, I nurtured a secret terrible anger against this loving man, and I used my anger as a molten wall that would keep him from ever getting close again. I had repressed the sexual incident, so that I did not know what my anger was about. I felt ashamed, not only for some unknown imagined transgression but for my wall of anger, which violated my conviction about the loving nature of life. The years in Europe had been a desperate attempt to get away from him (for which years of travel I fortunately had other more positive motives), and to my anger and poor self-concept was added the guilt of deserting an old and vulnerable man who had given his children what he could.

On the long drive home from the workshop I began to process the memory. I saw how my father had been caught by his own deep sexual needs, and I didn't blame him. And for the first time I saw completely clearly that I wasn't a bad person, that I hadn't done anything, and the love for myself, which I had struggled to feel, for a moment came shining around me like a bursting star filled with song.

Meanwhile, as I moved more consciously into a state of balance, I became aware that there was a shadow covering me with thin fingers of depression and low energy. The more I came into balance, the more clearly I sensed the shadow, and I knew that it had been there for a long time. I had been able to identify and deal with several other shadowings as I became aware of them. My experience had confirmed that molested children are open to shadowing and I was no exception, but I didn't know how to identify this one. I didn't know what question to ask to get the entity to declare itself.

Eventually, during the period when I was in Egypt riding a camel in the Sinai or floating down the Nile with a Brugh Joy group, I found the answer. It was triggered by releasement work I did with a member of the group to whom an entity had attached in the Cairo Museum (Chapter VI). He recovered immediately, but the entity did not go to the Light and instead began to obsess me when I became temporarily depressed. I had to pressure it again to leave, though at the time I felt so ill I simply told it to get lost rather than helping it make a proper transition. My own immediate recovery led me to wondering why I hadn't been able to deal with the entity that had shadowed *me* for such a long time. It occurred to me that I had never asked *why* this unknown entity had decided to stay with me. I framed this question and an answer immediately came back: "Because you are rather boring and I have to spark you up and make you interesting." It was a dead give-away—my father, the charismatic story teller! I was so provoked that I didn't make an attempt to do any healing but simply also told him, also, to "get lost," which he did, not a fair treatment for an already lost entity!

When I returned home my conscience got the better of me and I called the Egyptian entity first, explained his misconceptions, and took him to the Light, then returned to see what was holding up my father. When he had died I had perceived him going toward a fire, which I assumed was a substitute for the Light, but it turned out that my father saw the flames as hellfire, toward which he was forced to go by his guilt over me, reinforced by the exhortations of our fundamentalist pastor. Rather than go to hell, he had attached to me, which explained the jettison of my chosen lifestyle and the substitute direction of marriage, children, and profession, my father's choice. I was irritated about this but let it go and summoning up a more loving stance, took my father into the Light, where, much relieved, he was met by my mother and my two brothers who had gone ahead. After that I was totally clear of that shadowing.

Meanwhile, I came into a revised understanding of an attachment I had released sometime earlier. When at the age of four I visited a hospital for a tonsillectomy, an entity entered me. It did not seem particularly destructive, and eventually I found that an old man who died at the time I was there, still grieving over his lost little daughter, had attached to me as a substitute. When I finally identified this man and talked with him, he willingly and a little wearily went on to the Light, where he found his daughter waiting. As I looked back after this releasement I realized that since four I had never felt myself to be a child, always old, and it became clear that I had been carrying the energy of the old man.

When I thought about the attachment, I assumed that it had occurred simply because I was there and vulnerable as a result of the anesthetic. However, recently it has become apparent that I played a much more involved role. At the time of the attachment I was stricken because of my father's rejection and was open to a kind father. The old man's need and my need meshed. It is even possible that for a while he helped me to weather the trauma of my real father and supported my intellectual thrust that began at that time. Perhaps he even saved me from the lifetime of anger and chaos that often follows abuse—at the cost, however, of a more spontaneous childhood and adolescence and of the physical and emotional energy that was my birthright. This attachment also made it easier for later attachments to occur, first by my father and then by my husband. It is sad that we do not know more about shadowing—how to perceive entities and how to release them. The old man was so willing to move on, especially when he could see his own little daughter, that he would have left me at any time.

More and more pieces of the puzzle were appearing and were fitted into place. However, there were still those two past lifetimes, and I kept mulling them over and finally, knowing I could not bring myself to look while I was alone, I asked Chet Snow to regress me to Berlin. I warned him that he would have to make me stay in the experience, which he did.

I found myself at first as a young girl of about twelve living with busy professional parents. I spent my days alone reading, writing poetry, thinking, uninterested in other people, either relatives or friends. In my still and protected world the important things were bird song and images.

When I was 17 my parents were killed in a carriage accident. There was only a little money, but I found a room, spacious but dark and gloomy, dark walls, brown carpets, faded lace curtains. My lifestyle was not much different from what it had always been. There wasn't much in Berlin to spark up my existence, so I looked inward, as I always had, living the life of a nun without any commitment.

One day I was returning from buying provisions at a little store, which was also dark and without friendliness, when the net bag in which I was carrying my purchases broke and a loaf of bread and apples and vegetables fell on the sidewalk. I tied up the hole in my bag and was trying to scoop things up when a tall and friendly young man, immaculately dressed, came and offered to help me. Then he walked me home. He came in for a moment and saw my books, and after that he came more and more often. I enjoyed our conversations and his intellectual charm. He was the only young person I had ever known.

He came frequently, and like water in flood tide reaching a dark hole that has been empty for a long time, he filled my life with sparkling meaning. With the slow inevitability with which dawn comes upon the earth, sprinkling light here and there and after a pause moving on until everything is illuminated, we became lovers. I was at peace about it, not asking, or even wanting, more than he had available to give of his time and concern. And like the inevitable dawn, pregnancy followed.

I was not distraught about this until he reacted with alarm and concern. Planning for life's contingencies had never been a part of my lifestyle—I assumed that somehow things would unfold for us. He explained that much as he loved me he could never take me home to his parents as a wife; they had other plans for him. Our warm togetherness faded after that. Every visit gurgled with worry and consideration of alternatives, all unacceptable to him, and finally, as the baby neared the half-way mark in its preparation for being, I began to see that there was no way out.

At his prodding I finally went to see an uncle and aunt whom I had known as a child but who, I knew, had pitied my parents for having such an introverted daughter. I walked up the slate steps to the dark door of their apartment totally without hope. And I was right. I had no sooner told them stumblingly that I was pregnant than my aunt screamed at me that I was a "fallen woman" and pushed me out.

I did not see any way to go and almost without thinking I turned to the dark comfort of the winter river. It was the only answer. And as the river rushed over me and carried me and my baby to our deaths, my last thought was, "I am a fallen woman." From a high perspective I scanned that lifetime and this one and recognized that the warm-hearted aristocratic young man then was my charismatic, handsome father in this lifetime. And I knew that the events in this life were just one chapter in a longer saga and that to judge them without context was a grievous error.

There remained the recovery of the immediate past life. With no colleagues available I had to undertake this myself, and my first step was to put aside presuppositions. In an altered state I went immediately to the Yukon and to my surprise found myself as a young man in his early twenties. I tuned in on a scene up above Dawson where my father of this lifetime, J. Fred, and I were cutting timber, which we planned to float down the Yukon River to the mouth of the Eldorado River with the spring thaw. Timber for housing was much needed there. J. Fred could tack against any wind, no matter how frustrating, and he had chosen this way to survive after the mine had been sold that he had been working on a partnership basis but for which he had no legal claim. We slept in a snow hut shored up by timber we had cut and trimmed. My one possession was a team of Husky dogs to which I was deeply bonded, especially to the lead, an ingenuously lovely young bitch with dark face markings and black eyes. The dogs slept curled up around our dwelling with their noses under their tails.

I followed our life together there in the constant darkness. J. Fred was in his late thirties and with his kindness and charisma easily became the father I had never had. But it went beyond that. I felt more and more drawn to him and even with the gloves and heavy jackets wanted to be physically close to him. I didn't understand this and was especially perplexed because J. Fred seemed to be struggling against the same feelings and occasionally would erupt in violent spells of anger.

We were planning to make a raft and float our logs down as soon as the river was clear enough of ice, but after one especially severe burst of anger, J. Fred announced that we were going to leave. I protested about the ice but eventually did what he said and helped bind the logs together in an eddy of the river. Then J. Fred got aboard and I pushed him off and ran along the edge of the river with my team.

We were nearly there when the accident happened. The pile of logs headed between two mammoth cakes of ice and there was no way J. Fred could stop it. With a grating wrench the pile of logs broke up, spilling him into the frozen water. He was a strong swimmer and made the shore and we stopped long enough for him to put on dry clothes and dry his jacket. Discouraged, angry, and with nothing to show for our winter's work, we made our way to the Eldorado River and its little cluster of houses. Here J. Fred, without a word to me, entered a saloon. Again I felt that sense of abandonment and impotence that I had experienced in the earlier lifetime, now completely forgotten. And I chose the same solution. I decided to leave.

A part of the smaller river was still frozen and I called to my dogs, and though the opposite shore led nowhere, I started to cross, running alongside my lead dog. Part way across we hit thin ice and went through. As I tried futilely to save them, I saw the helpless looks in the eyes of the dogs who had trusted me. We all drowned, and my last thought was that I was guilty of their deaths; if I hadn't been angry, it wouldn't have happened. My last memory was of the eyes of my lead bitch searching for me. From an extended perspective I saw that J. Fred left the Klondike after a few more adventures and sailed back to Seattle, where he made his home. Ten years later at the age of 47 he married my mother and became my father in this current lifetime.

So sad a life. So sad were both these times, in the Klondike and before that in Berlin. But they were pieces in a broad pattern, and I knew I had to release the sadness and accept this. As I thought about it, the abuse in this current life no longer seemed like abuse but a pathetic seeking for something we had a long time ago. And I also saw that the pattern of feeling loved and valued and then rejected, though it is not an unusual one, was repeated with striking faithfulness, not only in those two lifetimes and in the current one but also in my tranferences on all my therapists. The first and the last analysts, though they could not comprehend the depth of the pattern, were able to deal with it therapeutically and so made it possible for me to release it.

A recollection of my father in a still earlier lifetime has surfaced recently. I had touched on that life a number of times in my meditations, feeling myself to be a child in a boat on a dark swamp hung with streamers of moss. I saw a younger sister with me and could sense the fetid muddy water, but that was as far as I got. It seemed a French scene, but I couldn't remember any part of France with such a swamp, so I decided, as I often do, that I was making it up. Recently with the help of my Dutch colleagues Tineke and Rob, I retrieved the memory. They took me back on a mental bridge: "There's no way out."

I found myself as a nine-year-old girl living with my younger sister and my parents in an isolated house on a Louisiana bayou. The cuisine, mode of living, and the language were French. Since my father was often away hunting alligators and other game, I was close to my mother, and she taught my sister and me. When she developed consumption and died, my world shattered. I wasn't allowed to go to the funeral and no one talked to me about what had happened. Shortly after my mother's death I overheard my father telling a visitor that he was going to send me away; he could only manage one child and my sister was easier.

In the regression I became almost a blank, unable to feel, and my colleagues helpfully recognized that I was in shock. Without feeling, I went out in the boat with my sister and slipped over the edge into the dark water and was drowned. I was oblivious to my younger sister and her fright and grief when I first recovered the memory, but from a higher vantage point I could see what I had done to her. However, I saw also that she adjusted in the following days and that in this lifetime she was my mother—not a surprise because I had known that in various lifetimes not yet completely recovered I have been her mother, her older sister, and her teacher.

What was surprising was that my father in this lifetime was that Louisiana father. From an enlarged perspective I could see that he had not meant to reject me; he had felt overwhelmed by the loss of his wife and felt

I needed to go where I could attend school. It was clear that his remorse over my death made him vulnerable to trying to care for me in our Berlin lifetime. But he had not been able to cope well in any of his lifetimes—any sudden shift of a situation found him impotent to move constructively. In this lifetime he struggled for 75 years, but in spite of his burden of guilt he never gave up, and I know that this was growth for him.

The pattern of suicide is also interesting. When in my early teens I lost my fundamentalist view of life and along with it all my friends and my life goals, and could for a time not find anything else that seemed valid, the impulse to walk out into Puget Sound and not come back threatened to overwhelm me again and again. This time I made the decision to keep on trying to understand, no matter how dark things seemed. I believe that when in any lifetime one gives up, the same sort of circumstances keep repeating until one learns to hold on. I wish I had realized that it is simpler just to learn it the first time.

More common threads and patterns keep revealing themselves, some of them amusing. In the Berlin lifetime my father, as a young aristocrat, was involved in dueling with sabers, and one of the most pathetic memories of my current life is standing in a class of young fraternity men in a Munich fencing salle, where I was already highly competent in foils, holding a saber. When I realized the young male fencers were all staring at me as "that strange American girl," I saw that I was out of step and never returned, but until the recovery of the Berlin memories of my father, who belonged to a dueling fraternity, I did not understand what had propelled me so inappropriately. Also, I now realize why my grief over my great bitch Devi in this life, who with her dark face markings, her jet black eyes, and her charisma, strikingly resembled my lead bitch in the Yukon, has never found an end. I have felt guilt over her death and over the deaths of all our great dogs without realizing that the guilt and the grief were carryovers from the disaster on the river. There is still an ache, but it is better.

The most profound transforming insight came from recovering the final affirmation in the Berlin lifetime that I was a "fallen woman." I have always felt that in a sense I was bad and never knew why. I have come to see that such a judgment is neither fair nor true, not then and not now, and my attempt to love and comfort myself is becoming easier. Judgments about my father and anger toward him shadowed me for a long time, though not so much since I wrote that story about him. Now I can think of him with warm appreciation. Most of the pieces of the pattern in my life with him seem to have been turned up and put into place. There may possibly be still earlier lifetimes that I shared with him, but to all intents I am at peace about him. I am sure that I could visit Berlin now and see it as it is, though unfortunately it is now a wounded city with traces of the scar of its division only just beginning to heal.

The healing of my self-concept has been difficult. Cognitive understanding that I was not a bad person, even the growing ability to merge with my Higher Self and not judge my limited self, did not immediately counteract the self-critical reactions that were reinforced over so many years. Also, there was sadness in me over what seemed so many wasted years—the body that was stiff and frozen by shame so that I could not become the dancer I so longed to be, the bright creativity that I felt unworthy to express. Knowledge came at times that this was my way, the way of my greatest soul growth, and such awareness would thin my regret temporarily, but always I returned to my perception that my life had not borne the fruit it might have: both flowering and fruit had been sparse.

I became patient with the long process of healing, not knowing how to heal myself further except through meditation. It was in this attitude of sad half-acceptance of so many damaged years that I accompanied a friend to visit Sai Baba in his ashram in Puttaparti. Since I was strictly against guru-chasing, I went with her only as a favor because she had accompanied me to unusual places where I had wanted to go. I didn't expect anything, and unlike nearly every other person of the thousands staying at the ashram, I did not seek an interview. However, just in case I had the opportunity for one, I formulated four questions I would ask Sai Baba. The major question concerned the healing of my self-concept. I could still feel the wound.

Four events divide a day in the ashram—two long periods of singing bhajans in the early morning and at mid-afternoon and two other extended periods of receiving darshan (blessing) from Sai Baba at mid-morning and early evening. For each of these events thousands of people seat themselves under the portico or on the ground in the enclosed area around the temple. I, along with other foreigners, mostly older, who were not brought up to sit comfortably on the ground for hours, moved to an area where a few chairs had been set up. Baba seldom went there as he moved about the enclosure giving darshan, so the chance of an interview was nil, but I was content with sitting absorbed in the heightened vibrations.

During both darshan and bhajans I always slipped into an altered state, and I found myself in a conversation with Sai Baba that went on throughout my days there. It was as though he spoke in my heart clearly and helpfully, and he addressed each of my four concerns—if I had had an interview there would have been nothing more to ask or say. He answered the first three concerns briefly but in perceptive and reassuring ways, telling me, for instance, that my body would remain well and support me for many years to come, and that my karmic interaction with my son was finished and I could let it go.

When we came to my wounded life he worked differently. As I was going over it with him I began to gag and found myself coughing up the image of an appallingly deformed fetus. All that remained was stripped muscles, a skeleton about 18 inches long, and a dark heart throbbing through a pool of black blood. "I am influenced by Baba's coughing up the Siva lingam," I told myself, sure that my image would dissolve if I admitted that. But it remained and became increasingly clear over the days.

I sat looking at it and said to Baba, "What can I do about this?"

His answer was immediate, "Grieve, you haven't grieved enough."

I thought of all the anger and all the sadness I had felt, and it seemed enough, but I believed Baba, and as I looked at the distorted fetus the tears came. Then over the days the fetus began to grow and became longer and longer until it reached the length of 18 feet. Each day I sat beside it weeping in my heart.

Every darshan and each singing of the bhajans I returned to live with this image, and Baba sat beside me. Finally, when I had wept enough, black fertile earth began to spread over the image, beginning at the head and feet and moving inward, and as the earth covered the distorted fetus with this growing blanket, delicate white fresias emerged and filled the air with fragrance. Finally only the dark heart moving sluggish black blood was left open. What to do?

"Should it die entirely?" I asked Baba. "Or should it somehow get better?" But there was no answer.

Since the fresias had been so healing, I decided to do some imaging on my own, and in the surging darkness of the heart I planted violets. I filled it with purple violets, feeling that they would bring healing. But the next darshan, when I went back to the image, the violets were not there, and the dark heart beat on. Then I knew that I had not created the image of the fetus—it had been given to me and represented a deep truth that had to work itself out in its own time.

When I left Puttaparti the heart was unchanged—it remained throbbing dully in the field of fresias. Since then the exposed areas have shrunk in scope, and the heart and blood are brownish instead of black, but I am still unsure what will be the resolution of this image.

I find that the memory of Baba walking serenely among the seated crowds, enveloped in a cloud of love that outshone even the brilliant Indian sun, is growing dimmer. But the form of him sitting beside me in my heart, in silent conversations transforming the image of my wounded self, becomes more clear. His tranquility is becoming my tranquility, and I am beginning to know that someday I shall watch in the depths of myself while the sadness of the darkly beating heart resolves itself.

Notes

Chapter I: Prenatal and Birth Work

1. Many of the elements of this induction are to be found on the reverse side of "The Golden Flower," a tape handled by the Association for Past-Life Research and Therapies.
2. Josephine Van Husen. "The Development of Fears, Phobias, and Restrictive Patterns of Adaptation Following Attempted Abortions," presented at the Symposium of the Society for Clinical and Experimental Hypnosis, Los Angeles, CA, 1977.
3. See Stanislav Grof's description of the per-natal matrices in *Beyond the Brain,* Chapter 2, pp. 98-117. Albany: State University of New York, 1985.
4. For comparable situations see this volume, Chapter IV, especially Hickman's section.

Chapter II: Regression to Childhood

1. See Alice Miller's *Thou Shalt Not Be Aware* (1984).
2. For earlier regression work with this patient see Vol. I, Chap. XXI.

Chapter IV: Varieties of Interlife Experience

1. James, William. *Varieties of Religious Experience.* New York: The New American Library, 1958.
2. For a discussion of the archetypal aspects of the interlife see Sanislav Grof *Beyond the Brain,* Chapter VI. Albany: State University of New York, 1985.
3. For a thorough explanation of the doctrine and process of rebirth, see *The Case for Reincarnation* by Joe Fisher, published by Citadel Press (1992).
4. This phenomenon has been extensively researched by Joe Fisher in his book *Hungry Ghosts* published by Doubleday (Canada) Ltd. (1990).
5. Sandweiss, Samuel. *Sai Baba: The Holy Man and the Psychiatrist.* San Diego, CA: Birth Day Publishing Company, 1975.
6. Karagulla, Sharifa. *Breakthrough to Creativity.* Marina Del Ray, CA: DeVorss, 1967.

7. Steiner, Rudolph. *Between Death and Rebirth.* London: Rudolph Steiner Press, 1975.
8. Bayless, Raymond. *The Other Side of Death.* New York: University Books, 1971.

Chapter V: Conversations with the Unborn

1. His paper, presented at the meeting of the Association for Clinical and Experimental Hypnosis in 1977, suggested some innovative techniques.
2. *Babies Remember Birth* touches on this cautiously.
3. See Thomas Verney's pioneer work in *The Secret Life of the Unborn Child* (1981).
4. Gladys McGarey presented her approach in an article "Let the Baby Decide," published in *Venture Inward* in 1990. The deluge of letters that resulted made clear that many women have used this technique in a helpful way.
5. See Findeisen's article in *The Journal of Regression Therapy,* Vol. II, No. 1, on rescripting in cases of attempted abortion.
6. See Louise Ireland-Frey's article "Clinical Depossession: Releasement of Attached Entities from Unsuspecting Hosts" in *The Journal of Regression Therapy,* Vol. I, No. 2, 1986.
7. See article by Clara Riley (Claire Etheridge).
8. This dialogue process is described by Ira Progoff in his *At a Journal Workshop.* New York: Dialogue House Library, 1975.
9. For additional examples of Balinese dialogue see Anne Hubbell Maiden, "Three Dialogues on Birth in Bali," unpublished paper, and "Continuity of Care: Seven Stages of Birthwork," presented at the Fourth International Conference on Pre- and Peri-natal Psychology, Amherst, MA, 1989, available from the author, Star Route, Box 232, Muir Beach, CA, 91965 or from Sounds Tapes, 1825 Pearl Street, Boulder, CO, 80302.
10. Anne Hubbell Maiden and Edie Farwell. *Tibetan Birth Wisdom: Birth Care from before Conception through Early Childhood.* (In Press)
    ———. "The Wisdom of Tibetan Childbirth" in *Context: A Quarterly of Humane Sustainable Culture,* No. 31, 1992.
11. See Anne Hubbell Maiden, "Preconception: The First Stage of Life" in *Journal of Pre- and Peri-natal Psychology,* Vol II, Issue 2, 1988.

Chapter VI: Contemporary Approaches to Releasement

1. See Annabelle Chaplin *The Bright Light of Death* (1977).
2. In this work I followed Enid Hoffman's techniques as she described them in *Huna: A Beginner's Guide.* Rockport, MA: ParaResearch, 1975.
3. Moody, Raymond. *Life After Life.* Georgia: Mockingbird Books, 1975.

4. Ring, Kenneth. *Life at Death: A Scientific Investigation of the Near-Death Experience.* New York: Coward McCann, 1980.
5. Sabom, Michael. *Recollections of Death.* New York: Simon and Schuster, 1982.
6. Karl Wickland. *Thirty Years Among the Dead* (1974).
7. Burr, Harold Saxon. *Blueprint for Immortality.* London: Neville Spearman, 1972.
8. Russell, Edward. *Design for Destiny.* New York: Ballantine, 1976.
9. Motoyama, Hiroshi. *Science and the Evolution of Consciousness: Chakras, Ki, and Psi.* Brooklyn, MA: Random House, 1978.
10. Unpublished communication.
11. Moss, Thelma. *The Body Electric.* Los Angeles: Tarcher, 1979.
12. Albertson, Maurice, Bill Baldwin, and Dan Ward. "Post Traumatic Stress Disorders of Vietnam Veterans: A Proposal for Research and Therapeutic Healing Utilizing Depossession." *The Journal of Regression Therapy.* Vol. III, No. 1, 1988.
13. Karl Wickland, *Thirty Years Among the Dead* (1974).
14. Raymond Moody, op. cit.
15. See William Baldwin, *Regression Therapy: Spirit Releasement Therapy* (1992).
16. For a delightful and informative fictional account of this process see Franklin Loehr, *Diary after Death.* Grand Island, FL: Religious Research Press, 1986.
17. Reynolds, Edward. "Humanistic Considerations in Regression Therapy," *The Journal of Regression Therapy.* Vol. II, No. 2, 1986. See also Chapter XVIII in Volume I.
18. Mehl, Lewis. "Improvement of Diabetes in Conjunction with Regression Therapy." *The Journal of Regression Therapy.* Vol. II, No. 2, 1987. See also his book *Mind and Matter.* Berkeley, CA: Mind Body Press, 1981.
19. See also the section on "Philosophical Hypotheses" in Vol. I, Chapter XI.
20. Shealy, Norman and Caroline Myss. *The Creation of Health.* Walpole, N.H.: Stillpoint Publishing, 1988.
21. See Bruce Hapferer, *A Celebration of Demons: Exorcism and Aesthetics of Healing in Sri Lanka* for extensive documentation on the training and process of releasement in Sri Lanka. In spite of the rather forbidding terminology, many of the concepts are similar to those presented in this section.

Chapter VII: Death, Dying and the Dead

1. See Bibliography.
2. Rogers, Carl. *A Way of Being.* Boston: Houghton Mifflin, Co., 1980.
3. See Jue's section in Vol. I, Chap. XI.
4. See Volume I, Chapter XXI.
5. See Snow's section in Vol. I, Chapter XV.
6. This was translated by Mueller in *The Teachings of the Compassionate Buddha* by E.A. Burtt. New York, 1955.

7. See Evans-Wentz, *The Tibetan Book of the Dead* (1960).
8. Denning suggests the following books as background reading:
   Raudive, Konstantine. *Breakthrough.* New York: Taplinger Publ., 1971.
   Greger, Johannes. *Communication with the Spirit World.* New York: John Felsberg, Inc., 1932.
   Randall, Neville. *Life After Life.* New York: Corgi Books, 1975.
9. Richard, Douglas. "Dissociation and Anomalous Perceptual States," Treat II Conference (Third Conference in Treatment and Research of Experimental Anomalous Trauma), Kansas City, MO, March 5-10, 1991.
10. Simonton, Carl, Stephanie Simonton, and Craig Stevens. *Getting Well Again.* Los Angeles: Tarcher, 1978.
11. For a technique of dialoging with the body see Ira Progoff. *At a Journal Workshop.* New York: Dialogue House Library, 1975, Chapter 14.
13. Boone, J. Allen. *Kinship with All Life.* New York: Harper and Brothers, 1952.

Chapter VIII: Progression to the Future

1. Moody, Raymond. *Life After Life.* Georgia: Mockingbird Books, 1975.
2. Ring, Kenneth. *Life at Death: A Scientific Investigation of the Death Experience* (1980).
3. Wambach, Helen. *Reliving Past Lives.* San Francisco: Harper and Row, 1978, and *Life Before Life.* New York: Bantam Books, 1979.
4. Snow, Chet B. *Mass Dreams of the Future.* New York: McGraw Hill, 1989.
5. For a thorough discussion of quantum mechanics in layman's terms see Fred Alan Wolff. *Taking the Quantum Leap.* New York: Harper and Row, 1981. See also Larry Dossey, *Time Space and Medicine.* Boulder, CO: Shambala, 1982.
6. For further reading on "Ageless Wisdom" see Alice Bailey, *Prophecies by D.K.,* compiled by Aart Jurriaanse, Craighall, S. Afr: World Unity and Service, 1988. *Mass Dreams of the Future* also discusses this material in detail.
7. The Association for Research and Enlightenment (ARE) founded by 20th century clairvoyant Edgar Cayce, sponsors local study groups as one way to venture inward in this quest. The Association for Past-Life Research and Therapies (APRT) also has a referral service for professional regression therapy (P.O. Box 2015, Riverside, CA 92516).

Index